D1196618

Stuart Atkins: Essays on Goethe

Stuart Atkins

Essays on Goethe

**Edited by Jane K. Brown
and Thomas P. Saine**

WITH A BIBLIOGRAPHY OF THE PUBLICATIONS
OF STUART ATKINS

CAMDEN HOUSE

Copyright © 1995 by
CAMDEN HOUSE, INC.

Published by Camden House, Inc.
Drawer 2025
Columbia, SC 29202 USA

Printed on acid-free paper.
Binding materials are chosen for strength and
durability.

ISBN:1–57113–027–6

Library of Congress Cataloging-in-Publication Data

Atkins, Stuart Pratt, 1914–

Essays on Goethe / Stuart Atkins ; edited by Jane K. Brown and
Thomas P. Saine ; with a bibliography of the publications of Stuart
Atkins.
    p.   cm. -- (Studies in German literature, linguistics, and
culture)
Includes bibliographical references and index.
ISBN 1–57113–027–6 (alk. paper)
1.–Goethe, Johann Wolfgang von, 1749–1832 -- Criticism and
interpretation.   I. Brown, Jane K., 1943–   . II. Saine, Thomas P.
    III. Title.   IV. Series: Studies in German literature, linguistics,
and culture (Unnumbered)
PT2177.A85 1995
831'.6--dc20   95-33327
                                                      CIP

Contents

Acknowledgments   v

Preface   1

The Apprentice Novelist: Goethe's Letters, 1765–67   4

J. C. Lavater and Goethe: Problems of Psychology and
Theology in *Die Leiden des jungen Werthers*   23

The Opening Lines of Goethe's *Iphigenie auf Tauris*   83

Goethe and the Poetry of the Renaissance   92

Goethe's Nausicaa: A Figure in Fresco   118

Wilhelm Meisters Lehrjahre: Novel or Romance ?   130

Die Wahlverwandtschaften: Novel of German Classicism   137

Italienische Reise and Goethean Classicism   182

Goethe's Last Play: *Die Wette*   198

"Das Leben ist ein Gänsespiel": Some Aspects of Goethe's
West-östlicher Divan   207

Goethe's *Novelle* as Pictorial Narrative   220

The Mothers, the Phorcides, and the Cabiri in *Faust*   230

The Visions of Leda and the Swan in *Faust*   239

Goethe, Aristophanes, and the Classical Walpurgisnight   243

Goethe, Calderón, and Faust: *Der Tragödie zweiter Teil*   259

Irony and Ambiguity in the Final Scene of Goethe's *Faust*   277

The Evaluation of Romanticism in Goethe's *Faust*   293

Bibliography   323

Acknowledgments

We would like to thank the journals and publishers where these essays first appeared for their kind permission to reprint them here. The essays were first published as follows:

1. "The Apprentice Novelist—Goethe's Letters, 1765–1767," in *Modern Language Quarterly* 10, no.2 (September 1949): 290–306. Copyright University of Washington, 1949. Reprinted with permission.

2. "J.C. Lavater and Goethe: Problems of Psychology and Theology in *Die Leiden des jungen Werthers*," reprinted by permission of the Modern Language Association from *PMLA* 63 (1948): 520–76.

3. "On the Opening Lines of Goethe's *Iphigenie*," in *Germanic Review* 24 (1949): 116–23. Reprinted with permission of the Helen Dwight Reid Educational Foundation. Published by Heldref Publications, 1319 18th Street, N.W., Washington, D.C. 20036-1802. Copyright 1949.

4. "Goethe and the Poetry of the Renaissance," translated by Jane K. Brown from "Goethe und die Renaissancelyrik," published in Hans Reiss, ed., *Goethe und die Tradition* (Frankfurt/Main: Athenäum, 1972) 102–29.

5. "Goethe's Nausicaa: A Figure in Fresco," in Hans-Joachim Mähl and Eberhard Mannack, eds., *Studien zur Goethezeit: Erich Trunz zum 75. Geburtstag* (Heidelberg: Carl Winter Universitätsverlag, 1981) 33–44.

6. "*Wilhelm Meisters Lehrjahre*: Novel or Romance?" in Peter Uwe Hohendahl, Herbert Lindenberger, Egon Schwarz, eds., *Essays on European Literature in Honor of Liselotte Dieckmann* (St. Louis: Washington University Press, 1972) 45–52.

7. "*Die Wahlverwandtschaften*: Novel of German Classicism," in *German Quarterly* 53 (1980): 1–45 and 347.

8. "*Italienische Reise* and Goethean Classicism," in Stanley A. Corngold, Michael Curschmann and Theodore J. Ziolkowski, eds., *Aspekte der Goethezeit* (Göttingen: Vandenhoeck & Ruprecht, 1977) 81–96.

9. "Goethe's Last Play: *Die Wette*," in *Modern Language Notes* 97 (1982): 546–55.

10. " 'Das Leben ist ein Gänsespiel.' Some Aspects of Goethe's *West-östlicher Divan*," in Egon Schwarz, Hunter G. Hannum and Edgar Lohner, eds., *Festschrift für Bernhard Blume: Aufsätze zur deutschen und europäischen Literatur* (Göttingen: Vandenhoeck & Ruprecht, 1967) 90–102.

11. "Goethe's *Novelle* as Pictorial Narrative," in Ursula Mahlendorf and Laurence Rickels, eds., *Poetry Poetics Translation: Festschrift in Honor of Richard Exner* (Würzburg: Königshausen & Neumann, 1994) 73–81.

12. "The Mothers, the Phorcides, and the Cabiri in Goethe's *Faust*," in *Monatshefte* 45 (1953): 289–96.

13. "The Visions of Leda and the Swan in Goethe's *Faust*," in *Modern Language Notes* 68 (1953): 340–44.

14. "Goethe, Aristophanes, and the Classical Walpurgisnight," in *Comparative Literature* 6 (1954): 64–78.

15. "Goethe, Calderón and *Faust: Der Tragödie zweiter Teil*," in *Germanic Review* 28 (1953): 83–98. Reprinted with permission of the Helen Dwight Reid Educational Foundation. Published by Heldref Publications, 1319 18th Street, N.W., Washington, D.C. 20036-1802. Copyright 1953.

16. "Irony and Ambiguity in the Final Scene of Goethe's *Faust*," in Gottfried F. Merkel, ed., *On Romanticism and the Art of Translation: Studies in Honor of Edwin Hermann Zeydel* (Princeton: Princeton University Press, 1956) 7–27.

17. "The Evaluation of Romanticism in Goethe's *Faust*," in *Journal of English and Germanic Philology* 54 (1955): 9–38.

Preface

Stuart Atkins has been the preeminent American Goethe scholar in the second half of this century, virtually since the appearance of his first essay on *Werther* in the late 1940s. His reputation rests in part on two books, *The Testament of Werther in Poetry and Drama* and *Goethe's Faust: A Literary Analysis*, but equally on some twenty definitive essays on Goethe's literary work. It is typical of his constant questioning and correcting, and of his humility, that these essays have never been collected, even though their conclusions have long since become a living part of our understanding of Goethe. To make them more readily accessible, and to mark their contribution to Goethe studies, we offer this volume.

As the bibliography at the end reveals, our collection contains a small but central group of essays selected by their author. It includes only those essays that have not already been reprinted, hence the absence of well-known ones on *Faust I*, on *Tasso*, and on classicism (see bibliography). Six included here are on *Faust*; some provide the detailed justification for positions alluded to only in passing in *Goethe's Faust*, some raise different issues altogether. None is in any way superseded by the book; the two most general ones, "Irony and Ambiguity. . ." and "The Evaluation of Romanticism. . ." offer more comprehensive views of the play even than the book itself.

Each essay establishes beyond question some significant, often quite surprising, point about the text under consideration. There can no longer, for example, be any argument about the importance of the Neolatin tradition for Goethe's lyric practice, or of the verisimilitude of *Die Wahlverwandtschaften*. Now that we know what "Gänsespiel" means, we can rethink the role of that poem in the *Divan*; once we understand what constitutes Aristophanic or Calderonian style in *Faust* we can begin to comprehend its irony and symbolic dramaturgy. The essays are definitive not because they close off discussion, but because they settle clearly some important basis for it.

Because the essays have been so effective in establishing bases, it is easy to forget how interesting and important their details are as well. But who else has seen all the paintings Goethe did? Who else reads Lavater's sermons, Rousseau and Prévost, and even Beaumont and Riccoboni, when working on *Werther*? All the romances of Wieland? and of Gerstenberg? Neolatin poetry? histories of board games? and all the Goethe scholarship? Who else offers statistics about the relative frequency of entries in Goedecke? The essay on Renaissance poetry is a tour de force, a fugue on Goethe's use of the Neolatin tradition: it moves from Goethe's knowledge of Renaissance poetry in each of the Western European vernaculars to his knowledge of Neolatin poetry on the basis of citations, works by friends, Latin translations of Oriental poetry, poets read by Goethe, Goethe's evaluations of them, to Goethe's use of Neolatin meters, stances (parody and allegory), motifs and images, etc. Each subtopic unleashes a cascade of references, names, titles. Whenever it seems there can't possibly be any more, it starts all over again. Even the concluding gesture, "Goethe's use of Renaissance ideas has been well documented," brings on another flood of names before we reach the final assertion that Renaissance influence has also been demonstrated in stylistic terms. The learning in these essays is staggering.

But all is presented with a dry blandness, a bemused irony that keeps it, like Goethe's own pedantry, in its place. A quintessential Atkins footnote: "*Die Wette* is not mentioned by Brandes, Friedenthal, Gundolf, Haarhaus, Lewes, Heinrich Meyer, R. M. Meyer, Staiger, or Viëtor, who represent a great range of methods and interests; Bielschowski gives an account of its composition, and Emil Ludwig discusses it briefly as a late improvisation which, as improvisation, recalls the much earlier *Clavigo*." Or the bibliographical note in the *Novelle* essay, which dispenses with full references to the scholarship cited on the grounds that they are available in the standard bibliographies—a rare marriage of *Akribie* and good sense. And this mass is artfully shaped, so that the generalizations seem to grow of their own accord from the details. We are always made to feel as if we ourselves have uncovered the pattern from the material so generously placed before us.

Equally characteristic is the precision in reading. Particularly the early essays distinguish differences in style (in the opening of *Iphigenie*, in the visions of Leda and the swan) or establish stylistic connections (*Werther* and Goethe's letters, *Faust* and Aristophanes, *Faust* and Calderón) with unparalleled specificity, concreteness and clarity. Here if anywhere we can see why rhetorical analysis should still be in the curriculum. Similarly works major and minor—the *Lehrjahre*, *Die Wahlverwandtschaften*, *Novelle*, *Die Wette*—take on new shape or significance by having their genre determined more precisely. But such determinations are flexible as well as judicious. *Goethe's Faust* reads the play a tragedy of character, while the essays in this volume, particularly the one on Calderón, show what it means to consider it rather as tragedy of theme. *Faust* is not exclusively the one or the other, but both genres are tools to extend our understanding of the drama. Similarly concepts like irony and ambiguity, precisely defined, are used to demonstrate that the last scene of *Faust* represents the realm of experience (not transcendence), a thesis essential to the understanding of Goethean classicism.

Indeed, if there is one central theme in the volume, it is the defense and clarification of the term classicism. We learn about a variety of classicisms, from antiquity to Renaissance Neolatinism to Romantic Neohellenism. And we learn in precisely what terms each is relevant and irrelevant to Goethe. The distinction between classicism and Romanticism is passionately defended in these essays, but the distinction is not an abyss. This is, after all, the teacher who began the Romanticism course I took from him with Goethe's *Märchen* and ended it with *Novelle*. While a title like "The Evaluation of Romanticism in *Faust*" may at first seem pedantic, our view changes dramatically when the question of terminology leads to a defense of the unity of the drama and transforms our understanding of its central issues. And when it tactfully critiques obfuscations in the German scholarship on national identity and on the post-war swerve into religious readings of *Faust* in the context of the Cold War, the essay shows us what Goethe stands for—and what Stuart Atkins stands for. Ultimately the issue is not the label but the virtues of clarity, good sense, tolerance, committed secularity, moderation—"humanism," in a word that the precision and integrity of the essays rescue from any sense of cliché. Classicism embraces style, motifs, modality, and ethics: in this amalgam the essays speak both for Goethe's and for Stuart Atkins's commitment to literary culture as a central element in our education as individuals and as citizens.

Jane K. Brown

The Apprentice Novelist: Goethe's Letters, 1765–67

Whereas Goethe's early development as lyricist and dramatist can be traced in a variety of completed as well as fragmentary works from his student days, there has been preserved no sufficiently extensive example of his literary efforts in narrative prose antedating the publication of *Die Leiden des jungen Werthers* to permit direct examination of his early development as novelist. One result of this fact has been the tendency to neglect, despite certain passages in *Dichtung und Wahrheit*, the possible significance of his early interest in the epistolary novel.[1] Indeed, criticism of no less important a work than *Werther* itself seems to reflect this neglect by overwhelmingly emphasizing biographical rather than literary antecedents in Goethe's development, and so the extraordinary technical achievement which the novel represents is as it were somehow taken on the faith due genius. The structure of *Werther* has, to be sure, been analyzed, and been found to be patterned on a psychic year of four seasons, or to comprise two parts (as printed—reflecting experiences of a Werther-Goethe and a Werther-Jerusalem), three parts, five parts (various schemes for dramatic analysis), and more (methods of analyzing novels); all such observations have aesthetic utility, for they make the reader aware of large compositional features and certain proportions which suggest that there is a total pattern to the novel's composition. For appreciation of Goethe's technical achievement as a storyteller, however, such observations are unsatisfactory: although they throw valuable light on the completed work, they fail to suggest why Goethe's first published novel, a work probably written with little revising and without a detailed compositional plan, should be the finished product which it is. Even Erich Schmidt's classic study, *Richardson, Rousseau und Goethe*, in which the relationship of *Werther* to the novels of some of Goethe's more important predecessors and contemporaries is carefully investigated, starts with the dangerous assumption that "die literarischen Voraussetzungen von Goethes Werther" can be

---

[1] Thus L. Spriegel treats only "Lyrik" and "Drama" in the section of her Tübingen dissertation, *Der Leipziger Goethe und Gellert* (Borna-Leipzig, 1934), which covers "Gellerts Bedeutung für Goethes Dichtung"; cf. also, e.g., H. Kindermann's essay, "Der Rokoko-Goethe," prefatory to Bd. II, Reihe Irrationalismus, Deutsche Literatur in Entwicklungsreihen (Leipzig, 1932).

understood simply in terms of Werther, some of the Goethe-Kestner correspondence, and a few rather famous novels, and leaves no impression that the style and technique of *Werther* might represent the fruit of a fairly long and gradual development.[2] In the following pages an attempt is made to trace the development of Goethe's narrative technique in some of his earliest preserved letters, especially those of his Leipzig years (which, as critics have occasionally noted, sometimes strike "a chord that foretells the strains of *Werther*"[3]); and since the subject has, as already indicated, particular relevance to problems which arise in connection with *Werther*, occasional technical comparisons with passages in that novel will be introduced.[4] As for the assumption with which I start, that such a great literary achievement as *Werther* can only be understood in terms of actual previous practice on the part of its author, let Dr. Johnson speak:

> A man should begin to write soon; for, if he waits till his judgment is matured, his inability, through want of practice to express his conceptions, will make the disproportion so great between what he sees, and what he can attain, that he will probably be discouraged from writing at all.[5]

Before Goethe's letters from Leipzig are examined, one earlier letter, that written to Cornelia from Wiesbaden on June 21, 1765, deserves to be considered in some detail. In it can already be discerned a preoccupation with literary narrative technique: two barely significant incidents are reported—one as a heroic adventure, the other as a sort of romantic encounter with primitivistic nature, and both together comprising the large category "einige absonderliche Schicksaale."

> Dencke nur wir haben allhier—Schlangen, das häßliche Ungeziefer macht den Garten, hinter unserm Hause, gantz unsicher. [...] Und heute, laß es dir erzählen, heute morgen, stehen einige Churgäste und ich auf einer Terasse,

---

[2] Jena, 1875, p. 1.

[3] E. Feise, "Critical Essay," appended to his edition of *Die Leiden des jungen Werthers* (New York, 1914) 243; cf. Kindermann 44: "Der Leidenschaftsstil vieler Leipziger Briefe. . . geht späterhin. . . ein in die dichterische Weltbewältigung: von der Leidenschafts-atmosphäre der ersten Götz-Gestaltung bis zu der noch der Werther-Briefe sind die Spuren bemerkbar," and Heinrich Meyer in his review of Günther Müller's *Kleine Goethebiographie* (*Monatshefte* 35 [1943]: 426–27): "Wie [Barker] Fairley scheint Müller die Behrischbriefe wörtlich zu nehmen, indem er verkennt, daß es sich da doch auch um 'Literatur' handelt, genau wie die Käthchengeschichte Goethes erste bekannte Wertheriade ist."

[4] Goethe's letters are quoted from the first volume of M. Morris's *Der junge Goethe* (Leipzig, 1909, subsequently cited as *DjG*). The 1774 edition of *Werther* is quoted from Festausgabe, Vol. 9.

[5] *Boswell's Life of Johnson*, Oxford Standard Edition (New York [1933]) 2:341f.

siehe da kommt ein solches Thier mit vielen gewölbten Gängen durch das Graß daher, schaut uns mit hellen funckelnden Augen an spielt mit seiner spitzigen Zunge und schleicht mit aufgehabenem Haupte immer näher. [Stones are hastily seized, a few hits are made] daß sie mit Zischen die Flucht nahm. Ich sprang herunter, riß einen mächtigen Stein von der Mauer, und warf ihr ihn nach. er traf und erdruckte sie, worauf wir über dieselbe Meister wurden. . . .

The effort to magnify this incident is evident in "Dencke nur," in the dash for suspense and surprise after "allhier," in the interruption "laß es dir erzählen" separating "heute" from the more specific "heute morgen," in the emphatic "vielen" of "mit vielen gewölbten Gängen," in the vivid description of the deportment of the ever-approaching serpent-basilisk-dragon with its "aufge-habenem" head—linguistically conservative and elevated, like Werther's hands in his final letter—and in the rapid change of situation from defense to attack as our young hero successfully hurls a mighty rock at the foe. There is something Wieland-like in the technique of trying to make something out of so very little, although the humorous effect of summer-resort heroism is unintentional and therefore unworthy of that master; the anecdote suggests rather the vacuous animation of the epistolary specimens which Gellert had first published in 1751. As for the other incident, it is poeticized by the introduction of "eine wohlthätige Fee" who had marked the path leading out of the Rhenish wilderness—a rationalistic poeticization which in no way conceals an anticlimax when it follows "Bald stellte sich uns ein umschatteter Fels dar, bald ein düstres Gesträuch und nirgends war ein Ausgang zu finden."[6]

If this letter is typical of Goethe's prose efforts before he went to Leipzig, it is easy to understand why he could sooner or later have destroyed them. It is, however, valuable as an earliest example of his narrative letter style, the only prose style apparently deliberately cultivated by him—the *Judenpredigt* can certainly be disregarded—in the years prior to his sojourn at Strasbourg. In view of the young Goethe's belletristic ambitions, his early love of storytelling, it was inevitable that he should wish to practice the most popular literary prose form of the time as well as the verse forms of eighteenth-century poetry and drama, and so it may be reasonably assumed that his early letters are in some measure prose exercises, or at least reflect what has been practiced in literary exercises. Indeed, Goethe's early correspondence often forces upon the informed reader, who can see contradictions between almost simultaneous letters, or who otherwise possesses corrective evidence, an impression of artificiality of manner,

---

[6] For the exoticism of this letter, cf. the Abbé Prévost's American scene in such works as his *Histoire de M. Cleveland*, Livre XIII of which takes the narrator through pathless wildernesses.

though not an impression of deliberate misrepresentation, even in many an apparent outburst of unfettered sentiment; only the letters from the first half of 1774, when Goethe is intensively cultivating the letter form for explicit literary purposes in *Werther*, can perhaps be considered both directly self-revealing and frankly self-concealing, representative of a period when literary expression in prose found a full outlet in a literary work rather than surreptitiously or unconsciously in personal correspondence.

In Goethe's first letter from Leipzig imaginary speeches, not suspense-filled narrative episodes, best serve to enliven the epistolary style, which is still also marked, however, by exclamatory elements in word (*da!*; *sieh*) and punctuation. That Goethe's self-interruptions in his truly chaotic second paragraph do not represent incoherent irrationality, as the naive reader might be tempted to believe, may be inferred from the letter writer's consciousness of his literary mission, twice explicitly alluded to (*wir Poeten*; *auf Dichter Parole*) in that paragraph. In Werther's first letter the uncompleted sentence and the deliberate breaking off of discussion of a topic allow the reader insights into various traits of Werther's character, into varied interests past and present, without destroying the illusion of actual epistolary communication. In his next letter, which is almost pure literary monologue, the device of self-interruption (*Mein Freund—Aber ich. . .*) forces Werther's religiously rhapsodic outburst back into letter form, preserving not only the literary fiction but also the lyric effect of the previous lines: in an unfinished letter the reader cannot demand, unless he is unreasonable, the normal prosaic characteristics of epistolary communication; these, presumably, would have come later, but they are hardly to be found in the "letter" as it stands.

Still not a month in Leipzig, Goethe began a letter thus:

Leipzig den 20 Ocbtr 1765
Morgens um 6.

Riese, guten Tag!

d. 21. Abends um 5.

Riese, guten Abend!

Gestern hatte ich mich kaum hingesezt um euch eine Stunde zu wiedmen, Als schnell. . . .[7]

---

[7] This letter is cited by R. Weißenfels, *Goethe im Sturm und Drang* (Halle, 1894), as illustration of Goethe's stylistic striving "nach nichts so sehr, wie nach Natur, nach natur-wahrem, unmittelbarem Ausdruck der Empfindung und Situation, aus der heraus er

There follows an amusing soliloquy as Goethe wavers between continuing the hardly started letter and going to the theater, and then an informative account of his academic and other life is introduced, enlivened only by a pun "köstlich—kostspielig," a figurative "march of coins," and (perhaps) a "catalogue" of fish, flesh, and fowl from the *Küchenzettel.* This game of starting a letter twice is played, with variations, by Werther when he describes under the date "am 16. Juny" his first hours with Lotte. Werther protests that he is "vergnügt und glüklich, und so kein guter Historienschreiber," and claims that he has overcome the urge to postpone his account. But then we learn "Ich hab's nicht überwinden können, ich mußte zu ihr hinaus." Now, after a few brief lines which reveal that evening has come, Werther gains self-control: "höre denn, ich will mich zwingen ins Detail zu gehen," and an extraordinarily clear narrative, even containing faithfully recorded direct discourse, is presented. This narrative, begun June 16 and essentially completed by 2 A.M. of the 17th (cf. "am 19. Juny"), is complemented and concluded by one paragraph of June 19 telling of the return from the ball—a paragraph which patently contradicts the earlier statement of the same date about the specific hour of completion of the preceding letter, for it contains also the statement, "seit der Zeit können Sonne, Mond und Sterne geruhig ihre Wirthschaft treiben, ich weis weder daß Tag noch daß Nacht ist." In other words, Werther, like Goethe, does not hesitate to exploit the letter-writer's poetic license, although his disregard of prosaic facts, here probably humorous, will, unlike Goethe's, become a pathological disorder.

   In a letter from the end of October and early November, to Riese, is "das wahre bild" (in German and Latin verse) of Gottsched—primarily a picture of external details. Writing to Cornelia a month later (Dec. 6–7, 1765), Goethe characterizes his host and two table companions far more succinctly and effectively: physical description is minimized; gesture, voice, facial expression, and dominant psychological characteristics are emphasized. Thus in the briefest of the three sketches: "Magister *Morus.* Ein Teolog. Ein sehr artiger und geschickter Junger Mann: er redet wenig allein sieht immer freundlich aus." With this can be compared the many "physiognomical" introductions of characters in *Werther*—e.g., young V.., "ein offner Junge, mit einer gar glücklichen Gesichtsbildung" (cf. 1. Theil, den 17. May). Indeed, the last of the three sketches in the Leipzig letter, that of "Magister Herrmann Ein Mediciner," which borders on Hogarthian caricature, is interesting as an early example of a Wertherian figure in Goethe's

schreibt, nach dramatischer Lebendigkeit" (1:43).

writings[8]—"Er flieht die Welt, weil sie sich nicht nach ihm richten will"—a character whose exaggerated subjectivism, as imagined by Goethe, unfits him for life. And this Leipzig letter is interesting as the first to contain any mention of Richardson and his novels, novels for which Goethe is willing to make an exception (at first, all three, then only *Grandison*) as he prescribes more instructive reading as the proper fare of Cornelia.

Hardly more than a month later, writing to Cornelia January 17, 1766, Goethe comments on the reaction to a satiric poem that he had mentioned on December 12:

> Je m'en rejouis fort, si ma satire a pu trouver des originaux, autant plus, que je suis sûr, que je n'ai eu que la nature et les fautes universelles devant les yeux, en peignant ces portraits, et non pas, comme on pouroit penser, quelques personnes en particulier.

It may well be deduced from this statement of compositional principle that the psychological details in such a characterization as that of Herrmann, which was composed about the same time as the satire alluded to, were intended to lend the truth of Nature to the grotesquely particular. In *Werther*, not only does the protagonist himself—despite, and even because of, his consciousness of uniqueness—represent a widely found type; he also cultivates the brief characterization of general types represented by the already mentioned paragraph on young V..; and in his account of the thunderstorm's effect on certain young women at the ball he even arranges *caractères* in a triadic tableau (cf. penultimate paragraph, 1. Theil, am 16. Juny: "Die Klügste sezte sich. . .")—a far cry from practice of the *Vorsaz* "mich künftig allein an die Natur zu halten" enunciated as basic (Storm-and-Stress) aesthetic principle two letters earlier in connection with his discussion of drawing.

In March Goethe reproaches Cornelia at the same time that he praises her account of a wedding celebration: "tu n'as pas sçu peindre toutes les circonstances, d'une maniere si vive et si exacte, que je l'avois souhaitte et que j'avois lieu de l'attendre de ton addresse." (The ideal of lively detail is usually achieved with unconscious ease by Werther whenever he reports narrative or conversation, although a peculiar Storm-and-Stress tendency to naturalistic realism will best explain his introduction of such a detail as a snotty nose.) Later in this letter, Goethe returns to his favorite theme of Cornelia's readings, and illustrates the consequences of feminine vanity— viz., the failure to cultivate good authors—with an account of one young

---

[8] Not the earliest suicide—cf. "Exemplum Avtocheiriae," *DjG* 1:30–32.

lady's social *maladresse* imagined in rapid staccato style. (This theme recurs in *Werther* in reversed form, for there Lotte has outgrown most novels, as is well known, and is, moreover, the very paragon of young womanhood.) One passage in the letter, that dealing with Mlle Brevillier, is clearly modeled after a type situation of sentimental novels, the moment when it is discovered that a worthy character has been (long) unjustly misvalued (e.g., Lord Seymour by Sophie von La Roche's Fräulein von Sternheim; with more serious permanent hurt, "die arme Leonore" by Werther). Goethe begins the passage with expressions of admiration of the said young woman's demonstration of character in having kept her word, recalls his previous sympathy and esteem, and then summarizes the development of events which has finally confirmed his original opinion; his account ends with the general observation, "si on fait le juge trop vite, on court risque de faire le juge injuste"—the kind of moralization with which a Julie Wolmar will end a letter (e.g., *La Nouvelle Héloïse*, IV, xii: "j'éprouve avec douleur que le poids d'une ancienne faute est un fardeau qu'il faut porter toute sa vie"). In concluding his longish letter, Goethe explains why, with "tant a faire," he writes "de si longues lettres": "C'est pour me divertir que je fais cela." Surely a case of literary-educational divertissement!

The letter to Riese, April 28, 1766, is the earliest in which tones of strong pessimism are found, and several scholars have pointed out the Wertherian elements: "Einsamkeit," the pleasures of recollection "entfernt von jedermann, Am Bache, bey den Büschen," the changing aspect of nature as "Traurigkeit" increases ("Der Bach rauscht jetzt im Sturm vorüber"; "Kein Vogel singt in den Gebüschen"), the theme of humiliation (here avowedly only of himself as a literary aspirant). Whatever the origins of Goethe's mood and the degree of literal truth in the statements,[9] the irony of the formulation in *genre mêlé* of his renunciation of literary ambitions should not be overlooked, nor the fact that the brief prose passages represent a new stylistic tendency: "Einsam, Einsam, ganz einsam. Bester Rieße diese Einsamkeit," "so fühle ich dennoch allen Mangel. . . , Ich seufze. . . und wenn ich fühle daß ich vergebens seufze," "Aber wie froh bin ich, ganz froh," and "Lebt Wohl. . . Schreibt. . . Lebt wohl. . . Gewöhnt euch keine *academ*istische Sitten an. Liebt mich. Lebt Wohl. Lebt wohl." These are not examples of repetition for the sake of colloquial clarity and animation, but of repetition which expresses intensity of feeling—the writer seeks for words and can only repeat himself as he realizes that anaphora alone best make clear his idea, or he is so perturbed and distraught (last example) that

[9] Adolescent homesickness, end-of-winter vitamin deficiency, recurrence of depressive period, physical consequences of lying on damp and chilly ground—as well as injured pride?

he repeats unconsciously insignificant epistolary formulas. Goethe is here already "à l'école de Rousseau," is mastering a style to be effectively exploited in letters to Behrisch of 1767—and in *Die Leiden des jungen Werthers*;[10] perhaps this fact, not simply a desire to keep the home folks reassured about himself, partly authenticates the often doubted statement to Cornelia (September 27, 1766): "Ce qui regarde ma melancholie, elle n'est pas si forte, comme je l'ai depeinte, il y a quelquefois des manieres poetiques dans mes descriptions qui aggrandisent les faits."

In the letters from the rest of 1766 which have been preserved, no great innovations can be traced in Goethe's epistolary style. The two long letters to Cornelia (March 30-May 31; September 27-October 18) continue the moral, didactic, and satiric manner of previous correspondence: a less mature Saint-Preux, the young Goethe prescribes further reading for his sister; describes the psychology of solitude—and the charms of a garden more formal than Rousseau would have liked it; treats more general topics such as female education, "klein"-Parisian manners (cf. Saint-Preux's various ethnographical letters), the philosophic problem of free will, or the advantages for a young man of "acquaintance of young virtuos and honest ladies"; and, in English and under English literary influences, writes in "A Song over The Unconfidence towards my self" of his melancholia, his jealousy, and his artistic (poetic) impotence.[11] With one possible exception, these are all themes more or less important in *Werther*. In the second of these letters, moreover, there is an intelligent analysis of the dangers which result when epistolary prose is written under the influence of verse or poetic prose, and after a parody of Fénelon's language in *Télémaque*,[12] Goethe observes, not without self-satisfaction, "Je ne crois pas manquer, en attribuant a cette lecture [of too elevated styles], la faute commune des jeunes gens, de ne savoir pas ecrire des bonnes lettres": he evidently considers that he has mastered the art of blending *utile dulci*, of presenting serious ideas in a genuine letter form.

Within the time span of these two letters to Cornelia fall the letters to Trapp, Moors, and Behrisch which tell the story of Goethe's "passion pour la belle Charitas" (so nobly tragic and so rapidly terminated!) and of the initial stages of his "roman" (October 10 or 11) with Käthchen. In Madame

---

[10] Examples of this practice can be found on almost every page of *Werther*, and scattered throughout *La Nouvelle Héloïse*, especially the first two-thirds; some of the more striking parallels between the two novels are presented by Erich Schmidt 247–50.

[11] Cf. *La Nouvelle Héloïse*: I, xii (readings); I, xxxiii (solitude); IV, xi (gardens); V, iii (education); II, xiv ([Parisian] manners); VI, vii (free will); I, xliv (jealousy); etc.

[12] Section of letter dated September 27. The letter concludes (October 18) with a shorter parodistic allusion to prose romance.

Elie de Beaumont's *Lettres du Marquis de Roselle*, which Goethe had read before the end of May and which he mentioned again to Cornelia in September, he found not only acceptable ideas on "l'erudition des filles," but also the story of a man who loved a woman beneath his class and was willing to sacrifice family name to his love of an (apparent) paragon of virtue. Among the lines addressed to Trapp on June 2 are: "Chassons le vil honneur! que l'amour soit mon maître. / J'ecouterai lui seul, lui seul doit me guider, / Au sommet du bonheur par lui je vais monter." This suggestion of egalitarianism, here half subordinated to the theme of the ennobling power of passion (cf. *La Nouvelle Héloïse*, II, xi, toward end), anticipates the passage to Moors (October 1) beginning "Was ist der Stand. Eine eitle Farbe die die Menschen erfunden haben, um Leute die es nicht verdienen mit anzustreichen"—a passage which recalls utterances of Mylord Edouard Bomston on behalf of Julie and Saint-Preux (cf. *Héloïse*, I, lxii), as well as of the misguided Marquis de Roselle. The influence of literature on life can be seen in many details of these various letters,[13] but for the writing of *Werther* the narrative skill which they reveal is more important than the fact that they happen to deal with "frustrated" passion, with "un amour" (to Trapp, October 1, of Charitas), with a lover who, professing to value virtue[14] more than "Stand," can write (on the same day, to Moors, of Käthchen) in anticipation of frustration: "Das fürtreffliche Herz meiner S. ist mir Bürge, daß sie mich nie verlassen wird, *als dann wenn es* uns Pflicht und Noht-wendigkeit gebieten werden uns zu trennen" (italics mine). Lotte will observe to Werther, "ich fürchte, es ist nur die Unmöglichkeit mich zu besizzen, die Ihnen diesen Wunsch so reizend macht," as she charges him with deceiving himself (2. Theil, am 20. Dec.); in the case of the young Goe-the the "passion" seems rather the answer to a poet's needs, for he had written to Cornelia on September 27, "Si j'avois une belle, peutetre Cupidon me feroit il chanter plus, et mieux," and to Behrisch he writes on October

---

[13] A. Letters meant for another than the addressee (to Trapp, June 2 and October 1—in the latter direct allusion to this fact). B. The language of passion: "mon coeur sensible et tendre," "ce coeur farouche," "cet amour ardent," "mes sentimens impeteux" (same letters); "jezo füle ich zum aller erstenmhale das Glück das eine wahre Liebe macht" (to Moors); the lines beginning "What pleasure, God! of like a flame to born" (to Behrisch). C. The writing, as the "correct" thing to do, of a letter—to Behrisch!—at Käthchen's desk (cf. *La Nouvelle Héloïse*, I, liv: Saint-Preux writes to Julie from her room; and *Lettres du Marquis de Roselle*, xxxvi: the marquis at Léonor's secretary—where he finds a letter guilefully left where he will discover it). D. "Correspondence secrete" with a beloved in the same house, a traditional motif of comedy (to Behrisch, October 12).

[14] "Ich habe die Gewogenheit meines Mädgens nicht denen kleinen elenden Trakas-serien des Liebhaber zu dancken, nur durch meinen Charakter, nur durch mein Herz habe ich sie erlangt"—cf. Werther's consciousness of his own virtue, and also his "Ach was ich weis, kann jeder wissen.—Mein Herz hab ich allein" (2. Theil, am 9. May, end).

12, after his lines "What pleasure, God! of like a flame to born": "Pardonnez moi, en pensant, que nous ne sommes jamais si fertiles en expressions, que quand notre coeur nous en fournit."

If, by the end of 1766, Goethe had practiced most of the variant types of expository-narrative letter, he had nevertheless failed to master them completely. For one thing, the habit of employing several languages in the same letter, which only ends after the middle of 1767, did not always contribute to unity of tone. Various attempts to build up romantic situations are ineffectual because the letter writer falls out of his role: for instance, in the letter from the "secretaire de ma petite," our hero tells how he has enjoyed the flavor of the two apples Käthchen has given him, and seems to have difficulty in filling the page and passing the happy hours until her return. And the greatest art of all, sympathetic self-portrayal which avoids the obviously egotistic—which Goethe will achieve in *Werther*—is hardly characteristic of any of the sentimental passages; Goethe still has to learn how to express himself less bluntly than he does here (to Cornelia, October 18, 1766):

> Noch eine andere Ursache warum man mich in der grosen Welt nicht leiden kann. Ich habe etwas mehr Geschmack und Kenntniß vom Schönen, als unsere galanten Leute und ich konnte nicht umhin ihnen offt in großer Gesellschafft, das armseelige von ihren Urteilen zu zeigen.

In Werther's early letters, which establish his attractiveness, similar ideas and revelations of character are far more subtly presented (cf. especially 1. Theil, 17. May).

For the period from October, 1766, until the following October, Goethe's epistolary style can only be studied in three letters to Cornelia, and there is a gap of seven months between the letter of May 11–15, 1767, and the previous one. This letter of May, 1767, not only reflects the writer's greater maturity and self-assurance—"Man lasse doch mich gehen, habe ich Genie; so werde ich Poete werden, und wenn mich kein Mensch verbessert, habe ich keins; so helfen alle Criticken nichts"; it also reveals an easy mastery of the letter form which would seem to indicate that earlier practice was finally bearing fruit, and therefore demands detailed analysis.

The opening paragraph is especially felicitous, for Goethe disarmingly balances the factual explanations of why he has failed to write, a too common theme of introductory sentences, with delicate flattery and irony; he is "beschämt" *and* "von allen Seiten beschämt" (i.e., he has been reproached by himself, and in oral *and* written messages—he thus even appears to deserve some pity as the victim of friendly persecution!), he reminds Cornelia of her "Güte" and "zärtliches Herz," appeals to her sympathy by recalling his (recent) illness and his (admirable) sensitivity to the charms of Nature (cf. the heroines and heroes of Rousseau and of Madame Riccoboni—the latter is named in the next paragraph!), mentions a relapse, suggests conscientious preparations for "das unwichtige Amt eines *Opponenten*," and only at the end of his paragraph admits to laziness (in a metaphor!—"die kleine Faulheit die manchesmal in meinen Händen liegt ist durch deinen letzten Brief gänzlich gehoben"). The final sentence, "Und ich hoffe daß du nach geendigter Lesung dieses Briefs, völlig mit mir ausgesöhnt seyn wirst," means that Goethe is sure that he has already more than half achieved reconcilement; at the same time the sentence motivates the reading of the rest of the letter, and even implies a large though loose compositional plan.

Continuing in French, Goethe devotes two paragraphs to reconciliation of his sister, whom he does not blush to call "un esprit mur, une Riccoboni"; in the second of these the still young author implies that he considers the letter an art form: "Je t'avoue, je ne saurois pas de tout mon art prodouire une scene, comme la nature t'en a dictée une." The theme of the incomparability of Cornelia affords a transition to a series of half a dozen *caractères* (next three paragraphs), only the first of which, Mlle Breitkopf, contains (in the middle sentence) a reference back to Cornelia (in her writing one notices "trop l'air etudié, faute de ce stile simple que j'admire en toi"). The cultivation of the *caractère* is a noteworthy characteristic of the novels of Madame Riccoboni, herself a disciple of the author of *Marianne*, herself also familiar with the *caractère* in dramatic literature by virtue of her earlier theatrical career; the opening pages of her admired *Lettres de Mylady Juliette Catesby* (1759) contain several letters in which two or three successive paragraphs, like Goethe's here, give pictures of two or three of Juliette's immediate associates. In his portraits of table companions of December 6–7, 1765, Goethe had emphasized externals; now he attempts, not unsuccessfully, to give a "portrait moral," to give in a brief compass some impression of the depths of character, and at the same time he relates the persons described to himself by indicating their reactions to him and his to them. The technique here mastered is also exploited in *Werther*, and Goethe's paragraph beginning "Quoique morte, j'aime, j'estime la conseillere Böhme, plus que touttes les belles vivantes" stands comparison very well with Werther's beginning "Ach daß die Freundin meiner Jugend dahin ist," despite the stronger emotional subjectivity of the latter (1. Theil, 17. May).

If Goethe has been warned from home against youthful infatuation, or has fears that rumors of such an infatuation have reached home, the series of character sketches purportedly introduced to allow Cornelia comparisons with herself is also meant to allow Goethe to write: "ie les aime touttes [mes connoissances. . . un peu bornees], sans m'attacher a aucune [etc.]."

Returning to German after this observation, Goethe immediately charges his sister with an indiscretion, and so at the same time as he quickly gets away from what may be a ticklish topic he completes the reversal of his and his sister's relative moral positions. The rest of the letter is an innocuous account of himself and his literary interests—in which, however, he does not neglect to insist *en passant* "Pour l'amour veritable, il ne faut pas, q'un Poete en sente."

If the foregoing analysis of this one letter is correct in its emphasis on conscious construction, organization, and thematic repetition, it would be misleading to say of the pre-Weimar Goethe that "It was obviously difficult, if not impossible, for him to sustain a letter at any rational level."[15] It might, on the contrary, be possible to claim that he had revealed a talent for prose composition comparable to the talent evident in so deceptively simple a dramatic composition as *Die Laune des Verliebten*. "Auch das Genie beginnt als Talent. Die Poesie hat so gut ein handwerkliches Abc, das es zu erlernen gilt, wie die anderen Künste; und die Kraft des ursprünglichen Erlebens entfaltet sich später als der Trieb und die Fähigkeit, fremde Denk- und Gefühlsgehalte aufzufassen und wiederzugeben."[16] Goethe's achievement in this letter to Cornelia is sufficient proof of talent; what he practices in 1767 will be second nature—"La coutume," wrote Pascal, "est une seconde nature"—when he writes *Werther* in 1774. His first completed novel will be a highly polished work chiefly because of the long apprenticeship begun years before; and though Gundolf may properly minimize "kluge Absicht der Komposition" in discussing characterization, motifs, and themes in *Werther*,[17] it would also surely be unjust to imply that Goethe's mastery of form in that novel was the result of almost effortless inspiration rather than the achievement of conscious efforts well spent at some earlier period or periods.

Between October, 1767, and May, 1768, Goethe's preserved letters are all addressed to Behrisch, with the exception of one letter of October 12–14 to Cornelia. If the biographical value of these letters is great, especially because of what they reveal of the personality of the young Goethe and the workings of his mind, they are not less important because of the way in which they do so: because of the skill at self-analysis which they demon-

---

[15] B. Fairley, *A Study of Goethe* (Oxford, 1947) 32; cf. also 4–26.

[16] K. Viëtor, *Der junge Goethe* (Leipzig, 1930) 7.

[17] Cf. F. Gundolf, *Goethe* (Berlin, 1920) 166ff., who is apparently attempting to counteract the effect of such observations as Morris's "hier beginnt die lange Reihe der kunstvoll eingefügten, sich immer steigernden Vordeutungen auf den Ausgang" (*DjG* 6:415) or Erich Schmidt's "Ich bemerke noch, daß diese prophetischen Andeutungen des Selbstmordes meist sehr wirkungsvoll an den Schluß der Briefe gestellt sind" (243).

strate, because of the ability to preserve complete (artistic) unity of theme which several of them exemplify.

The first of these letters to Behrisch begins: "Ich muß dir etwas schrif[t]lich sagen, weil ich mich für deinem Spott fürchte, wenn ich dir es mündlich sagen wollte. [...] Ich will kurz seyn. Ich verlange deine Ge-dancken deinen Raht. . . ." Then, after briefly indicating the circumstances of the arrival of a young man who may be a potential rival in love, Goethe describes his vacillation between suspicion and the will to faith. When the evidence for and against suspicion has been given, the letter ends: "Rahte mir im ganzen. [...] Nur spotte mich nicht, wenn ich's auch verdient hätte." This return to the opening tone of supplication rounds out the letter as a whole and insists on the essential epistolary character of what otherwise could be interpreted to be primarily an attempt at self-clarification; at the same time it changes the original request for counsel into a request for reassurance. The latter ironic function of the closing words of the letter is surely intended, and it would seem to indicate that even in the young Goe-the intensity of experience was accompanied by no loss of feeling for aesthetic or, at least, compositional values. A somewhat similar rhetorical pattern appears in *Werther*, where, for instance, one letter begins "Was man ein Kind ist!"—which seems to be a general statement connected with earlier utterances of Werther's on the subject of children and the childlike, as in the final sentence of the letter immediately preceding ("wir sollen es mit den Kindern machen, wie Gott mit uns")—and ends "O was ich ein Kind bin!" after an account of one lover's hopes and doubts (1. Theil, am 8. Juli). And Werther's last letter to Charlotte, like this one to Behrisch, is above all an attempt at self-clarification.

Literary antecedents for this type of letter are probably as common as the experience which it describes; it may be noted, however, that Madame Riccoboni was particularly adept at writing such letters for her heroines, and that about half those in her almost completely plotless *Lettres de Mistress Fanni Butlerd, à Mylord Charles Alfred, comte d'Erford* (1757) might be placed in this category.[18] The characters of Riccoboni—like Rousseau's Saint-Preux with his "que c'est un fatal présent du ciel qu'une âme sensible" (*Hé-loïse* I, xxvi; cf. opening lines of third ode to the departing Behrisch)—are fond of sententious generalizations in the midst of their emotional crises, and a careful reader will find at least three in this letter to Behrisch, al-though Goethe begs to be excused for but one. Whatever its appro-priateness to younger or more naive characters, the habit of making

---

[18] In her more eventful *Lettres de Mylady Juliette Catesby; à Lady Henriette Campley, son amie* (1759) letters of this type are also to be found (e.g., xxxv).

philosophical observations will be entirely proper in a character like Werther, who has been undermined, as Goethe wrote to Schönborn, by "Spekulation"; contemporary readers of *Werther*, accustomed to the directly didactic in novels, would not have minded sententious maxims delivered out of character—the review of *Werther* in *Der Teutsche Merkur* of December, 1774, contains the revealing observation, "Außer der Kunst des Verfassers, die Nüance aller Leidenschaften zu treffen, verdient die populäre Philosophie Lob, womit er sein ganzes Werk durchwürzt hat."

Goethe's two other letters to Behrisch before the latter's departure from Leipzig are very different in tone from the one just considered. The first is concerned chiefly with Goethe's poetic interests and local news, and contains but a passing reference to the affair of his heart. The second, composed the morning after the farewell celebration of the two friends, is a reminder to Behrisch of a promise to say certain things to Käthchen which will serve Goethe's cause; it is in the politic form of an amusing account of the uneasy night of "ein eifersüchtiger Liebhaber" who has drunk "ebensoviel Champagner" (in his friend's honor) "als er brauchte, um sein Blut in eine angenehme Hitze zu setzen und seine Einbildungskraft auf's äuserste zu entzünden"; and even the concluding invitation to a last farewell explicitly states "NB nach der *Affaire* von unten." That this letter is in a high degree dispassionate, as internal evidence suggests, is confirmed by what Goethe writes the same morning to Cornelia (October 12–14: 2nd day): "Im Vertrauen zu reden ich bin diesen Morgen sehr lustig ob gleich Behrisch diesen Abend fortgeht"—this in a letter in which once more Goethe advises Cornelia in matters of narrative style, demanding ideas less "brouillirt," "Empfindung" in addition to "nackte Erzählung."[19] The dreams of Goethe's "so eine Nacht, wie diese, Behrisch" hardly compare with those of Werther's "Diese Nacht!" (2. Theil, am 17. Dez.), but their exploitation apparently represents the introduction of a new device in Goethe's sentimental narrative style, although one long exploited in literature and one not neglected by sentimental novelists (e.g., *La Nouvelle Héloïse*, V, ix).

The next two letters to Behrisch are so interesting biographically that it is difficult to read them primarily as evidence in which developments in Goethe's narrative technique may be traced; they are, however, important entirely apart from problems of *Erfahrung*, *Erlebnis*, or *Erlebnisdrang*, or even of the constituent proportions of these elements.

In the letter of October 16–17 Goethe records "einen kleinen Dialog, mit meinem Mädgen." He no longer uses the direct discourse of animation of

---

[19] The leading exemplifier of the combination "ideas-feeling-narrative" at the time of Goethe's writing was certainly Rousseau, whose primitivistic paradox Goethe terms in this letter to Cornelia "die verehrungswürdigste Wahrheit."

earlier letters, but a mixture of indirect discourse and interpretative obser-
vation (e.g., "da drückte sie mir die Hände und hatte die Tränen in den
Augen die eigentlich deinem Abschiede bestimmt waren"). Intentionally or
not, the passage reveals the character of Käthchen better than any of Goe-
the's earlier analytical *caractères*; the method will be used again, in *Werther*,
when Lotte is introduced, although minor characters in the novel—and even
Albert when he first appears (1.Theil, am 30. Juli)—are disposed of in the
more wholly subjective manner of *caractère*. Later in the paragraph
containing the dialogue with Käthchen, though in another connection, is a
phrase ("da spielen wir einen Roman *vice versa*") which may perhaps
indicate that Goethe was in some degree conscious of a novelist's problems
as he wrote; earlier in the letter, certainly, a parallel is drawn between
scenes in life and in drama:[20]

Hernach geh ich einmal zu meiner Kleinen, spiele der Abwechslung wegen
einige Scenen aus des Goldonis Verliebten. . . . Ich habe heute wieder so
einen dummen Auftritt gehabt, über einen dummen Zahnstocher, das nicht
der Mühe wehrt war; aber heutzutage da's einem um die Situationen so
Noht tuht, sieht mann überall wo mann sie herkriegt, und die kriegt ich
nun vom Zahnstocher. Es ist eine schöne Sache um's Genie.

And it is surely in the tradition of the novel that an apparently sober writer
should declare, "Gute Nacht ich binn besoffen wie eine Bestie"; Saint-
Preux's weakness is well known (*La Nouvelle Héloïse*, I, l–lii and, with
"criminal" results, II, xxvi), and an alcoholic lapse like his is the key to the
plot of Madame Riccoboni's earlier *Lettres de Mylady Juliette Catesby*
(d'Ossery feels obliged to marry the Miss Jenny whom he had raped under
the influence of liquor); even Werther, whom we have not yet seen drunk,
will declare to Albert, "Ich bin mehr als einmal trunken gewesen" (1. Theil,
am 12. Aug.) and will later be reproached by Lotte for letting himself be
seduced at times by one glass of wine "eine Bouteille zu trinken" (2. Theil,
am 8. Nov.).

[20] This point is hardly brought out in the notes of Morris (*DjG*, 6:28: "in seiner Komödie
Gl'Inamorati [i.e., Gl' Innamorati] schildert Goldoni anschaulich und mit einer Fülle
naturwahrer Züge das Gebaren Verliebter, ihr Jauchzen und ihre Verzweiflung, ihre
Zärtlichkeit und ihre Wutausbrüche") or of Kindermann (p. 358: "Goldoni schildert in dieser
Komödie das seltsame Gebaren Verliebter"). More relevant to Goethe's situation is the
continued willful irritability of Goldoni's lovers, which seems eventually to serve only to
postpone the play's dénouement. This letter is the one from which Fairley, in "Inspiration
and Letter-Writing: A Note on Goethe's Beginnings as a Poet" (*Germanic Review* 24 [1949]:
161–67), cites at most length to demonstrate the "artlessness" and "uncouthness" (163) of
Goethe's pre-Strasbourg letters.

Goethe's next letter (October 24) suggests that he himself realizes that he writes his letters not merely as correspondence, but also as self-expression: the statement, "Dein Brief ist gut, denn er ist lang, meiner wird nach diesem Maasstabe nicht gut werden. Ich habe heut keine Schreib-laune," certainly lends itself to such an interpretation. Otherwise the letter offers nothing new, although it is interesting for containing sententious quotation (from *Die Laune des Verliebten*) not used for deliberate ironic effect (and the first Italian word in many months, *Vigliettis*, perhaps brought into use by the reading of Goldoni's *Gl' Innamorati*—where it occurs as early as I, 2).

An account of his serious fall from his horse opens the letter to Behrisch of November 2–3, in which Goethe attempts to analyze, more subtly than in any of his previous prose, problems of sentiment with special reference to love's misery and the pleasure of being miserable, to friendship and sympathy. Although the letter's speculative passage has a close thematic relationship to *Werther*—for instance, Werther, like Goethe here, develops a parallel between physical and psychic illness (1. Theil, am 12. Aug.)—it is stylistically remarkable because what gives the impression of associative thought apparently moving farther and farther away from the opening idea is effectively referred back to that idea by a closing comparison of the situation of "the friend" with that of "the lover." That Goethe is very conscious of the problem of form at the time of writing is evident from the observation earlier in his letter, "Das ist ein Paragraf in dem die Figur meines Gehirns modelirt ist, verwirrt, und unzusammenhängend." And serious as is his letter as a whole, Goethe the apprentice author seems unable to forget his mission entirely, for he concludes: "Du wirst über meinen Brief lachen, er ist sehr sententiös. Ich kann mir nicht helfen, ich habe viele gute Gedancken, und kann sie nirgends brauchen als gegen dich. Wäre ich Autor, da würde ich sparsamer seyn, um sie ans Publikum dermal-einst verschwenden zu können."

The euphoria of Goethe's next letter (November 7)—"Ja Behrisch ich habe meine Jetty eine halbestunde ruhig, ohne Zeugen unterhalten"—is expressed in the conventional language of sentimentality; most noteworthy is the fetishistic "diese Hand." The letter as a whole is significant chiefly because it seems to suggest that the writer is uncertain whether he will be a version of Saint-Preux or of Lovelace. The long letter of November 10–14, however, which represents the climax of Goethe's "Geschichte des Herzens" (cf. November 20), reveals that he is a virtuous lover who suffers very much in the tradition of the protagonists of such novels as Madame Riccoboni's *Juliette Catesby* and who is still so essentially Goethean as to bear striking resemblances to Werther (cf. 2. Theil, am 3. Nov.). As Goethe explains on the evening of the 11th:

Ich habe meinen Brief wieder durchgelesen und würde ihn gewiß zer-
reissen, wenn ich mich schämen dürfte, vor dir in meiner eigentlichen
Gestalt zu erscheinen. Dieses heftige Begehren, und dieses eben so heftige
Verabscheun, dieses Rasen und diese Wollust werden dir den Jüngling
kentlich machen, und du wirst ihn bedauern.

The first of these sentences expresses not only a normal youthful
preoccupation with self, but also a certain degree of self-satisfaction perhaps
meant to justify the preservation of the previous well-written pages; the
second recalls the introductory lines of *Werther*.

In this "Werckgen"—the term Goethe uses on the 13th—can be found
most of the stylistic and compositional elements which have been noted in
Goethe's previous letters; there they were often unassimilated to the whole
composition and even seemed at times incongruous, but here they are all
in the proper place and the previous practice of them explains how Goethe
could tell his by no means uncomplicated story, with its interruptions and
flashbacks, without need of revision. The stammerings of passion, the
exclamations, the rhetorical questions, the interruptions, the direct and
indirect discourse, the *Sentenz* and the sententious quotation—all these are
here, and one previously neglected device beloved particularly of the
heroines of Madame Riccoboni: the quotation (rather than the enclosure) of
another person's correspondence.[21] One direct comparison with an earlier
letter will show clearly that proper practice can lead to relative perfection:
on November 7 Goethe wrote "So eine Stunde! Was sind tausend, von den
runzlichten, todten, mürrischen Abenden gegen sie?" while on the 11th he
achieves the pregnancy of *"Ein* Augenblick Vergnügen ersetzt tausende voll
Quaal."[22]

With this letter a point in the development of Goethe's sentimental
narrative style is reached beyond which he will not seem to advance in the
next years, at least technically. If letters to Langer, to Herder, Kestner, Lotte,
and other new friends contain profounder self-analyses and more objective
tones of irony, it is because the writer is a more mature and more complex

---

[21] Cf. the quotation of Lotte's note to Albert in the revised *Werther* (Zweites Buch, am
5. September).

[22] That "So wird's seyn morgen, übermorgen, und immer fort" (November 11) is an echo
of Saint-Preux (*La Nouvelle Héloïse*, V, vii), has often been remarked. It may also be pointed
out that a jealous lover's suicide threat—Goethe's "weißt du was ich meyne" two
paragraphs later—is a motif of Goldoni's *Gl' Innamorati* (II, xiii). In his next letter
(November 20) Goethe makes reference to his and Behrisch's diagnosis of "Stolz" as a
motive of Käthchen's behavior; in Goldoni's comedy pride is the ultimate reason for the
erratic conduct of the heroine, Eugenia, and even in the first scene Flamminia observes,
"Un poco più d'umiltà, sorella."

person. What has survived of "Ariane an Wetty" does not substantiate any assumption that Goethe mastered the art of the large-scale epistolary novel with several successfully characterized correspondents, and it may well be doubted if the lost epistolary prose tales submitted to Gellert in Leipzig were better than reported in the sixth book of *Dichtung und Wahrheit*. What he adapted to the needs of his own correspondence, what he was able to make truly his own, that will reappear again and again in the years before *Werther*, and in *Werther*. And at the same time many of the more obviously mannered elements will tend to disappear from his personal letters, only to reappear for a last time and be objectivized in *Werther*: surely the letters to intimates written in the first half of 1774 are on the whole among the most un-Wertherian of the younger Goethe, while *Werther* itself is remarkable because of the "uncompromising realism"[23] with which it represents all the phenomena of sentimentality—those of language and style as well as those of idea and feeling.

The letters which have been discussed in the foregoing paragraphs are from a period of less than three years, and yet they reflect in miniature the variety of style which will be a noteworthy characteristic of Goethe's whole literary achievement. Most important, the later letters are frequently so unified in tone as not to give the effect of *pastiche* which so often mars experimental writing. Goethe seems to have learned empirically what contemporary novelists such as Richardson, Riccoboni, Gellert, Wieland, and La Roche had not: that artistic verisimilitude or, since these are primarily personal letters, effective self-communication is only possible if successive themes develop from their predecessors, or if they are immediately associated with a main problem of a central personality. Hence the disappearance of incongruous didactic, philosophic, and moralistic digressions, and perhaps of more obvious forms of irony, may be considered evidence of an increasing feeling for the interrelation of form and content that could hardly have been so rapidly achieved in a medium where direct self-reference was less possible. To paraphrase Egle's lines in Scene 4 of *Die Laune des Verliebten*: "Ein junges Herz nimmt leicht den Eindruck vom Roman, / Allein ein Herz das liebt, nimmt ihn noch *besser* an." It is not necessary to claim that in writing *Werther* Goethe consciously returned to the literary and personal experiences of his Leipzig years because certain analogies between that novel and letters of those years can be pointed out. But it is not unreasonable to believe that techniques the mastery of which he then came close to attaining stood him in good stead when the moment

---

[23] E.L. Stahl, in his edition of *Die Leiden des jungen Werthers* (Oxford, 1945) xxii, where the words are referred only to "Goethe's account of Werther's death."

came to write the magnificently objective novel of Storm-and-Stress senti-
mentality which he entitled *Die Leiden des jungen Werthers.*[24]

---

[24] The foregoing *rapprochement* of *Werther* and Goethe's Leipzig letters is not intended
to demonstrate that Goethe returned in 1774 to a pre-Storm-and-Stress style. Even the
number of pre-Wetzlar experiences incorporated in *Werther* is larger than has usually been
realized, however (cf. E. Beutler, "Wertherfragen," *Goethe Viermonatsschrift* 5 [1940]: 138–
60), and so such a *rapprochement* can perhaps help decompartmentalize and deperiodize
our picture of Goethe by bringing into relief another aspect of the cumulative pattern of
development of his artistic and total personality.

J.C. Lavater and Goethe: Problems of Psychology and Theology in *Die Leiden des jungen Werthers*

I.

Johann Caspar Lavater is one of the three writers personally known to Goethe whose names are mentioned most often in *Dichtung und Wahrheit*. The other two are Herder and Merck:[1] Herder, whose stimulating influence on Goethe may be easily discerned in countless passages of *Die Leiden des jungen Werthers* and whose *Vom Erkennen und Empfinden der menschlichen Seele* has been suggested as "a more probable (and more systematic) source of psychological information for Goethe than the vague 'Sturm-und-Drang-Psychologie' sometimes indicated as the framework of the novel";[2] Merck—"dieser eigne Mann, der auf mein Leben den größten Einfluß gehabt," Goethe declares in *Dichtung und Wahrheit*—who in 1772 played a role in Goethe's life very like that of the far blinder and less effectual Wilhelm in the story of Werther, and who in 1774 insisted that Goethe submit *Die Leiden des jungen Werthers* for publication without making any revisions in the manuscript.[3] Lavater, however, enjoys a

---

[1] Cf. R. Weber, "Personen- und Sachregister zu 'Dichtung und Wahrheit,' " Festausgabe 16: 633, 626, 638; and G. von Loeper's index to *Dichtung und Wahrheit* (Hempel edition).

[2] R.T. Clark, Jr., "The Psychological Framework of Goethe's *Werther*," *JEGP* 46 (1947): 273–78; for quotation cf. *PMLA* 61 (1946): 1366. H. Gose, *Goethes "Werther." Bausteine z. Gesch. d. dt. Lit.* XVIII (Halle a.S., 1921) 101ff., utilizes this essay as well as other writings of Herder's to demonstrate "daß auch der junge Herder die Pandynamische Denkart schon so früh in sich ausgebildet hatte, daß eine Beeinflussung des Wertherdichters möglich war." Since there was a certain estrangement between Herder and Goethe from May 1773 until the end of 1774, it may be doubted whether Goethe knew and was influenced by an essay the earliest preserved draft of which is dated 1774.

[3] Merck's not too effective attempts to get Goethe away from Wetzlar and Lotte Buff are described in *Dichtung und Wahrheit*, 12. Buch: "seine Gegenwart, sein Zureden, beschleunigte doch [because Goethe did not leave Wetzlar until three weeks after Merck had departed from Darmstadt] den Entschluß, den Ort zu verlassen." Several characters in *Werther* besides Wilhelm have Merckian traits: Merck tried to divert Goethe's attention from Lotte by praising "die junonische Gestalt einer ihrer Freundinnen" and scolded him "daß ich mich nicht um diese prächtige Gestalt bemüht, um so mehr, da sie frei, ohne irgend ein Verhältnis sich befinde" (*D.u.W.*); Lotte says, "Warum denn mich! Werther! . . . ich fürchte, es ist nur die Unmöglichkeit mich zu besitzen, die Ihnen diesen Wunsch so reizend macht," to which Werther's comment is, "sehr weise! hat vielleicht Albert diese Anmerkung

distinction which neither Herder nor Merck shares with him: his name appears twice in the pages of *Werther*. It is therefore somewhat surprising that Goethe's connections with Lavater have not been systematically examined to see whether they throw any light on the meaning of the novel as a whole.[4] To be sure, Goethe himself is partly responsible for this sin of scholarly omission, since in his own critical study of *Werther*—the relevant passages in *Dichtung und Wahrheit*—he makes no mention of Lavater; later writers have simply followed suit, forgetting that compositional logic rather than any principle of strict chronology determines the moment when Lavater begins to play as important a role in *Dichtung und Wahrheit* as he did in the life of the young Goethe.[5]

When Goethe wrote *Werther*, he had not yet met Lavater, but the two men had been active correspondents since over a year before.[6] Lavater had been impressed by Goethe's *Zwo biblische Fragen* (1773), although Goethe had already reviewed, not very approvingly, Lavater's *Aussichten in die Ewigkeit: 3. Band* in the *Frankfurter Gelehrte Anzeigen* for November 3, 1772. The written exchange of ideas on religion led to a friendship between Goethe and Lavater that was strengthened by their personal association in the summer of 1774 and that lasted for several years; Goethe's collaborative interest in Lavater's physiognomical studies is its best known fruit. The two mentions of Lavater in *Werther*, both favorable, are good evidence that its author appreciated the importance of what might be called his "Lavater experience" even in its pre-physiognomical stage. The first mention, made in Goethe's own person, is found in a footnote to a passage in Werther's letter of July 1, 1771, and reads: "Wir haben nun von Lavatern eine trefliche

gemacht?" (Dec. 20, 1772. All *Werther* references are to the text of the first edition by date of letter.) Werther puts Merck-like advice in the mouth of the philistine of his "Gleichniß" in his letter of May 26, 1771: "feiner junger Herr, lieben ist menschlich, nur müßt ihr menschlich lieben! Theilet eure Stunden ein. . . ." Goethe's powers of psychological observation and analysis can only have been strengthened by his association with a man of Merck's "Menschenkenntnis" (cf. H. Bräuning-Octavio, *Goethe-Handbuch*, ed. J. Zeitler, 2:586).

[4] Ernst Feise has suggested that Werther's letter of Nov. 15, 1772, "the theistic tone of which somewhat contradicts the earlier pantheism of Werther, is probably due to Goethe's disagreement with Lavater" (*Die Leiden des jungen Werthers von. . . Goethe*, Oxford German Series [New York, 1914] 213; cf. also his "Zu Entstehung, Problem und Technik von Goethes 'Werther,' " *JEGP* 13 [1914]: 1–36, n. 77, p. 29).

[5] *Werther* is treated in 12.–13. Buch (genesis, composition, reception of the novel). By composition *Werther* belongs to the spring of 1774. The 14. Buch of *D.u.W.* covers the summer of 1774, and introduces Lavater, whom Goethe then met for the first time; there is a brief retrospective survey of their relationship, for up to this point in *D.u.W.* there have been but three passing references to Lavater.

[6] Early 1773; cf. *Goethe-Handbuch* 4:424.

Predigt hierüber [i.e., über die üble Laune] unter denen über das Buch Jonas." The other mention is made by Werther in his letter of September 15, 1772, an account of his return visit to St. . . , the scene of the action of the July 1 letter: Werther reports that the new "Frau Pfarrern" has impiously had "die herrlichen Nußbäume" of cherished associations cut down, and excitably calls her "eine Frazze, die sich abgiebt gelehrt zu seyn, sich in die Untersuchung des Canons melirt, gar viel an der neumodischen moralisch kritischen Reformation des Christenthums arbeitet, und über Lavaters Schwärmereyen die Achseln zukt." For Werther the word "Schwärmerey" has no less positive a value than does "treflich" for Goethe, who, especially as author of the satirical *Prolog zu den neuesten Offenbarungen Gottes: Verteutscht durch Dr. Karl Friedrich Bahrdt* (certainly a "neumodischer moralisch kritischer Reformator des Christentums"), must be thought of as sharing, at least partially, Werther's scale of values. Since the first three volumes of Lavater's *Aussichten in die Ewigkeit* constitute the most important of his early (religious) "Schwärmereyen," and since Goethe's review of the third volume shows him to have been familiar with all three, it must be assumed that Werther—who is in a sense Werther-Goethe—has also read them.[7] And since the author of *Werther*, the Goethe of February, March, and April 1774, was still to a great extent the Goethe who read Lavater's *Aussichten* in the fall of 1772, it will be not unprofitable to point out briefly how certain ideas and attitudes which Goethe expressed when he reviewed the *Aussichten* reappear in *Werther*.

Although Goethe ends his review of the *Aussichten* with a conciliatory sentence,[8] it consists chiefly of objections. He disapproves of offering "nur Aussichten für *Denkende* und *Gelehrte*" (although this is Lavater's announced purpose), for, like Werther, he esteems feelings more than "Verstand und Talente."[9] He finds that the letters of the third volume "nach unsrer Empfindung sogar hinter den vorigen zurückbleiben," protesting: "Und wir haben in diesen Briefen nichts gesucht, als was uns der Verf. versprach, ausgegoßne Ahndungen, innige Empfindungen von Freund zu

---

[7] Cf. F. Buriot Darsiles, *Goethe: Les Souffrances du jeune Werther (Die Leiden des jongen* [sic] *Werthers)* (Paris, 1931) XVI*: "Quant aux extravagantes rêveries dont il est question ici, c'est sans doute une allusion à ses *Aussichten in die Ewigkeit*, dont les deux derniers volumes parurent en 1772. Goethe en rendit compte."

[8] "Der grübelnde Theil der Christen wird ihm immer viel Dank schuldig bleiben. Er zaubert ihnen wenigstens eine herrliche Welt vor die Augen, wo sie sonst nichts als Düsterheit und Verwirrung sahen" (M. Morris, ed., *Der junge Goethe* 3:96–97—this edition is hereafter referred to as *DjG*).

[9] *DjG* 3:94; *Werther*, May 9, 1772 ("Auch schäzt er [Fürst **] meinen Verstand und Talente mehr als dies Herz, das doch mein einziger Stolz ist. . . . Ach was ich weis, kann jeder wissen. —Mein Herz hab ich allein").

Freund, und Samenblätter von Gedanken; und statt allem diesem finden wir Raisonnement und Perioden, zwar wohlgedacht und wohlgesprochen; aber was soll uns das!"[10] This complete repudiation of alien ideas is very like Werther's almost automatic imperviousness to or immediate repudiation of ideas he does not like.[11] There is a sort of Wertherian "Tadelsucht" and "üble Laune" in a statement like the following:

> Schon da wir vor dem ersten Theile [der *Aussichten*] den Inhalt der zu-
> künftigen Briefe durchsahen, machte es einen unangenehmen Eindruck auf
> uns, die [drei] Abhandlungen von *Erhöhung des Geistes, sittlichen* und
> *politischen Kräfte*, in Briefe abgetheilt zu sehen. Was heist das anders, als
> durch gelehrtes Nachdenken sich eine Fertigkeit erworben zu haben, auf
> *wissenschaftliche Claßifikationen*, eine Menschenseele zu reduciren.[12]

Goethe continues to find fault as he comments on the separate letters of La-vater's volume: he objects to "logisch-metaphysische Zergliederungen der Geschäftigkeit unsers Geistes" in the thirteenth letter ("Doch das geht durchs ganze Buch durch") and to Lavater's insistence that the after-life will be like the present raised to the thousandth power—"als wenn," observes Goethe, "nicht eben in diesem *Mehr* oder *Weniger* das Elend dieser Erde be-stünde."[13] With this last observation Goethe touches on the problem of human happiness with which Werther was to wrestle: having apparently been exhorted by Wilhelm to disregard the "Weniger," Werther writes in his opening letter:

> O was ist der Mensch, daß er über sich klagen darf!—Ich will, lieber
> Freund, ich verspreche Dir's, ich will mich bessern, will nicht mehr das
> Bisgen Uebel, das das Schicksaal uns vorlegt, wiederkäuen, wie ich's
> immer gethan habe. Ich will das Gegenwärtige genießen, und das
> Vergangene soll mir vergangen seyn. Gewiß Du hast recht, Bester: der
> Schmerzen wären minder unter den Menschen, wenn sie nicht—Gott weis
> warum sie so gemacht sind—mit so viel Emsigkeit der Einbildungskraft sich

---

[10] *DjG* 3:95.

[11] E.g., Werther's "Ich ließ das gut seyn" at the end of his paragraph on the young V.. (May 17, 1771); his "Ich lies mich aber in nichts stören" when the physician finds it undignified of him to play with "Lottens Kindern" (June 29, 1771); his refusal to accept Wilhelm's "Entweder Oder" analysis of his position in relation to Lotte and Albert (Aug. 8, 1771); his refusal to do his secretarial work as his "Gesandter" wished (Dec. 24, 1771 ff.; esp. Feb. 17, 1772: "Seine Art zu arbeiten und Geschäfte zu treiben ist so lächerlich, daß ich mich nicht enthalten kann ihm zu widersprechen. . .").

[12] *DjG* 3:95. It is unlikely that the author of these lines used any systematic source of psychological information "as a framework" (Clark, loc. cit.) for Werther.

[13] *DjG* 3:95.

beschäftigten, die Erinnerungen des vergangenen Uebels zurückzurufen, ehe denn eine gleichgültige Gegenwart zu tragen.

For a time Werther will seem to achieve the "Mehr"—as he cultivates children, simple and seemingly childlike people, and the cradle-song (May 13, 1771) of Homer, poet of the childhood of the race. But the favorable balance is destroyed: frustrated in his love for Lotte and lured into social-political activity, he finds "glänzendes Elend" and there comes the day when, having awakened morning after morning "elend," he can cry, "Genug daß in mir die Quelle alles Elendes verborgen ist. . ." (Nov. 3, 1772).

In his criticism of the *Aussichten* Goethe attacks Lavater with Lavater's own theological weapon of scriptural quotation; commenting on the thirteenth letter, he observes:

> *Erkänntniß*[tritt] vornen an, die ewige *Wißbegierde*, das *systematisirende Erfahrungsammeln*. Hat er [Lavater] nie bedacht, was Christus den großen Hansen ans Herz legt: "Wenn ihr nicht werdet wie diese Kindlein" und was Paulus spricht: "Das Stückwerk der Weissagungen, des Wissens, der Er-känntniß werde aufhören, und nur die Liebe bleiben."[14]

Werther also quotes the Bible, and in a sort of apology for his manner of dealing with children even declares, "Immer, immer wiederhol ich die gold-nen Worte des Lehrers der Menschen: wenn ihr nicht werdet wie eines von diesen" (June 29, 1771). After resigning his ministerial secretaryship, Werther visits Fürst **, only to realize that the companionship of a man who considers "Erkänntnis," "Wißbegierde" and "das systematisirende Erfahrung-sammeln" important is intolerable to him:

> Er ist ein Mann von Verstande, aber von ganz gemeinem Verstande, sein Umgang unterhält mich nicht mehr, als wenn ich ein wohlgeschrieben Buch lese. . . . Und der Fürst fühlt in der Kunst, und würde noch stärker fühlen, wenn er nicht durch das garstige, wissenschaftliche Wesen, und durch die gewöhnliche Terminologie eingeschränkt wäre. (June 11, 1772)

Goethe also finds fault with Lavater for not introducing the concept "Liebe" (Christ; St. Paul!) until the fourteenth letter of the *Aussichten*, and then for so introducing it "daß alles zusammen auf das Herz gar keine Wirkung thut" (a use of the word "Herz" in the pregnant sense it has throughout *Werther*). Lavater's fifteenth letter seems to please Goethe no better: he reproves Lavater for assuming that there will be "Knechtschaft"

---

[14] This and following quotations from *DjG* 3:96.

and "Herrschaft" "dort, wo alles, Hinderniß und Trägheit wegfallen soll—!" Werther shares Goethe's dislike of class distinction, "die fatalen bürgerlichen Verhältnisse" (Dec. 24, 1771), even though he appreciates "wie viel Vortheile er [der Unterschied der Stände] mir selbst verschafft"; but when insistence upon it results in his own humiliation, he cries, "ich möchte mir eine Ader öfnen, die mir die ewige Freyheit schaffte" (March 16, 1772). And Werther, himself not unafflicted with "Trägheit," associates "Mißverständnisse und Trägheit" with the chief causes of human misery (May 4, 1771).

After disposing of the sixteenth letter in one short sentence ("Wohlgedachtes. . . , doch quillt auch da nichts aus der Seele, es ist so alles in die Seele hereingedacht"), Goethe half-grudgingly concedes that the seventeenth, "von den gesellschaftlichen Freuden des Himmels," possesses a certain merit ("viel Wärme durch Güte des Herzens, doch zu wenig um unsre Seele mit Himmel zu füllen"). Although this letter may not have filled Goethe's soul with heaven, it contains passages which must have won the cordial approval of a reviewer who had recently observed at first hand the shortcomings of social life in the provincial and class-conscious town of Wetzlar; for instance, Lavater makes a contrast between "weisen, mächtigen und liebevollen Gesellschaften" and

den faden, seelenlosen Alltagsgesellschaften müßiger Leute, die. . . sich größtentheils nur durch künstlichen Zwang und unnatürliches, verstelltes Wesen ein frostiges, seichtes, augenblickliches Vergnügen erarbeiten müssen; . . . Gesellschaften. . . , die man mit unruhigem Herzen besucht, denen man mit krummer und schiefer Seele beywohnt, und die man mit Leerheit und Eckel wieder verläßt. . . .[15]

These condemnatory observations are less impassioned, but no less sentimental, than those of Ministerial Secretary Werther reporting "die Langeweile unter dem garstigen Volke das sich hier [in dem traurigen Neste D.] neben einander sieht" ("Rangsucht," "die elendesten erbärmlichsten Leidenschaften, ganz ohne Rökgen," "die fatalen bürgerlichen Verhältnisse,"[16] "Menschen. . . , deren ganze Seele auf dem Ceremoniel ruht"[17]). In a letter to Lotte Werther expresses with metaphor and simile a reaction to social artificiality almost identical with the one revealed by this last quotation from Lavater; he writes:

[15] Op. cit., "Zwote verbesserte Auflage" (Hamburg, 1773) 3:60.
[16] Dec. 24, 1771.
[17] Jan. 8, 1772.

Wenn Sie mich sähen meine Beste, in dem Schwall von Zerstreuung! Wie
ausgetroknet meine Sinnen werden, nicht Einen Augenblick der Fülle des
Herzens, nicht Eine selige thränenreiche Stunde. Nichts! Nichts! Ich stehe
wie vor einem Raritätenkasten, und sehe die Männgen und Gäulgen vor
mir herumrükken, und frage mich oft, ob's nicht optischer Betrug ist. Ich
spiele mit, vielmehr, ich werde gespielt wie eine Marionette, und fasse
manchmal meinen Nachbar an der hölzernen Hand und schaudere zurük.
(Jan. 20, 1772)

An unnatural line of conduct like that which Lavater condemns is forced
upon Count v. C. and Fräulein B. by the "noble" and "vornehm" society of
D., and destroys Werther's pleasure in their friendship.[18]

Goethe comments only briefly on the last two letters of the *Aussichten*,
"von Vergebung der Sünden, und den seligen Folgen des Leidens,"
remarking: "werden hoffentlich die heilsame Würkung haben, gewisse
Menschen über diese Materien zu beruhigen." The doctrinal questions
which they raise are, as will appear later in this essay, of considerable
importance to a Werther who will seek "Beruhigung" before he returns
"unvermuthet" to his God; and who will swear never to commit the sin of
daring to kiss Lotte's lips (Nov. 24, 1772), yet will kiss them. It is not
surprising that thoughts which Goethe had expressed in his review of the
Aussichten should reappear in Werther's letters, which were all written less
than a year and a half later; not that Goethe, constantly exchanging views
with his friend Lavater, should endow Werther with a knowledge of Lava-
ter's "Schwärmereyen," particularly since he himself subscribed to some of
Lavater's opinions. Although in his review Goethe esteems the third volume
of the *Aussichten* less than its two predecessors, he undoubtedly read it
more carefully than the volumes he was not reviewing; and since it was,
moreover, a distinctly more Storm-and-Stress work than the other two,[19]
there is every reason for its not fading too rapidly from his memory.

The other of Lavater's published religious "Schwärmereyen" with which
the author of *Werther* was certainly acquainted is Lavater's *Predigten Ueber
das Buch Jonas*.[20] This work, read by Goethe either just before or while

[18] Mar. 15, 1772: On Jan. 20 Werther had written of Fräulein von B.., "Sie gleicht Ihnen
liebe Lotte. . . . [I]hr Stand ist ihr zur Last, der keinen der Wünsche ihres Herzens befriedigt.
Sie sehnt sich aus dem Getümmel. . . ."

[19] Cf. C. Janentzky, *J.C. Lavaters Sturm und Drang im Zusammenhang seines religiösen
Bewußtseins* (Halle, 1916) 47ff.

[20] *Die erste-zweyte Hälfte* (Zürich, 1773). A review of *Die erste Hälfte* which appeared
in the *Frankfurter Gelehrte Anzeigen* of 1773 is reprinted in the *Ausgabe letzter Hand*, vol.
33; it is not by Goethe (cf. G. Witkowski, WA I.38:306ff.), but Goethe's endorsement of
Eckermann's guess that it was by him—doubtless inspired by the *Werther* footnote, which,

writing *Werther*, can, better than any other contemporary document, help
the modern reader to understand certain aspects of eighteenth-century
psychology and theology, the ignorance or disregard of which has all too
often led to confusion and inconsistency in *Werther* criticism.[21] Lavater
delivered his sermons on *Jonah* (hereafter referred to as *Predigten*) in the
course of 1772; in a preface to the published sermons he states that they are
"unausgearbeitet."[22] Thus antedating the beginning of Lavater's correspon-
dence with both Goethe and Herder,[23] the *Predigten*, like the *Aussichten*,
represent relatively untutored "Schwärmereyen." Even before Lavater
became a member of the accredited circle of Storm-and-Stress authors, he
had, however, admired and absorbed many of Herder's ideas,[24] so that there
was good reason for his work to be not too displeasing in the sight of
Herder and Herder's disciples: "Was wäre mir der Mann [writes Herder in
his first letter to Lavater], der mir aus den menschlichen Stellen Ihrer 'Aus-
sichten,' aus Ihren Predigten und aus den oft verkehrtesten Zügen des
Gerüchts erscheint, was wäre mir der Mann für Anblick und Lehrer!"[25]

   Goethe's allusions, in *Werther*, to Lavater, seem to be little more than a
tribute from one Storm-and-Stress writer to another, at most, a special
gesture of friendship meant to atone in some measure for the unsympathetic
review of the *Aussichten* of two years before. Such a tribute or such a
gesture might well account for Werther's passing defense of Lavater's
"Schwärmereyen," but it hardly explains Goethe's remarkable editorial
reference to Lavater's "trefliche Predigt. . . unter denen über das Buch
Jonas." For Goethe's editorial footnote is like no other footnote in *Werther*:

---

however, refers to a sermon in *Die zweyte Hälfte*—would indicate that the title *Predigten
Ueber das Buch Jonas* still had strong associations for him in 1823. Cf. also *DjG* 4:84 (Lava-
ter's diary, summer 1774).

   [21] Editors and commentators seem not to have verified Goethe's reference: thus O.
Walzel, Festausgabe 9:292, writes: "Der 2. Teil von Lavaters 'Predigten. . . ,' der die
erwähnte Predigt enthält, trägt die Jahreszahl 1774, ist also wohl 1773 ausgegeben worden";
M. Herrmann, Jubiläums-Ausgabe 16:387, evidently had not seen the sermons. That both
volumes appeared in 1773 is further authenticated by the fact that they are reviewed in the
first number of the *Allgemeine dt. Bibliothek* for 1774. An exception is E. Beutler, "Wer-
therfragen," *Goethe* 5 (1940): 138–60, esp. 155. (Cf. also n. 25.)

   [22] Op. cit., 1, [XIV]—dated Nov. 1, 1772.

   [23] Herder's first letter to Lavater is dated Oct. 30, 1772; cf. n. 25.

   [24] Lavater praises Herder as early as July 12, 1767 (letter to F. Hess) and lauds him in
the first volume of the *Aussichten* (1768).

   [25] H. Düntzer, F.G. von Herder, *Briefe an Herder von Lavater, Jacobi, Forster u.A.*
(Frankfurt/Main, 1858) 23. The editors note *ad* "Predigten": "Lavater hatte 'Vermischte
Predigten' (1770) und 'Predigten über das Buch Jonas' (1772[!]) herausgegeben." Herder can
only be alluding to the former sermons, and he has seen only the first two parts of
Aussichten (cf. postscript of Lavater's reply, Nov. 10, 1772).

it does not explain that identifiable names have been disguised[26] or that irrelevant material has been suppressed.[27] Since it deliberately directs the reader's attention away from the immediate world of Werther and from his story, it would seem to be what the few critics who have given it any thought have suggested—an inept attempt by Goethe to introduce a realistic touch of a type very common in the eighteenth-century epistolary novel.[28] But appearances are notoriously deceiving. Perhaps Goethe had qualms of conscience about the morality of his novel—which many of his contemporaries, in fact, immediately denounced as immoral—and wanted to suggest a moral antidote to it. In any event, the reader with access to a copy of the *Predigten* who put *Werther* aside for a moment in order to see what Lavater had to say about "üble Laune" in the "trefliche Predigt" did not act ill-advisedly in following Goethe's hint, for he would take up the novel again much enlightened about the character of its hero and well prepared to understand the patterns of conduct which Werther exhibits. In the following sections of this study the implications of this footnote and the light which Lavater's *Predigten* shed on Werther's behavior are used as the basis for an aesthetic as well as psychological reinterpretation of *Die Leiden des jungen Werthers*.

II

Werther's letter of July 1, 1771, is of great importance for the structure of Goethe's novel. It is separated by two shorter letters from the long account of Werther's first meeting with Lotte (letters of June 16 and 19), and represents the first serious break in the mood of elation which has continued ever since that meeting. It contrasts with the shorter letters of June 21 ("Ich lebe so glükliche Tage, wie sie Gott seinen Heiligen ausspart") and June 29 (the physician finds Werther's playing with the children undignified—"Ich lies mich aber in nichts stören"), in which Werther preserves a tone of optimistic confidence despite speculative realization of human limitations and despite hostile criticism of his course of conduct. Chronologically the events of the letter of July 1 may antedate the letter of

---

[26] May 21, 1771; June 16, 1771; cf. use of disguised names, initials, asterisks, in text.

[27] June 16, 1771, Feb. 17, 1772.

[28] Buriot Darsiles, IX*, not the only critic misled by Düntzer's *Erläuterungen zu den dt. Klassikern (Goethes Leiden des j. Ws.*, 2. Aufl., Leipzig, 1880), is satisfied to comment: "Düntzer dit de la note. . . qu'elle n'était rien moins qu'indispensable et qu'en tout cas elle aurait dû, comme plus haut, l'éloge de Klopstock, être fondue dans le texte, mais que Rousseau aussi a des notes de ce genre." The realistic technique of *Werther* forbade the anachronism for one thing!

June 29 (referring to an incident of June 27—"vorgestern"), since it deals
with a visit to the pastor of St. . . . "vorige Woche," although this is not
necessarily so, since July 1 was a Sunday and June 27 the previous
Wednesday. Compositionally, however, the letter of July 1 serves to show
Werther once again overpowered by his feelings: Werther is carried away
by emotion as he discourses with the best of intentions against the
pernicious effects of "üble Laune"; the remembrance of his own past brings
tears to his eyes; and he is finally completely overcome when he describes
a death that has been ineluctably hastened and embittered by that "vice." In
a few lines at the end of the letter we are informed that Lotte has warned
Werther that he must spare himself lest he be destroyed by feeling
("Antheil"), and he concludes with the exclamation: "O der Engel! Um
deinetwillen muß ich leben!" Werther's letters from the following weeks
show him again resiliently but blindly optimistic until the very end of the
month, when Albert arrives; then, beginning with his letter of July 30, Wer-
ther exhibits the symptoms of "üble Laune" which are to mark his remaining
days. Thus does Werther succumb anew to the vice against which he had
spoken with such strong personal feeling in his letter from the first of the
month.

Werther's discussion of "üble Laune," inspired by Herr Schmidt's
obstinate and ill-humored jealousy of Werther's attentions to Friedrike, is
supposed to show that one should not willfully waste the opportunity to be
happy. Werther claims that a heart ready to appreciate the good things of
life will also have the strength necessary to bear misfortune. To the
objection that much depends upon physical health, Werther counters that
even if "üble Laune" is regarded as a disease, a cure for it can be outlined.
This cure is joyous activity, to which we must rouse ourselves. Herr Schmidt
protests that feelings cannot be commanded, but Werther assures him that
"üble Laune," being an unpleasant feeling, is something no one deliberately
wants to cultivate, so that the effort to cure it is natural. Now Werther terms
"üble Laune" a vice ("Laster")—at this point comes the footnote mentioning
Lavater's *Predigten*—and defends his use of the term "Laster" against
Schmidt's charge of exaggeration by delineating the suffering which "üble
Laune" can produce in the lives of those with whom one associates. Thus
the letter of July 1 foreshadows, even before Werther is clearly aware of the
dilemma into which his love of Lotte is leading him, the pattern of later
events: Werther will attempt to cure himself by seeking activity, he will fail
to evoke the joyousness which can make activity effective, the sickness will
accordingly be fatal, and he will have clouded the happiness of Albert and
Lotte through his behavior.

Goethe's editorial reference to Lavater's *Predigten* serves to emphasize
the lesson which Werther is preaching. The industrious collector of Wer-

ther's story, who knows that the grateful reader will love and admire Werther's mind and character, will weep at Werther's fate, will find consolation in Werther's suffering—this sympathetic editor carefully points out that a leading liberal Swiss divine has considered "üble Laune" a sufficiently serious moral phenomenon to treat it seriously from the pulpit. Although Werther fails when the time comes to put into practice what he has preached, that is because he is an exceptional case; the average, and grateful, reader may well take the lesson to heart. Certainly the reader who remembered that Werther had argued the curability of unhealthy mental states with Herr Schmidt would take with a grain of salt Werther's argument, later offered to Albert (Aug. 12, 1771), that an unhealthy mental condition could make the suicide of even an intelligent human being inevitable ("der Mensch ist Mensch, und das Bißgen Verstand das einer haben mag, kommt wenig oder nicht in Anschlag, wenn Leidenschaft wüthet"). Few readers seem to have paused to take in the meaning of the footnote referring to Lavater's *Predigten*, however, and Goethe added to the title pages of the *Zweyte ächte Auflage* of *Werther* (1775) the familiar stanzas, the second of which ends "Sey ein Mann, und folge mir nicht nach."[29]

If the irony of Werther's shift in point of view was missed by contemporary readers, so has the irony of the "nun" in "Wir haben nun [i.e., 1774] von Lavatern eine treffliche Predigt" been overlooked by critics of *Werther*, or else they would long since have discovered that in Lavater's *Predigten* "üble Laune" is not only discussed, but that it is discussed much as in *Werther*; and that in Lavater's moral psychology "üble Laune" is properly a vice because it can lead to the crime of suicide. The *Predigten*, fourteen in all, are models of homiletic effectiveness. Each section of the story of Jonah, taken separately, is made to furnish vivid illustrations of ever-repeated patterns of human conduct from which moral lessons can be drawn and of problems for which religious-theological solutions can usually be suggested with little inappropriateness. The constant emphasis upon the all-too-human

---

[29] If, as J. Wahle believes (Festausgabe 9:286), both pages of the first drafts of certain *Werther* passages published by Schöll in 1846 (cf. *DjG* 6:408–9, 4:219) date from 1774, Goethe must have decided that the prefatory paragraphs of the novel better suited the objective tone at which he aimed than did such a statement as: "schöpfe nicht nur wollüstige Linderung aus seinem Leiden, laß indem du es liessest nicht den Hang zu einer unthätigen Mismuth in dir sich vermehren, sondern ermanne dich und laß dir dieses Büchlein einen tröstenden, warnenden Freund seyn, wenn du aus Geschick oder eigner Schuld keinen nähern finden kanst, dem du vertrauen magst und der seine Erfahrungen mit Klugheit und Güte auf deinem Zustande anzupassen und dich mit oder wider willen auf den rechten Weeg zu leiten weis." There is no immoralism in these words, but, as is pointed out *infra* in the text, any emphasis on "Zustand," especially at the beginning of *Werther*, could easily disserve Goethe's aesthetic intention.

character of Jonah gives the sermons a more fundamental unity than that already partly achieved by the mere choice of a single well-knit narrative as framework within which to present a given interpretation of Christian doctrine. Lavater probably did not realize that he was presenting Jonah to his listeners and readers as the hero of a tale which has been elaborated into a study in psychological analysis;[30] but both his own gifts, and the tendency of eighteenth-century philosophy to emphasize problems of psychology above all else,[31] helped to produce a collection of sermons that could not fail to interest a Goethe about to portray, or already in the process of portraying, a complicated character marked with some of the same traits as Lavater's Jonah. The value of Lavater's psychological analyses, whether in the *Predigten*, or in his *Von der Physiognomik* of the same year and its more ambitious sequels, did not derive from any dependence upon philosophical systems of consistent theoretical psychology. Goethe, despite his collaboration in Lavater's *Physiognomische Fragmente*, soon had no illusions about the lack of significance, actual or potential, of this work as a contribution to pure or applied science. The following passage, taken from a section of *Dichtung und Wahrheit* in which Goethe analyzes Lavater's failure to achieve philosophic thinking and creative literary writing, will show that he nevertheless continued to appreciate the greatness of Lavater as a highly endowed and remarkably perceptive interpreter of human character:

Jedes Talent, das sich auf eine entschiedene Naturanlage gründet, scheint uns etwas Magisches zu haben, weil wir weder es selbst, noch seine Wirkungen einem Begriffe unterordnen können. [It is to be noted that in 1813, the earliest *terminus a quo* to be suggested for this passage, Goethe has not ceased being conscious of the limitations of "wissenschaftliche Claßifikationen."] Und wirklich ging Lavaters Einsicht in die einzelnen Menschen über alle Begriffe; man erstaunte, ihn zu hören, wenn man über diesen oder jenen vertraulich sprach, ja es war furchtbar, in der Nähe des Mannes zu leben, dem jede Grenze deutlich erschien, in welche die Natur uns Individuen einzuschränken beliebt hat. (Festausgabe 16:292)

---

[30] After Lavater has treated the general religious theme of his introductory sermon, he immediately turns his attention at the beginning of the second to the problems of character in action: "Der *Character* und das *Betragen* des Propheten Jonas ist nun das *erste*, das sich unserer weitern Aufmerksamkeit darstellt." Significantly, there is no corresponding "das *zweyte*." Cf. 1:43ff.

[31] An early work of Lavater's bearing on the themes of the *Aussichten* was his translation (1769) of the latter part of Charles Bonnet's *Idées sur l'état futur des êtres vivants, ou Palingénésie philosophique*. Developing ideas of Locke's empirical system, the Franco-Swiss naturalist and philosopher Bonnet had expounded a materialistic psychology (*Essai de psychologie, ou Considérations sur les opérations de l'âme*, 1755) with which he harmonized his teleological religious beliefs only with difficulty.

As much because of Lavater's emphasis upon elements in the Jonah story
that were congenial to his own intuitive psychological talent as because of
the skeleton of narrative around which his *Predigten* are ordered, these
represent to a remarkable degree an organic whole in which each sermon
has a place determined by the relation of its themes to the psychological
development of the biblical prophet as Lavater sees it. Each sermon stands
in definitely stated relationship to its predecessor or successor, and in it
subjects are treated which are logically connected with those of adjoining
sermons by the principles of similarity or of contrast. To some extent, the
very titles of the sermons make clear the pattern of *durchkomponiert*
organization,[32] so that a reader of *Werther* curious enough to wish to
examine Lavater's "trefliche Predigt" on the theme which Werther had so
passionately discussed would discover from the table of contents of the
Predigten that there was indeed one—the *Werther* footnote says "eine. . .
Predigt"—in whose title there occur the words "üble Laune," *viz.*, the
twelfth;[33] but unless this reader was wearing mental blinkers, he also
discovered that the "Unzufriedenheit" of the twelfth sermon's title is a
repetition from the title of the eleventh; and if he read any significant part
of the twelfth sermon, on the fifth page of which Lavater exhorts, "Sehet
hier das Bild des Ueberdrusses und der übeln Laune," he realized that the
thirteenth, entitled "Von dem Ueberdrusse des Lebens," must also have
some connection with Werther's theme in the letter of July 1. Goethe's
footnote is a valuable hint, but with its "nun" and its "eine[!] Predigt" it could
only fail to serve the less wary reader.

Lavater's *Predigten* are less fully representative of German Storm and
Stress than some of his subsequent writing was to be. Nevertheless, in
addition to an imaginative, subjective interpretation of a familiar Bible story,
they contain restatements of many ideas current in the century of enlighten-
ment, often with the special emphasis characteristic of the Storm-and-Stress

---

[32] If it is recalled that because of the 1770–72 famine special days of prayer were
obligatory in all churches, the titles are self-explanatory: 1. Von der Allgemeinheit der
göttlichen Fürsehung; 2. Das Fehlerhafte in dem Betragen Jonas; 3. Das Gute in dem
Betragen Jonas; 4. Die Schiffgefährten Jonas; 5. Jonas in und ausser dem Wallfische; 6.
Unwandelbarkeit der göttlichen Güte; 7. Vorbereitungs-Predigt auf den Communionstag vor
dem Bethtag [begins: "Wie mag dem Jonas zu Muth gewesen seyn, da er. . ."]; 8. Glauben
an Gott; 9. Bethtags-Predigt [begins: "So konnte doch Jonas seine Zuhörer nicht anreden,
wie ich diesen Augenblick Euch angeredet habe. . . . Ausrufen konnte er wol. . ."]; 10.
Nachlese zum Bethtag; 11. Jonas Menschenfeindliche, Ehrgeitzige Unzufriedenheit mit
Gottes Fürsehung und Güte; 12. Mittel gegen Unzufriedenheit und üble Laune; 13. Von
dem Ueberdrusse des Lebens; 14. Gottes Güte und Langmuth.

[33] See n. 32.

period. Throughout the eighteenth century, from Pope with his "The proper study of mankind is man" to the so-called classical period of German literature with its neo-humanism, anthropocentric thinking predominated, and even in the early Herder the term "Menschlichkeit" had acquired the slogan-like magic value which was to become even more important as the century drew to a close. In Lavater's two volumes of *Predigten* this value is regularly given to the word, and it is significant that in the *Vorrede* of November 1, 1772, written before the receipt of Herder's first letter to him, Lavater describes his collection as "Predigten, die so eigentlich zur Ausbreitung und Stärkung des Glaubens an Gott und seine Fürsehung und Güte,— und zur Beförderung der Menschlichkeit abzwecken." He thus anticipated by a few days a criticism of his *Aussichten [I, II]* which he was to find in that letter:

> Die Bibel hat uns vom ganzen künftigen Leben durchweg (ich nehme die "Offenbarung Johannis" als ein poetisches Buch aus, was ich nicht verstehe) nichts offenbart, als was sie für nöthig gefunden, *auf unsern moralischen Sinn,* hier würklich *auf unsre Menschlichkeit* zu *beziehen,* und was das Schönste ist, die Menschheit (ich rechne die speculative Neugierde und andre so abgerißne Zwirnsfäden aus diesem großen Bunde voller Kräfte nicht für Menschheit) ist auch würklich so gebaut, daß sie nur das *annimmt, fodert* und *will* und *genießt,* was sich darauf beziehet. Alsdann ist sie gleichsam gesättigt, sie läßt das andre als *caput mortuum* sinken, und einverleibet sichs nicht. So ists mir, liebster Lavater, mit Ihrem Buch gegangen, und, glauben Sie mir, so wirds allen, und Ihnen selbst einmal, wenn Sie nicht mehr Autor, wenn Sie so weit entfernt stehen werden, um es ganz als fremdes Werk anzusehen. . . . Ich spreche [writes Herder in another passage] noch immer als Theolog; weil ich nämlich sehe, daß Sie fast Allem theologischen und nicht bloß poetischen Werth geben wollen, und ich wahrlich wünschte, daß Sie ihrem Gedicht, was mehr als beides ist, *ewig menschlichen* Werth geben könnten. . . .[34]

In the only part of the *Predigten* volumes written after he had begun to correspond with Herder—in a dedication to Hasencamp dated February 18, 1773[35]—Lavater carefully iterates with pleonastic emphasis his devotion to the ideal of his times: "*Menschlichkeit* auszubreiten, lieber Freund, *Menschlichkeit,* diese erste und letzte Menschentugend ist einer meiner Hauptzwecke bey diesen Predigten. Dieß, lieber Bruder, sey dir ein Wink!" Since

---

[34] Op. cit., n. 25, 15–16, 19.

[35] This dedication is printed in a font otherwise not used for connected text in the *Predigten*; placed before the *Vorrede*, it authenticates with a high degree of probability the dating of the latter.

only the final sermons in Lavater's collection deal more exclusively with explicit themes of *Werther* and are the ones to which Goethe's footnote most specifically refers, a cursory mention of a few passages from the earlier part of the collection will suffice to demonstrate the degree to which there are common elements in the intellectual and psychological worlds of the author of the *Predigten* and of that of *Werther*; the adducing of verbal and other parallels from *Werther* is, however, in no way an attempt to ascribe to these passages any spurious significance as possible literary influences of which Goethe may or may not have been conscious, but is rather an attempt to point out certain patterns of thought current at the time that Goethe conceived and wrote the novel.

III.

In his dedication to Hasencamp, Lavater touches at one point upon an important article of his personal faith, *viz.*, the conviction that Christianity must center not about God but almost exclusively about Christ:

> Widersetze dich ferner, lieber Bruder, mit Weisheit, Sanftmuth, und leuchtender Stärke des Geistes und Herzens, den beyden grossen Feinden der Wahrheit und Tugend, die so sehr sie verschieden scheinen, einen gemeinschaftlichen Vater, den *Stolz*, und dieselbe Mutter, die *Unwissenheit* haben. Ich meyne das emporbrausende *Christusleere Christenthum* auf der einen, und die *vernunftlose Schwärmerey* auf der andern Seite.

The problem of "Christusleere Christenthum" was one to which Lavater constantly returned in his writings of the early seventies, and Goethe's double letter to Pfenninger and Lavater of April 26, 1774, with its marked similarities to Werther's letter of November 15, 1772, counters the attitude of Lavater represented by such statements as "Entweder Atheist oder Christ," "ich habe keinen Gott als Jesus Christus," and "Sein Vater! Grosser Gedanke—ist *mir* nur in ihm; ist mir in allem—wäre mir nirgends, wär' er mir nicht in ihm." In his letter, Werther, who has been urged by Wilhelm to find strength in religion—and, apparently, à la Lavater, in Christ—makes, in a spirit of contradiction, a distinction between God-Son and God-Father: "Sagt nicht selbst der Sohn Gottes: daß die um ihn seyn würden, die ihm der Vater gegeben hat. Wenn ich ihm nun nicht gegeben bin! Wenn mich nun der Vater für sich behalten will, wie mir mein Herz sagt!" Ernst Feise has ventured the opinion that the letter, with its "mehr der monotheistischen Gottesanschauung sich nähernden Stimmung," is "einer der uneingeschmolzenen Lebensreste" in *Werther*,[36] although Hippolyte Loiseau, in his *L'Évolution morale de Goethe*, had earlier noted in connection with the same passage that Werther's religion, if less profound than Faust's, is no more orthodox, stating:

> Que signifie ce dualisme, cette subtile distinction entre la religion du Père et celle du Fils, si ce n'est qu'il y a deux religions profondément différentes, l'une, la religion commune, extérieure, le Christianisme fondé par Jésus ou tel qu'il est sorti de sa doctrine, par voie de déformation, l'autre, la religion naturelle, la religion du Divin?[37]

(The relevance to *Faust*, ll. 3415ff., is obvious.)

This *Werther*-passage has, moreover, a compositional importance which makes it inomissible, for it alone makes fully understandable Werther's prayer at the end of his letter of November 30, 1772; having heard the story of the madness of Heinrich, but before learning that an unfortunate passion for Lotte has effected it, Werther cries:

> Gott im Himmel! Hast du das zum Schiksaal der Menschen gemacht, daß sie nicht glücklich sind, als eh sie zu ihrem Verstande kommen, und wenn sie ihn wieder verliehren! . . . O Gott! du siehst meine Thränen. . . . Vater, den ich nicht kenne! Vater, der sonst meine ganze Seele füllte, und nun sein Angesicht von mir gewendet hat! Rufe mich zu dir! . . . Und würde ein Mensch, ein Vater zürnen können, dem sein unvermuthet rükkehrender Sohn um den Hals fiele und rief: Ich bin wieder da mein Vater. Zürne nicht, daß ich die Wanderschaft abbreche, die ich nach deinem Willen länger aushalten sollte. . . . Und du, lieber himmlischer Vater, solltest ihn von dir weisen?

Regardless of what his religious beliefs may have been, Werther is portrayed as profoundly religious and endowed with reverent respect even for such manifestations of faith as popular superstitions (he has compared Malgen's washing away of his kiss with baptism and recorded his equal respect for both rituals—letter of July 6, 1771); he has to dispose of the widespread religious prejudice against suicide before he can, emotionally and reli-

---

[36] Cf. *DjG* 4:15–17. The parallels between the two letters have been pointed out by Feise (cf. n. 4, esp. *JEGP*, p. 29).

[37] (Paris, 1911) 281ff.; Loiseau's whole section must be read if his lucid and carefully documented analysis of the fundamental unity of Werther's religious utterances is to be appreciated. The assumption of various critics (e.g., Feise) that Werther's pantheism is incompatible with monotheism ignores the transcendental element in Storm-and-Stress pantheistic thinking; cf. A. Gillies, *Herder* (Oxford, 1945) 7, 59, 94.

giously, be ready to put his intention into effect without being inconsistent
with his own nature; for this reason, then, a religion of God the Father,
related by countersuggestion to the inconceivability of "Christusleere
Christenthum" not only for Lavater but for many others, is a highly plausible
and appropriate development or refinement of Werther's religious thinking
if he is to be able to envisage the act of suicide and still is to remain a
psychologically consistent character. As for Lavater's observation that
"Christusleere Christenthum" stands in a filial relationship to "Stolz," it may
be remarked in passing that Werther repeatedly shows a certain smug
superiority in his attitudes toward individuals less highly endowed than
himself (e.g., his tolerant indifference towards the would-be aesthetician
V..—letter of May 17, 1771; his dissatisfaction with Fürst**, already discussed
above; etc.), even toward those who are his actual social inferiors, in which
cases he does not successfully conceal a vanity flattered by ability to
understand the common man (the first of many instances of this comes at
the end of his first letter: "Bald werd ich Herr vom Garten seyn, der Gärtner
ist mir zugethan, nur seit den paar Tagen, und er wird sich nicht übel davon
befinden").

The pertinence to *Werther* of Lavater's observation that religious
radicalism can simply be an expression of intellectual arrogance may help
explain why Goethe—in his youth, at least, not without certain of Werther's
traits of character—should have declared in *Dichtung und Wahrheit*, "es
war furchtbar, in der Nähe des Mannes zu leben, dem jede Grenze deutlich
erschien, in welche die Natur uns Individuen einzuschränken beliebt hat."
Although Goethe-Werther would probably have hardly conceded that proud
"Christusleere Christenthum" was one of the two great enemies of "Wahrheit
und Tugend," he might have subscribed to Lavater's corollary that "vernunft-
lose Schwärmerey," mothered by "Unwissenheit," was the enemy of truth
and virtue; certainly Werther, especially as ministerial secretary, finds
himself repeatedly frustrated by official and social narrow-mindedness that
fails to appreciate his presumably more enlightened views. For Werther, as
for Faust, the *famulus* Wagner would have been merely "der trokne
Schwärmer" (*Urfaust*, l. 168): Werther, like Faust, is the creation of the same
young Goethe.[38] The truism that pride is an enemy of virtue, Goethe did
however accept when divested of the theological trimmings with which La-
vater had formulated it, for the dramatic catastrophe in the story of Wer-
ther's relation to Lotte is very clearly motivated by Lotte's pride. When,
disregarding her request not to come to the house again before Christmas

---

[38] Lavater's "emporbrausend" conveys a negative value judgment; Feise, *Die Leiden des
jungen Werthers* 177, correctly notes that *empörtes* (Werther, May 13, 1771) "is not to be
taken as an absolute expression of dissatisfaction." (The 1774 *Werther* has "empörendes.")

Eve, Werther calls at 6:30 on December 21, 1772, Lotte finds it impossible
to obtain chaperones from among her friends. Instead of calling a servant
girl into the room, "wie sie anfangs vorhatte," she remains alone with Wer-
ther, plays the piano, and then asks for the reading from Ossian which so
rouses Werther's emotions that he loses all self-control and so at last takes
her into his arms—all this because, informed that none of her friends could
or would join her and Werther, the news left her "einige Minuten nach-
denkend, bis das Gefühl ihrer Unschuld sich mit einigem Stolze empörte.
Sie bot Albertens Grillen Truz, und die Reinheit ihres Herzens gab ihr eine
Festigkeit [etc.]. . . ."

One further passage from *Die erste Hälfte* of Lavater's *Predigten* will help
to make clearer than could any generalization the significant fact that the
language and ideas of *Werther* reflect not only Goethe's great familiarity
with the Bible, so often noted by commentators, but also his mastery of the
logico-stylistic method of Protestant theological writing with which his own
theological studies had made him acquainted. If "the devil can cite Scripture
for his purpose," how much more effectively can those utilize it who, like
Lavater, consecrated to the service of Christianity, have authority to elucidate
biblical texts by paraphrase and other means which will bring Christian
doctrine nearer to the hearts and the understanding of men! Although the
scriptural bases from which ideas expounded by Lavater or Werther derive
can be discerned with little difficulty, the significance of these ideas lies
primarily in the peculiar twists which they contain as actually formulated.
Lavater declares:

> Wenn Gott gebeut, o mein Zuhörer! so ist es an dir zu gehorchen; Wenn
> er dir ruft, auf welche Weise er immer rufen will, so sollst du seinem Rufe
> folgen. Er fordert nichts von dir, das so schwer sey, wie das, was er von
> dem Propheten Jonas forderte [i.e., eine gottlose Stadt zur Busse zu
> erwecken[39]]; Wenn er aber auch etwas noch schwerers von dir fordern
> würde, so wäre es Pflicht, oder wenn du lieber willst, es wäre wahre
> Weisheit, es wäre deine höchste Glückseligkeit, ihm zu gehorchen, und
> seinen allerschwersten Willen, mit gänzlicher Aufopferung deines eigenen
> Willens, mit williger Folgsamkeit und kindlicher Freudigkeit zu thun.[40]

Lavater's insistence upon the complete subordination of one's own will to
the will of God recalls the heretical doctrines of Catholic quietists that had
been disseminated in Protestant Germany by the pietists; his formulation of
the necessity for "Gelassenheit" misses being heresy, however, because it

[39] Op. cit., 1:46.
[40] Ibid. 53.

clearly implies that "Aufopferung d[es] eigenen Willens" demands exertion of the individual will, and that passive submission to the Divine will does not lead only to quietistic passivity, but to effortful achievement of good works also.

With pastoral zeal, Lavater is simply using one of many available arguments in order to persuade members of his congregation, and his readers, that it is incumbent upon them to do their Christian duty. His argument, which allows the true Christian hardly more than the irreducible minimum of individual free will compatible with orthodox theology, is relatively innocuous for those who accept revelation and the teachings of Christ and the church fathers as their guide to conduct. For a deist, for one whose religion is "Christusleer," is unrevealed or, like Werther's, dispenses with Christ as mediator between man and God, Lavater's argument becomes an authorization to do only what the inner voice of conscience demands— which may be nothing at all. The doctrine of the wisdom of loving obedience to divine will is religious fatalism, a sort of *Amor divini fati*, even if the person who believes it is in direct communication with God; if this communication ceases, or if the ego is very strong, the will of the individual becomes the will of God and egocentric voluntarism vaunts divine authority.

Werther, who has proudly rejected revealed Christianity, exemplifies in his theistic religious thinking a kind of voluntary fatalism favorable to temporization, inactivity, inertia, feelings of irresponsibility and frustration, or, in one word, to "Trägheit." His theology allows him complete subjective freedom, and at the same time it is perhaps the only occidental one at all compatible with his pantheistic feelings. In any case, it is the nearest possible religious equivalent to his deterministic philosophy and to the fatalistic passivity reflected in his constant allusions to "das Schicksal." Thus on every level of his experience Werther denies the effectiveness of free human effort; he is "ein Leidender," to paraphrase the common noun in the title of Goethe's novel; he succumbs to the "Trägheit" of "üble Laune" against which he has so strong a prejudice; he lets himself be so undermined by "schwärmende Träume," emotions and "Spekulation,"[41] that he is unable to adjust himself to the world of practical activity in which he sought to counteract the passion for Lotte; he considers that he has never been a greater artist than at a time when he could not draw even a line,[42] but deceived himself into thinking that if he had clay or wax he could achieve something in a plastic medium;[43] he cannot keep his resolutions not to see

---

[41] Quotation from letter to Schönborn, June 1, 1774, in which Goethe characterizes his forthcoming novel (*DjG* 4:26).

[42] May 10, 1771.

[43] July 24, 1771.

Lotte, and is attracted to Wahlheim as by a magnet;[44] in one of his earlier
letters he rejects his mother's suggestion that he should seek "Aktivität" with
an argument—"ist's im Grund nicht einerley: ob ich Erbsen zähle oder
Linsen?"—that recalls philosophic efforts during the eighteenth century to
reduce human experience to a common denominator which left
individuation unjustifiable;[45] and, to note a last significant instance, which
illustrates his inability to evaluate activity, he can feel keenly as he shells
peas "wie die herrlichen übermüthigen Freyer der Penelope Ochsen und
Schweine schlachten, zerlegen und braten."[46]

Werther's passivity, his indifferentism, his "Trägheit"—these are corol-
laries of his tendency to minimize man's freedom for volitional action. He
has no motive to exercise his talents, and his energies, unlike those of so
many Storm-and-Stress heroes, are so consumed in inner processes, emo-
tional and speculative, that none remain for external activities. Werther
wants very little of life because his philosophic "Spekulation" has robbed life
of almost all desirable values: one cannot properly desire or want anything
if the human will is impotent. In his philosophy, Werther simply carries to
its logical conclusion the mechanistic determinism which caused Leibniz to
postulate monads acting only by virtue of preestablished harmony; which
inspired primitivistic theories, espoused by Werther also, according to which
the effort expended to produce highly evolved civilizations was wasted; and
which explains the trouble that exponents of empirical systems of philoso-
phy (including Charles Bonnet) had to explain how man could enjoy free
will—if they did not, like Lamettrie, actually believe in "L'homme machine."
Werther's early letters show how his philosophy has rendered him an
ineffectual member of society. Then he discovers that everything is not yet
"im Grund. . . einerley": he wants Lotte. But even as he has lost the power
to distinguish between desires that can possibly be realized and those that
cannot: he blithely ignores the fact that Lotte is "so gut als verlobt." When,
after long and painful suffering, he at last sees that his wish is unrealizable,
life loses its last remnant of value for him: the thought of death becomes his
constant preoccupation. The frustration of his desire for Lotte—and of his
half-hearted secretarial "Aktivität" undertaken as antidote to this
frustration—has destroyed whatever residual faith in volitional freedom he
may still have had.

In his letter of August 12, 1771, Werther gives an account of how, in a
memorable conversation with Albert, he had justified suicide to his own

[44] July 26, 1771.
[45] July 20, 1771.
[46] June 21, 1771.

complete satisfaction; his arguments are those of a deterministic philosopher-psychologist, and make the suicide a victim of emotions and thoughts over which he has no control. Some fifteen months later, at a moment when his letters contain little more than iterated negations of the value of life, Werther tells (letter of December 8, 1772) how the sight by moonlight of the flooded valley below Wahlheim inspired in him the longing to jump from his rocky vantage-point, "all meine Quaalen all mein Leiden da hinab zu stürmen, dahin zu brausen wie die Wellen"; but he has not followed what was clearly an almost overpowering impulse to commit pantheistic suicide because he feels ("ich fühl's," not the less vivid "ich fühlt' es"), "Meine Uhr ist noch nicht ausgelaufen." The only convincing reason that can perhaps be offered for Werther's failure to execute his impulse, and for his unelaborated statement to the effect that his time has not yet come, is that even a pantheistic determinist must do what Werther no longer can: of his own free will deliberately choose a course of action. Werther will not kill himself until he is satisfied that the volitional responsibility for his act does not rest with himself alone; in his subjective religion he finds the theological justification for his suicide.

It is fascinating to see how Werther the theist convinces himself that what he desires is really only to perform God's will "mit gänzlicher Aufopferung d[es] eigenen Willens, mit williger Folgsamkeit und kindlicher Freudigkeit." As early as November 3, 1772, Werther explains his present unhappiness, his vain prayers for tears, as the result of having been too strong-willed, of having lacked what pietists and others have called "Gelassenheit": "jene Zeiten, deren Andenken mich quält, warum waren sie so selig? als weil ich mit Geduld ['dulden' = '(still) leiden'] seinen Geist erwartete, und die Wonne, die er über mich ausgoß mit ganzem, innig dankbarem Herzen aufnahm." In his prayer of November 30 to the God-Father of his unorthodox religion Werther vehemently asks to be called to Him. Yet on December 8 he must still confess, "Meine Uhr ist noch nicht abgelaufen," although he has already assured himself (on December 4) that God would come around to his way of thinking—"Gott! du siehst mein Elend, und wirst es enden." Writing ambiguously to Wilhelm on December 20, Werther shows that he is not yet fully prepared to die when he declares, using a metaphor perhaps inspired by his reading of *Emilia Galotti* (its heroine, who has willed and effected her own death, describes herself as "Eine Rose gebrochen, ehe der Sturm sie entblättert"[47]), "Es ist nöthig, daß nichts

---

[47] Lessing, op. cit., V, vii. The metaphor common to both *Werther* and *Emilia Galotti* is not pointed out by E. Feise, "Lessings *Emilia Galotti* und Goethes *Werther*," *MP* 15 (1917): 321–38, who, to be sure, considers the death of Emilia to be a "Mord" which in *Werther* "wird. . . zum Selbstmord" (331); nor by R.T. Ittner, "Werther and *Emilia Galotti*," *JEGP* 41

gepflückt werde, eh es reif ist." From the account of how Werther conducts himself when he calls on Lotte later this same day, it is clear that he has still to achieve the calm of spirit which is the prerequisite of a suicide even on the purely non-religious plane of a materialistic philosopher like Addison's Cato.

The following morning, however, when he begins his last, long letter to Lotte, he writes "ohne romantische Ueberspannung gelassen ['gelassen' = 'geduldig, beherrscht, ruhig']" that he has had "eine schrökliche Nacht. . . , und ach eine wohlthätige Nacht, sie ist's, die meinen wankenden Entschluß befestiget, bestimmt hat: ich will sterben." God granted him "das lezte Labsal der bittersten Thränen [for which he had vainly prayed on November 3], und tausend Anschläge, tausend Aussichten wütheten durch meine Seele, und zuletzt stand er da, fest ganz der lezte einzige Gedanke: Ich will sterben!" If God has granted his prayer for tears, He has, by Werther's reasoning, inspired the chain of ideas which leads to the one whole, fixed, final thought "Ich will sterben!" Confirmation of the propriety of the thought is that

> Morgens, in all der Ruh des Erwachens, steht er [der Gedanke] noch fest, noch ganz stark in meinem Herzen: Ich will sterben!—Es ist nicht Verzweiflung, es ist Gewißheit, daß ich ausgetragen habe, und daß ich mich opfre für Dich, ja Lotte, warum sollt ich's verschweigen: eins von uns dreyen muß hinweg, und das will ich seyn.

Werther can conceive of his suicide as a sacrifice, which is a Christ-like action and a Christian duty, for "Greater love hath no man than this, that a man lay down his life for his friends." In Lavater's formulation, "Wenn er [Gott] dir ruft, auf welche Weise er immer rufen will, so sollst du seinem Rufe folgen," for it is "Pflicht. . . ihm zu gehorchen," there lies the loophole by which a Werther could evade the prohibition of suicide in orthodox Christian doctrine; "auf welche Weise er immer rufen will" is a phrase which leaves great freedom of interpretation to the individual, and it is characteristic of the kind of theological reasoning which Werther employs in finally justifying his suicide on the plane of theistic religion. The irony of it all is that he has not yet really achieved the complete quietude which he claims at the beginning of his letter to Lotte, for by the end of its first paragraph recollection of his having contemplated the murder of Lotte and Albert and a vision of Lotte at his grave have reduced Werther to tears: "Ich

(1942): 418–26, who accepts, as does the author of the present study, the interpretation of H.J. Weigand, "Warum stirbt Emilia Galotti?", *JEGP* 28 (1929): 467–81, but who seems not to know Feise's article.

war ruhig da ich anfieng, und nun wein ich wie ein Kind. . . ." Even in the
very last section of his letter ("nach eilfe"), in which Werther again insists
that his action has divine approval—"ich danke dir Gott, der du diesen
lezten Augenblikken diese Wärme, diese Kraft schenkest"—his opening
observation, "so ruhig [ist] meine Seele," is belied by over a score of
exclamation points alone, and almost his last words to Lotte—"sey ruhig! ich
bitte dich sey ruhig!"—have the simultaneous value of self-exhortation.

That Werther should have created a God in the image of his own
feelings is nothing unique, however subtle the process by which He is made
to harmonize with the world-outlook of Werther's highly complicated
personality; but that the Christ-conscious Lavater should have postulated a
theoretical case, although to him an improbable and impossible one, in
which the creation of another god than the God of Israel would be justified,
shows that Werther's method falls into an already existing pattern of
Protestant theological thinking:

> Eine Gottheit die nicht hilft, ist keine Gottheit. . . [writes Lavater]. Keine
> einzige Seele von dem Anfang der Welt her. . . wird auftreten und sagen
> können: "Ich habe zum Herrn gerufen, und er hat mir nicht, hat mir auf
> keinerley Weise geantwortet: Ich habe stark angehalten, und er hat mich
> nicht errettet, mich nicht getröstet, mir nicht einmal Muth eingeflößt. Keine
> wird sagen können: Ich habe mein Vertrauen auf ihn gesezt, und er hat mir
> nicht geholfen; Ich habe auf seine Hülfe geharret, und bin zu schanden
> worden."
> Wenn eine solche Seele, die das im Ernst, und bey gesunder Vernunft
> nach der Wahrheit sagen könnte; Kein Bedenken, M[eine]. Th[euersten].
> würde ich mir machen, hier öffentlich von der Kanzel ihr zuzurufen: Such
> einen andern Gott! Ruf einen Gott der Welt an! . . . Suche irgend etwas,
> mache irgend etwas zu deinem Gott, das sich in Noth und Gefahr
> freundlich zu dir wendet, daß du nicht verdärbest.[48]

In Lavater's sense, Werther could not properly say "Ich habe stark ange-
halten," nor could he, as the analysis of Lavater's psychology of "Überdruß
des Lebens" will demonstrate, say it "bey gesunder Vernunft," so that his
repudiation of the orthodox God and its consequences, while psychologi-
cally consistent with his character, would not in Lavater's eyes be an
instance of the valid applicability of the principle stated in the passage just
quoted. What is important for Werther, however, is that he, who is so well
aware of the good in children (à propos of whom he once quoted "die
goldnen Worte des Lehrers der Menschen: wenn ihr nicht werdet wie eines

---

[48] *Predigten*, 1:124–25.

von diesen!"), shall be able to present himself to a forgiving God-Father who
will not be able to chide "sein unvermuthet rükkehrender Sohn."[49] His
obviating of a God who presumably does not condone suicide permits him
to answer the call of his God-Father "mit williger Folgsamkeit und kindlicher
Freudigkeit," or, to use out of context another phrase of Lavater's, "sich. . .
dem allmächtigen und unendlichen Erbarmer mit kindlicher Zuversicht
darstellen."[50] On the eve of his first real separation from Lotte, he had
answered her "Wir werden seyn, . . . aber Werther, sollen wir uns wieder
finden? und wieder erkennen?" with an assured "wir werden uns wieder
sehn! Hier und dort wieder sehn!"[51] Writing to Lotte the morning of his last
full day of life, Werther the pantheist merely can say, "So traure denn, Natur,
dein Sohn, dein Freund, dein Geliebter naht sich seinem Ende," and Wer-
ther the speculative thinker declares, "Sterben! Was heist das? Sieh wir
träumen, wenn wir vom Tode reden. . . . Sterben! Grab! Ich verstehe die
Worte nicht!"[52] But the Werther who had dared ask barely a month before
if it would really be sin to fulfill himself by pressing a kiss on Lotte's lips[53]—
as he was finally to do—must still seek the meaning of his experience and
imminent death in theological terms. Lotte is his "auf ewig," and though his
love may be "für diese Welt Sünde," he goes with complete declared
confidence in his God-Father "zu meinem Vater, zu deinem Vater, dem will
ich's klagen und er wird mich trösten biß du kommst, und ich fliege dir
entgegen und fasse dich und bleibe bey dir vor dem Angesichte des
Unendlichen in ewigen Umarmungen." No less than Lavater's more
orthodox God, Werther's is "die gränzenlose Liebe"[54] and the "Vater der
Liebe und der Unsterblichkeit,"[55] for in the face of death Werther affirms his

---

[49] Nov. 30, 1772.

[50] *Predigten* 1:227–28.

[51] Sept. 10, 1771.

[52] Cf. also his undated comments on "Den Vorhang aufzuheben" (beginning of
"Herausgeberbericht").

[53] Nov. 24, 1772. Ittner (421) insists on Werther's "consciousness of guilt and. . . desire
to atone for such guilt. . . as the immediate, although not, of course, the primary and
ultimate cause of Werther's death." This explanation disregards the way Werther makes fate
responsible for the "unhappiness he caused through his guilt." Referring to "Sünde
abzubüssen—Sünde?" Ittner further declares that a "vow never to kiss Lotte is to be
considered as having been immediately retracted. Werther feels that he will kiss her and
he is ready to atone for this sin. . . . In his last letter his calm and resigned tone indicates
that he has continued to consider this ethical point; now he feels unequivocally that his
kisses are a sin,—and he is ready to pay the penalty" (422). In finding confirmation of his
interpretation in the words "Sünde? Gut! und ich strafe mich davor," Ittner ignores both
context and interrogation points.

[54] *Predigten* 2:19.

[55] Ibid., 27.

faith in immortality and repeats the words of the conversation of over fifteen months before, this time in the assurance of a clearer knowledge of God, "Ich träume nicht, ich wähne nicht! nah am Grabe ward mir's heller. Wir werden seyn, wir werden uns wieder sehn!" Although Werther had already justified his suicide as a Christ-like sacrifice at the beginning of this last letter to Lotte, he now repudiates the idea that it is to be regarded as atonement for sin:

> Und was ist das? daß Albert dein Mann ist! Mann?—das wäre denn für diese Welt [i.e., "when they shall rise from the dead, they neither marry, nor are given in marriage; but are as the angels which are in heaven"]—und für diese Welt Sünde, daß ich dich liebe, daß ich dich aus seinen Armen in die meinigen reissen möchte?

With its subjunctive of strong doubt, Werther's ironic rhetorical question expresses complete indifference to the standards of a world whose sense of values he has never accepted. So successful has been his self-justification that Werther boldly continues, "Sünde? Gut! und ich strafe mich davor," again using an interrogation point with pregnant irony. Later in the evening he writes dispassionately to Albert:

> Ich habe dir übel gelohnt, Albert, und du vergiebst mir. Ich habe den Frieden deines Hauses gestört, ich habe Mißtrauen zwischen euch gebracht. Leb wohl, ich will's enden. O daß ihr glüklich wäret durch meinen Tod! Albert! Albert! mache den Engel glüklich. Und so wohne Gottes Seegen über dir!

Here Werther mentions as a simple fact the trouble that he has caused his friends, and hardly more than ventures to express a vague hope that his death may (*n.b.* "wäret") help remedy matters.[56] Accordingly, in the final

---

[56] This passage is quoted by Ittner (425), who realizes that Werther "is not dying for Lotte," that "his vanity still leads him to feel that her calm and her happiness will not be restored." But Ittner vitiates the value of his observations by adding: "And so Werther dies, conscious of the guilt of his uncontrolled passion, conscious too, and remorseful over [!] the unhappiness and suspicion he has caused between Albert and Lotte." Ittner's assumption that he has refuted L. Simon's statement (*Verantwortung und Schuld in Goethes Roman* [Erlangen, 1934] 9), "Sozialethische Motive liegen Werthers Selbstmord nicht zugrunde," is therefore unjustified, as is his feeling of "a kind of admiration for this Werther who finally takes cognizance of the institutions and standards of the world, and who acknowledges them by sacrificing himself." He is, it may be hoped, speaking for the few when he says, "With respect to the tone of the last few pages of *Werther*, we are even reminded somewhat [!] of the transfiguration that takes place in Maria of *Maria Stuart*, in Johanna of *Die Jungfrau von Orleans*, and in Ottilie of *Die Wahlverwandtschaften*."

section of his letter to Lotte, Werther no longer maintains the pretense that his death is a sacrifice:

> Daß ich des Glüks hätte theilhaftig werden können! Für dich zu sterben, Lotte, für dich mich hinzugeben. Ich wollte muthig, ich wollte freudig sterben, wenn ich dir die Ruhe, die Wonne deines Lebens wieder schaffen könnte; aber ach das ward nur wenig Edlen gegeben, ihr Blut für die Ihrigen zu vergiessen, und durch ihren Tod ein neues hundertfältiges Leben ihren Freunden anzufachen.

Werther's *beau geste* is contrary-to-fact, and only potentially is his blood—like Egmont's "und vieler Edeln"—"nicht umsonst vergossen"; but the megalomania of these lines is certainly an aspect of the deeply-rooted pride that is also mirrored in Werther's religious thinking.

IV

The analysis of how Werther successfully rationalizes the conversion of his longing for death into a will to die leaves unexplained why *tædium vitæ* should have taken an extreme, fatal form in his case. As Ernst Feise has convincingly demonstrated in his careful analysis of "Goethes Werther als nervöser Charakter," the young Goethe and Werther had almost countless neurotic traits in common, and for this reason Goethe explained his reluctance to reread *Werther* with the words: "ich fürchte den pathologischen Zustand wieder durchzuempfinden, aus dem es hervorging."[57] Goethe did not die of Werther's disease, however, nor do the symptoms which Werther shows necessarily authorize a prognostication of suicide. This act is usually associated with endogenous melancholia (symptoms: feeling of worthlessness, brooding, *tædium vitæ*, ineffectiveness of attempts at distraction—a pattern distorted in Werther's case because he has successfully compensated his inferiority complex); in fact, Werther shows rather the patterns of paranoia and paranoid schizophrenia which lead first to violence like that of the discharged secretary Heinrich and like that attempted by the "Bauerbursch" of the second version of *Werther*, and then to a quiet indifference and dream-like existence corresponding to the state of Heinrich when Werther meets him (symptoms: suspiciousness, as when Werther charges Lotte with uttering Albert's rather than her own thoughts;[58]

---

[57] Op. cit., *GR* 1 (1926): 185–253, esp. II [.Teil], 221–53 (Goethe as quoted by Eckermann, Jan. 2, 1824).

[58] Dec. 20, 1772 (evening).

persecution complex—"Es hezt mich alles!";[59] illusions of grandeur, at least partly represented by Werther's various illusions of superiority already noted in connection with the moral concept "pride"; the sudden schizophrenic transitions from calm to excitement or to violence, a pattern "calm-excitement" very apparent in the passages discussed above in connection with Werther's claims that he has become "ruhig" enough to be able to commit suicide with justification). The end-state of schizophrenia is fully as tragic as the result of fatal melancholia, but as a state it is pathetic and undramatic. The abrupt ending of melancholia is startling and in this sense dramatic, however, so that there is good artistic reason for the dénouement of *Werther* even though Werther does not fit the typical symptomatic pattern of melancholia quite so well as does Jerusalem in Kestner's report to Goethe.

It would be presumptuous to assert that Goethe, when writing *Werther*, might have been consciously concerned with resolving the problem of how to join his own psychological experiences, the "autobiographical" element in the novel, to those very different ones of Jerusalem so as to guarantee the unity and psychological truth of Werther's character. An answer to the question of how Werther-Goethe can also be Werther-Jerusalem will be satisfactory only if it explains why the real Werther, the Werther of Goethe's novel, develops a fatal case of *tædium vitæ*; in other words, either Werther is a consistent character, and the novel a homogeneous work of art, or else he is made up of incongruous elements ("Lebensüberreste"), and Goethe failed to solve the problem of creating a whole, psychologically true character. It is not necessary to assume that Goethe consciously worked out a psychological explanation of how Werther-Goethe could also be Werther-Jerusalem. Indeed, the fact that Goethe's *Dichtung und Wahrheit* account of the writing of *Werther* contains a palpably erroneous statement to the effect that the news of Jerusalem's death crystallized the plan of the novel in Goethe's mind, would indicate that Goethe had not consciously spent time working out his novel during the year and more which elapsed between the receipt of that news and the composition of the novel.[60] It is,

---

[59] Mar. 16, 1772.

[60] The interpretation of passages in *Dichtung und Wahrheit* as historical evidence of the degree to which Goethe may have been conscious of how he created a given work is the one legitimate "use" of Goethe's autobiography for which Max Herrmann failed to allow when he condemned its "Überschätzung" by those who are blind to any but biographical interpretations of Goethe's works (*Das Jahrmarktsfest zu Plundersweilern: Entstehungs- und Bühnengeschichte* [Berlin, 1900] 5). The traditional biographical emphasis on "Goethe's Wetzlar experience," on "Kestner's account of Jerusalem's sad fate," and on "Goethe's experience in the house of the Brentanos" as the "three-fold inspiration" of *Werther* (Ittner 420), is not only inadequate, as many critics have long realized, but actually misleading.

moreover, unlikely that Goethe grafted experiences of whose emotional values he can only have been fully aware after his connection with Maximiliane La Roche and her husband Brentano on to any complete plan of his novel, for these experiences furnish the motive of destroyed domestic harmony which affords Werther a basis for equating his suicide with moral-theological atonement while leaving his love for Lotte only "für diese Welt Sünde." *Werther* must therefore properly be regarded as a work of the early months of 1774, at about which time the character of the real Werther assumed its definitive form.

When, many years later, Goethe wrote the thirteenth book of *Dichtung und Wahrheit*, which has been described by Ewald A. Boucke as "vollkommen von der *Wertherdichtung* beherrscht, deren psychologische und literarische Voraussetzungen so eingehend dargelegt werden, daß das persönliche Element fast ganz verschwindet,"[61] he gave an excellent symptomatology of *tædium vitæ*, especially as a cultural and literary phenomenon. His exposition of the psychology of *tædium vitæ* and its relation to suicide, although it reflects a sound understanding of human behavior, offers no explanation of a causal relationship between *tædium vitæ* and suicide. A careful reading of certain passages in this thirteenth book reveals that Goethe mentions symptoms not strictly applicable to Werther's case, and that he skillfully glosses over the lack of a necessary connection between *tædium vitæ* and suicide with the facile, somewhat tendentious, and certainly not absolute generalization offered in the subordinate clauses of the following sentence—the lack of grammatical emphasis allows the reader to take in the *non sequitur* without feeling that it is insistently being forced upon him:[62] "Dieses sind eigentlich die Symptome des Lebensüberdrusses, der nicht selten in den Selbstmord ausläuft und bei denkenden, in sich gekehrten Menschen häufiger war, als man glauben kann." The answer to the psychological problem which Goethe seems to avoid in *Dichtung und Wahrheit* must be sought in *Werther*; but how he could consciously or unconsciously derive the conduct pattern "*tædium vitæ*-suicide" may be more clearly brought out if Werther's behavior is also examined in the light of certain passages in Lavater's *Predigten*; for this purpose it does not matter whether Lavater's explanations

[61] Festausgabe 16:559.

[62] Goethe ambiguously uses "jener" without antecedent once in the paragraph here quoted from and once in the one immediately before it; Düntzer, *Goethes Dichtung und Wahrheit: Erläutert.* . . (Leipzig, 1881) 2:196–97, felt constrained to note, "*Jener Ueberdruß*, von dem bisher noch gar keine Rede war" and "*Jener Eekel*, im Uebergange, wie oben *jener Ueberdruß* fällt um so unangenehmer auf, als *jene* in anderer Beziehung bald folgt." The first "jener" is, of course, proleptic, but Düntzer at least felt the forced character of Goethe's transitions in these two paragraphs (Festausgabe 16:126f.).

of psychological phenomena were original with himself, or whether they were to some extent already common intellectual property in the period of Goethe's youth.

The distinction between a Werther-Goethe and a Werther-Jerusalem has been used up to this point because it conveniently represents a kind of thinking found too frequently in discussions of literary works by critics who, often despite the best of intentions, cannot help paying homage to the great nineteenth-century positivistic tradition of *Quellenforschung* which has left so deep a mark on Goethe studies. To subdivide Werther into a Werther-Jerusalem and into a Werther-Goethe, and then to subdivide the latter into Werther-Goethes standing in a relation to Lotte Buff and Kestner, to Maximiliane La Roche and Brentano, or to other historical figures, is deliberately to risk losing sight of the character Goethe created; such sub-characters are the creation of the critic and represent individuals—psychologically perhaps perfectly consistent in themselves—whom the critic or his reader tends to substitute, wittingly or unwittingly, for the character delineated in the original literary work, often with complete disregard of the invalidity of explanations offered after such a substitution has been made.[63] In criticism of *Werther* the most important source of confusion has been the tendency to identify Werther too closely with Goethe, that is, either with the young Goethe of Max Morris's six volumes, a historical figure, or with the young Goethe of *Dichtung und Wahrheit*, in no small measure a literary creation. It is, therefore, more than advisable when discussing *Werther* to give particular attention to the traits of Werther's character which distinguish him from "Werther-Goethe." In explaining the conduct pattern "*tædium vitæ*-suicide," however, only one difference between Werther and Goethe needs to be emphasized: the latter was never so completely demoralized by the defect of character which Werther calls "Trägheit" as is the former.

The two non-scientific equivalents of "Trägheit" given in so brief a dictionary as *Der Sprach-Brockhaus* are "Faulheit" and "Unbeweglichkeit," and the word can be translated into English by "laziness, indolence, remissness, sloth, slothfulness, sluggishness, inertness, idleness, slowness, etc." Werther-Goethe in the narrowest sense, the young Goethe of Wetzlar

---

[63] A recent instance of Werther compounded is found in J. Hennig, "Goethe's Translation from Macpherson's 'Berrathon,' " *MLR* 42 (1947): 127–30: "In its shortness the *Berrathon* passage illustrates even better than *Songs of Selma* the perfect harmony to which Goethe-Werther's mind had attained with that of Ossian" (p. 128; = Goethe-Werther-Ossian!). As a result of creating Werther-Emilia Galotti, Ittner interpreted Werther's conduct according to Lessing's rationalistic moral psychology—toward which Goethe was probably hostile (cf. Feise, "Lessings *Emilia Galotti* und Goethes *Werther*," 324–29, 337). For Werther-Spiegelbild der Charakterentwicklung Goethes, cf. n. 152, *infra*; and see n. 28, *ante*, for the result of having created a Goethe-Rousseau.

and Frankfurt between May 1772 and the beginning of 1774, led an active social life, did legal work, carried on a lively correspondence with a wide circle of friends and associates, composed or translated a score of poems, contributed eight times to the *Frankfurter Gelehrte Anzeigen*, wrote several essays and pamphlets, thoroughly revised *Götz*, completed five playlets, started *Mahomet* and *Prometheus*, and did some sketching besides. This is no example of a man in whose character "Trägheit" constitutes a dominant trait!—which does not mean that the young Goethe need have had no personal experience of the pleasures of idleness, of the demoralizing effects of sloth, or of periods of depression when he was haunted by fears of psychic paralysis; but that the degree of "Trägheit" in the young Goethe was incommensurable with that in the young Werther.[64] For Werther represents the extreme form of "Trägheit." The way his negatively fatalistic philosophical and religious speculations enhance inactivity with positive values has already been sufficiently indicated. Moreover, between May of 1771 and the end of the following year the sum total of his achievements is negligible: he did the (automatic[65]) drawing enclosed in his letter to Wilhelm of May 26, 1771, presumably settled the difficulties in the matter of the inheritance mentioned in his first letter, took part in some social activities despite a declared love of solitude[66] and a tendency to restrict his social intercourse to single individuals and small groups,[67] carried on a limited correspondence[68] and put in somewhat less than six months at unsatisfying gainful employment in a manner at least unsatisfactory to his immediate

---

[64] That some of the emotional experiences of the young Goethe are commensurable with those of Werther has been well demonstrated by Feise, "Goethes Werther als nervöser Charakter," 232ff., who analyzes, for instance, Goethe's appreciation of the psychological effects of loneliness and isolation in 1772 and 1773. Feise's purpose, however, is to show that Werther-Goethe has psychological traits in common with Werther-Jerusalem, that "was Kestners dem Schicksale Werthers 'angeklebt heissen, trutz ihnen und ander—eingewoben ist' (*DjG* 4:147), weil es aus derselben Quelle des Selbst- und Miterlebens stammt." This is psychoanalytical *Quellenforschung* and the technique of demonstrating that Goethe was ever writing fragments of his great confession.

[65] "Ich. . . fand nach Verlauf einer Stunde, daß ich eine. . . Zeichnung verfertigt hatte, ohne das mindeste von dem meinen hinzuthun."

[66] Delight in "Einsamkeit"—1st letter, ff.; neglect of Amtmann S.'s invitation—June 16, 1771; preference for the solitude of a "Bauernherberge" to life "in dem traurigen Neste D. . ."—Jan. 20, 1772, i.e., before Werther's "Verdruß" reported Mar. 15.

[67] Early cultivation of Lotte and her family circle to the exclusion of other social interests; while ministerial secretary Werther has only two intimates, *viz.* Fräulein von B. . and Count von C. . .

[68] Chiefly with Wilhelm; at a period when letters were faithfully preserved and wide correspondence was the rule, the editor of *Werther* has "mit Fleiß gesammelt" a number averaging less than one per week.

superior.[69] "Trägheit" is a negative concept, and it is easiest to state the tragedy of Werther's character in negative terms—a highly developed inner life not balanced by any corresponding degree of external activity. In the words which Goethe used when describing his forthcoming novel to Schönborn, Werther is a young man

> der mit einer tiefen reinen Empfindung, und wahrer Penetration begabt, sich in schwärmende Träume verliert, sich durch Spekulation untergräbt, biss er zulezt durch dazutretende unglückliche Leidenschafften, besonders eine endlose Liebe zerrüttet, sich eine Kugel vor den Kopf schiesst.[70]

The disproportion between speculation and activity *alias* non-"Trägheit" is fatal for Werther, and it is for this reason that Werther's letter of July 1, 1771, with its discussion of "üble Laune" (which, Werther specifically declares, "ist eine Art von Trägheit") and with the only footnote in the novel directing the reader's attention away from Goethe's text, assumes such great importance for the motivation in *Werther*.

On the strictly compositional level of plot Werther's discussion of "üble Laune" is significant because, as has been pointed out above, it associates tragic suffering and death with a pattern of conduct which Werther himself is going to exemplify. The intensity of Werther's inner life is revealed when, at the end of his discourse, overpowered by memories, he breaks down for the first time since he has met Lotte; even in a period of relative euphoria he lacks what he has just termed "ein offnes Herz. . . das Gute zu geniessen, das uns Gott für jeden Tag bereitet." The sensitive reader is therefore not surprised to recognize touches of "üble Laune" in the first letter Werther writes after Albert's arrival, in which he very successfully damns with faint praise that "braver lieber Kerl" whose "gelassene Aussenseite" (a sort of false front, Werther implies!) contrasts with Werther's "Unruhe" and in whom he finds, with unconscious irony, the qualified negative virtue of having "wenig üble Laune"—"und du weist, das ist die Sünde, die ich ärger hasse am Menschen als alle andre" (July 30, 1771). Werther's last statement refers the reader back to the themes of the letter of July 1. Goethe is here hardly more subtle than is Werther in his method of characterizing Albert; it was too important to establish a definite association with the earlier letter, apparently, for Goethe to risk obscuring his point by the use of over-

---

[69] There is no reason to credit Werther's account with Ossian translations; long before he declared "Ossian hat in meinem Herzen den Homer verdrängt" (Oct. 12, 1772) he had indignantly observed, "Neulich fragte mich einer, wie mir Ossian gefiele" (July 10, 1771).

[70] *DjG* 4:26.

subtlety. In "Trägheit" and "üble Laune" there lies the fatal germ of tragedy and death.

As Franziska observed to Minna von Barnhelm, "Man spricht selten von der Tugend, die man hat, aber desto öfter von der, die uns fehlt." This familiar psychological generalization sufficiently explains how Werther can properly speak in character of the virtue non-"Trägheit" which he certainly lacks. The uniqueness of the discourse against "üble Laune" cannot, however, be over-emphasized, for it offers a stumbling-block to modern psychoanalytical interpretation of *Goethes Werther als nervöser Charakter*, as Ernst Feise seemed to realize when he wrote:

> Ein einziges Mal scheint es, als ob Werther von seiner Überzeugung der schicksalsmäßigen Determiniertheit des menschlichen Willens abwiche, das ist in seiner Rede gegen den üblen Humor. . . . Das durchaus wertherische Argument der Pfarrerin, daß wir unser Gemüt nicht in unserer Gewalt hätten, muß er einräumen und will die Laune demnach als eine Krankheit ansehen. Dagegen müsse man sich ermannen. Dem wiederum wertherischen Einwande Herrn Schmidts, daß man nicht Herr über sich selbst sei und am wenigsten über seine Empfindungen gebieten könne, entgegnet er, daß man die bittersten Arzneien nicht abweisen würde, um seine Gesundheit zu erhalten, und daß niemand wisse, wie weit seine Kräfte gingen, bis er sie versucht hätte.[71]

What is a very natural situation by eighteenth-century standards of psychological truth (is a Werther-Franziska so much less plausible than a Werther-Emilia Galotti?), requires a very subtle explanation containing a "wohl" when discussed in connection with a Werther-"nervöser Charakter":

> Die Erklärung [to continue the previous quotation] für dieses Ausweichen aus seiner eignen Denkbahn finden wir dann wohl in Werthers Bezeichnung der bösen Laune als eines inneren Unmuts über uns selbst, d.h. als einer als unwürdig erkannten Entwertungstendenz, besonders aber in der Tatsache, daß "Die Erinnerung so manches Vergangenen"—nur so begreift sich Werthers gewaltige Bewegung und sein Ausbrechen in Tränen—ein Gedenken eigner Schuld bedeutet. Er bekämpft sich daher in dem Herrn Schmidt selbst, wie er auch seinen vorgeahnten Selbstmord im Gespräche mit Albert verteidigte.

Of this explanation it is necessary only to remark that "bekämpfen" and "verteidigen" are not synonymous, although both suggest to the reader of

---

[71] Op. cit., 209–10.

German some common concept such as "Kampf," and that "Schuld" is a very ambiguous term when applied to Werther, who consistently, and usually successfully, tries to evade acknowledging even to himself responsibility for his actions, as his final rationalization of his death and use of the phrase "für diese Welt Sünde" have shown.[72] Whatever guilt Werther may have felt, it is safe to assume that in his "Erinnerung so manches Vergangenen" there is a far greater degree of self-pity for remorseful suffering than any permanent remorse; this is an interpretation more consistent with his tendency always to justify himself in his own eyes, a tendency evident in his very first letter (having barely gotten away from the atmosphere of some Leonore tragedy, he can say "Und doch war ich unschuldig! Konnt ich dafür, daß. . ."; his subsequent halfhearted self-reproaches, beginning "Und doch—bin ich ganz [sic] unschuldig?" break off with the consoling generalization, "O was ist der Mensch, daß er über sich klagen darf!"

V

Werther's pivotal[73] discussion of "üble Laune" contains elements that can, for the purpose of convenient emphasis, best be elucidated by making a comparison, to which Goethe's own footnote invites the reader of *Werther*, with the intuitive Lavater's psychological analyses in the three sermons, "Jonas Menschenfeindliche, Ehrgeitzige Unzufriedenheit mit Gottes Für-sehung und Güte," "Mittel gegen Unzufriedenheit und üble Laune," and "Von dem Ueberdrusse des Lebens." The text of the first of these sermons shows Jonah's displeasure with divine providence. Although he should have been pleased, not angry, that God wished to spare Nineveh, "ein zur Unzu-friedenheit geneigtes Gemüthe ist nicht fähig, die Sachen nach der Wahrheit anzusehen und richtig zu beurtheilen."[74] Werther, who has a genius for dissatisfaction, neither sees clearly nor judges well. In his letters antedating the one of July 1, 1771, he expresses displeasure with (a) class-conscious condescension towards the common people;[75] (b) the senseless activity of the "rechte gute Art Volks" who surround him and (c) by whom he cannot

---

[72] The word "Schuld" has too strong moral or ethico-sociological overtones. In the final sentence of the paragraph from which these quotations are taken an aesthetic value judgment is introduced: "So gefaßt erhält diese ganze Episode erst [!] den Stempel tiefster tragischer Ironie." Surely Lessing's simpler psychology does not exclude ironic implications of tragic significance.

[73] Pivotal also by its physical position at the exact middle of the "Erster Theil" of *Werther* (in *DjG* the passage from "Wir Menschen beklagen uns oft" to the end of the letter is preceded and followed by 23+ pp. text; in Festausgabe by 25 1/2 pp.).

[74] Op. cit., 2:156.

[75] May 15, 1771.

be appreciated—in fact, (d) the futility of wanting "was hienieden nicht zu finden ist"; (e) academic learning, especially in the field of aesthetic theory; (f) the intolerable offers of friendship by "einige verzerrte Originale";[76] (g) the general futility of human activity, which contrasts with his own rich inner life ("Ich kehre in mich selbst zurük, und finde eine Welt");[77] (h) the purely negative value of rules for conduct and (i) artistic creation;[78] (j) the interest of women in dress and (k) their tendency to gossip (here Werther is only lightly ironic); (l) certain books (by approval of Lotte's opinions);[79] and (m) failure to appreciate children properly.[80] It is thus not surprising that he should fail to see the inconsistency of his preaching against "üble Laune," or that he should judge Albert to be a sort of clod. So long as Werther still lives not completely resolved to renounce and die, he will begrudge Albert Lotte; this is envy which springs from the proud assurance of being superior to Albert, and envy also is dissatisfaction with the way things are ordered.

Each of Lavater's sermons is divided into two parts, the second of which contains applications to everyday life. In the second part of this sermon, Lavater warns his listeners to examine themselves before they pass judgment on Jonah's dissatisfaction with God's providence—"ehrgeitzige Unzufriedenheit" because Jonah, in his pride of race, disapproves God's concern with a gentile people. Lavater asks,

> Hat es dich, Lehrer des Evangeliums, nie heimlich verdrossen,—wenn andere Menschen, durch andere Menschen als durch dich, besser geworden sind? . . . Bloß weil du etwa besorgest,—daß *dein* Ruhm, *dein* Ansehen dadurch vielleicht vermindert werden mögte?[81]

As Werther declares in his discourse:

> ist sie [üble Laune] nicht vielmehr ein innerer Unmuth über unsre eigne Unwürdigkeit, ein Misfallen an uns selbst, das immer mit einem Neide verknüpft ist, der durch eine thörige Eitelkeit aufgehetzt wird: wir sehen glükliche Menschen die wir nicht glüklich machen, und das ist unerträglich!

With the clairvoyance of one glorifying virtues that he does not have, Werther analyzes his own capacity for envy and dissatisfaction, and forgets for

---

[76] May 17, 1771.
[77] May 22, 1771.
[78] May 26, 1771.
[79] June 16, 1771.
[80] June 29, 1771.
[81] Op. cit., 2:165–66.

one moment that he in his pride ordinarily succeeds only too well in convincing himself that everyone else's "Unwürdigkeit" is far worse than his own. Proud sensitivity, whether one is aware of it or not, is a corollary of "Trägheit" and "üble Laune," so that the episodes in which Goethe shows Werther suffering from injured honor do not represent the superimposition of a second alien theme on some such fundamental theme as the "endlose Liebe" mentioned by Goethe when he wrote Schönborn that Werther undermines himself by speculation until, "durch dazutretende unglückliche Leidenschafften [plural!] zerrüttet," he puts a bullet through his head.[82] Well before the crisis of injured honor, the ministerial secretary Werther furnishes in his letters plentiful evidence of misanthropic dissatisfaction: Lavater can well exclaim,

> Du bist ein unergründlicher Abgrund der niederträchtigsten Menschenfeindlichkeit, menschliches Herz, wenn eine eigensüchtige Leidenschaft dich beseelet, oder vielmehr vergiftet.—Urtheile selbst, o mein Zuhörer, in einer ruhigen Stunde *ob es wol gethan sey, daß du so unzufrieden bist?*[83]

Werther never has the quiet hour for careful self-judgment that did Lavater's hearer: even when talking with philanthropo-didactic intent about "üble Laune" he lets himself be carried away by emotion, and the reader who might want to know what else Werther could have said about his theme has no recourse but to examine Lavater's *Predigten*.

Werther only describes the hurt which "üble Laune" can cause to one's associates and the remorseful pain which one may feel when the final results of one's "üble Laune" become apparent. Lavater, however, completes the picture:

> *Du schadest damit* [mit deiner Unzufriedenheit] *niemand mehr als dir selbst.* Schrecklich schadest du dir damit; Du erniedrigst und verunedelst deine ganze Seele; Du raubest dir selber alle Ruhe, allen Frieden, alle Heiterkeit der Seele; Raubest dir das allersüsseste, reineste, edelste,

---

[82] Feise, "Goethes Werther als nervöser Charakter," 192, notes that Werther's "Berufsauffassung" is "eine organische Äußerung seines Charakters"; he accordingly begins his discussion of "das Problem des nervösen Charakters" "von dieser Seite seines [Werthers] Wesens ausgehend, nicht von seiner Natur- und Liebesauffassung"—a very sound procedure.

[83] Op. cit., 2:171–72.

unsterblichste, göttlichste Vergnügen der menschlichen Natur,—*das Vergnügen der theilnehmenden, brüderlichen Menschenliebe.*[84] A rich emotional life need not exclude "alle Ruhe. . . der Seele," yet it does so in the case of the dissatisfied and steadily more misanthropic Werther. In his second letter he already reveals that for him "Ruhe" is passive enjoyment:

> Eine wunderbare Heiterkeit hat meine ganze Seele eingenommen, gleich denen süßen Frühlingsmorgen, die ich mit ganzem Herzen geniesse. Ich bin so allein und freue mich so meines Lebens, in dieser Gegend, die für solche Seelen geschaffen ist, wie die meine. Ich bin so glücklich, mein Bester, so ganz in dem Gefühl von ruhigem Daseyn versunken, daß meine Kunst darunter leidet. Ich könnte jetzo nicht zeichnen. . . .

But before the letter ends, he is overcome by theistic, erotico-mystic, almost pantheistic emotions and breaks off his wish-dream of expressing in picture form what he sees in nature, declaring, "ich gehe darüber zu Grunde, ich erliege unter der Gewalt der Herrlichkeit dieser Erscheinungen." Because of his dissatisfaction with the generally accepted scale of social values, he cultivates the common man, whose "Gelassenheit" he praises without sharing ("so linderts all den Tumult, der Anblick eines solchen Geschöpfs, das in der glüklichen Gelassenheit so den engen Kreis seines Daseyns ausgeht"),[85] and when the moment has come to introduce Albert, he succeeds in presenting what is a symptom of his potential moral disintegration as a trait which shows integrity of character: "seine [Albert's] gelassne Aussenseite sticht gegen die Unruhe meines Charakters sehr lebhaft ab, die sich nicht verbergen läßt." Werther's excitable irritability develops unchecked, so that when his mother and Wilhelm, putting their faith in activity as the allopathic cure for "Trägheit," have gotten him to take a ministerial secretaryship, he is making only a halfhearted attempt at self-cure. As he declares on February 17, 1772: "Die Ruhe der Seele ist ein

---

[84] Ibid., 175. There is a significant "einander" in the second sentence of Werther's answer to Herr Schmidt's objection to his use of the term "Laster": "Mit nichten. . . wenn das, womit man sich selbst und seinen Nächsten schadet, den Namen verdient. Ist es nicht genug, daß wir einander nicht glücklich machen können, müssen wir auch noch einander das Vergnügen rauben, das jedes Herz sich noch manchmal selbst gewähren kann." Werther's entire emphasis is on the hurt "üble Laune" causes others, and the "sich selbst" of one of his next statements, "Alle Geschenke. . . ersezzen nicht einen Augenblick Vergnügen an sich selbst, den uns eine neidische Unbehaglichkeit unsers Tyrannen vergällt hat," refers to the victim of some other person's "üble Laune." For the value of "neidisch" in this last quotation, cf. n. 123, *infra*.

[85] May 27, 1771.

herrlich Ding, und die Freude an sich selbst, lieber Freund, wenn nur das Ding nicht eben so zerbrechlich wäre, als es schön und kostbar ist." Less than a month later the insulting of his honor furnishes him with an excuse to hand in his resignation and to devote himself again to full-time dilettantism—and "Trägheit." When Werther pays his penultimate visit to Lotte he is just about to complete the final rationalization of his suicide, which he has envisaged accomplishing "mit der möglichsten ruhigen Entschlossenheit";[86] he is still anything but calm, and Lotte thrice urges him to get control of himself, for she realizes that he must have "a quiet hour" if he is to be able to correct the error of his ways: "Nur einen Augenblik ruhigen Sinn, Werther. . . . Fühlen Sie nicht, daß Sie sich betrügen, sich mit Willen zu Grunde richten?"[87] It is too late, however, and the only calm that Werther achieves is that of the cold suspicion that Lotte is merely repeating her husband's observations; it is a calm unrelieved by any degree of "Menschenliebe," and Werther tears himself away "in der fürchterlichen Empörung [s]einer Sinnen,"[88] to reach his final resolution that very night.

In his next sermon Lavater treats "Mittel gegen Unzufriedenheit und üble Laune." Jonah's irritability with God's mercy towards a gentile people is only part of his more general dissatisfaction "mit allem. . . wovon er nur die geringste Unbequemlichkeit hat." This fault is so "allgemein, und von so schädlichen und weitgreifenden Folgen," that an hour will be little enough time in which to expound the extirpation of a vice "von welchem"—and here Lavater seems to confirm the truth of Werther's observation that he had never heard of a sermon in which "üble Laune" was discussed—"in den öffentlichen Vorträgen, Predigten und Schriften so wenig geredet wird."[89] For the purposes of his discussion Lavater considers it sufficient to describe four commonest varieties of "Unzufriedenheit" and "üble Laune," although there are "andere Arten, höhere und seltnere Grade des Unmuths und Lebens-Ueberdrusses" of which he does not wish to say anything at this juncture.[90] Could Werther, who certainly considered himself a very superior sort of person, have compared himself objectively with Lavater's commonest types of "unzufriednen, launischen, überdrüßigen. . . Menschen,"[91] he would not have been pleased to discover that he shared a surprising number of

---

[86] 4th paragraph of "Herausgeberbericht."

[87] Evening of Dec. 20 (editor's account).

[88] Dec. 21, 1772 ("früh").

[89] Op. cit., 2:184–85.

[90] The terms "Type I–IV" in my text replace Lavater's enumeration of "der seltnen Menschen mancherley Arten" ("Einige," "Andere," "Wiederum andere," and "Noch andere" as the opening words of four successive paragraphs, 2:188–93).

[91] Ibid., 187–88.

traits of character with them. Werther and the members of Lavater's Type I "sind mit ihrem *Schicksal,* und der göttlichen Fürsehung über sie, niemals zufrieden," although Werther in his pride does not consciously share with them the subjective insufficiency of endogenous melancholy attributed to them by Lavater when he says, with eighteenth-century simplicity of language, "Sie verweilen sich mit ihren Gedanken immer nur bey den Mängeln ihrer Natur, den Wiederwärtigkeiten ihres Schicksals."[92] This type overlooks "das Gute, das Gott ihnen täglich erweiset"—Werther's "das Gute. . . das uns Gott für jeden Tag bereitet"—and although they may be "ausserordentlich fröhlich" for a few moments, "[sie] sinken aber bald wieder in ihre vorige Unzufriedenheit zurück."[93] Werther has shown traits of this type even before his first letter, in which he promises Wilhelm that he will try to apply some of the latter's good advice:

Ich will, lieber Freund, ich verspreche Dir's, ich will mich bessern, will nicht mehr das Bisgen Uebel, das das Schicksal uns vorlegt, wiederkäuen, wie ich's immer gethan habe. Ich will das Gegenwärtige genießen, und das Vergangene soll mir vergangen seyn. Gewiß Du hast recht, Bester: der Schmerzen wären minder unter den Menschen, wenn sie nicht—Gott weis warum sie so gemacht sind—mit so viel Emsigkeit der Einbildungskraft sich beschäftigten, die Erinnerungen des vergangenen Uebels zurückzurufen, ehe denn eine gleichgültige Gegenwart zu tragen.

Werther here repeats a lesson the meaning of which he does not feel, or he would not place all responsibility for "Uebel" on fate nor so depreciate the present; the constantly appearing expressions of dissatisfaction in his subsequent letters reveal that he is always sinking back into his "vorige Unzufriedenheit," and the manic-depressive pattern of extremes of feeling is not new, as he reminds Wilhelm as early as May 13, 1771: "so unstet hast Du nichts gesehn als dieses Herz. Lieber! Brauch ich Dir das zu sagen, der Du so oft die Last getragen hast, mich vom Kummer zur Ausschweifung, und von süsser Melancholie zur verderblichen Leidenschaft übergehn zu sehn." Two letters later, describing the social activities which have "eine ganz gute Würkung" on him, Werther instinctively characterizes them pessimistically as "die Freuden. . . die so den Menschen noch gewährt sind" and regrets "noch so viel andere Kräfte in mir. . . die alle ungenutzt vermodern, und die ich sorgfältig verbergen muß. Ach das engt all das Herz so ein—Und doch! Misverstanden zu werden, ist das Schicksal von unser einem." Werther is never long satisfied with his "fate," and he is able to

---

[92] Ibid., 188.
[93] Ibid., 188–89.

announce in the third sentence of the first letter of the *Zweyter Theil* of the novel, "Ich merke, ich merke, das Schiksal hat mir harte Prüfungen zuge-dacht," which is the clearest unconscious revelation of dissatisfaction become habitual.

Persons of Type II "sind nur mit *besondern Widerwärtigkeiten*, die ihnen begegnen, unzufrieden." Type II differs from Type I primarily in that Lavater does not attribute to its members anything that corresponds to "subjective insufficiency," which his other two types also lack, and it may be noted that except in this respect all his types overlap each other, so that he cannot here be either credited or charged with having reduced the human soul to "wissenschaftliche Claßifikationen." Under Type II Lavater enumerates certain forms of adversity which Werther also experiences:

> eine Verläumdung, ein Widerspruch, die Fehlschlagung einer süssen Hoff-nung, ein Verlust, ein Mißverstand, ein saurer Blick den man ihnen giebt, ein mißlungener Versuch, ein ungerechtes Urtheil oder Betragen, ein Mangel von Höflichkeit oder Ehrbezeugung, die sie erwarteten, und zu verdienen glaubten. . . . Sie kränken sich gar sehr darüber; Sie verlieren sich bisweilen in ängstlichen Klagen, und überlassen sich einer mürrischen *Ungeduld.* . .—und verlieren sich unter dem Gefühl der gegenwärtigen Widerwärtigkeit so weit, daß sie oft mit dem Propheten seufzen: *Mein Tod wäre mir besser als mein Leben. Ja, es ist wol gethan, daß ich zürne bis auf den Tod.*[94]

Even in the relatively happy month of June, 1771, Werther shows "üble Laune" when he refers to the physician who has spread the slander that Werther is spoiling the Amtmann's children completely as "eine sehr dog-matische Dratpuppe"; the physician has, moreover, contradicted some of Werther's favorite ideas (June 29, 1771). And even before his "sweet hope" of winning Lotte has been proved vain, Werther has known moments when in his anger or disgust he could say, with Jonah, "It is better for me to die than to live"; as when he reports how Lotte's piano playing often soothes him "zur Zeit, wo ich mir eine Kugel vor'n Kopf schiessen möchte" (July 16, 1771). Later the figure of speech acquires real meaning, as in the statement made exactly one month after Albert's arrival: "Ich seh all dieses Elends kein Ende als das Grab" (Aug. 30, 1771). After the "Verdruß" of insulted honor it occurs with great frequency: "Da möchte man sich ein Messer in's Herz bohren";[95] "Ach ich hab hundertmal ein Messer ergriffen, um diesem ge-

---

[94] Ibid., 189–90.
[95] Mar. 15, 1772 (because Werther's "Neider" are triumphing at the fall of an "Ueber-müthigen").

drängten Herzen Luft zu machen";[96] "Man möchte sich dem Teufel ergeben, Wilhelm, über all die Hunde, die Gott auf Erden duldet";[97] "Ich möchte mir oft die Brust zerreissen und das Gehirn einstoßen, daß man einander so wenig seyn kann";[98] and so forth, until preoccupation with suicide finally dominates Werther's thinking. The easily offended Werther truly complains with varying degrees of Lavater's "surly impatience," which once reaches the deliberately unparaphrased arrogance of "Mein Gott! Mein Gott! warum hast du mich verlassen?"[99]

To Type III belong those dissatisfied with "unangenehme Begegnisse, die sie mit andern Menschen gemein haben."[100] Theirs is a relatively mild form of "üble Laune," of which the worst that Lavater can say is that it comes very close to being a blaming of divine providence, and for which he gives instances of delay or inconvenience caused by bad weather. Werther, never unaware that he is an uncommon man, has little of this common kind of "üble Laune," and specifically points out that fact when, on November 3, 1772, he analyzes his complete misery: "O daß ich launisch sein könnte, könnte die Schuld auf's Wetter, auf einen dritten, auf eine fehlgeschlagene Unternehmung schieben." (At this period Werther most nearly corresponds with Lavater's Type I in the matter of subjective insufficiency; admitting to a feeling that "an mir allein alle Schuld liegt," he immediately corrects himself however with "nicht Schuld! Genug daß in mir die Quelle alles Elendes verborgen ist.") Later in the same letter, moreover, he explains God's failure to grant his prayer for the power still to enjoy nature—as he once could when "mit Geduld" he passively awaited the divine spirit—with the aid of an analogy that refers to the too-human tendency to be dissatisfied with the weather: "Gott giebt Regen und Sonnenschein nicht unserm ungestümen Bitten." Nevertheless, Werther occasionally takes to heart experiences which he shares with a whole community of people, as when he expresses his violent reaction to the cutting down of the two trees at S . .—a reaction far more extreme than that of the actual villagers, however, who merely grumble and, in the case of the schoolmaster, perhaps shed some gentle tears.[101] It is ironic that on the

---

[96] Mar. 16, 1772 (referring to the same triumph of "die schlechten Kerls alle").

[97] Sept. 15, 1772 (because the "Nußbäume" at St. . have been cut down).

[98] Oct. 27, 1772 (refers to Werther's realization in the preceding letter that his disappearance from the world of Lotte and Albert would not leave a permanent emptiness even though he is now "diesem Hause. . . Alles in allem").

[99] Nov. 15, 1772. The corresponding allusion in the last paragraphs of his farewell letter to Lotte is less bitter but hardly more patient: "Ich schaudere nicht den kalten schröklichen Kelch zu fassen, aus dem ich den Taumel [not 'Ruhe'!] des Todes trinken soll!"

[100] Op. cit., 2:191.

[101] Sept. 15, 1772.

occasion of his first visit to this village, fourteen and a half months before, Werther had assured Herr Schmidt that "üble Laune" was curable. Those who belong to Type IV are *"überhaupt zu allen Zeiten. . .* entweder gegen *alle Menschen,* oder nur gegen. . . gewisse Personen unzufrieden."[102] Lavater's examples of Type-IV behavior make clear the difference between this type and Type II:

> Sie haben sich angewöhnt, alles zu tadeln. . . . Sie sind unzufrieden. . . wenn man redet, "man redet ihnen die Ohren voll, man schwazt ins Gelag hinein"; Unzufrieden, wenn man schweigt, "man ist stolz, man mag sich nicht mit ihnen abgeben, man verachtet sie." Ihr Lob ist Unzufriedenheit, wie ihr Tadel. . . . Höchstens sind es gewisse wenige Menschen, oder noch viel geringere Dinge, womit sie sich bisweilen einigermaassen auf eine angenehme Weise beschäfftigen, mit denen sie, wenigstens eine Zeitlang, so ziemlich ordentlich, und ohne Streit, Vorwürfe, Argwöhne, Zwistigkeiten und Verdrüßlichkeiten, durchkommen können.[103]

Persons in Type IV consistently let others feel the effect of their "üble Laune"; they are deliberately guilty of destroying for other people the pleasure which each heart, to use the words of Werther's own discussion of this "Laster," "sich noch manchmal selbst gewähren kann." Werther not only has strong personal dislikes, which he reveals to Wilhelm by the liberal use of such terms as "verzerrte Originale, dogmatische Dratpuppe, eine Närrin, die alte Schachtel, die Kerls, die Thoren, die Schurken, die Hunde, ein Thier, eine Frazze, ein Ding"—this series mirrors his increasing ill-humor over a year and a half—; but that he also makes no efforts to conceal from others his indifference or displeasure is evident from statements like "Ich lies mich aber in nichts stören" and from his report, after the insult to his honor, of the triumph of those who have long condemned his "Uebermuth und Geringschäzzung andrer" (March 16, 1772). Although Werther knows "wie nöthig der Unterschied der Stände ist,"[104] the insistence upon social distinctions by the guests of Count v. C. seems to him a deliberate personal humiliation. Not only is his praise of Albert from the very first so faint as to be "Tadel"; less than two weeks after they have first met Werther shows how little he thinks of Albert's opinions by stopping him in the middle of a sentence and quitting his presence when in the midst of their discussion of suicide (Aug. 12, 1771). Although at one point he assures Wilhelm "Es war gewiß nicht auf dich geredt, wenn ich schrieb: schafft mir die Kerls vom

---

[102] Op. cit., 2:192.
[103] Ibid., 192–93.
[104] Dec. 24, 1771.

Hals, die sagen, ich sollte mich resigniren,"[105] when he has had his "Ver-
druß" he immediately blames Wilhelm and his mother for it.[106] And the
inconstancy of Type IV appears in such shifts of interest as the substitution
of Homer for his former book collection,[107] of Ossian for Homer, or,
potentially, of modeling for his suspended sketch-work;[108] and in the ease
with which he discards people, like Fräulein v. B. or Fürst **, for whom he
first has only kind words. Indeed, even with Lotte there comes a moment
of strained relationship and of suspicion expressed in a statement like
"Weise! . . . sehr weise! hat vielleicht Albert diese Anmerkung gemacht?
Politisch! sehr politisch!"[109]

    As Lavater makes clear, however, all types of "üble Laune," not merely
Type IV, hurt innocent victims:

> Es ist nicht auszusprechen, wie viel tausend Seufzer und Thränen durch
> eine so unzufriedene. . . Gemüthsart manchem unschuldigen Herzen alle
> Tage ausgepreßt werden; Wie viel tausend Beängstigungen dadurch
> veranlasset, wie viel tausend Leben und Gesundheiten dadurch aufge-
> opfert, abgeschlachtet und abgemartert werden,—eigne und anderer Leben
> und Gesundheiten. . . .[110]

Werther makes the same point when he bids Herr Schmidt name him the
person "der übler Laune ist und so brav dabey sie zu verbergen, sie allein
zu tragen, ohne die Freuden um sich her zu zerstören"; and when, after
crying "Weh denen. . . die sich der Gewalt bedienen, die sie über ein Herz
haben, um ihm die einfachen Freuden zu rauben, die aus ihm selbst hervor-
keimen," he affords a glimpse of his own past as the recollection "so
manches Vergangenen" brings tears to his eyes and he vividly describes the
pathos of the death scene at which he himself was present. In his farewell
note to Wilhelm, Werther asks his mother's forgiveness "wegen all des
Verdrusses, den ich ihr gemacht habe," and aptly sums up the effect of his
"üble Laune"—though not without remaining true to Type I—in the sen-
tence, "Das war nun mein Schiksal, die zu betrüben, denen ich Freude
schuldig war":[111] the fate with which he has been constantly dissatisfied can
assume his guilt; hence the assurance "du vergiebst mir" in his last lines to

---

[105] Aug. 8, 1771.
[106] Mar. 15, 1772 ("ihr seyd doch allein schuld daran").
[107] May 13, 1771.
[108] July 24, 1771.
[109] Evening of Dec. 20, 1772.
[110] Op. cit., 2:196.
[111] Dec. 20, 1772.

Albert. But Werther has clearly exemplified "die Tiefen des Jammers" and the "Elend" which, according to Lavater, "auf der Seele des Unzufriednen ruhet,"[112] and which he so vividly described in his letter of November 3, 1772 with such significant utterances as "Genug daß in mir die Quelle alles Elendes verborgen ist." And the months of his final deterioration have surely demonstrated the justness of Lavater's psychological observations:

> Fast kein Mensch kann ihm [dem Unzufriednen] beykommen; Er hat keine Ohren mehr für die Erinnerungen eines Freundes. Alles macht ihn nur bitterer, unzufriedner, mürrischer, womit man ihn zahm und zufrieden machen will. So schrecklich zerrüttet Unzufriedenheit und üble Laune das Herz, und den ganzen Character des Menschen.[113]

Perhaps one of Goethe's finest touches in *Werther* is the scene when, hearing Lotte play the tune which has long been associated with her beneficent influence upon him, Werther cries, "um Gottes Willen hören sie auf"; she stares, then says with a smile, "Werther, sie sind sehr krank, ihre Lieblingsgerichte widerstehen ihnen" (December 4, 1772).

VI

In Werther's discussion of "üble Laune" occurs the sentence, as answer to the objection of the pastor's wife that our disposition may be influenced by our physical condition: "Wir wollens also. . . als eine Krankheit ansehen, und fragen ob dafür kein Mittel ist!" The cure which Werther suggests, to rouse ourselves to activity, does not really answer her objection, since it implies that we always have some control of our feelings. Herr Schmidt senses the weakness of Werther's logic and protests against this implication, whereupon Werther again begs the question:

> Es ist hier die Frage von einer unangenehmen Empfindung. . . die doch jedermann gern los ist, und niemand weis wie weit seine Kräfte gehn, bis er sie versucht hat. Gewiß, einer der krank ist, wird bey allen Aerzten herum fragen und die größten Resignationen, die bittersten Arzneyen, wird er nicht abweisen um seine gewünschte Gesundheit zu erhalten.

Werther's own story gives the lie to his first statement; and the application of his medical analogy is never made, for Werther interrupts himself to explain to the deaf pastor the theme of his discourse: in so doing he terms

---

[112] Op. cit., 2:197.
[113] Ibid., 198.

"üble Laune" a vice, and when forced to justify his use of this moral-theological term to the ever-objecting Herr Schmidt, this new problem so interests him that he neglects to go back to where he left off.[114] To judge from Werther's method of reasoning in his later discussion of suicide with Albert, however, it is doubtful if his analogy would have held water. A psychic disorder cannot be treated like a physical disease, a fact familiar to modern psychiatrists, who warn, for instance, that it is futile if not harmful to try to distract a person afflicted with melancholia by giving him work or by having him change his environment unless the ultimate source of his disorder is also treated. The tragic fate of Werther would indicate that Goethe recognized this principle, although it is perhaps only intuition that caused him to include the passages in the second part of *Werther* which suggest that the germ of Werther's disease is to be found in childhood experiences.[115] Lavater's discussion of "Mittel gegen Unzufriedenheit und üble Laune" (the second part of his sermon) reveals equal insight.

Lavater concedes hardly more value to physical therapy than would a modern psychologist. Only for some cases would he hesitatingly recommend "cörperliche Arzneyen," which could render "nicht übele Dienste":

> Denn es ist nicht zu läugnen, daß sehr oft die Beschafenheit des Cörpers, und unsere Gesundheitsumstände, grosse Ursachen unsers mißvergnüg-ten. . . Betragens sind, —Arzneyen, Luftveränderungen, unschuldige Er-götzlichkeiten, leichtere und freudigere Beschäftigungen, der Umgang mit guten, geduldigen, aber dennoch klugen und beherzten Menschenfreun-den, das Lesen aufweckender Schriften. . .—alles das mögen zu gewissen Zeiten, und für gewisse Personen, ganz gute unverwerfliche Mittel seyn. . . .[116]

Werther was exposed to all these remedies, if Wilhelm's letters be counted as "aufweckende Schriften"; but to no avail. As Lavater declares: "diese Mittel alle sind ausser uns, sind nicht allgemein brauchbar, dringen bey weitem nicht tief genug, können in unzähligen Fällen nicht helfen, und können sehr oft nicht einmal angebracht werden."[117] Lavater accordingly

---

[114] Lavater, 2:194, also speaks of the "Lasterhaftigkeit" of "üble Laune."

[115] May 9, 1772. Early religious associations are immediately suggested by the beginning of this letter: "Ich habe die Wallfahrt nach meiner Heimath mit aller Andacht eines Pilgrims vollendet. . . ." Werther's love of children could have special significance if it had its source in a regretted, first, happier part of childhood; cf. Feise's modern-psychological interpretation of this episode ("Goethes Werther als nervöser Charakter," 202).

[116] Op. cit., 2:200–1.

[117] Ibid., 201.

proposes a more fundamental remedy, "der Glaube an die allesregierende göttliche Fürsehung," upon which he then elaborates. Some light is perhaps shed on Werther's compulsion to rationalize, no matter how, his suicide as an act in harmony with the will of his God-Father, if Lavater's insistence that with God's help man can escape from the vicious circle of ever more virulent "üble Laune" be remembered; for Lavater is the representative of a religious tradition with which Werther is familiar and which, moreover, as modern psychologists sometimes concede, had long experience in dealing with the problems of the human soul. Such a statement as "Die Unzufriedenheit und üble Laune sieht alles in der Welt verzogen, verwirrt, alles in der größten Disharmonie und Zerrüttung"[118] could stand as an apt characterization of the tone of some of Werther's later letters, in which, by pathetic fallacy, even nature assumes the hues of Werther's state of mind. And it is in these same letters that Werther justifies his suicide step by step until he has, with his own God's help, achieved a suitable adjustment. He has not, however, used the strength gained from God, as a Christian like Lavater would have expected, to adjust himself to his environment; but he nonetheless believes that he has somehow recaptured in a sense the spirit of "jene Zeiten, deren Andenken mich quält"—times which were "so selig. . . weil ich mit Geduld seinen [God's] Geist erwartete, und die Wonne, die er über mich ausgoß mit ganzem, innig dankbarem Herzen aufnahm" (Nov. 3, 1772).

The last of Lavater's three sermons here to be discussed is "Von dem Ueberdrusse des Lebens, oder von dem Verlangen zu sterben,"[119] into which "üble Laune" can easily degenerate.[120] After an exordium in which he emphasizes the great value of God's gift of life, Lavater first treats cases in which it is permissible, noble and magnanimous to repeat, "freylich in einem ganz andern Geist," Jonah's words, "Ach Herr, nimm meine Seele von mir, denn mein Tod wäre mir besser als mein Leben."[121] There is (a)[122] a natural, innocent and momentary kind of discouragement which does not last if it is not "wilder Art" and if it is balanced by "Gottesfurcht und Vertrauen." In all humility, without wrath or envy, in the weariness of an Elijah,

---

[118] Ibid., 204.

[119] With this expansion of his sermon's title Lavater announces (2:221) the topic on which he will talk. Although, exceptionally, this sermon has a tripartite division, it falls into Lavater's usual two-part pattern: parts I and II, dealing with the worth of human life and permissible forms of longing for death, are together no longer than part III with its countertheme of sinful *tædium vitæ*. The term "second part" is accordingly used here to refer to the latter half of this sermon.

[120] Op. cit., 2:220.

[121] Ibid., 229.

[122] This letter-classification is Lavater's: (a) = 2:229–31; (b) 231–33; (c) 233–36.

we may ask for death because "unser Elend" at moments seems insurmountable, "vielleicht mehr um anderer als unser selbst willen." Werther's discouragement is not of this variety, for it is more than momentary, it does lead to death, and it is embittered by envy—envy not of Albert or of Albert and Lotte's happiness, but the grudging envy of "üble Laune" which is envy without humility (Werther, confident in his own superiority, is sure that he alone is fully worthy of Lotte: "O er [Albert] ist nicht der Mensch, die Wünsche dieses [Lotte's] Herzens alle zu füllen."[123]). Nevertheless, he for a while maintains the pretense that he is sacrificing himself for Lotte and until the end protests his reverent confidence in God's approval of his suicide: "ich danke dir Gott, der du diesen lezten Augenblikken diese Wärme, diese Kraft schenkest."[124] There is (b) a noble *tædium vitæ*:

> Die Seele des Menschen kann zuweilen durch Betrachtung des zukünftigen Lebens, durch vertrauten Umgang mit der ewigen Liebe in Jesu Christo— durch lebhafte Empfindung der unaussprechlichen Liebenswürdigkeit Christi, in ein sehnliches Verlangen des Todes, in eine edele Verachtung des gegenwärtigen leiblichen Lebens mächtig dahingerissen werden. . . . Der Gott, der dieß Verlangen in uns wirkt, kann uns auch die Liebesvolle Ergebung lehren. . . .

In Werther's longing to go "zu meinem Vater, zu deinem [Lotte's] Vater" there is, unfortunately, no balancing element of loving submission, but at best only a selfish hope of eagerly anticipated "ewigen Umarmungen."[125] And there is (c) a magnanimous scorn of life:

> Wer seines Lebens um des Lebens, der Wolfahrt und Glückseligkeit anderer willen nicht achtet; Wer mit seinem Leben gern das Leben eines oder mehrerer Brüder erkaufen mögte: dessen Lebensüberdruß ist nicht nur edel sondern großmüthig und erhaben.

Lavater's use of "Lebensüberdruß" is here very loose, for he is referring only to the spirit of pure sacrifice. This Werther too clearly lacks.

---

[123] July 29, 1772. For the peculiar value of the word "Neid" in Werther's statement to Herr Schmidt, "ist sie [üble Laune] nicht vielmehr ein innerer Unmuth über unsre eigne Unwürdigkeit, ein Misfallen an uns selbst, das immer mit einem Neide verknüpft ist, der durch eine thörige Eitelkeit aufgehezt wird," cf. H.J. Weigand, "*Wandrers Sturmlied*—'Neidgetroffen,' " *GR* 21 (1946): 165–72, esp. 170 and n. 14; cf. also, S. Atkins, "Werther's 'Misfallen an uns selbst, das immer mit einem Neide verknüpft ist,' " *MLR* 43 (1948): 96ff.

[124] "nach eilfe."

[125] Farewell letter to Lotte (last morning).

It is rather in the second part of this sermon, "von dem sündlichen, unedeln, niederträchtigen, unverantwortlichen Ueberdrusse des Lebens," that Lavater really treats the factors which account for such a conduct pattern as Werther's "*tædium vitæ*-suicide":

> Sobald sich Zorn, Menschenfeindlichkeit, Neid, wildes ungeduldiges Wesen, Empörung gegen Gottes Führung und Schickung, in unsere Sehnsucht nach dem Tode, in unsere Lebensverachtung einmischet, sobald ist sie unedel, sündlich und niederträchtig.[126]

Lavater's is a moral, not a "reine Experimental Psychologie."[127] That is to say, although he possesses a keen insight into the motives of human conduct, he cannot eliminate, as a modern psychologist might, ethical and theological judgments from his thinking, for he is, however remarkable his talent, the representative both of his church and of an intellectual climate in which ethical issues were very much alive. The uttered wish to die characteristic of *tædium vitæ* need indeed not lead to suicide, but as the expression of a sinful attitude—ungratefulness for God's gift of life—it can, theologically, become identical with suicide, which is a gesture of contempt for the great gift of life. The following sentence reveals how *tædium vitæ* can be equated with suicide: "Wer sein Leben verwünscht, oder es sich gar vorsätzlich, es sey nun nach und nach, oder auf eine gewaltthätige Weise verkürzt. . .—der betriegt sich selbst auf eine entsetzliche Weise."[128] If *tædium vitæ* and suicide were for Lavater hardly distinguishable forms of the same sinful folly, failure to appreciate the value of life, it is understandable that he can treat suicide as the final manifestation of the process of disintegration which begins with "Trägheit und üble Laune" and which does certainly become "Ueberdruß des Lebens." And so the remedy remains the submission of individual to divine will "mit der Dehmuth und Zuversicht eines Kindes,"[129] the remedy which Werther's pride never permits.

The weakest point in Lavater's reasoning thus comes when he allows a ready-made conventional moral judgment to replace psychological analysis—at the moment, incidentally, when he introduces the theme of non-sacrificial suicide for which the story of Jonah, so long his inspiration, does not provide any relevant example or analogy. It is, moreover, possible that his own self-observed psychological experience did not extend to serious contemplation of suicide, so that he had no basis for an intuitive

---

[126] Op. cit., 2:237.
[127] Cf. n. 133, *infra*, and Goethe's full statement there referred to.
[128] Op. cit., 2:237.
[129] Ibid., 239.

analysis and accordingly speaks like Albert, who declares when discussing the problem with Werther, "Ich kann mir nicht vorstellen, wie ein Mensch so thörigt seyn kann, sich zu erschiessen."[130] Lavater also considers it "thörigt" and "Thorheit," "sich selbst sein Leben zu verwünschen oder zu verkürzen,"[131] using the very kind of verbalistic judgment against which Werther protests with Albert: "Daß ihr Menschen. . . um von einer Sache zu reden, gleich sprechen müßt: Das ist thörig, das ist klug, das ist gut, das ist bös! Und was will das all heissen? Habt ihr deßwegen die innern Verhältnisse einer Handlung erforscht?" But Werther, despite his greater experience of physical and emotional excess,[132] also falls into verbalisms when, not without a touch of megalomania, he gives to the ambiguous words "Leidenschaft! Trunkenheit! Wahnsinn" primarily positive connotations simply by declaring that he has learned "Wie man alle ausserordentliche Menschen, die etwas grosses, etwas unmöglich scheinendes würkten, von jeher für Trunkene und Wahnsinnige ausschreien müßte." Not all that is excessive and unusual is good and great, Albert implies when he charges Werther with exaggeration—and again lays himself open to a new attack from Werther by adding a platitude about suicide's being weakness.

Werther, very properly in view of his later inner conflicts, senses that suicide can be a difficult decision, but his first attempt to demonstrate this truth uses two examples of the strength of despair (a people revolting; a man saving his goods from a burning house) which correspond to some such logic as "If there is strength in despair, all despair is strength" but which Werther sums up in the even more illogical form "wenn Anstrengung Stärke ist, warum soll die Ueberspannung das Gegentheil seyn?" Werther's final analogy is his happiest one, for it in a sense balances out the impossible medical analogy he started on in order to give Herr Schmidt proof that persons wish to be rid of disagreeable feelings as much as they wish to be rid of a disease; it is illustrated with the story of a simple girl who is seduced, deserted, and who commits suicide, the lesson drawn from it being:

Wehe dem, der zusehen und sagen könnte: Die Thörinn! hätte sie gewartet, hätte sie die Zeit würken lassen, es würde sich die Verzweiflung

---

[130] This and ff. quotations from Werther's discussion of suicide with Albert: Aug. 12, 1771.

[131] Op. cit., 2:241–42.

[132] "Ich bin mehr als einmal trunken gewesen, und meine Leidenschaften waren nie weit vom Wahnsinne, und beydes reut mich nicht, denn ich habe in meinem Maasse begreifen lernen: Wie man [etc., as quoted in text]."

schon gelegt, es würde sich ein anderer sie zu trösten schon vorgefunden haben.

Das ist eben, als wenn einer sagte: der Thor! stirbt am Fieber! hätte er gewartet, bis sich seine Kräfte erhohlt, seine Säfte verbessert, der Tumult seines Blutes gelegt hätten, alles wäre gut gegangen, und er lebte bis auf den heutigen Tag!

And with true intuitive insight Werther can counter in one clear sentence Albert's objection that an educated person would not behave like this simple girl: "der Mensch ist Mensch, und das Bißgen Verstand das einer haben mag, kommt wenig oder nicht in Anschlag, wenn Leidenschaft wüthet, und die Gränzen der Menschheit einen drängen." By his new medical analogy Werther does not make clear why suicide rather than madness should be the psychic equivalent of physical death. But he does leave a convincing impression that the mental life follows its own laws, an impression which Goethe, by having Werther leave Albert before the latter can present any counter-arguments, allows to remain final in the reader's mind. Werther has by no means "justified" suicide except to the extent that he has stated that there are cases when it is inevitable—his own final subtle justification is, in fact, only rationalization—but he has corrected the impression, which he himself gave in his lecture to Herr Schmidt, that a mental disease like "üble Laune" is to be remedied by what Lavater calls "Mittel ausser uns."

Werther and Lavater see, each in his own way, the limitations of vulgar eighteenth-century psychology; and although Goethe, through Werther, shows at times more understanding than the one-time associate whose "Talent" he so fully appreciated, even he did not possess the systematic knowledge which would have made it possible for him to indicate definitely in *Werther* the ultimate sources of Werther's psychopathic condition. Werther can be understood in terms of eighteenth-century moral psychology; but Goethe has portrayed him without committing himself to the traditional terminology of the moralities which he, like other Storm-and-Stress thinkers such as Herder, was submitting to the sharpest critical scrutiny. Goethe's distrust of conventional verbalism, his faith that the eternal truths of human experience need not be expressed in hackneyed formulae, can be seen in his letter to Lavater and Pfenninger of April 26, 1774—a letter which not only recalls Werther's of November 15, 1772, but also passages in Werther's discussion of suicide with Albert:[133]

---

[133] *DjG* 4:15–16. When Albert questions the aptness of his "Beyspiele," Werther observes, "man hat mir schon öfter vorgeworfen, daß meine Combinationsart manchmal an's Radotage gränze!" and later he declares "der Mensch ist Mensch." Goethe's letter similarly emphasizes a peculiar way of thinking and a common human element. For the parallels

Ich bin vielleicht ein Thor dass ich euch nicht den Gefallen thue mich mit euern Worten auszudrücken, und dass ich nicht einmal durch eine reine Experimental Psychologie meines Innersten, euch darlege dass ich ein Mensch binn, und daher nichts anders sentiren kann als andre Menschen, dass das alles was unter uns Widerspruch scheint nur Wortstreit ist der daraus entsteht weil ich die Sachen unter andern Combinationen sentire und drum ihre Relativität ausdrükkend, sie anders benennen muss[.]

Significantly, this letter contains an allusion to the manuscript of *Werther*, which is to provide Pfenninger "viel Erläuterung" on Goethe's religious views. And Goethe's application of the principle, "der Mensch ist Mensch," is so successful that *Werther* remains psychologically verisimilar even when analyzed as a case history by Ernst Feise in his essay, "Goethes Werther als nervöser Charakter."

VII

Shortly after the publication of *Werther*, Lavater wrote to Hartmann, "Herr Jesu! welche Wahrheit!" and two years later he expressed in a letter to Wieland his full approval of the novel.[134] That Lavater, unlike so many of his moralistic and theological contemporaries, did not find *Werther* an immoral book, is not to be explained by any motives of friendship for Goethe, however important these might have been. Although Lavater was almost the complete antithesis of Werther,[135] he was able to appreciate psychological truth when he saw it. Moreover, if he applied to the novel the yardstick of his own moral psychology, he could only congratulate himself on the correctness of his views as to the dangerousness of Christ-less religious thinking, exemplified by Werther. On the other hand, it was not even necessary for Lavater to regard Werther as a horrid example, for Werther is not only pathological, but is so to a degree which would justify his Christian salvation, at least for a tolerant representative of the church. Goethe, to be sure, does not insist on this point—"Kein Geistlicher hat ihn [Werther] begleitet"—which would have aroused still more antagonism towards the novel than, certainly to Goethe's surprise, did exist after it appeared. But in a century when the slogan of liberals, including Christian ones, was

noted by Feise, cf. notes 4 and 36, *ante*.

[134] Letter to Hartmann, Oct. 10, 1774 (cf. Janentzky, op. cit., 97); to Wieland, Aug. 9, 1776 (cf. C.F. Schreiber, *Goethe's Works with the Exception of Faust: A Catalogue*. . . [New Haven, London, 1940], *item* 949a).

[135] This point is fully elaborated by O. Guinaudeau, *Études sur J.-G. Lavater* (Paris, 1924) 337ff.

tolerance, when "tout comprendre" was "tout pardonner," not only admiration and love for Werther's mind and character, not only tears for his fate, but also pardon for his suicide could have been asked; for his case comes very close to being the exception to deliberate sinful suicide for which Lavater allows even as he condemns "sein Leben zu verwünschen oder zu verkürzen" as the greatest of follies:

> Den Fall ausgenommen, daß es in einer ganz unverschuldeten und unüber-windlichen Schwermuth geschehe, in welchen Fällen dann freylich der Unglückliche, und am Verstand und Herzen Kranke, dem gnädigen Urtheil und Erbarmen des gerechten Richters, ohne lieblose und harte Urtheile zu überlassen ist. . . .[136]

With intuitive wisdom Goethe has left the ultimate motives, "die innern Verhältnisse," of Werther's conduct unstated, and presents at the very start of his novel a character who already shows the dangerous and significant symptoms: "Trägheit" and "üble Laune." What follows is a long catastrophe culminating in suicide, a narrative the hero of which seems to have freedom of choice, although his fate, like that of Schiller's Wallenstein, actually is determined by his earlier behavior. Werther seems guilty, seems to know the value of the words "Laster," "Sünde," "Schuld," but in the course of the novel it becomes evident that he has used these words in an arbitrarily subjective sense, that he is not, morally speaking, what Lavater would call a "gesunder vernünftiger Mensch."[137] The interest of the novel is not in why Werther behaves as he does, but in how he will behave under given conditions. Goethe leaves unanswered the question whether or not Wer-ther's disease is "unverschuldet," so that for much of the novel—and for some readers, all of it—Werther's conduct has the apparent suspense value of responsible free action. However, just as Werther almost immediately reveals symptoms of "Trägheit" and "üble Laune," and, in his very first letter, shows a suspiciously weak moral sense, so also is it soon suggested that he may be one of those who are "am Verstand und Herzen Kranke." There is strange logic, almost as peculiar as that of his discourse of "üble Laune" and of his discussion of suicide with Albert, in his second letter: "Ich könnte jetzo nicht zeichnen, nicht einen Strich, und bin niemalen ein grösserer

---

[136] Op. cit., 2:242.

[137] Ibid., 223. ("Es ist kein vernünftiger Mensch, der das Seyn dem Nichtseyn, das Leben dem Tode nicht vorziehe; Kein gesunder vernünftiger Mensch, der natürlicher Weise nicht eine Furcht, eine Abneigung vor dem Tode, vor der Zerrüttung und Zerstörung seiner Natur habe." Is Lavater's "Seyn-Nichtseyn" a *Hamlet* "Anklang," as critics have claimed Werther's of Nov. 15, 1772, to be? In *Werther* "zerrütten" and "zerstören" are also used synonymously; cf. text, next paragraph.)

Mahler gewesen als in diesen Augenblicken"; and the theme of his sick heart is first introduced in his fourth: "Auch halt ich mein Herzgen wie ein krankes Kind. . . ." This theme is more definitely stated in the opening sentence of the letter which records his sermon against "üble Laune": "Was Lotte einem Kranken seyn muß, fühl ich an meinem eignen armen Herzen, das übler dran ist als manches, das auf dem Siechbette verschmachtet." Before he offers Albert his imperfect analogy between physical and mental disease as an explanation of suicide, Werther has already implicitly compared to a physical disorder the emotional dilemma from which he suffers because of Albert's arrival: he has asked Wilhelm,

> Und kannst du von dem Unglücklichen, dessen Leben unter einer schleichenden Krankheit unaufhaltsam allmählich abstirbt, kannst du von ihm verlangen, er solle durch einen Dolchstos der Quaal auf einmal ein Ende machen? (Aug. 8, 1771)

Less than three weeks later Werther's condition has definitely become a disease, and all that remains uncertain—although for Werther only slightly more so—is whether it can be cured: "Es ist wahr, wenn meine Krankheit zu heilen wäre," writes Werther, reporting his birthday surprises, "so würden diese Menschen es thun" (Aug. 28, 1771). Werther's sickness is of the soul, of the "heart," primarily, and he never loses his ratiocinative faculties, although they only serve the desires of that heart.

Towards the end of *Werther* the distinction between sickness of mind and sickness of heart becomes minimal as the tyranny of emotion over reason reveals itself both in the violence of Werther's language, which gives the lie to assurances that he is "ruhig," and in the over-subtle rationalizations which he uses to justify his deeds and desires. In Werther's letter of November 30, 1772, the account of the mad Heinrich, who turns out to have been in love with Lotte, has been considered "fast stilwidrig episch" by more than one critic,[138] although the letter as a whole, in which almost as many lines are devoted to Werther's interpretation of the story's significance as to the narrative itself, shows no less than his shorter letters the ever-recurring pattern of would-be calm giving way to emotional turbulence. Whatever the stylistic virtues or defects of this letter, however, it serves a double purpose. On the one hand, Heinrich's story by itself is sufficiently like Werther's to suggest that what the latter suffers is only a more complicated form of madness, so that sympathy for a Werther who commits suicide need not be qualified by conscientious scruples in the case of readers too hasty with

---

[138] E. Feise, "Zu Entstehung, Problem und Technik von Goethes 'Werther,' " 29; cf. M. Herrmann, Jubiläums-Ausgabe 16:xviii.

moral judgments. On the other hand, Werther's general comments once more raise the question of how valid conventional terminologies are and remind the reader that they cannot explain "die innern Verhältnisse einer Handlung":

> Müsse der trostlos umkommen, der eines Kranken spottet, der nach der entferntesten Quelle reist die seine Krankheit vermehren, sein Ausleben schmerzhafter machen wird, der sich über das bedrängte Herz erhabt, das, um seine Gewissensbisse los zu werden und die Leiden seiner Seele abzuthun, seine Pilgrimschaft nach dem heiligen Grabe thut! Jeder Fußtritt der seine Solen auf ungebahntem Wege durchschneidet, ist ein Lindrungstropfen der geängsteten Seele, und mit jeder ausgedauerten Tagreise legt sich das Herz um viel Bedrängniß leichter nieder. —Und dürft ihr das Wahn nennen—Ihr Wortkrämer auf euren Polstern—Wahn!

What renders disservice to physical health can assuage "das bedrängte Herz," and so Werther demonstrates, more successfully than when discussing with Albert suicide, the ambiguous connotation of such a word as "Wahn," which belongs with the earlier group of "Leidenschaft! Trunkenheit! Wahnsinn." Werther's own sickness is primarily of the heart, but the lines just quoted follow a sentence in which "in deinem zerstörten Herzen" and "in deinem zerrütteten Gehirne" ("dein" refers to Heinrich) stand in immediate apposition, so that Werther's special disorder is equated implicitly with something called by another name—madness, the conventionally condonable "cause" of suicide. After an interval of three short letters Werther finally does equate his condition with madness: "ich bin in einem Zustande, in dem jene Unglüklichen müssen gewesen seyn, von denen man glaubte, sie würden von einem bösen Geiste umher getrieben." It is surely intentional that this statement is so formulated as to emphasize incidentally a truth which both Goethe and Werther perceive: that the nature of things is often obscured by the words applied to them. Standing as it does between these two equations of Werther's sickness with madness, Lotte's observation of December 4 assumes profound tragic-ironical significance: "Werther. . . sie sind sehr krank, ihre Lieblingsgerichte widerstehen ihnen."

After Werther's letter of December 17 ("Meine Sinnen verwirren sich. Schon acht Tage hab ich keine Besinnungskraft") he is no longer the sole narrator of his own story, but it is his own papers and last letters which contain his remarkable final rationalization of suicide, a display of virtuosity at (paranoic) self-deception far surpassing the delusion of the mad Heinrich that all *his* difficulties would be permanently solved if the "Generalstaaten" paid him moneys due. As always, the interest of the novel centers on the problem of how Werther will act, although at the beginning of the "Herausgeberbericht" an undated "Zettelgen" is quoted which for the last time directly reminds the reader that Werther may not be a responsible free agent and that there are definite limits to our conventionally formulated knowledge:

> Ihre Gegenwart, ihr Schiksal, ihr Theilnehmen an dem meinigen, preßt noch die lezten Thränen aus meinem versengten Gehirn.
> Den Vorhang aufzuheben und dahinter zu treten, das ist's all! Und warum das Zaudern und Zagen?—Weil man nicht weis, wie's dahinten aussieht?—und man nicht zurükkehrt?—Und daß das nun die Eigenschaft unseres Geistes ist, da Verwirrung und Finsterniß zu ahnden, wovon wir nichts Bestimmtes wissen.

"Aus meinem versengten Gehirn" echoes the earlier "in deinem zerrütteten Gehirne," while the doctrine of the finite limitations of human knowledge is now used, not to account for suicide, but to clear the way to it. To the very end of Goethe's novel the question of what are the ultimate causes of Werther's suicide is left unanswered. Werther is interred without sacrament in a corner of the churchyard, and finite man cannot say whether or not he will be reunited with Lotte "vor dem Angesichte des Unendlichen in ewigen Umarmungen." But Werther's logically twisted faith in a God-Father has enabled him to reveal the verbalistic insufficiency of the time-honored theological doctrine stated by Lavater in these words: "Wer sich sein Leben selbst verwünschet oder verkürzt. . . muß ganz und gar kein Zutrauen, keinen Glauben, kein Herz mehr zu seinem Schöpfer und Erlöser haben."[139] Werther does not heed the final injunction of Lavater's sermon "Von dem Ueberdrusse des Lebens"—"Verwünsche dir nie, noch vielweniger verkürze dir dein Leben"; perhaps, however, Lavater's preceding words do in some sense apply to him:

> *Gott ist die Liebe, und du bist sein Geschöpf, das Geschöpf der ewigen Liebe bist du:* Das ist unveränderlich wahr, du magst es glauben oder nicht glauben. Gott vergißt deiner nicht, wenn du gleich seiner vergissest.[140]

But Goethe left this for the reader to decide.

---

[139] Op. cit., 2:243.
[140] Ibid., 252.

VIII

Ever since *Werther* first appeared, it has been the subject of controversy. Readers of 1774 and 1775, accustomed to novels in which characters were well-defined, whether good, bad or mixed, were unable to accept Werther for what he was—a character upon whom no final moral judgment is passed. Many sentimentalists took him at his own evaluation, and apotheosized him; other critics, seeing only that he is a suicide, charged Goethe with deliberately trying to undermine the moral foundations of society by making him the hero of a novel. Hence poems like *Lotte auf Werthers Grab*, but also satires like Nicolai's *Freuden* or opinions like Bodmer's: "Ist nicht Wehrter [*sic*] der blödeste, feigherzige Mann? Aber es scheint, der Verfasser halte die Feigheit, welche den Schmerzen der Liebe durch den Tod entflieht, für Stärke der Seele."[141] It merely seemed "ganz kühn" to Nicolai's friend Bretschneider that Goethe maintained "man habe ihn nicht verstanden,"[142] but Goethe had already reported to Sophie von La Roche in December, 1774, the impression that was made upon him by finding in an "umgeliehen" copy of *Werther* the words, "Tais Toi Jean Jaques ils ne te comprendront point!"[143] The obstacle to understanding of *Werther* was an ingrained habit of passing moral judgments in terms which seem to have absolute values; it was the assumption that verbalistic definition can furnish the key to "die innern Verhältnisse." Goethe himself makes this point in one of his contributions to Lavater's *Physiognomische Fragmente*, in a passage curiously enough not indexed under "*Werther*" in M. Morris's *Der junge Goethe*:

Wie die Sachen eine Physiognomie haben, so haben auch die Urtheile die ihrige, und eben daß die Urtheile verschieden sind, beweist noch nicht, daß ein Ding bald so, bald so ist. Nehmen wir zum Beyspiel ein Buch, das die Freuden und das Elend der Liebe mit den lebhaftesten Farben schildert. Alle junge Leute fallen drüber her, erheben, verzehren, verschlingen es; und ein Alter, dem's unter die Hände kommt, macht's gelassen oder unwillig zu, und sagt: "Das verliebte Zeug! Leider, daß es in der Welt so ist, was braucht man's noch zu schreiben?"

Lassen Sie nun von jeder Seite einen Kämpfer auftreten! Der eine wird beweisen, daß das Buch vortrefflich ist, der andere, daß es elend ist! Und welcher hat Recht? Wer soll's entscheiden? Niemand, denn der Physiognomist. Der tritt dazwischen und sagt: begebt euch zur Ruh, euer

---

[141] *DjG* 5:269–70.
[142] Ibid., 245.
[143] *DjG* 4:157.

ganzer Streit nährt sich mit den Worten *fürtrefflich* und *elend*. Das Buch ist weder fürtrefflich noch elend. Es hat nur deine ganze Gestalt, guter Jüngling. . . und weil dir's gleich sieht. . . so nennst du's deines Gleichen, oder welches eins ist, deinen Freund, oder welches eins ist, fürtrefflich. Du Alter hingegen würdest ein Gleiches thun, wenn diese Blätter so viel Erfahrung, Klugheit, praktischen Sinn enthielten.[144]

Werther was not meant for those who were old, for those whose mental habits had become so set that they would be unable to bring understanding to its Storm-and-Stress relativism: "Und du gute Seele, die du eben den Drang fühlst wie er, schöpfe Trost aus seinem Leiden, und laß das Büchlein deinen Freund seyn, wenn du aus Geschick oder eigner Schuld keinen nähern finden kannst." The "Freund" of *Werther* would surely appreciate Goethe's parable of the controversial book, and if he had really understood it he could agree with the lesson Goethe draws from it:

Alles wirkt verhältnißmäßig in der Welt, das werden wir noch oft zu wiederholen haben. Das allgemeine Verhältniß erkennet nur Gott; deswegen alles menschliche, philosophische und so auch physiognomische Sinnen und Trachten am Ende auf ein bloßes Stottern hinauslauft.[145]

As Goethe came to realize that Lavater, too, was striving for an absolute of "wissenschaftliche Claßifikationen," his interest in physiognomy soon ended. One may even venture to doubt that he would have conceded more than relative value to any modern systems of psychology, for, although their analyses go far deeper into patterns of human behavior than did eighteenth-century efforts such as those of Lavater—or Herder—in the last analysis they also do not go beyond the "how."

The whole history of *Werther* criticism illustrates one ever-repeated pattern of human behavior: the tendency to fill the vacuum of relativism with absolutes; for relativism is, to use Lavater's words, "eine Gottheit die nicht hilft" and is so abhorrent to most men that they instinctively follow the advice, "Suche irgend etwas, mache irgend etwas zu deinem Gott. . . daß du nicht verdärbest"—which is what even the relativist Werther does in his own exceptional way. It cannot be too often pointed out that the interest of *Werther*is deliberately centered in the problem of how its hero will behave, not that of why he so behaves or that of what psychic disorder may account for his behavior; Goethe accordingly emphasized the impossibility of knowing "die innern Verhältnisse einer Handlung"—the story of Werther is an *action*

---

[144] Op. cit., 5:325.
[145] Ibid., 326; cf. also Faust's rejection of "Im Anfang war das *Wort*."

in the literary sense—and so understated the pathological element in Werther's character that countless readers have assumed Werther to be a morally responsible free agent.[146] (The understatement of the pathological is counterbalanced somewhat by the verses added to the "Zweyte ächte Auflage" of *Werther*, 1775, which contain the warning, "Sey ein Mann, und folge mir nicht nach"; and more fully in the 1787 version by changes and additions of a more drastic nature.) In many senses Werther is passive, but he is not static, nor is his story, which is a small part of the Erdgeist's "wechselnd Leben," of "der Gottheit lebendiges Kleid." Nevertheless, from 1775 until the present day even those critics who have fully realized that *Werther* can be properly understood only in terms of relativism have continued to offer interpretations of it which emphasize its static elements at the expense of the dynamic component: the story or action. The one contemporary reviewer who saw clearly that *Werther* could not be understood by critics who applied to it the criteria of conventional morality or of biographical-historical accuracy, managed to find the novel "die allervortreflichste Erläuterung durch ein Beispiel von dem Satze: Die Menschen werden zu ihren jedesmaligen Handlungen durch die zusammengesezte Wirkung der Umstände und ihres Charakters unwiderstehlich bestimt."[147] A modern critic credits this reviewer with having "den gedanklichen Schwerpunkt der Dichtung richtig erkannt, wenn er [so] schreibt"; which is to substitute arbitrarily a static general principle for the special problem that really holds the attention of the reader of *Werther*, the problem of how Werther will act next. This very critic, who belongs to the school of Franz Saran and who attempts, with praiseworthy humility, to interpret *Werther* "aus sich selbst" and to understand it "von innen heraus,"[148] so stresses the "Gedankengehalt der Dichtung" that any impression of the degree to which Werther's story mirrors the dynamic complexity of life in all its irrationality is destroyed:[149] because Werther is a "Naturalist" in all his

---

[146] A second reason for this understatement was the necessity of making Werther as likable a character as possible, lest "normal" readers take offense and decide that a mere psychopathic case was unworthy of their attention.

[147] Anonymous review, *Auserlesene Bibliothek der neuesten deutschen Litteratur* (Lemgo, 1775) 8:500–20; quoted by Gose (n. 2), 6.

[148] Gose, 1.

[149] Ibid., 11; cf., however, p. 2, where Gose justifies his procedure: "Da sich die Wertherforschung bisher vorwiegend mit den philosophischen, den stofflichen und den ästhetisch-formalen Fragen beschäftigt hat, eine methodisch erschöpfende Herausarbeitung des Gedankengehalts aber noch aussteht, so betont die vorliegende Arbeit mit bewußter Einseitigkeit das Gedankliche." "Damit," Feise observes ("Goethes Werther als nervöser Charakter," 185–86), "ist aber der Charakter Werthers noch nicht erschöpft. Denn aus der Idee allein wird noch kein Werk geboren. . . ." Feise wisely notes that *Werther* is no allegory, but then, by applying a negative value judgment to the term "allegory" and a

thinking, his "religiöse Auffassung" is stripped of its irrational inconsistencies as much as possible and defined as "ein mit biblischen Resten durchsetzter *dynamischer Pantheismus* von naturalistischer Färbung";[150] for the same reason, his method of rationalizing away such moral and religious scruples as stand in the way of his suicide is allowed to demonstrate that "Der Naturalist fühlt sich für den von Naturkräften bedingten Ablauf seines Lebens nicht sittlich verantwortlich"—which may indeed be true, but which minimizes the element of flux in Werther's character that is the essence of the (dramatic) suspense in *Werther*.[151] And in 1946, to offer a fully up-to-date example of the tendency to neglect the dynamic component in *Werther*, twenty-five years after the critic just quoted, still another scholar, discussing "Werther, Tasso und Wilhelm Meister als Spiegelbilder der Charakterentwicklung Goethes," practically reduces the novel to a series of expressions of "infantile Eigenschaften" corresponding to one (static?) stage of Goethe's development and observes that Werther's (one) neurosis might be described as masochism;[152] it is a far cry from applying moral yardsticks to literature to applying those of modern -ologies, yet will a critic ever understand a literary work if he approaches it with an irrelevant assumption, however true, such as "Nach künstlerischen Gesichtspunkten geformt. . . heißt. . . für den charakterologischen Deutungszweck deformiert"?[153]

---

positive one to "symbol," manages to find in the work symbolic value and to reach his absolute, "Typus": "Ist das Symbol ein menschlicher Charakter, so wird seine Einheit demnach nie in einer Idee aufgehen, auf einen Typus werden wir ihn trotz aller seiner Widersprüche zurückführen können, wenn er wahr und lebensfähig ist."

[150] Gose, 24. The concept of "dynamischer Pantheismus" as the fundamental "Anschauung von den letzten Dingen" in *Werther* is the premise of H. Schöffler's interpretation of Goethe's novel as "der Urfall eines Leidens in Sehnsucht nach unerreichbarem diesseitigem Werte" (*Die Leiden des jungen Werther: ihr geistesgeschichtlicher Hintergrund* [Frankfurt/Main, 1938] 29) and as a seriously intended parody of the Christian "Erlösungstod" (30)—"die erste nicht-dualistische Tragödie unserer Geistesentwicklung" (32) because "Die Geschlechterliebe ist der absolute Wert in diesem Kunstwerk, und kann dieser Wert nicht erlangt werden, so wird das Leben wert-los" (27). Schöffler, who finds Goethe-Werther of the "Erster Theil" "weit entfernt vom Jerusalem-Werther des zweiten Jahres" (7), calls it a "Tatbestand, daß Werther seinen Tod als Opfertod bezeichnet" (16); he is thus able to establish startling parallels between Werther's story and that of Christ as told by St. John.

[151] Gose, 65; his next sentence renders Goethe the further disservice of reemphasizing the static quality attributed to Werther's personality: "Im Ethischen bleibt also Werther seinem Naturalismus treu." Because of its component "natura," *ethischer Naturalismus* suggests a positive value judgment hardly inherent in its synonym: "egocentric voluntarism" (and Werther's desires are his only law!).

[152] Helmut Hirsch, *GR* 21 (1946): 247–56, esp. 247–50; in this interpretation Werther's suicide decision is evoked by Lotte's "Seien Sie ein Mann" (250) and really represents the conduct pattern "die bösen Eltern durch Selbstbestrafung zu rühren" (249).

[153] Hirsch, 247.

Perhaps "the vague 'Sturm-und-Drang Psychologie' sometimes indicated as the framework of the novel"[154] is, because of its very vagueness, the -ology which can be introduced into a discussion of *Werther* with the least danger of obscuring Goethe's artistic intention. After all, the words "vague" and "deformiert" convey the kind of value judgments against which both Werther and the young author of *Werther* so insistently protested. Helene Herrmann treated *Die psychologischen Anschauungen des jungen Goethe und seiner Zeit* in a dissertation of which only the introductory sections were separately published, and her husband incorporated several previously unpublished paragraphs of this work in his introduction to the 16th volume of the Jubiläums-Ausgabe of Goethe's works.[155] A few quotations from these paragraphs, which reflect an intimate knowledge of Storm-and-Stress literature in the widest sense of the word (*belles-lettres*, diaries, letters, theoretical writings such as Herder's, etc.), will serve to show that she, at least, succeeded in formulating the conclusions reached in her study of "die Sturm-und-Drangseele" without substituting terms with connotations of the static and absolute for ones with connotations of the dynamic and relative:

> Die unablässige Bewegtheit dieser Seelen macht ihnen eine Psychologie begreiflich, ja notwendig, die die Seele als einen Prozeß faßt.—Man fühlt sich als ein Wirksames, nicht als ein Leidendes.—Seelenwesen ist Wirken um des Wirkens willen. Jede Zielsetzung von außen ist Negation. Daher bei allen diesen Menschen der Haß gegen ein Amt. . . . Die Briefe des jungen Goethe seit 1771 enthalten implizite diese große Erfahrung, daß Wirkungs-streben, "Drang"[,] die Seele selbst sei, ohne bestimmten Inhalt, ohne sicheres Ziel, nur ein "*nisus* vorwärts." Das zeigt die damalige Art seiner Selbstbeobachtung. Weniger penible Zustandsanalysen als Angaben über Tempo und Stärke des inneren Erlebens.—Verstehen heißt ja dieser Psy-chologie: gleicherleben.[156]

Both the "psychology" and "theology" of Werther, and the aesthetics of *Werther*, foredoom to self-contradiction every interpreter of Goethe's novel who believes he has defined the content ("Inhalt") of Werther's psyche, who neglects to emphasize the process ("Prozeß") of Werther's sufferings, or who overstresses the leitmotifs in the novel[157] and the facets of Werther's

---

[154] Cf. notes 2 and 12, *ante*, and text.

[155] XIX–XXVI.

[156] XIX–XX, XXVI.

[157] Cf. M. Diez, "The Principle of the Dominant Metaphor in Goethe's Werther," *PMLA* 51 (1936): 821–41, 985–1006: "Werther's suicide is the principle theme, the most important event and climax of the whole development" (830). In this invaluable study can be found

character which seem to prove that the dramatic intention of *Werther* ("Ziel [der Handlung]") is beyond a shadow of doubt suicide. It will be the attempt of the just critic "Mitgeteiltes aufzunehmen, wie es gegeben wird" while trying to avoid any "Sich-mitzuteilen";[158] being only human, however, he may see—as the author of this present study no doubt at times has done— premises where there are only processes—as did even Max Herrmann, who clearly appreciated the great significance of his wife's findings in her study of Storm-and-Stress psychology, when he began his analysis of the psychological problem of *Werther* by assuming that "Ursprünglich ist Werthers Seele durchaus gesund."[159] In attempting to understand Werther the critic will nevertheless be wise who lets his "gleicherleben" remain vicarious, for then he will be able to give *ex post facto* his equivalent of Lavater's "Herr Jesu! welche Wahrheit!" After all, "Am farbigen Abglanz," too, "haben wir das Leben."

in systematic form plentiful evidence of the importance of non-static imagery in *Werther:* for instance, metaphors and similes classified together as relating to *death* (a "Zustand"!) more often than not refer to the processes of dying, killing, being killed or decaying (cf. 838–41); there is, moreover, full treatment of metaphoric use of words of *motion* (991–95).

[158] Cf. *Die Wahlverwandtschaften*, II. Teil, 4. Kap., "Aus Ottiliens Tagebuche."

[159] Jubiläums-Ausgabe 16:VIII; whether "ursprünglich" means at some point in Werther's past, or, as Feise ("Goethes Werther als nervöser Charakter," 202), repudiating Herrmann's assumption, seems to interpret this statement, at the time the novel begins, hardly affects the irrelevancy of the assumption.

The Opening Lines of Goethe's *Iphigenie auf Tauris*

It has so frequently been remarked upon that the opening lines of Goethe's *Iphigenie auf Tauris* serve to establish the tone of that drama that it may seem uncalled for to offer again a more detailed analysis of them. It would, indeed, be difficult to say something not already said by someone about what they mean, both literally and for such problems as the ideas of the drama, the character of its heroine, or the foreshadowing of its action.[1] On the other hand, except for rather general observations or for isolated comments on separate words and phrases, relatively little has been written about the style of these fifty-three lines: to the extent that what holds true for the language of *Iphigenie* as a whole is also valid for them, but to that extent only, have they been satisfactorily analyzed in point of style.[2] The following paragraphs therefore contain an attempt to define the peculiar stylistic quality of Iphigenie's monologue, and to determine its function not in terms of explicit meanings[3] but, at least primarily, simply as poetic language.

The spirit of *Iphigenie* is modern; essential features of classical Greek tragedy are wanting in it; and yet, thanks to "des particularités tout extérieures"—"surtout. . . la noblesse et la pureté du style, . . . le parfum d'archaïsme qu'il [Goethe] donne à sa langue, . . . l'imitation de certains procédés de la diction antique, . . . le vers, enfin, qui, par son allure régulière et aristocratique, rehausse la majesté et la sérénité de l'action"[4]—, it deliberately gives the impression of classical tragedy. Thus it opens, unlike *Götz, Clavigo, Stella,* or *Egmont,*[5] with a monologue, more or less Euripidean. The stage is set in the open air, and there is a certain amount of factual exposition, dramatically gratuitous for the most part since it will be recapitulated in subsequent dialogue: Iphigenie misses her Greek home (ll.

---

[1] James Boyd, *Goethe's "Iphigenie auf Tauris." An Interpretation and Critical Analysis* (Oxford, 1942), offers convenient surveys of critical opinion on disputed passages as well as detailed analysis of the text in its parts and as a whole.

[2] Cf., for example, H. Morsch, "Goethe und die griechischen Bühnendichter," *Königl. Realschule zu Berlin, Progr. Nr. 90* (1888), or the introductions of various editors.

[3] Cf. Boyd 21–25, or Walzel's commentary, Festausgabe 7:511–12.

[4] H. Loiseau, "Étude sur *Iphigénie en Tauride*," [Goethe's] *Iphigénie.* . . . (Paris, 1931) cxxi.

[5] But like *Satyros* and *Urfaust*—both, however, in (another) archaizing style.

1–14), does not enjoy her forced priesthood (ll. 33–42), and wants, as her prayer indicates, to return home given specific conditions (ll. 43–53); more important, she has faith in divinity (ll. 39–40) and cherishes an ideal of perfect ethical harmony (ll. 35–38). As monologue, Iphigenie's speech suggests a dramatic tradition deriving, at least ultimately, from Greek literature; in failing to state an immediate conflict—Iphigenie describes a situation and her reactions to it apparently extending over "so manches Jahr" (l. 7)—, it prepared the audience for a drama of simple and leisurely action, in externals marked by archaic "edle Einfalt und stille Größe" as characteristically Greek. More specifically classical is the impersonal style of just over a third of her speech (ll. 15–32), those lines first given as generalizations on the lot of the exile and of woman, and only afterwards specifically referred to herself—lines which evoke the Greek fondness for generalized comment, especially from the chorus. In the larger sense of dramatic style, then, this monologue can be said to help set the elevated tone which is to mark Goethe's whole drama.

It is in the narrower sphere of linguistic style, however, that Goethe effectually gives substance to the otherwise ambiguously suggested feeling of classical antiquity,[6] and he does so subtly yet unambiguously: without ambiguity because Iphigenie speaks a language which clearly echoes classical poetic diction even to the extent of Grecism and Latinism, and with subtlety because only gradually is the peculiar nature of her diction forced upon our attention. In tracing the process by which Iphigenie becomes, at least in diction, a figure from classical antiquity, it will be helpful to consider her monologue as comprising four stylistic sections, and to examine each one separately. Such a division may be arbitrary, and certainly cannot have been consciously intended by Goethe, but it provides a convenient pattern in large into which a necessarily great number of detailed observations can be fitted in the interest of surveyability.

In the first section of the monologue (ll. 1–14) Iphigenie's language is dignified without being necessarily classical. Various commentators notwith-standing,[7] it is impossible to associate *heilig* and *dichtbelaubt* (l. 2) with *hierós* and *puknóphullos* on a first hearing or reading, for they apparently only provide helpful information: *heilig*, particularly, is necessary to define the seemingly Klopstockian and biblical connotation of *Hain* at a time when

---

[6] There is ambiguity because of the ethical refinement, the absence of direct exposition, the (then novel) metrical form.

[7] In addition to commentaries already noted, those of H. Düntzer, P. Klaucke, Erich Schmidt, C.A. Buchheim, Max Winkler, C.A. Eggert, P.S. Allen, and L.A. Rhoades have been most frequently consulted. (In the introduction to the Rhoades edition is an observation that may once have been true: "Of the language it is scarcely necessary to speak" [xxix]).

the word was favored—as by Wieland, "Ein Hain, worin sich Amor gern verliert" (*Musarion*, l. 1405)—for "den kleinen, gehegten und gut gepflegten lustwald" (Grimm, *Deutsches Wörterbuch*, IV, 2:173). Figures of speech are few, and most of them are inconspicuous except in the last third of the section. The grammatical ones include two figures of etymology which represent standard German poetical usage (syncope in *heil'gen*, l. 2; apocope, ll. 4 and 11, in the interest of euphony—to avoid glottal stop) and one less usual figure of syntax, hypallage (*suchend*, l. 12, refers to an antecedent *ich*)—this, however, toward the end of the section.[8] The rhetorical figures are of the simplest: one simile (l. 5—the *wie* of l. 3 is as weak as *wie auch* in the sense of *und*[9]), personification of sorts (l. 1, *Wipfel*, half apostrophic; ll. 10 and 13, *mich trennt das Meer* and *bringt die Welle*, the former primarily impersonal for *ich bin*, etc., and the latter also a doubtful instance), and the onomatopoeia of ll. 13–14. There are no strong antitheses, except perhaps for the ambiguous *dumpfe. . . brausend* of the last line;[10] epithet is inconspicuous. The effect achieved is of regularity and simplicity: ellipsis and parataxis are apparently avoided (cf. notes 8 and 9 *supra*) as too insistent (l. 9 is softened by an adversative *doch*), and fullness of expression is preferred to sententious brevity.[11]

In the second section (ll. 15–32) the language becomes more stylized and is, indeed, so richly figurative and rhetorical as to force classical associations upon the reader or listener who was ever asked according to century-old custom to analyze and give name to every feature of Vergilian or Homeric poetic usage. Not only is the thought archaic—the picture of the status of woman is definitely classical, and the feeling of the terribleness of exile somewhat so—, but also the language in what is, it must be remembered, a deliberately regularized text: the ambiguity of the weak genitive singular *Frauen* (l. 24) is resolved by the singular *Mann* in the next line, and resolved with special emphasis because of the chiasmus in verb-noun patterns; the shorter adjectival forms *einsam* and *feindlich* (ll. 16 and

---

[8] *Brausend* (l. 14) is at least ambiguous, can be taken adverbially. "Gewöhnt sich hierüber" (l. 5) may represent an ellipsis, although *sich gewöhnen* can occur alone; in any case, the Klopstockian practice of compounding with *her-* was well-established when Goethe wrote.

[9] There is no conjunction in the earliest version.

[10] *heraus in. . . in* (ll. 1 and 3: stronger in the first version "heraus in. . . herein in"); *rege. . . stilles* (ll. 1, 3); *noch jetzt. . . zum erstenmal* (ll. 4–5); *höher. . . ergebe* (l. 8); *verborgen. . . fremd* (ll. 7 and 9)—all non-insistent.

[11] Expansion occurs twice: "mit schauderndem Gefühl" (l. 4), not so positive as "Schauer" (first version) and more exact psychologically; "das Land der Griechen" (l. 12), less etymological archaism for "Griechenland" than, because of emphasis on *Griechen*, an indication of racial and family feeling.

32) are at least poetically old-fashioned, although they serve no less to heighten the classically sententious tone of the utterances in which they occur; *abwärts* (l. 18) may possibly be intended to give a slight archaic flavor; and the three occurrences of prepositive genitives (ll. 19, 24, and 29—l. 3 contains the only "anastrophic hyperbaton" in section I), if not archaisms, at least emphasize archaic brevity. *Mitgeborne* (l. 21) is Grecism and Latinism—*súggonoi, cognati*—, and Greek is at least the compounding pattern of *eng-gebunden* (l. 29), while *Zu Haus' und in dem Kriege* (l. 25) recalls Latin *domi militiaeque* (used almost as synecdoche for "everywhere," since only "in der Fremde" is specifically excluded—l. 26). Syntactically, the regularized simplicity of the first section gives way in the second to a more emphatically elliptic pattern which underscores the antithetical sententiousness of the text. Counting *Weh dem* (l. 15) and *wie elend* (l. 31), which echo biblical and "beatus ille" patterns, there are thirteen co-ordinate and only four subordinate clauses, and two of the latter are half assimilated to *Weh dem* and *wie elend* with which they form sentences with a single inflected verb; the other two (ll. 19–22) fall together in referring to a single antecedent. The principle of emphatic ellipsis explains the asyndeton of lines 27–28, the absence of connectives (ll. 16, 18, 20, and 31), and the absence of possible adversatives (ll. 23—first clause; 25; 29). A climax of ellipsis is reached in line 31, which stands for "Ist *ihr eine* Pflicht und *ein* Trost; wie elend *ist es*, wenn sie gar"—a line in which the exclamatory *wie* repeats anaphorically the one of line 29; in which *ist* can be supplied from that line only by a kind of zeugma; in which *sie*, referring to [*das*] *Weib*, represents synesis; and in which *Pflicht und Trost* is hendiadys for "Pflicht, die (doch) Trost enthält." For completeness it may be noted that hypallage also occurs in this section (*spielend*, l. 21), more strikingly than in the first because the present participle here expresses not a present but a past tense; because this line also contains the already noted *Mitgeborne*; and because it further illustrates another form of enallage in *fest und fester* if *fest* be taken not as an apocopated form but as the positive for the comparative degree.

Rhetorically also this section is more emphatic than the first, as is most obviously apparent in its four exclamations (ll. 15–16, 27, 29, 31–32). Instead of simile there is vivid metaphor: "Ihm zehrt der Gram / Das nächste Glück vor seinen Lippen weg"—also the first instance of close alliteration—, deliberately stronger than the "Ihn läßt der Gram des schönsten Glückes nicht genießen" of the earliest version. Standing in a parallel construction to that of this clause,[12] *die Gedanken* (l. 18) seem half personified, while *die*

---

[12] The parallelism is deceptive: asyndeton makes the *ihm* (l. 18) seem anaphoric repetition (of *ihm*, l. 16); the first *ihm* (l. 16) is a dative of interest, the second also—but more specifically, in that it defines the "possessor" of *die Gedanken*.

Sonne (l. 19) is clearly so; personification occurs again in line 27 (twice) and, as is so common with a "fate," in line 32. Two instances of metonymy come close together—*Eltern und Geschwister*[*n*] (l. 15, for *Verwandte*, and perhaps also *Bekannte*) and *Hallen* (l. 19, for "home, dwelling"), the first of these synecdoches approximating elaborative paraphrase also; there is perhaps a third instance in *Glück* (l. 29; then not, as according to Winkler, Loiseau, and others, *Geschick*, but rather "sphere of happiness"). What seems to be the one admittedly personal statement in the section—"Ich rechte mit den Göttern nicht; allein. . . ."—has, in its *immediate* impersonal context, primarily the ironic value of oratorical *praeteritio*. Iphigenie's generalizations are no exception to the rule that a series of unqualified generalizations (cf. *immer*, l. 18) tends to suggest one-sided exaggeration,[13] and there is hyperbole in every superlative (cf. *nächste*, l. 17). The use of epithet becomes somewhat more striking than in the first section, especially with the oxymoron *Mit sanften Banden* (l. 22), and in addition to the large antitheses between home and exile, woman's lot and man's, there are lesser ones such as *Gram. . . Glück* (ll. 16–17); *Zu Haus. . . in dem Kriege* (l. 25)— if not opposed to each other, but only used as a formula, still contrasted with *in der Fremde* (l. 26); *eng-gebunden. . . Glück* (l. 29: at least if *Glück* has some of the meaning it has in l. 17); and, perhaps, *Eltern und Ge-schwistern. . . einsam* (ll. 15–16) and even *fern. . . nächste* (ll. 15 and 17: at most a purely verbal coincidence, but one allowed to stand). The broad-based pattern of line 30—"Schon einem rauhen Gatten zu gehorchen"—may be noted by ears which have heard the more obvious (and certain) onomatopoeia of line 14. And it is interesting that the two parallel relative clauses of the section—in the sentence ll. 16–22, the longest of the section by far—are poetic elaborations for "where he was born" and "where he spent his childhood"; by contrast with their environment of paratactic sententiousness they seem only the more ornate.[14]

In the third section (ll. 33–42) the style established in the second is, as it were, amalgamated with that of the first. Its first two lines—surely meant to be preceded by a thoughtful pause, but followed by an immediate self-reproach: hence my beginning of this section with l. 33—mark a return to simile in almost Homerically extended form as they incorporate the long preceding passage into Iphigenie's personal experience and so give it, as well as the whole monologue, greater unity. Sentences as short as "Ihn freuet der Besitz" (l. 27) are not used, and there is a greater balance in the

---

[13] Characteristic of an archaizing tradition? In no event can l. 25 or ll. 30–31 be said to describe the Age of Xanthippe.

[14] These two clauses are also striking for the somewhat polysyndetic repetition of *wo* in an otherwise asyndetic context.

use of main and subordinate clauses (four of the former to three of the latter). The use of grammatical and rhetorical figures of speech is less concentrated than in the second section, for which reason the language seems more regular, but enough of them are employed to preserve the classical tone. Thus *heil'gen*, recurring twice (ll. 34—in which it is strengthened by *ernst*—and 42) in the same syncopated form as in line 2, now becomes clearly both a Grecism and a repeated epithet in classical tradition.[15] Two other already used adjectives also appear again, *still* (l. 36; cf. l. 3) and *sanft* (l. 42; cf. l. 22)—both, significantly, suggesting so-called classic calm. Other verbal echoes include *noch jetzt* (l. 40; cf. l. 4) and, more important, the antithetical *-banden* and *fest* (l. 34; cf. ll. 21–22), at first referring back but later also opposed, together with *Widerwillen* (l. 36), to *freiem Dienste* (l. 38). There is also anaphoric repetition of *dir* (ll. 35 and 37)—not the sententious anaphora of the previous section, but deliberate repetition in the interest of full clarity. Fullness also marks the one exclamation of this section (ll. 35–38), the longest so far, with its clear instance of apostrophe, its highly informative compound apposition, and its complete lack of any ellipses (in contrast to the earlier complex exclamations—ll. 15–16 and 31–32).[16] The final sentence (ll. 39–42) illustrates particularly well the insistence on a clear yet elevated style: "und hoffe / Noch jetzt auf dich" is more important as epexegetic elaboration than as an occasion for grammatical antithesis of verb forms (*hab' gehofft. . . hoffe*) or for the weak chiasmus in *auf dich gehofft* and *hoffe. . . auf dich*; a full line—containing the "pleonastic" form *Königes*—is placed in apposition to the monosyllable *mich*, the more effectively because it follows the simple "dich Diana"; and the subordinate clause is the weightiest up to this point, less because it is slightly longer than that of lines 20–22 than because of the ellipsis of *hast* after *genommen*, which both emphasizes the literary quality of the diction and avoids the unemphatic intonation pattern otherwise characteristic of the end of such a clause.

The fourth and last section of Iphigenie's monologue (ll. 43–53) comprises one long and, by comparison with what has gone before, startlingly complex sentence—a rhetorical period which makes clear beyond any shadow of doubt the peculiar character of the intended style by its

---

[15] In the section where classical Greek and Latin names—one mythological—first occur (ll. 33 and 40).

[16] In view of the regularizing tendency of the stylistic context, *sollte* (l. 37) is not to be read as if it had the same time value as *gesteh'* and *diene* in this exclamation; it can only be a simple past tense and mean "[it] was [thy] intention" since the introductory *auch hab' ich* (l. 39) of the next following sentence clearly indicates a co-ordination extending to the parallel use of tenses.

insistently literary diction. Even more because of the language of the monologue than because of the monologue form itself we are prepared for the stylized drama which follows, for idealization of characters all of whom will in some degree be worthy of the nobility of their diction, for action which develops with leisurely fullness, and, above all, for preoccupation both with subtleties of psychology and with nice distinctions of idea. Although this sentence might end with an exclamation point, it is not, like previously so punctuated clauses, a simple exclamation: as an urgent prayer using imperative verb forms it must so end in modern print, however great Iphigenie's humility.[17] What most strikes the reader or listener is the length and involvedness of a protasis (ll. 43–50) that can be balanced by the simple clarity of "So gib auch mich den Meinen endlich wieder" (l. 51)—for the next two lines are only a restatement of the same thought in more ornate form (with the antitheses *rette. . . errettet* and *Tod. . . Leben*, the oxymoron *Leben. . . Tode*, the formal ellipsis of *hast* after *errettet*). In the protasis are the richly associative classical names Zeus, Agamemnon, Troy and, with half-Latin declension, Electra; the Grecism *göttergleich* (l. 45; cf. *isótheos*, etc.) and the Latinism, and Vergilian echo, of "von Trojas umgewandten Mauern" (l. 47; cf. "vertere ab imo moenia Trojae" and, also, *katastréphein*, etc.); the hypallage of line 44, again with past tense value, and, for the first time, the loose usage of an adverb for a phrase or clause (*rühmlich*, l. 47, is transferred from the normal agent-subject *du* to Agamemnon and means "mit Ruhm [gekrönt]" rather than *löblicherweise*); the synecdoche *umgewandten Mauern* for "ruins" in the three-word paraphrase for "Troy,"[18] the euphemistic paraphrase "zum Altare brachte" for "opferte" (l. 46: note the gain in number of broad vowels as result of this substitution), and, in the same line, the almost hyperbolic circumlocution "sein Liebstes"; the polysyndetic anaphora *wenn du* (l. 45; cf. l. 43) and the ellipses, or ellipsis and asyndeton, of *begleitet, die Gattin* (ll. 48–49: for "begleitet hast [cf. l. 50] und [wenn du <cf. l. 43>] die. . . ."); the re-use of *hoch* (cf. l. 8) in the paraphrase "den hohen Mann" (l. 43)—identified as Agamemnon (l. 45) in an appositive phrase separated from *Mann* by a line of relative clause. (The echo of earlier time statements contained in *endlich* [l. 51: cf. ll. 4, 7, 9, 40] comes only in the apodosis.)

With the resolution of this carefully constructed period after its eighth line in a prayer, the ethical theme already explicitly present in lines 35ff. is

---

[17] After this sentence has been heard the exclamation of ll. 35–37 acquires connotations of confessional prayer and a closer connection between these two sections of the monologue is established than the form of a most fervent wish could have created.

[18] A better Vergilian echo than the earlier "vom Felde der umgewandten Troja," yet also less elliptical.

raised to a religious level—but in such a way stylistically as perhaps to suggest that simplicity, here the truly *"sancta" simplicitas* of Iphigenie, will resolve the complications of the play's dramatic, psychological, and ethical actions. If it be too presumptuous to read such implications into the stylistic pattern of these opening fifty-three lines, it is still surely correct to see them as setting the tone of the play in matters of classicality and diction. By careful analysis of Iphigenie's language throughout the whole monologue it has been possible to indicate the poetic connotations of an occasionally neglected or misunderstood line, and to give a clearer impression of the density of the poetic texture of lines too often passed over with thin generalization. One much-disputed phrase in Iphigenie's speech—really the only one on which every commentator apparently feels obligated to take a stand, and one deliberately left unmentioned in the last paragraph—can be properly understood, I believe, only if the stylistic tendency of the language is taken into account: "die schönen Schätze" of line 50 has been held by many to be an appositive to "die Gattin ihm, Elektren und den Sohn" in the line before, and by a few to be the royal treasury. The former could evoke punctuation and the apparent termination of the enumerated series with "und den Sohn"; and the latter have only appealed to the singular form *Schatz* of earlier versions—which is a dubious critical procedure when trying to interpret a specific text in itself. From the foregoing analysis it is evident that "und den Sohn" need not be the end of the series in a text rich in syntactic variations, yet on the other hand the word order does not make it certain that *Schätze* is a new item in the series. The syntactic pattern of Iphigenie's last sentence, however, its "period-ness," demands that a climax be reached in the last line of the long protasis; there can be no parenthetical-appositive dropping of the voice between *Sohn* and *wohl erhalten hast* or the whole rising effect is destroyed too close to its end; and hence for stylistic reasons alone "die schönen Schätze" must be taken as the fourth member of a series which, by the addition, becomes longer and so underscores the periodic nature of the climactic sentence containing it.

That the tendency and function of the grammatical-rhetorical form of Iphigenie's monologue is to establish a particular style, is confirmed by reading immediately after it the next fifty-three lines of Goethe's drama. In this expository dialogue certain turns of diction already become familiar no longer are so striking as to distract or, better, divide the attention of the reader or hearer. Although sentence periods occur, the syntax of them is marked by a relatively clear ease. One revealing difference appears only on analysis, viz. the fact that a more common balance between varieties of word order, characteristic of the language of the play as a whole, first appears in them; in other words, in the opening monologue the principle of consciously elevated diction resulted in a somewhat abnormal preference for inversion.[19] There can be little doubt, then, that the opening lines of *Iphigenie* are deliberately complex—far more so, for instance, than those that follow directly upon them or such important speeches as those of Iphigenie in the last scene of the play. It would, however, be unjustified to pretend that any single feature of these lines was intentionally imposed upon them: some figures may merely have resulted from the process of versification, from the need of insistent establishment of a regular verse pattern at the beginning of a verse work;[20] some surely represent poetic licenses given currency by previous writers such as Klopstock and Voß; some are doubtless half-conscious echoes resulting from Goethe's immersion in Greek and Latin materials relevant to his subject; but taken all together they effectively create that very special world which Iphigenie and the rest somehow never seem to leave.

[19] In ll. 1–53 expressed subject of declarative sentences follows inflected main verb eighteen times out of twenty-two, while in ll. 54–106 the (more normal) proportion is eleven postpositive subjects to twelve prepositive ones. For further confirmation of this generalization, cf. also Iphigenie's next monologue (ll. 538–60), in which the expressed subject precedes five (seven, counting more generously) times, follows only three.

[20] The importance of metrical regularity may partly explain the absence of strong alliteration, which can be distracting to the ear, before ll. 16–17 (as noted above in text), as well as the apparent avoidance of caesura. (The fairly liberal use of enjambement does not, as is sometimes popularly assumed, diminish awareness of metrical pattern, but actually makes such pattern more obvious by forcing a distinction between sense and form.) The overwhelming majority of examples of alliteration comes ll. 29ff.

Goethe and the Poetry of the Renaissance

Durch Vernünfteln wird Poesie vertrieben;
Aber sie mag das Vernünftige lieben.
(*Sprichwörtlich*—WA I.2:243)

The topic Goethe and the Renaissance has been much studied—by Ludwig Geiger, Otto Harnack and many others.[1] Yet older scholarship has only occasionally emphasized the possible significance of the poetry of the Renaissance for Goethe's development as a lyric poet, even with respect to *Römische Elegien, Venezianische Epigramme*, and a very few other poems, particularly "An den Geist des Johannes Secundus"; examples of exceptions to this generalization are Georg Ellinger's studies and Adalbert Schroeter's *Beiträge zur Geschichte der neulateinischen Poesie.*[2] It is but recently that Arthur Henkel, in his stimulating monograph *Wanderers Sturmlied,*[3] called attention to the remarkable number of Goethe's poems characterized by symbolism in the tradition of Baroque emblematic poetry. Goethe composed such poems in every phase of his career: Henkel names—in addition to "Wanderers Sturmlied"—the first ode to Behrisch, "Adler und Taube," "Seefahrt," "Das Veilchen," "Amyntas," "Der Schatzgräber," the parables of the mosquito and the pearl in the *Divan,* various lyric passages in the second part of *Faust,* the song at the end of *Novelle,* and several explicitly emblematic poems such as "Leuchtender Stern über Winkelwage," "Blei und Zirkel," and "Beschilderter Arm gegen ein vorüberziehendes Wetter Bücher beschützend"; for each he can adduce appropriate emblems from Alciati or Sambucus, whose emblem collections Goethe owned. But Goethe was also familiar with other emblem books—in August 1826, for example, he borrowed from the Ducal Library *Catechismus imaginibus expressus* by the Jesuit Peter Canis(ius), a work doubtless

---

[1] "Goethe und die Renaissance," (1887), in Geiger, *Vorträge und Versuche* (Dresden, 1890) 281–318; "Goethe und die Renaissance," in Harnack, *Aufsätz und Vorträge* (Tübingen, 1911) 58–97.

[2] Berlin, 1909 (Palestra, 77).

[3] Frankfurt/Main, 1962.

already known to him. For each period of Goethe's literary development it would be possible to draw up a substantial list of poems featuring emblems reminiscent of the Renaissance tradition: from the 1770s "Mit einer Zeichnung" ("Sieh in diesem Zauberspiegel. . .") and "Gellerts Monument von Oeser"; from the 1780s "Die Nektartropfen," "Der Becher," and various, often epigrammatic poems "Antiker Form sich nähernd"; from the 1790s many of the epigrams and *Xenien*, especially among those included in "Weissagungen des Bakis"; and from the following decades not only riddles like the Herzlieb sonnet and "Magisches Netz," but also emblematic poems like "Gingo biloba," the "Loge" group, "Aeolsharfen," "Zu meinen Handzeichnungen," and *Wilhelm Tischbeins Idyllen*, to name only texts Goethe did not include under the rubric "Parabolisch." Since what Günther Müller, in his interpretation of the "Parzenlied," called "das Chiffrenhafte"[4] is a common, indeed essential characteristic of emblematic poetry, such poems often seem much less concrete than the symbols elaborated in them. Müller's observation is valid not only for the hymn "Das Göttliche," but also, to some extent, for a number of Goethe's emblematic poems: "['Das Göttliche'] ist. . . von einer asketischen Bildlosigkeit, einer begrifflichen Abstraktheit, die sich mit der gewohnten Vorstellung von Goethes Lyrik schwer vereinbaren läßt."[5]

In German literary history Baroque is commonly equated with the seventeenth century. It is therefore easy to forget, despite Karl Otto Conrady's informative monograph *Lateinische Dichtungstradition und deutsche Lyrik des 17. Jahrhunderts*,[6] that the Baroque, in literary-historical terms, can be considered, as it was in Goethe's times, an already extant variant of Renaissance style, and that it scarcely interrupted the great post-medieval development that later led to such different phenomena as French Classicism, German Classicism and (perhaps) romantic Hellenism. Goethe himself consistently emphasized the unifying force of the Renaissance tradition: "Es ist Zeit," he wrote to Iken in 1827,

daß der leidenschaftliche Zwiespalt zwischen Klassikern und Romantikern sich endlich versöhne. Daß wir uns bilden ist die Hauptforderung; woher wir uns bilden wäre gleichgültig, wenn wir uns nicht an falschen Mustern zu verbilden fürchten müßten. Ist es doch eine weitere und reinere Umsicht in und über griechische und römische Literatur, der wir die Befreyung aus mönchischer Barbarey zwischen dem 15. und 16. Jahrhundert verdanken!

---

[4] "Goethe: Das Parzenlied," in Benno v. Wiese, ed., *Die deutsche Lyrik: Form und Geschichte* (Düsseldorf, 1957) 1:243.

[5] Op. cit., 239.

[6] Bonn, 1962 (Bonner Arbeiten, 4).

Lernen wir nicht auf dieser hohen Stelle alles in seinem wahren, ethisch-ästhetischen Werte schätzen, das Älteste wie des Neuste.[7]

In the next sentence he applies these observations to his "Ausarbeitung der Helena," but the striking echo of the closing lines of "Unbegrenzt" from the *Divan*—"Nun töne Lied mit eignem Feuer! / Denn du bist älter, du bist neuer"—, together with the subsequent extension of the principle of repeated reflections (to explain other obscure passages in "früheren und späteren Gedichten") seems to justify the view that Goethe was consciously or semi-consciously much more often indebted to the tradition of Renaissance poetry than is admitted (on heuristically justifiable grounds) by those interpreters and historians of literature who emphasize a radical break in Goethe's poetic development with his Strasbourg lyrics. This view neither underestimates the originality of his lyric achievement nor does it overlook in his work the often significant moment of innate ineffability in modern poetry, of a symbolism inexpressible in words that points beyond itself.

Goethe's partiality for ottava rima, sestina, sonnet, terza rima, redondilla, etc. shows that he retains much more of the formal variety of the Renaissance tradition in lyric and lyrical epic than do other preromantic poets such as Wieland, Heinse, or Bürger. In his letters from Leipzig (and in *Dichtung und Wahrheit*) he repeatedly expresses his admiration for Ariosto—one thinks, also, of how Antonio evokes the spirit of the *Orlando furioso* in the first act of *Torquato Tasso*—and for Tasso; and he recommends to his sister Cornelia the *Pastor Fido* of their fellow Ferraran Guarini, from which Wilhelm Meister recites poems in both the *Sendung* and the *Lehrjahre*. Goethe owned the works of these poets, as well as those of Petrarch (documented already in the earliest catalogue of his library), Salvator Rosa ("La Pittura"—the [third] verse satire—in terza rima, in the 1785 edition), and Dante. He had the sonnets of Bendetto Varchi and Cellini translated by a "Kunstfreund" for *Benvenuto Cellini*. Despite his own sonnets he seems to have identified Petrarchism, known to him also in German at least since Klamer Schmidt's Petrarchan efforts in the Göttingen *Musenalmanach auf das Jahr 1773*, with the "Epoche der forcierten [i.e. romantischen] Talente," but he explicitly praised Cellini's terza rima poem 'In Praise of Prison' ("Chi vuol saper quant' è il valor di Dio") in his appendix to the autobiography.[8] For the second part of *Faust* he studied and made use of Lasca's large collection of carnival poems by Lorenzo de' Medici—

---

[7] WA IV.43:81f.
[8] Jubiläums-Ausgabe 32:279.

admired by Goethe in this genre[9]—and his contemporaries,[10] but as early as 1778 *Das Luisenfest* was originally planned as a "favola boschereccia," even though it was executed differently.[11] Goethe's report on his induction into the Arcadia[12] testifies to his knowledge of the development of Italian poetry in the seventeenth century (partly from G.M. Crescimbeni's *Istoria della Volgar Poesia* [1698], but probably also from anthologies such as the *Saggio di poesie di varii carattere recitate in diversi tempi nell' adunanza degli Arcadi in Roma* [Rome, 1761], which he borrowed from the Ducal Library in late April 1829). Among the earlier poets he was interested in were Aretino,[13] Francesco Berni,[14] Leonardo,[15] Michelangelo,[16] and Giordano Bruno (see below). He also knew Herder's translations[17] of Italian sonnets (from around 1780) by Petrarch (six), Faustina Maratti (more than 30), Frugoni, Michelangelo, Filicaja, and Vittoria Colonna and (in the *Adrastea*) Campanella.

The *Lusiads* of Camoëns, which Goethe probably read first in an excerpt translated by Wieland, then several times later,[18] belong in the tradition of Italian Renaissance poetry. From Spanish poetry, in addition to Herder's translation of the *Cid*, Goethe knew several romances by Góngora in Herder's collection of folk songs and was familiar with the richly lyrical dramas of Calderón, from which he took many Renaissance motifs and stylistic features for *Faust II*. As regards the Italian eighteenth century—besides the remarkable combination in "Rinaldo" (1811) of elements from Tasso, Baroque love poetry, and the operas of Metastasio, for whom he otherwise had little use—Goethe's positive judgments of G.-B. Casti's *Gli animali parlanti* and *Novelle galanti* (in ottava rima), from which he had heard the author read in Rome in 1787, are well known,[19] even if Ariosto is as likely a source for the content of "Das Tagebuch" (in ottava rima) as one of these

---

[9] Cf. *Anhang zur Lebensbeschreibung des Benvenuto Cellini*, X.

[10] Grazzini, *Tutti i trionfi*, 1559.

[11] *Biographische Einzelheiten*, 8 (Jubiläums-Ausgabe 25:223f.).

[12] *Zweiter Römischer Aufenthalt*, "Januar 1788."

[13] *DjG* 4:79; "Biographische Einzelheiten," 1 (Jubiläums-Ausgabe 27:201).

[14] Not the satires, but the sonnets (cf. WA III.3:286).

[15] A translation of a Leonardo sonnet by Gries seems to have stimulated him to an adaptation of his own in 1813—cf. WA I.5,2:394.

[16] Whose 7th madrigal may have influenced Epimetheus's sestinas which begin with the words "Der Seeligkeit Fülle hab' ich empfunden" (cf. Harnack 61).

[17] *Sämtliche Werke* (SW), ed. Bernard Suphan, vol. 27.

[18] E.g., in the German translation which he borrowed from the Weimar Library from 25 July to 11 August 1819.

[19] Cf. for example *Zweiter Römischer Aufenthalt*, "den 16. Juli."

novellas in verse. (He also knew well the verse novellas [*Novelle galanti*] of Domenico Batacchi, known as Verocchio.[20])

Although it is hardly appropriate to enumerate here Goethe's readings in world literature, it is necessary to recall what was and remained important for him of the Renaissance tradition—still important, especially, for contemporary French poets—in his pre-Leipzig years: in *Ephemerides* one may find an excerpt from Dorat's *Discours préliminaire des Baisers*,[21] and Fernand Baldensperger[22] has identified striking similarities between lyrics from both Leipzig and Strasbourg and poems in the *Almanach des Muses*—e.g., between Léonard's "Quelquefois en filant mon lin"[23] and "Meine Ruh ist hin," and between Gentil-Bernard's "Rien n'est si beau / Que mon hameau" and "Maifest" ("Mailied"). It is hardly necessary to surmise, with W.A. Nitze,[24] Ronsard's direct influence on Goethe's lyric (since his name does not occur in the literary works, the conversations, or the first edition of the *Goethe-Handbuch*), but we know that his library included Du Bartas's *Oeuvres poétiques*,[25] and that Marot was among the French poets (Montaigne, Amyot, Rabelais are also named) in whom he was interested in Strasbourg in 1771[26]—Marot, whom he also mentioned with praise along with Du Bartas in the notes to *Rameaus Neffe*[27] and into whose French he thought *Faust* might best be translated.[28] He first borrowed Marie de France, *Poésies ou Recueil de lais*, in an edition that had just appeared, from the Ducal Library in June 1820, but Boileau he had known well since childhood.[29]

The lyric of the Renaissance was thus a living force for Goethe, both directly and indirectly, and not just where—as in the sonnets of 1807–

---

[20] See the *Annalen* for 1812.

[21] Excerpted from *Mercure de France*, January, 1770.

[22] "L'Anacréonisme du jeune Goethe et la 'poésie fugitive' française," in his *Études d'histoire littéraire*, 4e série (Paris, 1939) 185–203.

[23] *Almanach*, 1771, p. 116.

[24] "Goethe and Ronsard," *PMLA* 59 (1944): 486–90. In Bertram Barnes, *Goethe's Knowledge of French Literature* (Oxford, 1937), Ronsard's name does not appear.

[25] Genève, 1615.

[26] Cf. *Dichtung und Wahrheit*, Book 11.

[27] Jubiläums-Ausgabe 34:163.

[28] Conversations with Soret on 13 April 1823 and V. Cousin on 28 April 1825. Cf. Richard Newald, *Probleme und Gestalten des deutschen Humanismus* (Berlin, 1963) 142: "Wenn... Goethe sich eine Übersetzung Homers in der naiv-lebendigen Sprache des Zeitalters der Reformation wünschte, so ahnte er, daß die naive Prosa der *Ilias* des Johannes Baptist Rexius (1584), obwohl dieser aus einer lateinischen Vorlage übertrug, vom Geiste des Originals stärker berührt war, als die kunstvolle Dichtersprache seiner Zeit. . . ." (Cf. letter to Knebel, 10 March 1813 and remarks to Eckermann, 8 April 1829.)

[29] Cf. *Goethe-Handbuch*, 2nd ed., "Boileau."

1808—Renaissance verse forms and style were exploited for specific purposes. Over and over he encountered aspects of the Renaissance in German poets of the Enlightenment, of Sensibility, of Storm and Stress, of early Classicism, not to mention the Romantics—e.g., in Ewald von Kleist (whose neologism "Blütendampf" appears in the Strasbourg poem "Maifest" and whose *Frühling*, as one of my students[30] once demonstrated, provided almost the entire vocabulary of the sentimental description of nature in Werther's first letters), in Wieland, in the writers of fables and the Anacreontics, in Heinse, Klamer Schmidt, and Bürger, and in Herder's collections and translations of songs, odes, and sonnets of the early, high and late Renaissance. How at ease Goethe felt with language of the pre- and early Enlightenment poets even late in life can be observed in his introduction of the somewhat old-fashioned word "Wohlredenheit" (instead of "Beredsamkeit") into the dialogue of the *Wanderjahre* shortly before he mentions the triumvirate Haller, Kleist, and Geßner.[31]

In listing Renaissance poets I questioned whether Ronsard ever influenced Goethe directly: Ronsard's name never appears in Fritz Strich's *Goethe und die Weltliteratur*, but he must have had some influence on Goethe both through later French poetry and, still more, through the Renaissance tradition of Neolatin lyric and the German-language poetry of the seventeenth century imitative of it. For that reason alone it is a regrettable simplification, indeed distortion, of the historical situation to conclude the article "Neulateinische Dichtung" in the Stammler-Kohlschmidt *Reallexikon* with the end of the seventeenth century. One should not forget that Greek poetry was read by Goethe and his contemporaries, i.e. well into the nineteenth century, primarily in or with the aid of Neolatin verse translations. Thus both the motto to *Dichtung und Wahrheit* and the content of the *zahmes Xenion* "Die Eiche fällt und jeder holzt sein Teil" derive from the *Excerpta ex tragoediis et comediis graecis. . . Latinis versibus reddita ab Hugone Grotio* (Parisiis 1626). The *zahmes Xenion*—" 'Anders lesen Knaben den Terenz, / anders Grotius.' / Mich Knaben ärgerte die Sentenz, / Die ich nun gelten lassen muß"—contains a characteristic identification of himself with Grotius which, however, is surpassed by Goethe's later equation of himself with Reuchlin in the xenion "Reuchlin! wer will sich ihm vergleichen" and of himself with Hutten in the *Divan* poem "Übermacht, ihr könnt es spüren." As a student of law he may well also have read parts of Hertius's *De selectis. . . ex jurisprudentiâ universali. . . argumentis tomis*

---

[30] Mr. Francis Thompson, Cambridge, Mass.
[31] Book 3, chapter 13 (HA 8:421).

tres.[32] In these tractates are routinely cited not only Neolatin poets like van Barle[33] and Owen, but also Greek poets in the translations of Saumaise and Buchanan (Euripides), for law was, not so long before Goethe's own university years, at least theoretically an ethical, humanistic field of study. Later he used the Παροιμίαι ἑλληνικαί of Andreas Schottus, in which the *Stromateus*, in a translation by Justus Scaliger into various Latin meters, constitutes an important group of adagia.

It should also not be forgotten that all his life Goethe regularly received Latin poems from his contemporaries, read them—and occasionally valued them highly. In *Dichtung und Wahrheit* (Book 12) he mentions "die geistreichen lateinischen Gedichte" by Hieronymous Peter Schlosser, of whom he owned "noch verschiedene scherzhafte Distichen" and in whose *Poemata*[34] his lines of thanks, "Du, dem die Musen von den Acten-Stöcken," were first published. The French Hellenist Villoison (editor of *Daphnis and Chloe*, 1777, and later of Homer) was at the Weimar court in 1782, where he responded to Herder's and Goethe's renewed interest in epigram by composing Latin distichs for several busts, among them the lines that begin "Augusto & Musis charus, tractavit amores / Lethiferos iuvenum. . . ." (Goethe later mentions Villoison in conjunction with these busts in a paralipomenon to the *Propyläen*.[35]) Along with many older Latin poems in the modus alternus Goethe's library contained *Epistola poetica* (1806, about the Cologne cathedral), which he had surely read, given his great interest in the valuable if "chaotic"[36] art collection of its author, Canon (F.F.) Wallraf.

From the *Briefe die neueste Literatur betreffend*,[37] if not also from Lessing's less belletristic writings, Goethe might well have known, in addition to Lessing's own Latin epigrams, selections from works like Klotz's *Opuscula poetica*[38] and K.C. Schilling's *Carminum Libri duo*;[39] the latter was a profound admirer of Neolatin writers such as Poliziano, Lotichius, Everard (Johannes Secundus), Marull (Tarc[h]aniota), Pontano and Georg Sabinus. He must also have read poems like Michael Denis's "Symbolum"[40] or his "Mors Oscaris,"[41] after Ossian.

---

[32] Frankfurt/Main, 1700.
[33] Caspar Barlaeus, 1584–1648.
[34] Frankfurt/Main, 1775.
[35] WA I.53:400 (number 108).
[36] Cf. WA IV.26:133.
[37] Cf. number 212 (by Abbt).
[38] Lipsiae, 1761.
[39] Also 1761.
[40] In his *Carmina quaedam* (Vindobonae, 1794) 174.
[41] Ibid., 132–34.

Yet more important for Goethe than such learned exercises were Neolatin verse translations from oriental languages, for they encouraged an extensive identification of oriental epigram, love poem, and drinking song with classical counterparts. In the "Prœmium" to his *Poeseos asiaticæ commentariorum libri sex, cum appendice; subjicitur Limon, seu Miscellaneorum liber* (including the author's own Latin odes)[42] Sir William Jones declares not without some pride, "fateor me librum versibus conspersisse, ut lectores varietate rerum allicerentur; fateor me in Latinis Horatii, Ovidii, Vergilii, Phædri, in Græcis, Theocriti, Anacreontis, Callimachi, *numeros* (vim et copiam non dico) imitatum fuisse, feliciter necne alii judicent" (xii). Thus we find *Ebni'l Faredhi elegia, metro Ovidiano, Latinè reddita* (98–100) and an episode from Ferdusi's *Shah nama* in Vergilian hexameters (304–8); one of Hafiz's love songs is rendered in Greek "versibus Anacreonteis" (215f.) and a love poem from the *Hamasa*[43] is transformed into a Latin ode in three-line stanzas complete with Luna, Cupido, and Zephyri, and with an address to a Fabellus who corresponds to no figure in the Arabic text. For purposes of comparison Jones includes verse translations from the Greek by Neolatin poets like Grotius and even cites modern works like *Der Tod Abels*, the *Lusiads*, etc.

Herder proceeds in similar fashion when he renders into German distichs and hexameters not only Neolatin poems such as the ode "Deo" by the Italian free-thinker Lucilio Vanini,[44] de Thou's "Gebet an die Wahrheit"[45] and much of Jacob Balde's poetry,[46] but also, in *Zerstreute Blätter*, oriental verses,[47] which are thus assimilated to the style of the modus alternus of Hutten, Melanchthon, and Lotichius that also appear there as German distichs.[48] It is thus hardly surprising that Goethe formulated his praise of Kālidāsa's drama in distichs: "Will ich die Blumen des frühen, die Früchte des späteren Jahres, / Will ich was reizt und entzückt, will ich was sättigt und nährt, / Will ich den Himmel, die Erde mit Einem Namen begreifen; /

---

[42] London, 1774.

[43] In Jones's *Poems in Three Parts* (Calcutta, 1800), under the title "Ode arabica. Ad Fabellum."

[44] *Gott, Erstes Gespräch*, 1787 (SW 16:318ff.).

[45] *Briefe zur Beförderung der Humanität*, Nr. 47 (SW 17:235ff.).

[46] *Terpsichore* (SW 27).

[47] *VI*, II, "Das Land der Seelen" (Arabic poems); *II*, "Spruch und Bild, insonderheit bei den Morgenländern" (Persian poetry by Saadi); *IV*, I, "Über Denkmale der Vorwelt" ("Jehuda [ben Samuel] Halevis Seufzer nach den Denkmalen des Heiligen Landes"); *VI*, "Über ein morgenländisches Drama" (introduced by Goethe's *Sakuntala*-Motto: "Kamas Erscheinung").

[48] *V*, VI: "Denkmal Ulrichs von Hutten."

Nenn ich Sakontala dich, und so ist alles gesagt."[49] Anyone familiar with Hammer-Purgstall's translation of Hafiz knows how often he adduces Latin quotations from Horace, Tibullus, Martial, Anacreon, etc.; how much—probably more significant—his diction (which is certainly not always "vollends rhapsodisch," as Emil Staiger claimed[50]) owes to unrhymed German poetry of the eighteenth century; and how often he uses fully regular, stichic verse and regular four-line strophes adapted more or less freely from classical models. Page after page sounds dactylo-epitritic,[51] but even where Hammer alternates four-foot and three-foot iambic lines in four-line strophes the effect is more classicizing than popular because there is no rhyme.[52]

But even if we ignore translations, the evidence for Goethe's life-long reading of Renaissance Neolatin poets outweighs that for his reading of vernacular poets of the same period. In *Über Kunst und Altertum* he praises "das wahrhaft poetische Verdienst. . . , welches deutsche Dichter in der lateinischen Sprache seit drei Jahrhunderten an den Tag gegeben,"[53] and in referring to Georg Agricola, whose *De ortu et causis subterraneorum* he read, according to the *Annalen*, in 1806, he calls the sixteenth century a "Zeit der. . . ihren höchsten Gipfel erreichenden Kunst und Literatur."[54] Notable too is the *Faust* parallel in the eulogy—an elegy by Adam Siber dedicated to Valentin Hertel—that introduces Agricola's book: "Gloria te leuet ut terra sublimis, ut inter / Non fastiditos annumere uiros. / . . . procul absit inertia. . ." (ll. 33ff.).

---

[49] WA I.5, 2:341.

[50] *Goethe*, vol. 3 (Zürich, 1959) 18.

[51] E.g., Ta XLI (Joseph von Hammer, *Der Diwan von Mohammed Schemseddin Hafis* [Stuttgart and Tübingen, 1812f.], also quoted in Hammer's introduction (1:xxxii): "Wende die Schritte nicht ab / Vom Grab' Hafisens, / Wenn gleich in Sünden verstrickt / Harrt er des Himmels"; also Elif I: "Reich mir, o Schenke das Glas, / Bringe den Gästen es zu, / Leicht' ist die Lieb' im Anfang, / Es folgen aber Schwierigkeiten." (For these last four verses Hammer adduces two parallels from Anacreon and one from Horace.)

[52] E.g., Elif II: "Der Mond der Schönheit borgt sein Licht / Von deiner Wangen Strahlen, / Der Glanz der Armuth strahlet aus / Von Deines Kinnes Grübchen." Hammer's unrhymed trochaic four-line stanzas also have a classical-archaic effect, e.g., Ja LXXII: "Schenke, sieh' die Rosen haben / Fluren Eden gleich gemacht; / Setz' dich auf das Rosensoffa / Aufgestellt am Bachesufer." Only rarely does he offer rhymes, for example Dschin I, where, in addition to his own translation, he prints sestinas by Carl von Harrach.

[53] I (3), 1817 (Jubiläums-Ausgabe 37:92). The letters to A.O. Blumenthal (10 April and 28 May 1819) are further evidence that Goethe had extensive knowledge of Neolatin elegiac and didactic poetry and that he appreciated the importance of historical understanding of German Neolatin poetry.

[54] *Zur Geschichte der Farbenlehre* (Jubiläums-Ausgabe 40:199). Cf. also *Dichtung und Wahrheit*, Paralipomenon 77 (WA I.53:379): "Das Frische des 15. und 16. Jahrhunderts in allen Dingen."

That several German Neolatin poets are represented in Goethe's autograph collection[55]—Flacius Illyricus, Taubmann, Sturm, Melanchthon (and the Dutchman Janus Gruter)—is perhaps only secondary evidence from his later years for his high regard for Neolatin poetry. Although Harnack claimed, "Am wenigsten konnte natürlich ihn [i.e. Goethe] jene Literatur anziehen, die sich rein nachahmend gegenüber dem Altertum verhielt, wie es die neulateinische Poesie tat,"[56] in *Ephemerides* he already explicitly prefers the Frenchman Calvidus Letus (Claude Quillet) to the Roman Manilius,[57] and excerpts several works in which Neolatin poems occur—among others the *Processus juris joco-serius* (Hanoviae 1611), with verses by John Barclay (whose *Icon Animorum* in French translation is alluded to a few pages later). Goethe would have undervalued the Neolatin poets only in his Strasbourg period or immediately thereafter, when he was to some extent under the influence of a Herder, who inveighed against Latinism in the *Fragment* "Von der neuern Römischen Litteratur."[58] But Herder soon realized that the principle articulated there, "Die Sprache in der ich erzogen bin, ist *meine* Sprache" must also be valid for authors like Erasmus, Montaigne, and Balde, who spoke and thought in Latin, and from the unpolemical tone of the relevant passage in A.W. Schlegel's *Geschichte der Elegie* it seems clear that the originality of the Neolatin poets was also scarcely questioned in the age of German classicism and Romanticism.[59]

Goethe's early receptivity for the Neolatin corpus doubtless has to do with the pedagogical system of his Latin teacher J.J.G. Scherbius, who—partly with the aid of colloquies reminiscent of Erasmus (Goethe's *Labores Juveniles*)—taught Goethe Latin from the beginning as a living language,[60] which he then wrote and spoke easily in Leipzig. As a matter of family pride he had doubtless carefully read the volume of Neolatin poems published in the seventeenth century in honor of Johann Wolfgang Textor.

In the edition Goethe used of Hederich's *Mythologisches Lexicon* (1770) Alciati, Barth, Jacob Mycillus, Frischlin, J.C. Scaliger, Taubmann, and Zesen are among Neolatinists cited; it is also highly probable that Goethe read attentively Lilio Gregorio Giraldo's (Gyraldus) Latin version of a Greek mnemonic epigram in the article "Musae"—an article he would scarcely have failed to read when, following the example of various Italian Neolatin writers (e.g., Filelfo, whose unnumbered books of odes are named for

---

[55] Cf. H.J. Schreckenbach, *Goethes Autographensammlung. Katalog* (Weimar, 1961).
[56] Harnack 61.
[57] *DjG* 2:40.
[58] *Fragmente, Dritte Sammlung* (SW 1:361ff.).
[59] *Kritische Schriften und Briefe*, vol. 3, ed. E. Lohner (Stuttgart, 1964) 241.
[60] Cf. Elisabeth Mentzel, *Wolfgang und Cornelia Goethes Lehrer* (Leipzig, 1909).

muses), he was naming each canto of the extended idyll *Hermann und Dorothea* after one of the nine muses.

In Achilles August Lersner's *Frankfurter Chronica* (1706, 1734), which Goethe was reading when he composed the opening books of *Dichtung und Wahrheit* (above all as a source for his description of the imperial coronation), some fifty Neolatin poets are represented with poems—among the best known are Celtis, J.C. Scaliger, Camerarius, Caspar Brusch, Georg Fabricius, and Melissus, to name only poets of the sixteenth century. A much larger compendium, and one whose 22 volumes Goethe regularly perused for years, was the *Historische Münzbelustigungen* (1729–50) of Johann David Köhler, a part of whose coin collection later came into Goethe's possession; in a single volume (the 22nd) of this work poems by Adam Siber, Sambucus, Chytraeus, Dantiscus, Sabinus, Lotichius, Eoban Hessus, Giovanni Piero Valeriano, and others are reprinted, mainly as biographical background.

It would be simple, but certainly incorrect, to assume Goethe read Neolatin poems only as historical texts without regarding them as literature. In the *Materialien zur Geschichte der Farbenlehre* he expresses his appreciation for the poetic value both of Antonio Thylesius's small Danae drama *Imber Aureus* (1529) and of his eclogues "Cyclops" and "Galatea,"[61] and he observes in connection with Latin hexameters cited from the end of *De Cicindela* ("Vom Leuchtwurm"): "in der Mittelgattung der Dichtkunst, in der beschreibenden, [hätte er] noch manches Erfreuliche. . . leisten können." In Thylesius's *De coloribus*, published in 1549 together with Baïf's *Annotationes*, he doubtless read *sub voce* "viridis" (immediately following "fulvus," which he discusses in detail), a ten-line epigram in distichs about scarabs as well as its "Epilogus," which narrates in 18 choriambic lines the invention of purple by Hercules.

In 1818[62] Goethe cites in (his own?) translation Gilles Ménages's neo-Greek epigram about Myron's cow[63]—Χαλκοῦν σεῖο, Μύρων, Ἥρη ποτὲ πόρτιν ἰδοῦσα, Ζηλοτύπησεν, ἰδεῖν Ἰνάχιδ' οἰομένη—and in the popular *Menagiana* (three, sometimes four, volumes) several Neolatin poets are represented, including Uberto Folieta, Jérome Amalthée, Quillet, Vavasseur, and of course Ménage. Much earlier, at the time of his journey to Italy, he had attentively studied Serassi's biography of Tasso, which

---

[61] Thylesius, *Poemata* (1531 edition).

[62] WA I.49:13—cf. WA I.5, 2:243: "nach dem Französischen des Menage," a misleading statement which presumably explains why, in the Hamburger Ausgabe (12:610), only the name "Menage" is annotated as "französischer Dichter und Gelehrter."

[63] *AEgidii Menagii Poëmata*. Quarta editio (Amstelodami, 1663) 122 (slightly changed in Quinta editio [Parisiis, 1665] 108).

contains Neolatin texts like the satire attributed to Niccola Villani,[64] Agostino Mosti's eulogy of Ariosto,[65] and Tasso's famous ode "Ad Nubes."[66] It is hardly likely that he would have ignored the Latin poems in Tasso's œuvre—the various distichs and the hexameters "In die festo coronationis [Clementis octavii]"—since they were especially appropriate sources for characterizing in *Torquato Tasso* papal Rome and the court life of the Renaissance.

Although the second *Caput* of Girolomo Cardano's *De propria vita liber* is but one among several models proposed for the astrological interpretation of the hour of his birth at the beginning of *Dichtung und Wahrheit*, Goethe's great interest in Cardano, documented in the letters to Frau von Stein[67] and in the *Geschichte der Farbenlehre*, testifies amply that later too he would have read with great sympathy the biography of that successful and famous, but nevertheless by his own account rarely happy man, and his hexameter "Nænia in morte filii."[68] (In Cardano's *De Subtilitate libri xxi*, which he would have had to look at during his color studies, Goethe will have noticed the irony of the motif of fame in the distichs that begin: "Non me terra teget, coelo sed raptus in alto / Illustris vivam docta per ora virum.") And in his early years he presumably knew Lessing's *Rettung* of Cardano, since he too was interested in the Koran as the expression of universal-human religious sensibility.

Goethe not only composed poems that contained emblems from Alciati and owned his collection; from the 14th *Nachtrag* to the *Farbenlehre*[69] it is also clear that he had read him more than superficially, for he mentions with approval a remark about the color yellow in Claude Mignault's[70] commentary on emblem 117 "In colores."[71] It is just as likely that he read the Latin verses mentioned around 1820 in "Erfinden und Entdecken," in which Galileo anagramatically hid away his scientific results, "um sich die Priorität zu bewahren einer Entdeckung, die er nicht aussprechen wollte," as that he read those of Thomas More cited in *Caput* XXXI ("De Astrologia") of Agrippa von Nettesheim's *De incertitudine et vanitate omnium scientiarum*

---

[64] P.-A. Serassi, *La Vita de Torquato Tasso* (Roma, 1785—in the 1790 Bergamo edition, 2:199).

[65] 2:39 (in dodecasyllables).

[66] 1:184.

[67] Goethe read the *Vita* in 1777 and again in 1778.

[68] *Vita*, Caput L.

[69] *Goethes Werke*, Cottasche Gesamtausgabe 22:918.

[70] *Omnia. . . Alciati . . . emblemata, cum commentariis. . .* per Clavdium Minoem (Antverpiae MDLXXVII) 399ff.

[71] "Index mæstitiæ est pullus color. . . ."

& *artium liber*, a work mentioned in the fourth book of *Dichtung und Wahrheit* as childhood reading.

Even when classicizing translations were available, Goethe at least occasionally looked up the relevant Neolatin texts: the motto to "Calderons Tochter der Luft"[72] derives from "Ludus Palamedes," the thirteenth ode in the third book of Balde's *Lyrica*. In *Die Geschichte der deutschen Ode*[73] Karl Viëtor cites Goethe's remarks on Balde—"Er bleibt bei jedem Wiedergenuß derselbe, und wie die Ananas erinnert er einen an alle gutschmeckenden Früchte, ohne an seiner Individualität zu verlieren"—and takes them to be negative: "Aber hätte Goethe neben Baldes Werk die Leistungen seiner neulateinischen Vorgänger vergleichend halten können, er würde seine Wertung positiver ausgedrückt haben. . . ." But I think that on the basis of his extensive knowledge of Neolatin poetry Goethe was only trying to emphasize the presence in Balde of what according to his classical theory of art is an important characteristic of all good and original poetry. There was, after all, great and widespread interest in and understanding of Neolatin poetry at the end of the eighteenth century, as is proved by the publication in Schiller's *Musenalmanach auf das Jahr 1796* and in the *Neue deutsche Monatsschrift* (1795) of a half dozen of Herder's translations of odes by Sarbievius in unrhymed German strophes.[74]

In the essay of 1817 already referred to, "Deutsche Sprache," in which Goethe speaks of the achievements of German poets in the Latin language, he mentions Johannes Secundus and Balde together. Balde he probably first became aware of through Herder's *Terpsichore*, but in his youth he had already known Everard, "den lieben, heiligen, großen Küsser" of the poem preliminarily titled "Ad Manes J.S." in 1776. Secundus's *Opera*[75] were in Goethe's library, and his name comes up early and late—both 1 November 1776 and 31 March 1820 in the diaries, as well as in the essay already mentioned. Goethe also acquired the translation by Franz von Passow that appeared in 1807 and the new Latin edition of 1821.

The Hamburger Ausgabe calls attention to the relationship of the eroticon "Morgenklagen" of 1788 ("O du loses, leidig liebes Mädchen") to the poems of Everard: Erich Trunz refers there, as in his commentary on *Römische Elegien*, to Ellinger's essay, "Goethe und Johannes Secundus."[76] In

---

[72] (1822): "De nugis hominum seria veritas / Uno volitur assere."

[73] (München, 1923) 36.

[74] SW 27:313–16 and notes. Still another ode appeared in 1794 in *Briefe zur Beförderung der Humanität* (Nr. 35)—cf. SW 17:173 and 244, and *Musenalmanach*, p. 54 ("Die flüchtige Freude").

[75] Paris, 1748.

[76] *Goethe Jahrbuch* 13 (1892): 199–210.

most, if not all, of the reminiscences of Secundus identified by Ellinger in the elegies, we may, with Adalbert Schroeter, see only the consequence of dependence on common sources and of similarity in the situations treated. But there is no mistaking that Goethe's treatment of classical motives is by and large not very different from that of the Neolatin poet, for both have drawn on the same Latin traditions, old and new, without slavish imitation. Even Schroeter admits the possibility that Everard directly influenced Goethe; but he finds it less in the aspects of content noted in passing by Ellinger—in the "gewisse Ähnlichkeit" of ideas in "Grenzen der Menschheit" and at the beginning of Eleg. II, 9, or in the fact that the mood of that poem and of "Gesang der Geister über den Wassern" and related poems is reminiscent of Everard's "In vicissitudinem rerum instabilemque fortunam" (in the Silvæ)—than in the "weihevollen hymnenhaften Tonfall" of the latter poem, whose versus adonius Goethe likes to use for his odes from the early eighties to the Chorus mysticus of Faust. That Herder designated Goethe as Johannes Tertius in the poem he sent him for his birthday in 1788 is valuable as contemporary evidence for Goethe's unmistakable affinity with the (Neolatin) Renaissance.

There is general recognition of the importance of Giordano Bruno for Goethe, who as early as Ephemerides defended him against Bayle's criticism. H. Brunnhofer has pointed out echoes in Faust and "Vermächtnis" of the poem De Immenso et innumerabilibus,[77] and we must not forget that in the Italian works of Bruno known to Goethe all the popular Renaissance verse forms are represented. Goethe seems to have known even the Carmina of Bembo, author of the Asolani and the Rime, for in the diary of his journey to Italy[78] he comments with regard to Cattaneo's verses about him, entirely in the spirit of Renaissance humanism, that Bembo "nicht gern in der Bibel las, um seinen lateinischen Stil, wahrscheinlich auch, um seine Imagination nicht zu verderben." In any case he read the Italian Neolatin poets repeatedly, and in 1809 he borrowed for more than three months the small collection Practica artis amandi,[79] which contains not only the Latin version in distichs of a Boccaccio novella by the highly respected lyric poet Philippus Beroaldus,[80] but also among other epigrams the "In effigiem amoris" of Enea Silvio, some facetiae in verse and, by Beroaldo, "Dirae in maledicam Lenam." (There are also verses by Baptista Mantuanus—from the first and fourth eclogues—included in a prose text by Kinthisius Agricola.) Goethe also knew Sannazzaro's De partu virginis, as is clear from the

---

[77] Goethe Jahrbuch 7 (1886): 241–50.
[78] Jubiläums-Ausgabe 27:296, "Padua, den 27. September."
[79] Ursel, 1606, edited under the pseudonym "Hilarius Drudo."
[80] "Amores Guiscardi & Gismundeæ."

passage in Book 14 of *Dichtung und Wahrheit* in which, with reference to Lavater, he elaborates on the psychology of the cult of the Virgin.

As one might expect, Goethe's interest in the German Neolatin poets seems never to have abated. In 1819 he borrowed Locher's translation of the *Narrenschiff* for a few days,[81] but he had probably read Locher's own poems at the time of *Ephemerides*, in which he refers to the second volume of Schelhorn's *Amœnitates litterariae*, a work containing letters by Locher and Rychardus, with passages in elegiac verse, about Luther and the events of the Reformation. (In Schelhorn he could also read H. Meibom's elegy on the death of Borchold and other Neolatin poems.) And little more than a year before his death, after reading Boguslaw Lobkowitz's ode on Carls-bad,[82] he borrowed from the Weimar library the latter's *Farrago poematum*, in the Prague edition of 1570, the very next day.

The largest collection of Neolatin poetry Goethe seems to have looked at was the *Amphitheatrum sapientiœ socraticœ joco-seriœ, hoc est, encomia et commentaria avtorvm, qva vetervm, qva recentiorvm prope omnium: qvibus res, avt pro vilibvs vvlgo aut damnosis habitœ, styli patrocinio vindicantur, exornantur: Opus ad mysteria naturœ discenda, ad omnem amœnitatem, sapientiam, virtutem, publice priuatimque vtilißimum: in dvos tomos partim ex libris editis, partim manvscriptis congestum tributumque, à Caspare Dornavio [Dornau] Philos. et Medico*[83] that he borrowed from the Weimar library in January 1809. Arranged by themes, it included texts by several hundred poets, among them also Latin verse translations of various Greek poems and metrical versions of Neolatin prose texts. All possible genres seem to be included: e.g., *sub voce* "Vita Rustica"—to let one group stand for all—one finds Lipsius, Thomas More, Lotichius, Nicolaus de Clamengiis, Joh. Aurelius Augurellus, Julius Aelius Crottus, Antonius Faminius, Pontano, du Bellay, Joh. Stigelius, Boissard, Henri Etienne, Camerarius, Lauterbach, Flor. Schoonhovius, Buchholzer, Du Bartas, Janus Douza, Stephanus Forcatulus, Bendecius Jovus, and Laurentius Lippus, each represented by one or more, often page-long poems. It would be pointless to recite the names of all the poets included in Dornau, since we cannot know which themes or poets interested Goethe; the most significant and famous other Neolatin poets are Micyllus, Bembo, Joseph Scaliger, Taubmann, Siber, Heinsius, Johannes Secundus, Buchanan, Chytraeus, Vida, Eoban Hessus, Euricius Cordus, Postius, Gruter, Stigelius, Melanchthon,

---

[81] Cf. E. v. Keudell, *Goethe als Benutzer der Weimarer Bibliothek* (Weimar, 1931) Nr. 1237.

[82] Diary entry of 30 January 1831.

[83] Hanoviae, MDCXIX, 854 and 305 folio pages in double columns.

Sannazzaro, Alciati, Poliziano, Schede-Melissus, Douza, Caspar Sturm, Kepler, Hutten, Frascatori, Strozzi, Angeriano, and Beroaldus Junior.

It cannot, then, be denied that Goethe's knowledge of the Neolatin poetic tradition must have been extraordinarily extensive. But anyone familiar with this tradition knows how classical, late medieval, Petrarchan and modern elements blend with one another to produce an amalgam of old and new that is often strongly reminiscent of Goethe's deliberately "classical" writing. The motif of ruins and archeology in the *Römische Elegien* is a prime requisite of both Latin and vernacular Renaissance poetry; these poems' dedicatory addresses to gods and spirits, for which the most thorough study of Goethe's sources was unable to discover classical models,[84] have close analogies in the invocations of *genii loci* in Neolatin onomastic poetry; similarly the humorous personification of boredom as the mother of the Muses in the *Venezianische Epigramme* wittily recalls the popularity of such allegories in Renaissance poets. Even more frequently than do the *Römische Elegien* the *Venezianische Epigramme* recall the often artificial freedom of—sometimes free-thinking—Renaissance poets who exploited the high standing of any remnant of ancient poetry as pretext to violate tabus, just as the westernizing of oriental poetry in Neolatin translation similarly rendered its themes, if not more decent, at least more acceptable to polite literary society. The second of Goethe's posthumously published Roman elegies, which begins, "Zwei gefährliche Schlangen, vom Chore der Dichter gescholten,"[85] takes as its theme the illness that was only first identified in the Renaissance and received its first poetic discussion (ca. 1494) in the Neolatin poetry of Pontano, then again in 1522 and yet again in 1530 in the physician Geralomo Frascatori's allegorical didactic poem, frequently translated into the vernaculars, *Syphilis, sive morbus gallicus, ad Petrum Bembum.*[86]

Goethe's less classical and even non-classical poems, above all the love lyrics and reflective poems of his later years such as those in the *Divan* and "Trilogie der Leidenschaft," contain Orphic and Neoplatonic motifs that do not occur in the lyric poetry of antiquity but do play a significant role in the poetry of the Renaissance. Because the preciosity of Renaissance vernacular

---

[84] F. Bronner, "Goethes römische elegien und ihre quellen," *Neue Jahrbücher für Philologie und Pädagogik* 148 (1893), *passim*.

[85] WA I.53:4ff.

[86] Excerpts in Teodoro Pennacchia, *Storia della Sifilide* (Pisa, 1961 = Scientia Veterum, 17), who also offers information about Massimo Pacifico d'Ascoli's "De gonorrhea violenta," which is composed in hexameters.

poetry,[87] which still echoes in the language of Sensibility (as it was cultivated by Goethe above all in *Stella*, his "Schauspiel für Liebende"), exerted a strong influence on Neolatin poetry, the effect of classicizing translations from the Persian into Latin was much less alien than if they had appeared first in the stylistically more uniform poetic vernaculars of the age of Enlightenment: Goethe could also have claimed, "Nur wer weiß, was Calderon gesungen, wird auch Hafis' Wert erkennen."

If, as I am inclined to believe, the tradition of Renaissance poetry was important for Goethe all his life, it must be even more relevant for his song-like and gnomic poetry than for the smaller body of his poetry in classical forms. In the *West-östlicher Divan* especially, the number of motifs and techniques for which there are correspondences in Renaissance poetry is astonishing,[88] and in this work the relatively large number of short poems is reminiscent of the importance of epigram in the collections of Renaissance love poets. The use of lyric to record biographical events of whatever kind, for which antiquity provides only the sketchiest of precedents, is fully developed in poets like Petrarch, Campano,[89] Celtis, and Pontano—in the latter case even with the motif so important for Hafiz and for Goethe's *Divan*, that of the aging and finally old man who can still love passionately. Even if Goethe did not imitate the etymologizing meta-morphoses of the Neolatin poets as they invented more and more new local *genii*—like Pontano's inventions in the *Eridanus* and the Lepores (the bay of Naples) in his *De amore conjugale* II, vii—nevertheless he did engage in the transformation and re-creation of classical myths that so often accompanied their doing so: he does this not only in *Faust*, but also in poems like "Ganymed," which does not lack its euhemerist aspect, and the epigram of the 1790s "Phöbos und Hermes," in which the allegorical appearance of Ares—War, who violently breaks the lyre of Poetry—seems to lack any classical precedent. (The personification of the birches in the Leipzig song "Die [schöne] Nacht," and also that of the night as mother of

---

[87] Two well-known representatives of Neolatin Petrarchism are Giovanni Marrasio, the author of "Angelinetum" (ca. 1420), and Ugolino Verino, whose poetry however is at the same time imbued with the spirit of Tibullus and Propertius. Two *concetti* which the editors of the Weimarar Ausgabe (I.53:424) try to link to an unidentified dramatic project are probably just preciosities which Goethe found worth noting: "Du weinst—doch fliesen deine Trähnen nur mein Herz mit den Pfeilen deiner Augen zu verwunden"; "Mein Herz, das schon zu Stücken gebrochen am Todte liegt."

[88] To demonstrate the principle of anthithetical thought structures with a more recent text while interpreting Gryphius's sonnet "Es ist alles eitel," Wilhelm Schneider quotes the *Divan* poem, "Die Jahre nahmen dir, du sagst, so vieles" (*Liebe zum deutschen Gedicht* [Freiburg, 1952] 295).

[89] Ed. Burkhard Menken (Lipsiae, 1707).

monsters in "Willkommen und Abschied," are similarly inventive.) Such motifs occur more frequently after the turn of the century, after Goethe had briefly occupied himself, not too successfully, with efforts in the middle—didactic—genre based less on classical than on Neolatin and vernacular models, such as his fragment on Jussieu's *Genera*.[90] Goethe's poetry becomes ever more explicitly symbolic: in addition to the serious poems in "Gott und Welt" deserving of special mention are the *Divan* poems "Hochbild," with the otherwise seriously used topos of the eternally unreachable daughter of the clouds,[91] and "Sommernacht," in which its kindly poet, wanting to persuade his cup-bearer to go off to bed, represents Aurora as a grass widow making eyes at the sleepy boy.

It is not only in the Leipzig poems and those of the pre-Weimar years in Strasbourg and Frankfurt that anacreontic motifs play a significant role. Goethe wrote occasional poetry in much greater quantities afterwards, and in the best of these poems combined personal moments with timeless elements of broad, general interest. Many of the poems in the *Divan* were written for a particular occasion and inserted into the framework of the cycle with little or no revision; indeed, the women addressed, even within the "Buch Suleika," constitute a biographical plural, which is once again typical of the Renaissance tradition: Lesbia was a single person, but it was no secret that the Neæra of Marullo and the Flametta of Verinus represented different individuals in different poems.

What most distinguishes the *Divan* formally from both Goethe's earlier cycles of poems and from his primary model, the Divan of Hafiz, is its variety of verse forms. In this respect Goethe has followed Neolatin example (and the practice of Hammer's translation), not that of classical and vernacular poets, who preferred to use elegies (or songs, sonnets, dizaines, etc.) in unbroken series for cyclical works. The constant metrical variation of the *Divan* evokes most nearly the occurrence of hendecasyllabics and sapphic strophes among the distichs of the *Xandra* of Cristoforo Landino, the half dozen recurring meters of the *Parthenopeus sive Amores* by Pontano, and the wealth of forms in Secundus's *Basia* (distichs, Horatian epode meter, hendecasyllabics, anacreontica, asclepiadian strophes, and one strophe form apparently of his own invention). One might well claim that the greater freedom Goethe derived from his Neolatin models—including

---

[90] WA I.5, 2:405.

[91] Cf. Lohenstein, *Agrippina*, III, ll. 187–88: "Die Sonne rennet stets der Morgenröte nach, / Und ihrer Mutter Schoß ist auch ihr Schlafgemach."

sudden rhythmic shift within a poem[92]—helped him avoid in the *Divan* a monotony that could be tiresome to a western reader of a cycle of more than a hundred poems.

Thus it is not only the oriental elements that place the *West-östlicher Divan* in an older and, for the cosmopolitan European, more generally valid poetic tradition than that of the Storm und Stress or even of the Romantics with their interest in so much that was old or exotic. The harmonious blend of styles and forms from works of several cultures and periods is entirely in Goethe's anti-purist spirit—and that of many Neolatin poets! What in many early poems is perhaps properly excused as remnant of the Rococo and of *poésie fugitive* seems after the early 1780s to be used as a means to balance tendencies to strict classicism—in this spirit at least may be understood the assertion about theater in the *Sendung* that imperfection is the quality of a living art: "Es scheint mir, wenn ich ein Gleichnis brauchen darf, wie ein Teich zu sein, der nicht allein klares Wasser, sondern auch eine gewisse Portion von Schlamm, Seegras und Insekten enthalten muß, wenn Fische und Wasservögel sich darin wohl befinden sollen."[93] And more than two decades later, at the high point of his most consistent classicism, Goethe wrote in the commentary to *Rameaus Neffe sub voce* "Geschmack" (which is itself a Renaissance concept): "Wohl findet sich bei den Griechen, sowie bei manchen Römern eine sehr geschmackvolle Sonderung und Läuterung der verschiedenen Dichtarten, aber uns Nordländer kann man auf jene Muster nicht ausschließlich hinweisen: wir haben manch anderes Vorbild im Auge. Wäre nicht durch die romantische Wendung das Ungeheure mit dem Abgeschmackten in Berührung gekommen, woher hätten wir einen Hamlet, einen Lear, eine Anbetung des Kreuzes, einen Standhaften Prinzen?"

Although Goethe displayed little enthusiasm for the classical strophes of Klopstock's imitators, in the Storm-and-Stress period he wrote not only hexameters in the style of the *Messias*,[94] but also asclepiadian-like strophes for the ode of the young Mahomet "Teilen kann ich euch nicht dieser Seele Gefühl," which seems to demonstrate an early subjective equivalence for Goethe of oriental and classical elements of style. It is of course not possible to say if the weaknesses criticized by Emil Staiger in Goethe's ionics and choriambs and in his early unclassical use of the caesura in hexameter[95] become pardonable simply because, in the period before *Römische Elegien*,

---

[92] E.g., Filelfo, "Apollo," IX, 57f. Presumably such rhythmic shifts were conceived during the Renaissance, as later during the Storm and Stress, as an expression of Pindaric "Oden-freiheit."

[93] *Wilhelm Meisters theatralische Sendung*, II, 5.

[94] Cf. WA I.53:359, paralipomenon 33.

[95] "Goethes antike Versmaße," in *Eumasia [E. Howald-Festschrift]* (Zürich, 1947) 175–91.

he had devoted more attention to Neolatin and to classicizing German poetry than to the Roman poets: in a paralipomenon to *Dichtung und Wahrheit*[96] he in any case notes a Leipzig or pre-Leipzig "Gewandheit den Homer aus dem Text deutsch in Klopstockischen Hexametern abzulesen," and his later classical meters were almost always rhythmically more effective before he attempted to bring them into conformity with Voß's and Humboldt's standards of correctness.

Since these meters play such a relatively small role in Goethe's total lyric oeuvre we may ascribe, with the musicologist F.W. Sternfeld,[97] greater significance to those rhythmic elements that are common to Neolatin and vernacular poetry and that persisted in folksong and in the Renaissance tradition, still practiced at the time of Goethe's journey to Italy, of responsive singing and recitation to lute accompaniment—especially of Ariosto's ottava rima. According to Sternfeld the Serbo-Croatian *deseterac*, madrigal verse, German octasyllabics of the sixteenth century, the emphatically rhythmic short lines of Johannes Secundus, and the hendecasyllabics of the *canzoni di ballo e potatoria* all had, as metrically related forms, strong influence on Goethe's unrhymed verse. I believe, in any case, that I speak for most non-German readers when I dare to assert that both the *Römische Elegien* and the *Venezianische Epigramme*—in contrast to *Hermann und Dorothea*—sound more like German pastiches of Neolatin poetry than like renewals of classical models: their basic rhythm is too subjective, too Goethean, and their outlook too much that of the Renaissance and after. Even in a poem so perfect as "Euphrosyne" the structural complexity, its rhetorical, didactic aspect, and the important role played by biographical details and by the occurrence of literary and mythological motifs from several spheres remind us more of the Neolatin writers than of Propertius and other philologically demonstrable Roman models. And indeed from "Ilmenau" and "Zueignung" until "Urworte Orphisch" and "Marienbader Elegie," without interruption, Goethe's poems in sestina and ottava rima share the melodic and rhythmic qualities of Italian models stretching back to the Renaissance.

Goethe is also close to poets of the Renaissance in his lifelong cultivation of serious parody and adaptation: this is true not only for several of his Leipzig lyrics, but also for the Strasbourg "Erwache, Friederike" and (presumably) for certain songs in his pre-Italian *Singspiele*. From the 90s there are "Ich denke dein" and "La Biondina,"[98] from the following decade "Nachtgesang" and—after Johann Leon's "Ich hab mein Sach Gott heim-

---

[96] WA I.53:382.
[97] "Renaissance Music in Goethe," *Germanic Review* 20 (1945): 241–60.
[98] An adaptation of the translation by Gries (cf. WA I.53:355).

gestellt" (or Pappus's ". . . angestellt," 1610)—"Vanitas! vanitatum vanitas!" The number of such texts from later years is even greater, especially in the category of epigrams and aphorisms revised with lyric inserts, in which one ought also to include little known poems like his continuation of Bürger's "Mollys Werth"[99] and his revision of a sonnet by Nicolaus Meyer. [100]

Many motifs in Goethe's lyric seem to have Renaissance rather than classical precedents. Children's and parlor games as motifs for Rococo poetry were familiar to the young Goethe—consider "Blinde Kuh" and "Stirbt der Fuchs, so gilt der Balg"—but their metaphoric, often emblematic application seems to derive from an older, originally Neolatin, poetic tradition. Here, in addition to the purely gnomic symbolic and emblematic poetry already sufficiently considered, one might mention poems like the 90th Venetian epigram and the *Divan* poem "Das Leben ist ein Gänsespiel." In Hugo Grotius's *Poemata* (1670), which Goethe borrowed from the Weimar library from mid-December 1812 until the end of August 1813, there is a group of epigrams on toys "ad imitationem apophoretôn Martialis": *Turbo. Werp-tol* ("Vertitur orbe brevi puerili missus habena, / Et moritur turbo deficiente manu"), in contrast to Goethe's epigram, is without (erotic) metaphorical application, but *Ludus anseris. Jeu des oyes* ("Sorte quidem varia, metam tamen imus ad unam: / Votaque mors rumpit: quis putet esse jocum?") is strongly reminiscent of Goethe's "Gänsespiel" poem.[101]

Adducing such parallels proves only that Goethe—in the event that he wanted to compete in such cases with antiquity and with the East—was also influenced by modern literary traditions. So too the aspect of rather broad allegorical narrative in the first poem of the section "Kunst," "Die Nektar-tropfen" (from the pre-Italian years), and in the late "Deutscher Parnaß," that seems to have no classical models, evokes Renaissance and Baroque poetry, from which derive the allegorical personifications in "Hans Sachsens poetische Sendung," "Meine Göttin" (Phantasy, as the sister of Hope and daughter-in-law of Wisdom—inspired in 1780 by the ottava rima of Wieland's *Oberon*), "Zueignung," and "Die Geheimnisse." The same is true for the poem from the late 90s, "Die Musageten," whose irritating flies are celebrated as the true leaders of the Muses—a twist owing rather to the tradition of *concetto* than to the Rococo, to which it has recently been commonly and exclusively attributed (as by Richard Friedenthal also). There are certainly Rococo elements in "Deutscher Parnaß," as also in the rather anacreontic allegory of the Muses as the sisters of Spring in "Frühzeitiger

---

[99] WA I.5, 2:357.

[100] Ibid., 394.

[101] See in this volume " 'Das Leben ist ein Gänsespiel.' Some Aspects of Goethe's *West-östlicher Divan*."

Frühling" (ca. 1801), but the play on numbers (with the Roman numeral L) in the *Zahmen Xenien*—"Wer mit XXII den Werther schrieb, / Wie will der mit LXXII leben" ("Du hast dich dem. . .") and "Doch sieht es schon bedenklich aus, / Wird aus dem Hirsch ein HirscheL. . . // Das geht auf eine HirscheLL hinaus— / Heil unsern alten Tagen!!!" ("Erst singen wir. . .")—depends on Shakespeare and the tradition of chronogram that flourished in the sixteenth and seventeenth centuries (but not in the eighteenth), even though their lyric-ironic tone makes Goethe's epigrams more interesting and significant than the majority of impersonal epigrams by his Renaissance predecessors, who, compared with their classical models, seem rather to describe than reflect.

What first called my attention to Goethe's possible relationship to Renaissance poetry is the astronomical aspect of the poem "Ein zärtlich-jugendlicher Kummer / Führt mich ins öde Feld. . . / Und die Natur ist ängstlich still und trauernd. / Doch hoffnungsvoller als mein Herz. // Denn, bald gaukelt dir, mit Rosenkränzen / In runder Hand, du Sonnengott, das Zwillingspaar / Mit offnem blauen Aug', mit krausem goldnen Haar / In deiner Laufbahn dir entgegen." The allegorical-symbolical motif of the Zodiac is taken—as recently by Detlev Schumann—to be anacreontic, and so Hermann Baumgart,[102] Schumann and others have rejected Max Morris's dating "Aus dem März 1772" and naturally also Ewald A. Boucke's assumption that the poem originated in Goethe's early Weimar years,[103] and instead suggested, at least for the lines cited, the date 1768. The harmonious blend of elements of Sensibility and Neoclassicism—these would include the echoes of Thomson's *The Seasons*, or at least of Ossian—is reminiscent of many of the elegies of certain Neolatin poets, who repeatedly reveal through such details the Renaissance interest in astronomy; examples are offered by Lotichius in the vigil of his elegy "Ad Lunam. Cum noctu iter faceret,"[104] by Giovanni Antonio Campano in "De discessu amasiae,"[105] and by Pontano in the *Parthenopeus* (II, V) and *De amore conjugali* (IX), to name but a few of them. In these texts the (favorable or inimical) hour and the passage of time—more rarely, the season—are not indicated by stars or constellations, as in classical elegies, but the season is identified by images from the Zodiac. Even more similar to the Goethe passage are the metaphoric lines in Opitz's *Trostgedichte in Widerwärtigkeit des Krieges*:

---

[102] *Goethes lyrische Dichtung in ihrer Entwicklung und Bedeutung*, I (Heidelberg, 1931) 97f. Detlev Schumann's dating in *Goethe. Viermonatsschrift der Goethegesellschaft* 25 (1963): 182–91.

[103] Festausgabe 2:488. Morris's dating in *DjG* 5:187.

[104] Lib. I, V.

[105] Carmina, II, X.

"Was hilft es, daß jetzund die Wiesen grüne werden / Und daß der weiße Stier entdeckt die Schoß der Erden / Mit seiner Hörner Kraft. . . ."[106] Most closely related to the elegiac tone of Goethe's poem, however, are several bucolic passages in Landino's *Xandra*, where the two other spring signs, Ram and Bull, serve the same function as Goethe's Twins.[107] If any single text has served as Goethe's model here, it is probably the *Callipædia* of Quillet, which Goethe first read in 1770 and praised in *Ephemerides*: in its second book the Twins are recommended as particularly efficacious for the begetting of beautiful children. That Goethe never fully distanced himself from the Renaissance tradition of seasonal poetry is shown by both the arrangement of ninety-nine xenien under the rubrics "Frühling," "Sommer," "Herbst," and "Winter" (ca. 1800) and by the later arrangement "Immer und überall—März—April—Mai—Juni—Frühling übers Jahr," for a whole group of lyrics.

Goethe's affinity with the gnomic and didactic aspects of Renaissance poetry could be demonstrated by further examples of parallel passages in Renaissance texts, although to do so here would be superfluous. But the existence of such sources has been shown often enough, as in the case of the ballad "Der Schatzgräber," based on material from Petrarch, or of the lines from the *Divan* "Mein Erbteil wie herrlich, weit und breit, / Die Zeit ist mein Besitz, mein Acker ist die Zeit," which has been connected with the symbolum "Tempus divitiae meae, tempus ager meus" cited by Goethe in a letter of 26 April 1797 to Fritz von Stein. (The couplet "Was uns gefällt und scheinet fein, / Muß erst mit Müh erworben sein" is also the versification of a symbolum—the emblematic motto "Difficilia quae pulchra."[108]) As for the Rector Siegfried in Georg Rollenhagen's *Propempticon*[109] so too for Goethe agriculture and gardening are the most natural symbols of training and education: "Weiß doch der Gärtner, wenn das Bäumchen grünt, / Daß Blüt' und Frucht die künft'gen Jahre zieren." What Hellmut Rosenfeld[110] said about Goethe's poems on works of art generally applies to his use of symbol and emblem as well: "hier wie auch sonst bei den Neuhumanisten

---

[106] Cf. Albrecht Schöne, ed., *Das Zeitalter des Barock* (München, 1963) 701 (ll. 1ff.).

[107] Lib. I, III, 21f.: "Aurea Phrixei nam tum per vellera signi / maxima lux mundi sol agitabat equos"; III, XVII, 17f.: "Quam variis redmita novi sub sidera Tauri / floribus in verno tempore ridet humus."

[108] WA I.53:353.

[109] 1568—quoted by Ellinger, *Deutsche Lyriker des sechzehnten Jahrhunderts*, Lat. Litteraturdenkmäler des XV. und XVI. Jhs., vol. 7 (Berlin, 1893) xxv–vi: "Ac veluti cultor fragrantis rusticus horti / Ponit odoratas vario discrimine plantas / Et rigat et dulces sperat decerpere fructus."

[110] *Das deutsche Bildgedicht, seine antiken Vorbilder und seine Entwicklung bis zur Gegenwart* (Leipzig, 1935 = Palaestra 199) 125.

[ist] es nicht eigentlich ein Ringen um das Bildwerk als Eigenwert. . . . , sondern der Drang, von dem Bild eine Brücke zum Menschen zu schlagen, . . . den Menschen im Bildwerk sich selbst in geläuterter vollendeter Existenz wiederfinden zu lassen." Thus in most of the epigrams in the group "Antiker Form sich nähernd" there is an unmistakable lyric moment, and in many later poems—in the *Divan*, e.g., "Abglanz" ("Ein Spiegel, er ist mir geworden") and "Gingo biloba"—subordinate epigrammatic or emblematic and major lyric elements are indissolubly linked. As in the case of the great Renaissance poets, it is difficult to distinguish clearly between surface—ornament, mask, costume, jest—and essence—experience, reality, seriousness. Even in *Ephemerides* Goethe had already noted the following sentence from Giordano Bruno, whom he found particularly sympathetic: "E quello che fa la multitudine nelle cose, non è lo ente, non è la cosa: ma quel che appare, che si rappresenta al senso e nella superficie della cosa."[111] As Günther Müller remarks at the end of his discussion of Goethe's so-called Storm-and-Stress lyrics[112]: it would be erroneous to characterize Goethe's lyric poetry as popular, for (even in that period) it was "Standesdichtung, . . . die aus dem Boden hochgezüchteter Bildung hervorging." It is for precisely this reason that such a large role is played in Goethe by the gnomic moment that so struck Friedrich Schlegel in early poems like "Willkommen und Abschied" and "Neue Liebe, neues Leben," and that he felt produced in other poems ironic, if not prosaic, conclusions. Considered without the prejudices of a vulgar romanticism, Goethe's lyric poetry is no less *Kunstdichtung* than that of the best Renaissance poets: hence he could assert with full consistency in *Maximen und Reflexionen*:[113] "Alles Lyrische muß im Ganzen sehr vernünftig, im Einzelnen ein bißchen unvernünftig sein"—a reflection that, so to speak, generalizes the apparent impossibility of the Baroque's "beau désordre."

The strong influence of Renaissance ideas on Goethe's thought has been impressively demonstrated, by Geiger and more thoroughly by Harold Jantz,[114] while R.D. Gray[115] and others claim to have discovered in Goethe's early engagement with the symbolic and allegorical alchemical writings of the Renaissance significant influences on the development of his scientific, aesthetic, and critical concepts and methods. If the young Goethe identified himself as a chameleon, the term is not necessarily to be understood as partly negative, as by Barker Fairley, for man as Proteus or—in Pico della

---

[111] *DjG* 2:27.

[112] *Geschichte des deutschen Lieds*, 242.

[113] Jubiläums-Ausgabe 38:255.

[114] *Goethe's Faust as a Renaissance Man: Parallels and Prototypes* (Princeton, 1951).

[115] *Goethe the Alchemist* (Cambridge, 1952).

Mirandola's synonym—chameleon, as a being capable of transformation and education, is a topos and central concept of Neoplatonism. In Faust's "Dem Tüchtigen ist diese Welt nicht stumm" and in the comment in the foreword to the *Farbenlehre*, "von dem leisesten Hauch bis zum wildesten Geräusch, vom einfachsten Klang bis zur höchsten Zusammenstimmung, von dem heftigsten leidenschaftlichen Schrei bis zum sanftesten Worte der Vernunft ist es nur die Natur, die spricht,"[116] we seem to hear the echo of Eusebius's speech at the beginning of Erasmus's *Convivium religosum*: "Est nonnihil, quod dixit Socrates, si solus obambules in agris. Quamquam sententia, non est muta rerum natura, sed undiquaque loquax est, multaque docet contemplantem, si nacta fuerit hominem attentum ac docilem." Goethe however knew and valued the advantages of a later, more scientific and methodical, and more fruitful understanding of nature. Hence the catchword "Goethe, the last Renaissance man" remains only a topos, for in both his genetic, historical, relativistic thinking and in his philosophical, ethical idealism he belongs unmistakably to the later age of Enlightenment and Romanticism.

Yet as *poet*, and in his understanding of the poet's role, Goethe is bound, despite all his originality and highly individual artistic profile, far more closely and faithfully to earlier literary traditions than most of his pre-romantic, romantic, and romantic-hellenizing contemporaries. As Ludwig Geiger understood, even his youthful rebellion against tradition was at bottom related to the revolutionary rejection of the Middle Age by humanists who championed not only classical but also modern values. For the older Goethe "Original" could be "geradezu ein Schimpfwort," as Friedrich Sengle put it in his essay "Konvention und Ursprünglichkeit in Goethes dichteri-schem Werk."[117] His early "Hauptaperçu, daß zuletzt alles ethisch sei," [118] is in the profoundest sense classical-neoclassical, and I would argue that an uninterrupted, if not always conscious, continuation in principle of the tradition of Renaissance poetry provided his lyric production a unity in diversity lacking in his dramatic and narrative oeuvres as totalities—despite many magnificent single works and often brilliant sections within larger works in forms less tied to tradition and therefore potentially more eclectic in effect. Thus he referred not only to his contemporaries, but also to himself, when he said to Heinrich Voß in 1804: "Was sind wir doch gegen die Künstler des 15. und 16. Jahrhunderts? Wahre Taugenichtse! Was ist

---

[116] Jubiläums-Ausgabe 40:61f.
[117] *Studium Generale* 2 (1949): 369ff.
[118] Paralipomenon to *Dichtung und Wahrheit*, WA I.53:384.

unser Jahrhundert gegen dieses kraftvolle!"[119] But as poet he is inferior to no poet of the Renaissance in either energy or artistry.

(Translated by Jane K. Brown)

[119] 6 May 1804; Gedenkausgabe 22:353.

Goethe's Nausicaa: A Figure in Fresco

In *Italienische Reise*, in his account of the dramatic fragment ultimately given the title *Nausikaa*, Goethe so much stresses the importance of Mediterranean landscape as evoked by the paintings of Claude Lorrain— and himself so successfully evokes that landscape—that in brief discussions of *Nausikaa* the figures in its landscape understandably receive little, and sometimes no, attention.[1] When Goethe describes the tragedy he began writing in Palermo,[2] he does not mention what we know from his Italian diary for Charlotte von Stein, that he first had the idea of a *Ulysses auf Phäa* almost six months earlier. For this silence there are valid compositional reasons. Since the drama was never completed, since the short-lived impulse to execute it was strong only in Palermo and Taormina, and since his readers did not even know the fragments of it he would publish in 1827, Goethe mentions it only in the section of *Italienische Reise* captioned "Sizilien."[3] As an unrealized poetic vision ("meine dichterischen Träume"), moreover, *Nausikaa* makes an effective contrast to "ein anderes Gespenst, . . . die alte Grille. . . , ob ich nicht. . . die Urpflanze entdecken könnte" (11:266), and the first interruption of its execution in Palermo nicely

---

[1] So sensitive and judicious a critic as Karl Viëtor, *Goethe: Dichtung, Wissenschaft, Weltbild* (Bern, 1949) 101, limits his account of *Nausikaa*—this is obviously deliberate simplification—to elements that relate to Sicilian landscape, neither discussing plot and characters nor mentioning that the original conception can be dated half a year earlier than *Italienische Reise* would indicate.

[2] HA 11:266. In the following for volume 5 only the 8th ("völlig neubearbeitete") edition is used. When Br. precedes the volume number, *Goethes Briefe*, HA, is to be understood. Brief references to these editions, and to other works cited, are given parenthetically in my text whenever this practice is more convenient than numbered notes.

[3] An evident compositional principle of *Italienische Reise* is that works on which Goethe worked in Italy and which are already known to his readers (e.g., *Iphigenie auf Tauris*, *Torquato Tasso*) receive leitmotif-like mention; there is no such mention of works as yet not published in any form (e.g., "Der ewige Jude") or of works Goethe never executed (e.g., *Iphigenie auf Delphi*). It may therefore not be fortuitous that in *Italienische Reise* the first allusion to *Nausikaa*, "ein ander Denkmal dieser meiner glücklichen Stunden" (11:232) is—whether or not originally so—deliberately vague, letting Goethe concentrate his Palermo mentions of *Nausikaa* in two consecutive, successively dated sections of his text (11:266: "Montag, den 16. April 1787" and "Dienstag, den 17. April 1787").

adumbrates what will prove to be its abandonment in Taormina. Goethe's failure to include in *Italienische Reise* his first reference to "a drama about wandering Ulysses, . . . for whom he felt he had gained new understanding,"[4] does not represent significant autobiographical distortion, since his early Italian self-identification with Ulysses is established as of 26 October 1786 in a passage taken almost verbatim from his Italian diary— "Hier in Foligno, in einer völlig homerischen Haushaltung. . ." (11:120)— which to all intents and purposes is there its only important expression apart from the mention of the drama itself four days earlier.

The original title *Ulysses auf Phäa* has permitted the inference that what became *Nausikaa* was conceived as a play primarily about Ulysses: "Glücklich darüber, daß die Gegenwart ihn an die Antike erinnerte, sich selbst [sc. in Foligno and earlier] Odysseus vergleichend, dies ist der für uns erkennbare Ansatz für Goethes Plan, den Aufenthalt des Odysseus bei den Phäaken dramatisch zu behandeln."[5] Goethe's characterization of the play, from the very beginning, as a "Trauerspiel" does not, however, support the inference. As a tragedy it can only have had as its theme what Goethe subsequently identified as the fatal "Rührung eines weiblichen Gemüts durch die Ankunft eines Fremden" (5:487), and its heroine can only have been the daughter of King Alcinous. (The fact that the theme had less immediacy the longer he was away from Charlotte von Stein helps explain both Goethe's apparent loss of interest in *Ulysses auf Phäa* and his failure to complete *Nausikaa*.) As we know from the repeated occurrence of "Arete" in H², it was only after rereading the relevant books of the *Odyssey* in Palermo that Goethe was able to give his heroine her correct name; until then, unable to remember it, he gave her the name of her mother. He made the substitution, I believe, not—as is usually stated despite the lack of any direct written or oral confirmation by him that this was the reason—because he believed Arete to be Alcinous' daughter, but simply in order to have a

---

[4] H.G. Haile, *Artist in Chrysalis: A Biographical Study of Goethe in Italy* (Urbana, 1973) 21.

[5] Helmut Mainzer, "Zu Goethes Fragmenten 'Ulyß auf Phäa' und 'Nausikaa,' " *Goethe-Jb.* 80 (1963): 167. Mainzer's inference (or what his almost telegraphic style permits to be taken as such) is far less incautious than Julius Zeitler's speculation, *Goethe-Handbuch* 3:20, "Vielleicht strebte die Handlung von der *ursprünglichen* herrlichen Anlegung auf das 'Meer- und Inselhafte'. . . bei weiterem Durchdenken zu schärferer Charakterisierung des Ulyß" [emphasis added], which hardly fits with a North Italian genesis "in denselben Tagen, wie die Pläne zum 'Ewigen Juden', zu 'Iphigenie in Delphi' in ihm [i.e., Goethe] auftauchte" (18). In October 1786 "Homeric" did not yet mean "Mediterranean," but only "simple"; the already cited passage for 26 October continues "wo alles um ein auf der Erde brennendes Feuer in einer großen Halle versammelt ist, . . . am langen Tische speist, wie die Hochzeit von Kana [e.g., variously by Tintoretto] gemalt wird. . . ."

name to work with provisorily. (Why the name Nausicaa eluded him can, I think, also be explained plausibly, but the explanation is best left until later, since it is incidental to the final theme of this essay, the possible importance of Nausicaa as a figure in fresco for Goethe's impulse to make her a tragic heroine.) It was to avoid the provisory name Arete that he thought of his play about The Daughter of Alcinous and Ulysses simply as *Ulysses auf Phäa* and so entitled it in the diary to be sent back to Weimar.

Why *Ulysses auf Phäa* remained little more than an idea until Goethe reached Sicily is easily understood. Revision of *Iphigenie auf Tauris* demanded all his creative energies until its completion at the end of December. Then *Torquato Tasso* became the first item on his poetic agenda and was accordingly the only literary project to accompany him to Naples and Sicily (11:176). The difficulties which it caused him—less than a week before leaving Rome he asked "Tät' ich nicht besser, 'Iphigenie auf Delphi' zu schreiben, als mich mit den Grillen des 'Tasso' herumzuschlagen?" (11: 170)—were such that with the exception of *Faust* it was the last completed of all the works Goethe had undertaken to revise and finish in Italy, being in fact completed (unlike *Egmont*, *Erwin und Elmira*, or *Claudine von Villa Bella*) only after his return to Weimar. Although Goethe claimed and perhaps believed that during the voyage from Naples to Palermo the "Plan" of his Tasso drama "war. . . ziemlich gediehen" (11:228), failure to mention *Tasso* again until 11 August 1787, when he promises it for early in 1788 (11: 383), suggests that ideas which had seemed viable to a half-awake seasick poet "im Walfischbauch" and until he went ashore at Palermo on the morning of 2 April soon seemed less so in fully waking hours on the brightly-lit terra firma of Sicily. By evening of the same day, as Goethe declares "nachträglich," he has begun to work on "ein ander Denkmal dieser meiner glücklichen Stunden" (11:232) and has once again put *Tasso* aside.

Since we know nothing of *Ulysses auf Phäa* except that it was to be a tragedy, and since Goethe was not to read Homer and be able to re-entitle that tragedy *Nausikaa* until over a week after his arrival in Palermo (11:631 [n. to p. 241, l. 8]), it is natural to assume that both H² and the two opening scenes of the fragment, both lacking the name of Nausicaa, substantially correspond to Goethe's original "Plan" of the preceding October. There are then only two *Nausikaa* plans, one represented by manuscripts originally Sicilian (and possibly Neapolitan), the other that much later sketched "Aus der Erinnerung" for *Italienische Reise*. The differences between these two distinct plans have so often been thoughtfully examined and evaluated— most recently by Dieter Lohmeier in the newly revised fifth volume of the Hamburger Ausgabe—that only the first immediately concerns us here. But it is legitimate to ask whether *Ulysses auf Phäa* and this Siculo-Neapolitan (manuscript) material, which for brevity I shall simply call *Nausikaa*, may have differed in any important ways.

As in 1786, in 1787 Goethe is still the *Wanderer*; he can still identify himself with Ulysses, and Ulysses with a sometimes idyllic, sometimes heroic, primitive-patriarchal world. The identifications are reawakened after several months of modern-urban life in Rome and Naples by a not unadventurous sea voyage that takes him to Sicily, the land of Charybdis and the Cyclopes. Sicily was exotic not only by virtue of its vegetation but also because, as Goethe could expect from accounts he had read by earlier eighteenth-century travelers who had thought to discern Homeric survivals in Sicily, he would find there ways of life often simpler than those he had recently known in Italy.[6] *Nausikaa*, in reflecting such elements, can differ from *Ulysses auf Phäa* only in minor details of natural and Claude Lorrainian landscape, and so critics have rightly stressed the play's affinity to *Iphigenie auf Tauris*, particularly since Goethe was completing the latter, still a drama of Winckelmannian "Frühklassik," when he conceived *Ulysses auf Phäa*.[7]

But is it entirely proper to claim that what Goethe wrote in 1787 indicates that "die *Nausikaa*-Tragödie als ein klassisches Versdrama in dem soeben durch die Umarbeitung der *Iphigenie* erprobten Stil geplant war?"[8] If by "Nausikaa-Tragödie" is meant *Ulysses auf Phäa*, the answer must be:

---

[6] A Sicily still often Homeric was not Goethe's private discovery. In his *Lettres sur la Sicile. . . écrites en 1777* (Turin, 1782, 2 vols.) Michel-Jean de Borch, who shared Goethe's interest in mineralogy (cf. Borch's *Lythologie sicilienne* [Rome, 1778]) and who in the *Lettres* signals the "richesses pour la Botanique" of the Kingdom of the Two Sicilies (1:19), emphasizes the primitiveness of life once Calabria is reached (1:16f.); Borch nevertheless criticizes (1:xii) Johann Hermann Riedesel, the author of *Reise durch Sicilien und Groß-griechenland* (Zürich, 1771), for a—Winckelmannian—blindness to all but evidences of classical antiquity and its survival which constrains Riedesel to see even what is modern through the eyes of Theocritus. Perhaps the most "unmodern" Sicilian custom noted by Borch is the nude sea-bathing of young women (2:142f.). (René Michéa, *Le "Voyage en Italie" de Goethe* [Paris, 1945], also notes Borch's and Goethe's common scientific interests, but Michéa cites only Borch's *Lythologie sicilienne* [Rome, 1778], the original edition of which, *Lythographie sicilienne* [Naples, 1777], has as its motto the first three of the nine lines cited from Thylesius—for which Borch's source is "Thylesius Carm. VIII. lib. I"—by Goethe in *Materialien zur Geschichte der Farbenlehre* 14:72.) J.-P.-L. Houel, whose *Voyage pittoresque des Iles de la Sicile* (Paris, 1782–1787, 4 vols.) had Goethe's approval—cf. Goethe: *Begegnungen und Gespräche*, vol. 3, ed. Renate Grumach (Berlin, 1977) 392—, similarly thought to discern survivals of Homeric (primitive and ancient Greek) manners and customs among the Sicilian lower class, but Riedesel (137), disregarding Roman, Christian, Norman, Moslem, and Spanish influences in Sicily, even explained the great virtuousness of Sicilian women as demonstrating a survival of ancient Greek moral values.

[7] Cf. Werner Kohlschmidt, "Goethes 'Nausikaa' und Homer," in: Kohlschmidt, *Form und Innerlichkeit* (Bern, 1955) 33–49 (esp. 36 and 49); also Lohmeier, HA 5:491f.

[8] Lohmeier 491.

quite probably, since all we can assume with any certainty is that it was a play with the tragic motif of the fatal desertion of the girl who has befriended the stranded Ulysses. Despite its—working—title, like *Iphigenie auf Tauris* and what possibly was its immediate predecessor by a few days, the also never realized plan of an *Iphigenie auf Delphi,*[9] *Ulysses auf Phäa* was to have had as its protagonist a mythical Greek heroine. Unlike these plays, it was to have been a tragedy in the strict sense of the term (not a "Schauspiel" but a "Trauerspiel"[10]), but its temporal closeness to them justifies the inference that it too was to have been formally "une tragédie tout à fait selon les règles," to use the phrase with which Goethe in 1823 characterized *Iphigenie auf Tauris* in contrast to a *Torquato Tasso* that because of its changes of scene could only qualify as a "tragédie selon les règles."[11] That the neoclassical principle of unity of place so effectively sustained in *Iphigenie auf Tauris* and implicit in Goethe's plan of *Iphigenie auf Delphi*—which was to be a companion-piece to that play and to Euripides' *Iphigenia at Aulis*—was to be strictly observed in *Ulysses auf Phäa* also seems indicated by the "auf" of its title. Goethe's "Phäa" is Scheria, unequivocally identified since early classical times with Corcyra (Corfù), an Ionian island small enough to be 'one' place taking, like Delphi alias Delphos, the preposition "auf" and not, like Sicily (titularly half of the large Kingdom of the Two Sicilies), the preposition "in" that Goethe uses in such phrases as "auf dem bisherigen Wege in Sizilien" (11:281). *Ulysses auf Phäa* was to be one of three plays all of whose titles announce unity of place.

After his arrival at Palermo Goethe identifies Sicilian landscape with that of Scheria—"alles rief mir die Insel der seligen Phäaken in die Sinne" (11: 241)—and soon names his play after its heroine. The main action (Acts II–V) will take place in the great hall of Alcinous' palace, but strict unity of place is now sacrificed for the sake of an effective opening scene on the shore of the Mediterranean, so that *Ulysses auf Phäa* becomes formally less like *Iphigenie auf Tauris* and more like *Torquato Tasso*. But the price of this scene is the three "Mädchen" of H[2] (in the text printed in 1827 "Aretens Jungfrauen"), who increase the number of speaking actors beyond the neoclassical limit of five so carefully observed in the two Iphigenie and the Tasso dramas.[12] *Ulysses auf Phäa* has thus not only become *Nausikaa*, but it also has ceased, by Goethe's self-imposed standards, to be even a

---

[9] 18 October (cf. HA 11, n. to p. 107, l. 30).

[10] Neither in Goethe's diary nor in *Italienische Reise* is *Iphigenie auf Delphos* (. . . *Delphi*) ever called a "Trauerspiel."

[11] WA I.53:208f.

[12] H[2] has a sixth speaker, the Messenger of V.v.

"tragédie selon les règles."[13] Although in H[2] the wooers of "Aus der Erin-nerung" have not yet appeared, there is no longer any formal principle that excludes their introduction.[14] *Nausikaa* still belongs to the group of classicizing verse dramas which Goethe planned or worked on in Italy, but in its treatment of place it is now less close to *Iphigenie auf Tauris* than to *Torquato Tasso*, and in its disregard of a five-actor limit less close to either of these two plays than to the next text—also a "Trauerspiel"—to which Goethe was to turn in Italy, his *Egmont*.

Until landscape that recalled Claude's landscapes gave Goethe the impetus to begin the actual writing of *Ulysses aus Phäa*, its entire action can only have taken place in the great hall of Alcinous' palace, with the original meeting of Nausicaa and Ulysses there reported by one of the play's five speaking actors—perhaps by her to her confidante Xantha/Eurymedusa in a scene partly corresponding to I.iii,[15] perhaps by Ulysses in an expository monologue similar in function to that of Iphigenie in the grove before the Temple of Diana. (If for Ulysses, as has been suggested, there was "eine tiefere Wurzel. . . in der vordeutenden Pyladesgestalt der 'Iphigenie auf Tauris,' "[16] the major burden of exposition might properly have fallen on him, since he would, like Clavigo in relation to Weislingen, have been Pylades "in der ganzen Rundheit einer Hauptperson" [HA 4, 1. Aufl., 544].) Despite new formal and substantive—chiefly landscape—elements, however, in plot *Ulysses auf Phäa* cannot have been fundamentally different from *Nausikaa*, and what Goethe later declared to Schiller, that the motif was "nach der Nausikaa [sc. of the *Odyssey*] gar nicht mehr zu unternehmen" (HA Br. 2:331), holds true as much for the earlier as for the later play.

[13] If *Ulysses auf Phäa* followed the pattern of the other two works of which Goethe was thinking when it was first conceived, the report of Nausicaa's (Arete's) death could have been brought by her brother (Neoros) or by her confidante-maid (Xantha/Xanthe, Eurymedusa).

[14] The generally accepted opinion that a scene with Nausicaa's wooers (cf. "Aus der Erinnerung") was a later—perhaps "Shakespearian"—afterthought seems to be confirmed by H[2], but such a scene was no longer inconceivable once unity of place and the five-actor rule had been abandoned. "Aus der Erinnerung" could therefore represent ideas considered by Goethe, if not in Taormina, at least in Naples just before he finally abandoned his dramatic project for ever (cf. also Lohmeier's recognition, p. 491, of "Betonung der Sitte" as a possibly Sicilian motif).

[15] That in 1827 Goethe published nothing of *Nausikaa* after I.ii may indicate awareness that what we now have as I.iii is not quite of a piece with I.i and I.ii. I.iii opens (ll. 61–76) with references to I.i, but it is technically clumsy to have Nausicaa recount late in the day what she would more naturally have reported in the circumstance implied by her words "Gesteh ich dir geliebte Herzensfreundin / Warum ich heut so früh in deine Kammer / Getreten bin. . ." (ll. 77ff.).

[16] Zeitler 18.

What also holds true for both plays, I believe, is that much of the creative impulse behind each of them is Goethe's "alte Gabe, die Welt mit Augen desjenigen Malers zu sehen, dessen Bilder ich mir eben eingedrückt" (11:86). Goethe recalls in the already cited letter to Schiller that when he was reading books of the *Odyssey* in Sicily and Naples it was "als wenn man ein eingeschlagnes Bild mit Firnis überzieht, wodurch das Werk zugleich deutlich und in Harmonie erscheint," and from *Italienische Reise* we know that for this simile of a picture it is a Claude Lorrain landscape that must be supplied. A pictorial impulse did not suffice to sustain Goethe's interest in a motif the limited dramatic potential of which he must soon have begun to sense in October 1786, and, more keenly, in April and May 1787, however unsystematically he had yet reflected on the differences between epic and dramatic poetry that were later to occupy so much of his and Schiller's attention.[17] Although Claude's "Bilder" as it were explain *Nausikaa*, Claude does not become important for the Italian Goethe before Rome—he is first mentioned in *Italienische Reise* under the date 19 February 1787 (11:174)— and so we must seek another painter as the possible inspiration of *Ulysses auf Phäa*.

When Goethe conceived his original "Plan," "Bilder" important for him were, with the notable exception of Mantegna frescos in Padua, almost exclusively paintings by either Cinquecento or later artists—in mid-October 1786 these were chiefly Guercino and other Bolognese eclectics—in whose work landscape was never the major theme. Although Goethe does not mention their fresco painting, his enthusiastic comments on Mantegna permit the assumption that during this period, as subsequently throughout his stays in Rome, significant examples of it did not escape his attention. It is therefore possible that *Ulysses auf Phäa* was, consciously or unconsciously, a response to Bolognese frescos of scenes from the *Odyssey*, the two major North Italian examples of which were, and still are, to be found in Cento and Bologna.

---

[17] In "Aus Goethes Brieftasche" (1775) Goethe had already protested against the practice "jede tragische Begebenheit zum Drama zu strecken" (12:22). It is in part on Goethe's and Schiller's discussions of the difference between narrative and drama that the doubts expressed by Nietzsche in *Die Geburt der Tragödie* about the dramatic potential of *Nausikaa* are based: "Welche Form des Drama's blieb noch übrig, wenn es nicht aus dem Geburtsschoosse der Musik, in jenem geheimnisvollen Zwielicht des Dionysischen geboren werden sollte? Allein *das dramatisirte Epos*: in welchem apollinischen Kunstgebiete nun freilich die *tragische* Wirkung unerreichbar ist. Es kommt hierbei nicht auf den Inhalt der dargestellten Ereignisse an; ja ich möchte behaupten, daß es Goethe in seiner projectirten 'Nausikaa' unmöglich gewesen würde, den Selbstmord jenes idyllischen Wesens—der den fünften Act ausfüllen sollte—tragisch ergreifend zu machen. . ." (Nietzsche, *Werke*, ed. G. Colli and M. Montinari, 3. Abt., 1 [Berlin, 1972] 79).

In Cento, where Goethe devoted the day of 17 October to Guercino, are the Ulysses frescos of Guercino (and assistants), then in the Odyssey Room of the Palazzo Chiarelli-Pannini but since 1840, when they were transferred to canvas, in the Pinacoteca Civica. These he is not likely to have seen, since neither the palazzo nor its frescos are noticed—perhaps its owners did not welcome visitors—by Volkmann, whose *Historisch-kritische Nachrichten von Italien* was his chief guidebook,[18] and since if he had seen them he would surely, in his then immoderate admiration of Guercino, have recorded the fact. It is highly probable, however, that at some point during his stay in Cento these not too remarkable frescos and some of their themes—the first of the series is "Ulysses before Arete"—were referred to in his presence, and in this case the idea, or the germ of the idea, of a Ulysses play may antedate by part of a day the conception of *Iphigenie auf Delphos*, which his (evening) diary entry of 18 October places very early that morning. But in any event the "schon" four days later of Goethe's only mention of *Ulysses auf Phäa*, "Sagt' ich Dir schon. . . ?" conveys a vague awareness of having forgotten to record it as the other and, as his "der vielleicht glücken könnte" suggests, perhaps less promising of two plans conceived almost simultaneously.

Whether or not on 17 October he learned in Cento of the existence of Guercino's Ulysses frescos, during the afternoon of 18 October Goethe certainly did see in Bologna far more important frescos with themes from the *Odyssey*. (If these, rather than Guercino's, inspired the plan of his tragedy, the plan followed rather than preceded the idea of an *Iphigenie auf Delphos* by an almost exactly equivalent time interval, and the quasi-simultaneity of both conceptions remains a valid inference.) Under "d. 18. Bologna. Abends," an understandably tired Goethe announces his resolve to proceed from Bologna to Rome without further stopovers—"ich muß Florenz liegen lassen und es auf einer frohen Rückreise mit geöffneten Augen sehen"—and then adds, "Auch hier in Bologna müßte man sich lange aufhalten. Siehe nunmehr Volkmanns ersten Teil, von S. 375 bis 443." Specific references by page number follow (402, 403, 425, 387), indicating that what Goethe comments on was seen in the order given. Each of these numbers refers to more than one page (402 = 401f., 403 = 402f., 425 = 424f.), the last, however, to a whole section in Volkmann, "Von dem Institut zu Bologna und der bolognesischen Malerschule" (387–401): "Ich war im Institute. Davon will ich Dir nichts sagen. Es ist eine schöne edle Anlage. . . ." In *Italienische Reise* this is expanded to:

[18] Leipzig, 1770, 3 vols.

Nun war Ich auch in der berühmten wissenschaftlichen Anstalt, das Institut oder die Studien genannt. Das große Gebäude, besonders der innere Hof, sieht ernsthaft genug aus, obgleich nicht von der besten Baukunst. Auf den Treppen und Korridors fehlt es nicht an Stukko- und Freskozierden; alles ist anständig und würdig, und über die mannigfaltigen schönen. . . Dinge, die hier zusammengebracht worden, erstaunt man billig. . . . (11:109)

Volkmann mentions the only two important groups of frescos in the Institute. The first, four simply placed wall-frescos of charming *scènes galantes*, receives a single sentence: "In dem einen der für die Physik bestimmten Zimmer und in dem von der bürgerlichen Baukunst bemerkt man gute Freskomalereyen von Niccolo dell Abbate" (1:394). The second, more memorable by virtue both of its greater scope and its integration with architectural and ornamental elements (Goethe's "Stukkozierden"), receives a whole paragraph, which constitutes the conclusion of Volkmann's account of the Institute's "Malerakademie" (1:396–98):

In dem Versammlungssaal der Akademie befindet sich eine schöne Decke vom Pellegrino Tibaldi, worauf verschiedene Stücke aus der Odyssee vorgestellt sind. Man bemerkt darinn eine treffliche Zeichnung, und geschickte Verkürzungen. Ueberhaupt muß man sich wundern, daß der Künstler so viel große Figuren in einen so kleinen Raum bringen können. Von Tibaldi lernten die Caracci den großen Geschmack in der Zeichnung, den sie in ihrer Schule einführten. Er zeichnet in einer ebenso edlen Manier als die Caracci; und weiß die kühnsten Verkürzungen mit der richtigsten Zeichnung anzubringen.[19]

(Volkmann fails to indicate that the series of frescos only begins in the "Versammlungssaal," and ends in a somewhat smaller, but still large,

---

[19] Volkmann 1:398. In the 18th century still, as ever since the time of the Carracci's, the two Ulysses rooms were for Bolognese art students what Giuliano Briganti, *Il Manierismo e Pellegrino Tibaldi* (Roma, 1945) 79, calls "una specie di piccola Sistina." In his "Chronologisches Verzeichniß der Maler in Italien nach den verschiedenen Schulen" Volkmann states: "Seine [i.e., Tibaldi's] ersten in den Kirchen von Bologna befindlichen Gemälde haben ein schönes Kolorit, eine gute Zusammensetzung und richtige Zeichnung; dem ungeachtet konnte er kaum davon leben, bis ihn Pabst Gregorius XIII. [the pope whose sometimes forgotten patronage of the arts is mentioned in *Tasso*, ll. 667ff.] und nachgehends Philipp II. König in Spanien an ihren Hof beriefen. . ." (1:107f.). *Allgemeines Lexikon der bildenden Künstler von der Antike bis zur Gegenwart*, ed. U. Thieme and F. Becker, 33 [Leipzig, 1939] 129, characterizes Tibaldi's ceiling frescos, which Briganti (p. 77) calls "l'opera maggiore del. . . artista" and says represent "il momento il più felice della sua lunga operosità," as belonging to "den originellsten u. bedeutendsten Leistungen des Manierismus in Italien."

adjacent room which enjoys better natural light. He also completely disregards what would have been important for Goethe, coloration, which becomes more splendid as the series reaches the second room.[20])

The last and—this makes it most immediately accessible to the amateur of art whose taste, as Goethe's still was at this time, has been formed by paintings of or inspired by the High Renaissance—least manneristic of Tibaldi's *Odyssey* frescos is "Ulysses Introduced to Alcinous by Nausicaa."[21] The picture, whose coloring recalls the delicacy of Veronese's frescos at Villa Maser, is also the only one to represent a room, the pillared and pilastered hall of Alcinous' palace, in stage-design perspective. In the foreground Ulysses kneels behind Nausicaa, who stands before her father, an aged king wearing a modest crown, and points over her shoulder at the bearded, scantily garbed stranger she is introducing. Here vigorous maturity, youthful beauty, and the subdued spirit of old age are powerfully counter-posed with a classical restraint emphasized by Tibaldi's tribute to Raphael in the pose of Nausicaa, which is adapted from that of the young woman who kneels in Raphael's "Transfiguration."[22] Goethe could rightly say, after his one mention of *Ulysses auf Phäa* in his diary entry at Giredo (Ponte Ghiereto) on 22 October 1786: "In Bologna habe ich noch so manches gesehen von dem ich schweige."

---

[20] Cf. Briganti 79f.: "Nella piccola sala specialmente, la stessa forma colorata trasuda da tutti i pori la vivacità incredibile delle tinte: squillano impensati colori, accentuatamente 'artificiali', rossi indicibilmente rossi, gialli enormemente gialli; le finte colonne coperte di drappeggi sono verdi, viola, rosse, azzurre, gialle, appaiono qua e là figure intensamente colorate, disposte, in ragione del loro colore, con vivissima immaginazione compositiva." Johann Heinrich Meyer, *Geschichte der Kunst*, ed. H. Holtzhauer and R. Schlichting (Weimar, 1974) 215, characterizes Tibaldi with greater, almost late-Goethean, caution: "Unter den Künstlern, die Michelangelos mächtigen Stil nachzuahmen strebten, ist Pellegrino Tibaldi. . . einer, dem es beinahe am besten gelang. Fruchtbar an Erfindungen, wild und kühn in der Darstellung imponieren seine Werke dem Beschauer mehr, als daß sie ihn ergötzen. . . . Im Institut zu Bologna ist ein beträchtlicher Saal und ein an demselben liegendes Zimmer von diesem Künstler mit Geschichten des Ulysses in Fresko gemalt." Although Goethe himself apparently never mentioned Tibaldi, he owned one pen drawing by him—cf. Christian Schuchardt, *Goethe's Kunstsammlungen* (Jena, 1848) 1:352 (nr. 191)—and a charcoal and white drawing attributed in Schuchardt 1:243 (nr. 109) to Andrea Pellegrini which may actually be by Tibaldi (cf. Thieme-Becker, *s.v.* Andrea Pellegrini).

[21] Briganti, pl. 127. Although there exist reproductions of Tibaldi's "Fatti di Ulisse" in color, the best—especially by virtue of their large format—are those in black and white in Briganti (pls. 114–27); smaller black and white reproductions are most conveniently found in A. Venturi, *Storia dell'Arte Italiana*, 9, Parte 6 (Milano, 1933) 530–47.

[22] This is noted by Briganti 110, n. 88.

It is to Tibaldi, I believe, that the first strong—pictorial—impulse to write *Nausikaa*, alias *Ulysses auf Pbäa*, must be credited. But Goethe's three-day visit was too crowded and, as he said in his only subsequent mention of Bologna in *Italienische Reise* after his stay there, too "flüchtig" (11:125) for the impression of Tibaldi's fresco to be long-lasting, and so the completion of *Iphigenie auf Tauris* was not long threatened by either *Ulysses auf Pbäa* or *Iphigenie auf Delphi*. Why Goethe so long called his play after Ulysses rather than its heroine, however, now becomes explicable. The motif of the contrast in Tibaldi's fresco of three stages of life gave added meaning to the theme of Ulysses at Scheria, for Goethe was not only the "wandering Ulysses," but was also experiencing a rebirth, the rejuvenation of an again vigorous maturity, to which he repeatedly testifies in letters from Italy and in *Italienische Reise*. But this is not the whole explanation of his play's original title: in the eighteenth century—and in the most learned account of Tibaldi's frescos then available, Giampietro Zanotti's large folio volume *Le Pitture di Pellegrino Tibaldi e di Niccolò Abbati esistenti nell' Instituto di Bologna*(Venezia, 1756)—Tibaldi's fresco was called "Arete and Alcinous." Goethe must have known that the young princess of the fresco was not Alcinous' wife, whatever his cicerone may have said when showing him Tibaldi's "Fatti di Ulisse." But a false name all too easily blocks out the name one tries, however desperately, to remember, and so it was only in Sicily, and then only after he had Homer in hand, that he was finally able to give his play its title *Nausikaa*.

Despite the distinctive character of "Ulysses Introduced to Alcinous by Nausicaa," the total effect of Tibaldi's Ulysses is too Michelangesque to have left an enduring impression on a poet to whom Raphael, Giulio Romano, Guercino, and Guido Reni were more congenial, and there is little reason to lament Goethe's first brief and fruitless interest in the Nausicaa theme. But neither, I think, should we too much lament, despite the greater congeniality of Claude Lorrain and despite his own unsurpassed ability to evoke landscape, Goethe's failure to complete a *Nausikaa* in which all acts after that which opens the play were—still—to take place in the great hall of Alcinous' palace. Goethe nevertheless did convey (no doubt unconsciously) some of the spirit of Tibaldi's "colorata narrazione favolosa, ironica, quasi ariostesca degli errori di Ulisse," of Tibaldi's "avventuroso romanzo figurato, popolato d' un' umanità vivacissima, gesticolante, agitata, frettolosa. . . ,"[23] in Antonio's just and sympathetic characterization of Ariosto in *Torquato Tasso* (ll. 711–33).[24]

---

[23] Briganti 79.

[24] Other affinities of *Nausikaa* to *Tasso* (and *Iphigenie auf Tauris*) have occasionally been noted, e.g., by Robert Petsch, in Festausgabe 8:464: "Wie die Prinzessin. . . mit einer ahnungslosen Entdeckung ihrer Neigung und ihres Abschiedsschmerzes Tasso zu einer wilden Äußerung seiner Liebe anfeuert, wonach es für ihn keine Rückkehr mehr in seinen bisherigen Lebenskreis gibt, so verführt Ulyß das holde Mädchen. . . zu einem großartigen Geständnis ihres Sehnens; einer Tat, die vielleicht dem großen Bekenntnis der Iphigenie zu vergleichen ist." In her instinctive openness and strength of character, however, the heroine of *Ulysses auf Phäa* is closer to Goethe's Taurian and Delphic Iphigenias and— despite the modern-private motivation of her conduct—to Euripides' Iphigenia at Aulis (cf. Lohmeier 492) than to the Princess of *Tasso*. It was on the day after his visit to the Institute that Goethe saw in Bologna the painting, which he originally believed to be by Raphael, of a St. Agatha whose "gesunde, sichre Jungfräulichkeit" his Taurian Iphigenia was to share; it was the day before his visit to Cento that he saw at Ferrara the tomb of the poet-statesman Ariosto (in the church of the Augustinians—cf. Volkmann 3:488, who cites the inscription enumerating Ariosto's public services) and the "Holzstall. . . , wo er [i.e., Tasso] gewiß nicht aufbewahrt worden ist" (11:100).

Wilhelm Meisters Lehrjahre: Novel or Romance?

I t will soon be two hundred years since readers admiring the merits of *Wilhelm Meisters Lehrjahre*—what in old-fashioned language might have been called "The Beauties of *Wilhelm Meister*"—first systematically offered illuminating interpretative and critical insights into that work's form and meaning. Subsequent critics and scholars, among them Liselotte Dieckmann with her essay "Repeated Mirror-Reflections: The Technique of Goethe's Novels," have deepened these insights in various ways, of which not the least important has been to draw attention to the wealth of patterned or pattern-creating elements—points of view, themes, motifs, images, the use of sententious generalization, multiple dimensions of reality, etc.—that contribute substantive and structural density to the *Lehrjahre*. Such elements are typical features of the literarily important novel since Goethe, and so it has become customary to think of a work in which they fulfill essential functions as being a novel in the broad modern sense of the term.

That *Wilhelm Meisters Lehrjahre* is a "Roman" cannot be gainsaid. It is so called on the title pages of the first three editions that Goethe authorized, one published by Unger in 1795–1796 and the other two by Cotta in 1806 and 1816. In the *Ausgabe letzter Hand*, however, the words "Ein Roman," which had previously followed the title, were omitted, although no reason for this omission seems to be recorded in Goethe's letters or conversations. (This last assertion is based on negative findings in the relevant section of H.G. Gräf, *Goethe über seine Dichtungen*, in which here unprovided references to the exact sources of utterances by Goethe on the *Lehrjahre* are easily located.) It is possible that the elimination of "Ein Roman" in 1828, when the three volumes with the *Lehrjahre* appeared, was unintentional, but it is not probable, since for the second version of *Wilhelm Meisters Wanderjahre oder die Entsagenden* (1829)—a title followed in 1821 by the words "Ein Roman von Goethe" and still so followed when Goethe submitted it to Cotta for the *Ausgabe letzter Hand* in September, 1828—Goethe authorized Reichel (in January, 1829) to delete those words as superfluous. Gräf's explanation, "Weil der Roman in 'Goethes Werken' enthalten," is insufficient, since it applies logically only to the words "von Goethe," and not to "Ein Roman."

If one examines Goethe's mentions of and statements about *Wilhelm Meisters Lehrjahre* and the antecedent *Theatralische Sendung* from 1777 until he writes Göschen on July 4, 1791, to inform him that he may be able to offer him "einen größeren Roman," it will be discovered that he normally refers to the work—I disregard inflections—as "Wilhelm Meister" (so in the first diary mention, February 16, 1777), "Meister," or "Wilhelm," although in 1777 he writes of "mein Roman," and once again in 1778. (The statement of 1780, "Früh hab' ich einige Briefe des großen Romans geschrieben," though also listed by Gräf under "Wilhelm Meister," more probably refers to the never executed "Roman über das Weltall," since there is no letter in the *Sendung*'s "Zweites Buch," on which Goethe was still to be working in late August, 1782.) Again in 1782 there is a single mention of the work as "mein Roman," but from then until 1791 it is always called simply "Wilhelm" or "Wilhelm Meister," unless the humorous remark of January 25, 1788 ("meine Existenz ist wieder auf eine wahre Wilhelmiade hinausgelaufen") be regarded as containing a title-reference.[1] After the letter to Göschen, there is over a year's interval before "Wilhelm Meister" is again alluded to by Goethe as "mein alter Roman" (the only reference of 1793), but from 1794 until the end of the epistolary exchanges about it between himself and Schiller in late 1796, Goethe refers frequently to it as "(mein) Roman."

Subsequently, however, Goethe returned to the custom of referring to the work not as a *Roman*, but only by some form of its title (e.g., in the "Annalen"). That this is no mere chance emerges from an examination of his practice or usage in connection with the other long prose narratives that do not have the words "Ein Roman" after their titles in the *Ausgabe letzter Hand*. (Only *Die Wahlverwandtschaften*, its title always followed by "Ein Roman," and a work Goethe referred to both at the time of its composition and later, e.g., in the "Annalen," as a *Roman*, does not belong to this group of writings.)

Although *Die Leiden des jungen Werther(s)* is patently an epistolary novel, from the time of its conception until after the slightly tardy publication in 1825 of the fiftieth-anniversary edition of it, Goethe never calls it a *Roman*.[2] It is first mentioned, in 1774, as "eine Arbeit," then as a

---

[1] It is in 1794, when Goethe most often terms the work "mein Roman," that he writes to Schiller of "Wilhelm Schüler, der, ich weiß nicht wie, den Namen Meister erwischt hat," but the similarly wry false title is also merely humorous.

[2] Although Gräf cites under "Werther" the sentence in Goethe's letter to Kestner of June, 1773, "Und so träum ich denn und gängle durchs Leben, führe garstige Prozesse schreibe Dramata, und Romanen und dergleichen," neither Max Morris (*Der junge Goethe* 6:264) nor Hanna Fischer-Lamberg (*Der junge Goethe* 3:420) includes Werther among the "Romane" possibly alluded to. Morris in fact says, "nicht Werther. Vielleicht die Fortsetzung des Straßburger Briefromans," while Fischer-Lamberg provides, without further explanation of

"Geschichte" (in the letter to Schönborn, echoing the usage of the introductory words of the novel: "Was ich von der Geschichte das armen Werthers. . ."), and then variously as "Die Leiden des lieben Jungen," "Werther," or by full title. In subsequent years Goethe most often calls the work simply "Werther" or "mein Werther," although he occasionally writes "Werthers Leiden" and once, in 1781, alluding to the Italian translation published that year, of the "Briefe Werthers." Thus in 1824, in connection with the practical arrangements for the edition of 1825 (i.e., October, 1824), he refers to it only as "das Werk," "Werther," and "Werthers Leiden." These last two short titles are the ones he alone uses in the remaining years of his life, with the sole exception of the 1826 announcement of the *Ausgabe letzter Hand*, which states that Band 13 will contain "Romane und Analoges: Leiden des Jungen Werther. . . ."

In his references to *Wilhelm Meisters Wanderjahre*, published in 1821, as has been noted, with the word "Roman" on its title page, Goethe normally avoids using that term, except in two diary entries of 1810. Before 1821 he variously writes of "Wilhelm Meisters Wanderjahre," "Wilhelms Wanderjahre," "Wanderjahre Wilhelm Meisters," "alter Wilhelm," and, most frequently, "Wanderjahre" (all these forms actually occur in 1810 and 1811); later we usually find simply "Wilhelm Meister" or "Wanderjahre," although "(mein) Wand(e)rer" occurs in 1821 and "Reise-Jahre" in 1828, and then, especially in 1829, when the revised text appeared, "neue Wanderjahre," "meine Wandernden," and—in discussions of this text with correspondents—"das Werk," "das Buch," and "das Büchlein."

Except, then, in connection with *Die Wahlverwandtschaften*, and during the often very practical discussions of the *Lehrjahre* with Schiller, Goethe can be said to avoid applying the word *Roman* to any of his own writing. That this is not simply an idiosyncratic preference for specific titles or short titles instead of generic terms becomes obvious from the most cursory examination of his references to his dramatic works, in which frequent use is made of "Trauerspiel," "Drama," "Schauspiel," "Tragödie," "Stück," "Farce," "Fastnacht(s)spiel," "Komödie," "Lustspiel," etc. It is, then, not surprising to discover that in *Dichtung und Wahrheit* not only is *Werther*—alias "das Buch," "das Werk," "das Büchlein," "das Manuskript"—not called a *Roman*, but that apart from two mentions of "die Richardsonschen Romane" (one in the sixth, the other in the thirteenth book) the word is conspicuously absent. Goethe succeeds in discussing *The Vicar of Wakefield* at considerable length (in book ten) without employing the term; *Robinson*

her early dating of the *Theatralische Sendung*, the note: "Arbeit am Urmeister; vielleicht auch die Wiederaufnahme des Briefromans aus der Straßburger Zeit Arianne an Wetty."

Crusoe, Telemach, Die Insel Felsenburg, Agathon,[3] and *Die Abenteuer des Don Sylvio* are referred to only by title; there are allusions to *La Nouvelle Héloïse,* but it is never named; although Lenz, Marivaux, Sophie von La Roche, and Voltaire are discussed, some at considerable length, their novels or prose narratives (e.g., *Der Waldbruder, La Vie de Marianne, Die Geschichte des Fräuleins von Sternheim, Candide*) receive no mention; and Fielding, Smollett, and—most surprisingly, in view of Goethe's lifelong admiration of his work—Sterne, all novelists the young Goethe had read, do not appear at all in *Dichtung und Wahrheit.*

Goethe's reluctance to employ the word *Roman* except in special circumstances and connections reflects, I believe, several partially related facts and factors. Most obvious is the imprecision of the term itself, used in German since the seventeenth century for any type of prose narrative, whether it be "Schelmenroman," "Politischer Roman," "Satirischer Roman," "Schäferroman," "Reiseroman," "Abenteuerroman," "Galanter Roman," "Höfisch-Historischer Roman," "Allegorischer Roman," "Schlüsselroman," "Utopischer Roman," "Familiengeschichte," "Ritterroman," "Schauerroman," or some other kind of story.[4] Unmodified, *Roman* in Goethe's day and long after meant simply an "erdichtete oder dichterisch ausgeschmückte erzählung gröszeren umfanges in prosa, deren kern gewöhnlich ein liebesvorgang ist" (Grimm, *Deutsches Wörterbuch* 8:1152). Of Goethe's longer prose narratives, *Die Wahlverwandtschaften*—though obviously also a "Sittenroman"—most closely meets in its intention this definition, which is surely one reason why Goethe continued to let its title be qualified by the words "Ein Roman."[5]

---

[3] It may be regarded as a *tour de force* that in "Zum brüderlichen Andenken Wielands" Goethe succeeds in referring to "Agathon" and other narrative writings without using either *Roman* or (full) titles.

[4] Max Wundt, in *Goethes Wilhelm Meister und die Entwicklung des modernen Lebensideals* (Berlin und Leipzig, 1913), emphasizes the emergence of "Sittenroman," "sentimentaler Roman," "Bildungsroman" (as pedagogical form of the "Sittenroman"), and "Kulturroman" as developments in the history of the eighteenth-century novel especially important for the *Theatralische Sendung* and *Lehrjahre.* Less content-determined categories are "Ichroman," "Briefroman," "Memoirenroman," "Dramatischer Roman," elements of which are also found in *Wilhelm Meisters Lehrjahre.* (For the 1770's Robert Riemann, in *Goethes Romantechnik* [Leipzig, 1902], stresses the new significance of "Charaktergemälde," autobiographical novel, and "Mischgebilde von Roman und Drama.")

[5] Although *Die Leiden des Jungen Werthers* was universally read as, and called by all readers, a *Roman,* Goethe never conceded that the love story was its "Kern"—thus even in writing to Schönborn in early July, 1774, he emphasizes character portrayal of a talented young man "der. . . sich in schwärmende Träume verliert, sich durch Spekulation untergräbt, bis er zuletzt durch *dazutretende* unglückliche Leidenschaften, *besonders* eine endlose Liebe zerrüttet, sich eine Kugel vor den Kopf schießt" (my italics). *Die Wahlver-*

Although some critics consider Goethe's novels "deficient in plot and invention,"[6] *Wilhelm Meisters Lehrjahre* contains a wealth of motifs all too familiar in every sort of eighteenth-century "Trivialroman." There are several confusions of identity (including a disguised Wilhelm's being taken by the Count for his apparitional double and the wandering actors' being mistaken for richer victims by brigands); amorous encounters and love stories; an elopement; broken engagements; doubtful parentages (one leading to Jarno's revelation that "Therese ist nicht die Tochter ihrer Mutter"); several marriages, some of which are even *mésalliances*; an incestuous relationship; "falsche Tatsachen" like the poisoning of Felix, like Mariane's infidelity, and like Wilhelm's impression that Jarno may be a recruiting officer; an active secret society; and the usual vows (to the Harper, to the actors, and to Aurelie), dreams, and omens that are traditional in romance. And although it is usually asserted that the *Lehrjahre* is structurally more taut than the *Sendung*, it is, if anything, more complex and adds new motifs and narrative techniques (e.g., the *in-medias-res* opening, with its long "Ich-Erzählung"; Wilhelm's fictitious travel letters; the parallel life represented by "Bekenntnisse einer schönen Seele") to those of the already complex earlier work. The amazing thing is that despite, or perhaps thanks to such elements (since by their very frequency and quantity they, as it were, neutralize each other and cease to startle), Goethe is able to create a *Roman* whose ultimate effect is almost completely harmonious and which has conveyed to many different kinds of reader the impression of "ein harmonisches Weltbild."[7]

Such an impression few eighteenth-century novels had produced, and Goethe therefore rightly hesitated to refer to the *Lehrjahre* by the only German word available to him to denote both such novels and his own very different and far superior work. Although the English word *novel*—previously equivalent to French *nouvelle*—had begun to acquire its modern value by the mid-seventeenth century, over a century later it still competed with *romance*, and in the year that the fourth and final volume of the *Lehrjahre* appeared, the English-German dictionary of Nathan Bailey ("Neunte Auflage gänzlich umgearbeitet von Johann Anton Fahrenkrüger"

wandtschaften, however, is also a "tragischer Roman," a term Goethe actually uses, with highly positive connotations, in "*Gabriele* von Johanna Schopenhauer" (cf. Goethes Werke, Jubiläums-Ausgabe, 37:224ff.), whose novel he discusses without avoidance of the word *Roman*.

[6] So E.L. Stahl notes in "Goethe as Novelist," p. 46 (in *Essays on Goethe*, ed. W. Rose [London, 1949] 45–73), himself finding that "the artistic value" of the *Lehrjahre* "suffers from the addition of the final portion. The plot becomes tenuous and Goethe's invention pedestrian. . . ."

[7] Cf., for example, Hans Reiss, *Goethes Romane* (Bern und München, 1963) 129, and his reference to Emil Staiger.

[Leipzig und Züllichau, 1796]) defined *novel* only as "die Novelle; der kleine Roman, die Erzählung," while giving for *romance* the German equivalents "der Roman; die Erdichtung, das Märchen." (In the corresponding German-English volume of the following year, *Roman* is translated "romance, tale.") And even as late as 1830, in Oertel's *Grammatisches Wörterbuch der Deutschen Sprache* (München, 1830, 2, 1. Abt.:245), *Roman* is still defined as "1) erdichtete, meistens wunderb. Geschichte, bes. 2) erdichtete, verwickelte Liebesgeschichte."

On the one hand, then, *Roman* could mean "Liebesabenteuer" (fictitious or real, cf. *Faust*, 11. 160–65), and on the other—to return to the Grimm *Wörterbuch*—"erdichtetes. . . das den bedingungen der wirklichkeit nicht entspricht," as in *Wilhelm Meisters Lehrjahre* itself when it is reported of Wilhelm (1. Buch, 14. Kapitel): "Ein ganzer Roman, was er an der Stelle des Unwürdigen morgenden Tages tun würde, entwickelte sich in seiner Seele, angenehme Phantasien begleiteten ihn in das Reich des Schlafes sanft hinüber und überließen ihn dort ihren Geschwistern, den Träumen, die ihn mit offenen Armen aufnahmen und das ruhende Haupt unsers Freundes mit dem Vorbilde des Himmels umgaben." That Goethe on various occasions uses "Romanschreiber" scornfully and writes or speaks of "Journale und Romane" together is evidence enough, in view of his low opinion of journalists and journalism, of the pejorative associations *Roman* had for him.

Only in connection with the comparison of *Roman* and *Drama* (5. Buch, 7. Kapitel) is *Roman* used in the *Lehrjahre* with reference to literary works of high quality—works of Richardson, Goldsmith, and Fielding are specifically named, but the statements made here about the genre apply also to the *Lehrjahre* itself and are usually so applied by its interpreters, although they have also influenced many later general theories of the novel.

Writing to Schiller after the *Lehrjahre* had appeared, in connection with the discussions that eventuated in "Über epische und dramatische Dichtung von Goethe and Schiller" as published in 1827 in *Über Kunst und Altertum*, Goethe declared in his letter of December 23, 1797:

Es ist mir dabei [i.e., beim Lesen der Ilias und des Sophokles] recht aufgefallen wie es kommt, daß wir Modernen die Genres so sehr zu vermischen geneigt sind, ja daß wir gar nicht einmal imstande sind, sie voneinander zu unterscheiden. Es scheint nur daher zu kommen, weil die Künstler, die eigentlich die Kunstwerke innerhalb ihrer reinen Bedingungen hervorbringen sollten, dem Streben der Zuschauer und Zuhörer, alles völlig wahr zu finden, nachgeben. . . . So sieht man auch im Gang der Poesie, daß alles zum Drama, zur Darstellung des *vollkommen Gegenwärtigen* sich hindrängt. So sind die Romane in Briefen völlig dramatisch, man kann deswegen mit Recht förmliche Dialoge, wie auch

Richardson getan hat, einschalten; erzählende Romane mit Dialogen untermischt würden dagegen zu tadeln sein.

By Goethe's own standards as here formulated, *Wilhelm Meisters Lehrjahre* could only be an imperfect work, for it is surely simultaneously novel and romance, and so, in his letter of March 29, 1801, he could confess of it to Friedrich Rochlitz: "Die Form behält immer etwas Unreines und man kann Gott danken, wenn man imstand war so viel Gehalt hinein zu legen, daß fühlende und denkende Menschen sich beschäftigen mögen, ihn wieder daraus zu entwickeln."[8] Here the word "Form" applies to the many different narrative traditions and techniques represented in the *Lehrjahre*. That they are used, however, with unique contrapuntal skill and blended to create a work in an entirely distinctive style, Goethe also surely knew. And so he could declare in a "Spruch" published in 1821 in *Über Kunst und Altertum* (3. Bandes 1. Heft): "Der Roman ist eine subjektive Epopee, in welcher der Verfasser sich die Erlaubnis ausbittet, die Welt nach seiner Weise zu behandeln. Es fragt sich also nur, ob er eine Weise habe, das andere wird sich schon finden."[9] In this statement "Weise" is distinctive style, the force which welds the disparate elements of the romance *Wilhelm Meisters Lehrjahre* into a unity with more "Gehalt" than any single work that can be called a novel written before or since, and which lets it simultaneously satisfy Goethe's belief, expressed in 1812 in *Dichtung und Wahrheit* (7. Buch), that "der innere Gehalt des bearbeiteten Gegenstandes ist der Anfang und das Ende der Kunst."[10]

[8] By this date theories of Romanticism immoderately exalting the *Roman* had been proclaimed, a factor that may explain his avoidance of that term in these years and later.

[9] In *Maximen und Reflexionen* as No. 133 (Hecker's numbering). Two posthumously published definitions from the 1790's (op. cit., Nos. 1046 and 1047) show how close for Goethe the value of *Roman* was to that of the English word *romance* (story) at the time he was completing the *Lehrjahre*: The first, "Märchen: das uns unmögliche Begebenheiten unter möglichen oder unmöglichen Bedingungen als möglich darstellt"; the second, "Roman: der uns mögliche Begebenheiten unter unmöglichen oder beinahe unmöglichen Bedingungen als wirklich darstellt."

[10] The Chinese stories to which Goethe at various times referred with the term "Roman"—cf. Eric A. Blackall, "Goethe and the Chinese Novel," in *The Discontinuous Tradition: Studies in German Literature in Honour of Ernest Ludwig Stahl*, ed. P.F. Ganz (Oxford, 1970) 29–53—are all romances, as Blackall's plot summaries make clear.

Die Wahlverwandtschaften: Novel of German Classicism

Sich mitzuteilen ist Natur; Mitgeteiltes aufzunehmen,
wie es gegeben wird, ist Bildung. (II 4/384)

G oethe first formulated his classical concept of style in 1788, shortly
after his sojourn in Italy. Reflecting his enduring admiration of the
idealized naturalism of Renaissance art and its Graeco-Roman
models, it expressed a conviction that the highest concern of the serious
artist is imitation of nature's "charakteristische Formen" in such a way that
the essence of things—"die Eigenschaften der Dinge und die Art, wie sie
bestehen"—will be faithfully revealed.[1] From this time on all Goethe's
literary work reflects a conscious desire to convey the broad, even universal
significance of themes treated with scrupulous attention to truth of detail,
yet only in *Die Wahlverwandtschaften* did he sustain at such length and
with such rigor the principle of depicting significant detail only. The
consequence is a novel so tightly knit and dense in texture—Goethe himself
said that to be understood it must be read three times (645)—that it remains
his one major work still eluding some approximation of a critical consensus.
The following observations seek to clarify the function of verisimilitude in
this text by identifying elements that by virtue of their verifiability must be
regarded as embodying significant truth, be this fact or what Goethe is
known to have believed fact. Such clarification will obviate many

---

[1] "Einfache Nachahmung der Natur, Manier, Stil" (HA 12:32). (Goethe alluded to this
conviction or principle while writing *Die Wahlverwandtschaften* when in a letter of 9 June
1809 he characterized the work as a novel "der sich zwar nur um einen besonderen
Gegenstand herumdreht, doch aber auf manches allgemeine menschliche Interesse
hinzieht" [WA IV.20:358f.]). Hereafter references to HA are given as parenthetical volume
and page numbers (whereby Br. refers to the four HA volumes of Goethe's letters, ed. Karl
Robert Mandelkow), except that page references only are given for material in Vol. 6:
Romane und Novellen, I (9. Aufl., München: Beck, 1977), which includes *Die Wahlver-
wandtschaften*, ed. Benno v. Wiese. Book and chapter numbers precede references to the
text of this novel (e.g., II 12/451, but these are not repeated before an immediately
following page reference to the same chapter (e.g., 452).

misapprehensions about the novel and, I hope, make possible adequate interpretation of it as an expression of Goethe's classicism.

That verisimilar detail may be fraught with meaning is soon noticed. Even on a first reading it is possible to be impressed, as was Wieland (652), by the brief but revealing exchange between Eduard and Charlotte on the morning after Ottilie's arrival: " 'Es ist ein angenehmes, unterhaltendes Mädchen.' 'Unterhaltend?' versetzte Charlotte mit Lächeln; 'sie hat ja den Mund noch nicht aufgetan.' 'So?' erwiderte Eduard, indem er sich zu besinnen schien, 'das wäre doch wunderbar!' " (I 6/281). Descriptive details that in a less "classical" work might be merely incidental to the creation of atmosphere or local color are soon recognized as having plot-related and other functions. Only on a second reading, however, can the reader verify, as Walther Killy has done through close analysis of fifteen lines of landscape description,[2] the gradually established impression that no such details are ever superfluous and that many are multiply functional. But even then, because analysis of character and motivation is usually direct—it is as often accompanied by authorial generalization as it is complemented by information conveyed through such means as revealing turn of phrase or telling gesture—he may not notice that non-descriptive details are also multiply significant.

Recognition of the multiple significance of non-descriptive detail frequently depends on information extrinsic to the text (on factual knowledge today's reader may no longer possess), but that it need not is nicely illustrated by an unobtrusive phrase in the action-packed account of the festivities (*Richtfest*) on Ottilie's birthday (I 15). When the Surgeon—a paramedic, not a fully trained physician—takes charge of the boy rescued by the Captain after the partial collapse of the new dam under the press of people awaiting Eduard's firework display, Charlotte urges the Captain, whom she already respects and loves more than her husband, to return to the manor house for dry clothing. As he does so on being assured that everyone who fell into the lake is saved, she remembers "daß Wein und Tee und was sonst nötig wäre, verschlossen ist. . ." (337). The 'other necessaries' are medicaments in the *Hausapotheke* which had been augmented with the Captain's advice shortly after his, but before Ottilie's arrival—this was when his suggestion that the manor have a resident surgeon was adopted and when Charlotte's concern about dangerous substances led to the discussion of elective affinities in which Ottilie seemed destined to become his partner (I 4/267–76). The detail that evokes all these associations also demonstrates

---

the presence of mind and sense of responsibility even under stress and despite emotional involvement of the careful mistress who keeps all stimulants under lock and key; in addition, it provides a compelling reason for her to follow the Captain and by her example motivate a general departure that Eduard keeps Ottilie from joining, thereby gratifying his now inappropriate wish to entertain her with fireworks (I 15/338f.).

The contemporary reader of *Die Wahlverwandtschaften*, however, not only noticed the meticulous accuracy with which the immediate environment and the thoughts, feelings, motives, and actions of its human figures are recorded; he also recognized how faithfully the larger worlds to which these relate are depicted. Singling out for mention the fashionableness of landscaping in the English manner, of medieval art, and of *tableaux vivants*, K.W.F. Solger could accordingly declare that the novel afforded a complete picture of its age: "In diesem Roman ist. . . alles, was die Zeit Bedeutendes und Besonderes hat, enthalten, und nach einigen Jahrhunderten würde man sich hieraus ein vollkommenes Bild von unserem jetzigen täglichen Leben entwerfen können" (637). Solger had no need to mention that the novel's milieu is Germany in the Napoleonic period,[3] or that the particular part of Germany is a Protestant region under Prussian suzerainty,[4] although both political facts are far more important than any

---

[3] The action is most often said, as by Hans Reiss, *Goethes Romane* (Bern: Francke, 1963) 173, to take place in the late eighteenth century, although Peter Suhrkamp, "Goethes 'Wahlverwandtschaften,' " in *Goethes Roman "Die Wahlverwandtschaften"*, ed. Ewald Rösch (Darmstadt: Wissenschaftliche Buchgesellschaft, 1975) 197—this volume is hereafter cited as Rösch—gives the time as "um die Mitte des achtzehnten Jahrhunderts." In his chapter "Place and Time," H.G. Barnes, *Goethe's* Die Wahlverwandtschaften: *A Literary Interpretation* (Oxford: Clarendon, 1967), does not discuss historical contexts, but his note, p. 72, that the mansion of Eduard and Charlotte "symbolizes everyday life rather than the effete rococo society of some interpretations," insists on the action's contemporaneity. Important allusions to post-Revolutionary developments are: the Assistant Headmaster, despite being a commoner, can hope to woo and win Ottilie because differences of social class are easily reconciled by "die Denkart der Zeit" (II 7/413); Luciane's good figure is advantageously shown off when for a *tableau vivant* she wears seventeenth-century dress, although it is normally concealed by Empire fashions, "den modernen antikisierenden Bekleidungen der Frauenzimmer" (II 5/394); Charlotte laments the increase of animosity in private and public life since the Revolution (II 1/365); and it is primarily the greater acceptability of divorce in consequence of recent French legal reforms that Eduard has in mind when, justifying to the Captain his resolve to marry Ottilie, he rhetorically asks whether one should deny oneself "dasjenige. . . , was uns die Sitten der Zeit nicht absprechen" (II 12/448).

[4] This fact, which permits dating Eduard's military service, is established some three months (seven chapters) before Eduard, despairing of divorce because Charlotte is carrying his child, without notice joins the forces of a commander under whose leadership he believes death probable and victory certain. (The commander may have been Prince Louis Ferdinand of Prussia, who was slain in the engagement at Saalfeld, 10 Oct. 1806.) In early July, reminiscing about obstacles to Eduard's original courting of Charlotte before their first

geographical locating of the novel's manor at Wilhelmsthal in Saxe-Weimar because they permit Eduard's military service and the illumination of his character in connection with that service. The second fact was so strongly sensed by Thomas Mann that as a North German Protestant he charged Goethe with a lack of "protestantische Charakterstärke" because he "die Nachgiebigkeit gegen das Katholische so weit treibt, mitten in protestantischer Sphäre eine Heilige zu kreieren, zu deren Leichnam das lutherische Landvolk sich wundergläubig in die Kirche drängt!"[5] The novel's Protestant locale is essential, however, for establishing a milieu in which art will be dissonant (II 2/368) and monastic withdrawal—by Ottilie—anomalous or idiosyncratic (II 15/466).

Although time is treated in *Die Wahlverwandtschaften* with the same verisimilar exactitude as all other elements, even critics aware of how its carefully measured passage underscores the symbolic significance of seasonal changes fail to remark that the novel's action largely coincides with the latter part of the War of the Third Coalition, viz., the war of Prussia and Russia against France in 1806–07. For this war Prussia, supported by Electoral Saxony and Saxe-Weimar, mobilized its forces as of 9 August 1806, which explains Eduard's rejoining the Prussian army in late summer of the novel's first year (II 18/359). Before his birthday in mid- or late autumn (II 3/374) he has distinguished himself in a "bedeutende Kriegsangelegenheit" (371), which is identifiable as the first important military action of the war, the Franco-Prussian engagement at Saalfeld (10 October 1806). (Four days later came Napoleon's victory at Jena and Auerstädt; Napoleon occupied Berlin after thirteen more days and on 21 November issued the Berlin Decree.) Prussia fought on until the Russian defeat at Friedland, 14 June 1807, but within three weeks had signed the Treaty of Tilsit (supplemented

---

marriages to other partners, the visiting Count begins to tell an otherwise apparently insignificant incident that occurred during a state visit by his and Eduard's "höchsten Herrschaften" (I 11/317); after the Count has recalled an evening spent with Charlotte and her chaperon (the Count bored by his very unattractive partner, Eduard and Charlotte happily entertaining each other) in the apartments of the ladies-in-waiting, Eduard continues the story, describing how the two friends get lost on the way back to their own quarter of the palace and find themselves at what they recognize is the door of the guardroom; by going through this hall they will reach familiar territory, but they discover their path blocked by mattresses with rows of sleeping "Riesen," snoring "Enakskinder"—cf. Deut. 9:2, "a people great and tall, . . . the children of Anak"—none of whom awakens as they continue on (318). The guardsmen all above normal height are a Prussian tradition and identify Eduard and the Count as subjects of Frederick William II at the time of the anecdote and, at the time of its recounting, Frederick William III.

[5] Thomas Mann, "Phantasie über Goethe," *Gesammelte Werke* (Frankfurt/Main: Fischer, 1960) 9:743. What to Mann is incongruous is Goethe's way of indicating that no church or culture is without its credulous.

12 July by the Treaty of Königsberg). Only the events of the novel's last seven chapters (its final half year) can therefore be said to take place in time of peace, established coincidentally with Eduard's return from the army in late spring after just under a year of service (II 12/446).[6]

Failure to recognize the significance of these and related historical facts has resulted in serious misinterpretation of two of the novel's major characters, Eduard and the Captain. The inference that at the opening of the novel the latter is unemployed "because there is no need for soldiers in a time of peace"[7]—dubious if only because he seems to be a civil engineer in government service (hence his rank and continuing civilian status after Prussia's mobilization)—attaches misleading importance to the brief cessation of hostilities between the first and second parts of the War of the Third Coalition. To say that the novel offers no explanation "why so able a man should be left without satisfactory employment in civil life,"[8] is to disregard not only the fact that it nowhere states he is a military officer, but also Eduard's mention of "die traurige Lage, in die er, wie so mancher andere, ohne sein Verschulden gesetzt ist" (I 1/243)—an unambiguous reference to the layoff of public servants in every part of Germany consequent to the *Reichsdeputationshauptschluß* of 25 February 1803, which executed the Treaty of Lunéville by radically reducing the number of German political entities and so made state employment difficult to obtain for many years.

[6] The narrator's explanatory "Der Hauptzweck des Feldzugs war erreicht," true for Napoleon but not for Prussia, is not noted in the valuable survey of the use of irony in Goethe's novel offered by H.B. Nisbet and Hans Reiss in the introduction to their edition of *Die Wahlverwandtschaften* (Oxford: Blackwell, 1971) xx–xxvi; its irony probably reflects not so much Goethe's well known respect for Napoleon as his disapproval, since the mid-1780's, of what he regarded as the unwisely pro-Prussian foreign policy of his friend and patron Charles Augustus of Saxe-Weimar, the militarily over-ambitious ruler of an unprosperous duchy with a scant 100,000 population. The spring date of Eduard's discharge excludes the possibility of his having served in the War of 1805 (in which Austria was the sole German participant), since it did not end until 2 Dec. 1805 with the Battle of Austerlitz (Peace of Pressburg, 26 Dec.); there is no later war or campaign in which Eduard can have served by the time Goethe wrote (1808f.) and published (1809) his novel, nor was there one in 1804, the year of Alexander von Humboldt's return to Europe from his four-year stay in the Americas, allusion to which in a diary entry of Ottilie (II 7/416) excludes earlier dating of Eduard's military activity.

[7] Eric A. Blackall, *Goethe and the Novel* (Ithaca: Cornell University Press, 1976) 169.

[8] Nisbet and Reiss xxxiii. That the Captain is not a soldier emerges from the civil—perhaps diplomatic—assignment entrusted to him by the prince he serves when Major (II 17/476).

To speak of "a time of peace" is also to minimize grim realities[9] that permit an otherwise often feckless-seeming Eduard to demonstrate positive qualities of character; its corollary can be the assumption, incongruous with a principle of stylized realism otherwise meticulously sustained, that the novel's war is merely convenient literary invention.[10] In war, through self-imposed ordeals and courageous risks on behalf of others, Eduard overcomes what was originally a Wertherian death-wish—"Er sehnte sich nach dem Untergang, weil ihm das Dasein unerträglich zu werden drohte; ja es war ihm ein Trost zu denken, daß er nicht mehr sein werde und eben dadurch seine Geliebten, seine Freunde glücklich machen könne" (I 18/ 359)—and achieves a sense of worth that allows him to feel justified in seeking happiness even if its price must be divorce (II 12/449). In war, moreover, he demonstrates genuine selflessness off the battlefield as well as on it,[11] and so is especially welcome at the inn, where he hopes to dissuade Ottilie from returning to her school, because he has obtained for

[9] Realities of war explain why, during Luciane's stay at the manor, officers from *remote* (cf. n. 17, below) garrisons constitute a significant part of the spate of guests (II 5/390); the embittered young man she helps readjust to life had lost his hand in a real battle (II 5/386); only a real campaign justifies Ottilie's tears when she imagines the hardships Eduard endures in the army (II 10/433); only in real battle can Eduard have heard cannonades and whistling bullets, have had his hat riddled and his horse shot from under him, and have seen comrades fall (II 12/448f.); and only in a real military engagement can his bravery have gained him the early commendation the newspaper report of which first informs Charlotte that he has gone off to war.

[10] Oskar Walzel—whose essay of 1906, "Goethes 'Wahlverwandtschaften' im Rahmen ihrer Zeit," in Rösch 35–64, remains the standard treatment of the novel as a document of its age—states in Festausgabe 11:593, in a note to *Wilhelm Meisters Lehrjahre*, that the war in which Eduard serves "nicht näher zu bezeichnen ist, sondern zu einem brauchbaren Requisit des Erzählers wird"; in a note, 13:267, to a passage (II 18/359) in *Die Wahlver-wandtschaften* he makes the same assertion but adds "Immerhin war der Anfang des 19. Jahrhunderts reich an Kriegen."

[11] One of the few critics to emphasize Eduard's positive qualities is Hans Reiss, "Mehrdeutigkeit in Goethes *Wahlverwandtschaften*," *JDSG* 14 (1970): 366–96, who notes but, exceptionally, fails to refute the charge that Eduard "nie an andere denkt, nur an sich selbst" (374). Eduard may in some degree share Ottilie's fault of naiveté—the narrator refers to the "Unschuld seines Herzens" (I 10/314)—but this "innocence in his attitude," as Barnes calls it (109), is not the amoralism Barnes would make it out to be. Barnes states: "After committing spiritual adultery, he sees it as a crime against his love for Ottilie, not as an act of infidelity towards his wife"; the reflection from which he draws this inference—"Denn so ist die Liebe beschaffen, daß sie allein recht zu haben glaubt und alle anderen Rechte vor ihr verschwinden"—and which he says is "directed against Charlotte as well as Eduard for their attitude after the night of spiritual adultery" (109) refers, however, not to them but to the Count and Baroness; in contrast to Charlotte and Eduard, who are specifically described as "gleichsam beschämt und reuig," this pair meets at breakfast "mit dem heitern Behagen, das ein Paar Liebende empfinden, die sich nach erduldeter Trennung ihrer wechselseitigen Neigung abermals versichert halten" (I 12/322).

the Hostess' son, "der als Soldat sich sehr brav gehalten, ein Ehren-
zeichen. . . , indem er dessen Tat, wobei er allein gegenwärtig gewesen,
heraushob, mit Eifer bis vor den Feldherrn brachte und die Hindernisse
einiger Mißwollenden überwand" (II 16/471).

The demonstrable importance of realistic historical detail vitiates the now
popular thesis that the novel cannot be adequately interpreted as an
expression of Goethe's classical concept of style, that it must be read as
exemplifying a hypothetical later manner which is ironic and symbolic to a
degree excluding consistent verisimilitude, be it that of what von Wiese
terms "psychologischer Perspektivismus" (655), or that of a fully informed
narrator.[12] A discreet avoidance of journalistic explicitness cannot be
intended to prevent the reader who may be assumed to share the narrator's
knowledge from recognizing the factuality of easily identifiable recent
events, yet it is to such knowledge—and to shared moral and aesthetic
views, not private matters or Weimar personalia about which his Berlin
correspondent Zelter had never been informed by himself or others—that
Goethe alluded when he declared of his novel during its writing: "Ich habe
viel hinein gelegt, manches hinein versteckt. Möge auch Ihnen dies
offenbare Geheimnis zur Freude gereichen" (621). Deprived of their
historical context, however, elements in the novel that should be self-
explanatory constrain the reader to discern in them non-existent incon-
sistencies and ambiguities which he will be tempted to interpret as ironic
and symbolic or may seek to resolve by attaching to them values they could
not have for Goethe or the audience addressed by the narrator.

No longer self-explanatory, for example, is the patriarchal social order
of Germany in the Napoleonic era. From a late twentieth-century
perspective it may seem archaic, but it enjoyed what was tantamount to
unquestioned acceptance at a time when, in good part because a respon-
sible landowning class had corrected many of the social and economic
inequities that prevailed in France, changes reflecting the spirit of the French
Revolution were not yet widely demanded. Except as barriers to marriage,[13]
class differences were as much taken for granted as when Werther, having

---

[12] Cf. Blackall 172: "The narrator. . . is trying to describe something that is really beyond
him"; Gonthier-Louis Fink, "Goethes 'Wahlverwandtschaften': Romanstruktur und
Zeitaspekte," in Rösch, 452: "Da die Welt rätselhaft geworden war, verzichtet der Erzähler
darauf, sie zu verstehen und zu deuten."

[13] Since the novel's four main characters, despite differences of material wealth, are of
the same social class, the issue of misalliance does not arise. Charlotte had originally
intended that Ottilie be Eduard's second wife (I 2/253), and Eduard first thinks of her as
a suitable match for the Captain (I 4/276); only if she were to marry the Assistant
Headmaster would the—no longer serious (cf. n. 3, ante)—obstacle of class difference have
to be reckoned with.

condemned those who treat the common people with exaggerated aloofness or arrogant condescension, declared on the eve of the American Revolution: "Ich weiß wohl, daß wir nicht gleich sind, noch sein können" (11). Nevertheless, Eduard—at least after his war experiences—is not so hostile to liberal ideas as to assume that inherited wealth is *per se* good, declaring to the Captain:

> . . . wenn der Sohn nach dem frühen Tode des Vaters keine so bequeme, so begünstigte Jugend hat, so gewinnt er vielleicht ebendeswegen an schnellerer Bildung für die Welt, durch zeitiges Anerkennen, daß er sich in andere schicken muß, was wir denn doch früher oder später alle lernen müssen. Und hievon ist ja die Rede gar nicht: wir sind reich genug, um mehrere Kinder zu versorgen, und es ist keineswegs Pflicht noch Wohltat, auf Ein Haupt so viele Güter zu häufen. (II 12/448)

There is thus little plausibility in the claim—contradicted by the simultaneous observation that "Charlotte, who belongs to the same class [sc. as Eduard], exhibits exemplary devotion to duty"—that in *Die Wahlverwandtschaften* "the social life of a rich landed nobleman, his lack of responsibility. . . are implicitly criticized."[14] Eduard's military record also makes dubious the assertion that he "appears as a dilettante unwilling or unable to pursue any task seriously and consistently, the prototype of the self-seeking aristocrat."[15] As a musician Eduard is certainly the incompetent amateur, and as landscape architects both he and Charlotte are more or less inadequate, but dilettantism is not necessarily irresponsibility, let alone a serious flaw of character. As Goethe's narrator carefully insists in "billigen Gesinnungen" apropos of the chapel decorations of the highly qualified Architect who has replaced the Captain at the manor:

> Es ist eine so angenehme Empfindung, sich mit etwas zu beschäftigen, was man nur halb kann, daß niemand den Dilettanten schelten sollte, wenn er sich mit einer Kunst abgibt, die er nie lernen wird, noch den Künstler tadeln dürfte, wenn er über die Grenze seiner Kunst hinaus in einem benachbarten Felde sich zu ergehen Lust hat. (II 3/370)

---

[14] Nisbet and Reiss xli.

[15] Nisbet and Reiss xxxif. What Eduard suggests as a better alternative to the Captain's plan for financing estate improvements may not be as liberal or progressive as that plan, but it is acknowledged to be "eine vernünftige, gemäßigte Einrichtung" (I 7/294) and thus cannot be improperly "self-seeking."

To say that Eduard's "only interest is amateur gardening"[16] not merely exaggerates his dilettantism; it also depreciates the very activities that demonstrate his sense of social responsibility. Significantly, the novel begins as his participation in early-spring implanting of new grafts is favorably noted by the manor's Gardener, who also expresses approval of Charlotte's modest landscaping efforts (I 1/242). As these efforts become more ambitious and Eduard more involved in them, they afford him a welcome opportunity to provide the estate's village with improved hygiene and flood protection (I 6/285 and 9/304). Until Ottilie's self-imposed asceticism definitively frustrates their hopes of divorce, Eduard and Charlotte regularly devote their energies to constructive activities. Even after this, however, as in the moment of stress created by Ottilie's unexpected return to the manor after her chance encounter with Eduard, Charlotte still demonstrates her ability to do "was der Augenblick fordert" (II 17/475), can fulfill what is for Goethe always—"Was aber ist deine Pflicht? Die Forderung des Tages" (HA 8:283)—the first obligation of a responsible human being. All these facts are inconsistent with the view, which derives from historical misconceptions rather than textual evidence, that the world of Eduard and Charlotte is an "aufgeklärt-frivole Gesellschaft" of nobles whose aristocratic mode of existence is "inselhafte Abriegelung."[17] Their manor does not symbolize a

---

[16] Karl Viëtor, *Goethe the Poet* (Cambridge: Harvard University Press, 1949) 184; in his simultaneously published *Goethe: Dichtung, Wissenschaft, Weltbild* (Bern: Francke, 1949) 209, "Beschäftigung" (occupation) is used instead of "interest." Constructive activity is the one value esteemed in the novel not only by Charlotte, Eduard, and the Captain but by all important characters regardless of class, religion, or education: Mittler insists "Der Mensch ist von Haus aus tätig. . ." (II 18/481); Ottilie claims "Die schätzenswerteste Freistatt ist da zu suchen, wo wir tätig sein können" (II 15/466); the Count admires the Captain's "Tätigkeit" (I 10/313); everyone except her rival Luciane notes approvingly Ottilie's "ruhige, ununterbrochene Tätigkeit" (II 5/388); and the Assistant Headmaster proclaims "Das Höchste am Menschen. . . ist gestaltlos, und man soll sich hüten, es anders als in edler Tat zu gestalten" (II 7/407).

[17] Werner Danckert, *Offenes und geschlossenes Leben: Zwei Daseinsaspekte in Goethes Weltschau* (Bonn: Bouvier, 1963) 68 and 92. Danckert also denigrates Eduard's well-attested feeling for nature and landscape (cf. I 14/334) by calling him (81f.) "ein Mensch ohne innere Beziehung zur Erde und ihren Mächten" and by labeling his and Charlotte's efforts at estate improvement "Basteleien." Emil Staiger, *Goethe 1786–1814* (Zürich: Atlantis, 1956) 480 similarly exaggerates the manor's supposedly symbolic apartness: "Die Gesellschaft, die das Paar Charlotte und Eduard repräsentiert, ist wie durch eine unsichtbare Schranke von ihrer Umgebung getrennt," but his illustration of this thesis by Eduard's readiness "sich die Bedürftigen durch eine von dem Hauptmann empfohlene kluge Einrichtung, die sein Gewissen beschwichtigt, vom Leibe zu halten"—the reference is to I 6/286—unduly minimizes the fact that his dislike of impudent beggars is shared by Goethe, who declared in a book review of 1821, "Eigentlichen Bettlern. . . habe ich niemals gern gegeben" (Festausgabe 16:393). That the efforts to improve the manor and create an English-style park are to be regarded as worthwhile is evident from the willing cooperation of the

world of irresponsible aloofness, and before Ottilie's arrival—but when enough is known of her temperament to guarantee that she will introduce no careless gayety—the open sociability of landed-gentry life, as well as the predominantly serious interests of Eduard, Charlotte, and the (more obviously sober-minded) Captain, are noted in the same sentence:

> Fand sich keine Gesellschaft von benachbarten Orten und Gütern, welches öfters geschah, so war das Gespräch wie das Lesen meist solchen Gegenständen gewidmet, welche den Wohlstand, die Vorteile und das Behagen der bürgerlichen Gesellschaft vermehren. (I 4/267)

By identifying these interests as ones shared by citizens of all classes, the sentence further indicates not only that in *Die Wahlverwandtschaften* social tensions or conflicts are not to be important, but also that the novel's socially responsible aristocrats are at least adequate representatives of the well-established enlightened ideal of a class-transcending humanism to which Goethe gave full allegiance.[18]

Captain, a man who has chosen to work for respected friends rather than take less suitable but more gainful employment (I 2/256); that they succeed is indicated by the approval of the English lord who—like the Weimar park planner Goethe—is a connoisseur in such matters (II 10/429). Luciano Zagari, "Gusto psicologico e stile simbolico nelle "Affinità elettive," " *Annali* (Napoli: *Sezione Germanica* 5 [1962]): 183–212, commenting on critics (including Walter Benjamin) who unduly minimize the value of practical activity in Goethe's novel, notes (201) that the passages describing such activity are the most poetic in the text (are lyric and non-ironic); similarly Irvin Stock, "Goethe's Tragedy: A View of *Elective Affinities*," *Mosaic* 7, No. 3 (1974): 17–27, observes (20) that "the work on the estate. . . is presented as a perfectly adequate occasion for the exercise of Goethe's favorite virtues: industry, skill, taste, wisdom."

[18] For the ideal, cf. Friedrich Sengle, "Die klassische Kultur von Weimar, sozialgeschichtlich gesehen," *IASL* 3 (1978): 68–86, esp. 81. It is voiced in the text by Charlotte in her discussion (with the lawyer for the family seeking to revoke an endowment because she has had monuments moved to make the churchyard less desolate) of suitable memorials to the dead: "Das reine Gefühl einer endlichen allgemeinen Gleichheit, wenigstens nach dem Tode, scheint mir beruhigender als dieses eigensinnige, starre Fortsetzen unserer Persönlichkeiten, Anhänglichkeiten und Lebensverhältnisse" (II 1/363). It is also to some extent realized in social practice: civilians and officers—in the Prussian army: casteconscious nobles—are guests together at the manor house (II 5/390), where Mittler, the Assistant Headmaster, and the Architect (presumably a commoner too) are treated without any condescension. Informality also prevails in conversation: Mittler addresses Eduard and Charlotte, and is addressed by them, with the semi-intimate second-person plural pronoun (I 2/254ff.) whose use corresponds to Anglo-American address by given name or surname without title; the fact that when speaking to Mittler Eduard refers to his wife not as "meine Frau" or "meine Gattin," but as "Charlotte" (254), indicates that use of the pronoun is the consequence neither of Goethe's classicizing avoidance of any surname but Mittler, nor of the frequent (also classicizing) substitution of titles of rank and position for names. Mittler also addresses Eduard as "Sie," but as one speaking to a friend, "Freund" (II 16/470f.).

Neither aristocratic nor idiosyncratic withdrawal from normal human contacts is a general theme of *Die Wahlverwandtschaften*—hence the indispensable function of visits and visitors in the novel's action. At the laying of the cornerstone on Charlotte's birthday the example of the many guests who cast trinkets into the hollow stone occasions Ottilie's symbolic total acceptance of Eduard, her placing on their contributions the chain from which she had at his urging earlier removed her father's miniature (I 9/ 301f.). The count and Baroness make two visits—the first awakens the erotic impulses leading to the quasi adulterous conception of Eduard's and Charlotte's child (I 9–12); the second, coming when their marriage has at last become possible, is for Ottilie a depressing reminder of how remote has become hope of happiness with Eduard (II 5/390)—and immediately after their first departure there is "wieder neuer Besuch" which, because of the emotions they have unwittingly animated, is "Charlotten willkommen," "Eduarden ungelegen," and "Ottilien gleichfalls unerwünscht" (I 12/322). The presence of "viele Gäste" (I 15/335) at the *Richtfest* causes the dam to collapse, and their withdrawal to the mansion before the firework display underscores the pathos of what is the beginning of Eduard's and Ottilie's social isolation. Because visits are a regular occurrence, during Charlotte's pregnancy (and in Eduard's absence) it is the Architect's responsibility to receive strangers and decide which unexpected callers will be welcome (II 1/360), and during Luciane's stay (II 4–5) it is possible to accommodate an almost constant 'flood' of guests and visitors (II 5/390). The Assistant Headmaster is a house guest from before Christmas until late winter (II 6–8), and in the spring Charlotte's delivery of a son is the occasion for many congratulatory calls, the first being that of Mittler triumphant (II 8/420). Shortly after the next visit, that of the English Lord and his traveling companion which is important for the story "Die wunderlichen Nachbarskinder" and for recognition of Ottilie's abnormal psychic sensibilities (II 10–11), comes the novel's dramatic climax: during Charlotte's absence on a neighborhood call Eduard returns, sees Ottilie again and, for the first time, his child; delayed by her encounter with Eduard, to save time Ottilie rows across the lake, loses her balance, and lets the infant fall into the water; news of the drowning is Charlotte's welcome on her return home (II 13–14). Add to this catalogue Mittler's increasingly frequent visits (II 17/479 and 18/ 481)—the last two of his five major appearances (I 2, 9, and 18; II 8 and 18) occasion the respective deaths of the pastor who baptizes Otto and of Ottilie—and it is evident that even F.J. Stopp's exceptionally cautious

148   *Die Wahlverwandtschaften*: Novel of German Classicism

formulation "the half-isolation of a country estate"[19] does not fairly describe manor life in the novel.

There is, moreover, no indication that, because it is rural, the world of *Die Wahlverwandtschaften* is geographically isolated to any unusual degree. In fact, the novel situates its manor near a small city (II 13/453) and at what must, since its towers are possibly visible from an ideal vantage point (I 9/303), be considerably less than a day's distance from the provincial capital.[20] Even if the estate were further from urban centers, however, neighbors would entail the involvement of those living on it in the kinds of social activity depicted in Eichendorff's novel *Ahnung und Gegenwart* and other accounts of the life of the German landed gentry in the Napoleonic era. Eduard and Charlotte are urbane representatives of their social class, not withdrawn eccentrics in traditions so alien to Goethe's classicism as humorous grotesque or gothic romance, and they live, not isolated at some Wuthering Heights, but in easy and open contact with people of every kind (domestic, gardener, innkeeper, schoolmaster, ex-cleric, architect, and so on up the scale). In such a social milieu as theirs, private matters are more or less public knowledge, as the narrator ironically explains:

> . . . freilich waren die bisherigen leidenschaftlichen Vorfälle dem Publikum nicht entgangen, das ohnehin in der Überzeugung steht, alles, was geschieht, geschehe nur dazu, damit es etwas zu reden habe. (II 8/421)

This is why Mittler is so eager to announce the birth of a son to Eduard and Charlotte (it will allay malicious gossip), why Charlotte feels "keinen besondern Schmerz" when the English Lord unwittingly makes comments that might be interpreted as allusions to Eduard's absence (II 10/431f.), and why Eduard in his newly gained self-assurance can clinch his arguments against the Captain's many objections to a hasty divorce with the words:

> Laß dich durch keine Betrachtungen abhalten; wir haben die Welt ohnehin schon von uns reden machen; sie wird noch einmal von uns reden, uns sodann, wie alles übrige, was aufhört neu zu sein, vergessen und uns gewähren lassen, wie wir können, ohne weitern Teil an uns zu nehmen. (II 12/450)

[19] "Elective Affinities," rev. of H.G. Barnes, *Goethe's "Die Wahlverwandtschaften": A Literary Interpretation* and Hans Jürgen Geerdts, *Goethes Roman "Die Wahlverwandtschaf-ten"* [unsigned], *TLS*, 28 Sept. 1967: 914.

[20] The "remote" garrisons of n. 9, above, are wartime camps, not the standing garrisons in the two nearby cities, the lesser of which seems to be the little city (II 13/453) between the manor and the small estate to which Eduard withdraws after separating from his wife (I 18/352), and to which he returns after his military service (II 12/446).

The view that the manor symbolizes an abnormal degree of isolation is also irreconcilable with the classical principle—its violation was the aesthetic basis of Goethe's aversion from many manifestations of romanticism—of treating only themes with broad human significance. For Goethe, to live withdrawn from human society was always aberrant, as it is in his "Harzreise im Winter" of 1779 (HA 1:50ff.) and still is in *Faust II* (e.g., l. 7379: "Gesellig nur läßt sich Gefahr erproben"), and when he met Beethoven in 1812, what most concerned him was the fact that "ihn sein Gehör verläßt, das vielleicht dem musikalischen Teil seines Wesens weniger als dem geselligen schadet. Er, der ohnehin lakonischer Natur ist, wird es nun doppelt durch diesen Mangel" (Br. 3:200). Only when, toward the end of the novel, their misfortunes make Eduard, Charlotte, and Ottilie more exclusively dependent upon each other than ever before, does isolation become important, but it can only be so by contrast with the social norm already firmly established. That Goethe indeed realized in *Die Wahlver-wandtschaften* his announced intention to depict human conflicts—"sociale Verhältnisse und die Conflicte derselben symbolisch gefaßt" (620)—with no unclassical distorting of reality and with no undue emphasizing of aberrancy, is attested by Solger's confident assertion that the novel offers a true picture of contemporary daily life. In Germany before the Industrial Revolution, when all cities remained to some extent agricultural centers, the norm was sociable rural life, and it is a sociological or socio-historical anachronism to see the world of Charlotte and Eduard as representing a significant deviation from it.

When "sociale Verhältnisse" in *Die Wahlverwandtschaften* are not recognized as typical human relationships in a typical milieu, individual character traits are mistakable as class characteristics, and false significance is liable to be attached to what actually represents ordinary modes of behavior and feeling. To call Eduard's obstinacy a "class characteristic"[21] is to attribute to Goethe a social bias inconsistent with his conciliatory humanism and unsubstantiated by either his life or any of his works, including *Die Wahlverwandtschaften*, in which Mittler, who so obstinately refuses to concede that divorce may ever be justified, is a commoner of poor and—given his first small parish—presumably humble origins (I 2/255). Eduard's loyalty as a friend and his envy-free appreciation of merit (I 1/243f.), like his concern to manage the manor responsibly and his selfless courage in battle, are character traits more important for his stature as hero of a tragic novel than the moral blemish of fecklessness or the venial

---

[21] Nisbet and Reiss xli.

aesthetic fault of dilettantism. His virtues are unduly belittled when, without regard to the use of professional and specialist services among all social and economic classes, it is claimed "his dilettantism and his lack of purpose in social life constitute a tacit indictment of the social situation in the late eighteenth century, where a man without specific training was able, on grounds of social rank and wealth, to employ more gifted and better trained men such as the *Hauptmann* and the architect. . . ."[22] But once it has been wrongly inferred that "the whole novel. . . could be seen as a study in the decline of the aristocratic way of life,"[23] the almost adolescent purity of Eduard's infatuation with Ottilie and his always tender respect for her are apparently no longer recognizable as such, but only as his "licentious ways,"[24] for although moral corruption might not seem to be a capitalist monopoly, it is obviously a literary-sociological truism that all decadent aristocrats must be morally corrupt.

If it is furthermore assumed that aristocratic corruption is contagious, not only venial faults but even exemplary conduct may lose their ordinary significance. Nowhere in *Die Wahlverwandtschaften* is impropriety of thought or deed ever attributed to the Captain, whose embodiment of such virtues as competence, foresightedness, and tact, whose untiring dedication to productive activity make him recognizable as Goethe's alter ego: "weniger Schlaf als dieser tätige Mann bedurfte kaum jemand, so wie sein Tag stets dem augenblicklichen Zwecke gewidmet und deswegen jederzeit am Abende etwas getan war" (I 4/266). Nevertheless, Nisbet and Reiss hesitate to give him a clean bill of moral health—"His remarkable self-control may exhibit signs of pedantry, his apparent selflessness may be counterbalanced by egotism and poverty of feeling"[25]—although for Goethe a touch of pedantry would be no fault, and poverty of feeling is hardly what the Captain displays when he first has occasion to hold Charlotte in his arms (I 12/326). And so they conclude their case against him, which up to this point has been purely speculative, with what they must regard as positive

[22] Ibid., xlif.

[23] Ibid., xlii. The sentence cited ends "but it could also be seen as depicting the individual's problems in a society dominated by aristocrats," an alternative that hardly follows logically from the earlier, more cautious statement (xli): "It is difficult to accept the view that *Die Wahlverwandtschaften* is, in the main, a novel of social criticism."

[24] Ibid., xxx, n. 3. As von Wiese notes with reference to II 13/453: "In dieser Atmosphäre der Liebe gibt es nichts Schwüles oder Laszives. Nur ein einziges Mal im ganzen Roman, bei der leidenschaftlichen Wiederbegegnung am See, bricht das Erotische unmittelbar durch. Aber auch dort wie rein, wie kindlich!" (659).

[25] Nisbet and Reiss xxxiv. The narrator, however, significantly comments that the reciprocal affection of the Captain and Charlotte is "vielleicht noch gefährlicher" than that of Eduard and Ottilie (I 8/298).

evidence: "This man who appears to be a model of rectitude applies to Eduard's flute-playing the unfortunate expression *Flötendudelei*. His attitude towards the child's death seems to lack humanity; for it very soon makes him think of his own hope of marrying Charlotte, who is, after all, the dead child's mother."[26] To dislike hearing an instrument badly played is no fault of character: when Wilhelm wonders in *Wilhelm Meisters Wanderjahre* why he hears no instrumental music at the boarding school he visits, he is told music students must practice in a remote valley, "denn Ihr werdet selbst gestehen, daß in der wohleingerichteten bürgerlichen Gesellschaft kaum ein trauriger Leiden zu dulden sei, als das uns die Nachbarschaft eines angehenden Flöten- oder Violinspielers aufdringt" (HA 8:152). The Captain's comment to Charlotte on his friend's musicianship is significant only because Ottilie, who overheard it by chance, eventually relays it to Eduard, demonstrating how his bitterness toward Charlotte and the Captain has so infected her (I 13/339f.) that she becomes guilty of the fault he earlier displayed when, against the Captain's express wish, he informed Charlotte of his criticism of her landscaping (I 3/261f.). As for the Captain's nourishing hopes of marriage soon after the child's death, so exemplary a figure as the protagonist of the *Wanderjahre* novella "Sankt Joseph der Zweite" honestly admits that he hoped for the widowhood of Elizabeth while still uncertain whether her first husband had survived their encounter with marauders: "Ich gönnte und wünschte dem guten Ehemann das Leben, und doch mochte ich sie mir so gern als Witwe denken" (HA 8:25).

The function in *Die Wahlverwandtschaften* of social realism is thus not ideological but, like that of historical, geographical, and other detail, to heighten verisimilitude by setting more or less ordinary psychological confrontations in what once were readily identifiable contexts. By Goethe's standard of idealized naturalism and his definition of style, realistic elements ("charakteristische Formen") are incidentals important only insofar as they facilitate recognition of essential qualities and their mode of existence. Goethe's announcement of his novel clearly states that what concerned him was human freedom and the constraints imposed upon it not only by social forces but also, and more importantly, by individual passions so elemental as to justify the chemical analogy in its title. The medium in which these passions operate is "das Reich der heiteren Vernunftfreiheit" (621), a realm of rational, moral, and aesthetic freedom which, in an age of conflicting ideologies (e.g., rational classicism—romanticism, orthodoxy—enlightened humanism), allows no verifications as certain as those applying to the novel's social (sociological) and historical elements. Romanticism, however,

[26] Loc. cit.

as the newest development in philosophy, science, religious thought, art, and literature, is necessarily a major component of reality in 1806 and 1807. Accordingly, romantic motifs have a large place in *Die Wahlverwandtschaften*, but they function as verisimilar incidentals, no more representing authorial sympathy with romanticism than Eduard's laudable military career conveys authorial approval of Prussian or other militarism.[27]

The three aspects of romanticism important in the novel are its speculative science, its art, and its religious thought, all used though not always evaluated with neutral objectivity. Its science, having to all intents and purposes become historical fact only, is most easily seen by the modern reader to have a merely incidental function.[28] Ottilie's anorexia nervosa—at the time apparently still as mystifying a cause of death as is spontaneous combustion in *Bleak House*—illustrates a kind of psychosomatic disorder for which romantic physicians had more understanding than their materialist-rationalistic elders. Her headaches are diagnosed by the English lord's companion as curable with mesmerism, the new mode of treatment which the perhaps wisely cautious Charlotte will not let him use (II 11/445), but like her reaction to subterranean deposits and metals (443f.) they are significant only as symptoms of a dangerously heightened sensitivity. Prenatal influence (congenial to romantic speculation simply as a popular

---

[27] Staiger 509ff., recognizing with Walzel that they represent "Dinge, die er [i.e., Goethe] sonst nur mit grimmigem Spott erwähnt," calls the romantic motifs of *Die Wahlverwandtschaften* "Intarsien," but he infers from their importance in the novel that they have great private significance for Goethe—although one hardly attested unless "in dem oft übertriebenen, ungeduldigen Ton, mit dem er sie abzuwehren versucht"—and presage a subsequent turning toward romanticism. (In the text of the novel neither the narrator nor any character ever inveighs against what might be considered manifestations of romanticism, and the former's few occasional comments on them are tolerantly ironic or gently humorous.) Because he accepts Staiger's false inference, Rösch, in his Introduction (19), suggests that inconsistencies in Staiger's interpretation of the novel are explained by the difficulties "die einem auf das klassische Goethe-Bild ausgerichteten Forscher an diesem nachklassischen Werk erwachsen." Danckert, however, who as author also of *Goethe: Der mythische Urgrund seiner Weltschau* (Berlin: de Gruyter, 1951) might be expected to be more aware than other critics of romanticism in Goethe, states without qualification, op. cit. (n. 17, above) 52, that in *Die Wahlverwandtschaften* romantic elements produce "keinen wesenhaft romantischen Gehalt" and are "alles andere als bloße Stimmungskulisse" (which they might be in a romantic work): "Den festen, ordnenden Griff des klassischen Gestalters verrät jeder Satz."

[28] The aspects of romantic science important for *Die Wahlverwandtschaften* have been identified by Walzel (cf. n. 8, above). Although Walzel 44f. explains Ottilie's 'halber Totenschlaf' (II 14/460) as "ein Phänomen aus dem Gebiete der 'Nachtseite der Naturwissenschaft,' " he notes that nothing resembling "dieser (kataleptische?) Zustand" is described in romantic-scientific writings. That sleeping persons hear—and may remember on awaking what they have heard—is an ancient belief frequently exploited by poets, especially in the Renaissance.

belief) is even less an empirical fact than in Thomas Hardy's story "An Imaginative Woman," since the function of the physical resemblances of Eduard's and Charlotte's child to Ottilie and the Captain is to insist on the no longer valid marriage in which the ill-fated infant was conceived.[29] Despite some critics,[30] these miraculous-seeming elements are only incidental motifs. The science they represent is important in the novel solely as metaphor—what Eduard in the text twice (I 4/270 and 276) and Goethe in his announcement of it (621) both call "Gleichnisrede"—for social and psychological interaction, so that the otherwise potentially vexing question of its verisimilitude is moot.

Only indirectly, as an influence on artistic taste, does romantic religious thought affect the world of *Die Wahlverwandtschaften*. Not merely is it basically alien to Goethe's secular, strongly ethical humanism, but it would also be incongruous in a milieu of enlightened Protestants for whom religious rituals are ceremonial only. The baptism of Otto (II 8) and the funeral of Ottilie (II 18) are the only services depicted in the novel; the former was to have been "würdig, aber beschränkt und kurz" (II 8/421), although Mittler's loquacity lengthens it catastrophically for the officially officiating clergyman; the latter, because of Eduard's refusal to accept Ottilie's death, is an idiosyncratic rite described with no mention of clerical participation (II 18/484ff.). In this Protestant milieu, where the goblet that the mason intends to destroy is caught by Eduard not miraculously but "ohne Wunder" (I 9/303), the propriety of divorce is never questioned on

---

[29] I find no evidence that Goethe regarded prenatal influence as verifiable fact. That little Otto has Ottilie's eyes is naturalistically explicable, since she is his mother's niece; he may have the Captain's features because Eduard and the Captain—the latter, whether loser or winner (II 11/442) of the heroine of "Die wunderlichen Nachbarskinder," is a member of a 'bedeutendes Haus' (II 10/434f.)—belong to families likely to have intermarried. (The antecedents of the Captain, in contrast to those of other major figures of the novel, are deliberately obscured, as Barnes 189 notes without suggesting why. Goethe can have chosen to avoid the cumbersome technique of connecting all major characters genealogically or by marriage either because he had already used—or overused—it in *Wilhelm Meisters Lehrjahre*, or because it had been vulgarized since that work by novelists of minimal talent.)

[30] E.g., von Wiese: "Gegenstand des Romans ist. . . sogar das Wunder" (659). Commenting on Ottilie's "magnetic" sensitivity, Walzel, in Rösch 43, cites from a letter of Hegel, 23 Feb. 1807, to Schelling (whose accounts of such phenomena Goethe had just read): "Goethen habe ich neugierig darauf gemacht, der einstweilen seine Späße dabei anbrachte." Nevertheless, Walzel infers from *Die Wahlverwandtschaften* that Goethe came to take magnetism more seriously, at least to the extent of considering it "dichterischer Verwertung. . . würdig." Poetic use of mythology, legend, or superstition is not, however, evidence of serious belief, as *Faust* sufficiently demonstrates.

theological grounds,[31] and even for the ex-clergyman Mittler the sanctity of marriage is founded not on divine law but on the moral principle of conscience (I 10/307). Mittler's abandonment of his pastoral calling so that he may devote himself completely to social service (I 2/255) is an act of secularized Protestant consistency that adequately explains his friendly welcome in the circles to which Eduard and Charlotte belong, and it is perhaps because the novel's usually neutral narrator is primarily addressing members of such a milieu that he occasionally allows himself humorous or ironic tones when mentioning what might seem naive religious beliefs.[32] Ethics have here supplanted ecclesiastical, supernatural, perhaps even transcendent authority, and although Mittler is the extremist spokesman for this secularization of religion—most obviously in his reinterpretation of the Commandments and catechism (II 18/481ff.)—never in the novel does the narrator or any character take issue with his ethical views, however ill-timed their expression may be.[33] Indeed, when the narrator for the last time

---

[31] The Baroness and Count who, when they first appear, live together unmarried, do so because he cannot obtain a divorce, although it has been thought of (I 10/304); since no religious obstacle is mentioned, it must be inferred that no grounds have been furnished by his wife, whose death will make marriage possible when the couple again appears (II 5/390). A laconic remark reported by Eckermann (30 March 1824), who apparently missed its irony, records Goethe's amused reaction to interpretations of *Die Wahlverwandtschaften* that saw expressed in it a rigorism inconsistent with his usually liberal attitudes: "Der selige Reinhard [i.e., the clergyman F.V. Reinhard] in Dresden wunderte sich oft über mich, daß ich in bezug auf die Ehe so strenge Grundsätze habe, während ich doch in allen übrigen Dingen so läßlich denke." More obviously, and bitterly, ironic in tone is a conversation with Chancellor von Müller (7 April 1830), in which Goethe not only calls marriage, a Christian sacrament, "eigentlich unnatürlich," but also rhetorically asks: "Was liegt daran, ob einige Paare sich prügeln und das Leben verbittern, wenn nur der allgemeine [i.e., 'vulgar'] Begriff der Heiligkeit der Ehe aufrecht bleibt?" Further evidence of Goethe's tolerance of divorce is offered in the article by Hatfield cited below, n. 44.

[32] In the neologism for 'churchyard' "Auferstehungsfeld" (II 2/366) the combining of abstract ('Resurrection') and concrete-homely ('field,' 'yard') elements parodies Protestant-Pietistic usage (cf. Klopstock, *Der Messias*, 5:716: "das rauschende Feld voll Auferstehung"); at the end of Eduard's account of his and the Count's passage through the sleeping Anakim (cf. n. 4, above), the latter had already punned on "Auferstehung": "Ich hatte große Lust zu stolpern, . . . damit es Lärm gegeben hätte; denn welch eine seltsame Auferstehung würden wir gesehen haben!" (I 11/318). The initial reaction of the villagers to Nanny's ecstatic attribution to Ottilie of her harmless fall from the loft window depicts Protestant discomfort in the presence of faith in the miraculous (II 18/486)—Thomas Mann's failure to notice this partly explains his unfounded charging of Goethe with an incongruous lack of "protestantische Charakterstärke." The formula 'another world' is used in the text for the realm of art (II 5/393) and for a *locus amoenus* (I 7/295), but not for 'afterlife.'

[33] Like Goethe, Mittler regards marriage not as a sacrament but as a purely human tie (II 18/482f.); his rejection of injunctions against evil for encouragement of good is also Goethean, coinciding with Goethe's views in even so minor a detail as his wish that those guilty of adultery not be publicly shamed by church or state (soon after his arrival in

generalizes about human destiny, religion receives no mention; what count are "Charakter, Individualität, Neigung, Richtung, Örtlichkeit, Umgebungen und Gewohnheiten" (II 17/478). In this Protestant world the novel's concluding apotheosis cannot be taken literally and simply provides what Goethe, interpreting catharsis in his "Nachlese zu Aristoteles' Poetik" with reference to both tragedies and tragic novels, later called the "aussöhnende Abrundung, welche eigentlich. . . von allen poetischen Werken gefordert wird" (HA 12:343).

It is less easy, however, to distinguish—in part because of a subsequent rise of literary- and art-historical eclecticism, in part because romanticism is a timeless mode of feeling—incidental aspects of romantic art and aesthetics in *Die Wahlverwandtschaften* from those which in the larger context of Goethe's classicism may also represent essential values. This difficulty is aggravated by the fact that for a Goethe consciously hostile to much that is romantic, and hence for his narrator, what is as it were aesthetically incidental may nevertheless be otherwise significant, introducing an element of ironic ambiguity which would not have existed for the informed and enlightened audience originally addressed. In the novel's Protestant milieu, in what Aurelie in *Wilhelm Meisters Lehrjahre* calls "den gebildeten, aber auch den bildlosen Teil von Deutschland" (HA 7:271), art has no romantic-religious connotations, as is evident from the purely secular motives behind Charlotte's beautification of the churchyard and, even more, from those behind the Architect's of the church and its chapel. Moreover, the novel's very title helps establish a fundamental premise of Goethe's classical aesthetic, that every work of art is analogous to, though never identical with, what nature may produce; in this aesthetic, mimesis cannot be an end in itself either as naturalistic imitation of an immediate reality or as literal

Weimar Goethe sought to end state-church humiliation of unmarried mothers). In Goethe's thought, religion itself is a construct of human rationality, and in *Dichtung und Wahrheit*— the date of composition is 1813—he characterizes *taedium vitae* as "dieses traurige Gebiet, wo dem Verstande eine Aufgabe zugewiesen ist, die er zu lösen nicht hinreicht, da ihn ja selbst die Religion, *wie er sich solche allenfalls erbauen kann*, im Stiche läßt" (HA 9:581— emphasis added); the narrator of *Die Wahlverwandtschaften*, explaining how Nanny's belief in Ottilie's miraculous powers is soon shared by others, similarly observes: "Jedes Bedürfnis, dessen wirkliche Befriedigung versagt ist, nötigt zum Glauben" (II 18/488). Commonsense, but not extreme, rationalism, is the religious-intellectual stance of the novel's narrator and hence of most of its major characters: Mittler, the most fanatical enemy of "Aberglaube" (I 18/357), concedes, "Das Vernünftigste habe ich mißlingen sehen, das Abgeschmackteste gelingen" (I 2/256); Charlotte explains premonitions as "unbewußte Erinnerungen" (I 1/248); and the narrator carefully distances himself from superstition when he refers to "Diejenigen, die auf die Namensbedeutungen abergläubisch sind" (I 2/255), even though he recognizes that it is only rationalization to believe that reason can turn time back and "ein gewaltsam Entbundenes. . . wieder ins Enge bringen" (I 13/329).

recreation of an art belonging to a past age. The Architect's enthusiasm for German art of the Renaissance can be shared by Goethe's narrator, who as it were commends unqualifiedly the power to recognize and appreciate high artistic achievement of a world so different from one's own as to seem "ein Traum" (II 2/367).[34] But no greater intrinsic worth is attached to the Architect's imitation, with Ottilie's assistance, of primitive features of this art than to its imitation by Nazarene painters whose works Goethe disliked. And so the narrator humorously notes that his painting merely serves to reveal his obsession with Ottilie (II 3/372), then later remarks more grimly that the chapel they have restored will remain a pointless "Künstlergrille" unless used as a tomb (374), which is in fact its final function (II 15/464 and 18/485 and 490).

In contrast to the narrator's negative or at best neutral evaluation of romantic art as cultivated by Ottilie and the Architect, is his explicit approval of Charlotte's less pretentious but more traditional aesthetic taste. Although critics have often interpreted negatively her simultaneous use of natural and artificial flowers and greenery to decorate her garden house, the effect is actually said to do her "Kunstsinn" great credit (I 3/258), and although her beautification of the churchyard has been called an act of impiety by even non-Christian standards,[35] the narrator has only positive words for what she achieves:

[34] Paul Stöcklein, *Wege zum späten Goethe*, 2. Aufl. (Hamburg: Schröder, 1960) 20, identifies Ottilie with "mädchenhaften Madonnen der Frührenaissance" by omitting the important "vielleicht" in his paraphrase of "Nur vielleicht Ottilie war in dem Fall [scil. when among these Renaissance-art figures], sich unter ihresgleichen zu fühlen" (II 1/368). Predating the figures and ignoring the "vielleicht," von Wiese states: "Ihr Weltgefühl wurzelt in der Epoche des späten Mittelalters. . . . Darum vermag sie auch ohne Blasphemie die Himmelskönigin als lebendes Bild darzustellen" (667), but only Ottilie's beauty and possibly her religious naiveté, certainly not her exemplary worth, can be inferred from the cited passage—and as a Protestant she is keenly aware "wie wenig wert" she is "unter dieser heiligen Gestalt. . . zu erscheinen" (II 6/405). Barnes 99, n. 1 also confuses the Architect's Renaissance collection with his "medievalizing activity which she [*actually*: the narrator!] characterizes as 'eine Künstlergrille' (II 2)." Staiger 489f. first speaks of "Umrißzeichnungen nach Gemälden alter deutscher Meister" but then exclaims that Ottilie's counterparts are found "Im *gotischen* Mittelalter also!" (emphasis added), and although he recognizes that they recall "die Steine im Maffeianum zu Verona" that in *Italienische Reise* symbolize for Goethe healthy non-transcendentalism—the figures "falten nicht die Hände, schauen nicht in den Himmel" (HA 11:42)—he still thinks them "unverkennbar gotisch."

[35] E.g., Danckert 88 and Wilhelm Emrich, *Die Symbolik von Faust II: Sinn und Vorformen* (Bonn: Athenäum, 1957) 162; Emrich calls the graveyard "die mythisch ortsgebundene Erinnerungsstätte" whose transformation "die urgewaltigen Gesetze des Lebens unterhöhlt."

Mit möglichster Schonung der alten Denkmäler hatte sie alles so zu vergleichen und zu ordnen gewußt, daß es ein angenehmer Raum erschien, auf dem das Auge und die Einbildungskraft gerne verweilten. (I 2/254)

Only in her rejection of the Architect's—and Goethe's[36]—opinion that the best memorials to the dead are portrait busts does Charlotte's Protestant hostility to religious art outweigh her aesthetic feeling (II 2/365), but her weakness has its counterpart in the Architect's elegiac preference for urn burial (363), the manifestation of a hellenism no less romantic and other-timely than the medievalism of his painting.[37]

That romantic art-motifs in *Die Wahlverwandtschaften* are incidentals, is confirmed by Goethe's objection to a picture of Ottilie lying on her bier for emphasizing too much a Madonna and not enough the dead, and real, Ottilie.[38] Significantly, the novel's last *tableau vivant* (the second nativity scene), the least realistic of the five described, is the one least sympathetically characterized by the narrator. His phrase "fromme Kunstmummerei" (II 6/405) supports Ronald Peacock's rejection of the thesis that Ottilie as the Madonna in glory is "a pre-figuration of the final events of the novel, indicating that she fits the tableau perfectly," and confirms Peacock's insistence that Ottilie's sense of the incongruity of her role marks her becoming "for the first time. . . keenly conscious of the *latent* elements of guilt in her situation in the Eduard-Charlotte household."[39] To say, as does

---

[36] In "Bedeutung des Individuellen," Festausgabe 16:333f., Goethe expresses approval of Lavater's liking to have himself portrayed and of Aretino's commissioning of medallions with his portrait; in "Gehorsamstes Promemoria," WA I.48:141f., he rejects "bildlose allgemeine Formen" as suitable monuments to the dead—"Wie man es denn, so lange die Welt steht, nicht höher hat bringen können, als zu einer ikonischen Statue."

[37] The narrator's already noted preference for Renaissance art reappears when he characterizes Ottilie, "das Kind auf dem Arm, lesend und wandelnd," as "eine gar anmutige Penserosa" (II 11/446), a motif deriving not from medieval but Renaissance painting (e.g., Pinturicchio) and sculpture which also appears with allusion to Michelangelo's Medici Tomb in *Faust* (l. 8677). Less striking, but serving to counter an exclusively Nazarene interpretation of Nanny's vision of a celestial Ottilie, is the phrase "wie auf Wolken oder Wogen getragen" (II 18/486), in which Renaissance tradition conflates cloud-borne madonna or saint with Venus or Galatea.

[38] WA IV.21:249f. The language in the letter to Heinrich Meyer is forceful: "hole der Teufel das junge künstlerische Mädchen, das mir die heilige Ottilie schwanger auf's Paradebett legt. . . . Das todte, wirklich todte Kind gen Himmel zu heben, das war der Augenblick, der gefaßt werden mußte, wenn man überhaupt solches Zeug zeichnen will."

[39] Ronald Peacock, "The Ethics of Goethe's 'Die Wahlverwandtschaften,' " *MLR* 71 (1976): 336. Peacock's corollary (339) that Ottilie "contains Goethe's faith; she *is* what he admires," is confirmed neither by the text of the novel nor by any statement made elsewhere by Goethe. Ottilie's faith is correctly identified by André François-Poncet, "Der sittliche Gehalt der 'Wahlverwandtschaften': Das Schicksalhafte" [chapter 6 of his

von Wiese (667), that by virtue of resembling virginal madonnas of the Early Renaissance Ottilie can appropriately pose as Queen of Heaven, is to ignore the Assistant Headmaster's indirect gloss—his very Protestant disapproval of the restoration of church and chapel—on what he terms "diese Annäherung, diese Vermischung des Heiligen zu und mit dem Sinnlichen" because it obscures the important principle "Das Höchste, das Vorzüglichste am Menschen ist gestaltlos, und man soll sich hüten, es anders als in edler Tat zu gestalten" (II 7/407). What this gloss says with decorum is also the sentiment of the narrator who has ironically spoken of "fromme Kunstmummerei," and of the Goethe who angrily wrote an old friend just over a month before he began *Die Wahlverwandtschaften*:

> Bei den Alten, in ihrer besten Zeit, entsprang das Heilige aus dem sinnlich faßlichen Schönen. . . . Das Moderne ruht auf dem sittlich Schönen, dem, wenn man will, das sinnliche entgegensteht; und ich verarge Dir's gar nicht wenn Du das Verkoppeln und Verkuppeln des Heiligen mit dem Schönen oder vielmehr Angenehmen und Reizenden nicht vertragen magst: denn es entsteht daraus. . . eine lüsterne Redouten- und Halb-Bordellwirtschaft, die nach und nach noch schlimmer werden wird. (Br. 3:66)

Ottilie's sensing of the discrepancy between her role as Madonna and the fundamentally non-aestheticizing Protestantism in which she has been raised marks a religious awakening that will henceforth determine her conduct. Until little Otto is no longer regarded as an obstacle to divorce, she can gracefully accept renunciation of Eduard and in adolescent idealism even believe "daß ihre Liebe, um sich zu vollenden, völlig uneigennützig werden müsse" (II 9/425). But when she has been the cause of the child's death, by virtue of her sense of remorse (II 15/464) renunciation becomes atonement. She resolves—with some uncertainty at first, as her "vielleicht" betrays—to be "eine geweihte Person. . . , die nur dadurch ein ungeheures Übel für sich und andre vielleicht aufzuwiegen vermag, wenn sie sich dem Heiligen widmet, das, uns unsichtbar umgebend, allein gegen die ungeheuren zudringenden Mächte beschirmen kann" (467f.). As Peacock notes, this is "the natural naive religious language. . . of a woman who declares her resolve to be pure in heart and action amid misfortune and is for that

---

monograph *Les Affinités Électives de Goethe* (Paris, 1910)], in Rösch 74, as (a form of unsophisticated) Christianity: "Ottilies Vorstellung von den übernatürlichen Mächten entspricht. . . ganz den Vorstellungen des Christentums. Über die Menschen erhaben sind nur Gott und die Geister der Finsternis." Inasmuch as there underlies *Die Wahlverwandtschaften* not a Christian-transcendental, but an ethical-religious viewpoint, H.S. Reiss, *Goethes Romane* 194, can legitimately say that "die Religion. . . ist niemals unmittelbar das Thema des Romans."

reason, apart from religion, an ethical power."[40] It is, however, also the biblical language of Ottilie's Protestant upbringing, to which she had already reverted when, on the morning after Otto's drowning, she used the words "ich bin aus meiner Bahn geschritten" as synonymous with an appositive "ich habe meine Gesetze [i.e., principles of humility she had vowed to follow] gebrochen" (II 14/462). She repeats the first phrase, in which "Bahn" is the "paths of uprightness" of Proverbs 2:13, in the letter informing her friends of her vow of silence and abstemiousness: "Ich bin aus meiner Bahn geschritten, und ich soll nicht wieder hinein. Ein feindseliger Dämon, der Macht über mich gewonnen, scheint mich von außen zu hindern, hätte ich mich auch"—i.e., she has not—"mit mir selbst wieder zur Einigkeit gefunden" (II 17/476f.). As in that most secular of Goethe's poems "Das Tagebuch," written barely a year later than this passage and containing the lines "Denn zeigt sich auch ein Dämon, uns versuchend, / So waltet Was, gerettet ist die Tugend," here *Dämon* is only 'diabolic creature' or 'diabolic temptation' in a naive Christian-religious sense. Although Ottilie's "Dämon" has often been incautiously identified with a concept of the daemonic Goethe had not yet formulated when writing *Die Wahlverwandtschaften*, the identification attributes to her a verbal sophistication inconsistent with her character and upbringing and hence with the principle of verisimilitude that controls every detail of the text.[41]

[40] Peacock 339f. In her use of "Bahn" for the Lutheran-biblical "rechte Bahn" (Prov. 2:13) Ottilie adopts the language of Protestant homiletics created by Luther, who writes "der tritt freilich aus der ban und ist des teufels" (cited, Jacob and Wilhelm Grimm, *Deutsches Wörterbuch*, 1 [Leipzig, 1854], col. 1077); this language is found in such hymns as Paul Gerhardt's "Sollt ich meinem Gott nicht singen," which assures us that a father never entirely withdraws his heart from his child "Ob es [i.e., the child] gleich bisweilen Sünde / Thut und aus der Bahne weicht. . . ." It is thus incorrect to say, as does Stöcklein 65, interpreting Ottilie as "Eine Heilige die keine scheint": "Niemals benützt sie herkömmliche Worte der christlichen Terminologie, *bis* auf ihr letztes Gespräch."

[41] The earliest mention by Goethe of "Dämonisches" is that of 1810 (HA 4:590, "Schemata zu 'Dichtung und Wahrheit,' 20. Buch, 1810"), but elaboration of the concept in connection with the discussion in *Dichtung und Wahrheit* of the figure of Egmont is usually dated 1813 (cf. HA 10, note to 176,34): until 1810 Goethe uses "Dämon" and "dämonisch" only in literal senses, as in "Das Tagebuch" or as in the sonnet "Mächtiges Überraschen," which refers the adjective to an oread (a nature spirit, a 'daimon'). Critics already mentioned—there are many more like them—who intrude the concept into discussion of *Die Wahlverwandtschaften* include von Wiese (662); Hankamer, loc. cit.; Blackall 183 ("this daemon"); Barnes—cautiously—124 ("The mysterious traits of Ottilie's character have tempted critics to exaggerate the 'daimonic' element in her make-up") and 206 (Ottilie's "belief. . . that holy love alone can safeguard us against the daemonic powers of fate"); Reiss—also cautiously—*Goethes Romane* 201; and Killy 30 ("Skala des Dämonischen"). Viëtor and Staiger, however, avoid the concept.

Ottilie's belief in supernatural beings is naive, childlike, and, by enlightened Protestant standards, almost primitive. It is shared in the novel by no one of her own educational or social background, not even by the one adult said—"Eduard hatte bei zunehmenden Jahren immer etwas Kindliches behalten, das der Jugend Ottiliens besonders zusagte" (I 7/289)—to be also somewhat naive, but only by Nanny and by the credulous hoping for miraculous relief who so crowd chapel and church that the chapel must be kept permanently locked and the church can be opened only for divine service (II 18/488f.). As faith, however, it commands a frustrated Charlotte's tolerant respect, and even its most primitive counterpart, Nanny's conviction that Ottilie still lives and works "in einer höhern Region," can help assuage the Architect's grief for what to him is a life totally ended (487f.). Ottilie's sense of "das Heilige," however, is shared as the voice of conscience by other main characters, since it is an integral element of both secularized Protestantism and ethical humanism. Nevertheless, but appropriately in the case of one named after a saint born blind, for her "das Heilige" has a component of the supernatural which, to use Goethe's own language in a *Reflexion* of 1825, is her blind spot:

> Alle gesunde Menschen haben die Überzeugung ihres Daseins und eines Daseienden um sie her. Indessen gibt es auch einen hohlen Fleck im Gehirn, das heißt eine Stelle, wo sich kein Gegenstand abspiegelt, wie denn auch im Auge selbst ein Fleckchen ist, das nicht sieht. Wird der Mensch auf diese Stelle besonders aufmerksam, vertieft er sich darin, so verfällt er in eine Geisteskrankheit, ahnet hier Dinge aus einer andern Welt [e.g., "die ungeheuren zudringenden Mächte" and the "Dämon" of Ottilie], die aber eigentlich Undinge sind. . . . (HA 12:373)

It is Ottilie's tragic flaw that she confuses "das Heilige" of conscience with external forces—"Auf eine schreckliche Weise hat Gott mir die Augen geöffnet, in welchem Verbrechen ich befangen bin," she declares when definitively renouncing Eduard (II 14/463). In Goethe's Weltanschauung, however, there are but two true forms of religion, "die eine, die das Heilige, das in und um uns wohnt, ganz formlos [i.e., invisible], die andere, die es in der schönsten Form anerkennt und anbetet. Alles was dazwischen liegt, ist Götzendienst" (HA 12:372).

In *Die Wahlverwandtschaften* Goethe's view that, when not the glory of things seen, "das Heilige" is an invisible realm of ethical values, finds its most eloquent spokesman in Charlotte. It lies behind her rejection of portrait memorials to the dead that turn our thoughts to the past "und erinnern. . . , wie schwer es sei, die Gegenwart recht zu ehren" (II 2/365). It is, however, given clearest expression shortly before Ottilie invokes its authority when, finally consenting to a divorce that Ottilie's remorse will frustrate, Charlotte says of "Schicksal,"[42] the circumstances that have led to her child's death: "Vergebens, daß Vernunft und Tugend, Pflicht und alles Heilige sich ihm in den Weg stellen" (II 14/460). "Das Heilige" is that which is vital and life-giving, and in *Wilhelm Meisters Lehrjahre* there can be read on the roll held by the Uncle's funerary statue the quintessentially Goethean injunction "Gedenke zu leben" (HA 7:540). Human life at its fullest is, moreover, social, and so in *Vier Jahreszeiten* Goethe defines "das Heilige" as that which "viele Seelen zusammen / Bindet" and "das Heiligste" as that which "heut und ewig die Geister, / Tief und tiefer gefühlt, immer nur einiger macht" (HA 1: 227). The "nächste Nähe" in which toward the end of *Die Wahlverwandt-schaften* Ottilie, Eduard, and Charlotte exist, "aber selbst ohne gerade aneinander zu denken" (II 17/478), is thus only a sad counterfeit of "das Heilige" as Goethe envisioned it. And nothing casts a more dubious light on the seemingly saint-like death of Ottilie and the doubtful miracles attributed to her saintliness than that her last words should be her dying injunction to Eduard—"Versprich mir zu leben!" (II 18/484)—to continue such an existence. There is bitterest irony in the fact that these words are spoken by one whom the narrator calls, as he has before (II 15/464), "das. . . himm-lische Kind," for the apparently religious epithet *himmlisch* like its secular synonym *herrlich*[43]—e.g., in "das herrliche Kind" (II 14/462)—represents a fashionable usage that has lost all associations with the celestial or, in the case of *herrlich*, the sublime.[44]

---

[42] In Goethe's usage 'Schicksal' is indistinguishable from character: writing to Schiller in 1797 he uses the formula "das Schicksal oder, welches einerlei ist, die entschiedene Natur des Menschen" (Br. 2:267), and he approved the essay "Über die Wahlverwandtschaften" in which Solger declares, "Jede einzelne Regung oder Bewegung in dem ganzen Verlauf ist unmittelbar in dem Charakter der Personen gegründet" (636).

[43] For contemporary usage, cf. E.F.C. Oertel, *Grammatisches Wörterbuch der Deutschen Sprache* (München, 1829) 2:231 ("himmlisch") and 225 ("herrlich"); both words illustrate the same debasement of language as do their best English equivalents 'lovely' and 'divine.'

[44] Nisbet and Reiss xliii believe "Ottilie's attitude at the end of the novel may be called religious" since the narrator calls her " 'die Heilige' and 'himmlisch.' " To infer from the recurrent epithet "himmlisch" that the narrator believes Ottilie has achieved her ambition of becoming a saint-like lay-sister, "eine geweihte Person," is to disregard the fact that in a consciously "classical" text set epithets will appear in more or less appropriate contexts. (Gerwin Marahrens, "Narrator and Narrative in Goethe's *Die Wahlverwandtschaften*," in M.S. Batts and M.G. Stankiewicz, eds., *Essays in German Literatur in Honour of G.J. Hallamore* [Toronto: University of Toronto Press, 1969] 94–127, concedes [119] that what he terms the narrator's "eulogistic expressions" for Ottilie "far exceed what the reader, examining Ottilie's life, might be prepared to say," then incautiously infers that they are meant to have "a persuasive effect.") Given Ottilie's misuse or abuse of religious language, terms used to describe and characterize her must be interpreted carefully. This is especially necessary in a text in which the death of a child heralded as "den Heiland dieses Hauses"

Failure to see and interpret reality objectively is not, however, a weakness unique to Ottilie. Her blindness is shared in greater or less degree by the other major characters of the novel, though not by its narrator. This is especially true when they view Ottilie, and in the case of Eduard, blinded by wishful or fatalistic thinking, the all too human inclination to see only what one wants to see is unusually strong. Headmistress, Assistant Headmaster, and Charlotte are all aware of Ottilie's lack of appetite without recognizing how serious a symptom it is of anorexia nervosa. That her helpfulness—from her arrival on, Ottilie is "gegen jedermann. . . dienstfertig und zuvorkommend" (I 7/289)—is a form of self-abasement inappropriate to a girl her age, is conveniently ignored and, if not consciously exploited, at least taken for granted by everyone. Ottilie's conduct to all intents and purposes never violates adult standards of decorum, and the Architect even tells her "das Schickliche ist mit Ihnen geboren" (II 6/401). Inappropriate decorum, however, can be the symptom of dangerous neurosis—Luciane, whom the Architect is indirectly criticizing, has the healthy vitality Ottilie lacks, and in *Wilhelm Meisters Lehrjahre* that novel's true "schöne Seele" Natalie can be overjoyed to report to Wilhelm that his son's "Unart [i.e., his drinking directly from a bottle] hat ihn gerettet" (HA 7:604).

Ottilie herself, however, is chiefly responsible for Charlotte's failure to attach proper importance to what is symptomatically strange behavior. Her first act on arriving at the manor is her kneeling before Charlotte, whose disturbed "Wozu die Demütigung!" she assuages by explaining that to kneel is a pleasurable way of recalling the time "da ich noch nicht höher reichte

(by a sometime servant of the Lord whose wish for the officiating clergyman "Herr, laß deinen Diener in Frieden fahren" is literally fulfilled before he can complete his baptismal sermon) brings anything but salvation—even though Zacharias Werner, in his sonnet "Die Wahlverwandtschaften," calls the girl who takes such careless care of that child, "den Sohn der Sünden," an angel of salvation (647). As for the one reference to the dead Ottilie as a saint—"wie er [i.e., Eduard] in Gedanken an die Heilige eingeschlafen war, so konnte man wohl ihn selig nennen" (II 18/490)—its "wohl," its puns on 'sainted' and 'blessed' as two euphemisms for 'dead,' and the inverted commas that have to be supplied because "die Heilige" is also a reference to popular belief that her corpse has miraculous powers, cast serious doubt on Barnes's statement, op. cit. 159: "One can perhaps dismiss the postulation of Eduard's bliss as a stylistic flourish of the narrator, but not his use of the term 'die Heilige.' " Kurt May, "Goethes 'Wahlverwandtschaften' als tragischer Roman," in Rösch 267f., is thus more judicious when he states "Jedenfalls wandelt sich Ottilie keineswegs in das Urbild einer christlichen Märtyrerin" than when he declares, "Sie vernimmt im Gewissen die Stimme des Göttlichen." Ottilie's God is not Goethe's but that of biblical Christianity, for which Goethe—this is well documented by Henry Hatfield, "Zur Interpretation der 'Wahlverwandtschaften,' " in Rösch 181—expressed as little sympathy during the writing of *Die Wahlverwandtschaften* as at most other times. It is thus not, as Gonthier-Louis Fink claims (475), "die zwingende Kraft des Heiligen, das von Ottilie ausging" that keeps Eduard's passions in check, but his gentlemanliness and her Christian morality.

als bis an Ihre Kniee und Ihrer Liebe schon so gewiß war" (I 6/281). And although her "anständige Dienstfertigkeit" soon wins her Charlotte's approval, the latter is again—or still—disturbed by her unseemly readiness to pick up things men drop; but again Ottilie, who this time promises to refrain henceforth from this impropriety, has a ready explanation: the distress she felt in history class on hearing how when on trial Charles I of England himself had to stoop to pick up the knob that fell from his cane (284f.). As we however learn only when, after the novel's catastrophe, she resolves to renounce Eduard for ever, these explanations are only half-truths. Ottilie's humility is the consequence of a childhood decision made when she overheard—or heard while apparently asleep—Charlotte express concern that her impoverished orphanhood would doom her to a life of dependency unless fortune especially favored her: "Ich machte mir nach meinen beschränkten Einsichten hierüber Gesetze; nach diesen habe ich lange gelebt. . ." (II 14/462). And the fatal consequence of this humility is Eduard's love for her.

As a defense mechanism Ottilie's humility may ultimately be self-serving, but it is legitimately so because she remains a child from her entering the manor as "das liebe Kind" (I 6/281)—each time 'Kind' is the narrator's word—until her departing it and this world as "das bleiche himmlische Kind" (II 18/482). It is also the explanation, both as attentiveness to others and as a childlike quality, of why Eduard is attracted to her: "Gegen jedermann war sie dienstfertig und zuvorkommend; daß sie es gegen ihn am meisten sei, das wollte seiner Selbstliebe scheinen" (I 7/289). Why Charlotte and the Captain, similar in temperament and equal in age, are attracted to each other, is as evident to themselves as it is to narrator and reader; but the affinity between Ottilie, in the best or kindest sense of the words innocent and naive, and a much older man of considerable, even sophisticated, experience is something these two never understand even when, at the end of the novel, they have finally become as it were one: "es war nur Ein Mensch im bewußtlosen, vollkommnen Behagen, mit sich selbst zufrieden und mit der Welt. [...] Das Leben war ihnen ein Rätsel, dessen Auflösung sie nur miteinander fanden" (II 17/478). Only the narrator and the reader know that self-interest and self-love are electively affinitive, and they alone see the total verisimilitude of the analogy between elemental and psychological affinity that justifies the novel's title and Goethe's announcement of his intention "in einem sittlichen [i.e., psychological-moral] Falle eine chemische Gleichnisrede zu ihrem geistigen Ursprunge zurück[zu]führen" (621).

As Ottilie is blinded by her own naiveness, Charlotte—with Ottilie's assistance—by the benefits of Ottilie's humble service, and Mittler—most notably when he observes too late what proves to be the fatal weakness of the aged clergyman at Otto's baptism (II 8/422)—by his *idées fixes*, so

Eduard is blinded by affinities which, had he recognized their nature, might have exerted little or no power over him. This is moreover hinted, if not stated, by Goethe's narrator in the already cited "das wollte seiner Selbstliebe scheinen," for only here in the text is "scheinen" not the narrator's literal 'to appear, to put in an appearance' or his figurative, often cautious or ironic, 'to seem,' but the verb, already archaic in Goethe's day, that Luther had used in the sense "erhellen, klar sein" ('to be evident'). Elsewhere "scheinen" refers only to appearances, and for most of the novel almost exclusively to verifiably deceptive ones: the Assistant Headmaster reports that Ottilie, when taunted at school by Luciane, "schien gelassen für jeden andern, nur nicht für mich," for he has observed a change of color on one side of her face (I 5/279); when the occupants of the manor house retire on the night when Otto will unfortunately be conceived, the narrator ambiguously remarks, "so schien dieser Tag abgeschlossen" (I 10/317); when Ottilie's handwriting has so come to resemble Eduard's that Charlotte thinks a note from her to him is something he has written, he suspects his wife of deviousness and disregards graphological evidence of Ottilie's unhealthy over-adaptiveness, for "diese sonderbaren, zufälligen Zeichen, durch die ein höheres Wesen mit uns zu sprechen scheint, waren seiner Leidenschaft unverständlich" (II 13/331); after Eduard leaves, Charlotte is "ruhig und heiter; Ottilie schien es nur" (I 17/348); etc. In the novel's final chapter, however, "scheinen" (which in the last sentence of the preceding chapter means 'put in an appearance') chiefly connotes dubiety: when Ottilie collapses, to the manor's medical advisor what is actually her agony "scheint. . . nur eine Erschöpfung," and she is "sich selbst bewußt, wie es schien" (II 18/483f.); when a funeral to his liking has been arranged, Eduard "schien sich in alles ergeben zu haben"; when to Nanny the corpse of Ottilie "schien. . . zu winken," she falls and we are told "Das Kind. . . schien an allen Gliedern zerschmettert. Man hob es auf; und zufällig. . . lehnte man es über die Leiche, ja es schien selbst noch mit dem letzten Lebensrest seine geliebte Herrin erreichen zu wollen" (485f.); Eduard soon seems impassive—"er schien keine Träne mehr zu haben, keines Schmerzes weiter fähig zu sein"—and "Nur noch einige Erquickung scheint er aus dem Glase [i.e., the goblet he caught and saved from destruction at the *Richtfest*] zu schlürfen, das ihm freilich kein wahrhafter Prophet gewesen," but when he realizes that he is only drinking from a replacement of the recently broken original, "Der Trank scheint ihm von nun an zu widerstehen; er scheint sich mit Vorsatz der Speise, des Gesprächs zu enthalten" (489) and what has seemed submissive acceptance of the irremediable proves to be the same fatal apathy that has destroyed Ottilie.

As goodness is relative, so is self-interest, which is hardly a moral blemish unless consciously pursued. It may be more or less enlightened,

more or less naive, according to the state of self-awareness and respon-
sibility an individual has achieved. Charlotte and the Captain, who weigh
self-interest against the values of family obligation, are willing to renounce
each other until persuaded by Eduard that his child may be better off with
them as parents (II 12/448), and like Eduard, though less hastily, they accept
the child's death as removing the barrier to eventual marriage (II 14/461).
All three, however, are frustrated in their various hopes by Ottilie, who is
accordingly the central dramatic figure of the novel—not, as is sometimes
said, because she represents an ideal,[45] but because she is the unwitting key
to its plot and alone has the power to resolve the "Conflicte" of its "sociale
Verhältnisse." This is why Goethe could approve without the usual
overtones of ironic qualification (624) Reinhard's interpretation of her—and
Eduard's—character:

> Dieses liebliche Wesen steht unter einer Art von Naturnotwendigkeit, die
> von ihr auf alle ihre Umgebung ausgeht. . . . Weder in ihrem Wirken noch
> in ihrem Leiden ist volles, helles Bewußtsein; sie handelt und empfindet,
> sie lebt und stirbt so und nicht anders, weil sie nicht anders kann. . . . Was
> Eduard betrifft, so versieht er sich freilich darin, daß er sich etwas
> nachsieht, aber wer sieht sich nicht etwas nach, und wer hätte darum das
> Recht, ihn einen ärmlichen Charakter zu schelten? (651)

Ottilie's single-mindedness is a fault that both constrains respect and evokes
pity, and so she can be the novel's tragic heroine, can produce that catharsis
which "wirklich. . . oder durch ein Surrogat"—so Goethe, with reference to
"Tragödien und tragische Romane," in his "Nachlese zu Aristoteles'
Poetik"—"geschieht. . . durch eine Art Menschenopfer" and is demanded

---

[45] In his reply to the letter of Reinhard immediately cited in my text, Goethe refers to
Ottilie as "meine liebe Ottilie" (624), but to pity or love a person faulted is not necessarily
to condone his faults; what the narrator carefully calls Ottilie's "Gefühl ihrer Unschuld" (I
13/331) is not the same as innocence itself. Grete Schaeder, "Die Idee der Wahlverwandt-
schaften," in Schaeder, *Gott und Welt: Drei Kapitel Goethescher Weltanschauung* (Hameln:
Seifert, 1947) 276–323, persuasively argues that the novel contains "keine Idealgestalt" (304)
by demonstrating that no character seems to achieve what from his own utterances Goethe
is known to have regarded as (and what in the text is implied to be) full moral and
intellectual understanding. That, moreover, Ottilie approximates an ideal to a lesser degree
than do several other characters in the novel is convincingly inferred from the text itself by
Marahrens; taking as his cue Walther Killy's observation, op. cit. 30, "je freier, das heißt in
Goethes Sinn je sittlich bedeutender ein Mensch ist, um so mehr bleiben sein Äußeres und
seine persönliche Redeweise unserer Imagination überlassen," he notes that, although
Luciane, the child, the Count, the Baroness, and in some degree Ottilie are all physically
described, "Of the appearance of Charlotte and the Captain the reader is told nothing at all"
(118).

only when a tragic figure is "weder ganz schuldig noch ganz schuldfrei" (HA 12:343ff.).

Ottilie is thus not simply "das gute, reine Kind" she seems to Charlotte when the latter regrets that the (first) visit of the Count and Baroness will expose her ward at too early an age—"so früh"—to an unsuitable example of social impropriety (I 9/305).[46] Even if not all her curious psychological symptoms are to be rationalistically derived from the unhappy fear of poverty accidentally instilled in her when newly orphaned, at least her anorexia nervosa is consistent with a fear that she might at some future time be in circumstances not permitting her to eat properly, can be a suppressed form of the fear that explains her humble helpfulness. Before her arrival at the manor her "große Mäßigkeit im Essen und Trinken," her "Dienstbarkeit," and her "Kopfweh" have been noted as disturbing in the headmistress' report on Luciane's good progress. Only the first of these, however, is again mentioned, presumably because her explanations of her humility have been taken at face value: when, soon after her arrival, Charlotte responsibly re-examines her school reports "Sie fand. . . nichts Neues, aber manches Bekannte ward ihr bedeutender und auffallender. So konnte ihr zum Beispiel Ottiliens Mäßigkeit im Essen und Trinken wirklich Sorge machen" (I 6/283).[47] Saints may die of anorexia nervosa, and—like Heathcliff—Eduard too when his life becomes empty of meaning; moderately well adjusted young women do not, and so it is to this disorder that the greatest significance is attached at the very start of the novel. Ottilie's headaches are diagnosed as curable (although the cure would be only of symptoms, not

---

[46] Even if the words "das gute, reine Kind" were not "erlebte Rede" of Charlotte but the narrator's—and so ultimately Goethe's—they do not represent highest ethical approval. The innocence of inexperience is all too dangerous (fatally for Margarete in *Faust*, whose Lord proclaims "Es irrt der Mensch solang' er strebt"), while purity can be merely a lack of vitality (cf. Wilhelm's observation in *Wilhelm Meisters theatralische Sendung*, Festausgabe 10:103, on what happens when "das Theater gereinigt wird": "Es scheint mir. . . , wie ein Teich zu sein, der nicht allein klares Wasser, sondern auch eine gewisse Portion von Schlamm, Seegras und Insekten enthalten muß, wenn Fische und Wasservögel sich darin wohl befinden sollen").

[47] Barnes 157 erroneously claims that "the narrator makes comparatively little of Ottilie's fasting in his account of her life at the mansion. [...] There are but three quite casual references to her by no means total abstention from food (II.17 and 18)." Although Barnes (23) rejects "the belief that Ottilie seeks her death," he later seems to label her death a suicide in the comment (202): "the close linking of suicide and sanctity must strike the reader as paradoxical." He claims (158) that "The references to her fasting. . . suggest that she feels the need, not to placate these powers [i.e., the "daemonic powers" that threaten "herself and those she loves"] since they are implacable (II.15), but to offer satisfaction in order to atone for her crime ('Verbrechen'; II.14), which only the death of the child could make her realize." (For Barnes, as for many English critics, Ottilie's crime seems to be that she has fallen in love with a married man.)

causes), her humility is explained, but what has been the symptom of the guiltless crime of being poor remains, even when its cause is known, because it becomes instead the ultimately fatal symptom of crimeless guilt for Otto's accidental death.

There is pathetic irony in Ottilie's helpless blindness to her own motives, in what Reinhard called the lack of "volles, helles Bewußtsein" in both "ihrem Wirken" and "ihrem Leiden." It appears nowhere with more childlike inconsistency than in her two renunciations of Eduard. "Gott hat mir die Augen geöffnet, in welchem Verbrechen ich befangen bin," she declares after her first self-condemnation for having cherished the hope of marrying Eduard and escaping poverty, then threatens the un-Christian act of suicide should Charlotte agree to a divorce and marry the Captain: "In dem Augenblick. . . büsse ich in demselbigen See [i.e., the lake in which she let Otto drown] mein Vergehen, mein Verbrechen" (II 14/462f.). And when she reiterates in writing her "Ich bin aus meiner Bahn geschritten," it is an incongruous expression of un-Christian despair to claim "ich soll nicht wieder hinein" because "ein feindseliger Dämon" seems to have taken possession of her. In the same letter, moreover, she announces her "Ordensgelübde" of silence and abstemiousness, which is tantamount to a renunciation of life, yet inconsistently adds a reassuring—this recalls her 'explanations' of her self-abasement and her servility—"Ich bin jung, die Jugend stellt sich unversehens wieder her" (II 16/476f.).

To speak, like von Wiese, of Ottilie's "Tragödie" (669) is thus proper only if it is recognized that her resolve to dedicate herself to "dem Heiligen" and diminish Eduard's passion by having him come to see her as "eine geweihte Person" (II 15/467) is tragic—and youthfully romantic—self-delusion. To interpret positively her renunciation of life—"damit die *Geisteskraft* noch über alle *Schwachheit* des Leibes triumphiere" (669)—is to endow her with a "Geisteskraft" that only she attributes to herself and is nowhere in the text (nor by Goethe elsewhere) ever attributed to her; is to read into the novel a transcendentalism irreconcilable with the fundamentally enlightened ethical Protestantism of its narrator and its author as well as with the latter's secular concept of tragedy. The most famous utterance credited to Ottilie's saintly namesake, "La vie solitaire est le principal moyen de la perfection," is alone so alien to the novel's concern with "sociale Verhältnisse" as to make untenable the inference that the parallel between her and Ottilie implies exemplariness.

That Ottilie does not typify for Goethe a high form of saintliness is evident from the contrast between her and the three "saints" depicted by him with personal sympathy in his works. The first, never sanctified, is the founder of the Medici line, Giovanni di Bicci, whom Goethe admires "als einen Heiligen; gute Gefühle, gute Handlungen sind bei ihm Natur. [...]

Unaufgefordert eilt er den Bedürfnissen anderer zu Hülfe, seine Milde, seine Wohltätigkeit erregen Wohlwollen und Freundschaft. . . ."[48] (Luciane has more of these qualities than Ottilie.) The second is St. Philip Neri, "der humoristische Heilige" whose life Goethe sketches in *Zweiter Römischer Aufenthalt*; as a young man he is not only devout and socially concerned, but also vigorous, enthusiastic, sociable, and aesthetically responsive, and after he is ordained we find in the humble priest, except in moments of mystic ecstasy and levitation, "zwar immer einen leidenschaftlich wundersamen, aber immer höchst verständig praktischen Mann" (HA 11:465) whose unconventionality is a major source of the effectiveness that in Goethe's eyes warrants his sanctification. (Vigor, humor, sociability, and the ability to have enthusiasms are not qualities Ottilie notably possesses.) The third is St. Roch, whom Goethe characterizes with clearly personal emphasis in his report of the sermon given by the venerable priest of "Sankt-Rochus-Fest zu Bingen," which stresses not only "unbedingte Ergebenheit in den Willen Gottes" but also selfless love of sacrifice for others (HA 10:424ff.). What most distinguishes this saint, and the two others, from Ottilie is an ability to rise above introspective self-concern, and so there is no substantiation for the view that although no real miracles occur in *Die Wahlverwandtschaften* "Goethe will offenbar auch bekennen, daß er in Ottilie alle Voraussetzungen erfüllt sieht, die zu einem Leben und einem Tod im Geiste der Acta sanctorum gehören: höchste Liebesinnigkeit, die Prüfung der Sünde und die Entsagung."[49] There is, rather, a stronger component of truth in the acerbic comment, "her end appears just as inconsiderate and as unloving as Werther's,"[50] however unreasonable it may be to expect the strength of will and degree of self-understanding even Werther possesses in a girl conditioned early in life to an abnormally passive role and tragically failing, largely though perhaps not exclusively because of fatal circumstances, to achieve mature adulthood.

Since for Goethe tragedy is not transcendental but human, is concerned with autonomous acts in psychological, social, and, in the broadest sense, moral contexts, what Goethe called a tragic novel cannot be a fate tragedy, a drama of fatal or "daemonic" coincidence, in narrative form. In *Die Wahl-*

---

[48] "Anhang zur Lebensbeschreibung des Benvenuto Cellini," WA I.44:343.

[49] Staiger 507. In none of Goethe's three cited accounts of "saints" is "Sünde" or its "Prüfung" mentioned; when Goethe does use *Sünde*, it most often has, as in *Faust*, l. 3384, the value "(destructive) consciousness of guilt" (cf. also the final paragraph of this essay).

[50] Ronald Gray, *Goethe: A Critical Introduction* (Cambridge: University Press, 1967) 224. Hans M.. Wolff, *Goethe in der Periode der Wahlverwandtschaften* (Bern: Francke, 1952) 212, interpreting Ottilie's death as "eine Anklage jener überstrengen Ethik, die ihr das Leben unerträglich gemacht hat," also draws attention to how "Indem sich Ottilie dem Gesetz opfert, opfert sie gleichzeitig ihre Freunde" and "vereitelt alle ihre Hoffnungen."

verwandtschaften tragedy ensues as the consequence of abdication of moral autonomy by Eduard—who in his clearest moment knows that it is "ein sträflicher Selbstbetrug" to hope or expect "daß der Zufall uns leiten und begünstigen solle" (II 12/450f.)—when under the sway of passion, but even more by Ottilie under the double constraint of poverty and an impoverished religion. The opening words of the novel, "Eduard—so nennen wir einen reichen Baron. . . ," are usually only taken to refer to the fact that Eduard, out of friendship for the Captain, has given up using the given name Otto which is also the latter's. But they also refer to the independent fortune that, because it is enough for several heirs, obviates an often important obstacle to divorce (II 12/448). Although Ottilie never consciously thinks of hope of marriage with Eduard as an escape from poverty until the child's death, this hope—and not, of course, the accidental death of the child who was the obstacle to the marriage—is the "Verbrechen," the violation of her childhood vow of humble poverty, to which she believes God has finally opened her eyes (II 14/463). But when walking earlier with the child in her arms about the manor, "verbarg sie sich nicht, zu welchem großen, reichen Zustande das Kind geboren sei; denn fast alles, wohin das Auge blickte, sollte dereinst ihm gehören," although in her adolescent idealism the child's welfare and his reconciliation of his parents inspires at the time a conviction "daß ihre Liebe, um sich zu vollenden, völlig uneigennützig werden müsse" (II 9/425). The fact that Ottilie knows what it is to be poor among the rich has led more than one interpreter of *Die Wahlverwandtschaften* to compare or contrast her with Jane Austen's Fanny Price;[51] that she so long lacks the "helles Bewußtsein" of what she knows is what makes *Die Wahlverwandtschaften* not simply a novel of manners but a tragic novel.

Despite Walter Benjamin, H.A. Korff, and the many others who have emphasized her inadequacies to a degree that is tantamount to hostile denigration of her character,[52] Ottilie is, as she is repeatedly called, a "Kind." To children adult standards do not apply, and in them faults must be

---

[51] *Mansfield Park* is mentioned by Peacock 341f., and by Jane K. Brown, *"Die Wahlverwandtschaften* and the English Novel of Manners," *CL* 28 (1976): 97–108.

[52] Cf. Caroline Snyder, "The Helmsman-Rescue Motif in Goethe's 'Die Wahlverwandt-schaften,' " *MfdU* 63 (1971): 41–47, and Patricia Drake, "Ottilie Revisited," *GQ* 26 (1953): 243–57; the latter oversimplifies in interpreting Ottilie's anorexia nervosa simply as "an extremely effective attention-getting device," although Ottilie's other behavior—especially her making herself seem almost indispensably useful to others—often seems to draw attention to herself deliberately. Whether or not Ottilie is simply compensating for "a sick sense of inadequacy" (Drake 251), her successful establishing of herself at the manor does demonstrate the truth of the Protestant-homiletic maxim with which she countered Luciane's taunts after failing her school examinations: "Es ist noch nicht der letzte Prüfungstag" (I 5/279).

tolerated that in mature persons would rightly call for severe disapprobation. This, and not condonement of Ottilie's foibles, explains both the forbearance with which Charlotte treats her even in moments of greatest stress or anguish and the kindly tone in which the narrator reports even her shortcomings. He notes, for instance, that after Eduard's departure she has become—it is as if she were sympathetically infected with his neuroticism— "klug, scharfsinnig, argwöhnisch," then objectively adds: "ohne es zu wissen" (I 17/348). He scrupulously records the beneficent effect of her abnormally unflagging helpfulness, and he never disparages (as a less liberal Protestant might) what is after all her merely physical attractiveness, noting that in the new styles Charlotte soon encourages her to adopt she becomes "den Männern, wie von Anfang so immer mehr. . . ein wahrer Augentrost" while also insisting by elaborate emblematic simile that 'a sight for sore eyes' is not ironically trite metaphor:

> Denn wie der Smaragd durch seine herrliche Farbe dem Gesicht wohltut, ja sogar einige Heilkraft an diesem edlen Sinn ausübt, so wirkt die menschliche Schönheit noch mit weit größerer Gewalt auf den äußern und innern Sinn. Wer sie erblickt, den kann nichts Übles anwehen; er fühlt sich mit sich selbst und mit der Welt in Übereinstimmung. (I 6/283)

The power to exert a harmonizing influence on others Ottilie never loses, but her inner disharmony already becomes "eine dunkle Fühllosigkeit" when she has learned during Eduard's long absence that he "sich dem wechselnden Kriegsglück überliefert habe." What enables her to escape, at least temporarily, from this neurotic apathy is her youthful ability to rise to the stresses created by Luciane's arrival:

> Es war daher, als wenn ein guter Geist für Ottilie gesorgt hätte, indem er. . . ein wildes Heer hereinbrachte, das, indem es ihr von außen genug zu schaffen gab und sie aus sich selbst führte, zugleich in ihr das Gefühl eigener Kräfte anregte. (II 4/376)

It is thus untrue that Luciane, as we are told for example by von Wiese, is simply a negative foil to "die himmlische Ruhe Ottiliens" (660), and what he calls "das Morbide, Unfromme, Künstliche [der] Gesellschaftsordnung" to which she belongs has a not unhealthy vitality. Her jealousy of Ottilie (II 6/402) is no admirable trait, and her efforts to perform good works are not always lasting in their results (II 5/386), although they are sometimes successful, as with the young officer who has lost his hand, sometimes disastrous, as with the young woman who has withdrawn from life because she is responsible for the death of a younger child in her family (I 6/399f.).

Nevertheless Charlotte, who in the late months of her pregnancy is anything but blinded by maternal love, "hatte. . . aus der Erfahrung, daß solche Personen [sc. as her somewhat eccentric daughter, a "seltsamer Charakter"], durch Leben. . . gebildet, eine sehr angenehme und liebenswürdige Reife erlangen können, indem die Selbstigkeit gemildert wird und die schwärmende Tätigkeit eine entschiedene Richtung erhält" (398f.).

These words or musings of an afflicted parent on what children may become when they have at last matured touch on a central, but too often ignored, theme of Goethe's thought which also is central in *Die Wahlverwandtschaften*. Even before Ottilie has come to the manor, Charlotte realistically interprets the headmistress' "Hymnen. . . über die Vortrefflichkeit eines solchen Kindes" as "Entschuldigung auf Entschuldigung, daß ein übrigens so schön heranwachsendes Mädchen sich nicht entwickeln. . . wolle" (I 2/251). The Assistant Headmaster, who is smitten with Ottilie's beauty, also glosses over her failure to develop normally, and hopefully interprets it as illustrating the principle that there are "verschlossene Früchte, die erst die rechten kernhaften sind, und die sich früher oder später zu einem schönen Leben entwickeln" (I 3/264). Charlotte's pregnancy, however, halts any development—"Ottilie, nachdem. . . ihr Charlottens Geheimnis bekannt geworden. . . , ging in sich zurück" (I 18/359)—and so, at the novel's dénouement, in a pose recalling the Belisarius tableau, the Architect ponders the dead Ottilie:

Auch hier war etwas unschätzbar Würdiges von seiner Höhe herabgestürzt; . . . [hier] waren soviel. . . stille Tugenden [the word has the older meaning *potential qualities, potentialities*], von der Natur erst kurz [i.e., recently, in connection with someone still relatively young] aus ihren gehaltreichen Tiefen hervorgerufen, durch ihre gleichgültige Hand schnell wieder ausgetilgt, seltene, schöne, liebenswürdige Tugenden, deren friedliche Einwirkung die bedürftige Welt zu jeder Zeit mit wonnevollem Genügen umfängt und mit sehnsüchtiger Trauer vermißt. (II 18/487f.)

The tragedy in *Die Wahlverwandtschaften*, and of Ottilie, is failure—as much the stunting of growth as consequent inability to summon up the moral strength to live maturely—to advance from one normal stage of development to the next, to complete what in "Metamorphose der Tiere" Goethe calls the "heiliger Kreis lebendiger Bildung" (HA 1:202). Although the novel's title is taken from the science of physical chemistry, there is as Goethe declared in his announcement "doch überall nur *eine* Natur" (620); what is metaphor for that science is truth in a biology whose fundamental principle is metamorphosis. The pathos of unfulfilled potential, of the inability to realize the imperative "Stirb und werde!" (HA 2:19), is heightened by the fact that, when she first resolved to renounce Eduard and remain a spinster (II 9/425), Ottilie herself had been vouchsafed a glimpse of this universal potential, had recorded in her diary: "Alles Vollkommene in seiner Art muß über seine Art hinausgehen, es muß etwas anderes, Unvergleichbares werden" (427). At the same time, her illustration of this insight with the nightingale and its song insists that this development or metamorphosis—this *Über-seine-Art-Hinausgehen*—takes place within a natural, not a transcendent, order.

Special significance is attached to Ottilie's diary entry by virtue of its position in the novel. It is the extension of four preceding, more specific observations on seasonal growth patterns that begin "So wiederholt sich denn abermals das Jahresmärchen von vorn" (426f.) and that reflect the thoughts, at the opening of the same chapter, of the manor's Gardener. When Ottilie seeks to console him for the damage wreaked by Luciane's lavish winter cutting of trees and potted plants, the narrator explains why it is in vain: "So wenig der Gärtner sich. . . zerstreuen darf, so wenig darf der ruhige Gang unterbrochen werden, den die Pflanze zur dauernden oder zur vorübergehenden Vollendung nimmt" (423). And the next chapter restates the point with the novella "Die wunderlichen Nachbarskinder," whose hero and heroine pass successfully through their adolescent crises and cheerfully embrace in the wedding clothes of the young couple who shelter them (II 10/441). "Die Kraft der Jugend und die Regsamkeit der Liebe stellten sie in wenigen Augenblicken völlig wieder her," comments the English lord's traveling companion matter-of-factly, for the point (or at least one point) of his story is that such crises, however 'wunderlich,' are stages of normal growth. For Ottilie, who lacks youthful resilience, and who is already badly shaken by Mittler's glosses on the commandment against adultery, Nanny's description of the finery she plans to wear on Eduard's birthday as "ein Brautschmuck, ganz Ihrer Wert" (II 18/483) is the *coup de grace*; she dies with her feet resting on Eduard's first present to her, the chest filled with unused items that, like the one dress she has made from its contents (480), symbolizes the pathos of hopes of life never fulfilled.

To recognize the significance of the theme of growth patterns is far more fruitful for understanding *Die Wahlverwandtschaften* than to speculate about "das Dämonische" or to seek to distinguish between its "Novelle" and "Roman" components. Over-concern with novella-like elements only diverts attention from the major theme of the only work Goethe actually subtitled "Ein Roman,"[53] and even obscures the fact that this theme is treated not—as it would be in a novella—simply in connection with the story of a

---

[53] See "*Wilhelm Meisters Lehrjahre*: Novel or Romance?" (in this volume).

threatened marriage, but also with reference to manners, ethics, landscape, music, acting, architecture, art, social pastimes, scientific and educational ideas, and socio-economic activities (social work, village betterment, estate improvement). If the novel is read as a novella, what Eduard in moral scrupulousness calls double adultery (II 13/455) usually becomes the "unerhörte [i.e., novel] Begebenheit" that for Goethe (663) and many others etymologically defines *Novelle*.[54] Such adultery—Geiler of Keisersberg defined it as "turpiter uxorem in actu carnali tractare, aut de alia non sua tractare"—is, however, so little 'unerhört' that it was a common theme in Renaissance (sermonizing) authors[55] and occurs at least twice before *Die Wahlverwandtschaften* in Goethe's literary writings.[56] Even less fruitful is to find novel or novellistic the re-pairing of two couples, a tired motif of novella—and pastoral comedy—that Wieland had made slightly less unnovel by reduplicating it in a short story (first published in 1803) about two couples whose four divorces are possible because of the liberalized laws of post-Revolutionary France.[57] As for a child's conception becoming the obstacle to a divorce (presumably with *adulteria* in Geiler's sense), it is also not *per se* a novella motif and is centrally important in Mme de Staël's *Delphine*, a novel Goethe read when it appeared in 1803.[58]

[54] Cf. von Wiese: "Die *unerhörte Begebenheit*. . . kann nur jene verhängnisvolle Nacht sein, in der das seltsame Kind gezeugt wird. . . . Paul Stöcklein hat den unerhörten 'Fall' als echtes Novellenthema gesehen" (664).

[55] Cf. Friedrich Zarncke, *Sebastian Brants Narrenschiff* (Leipzig, 1854) 368, who states, citing Geiler, "Ich vermuthe, dass im canonischen recht eine ähnliche stelle vorkommt, denn ich finde alss selbe verbrechen noch öfter auch bei andern schriftstellern erwähnt. Sicher kannte Goethe eine dieser stellen."

[56] Cf. the withheld epigram "Zürnet nicht, ihr Frauen, daß wir dies Mädchen bewundern: / Ihr genießet des Nachts, was sie am Abend erregt" (WA I.5,2:380), and Barbara's reassuringly intended question to Mariane in *Wilhelm Meisters Lehrjahre*, "Wer wehrt dir, in den Armen des einen an den andern zu denken?" (HA 7:46).

[57] "Freundschaft und Liebe auf der Probe," in *Taschenbuch auf das Jahr 1804* (Tübingen, 1803), ed. [C.M.] Wieland and [J.W. v.] Goethe—in Wieland's *Das Hexameron von Rosenhayn* (Leipzig, 1805) with the title "Liebe und Glück auf der Probe."

[58] The conception of a child by Léonce and his wife Mathilde prevents a planned divorce that would have permitted him to marry Delphine (Quatrième Partie, Lettre XXVII). Mme de Staël's *Corinne*, however, which Goethe also read on its appearance and of which—though it contained praise of himself—he observed that talent is needed "auch das, was nicht recht ist, hervorzubringen" (Br. 3:51), may have suggested the miniature of her father which Ottilie wears until she begins to reciprocate Eduard's love; its counterpart in *Corinne* symbolizes the major obstacle to Oswald Lord Nevil's marriage to Corinne: after recovering from his exhausting rescue of a man drowning in the bay of Naples, Oswald first begs Corinne's forgiveness for having given her cause to fear for his life, then his "second mouvement. . . fut de porter sa main sur sa poitrine, pour y retrouver le portrait de son père. . . . il était à peine reconnaissable. Oswald s'écria: Mon Dieu! vous m'enlevez donc jusques à son image" (Livre XIII, Chapître 7).

Although Goethe's earliest known reference to *Die Wahlverwandtschaf-ten*—"An den kleinen Erzählungen schematisirt, besonders den 'Wahlver-wandtschaften' und dem 'Mann von funfzig Jahren' "[59]—is usually taken to mean that the novel was originally planned as a novella and converted into a novel, this is irreconcilable with both his classical aesthetic and his classical practice.[60] From the time he and Schiller in their discussions and correspondence agreed on the classical principle that genres should ideally be kept distinct, Goethe conceived all his works with simultaneous reference to both theme and genre. As is indicated by the posthumously published maxim, "Bei jedem Kunstwerk, groß oder klein, bis ins Kleinste kommt alles auf die *Konzeption* an" (HA 12:482), this principle applies to every formal and substantive detail of a text, and when Goethe found it impossible to follow it, as was the case with the planned verse-tale *Die Jagd* (whose theme and motif he recognized, three decades after he had gotten nowhere with the work, were suitable for a prose-tale—his *Novelle*), he would abandon a project as ill-conceived. The classical ideal of harmony of form, style, and substance ("Gehalt") extends "bis ins Kleinste," so that what Goethe called the decorum of the milieu depicted in *Die Wahlverwandt-schaften* (622) is also mirrored both in the structure of the novel and in many of its rhetorical elements. On the level of rhetoric it serves the fundamental aim of achieving stylized naturalism, and it explains such textual features as the deliberate suppression of irrelevancies[61] and a normalization of diction which even transforms verse into the measured

---

[59] WA III.3:327 (11 April 1808). The next diary mention of the novel refers to its "erste Hälfte" (1 May); after four more mentions of planning (in May), Goethe begins on 1 June to dictate "Die zwei ersten Capitel" (ibid., 341). Goethe did not use chapter divisions in his novellas, and in all specific allusions to *Die Wahlverwandtschaften* employs the terms "Roman" or 'kleiner Roman' (cf. Br. 3:86: "So habe ich meine Gedanken auf kleine Romane. . . gewendet").

[60] E.g., von Wiese (663); Barnes 5: "Much that is mysterious in *Die Wahlverwandtschaf-ten* seems to derive from its original *Novelle* form" which "shares the strict economy of the drama"; Blackall 167 entitles his chapter "Novella into Novel" and seems to accept, p. 307, n. 1, Paul Hankamer's description of "the special structure of the finished work as growing out of the tension between the expansive tendencies characteristic of a novel and the swift and inexorable plot-movement that is characteristic of a novella (*Spiel der Mächte*, 5th ed., Stuttgart, 1960, p. 243)"; Hans M. Wolff, *Goethes "Die Wahlverwandtschaften": Ein Rekon-struktionsversuch* (Bern: Francke, 1955).

[61] We are thus not told how, during the Count's and Baroness' first visit, Charlotte changes the subject of conversation from trial marriage, or to what, but only that "In diesem Augenblick machte Charlotte, die ein für allemal dies Gespräch abbrechen wollte, von einer kühnen Wendung Gebrauch; es gelang ihr" (I 10/313). (This technique is deliberately undramatic.)

prose used for narrative, dialogue, and reflective commentary.[62] Despite
René Wellek's claim that *Die Wahlverwandtschaften* illustrates Goethe's
"late, pompous, and involved manner,"[63] in clarity its diction is no less
exemplary than the meticulous verisimilitude with which every detail of
motivation and milieu is recorded. Conscious classicization appears chiefly
in the use of set epithet—in ironic passages a device especially confusing
for the unwary reader[64]—and of the euphuistic vocabulary of enlightened
Protestantism,[65] although it may also be evident in the use of sententious
observation as a means of generalizing (giving larger significance to)
psychological motives, a device that recalls the French classical novel.[66]

[62] Although it is said that at the *Richtfest* the young mason "hielt in Reimen eine
anmutige Rede, die wir in Prosa nur unvollkommen wiedergeben können" (I 9/299), given
Goethe's facility with such Poetry for Occasions—e.g., "Die ersten Erzeugnisse der
Stotternheimer Saline, begleitet von dichterischen Dialogen zwischen dem Gnomen, der
Geognosie und der Technik, überreicht zum 30. Januar 1828 mit getrostem Glück auf! C.
Glenck, Salinendirektor, untertänigst"—it is obvious that "können" is fictive for 'wollen.' In
his more romance-like Wilhelm Meister novels Goethe allows himself the introduction of
lyric and other kinds of verse.

[63] René Wellek and Austin Warren, *Theory of Literature*, 3rd ed. (New York: Harcourt
Brace, 1956) 181.

[64] In addition to the regular association with Ottilie of the epithets 'herrlich,' 'himmlisch,'
'gut,' and 'lieb,' there is also 'schön,' which is transferred to her "Gemüt" when she is
becalmed on the lake after pulling the dead child into her boat: "auch hier läßt ihr schönes
Gemüt sie nicht hülflos. Sie wendet sich nach oben. . . . Auch wendet sie sich nicht
vergebens zu den Sternen, die schon einzeln hervorzublinken anfangen. Ein sanfter Wind
erhebt sich und treibt den Kahn nach den Platanen" (II 13/457f.). (The drop in temperature
at nightfall, not Ottilie's "Gemüt," raises the breeze that brings her back to land.) Goethe
repeatedly expressed scorn of "Gemüt": "Ohne Umschweife / Begreift, / Was dich mit der
Welt entzweit: / Nicht will sie Gemüt, will Höflichkeit" ("Sprichwörtlich," [1815], ll. 578–81
= Festausgabe 2:60); "Gemüt wird über Geist gesetzt, Naturell über Kunst, und so ist der
Fähige wie der Unfähige gewonnen. Gemüt hat jedermann, Naturell mehrere; der Geist ist
selten, die Kunst ist schwer" ("Letzte Kunstausstellung. 1805," HA 12:129); "jetzt heißt es
[i.e., Gemüt] nur: Nachsicht mit Schwächen, eignen und fremden" (HA 12:386).

[65] In addition to Ottilie's use of "Dämon" for the more sectarian word *Teufel* there is a
noticeable avoidance of 'God'—the narrator uses for example the periphrasis "ein höheres
Wesen" (I 13/331)—in serious discussions, even of religious matters (e.g., Charlotte's
already cited "alles Heilige" and the narrator's "nach oben," n. 64, above); the most striking
avoidance of Christian terminology, however, occurs in a sentence omitted in n. 64: "Mit
feuchtem Blick sieht sie empor und ruft Hülfe von daher, wo ein zartes Herz die größte
Fülle zu finden hofft, wenn es überall [i.e., completely] mangelt" (II 13/458)—here "Fülle"
is a neutral equivalent of *Gnade*.

[66] Cf. the beginning of a paragraph in Madame de La Fayette, *La Princesse de Clèves*
(Paris: Tallandier, 1925) 1:25: "Les personnes galantes sont toujours bien aises qu'un
prétexte leur donne lieu de parler à ceux qui les aiment. Sitôt que le vidame eut quitté
Madame la dauphine. . . ."

Dramatic elements are subordinated to a deliberately epic tone in accordance with the principles of Goethe's and Schiller's essay "Über epische und dramatische Dichtung" (HA 12:249ff.), and an unhurried, steadily progressive mode of narration[67] serves to minimize drama-like effects in passages of dialogue (speeches, however, are legitimate epic devices) or in climactic episodes. This last principle is sustained with such rigor that when there is a moment of concentrated, eventful external action—examples are: the *Richtfest*; the day of the encounter of Eduard and Ottilie that ends with Otto's death and is followed by her revelation of the motives behind what has always seemed her innately agreeable behavior; the day of Ottilie's death—the pages suddenly become packed with narrative detail and as it were visibly mirror the intensity of such a climax. The almost always preannounced appearance (prepared entrances) of characters recalls neoclassical drama, and theater practice in general when accompanied by description of significant gesture or mode of conduct, but the technique actually serves to minimize theatricality (surprise elements) in a plot so tightly knit as to resemble that of a nineteenth-century *pièce bien faite*.[68] Retrospective exposition is used with epic restraint,[69] but as in

---

[67] Cf. Goethe's criticism to Schiller (letter of 3 Feb. 1798) of Caroline von Wolzogen's novel *Agnes von Lilien*: "Die summarische Manier, in der die Geschichte vorgetragen ist und die, gleichsam in einem springenden Tact, rhythmisch eintretenden Reflexionen lassen einen nicht einen Augenblick zur Behaglichkeit kommen, und man wird hastig ohne Interesse." (Blackall does not discuss Goethe's many revealing comments on *Agnes von Lilien* in his correspondence with Schiller.)

[68] Marahrens 115 notes that the only (main) character introduced by the narrator himself is Eduard, and that the coming of all others is announced before they appear. (He could have added that the narrator also motivates and announces beforehand all exits and departures.) That meticulously verisimilar motivation is "untheatrical," that a work true to life—and hence this novel too—cannot be in the vulgar sense "theatrical," is one point of the Count's disparaging reference to the theater ("Komödie") as a place where happy marriage is the ending of comedies that falsify reality (I 10/309); it is to such carelessly constructed and motivated plays that allusion is also made in Ottilie's diary entry "Ein Leben ohne Liebe. . . ist nur eine 'Comédie à tiroir'. . ." (II 10/427).

[69] The dramatic device of depicting two simultaneous actions in one scene (as in the first garden scene of *Faust I*) is avoided. Marahrens 111 gives as examples of "simultaneous happening" subsequently reported "Luciane's engagement: II, 4:153, conversations with Mittler and the Major: II 15:252, Nanny's disappearance: II 18:269," but there are many others—e.g., Charlotte's morning conversation with the Baroness (I 10/315) follows evening discussions of trial marriage and other topics, and Luciane's disastrous failure with the girl who is guilt-stricken because of her responsibility for a younger sibling's death is related only when, after Luciane's departure, the girl's aggravated condition has necessitated her institutionalization (II 6/399f.). The most striking avoidance of simultaneous exposition, however, is that Eduard's declaration of love to Ottilie (I 12/324) comes during the account of the two couples' walk, while the Captain's embrace of Charlotte (326) is reported in Charlotte's after-supper recollections of "was diesen Abend zwischen ihr und dem

the epic unity of place is discretionary (rather than absolute[70]) in that almost all the action takes place on parts of Eduard's estates, although a few episodes and most retrospective scenes have other settings—the boarding school, the palace, the inn, etc. Also epic-like, rather than theatrical, is the use of both serious and comic irony, a combination that helps counter any effect of sentimental, tragicomic, or melodramatic theatricality. Although humor—"Der Humor ist eins der Elemente des Genies, aber, sobald er vorwaltet, nur ein Surrogat desselben" (HA 12:472)[71]—is used decorously, it is healthily evident, serving also to provide the breadth of perspective and variety of tone which are features of the novel rather than of novella or drama.

Over-attention to novellistic details leads back to reading *Die Wahlver-wandtschaften* as an "Eheroman," even by those who insist that marriage is merely an occasion for social criticism;[72] but if the theme of the novel were marriage, Ottilie's return to the manor, which excludes all further hope of

---

Hauptmann vorgegangen war" (324).

[70] Although Marahrens 105ff. seems to accept the common opinion "that the narrator of *Die Wahlverwandtschaften* adheres as strictly as a playwright to the Aristotelian unities," his careful analysis demonstrates only that the novel has what he calls "a unilinear plot." Fink 438f., whose thesis is that the novel is post-classical and its classicism hence largely "vordergründig," explains unity of place—he finds this violated only in I 18 and in II 12 and 16—as the consequence of a "Streben nach klassizistischer Vereinfachung."

[71] The maxim is from the 1829 version of *Wilhelm Meisters Wanderjahre*. Jürgen Kolbe, "Die 'Wahlverwandtschaften' und die Romane Fontanes" [chapter 9 of his *Goethes 'Wahlver-wandtschaften' und der Roman des 19. Jahrhunderts* (Stuttgart: Kohlhammer, 1968)], in Rösch 408, claims that "das Komische" is completely lacking in Goethe's novel, while Stöcklein, "Stil und Geist der 'Wahlverwandtschaften,' " in Rösch 230, speaks only of "der versteckte Humor des Erzählers" which is "manchmal grimmig." Apart from the puns and many *bons mots* of its characters and its narrator, the novel contains a goodly number of straightforwardly humorous moments; examples are: Mittler's ridiculous tirade at being asked to give advice on so minor a matter as inviting the Captain and Ottilie to the manor (I 2/255f.); Eduard's belief that a silent Ottilie has been "unterhaltend"; the Architect's populating of the chapel ceiling with beings whose faces "fingen sämtlich an, Ottilien zu gleichen" (II 3/372), although even the best likeness is still only—note the use of a diminutive, rare in this text—a "Gesichtchen"; the distress of the pianist playing a funeral march who begins to run out of modulations because the Architect takes so long to sketch the tomb of Mausolus while Luciane stands impatiently as Artemesia (II 4/381); the shout "Tournez s'il vous plaît" when Luciane poses in the tableau after Terborch (II 5/394); Mittler's long-windedness and tactlessness—here the humor is also "grimmig"—at the baptism of the child (II 8/422); the gardener's dissatisfaction with botanical novelties pushed by nursery owners (II 9/424); and Nanny's naive conviction that her vision of Ottilie has been seen and heard by all (II 18/486).

[72] E.g., von Wiese (655), who nevertheless then discusses the marriage theme as if it were centrally important (659–61).

divorce, would be the end of the action.[73] Although Goethe, in an often adduced letter, wrote a Catholic admirer "Der sehr einfache Text dieses weitläufigen Büchleins sind die Worte Christi, 'Wer ein Weib ansieht, ihrer zu begehren pp.,' " he did so only after asserting that the true poet seeks solely to show "das Gefährliche der Gesinnung an den Folgen. . ." (625).[74] The correctives to this simplification are Goethe's statement of 1809 to Riemer that "Der Kampf des Sittlichen eignet sich niemals zu einer ästhetischen Darstellung" (623); his declaration to Georg Christian Müller that the novel demonstrates "wohin er [i.e., der Mensch] durch das natürliche Triebwerk eines zwar unverdorbenen, aber nicht sittlich geschützten Herzens geleitet wird";[75] and the wry confession to Zelter, in a letter of 1830, that he has no illusion that "irgend ein hübscher Mann könne dadurch [i.e., because of the novel's cathartic ending] von dem Gelüst, nach eines Andern Weib zu blicken, gereinigt werden" (626). By virtue of the innocence of inexperience Ottilie is 'unverdorben,' but for the same reason she is not 'sittlich geschützt' and with childlike inconsistency can support her Christian resolve to atone ("büßen") the crime she believes God has let her recognize by threatening to expiate ("In dem Augenblick. . . büße ich") her "Vergehen" and "Verbrechen" by suicide in the very lake in which Otto died (II 14/463).

The three other main figures of the novel, who all are in greater or less degree 'sittlich geschützt' (even Eduard never considers the possibility of an extra-marital liaison), are rendered helpless by Ottilie's disproportionate sense of guilt, and when it has been fatally aggravated by her hearing Mittler's interpretation of "Du sollst nicht ehebrechen" as "Du sollst Ehrfurcht haben vor der ehelichen Verbindung," she herself is its first victim. At this point, however, she enters too late to hear what is far more applicable to her exaggerated guilt feelings, Mittler's introductory comments on why he finds "ganz abscheulich" a Commandment that can "Die Neugierde vorahnender Kinder auf gefährliche Mysterien reizen, ihre Einbildungskraft zu wunderlichen Bildern und Vorstellungen aufregen, die gerade das, was man entfernen will, mit Gewalt heranbringen" (II 18/482). Destructive

[73] This point seems to be made only by Giuseppe Gabetti, *Le "Affinità elettive" del Goethe come espressione di una crisi pessimistica* (Milano: Lombardo, 1914) 99.

[74] Goethe is thanking an Augustinian canon, J.S. Zauper, for defending him from often made charges that his works demonstrate a lack of moral concern: "Zunächst aber sollen Sie gelobt sein, daß Sie des Dichters sittliche Tendenz und Verfahrungsweise so gut ins Licht setzen" (Br. 4:8); the letter has long been recognized as a "bewußt 'katholisierende Antwort' "—K.R. Mandelkow (Br. 4:522)—and is for example so interpreted by Peacock 332.

[75] G.C. [or B.] Müller ("Prediger in Neumark bei Zwikkau"), *Zwey Bücher vom Wahren und Gewissen* (Leipzig: Lehnhold, 1822) 213, cited *Jb. S. Kipp.* 4 (1924): 326.

feelings of guilt are far more important in *Die Wahlverwandtschaften* than any demonstration that "in this life. . . the sanctity of marriage is absolute,"[76] which is why the Count and Baroness can finally regularize their relationship happily, and why there is never a suggestion that, without Ottilie's moral scruples as intensified by naive religious beliefs, the divorce to which Charlotte consents after Otto's death is an unreasonable way to end a hopeless unhappiness. What Schiller wrote Goethe about "das Pathetische im Schicksal Mignons und des Harfenspielers" is also—as Wieland implied by asking "wie sollen wir nicht merken, daß diese *Ottilie* nur eine neue Auflage, oder vielmehr die Carricatur einer Kopie seiner [i.e., Goethe's] Mignon. . . ist. . . ?"[77]—applicable to Ottilie: "Nur im Schoß des dummen Aberglaubens werden diese monstrosen Schicksale ausgeheckt" (HA 7:629). That this was Goethe's tacit stance in *Die Wahlverwandtschaften* intelligent Christian readers immediately sensed, and it explains the hostile reactions of Fritz Jacobi, Jacobi's sisters, and Thümmel (644f.). Carl Ernst Schubarth, however, whose humanistic interpretations of his works Goethe approved, recognized that in the novel is represented the threat "daß das Gefühl und Bewußtsein von der Gottheit und dem Göttlichen für den Menschen. . . verderblich werde, ihn verwüste und zerstöre," although he perhaps somewhat naively assumed that it could be warded off simply by "Übung der Tugend und höchsten Pflicht" (653). Goethe, who much earlier had depicted in *Der Großkophta* the consequences of innocent credulity, had long been less optimistic and by not later than the early 1790's had begun to lament (as he would still in *Dichtung und Wahrheit*) "Die Beschränktheit worin die Menschen leben" which makes mortals vulnerable to "die Sehnsucht. . . nach fernen, unechten, unvernünftigen Mitteln."[78]

In view of the fact that Goethe's moral and psychological skepticism (not to say pessimism) is not new when he writes *Die Wahlverwandtschaften*, Gonthier-Louis Fink's question "Inwiefern spiegelt er [i.e., the novel] noch die Harmonie der Welt?"[79] is relevant only to the false assumptions that the novel no longer represents Goethe's classicism and that such classicism represents a shallow optimism. Significantly, however, the critique of his

[76] Henry Hatfield, *Goethe: A Critical Introduction* (Norfolk, Conn.: New Directions, 1963) 105f. The statement seems inconsistent with evidence Hatfield marshals in the article cited above, n. 44.

[77] Albert R. Schmitt, "Wielands Urteil über Goethes 'Wahlverwandtschaften,' " *JDSG* 11 (1967): 54, notes that the same charge was brought against Goethe by A.W. Rehberg in a review of the novel published in *Allg. Lit.-Zeitung*, 1. Jan. 1810.

[78] From manuscript notes on the Contra-Talmudist Jakob Frank, *Goethe-Jb.* 48 (1928): 100; for similar sentiments—some in the text of *Die Wahlverwandtschaften*—cf. n. 33, above.

[79] Fink 438.

newly published novel to which Goethe responded most warmly—"Ich danke Ihnen dafür auf das herzlichste" (Br. 3:115)—was that of Rochlitz, who declared that "classische Gediegenheit, Rundung, Sicherheit und Harmonie" effectively made *Die Wahlverwandtschaften* the most perfect of Goethe's narrative works (640). It is still the author of *Faust* and *Wilhelm Meisters Lehrjahre* who resignedly observes in 1826, "Wie in Rom außer den Römern noch ein Volk von Statuen war, so ist außer dieser realen Welt noch eine Welt des Wahns, viel mächtiger beinahe, in der die meisten leben" (HA 12:520). But it is also the author of *Winckelmann*, the Goethe who in 1805 asked in all seriousness, "wozu dient alle der Aufwand von Sonnen und Planeten und Monden, von Sternen und Milchstraßen und Nebelflecken, von gewordenen und werdenden Menschen, wenn sich nicht zuletzt ein glücklicher Mensch unbewußt seines Daseins erfreut?" (HA 12:98). When referring to *Die Wahlverwandtschaften* Goethe rarely used such impatient phrases as Schiller's "(der) Schoß des dummen Aberglaubens" (although he published his and Schiller's not always discreet correspondence), but his ironic questions to General von Rühle—"Ich heidnisch? Nun, ich habe doch Gretchen hinrichten und Ottilien verhungern lassen, ist das den Leuten nicht christlich genug?" (623)—reveal the impatience of a humanism taxed to its limits.

Although Wieland was not to remain an unqualified admirer of *Die Wahlverwandtschaften*,[80] his earliest recorded reaction—he was seventy-seven at the time—indicates that he, at least, understood it:

> Mir schauderte innerlich davor, daß ein so reines und unschuldiges *Kind* als diese Ottilie so verstrickt werden konnte. . . . Er [i.e., Goethe] schildert ihn [i.e., Eduard] *wie alle übrigen Personen* mit allen Mängeln und Gebrechen und allen liebenswürdigen Eigenschaften. . . und ich gestehe. . . , daß ich dieses wirklich schauerliche Werk nicht ohne warmen Anteil zu nehmen gelesen habe. (647f.—emphases added)

Schiller, the moral conclusion of whose *Die Braut von Messina* insists that the greatest human evil is a destructive sense of guilt, could also have found 'horrifying' the fatal introversion of so promising a 'child' as Ottilie—though with perhaps still undiminished intolerance of the specific form of 'superstition' on which the blame for that introversion is, albeit with decorous discreetness, in large part placed. Wieland seems to have recognized, like Solger, that what is centrally important in the novel is an innocence of immaturity and of that fatally stunted growth to which Solger's "diese reine *verschlossene* Knospe" (638—emphasis added) alludes. The failure of

---

[80] Cf. Schmitt 47–61, who reproduces all of Wieland's comments on the novel.

potential becomes the novel's irremediably tragic dénouement—Knebel asked rhetorically, "Was soll ich. . . sagen. . . zu der schaurigen Ruhe, zu der die Geschichte gegen das Ende steigt?"[81]—and is the ultimate explanation of the 'Erschütterung' or 'Ergriffenheit' to which Wieland, Rochlitz (639), Caroline von Wolzogen (643), and so many contemporary readers testified. 'Schauerlich,' however, most exactly describes the sense that Goethe's novel conveys of the forces—religious, social, ethical, emotional, psychological, and physical—that limit human freedom. And by virtue of its unemphatic but always significant verisimilitude it is a more awesomely tragic work than the story of Werther's fatalistic apathy, than the tragedy of Egmont's idealistic confidence, and than the tragic episode of a Gretchen who, however disproportionate *her* sense of guilt, achieves a recognizable measure of adult moral autonomy.

---

[81] *Briefwechsel zwischen Goethe und Knebel* (Leipzig, 1851) 1:358—cited in Hans Gerhard Gräf, *Goethe über seine Dichtungen*, 1. Teil, I (Darmstadt: Wissenschaftliche Buchgesellschaft, 1968) 415.

Italienische Reise and Goethean Classicism

G oethe's first visit to Italy is an essential part of his biography, and his *Italienische Reise*[1] its major record. In both popular and scholarly treatments of Goethe, whether or not these grant either the visit or his account of it the significance he attached to them,[2] "italienische Reise" is often equated with *Italienische Reise* or distinguished from it so slightly as to suggest that differentiation between the one and the other is unimportant.[3] The *Reise*, however, a mosaic of writing from over forty years

---

[1] The "Ausgabe letzter Hand" volumes *Italiänische Reise. I, Italiänische Reise. II*, and *Zweyter Römischer Aufenthalt von Juny 1787 bis April 1788* ("Zweyter Aufenthalt in Rom") are here called *(Italienische) Reise*; when separate mention is necessary, *Zweiter Römischer Aufenthalt* will be referred to as *Reise III*, and the first two volumes as *Reise I–II* or *Reise I* and *Reise II*.

[2] George Henry Lewes, *The Life of Goethe*, 3rd ed. (London, 1875) 296: "in the decline of his great powers he collected the hasty letters sent from Italy. . . and from them he extracted such passages as seemed suitable, weaving them together with no great care or enthusiasm"; in 1935 E.M. Butler was hardly more positive (cf. *The Tyranny of Greece over Germany* [Boston, 1958] 105f).

[3] Friedrich Gundolf treats Goethe's Italian sojourn at length, but devotes only a brief paragraph to the *Reise* (*Goethe* [Berlin, 1930] 637f.,); in *Goethe, 1786–1814* (Zürich, 1956), Emil Staiger discusses the *Reise* almost solely with reference to Goethe's first trip to Italy; and Richard M. Meyer, *Goethe* (Berlin, 1895) 417 writes of the first three parts of *"Dichtung und Wahrheit* (1811 bis 1814), denen sich bald die 'Italienische Reise' anschließt," "bald" being subsequently explained as March, 1816, publication date of *Reise I*. (Meyer's final reference to the *Reise* is typical of the liberties of chronology that biographers and others allow themselves. Discussing Goethe's historical thought, Meyer quotes a maxim from *Reise II* and comments, p. 588: "eben damals, als Goethe in Italien dieser Wahrheit Ausdruck gab, sprach Iphigenie die Worte: 'Es erzeugt nicht gleich / Ein Haus den Halbgott noch das Ungeheuer; / Erst eine Reihe Böser oder Guter / Bringt endlich das Entsetzen, bringt die Freude / Der Welt hervor.' " Iphigenie's words versify a prose formulation of 1779, and the maxim under the date "Palermo. . . den 9. April 1787"—over four months after Goethe finished with *Iphigenie*—could have been written in the mid-1810's.) Similarly, in *Goethe, a Critical Introduction* (Cambridge, 1967), Ronald Gray treats the *Reise* ("begun 1813") only as one of a series of works of self-record that runs from *Dichtung und Wahrheit* via *Annalen* and *Italienische Reise*—in this order—to Eckermann's *Gespräche mit Goethe*; in Liselotte Dieckmann's *Johann Wolfgang Goethe* (New York, 1974) 23 "the Italian journey, . . . written in 1814–1816," precedes *Dichtung und Wahrheit*, "written rather rapidly, in 1822–1823," and (p. 185, n. 4) is "published in 1817"; Horst Althaus, "Goethes

$(1789-1829^4)$, is a work usable only with caution to illustrate Goethe's development as poet or thinker, and it is to heighten awareness of this that I offer the following observations.[5]

Classicism—and Primitivism

"Goethes Kunstschriften. . . der mittleren Zeit (1788–1805) setzen die italienische Wandlung voraus. Man muß die *Italienische Reise* gelesen haben, um sie in ihrer Haltung und Zielsetzung verstehen und würdigen zu können."[6] The *Reise*, then, should answer many questions, including whether Goethe's Italian and post-Italian classicism was a slight variant of eighteenth-century neoclassicism, or represented a distinctive position properly labeled "(Deutsche) Klassik." Moreover, since it includes material written long after 1805, it should also help decide whether this classicism (or neoclassicism) subsequently underwent radical modifications—whether it is proper, for example, to discern a "gegenklassische Wandlung" in Goethe's writing after Schiller's death or beginning with *West-östlicher Divan* and the interest in early German painting aroused in 1815 by Goethe's knowledge of the Boisserée collection. Although to distinguish satisfactorily between neoclassicism and "Klassik" must be beyond the scope of a short essay, the *Reise* can afford evidence both of what the classicism was with which Goethe was imbued in Italy in 1786–1788 (and perhaps before Italy) and of how he subsequently regarded or adhered to that classicism.

'römisches Sehen,' " in his *Ästhetik, Ökonomie und Gesellschaft* (Bern, 1971) 160, gives 1819 as the date of *Reise III*; and Arthur R. Schultz, "Goethe and the Literature of Travel," *JEGP* 48 (1949): 452 states that the *Reise* was "prepared for printing in 1813." The simple confusion of "Reise" and *Reise* is nicely illustrated by Heinrich Meyer, *Goethe: Das Leben im Werk* (Hamburg-Bergedorf, 1951) 355f.: "Goethes 'Italienische Reise' und die während derselben geschriebenen Briefe."

[4] This time span is surpassed only by that of *Faust*; *Dichtung und Wahrheit* occupied Goethe from 1809 to 1831, and *Campagne in Frankreich 1792* and *Belagerung von Main* together from 1792 through 1822. (Comparable dates for *Wilhelm Meisters Lehrjahre* and the *Wanderjahre* are 1777–1796 and 1807–1829.) It is never stressed that *Reise III* was composed by the Goethe of *Faust II* and the final version of *Wilhelm Meisters Wanderjahre*, although *Reise I–II* is often related to Goethe's interest in autobiography and the concerns of *Über Kunst und Altertum*.

[5] Most introductions to editions of the *Reise* adequately explain its genesis and composition—exemplary is Herbert von Einem on " Die Veröffentlichung" in HA 11:572–77 (München, 1974—8. Aufl.)—but the implications of their information (except for Goethe's interest in his own past) are usually developed only in connection with *Reise I–II*.

[6] H. von Einem, HA 12:574 (München, 1973—7. Aufl.).

In the same year as *Reise II* Goethe published Heinrich Meyer's *Neu-deutsche religios-patriotische Kunst*—its concluding paragraphs are by Goethe—as a reaffirmation of his classicism, and von Einem observes:

> Beide Schriften muß man also zusammen sehen. Seine italienischen Bekenntnisse hatten für ihn nicht nur historischen, sie hatten Gegenwartswert. Zugleich lag ihm daran, in der Darstellung seines Ringens noch einmal die Lebenstiefe und Bedeutung der Idee des Klassischen sichtbar zu machen. So gewann die *Italienische Reise* programmatischen Charakter.[7]

But *Reise III* also reaffirms Goethe's classicism. In a passage of retrospective narrative probably written in 1828 (and not singled out by von Einem for commentary[8]) Goethe, recalling how the Sistine Chapel—and the Vatican *Stanze*—provided refuge from the heat of August, 1787, records:

> . . . es wurde Mode, zu streiten, ob er [Michelangelo] oder Raffael mehr Genie gehabt. Die Transfiguration des letzteren wurde mitunter sehr streng getadelt und die Disputa das beste seiner Werke genannt; wodurch sich denn schon die später aufgekommene Vorliebe für Werke der alten Schule ankündigte, welche der stille Beobachter [Goethe] nur für ein Symptom halber und unfreier Talente betrachten. . . konnte.[9]

The *Disputa* (1508), the first work Raphael executed in the *Stanze*, has quattrocento elements or features, does not yet represent the High Renaissance style Goethe most admired (e.g., in *The Transfiguration*, a work whose unity he subsequently argues in "Bericht. Dezember [1787]"), and so Goethe's account is not, as it might at first seem, intended to warn against overenthusiasm for Michelangelo (less to neoclassical taste than Raphael[10]), but against the use of Raphael in the behalf of a romantic cult of the pre-classical.[11]

---

[7] HA 11:577. H. Meyer, *Goethe: Das Leben im Werk* (n. 3 above) 359, though interpreting Goethe's (neo)classicism less positively, insists that Goethe's art theory underwent no significant modifications after Italy.

[8] To the art historian the implications were obvious, but Robert Weber (Festausgabe 17: 642) helpfully noted: "Worte. . . gerichtet gegen die späteren jungdeutschen Maler in Rom, die sog. 'Nazarener.' "

[9] HA 11:389f.

[10] The ultimately negative value that *maniera* acquired (cf. Bellori, Malvasia, Mengs, etc.) had led to widespread neoclassical depreciation of Michelangelo in the 18th century.

[11] Cf. Madame de Staël's Corinne (*Corinne, ou l'Italie*, Livre VIII, Ch. 3): "Elle admirait la composition sans artifice des tableaux de Raphaël, surtout dans sa première manière."

If by classicism is meant not simply Graeco-Roman revival but that "néo-humanisme cosmopolite" whose interest *inter alia* embraced Egyptian and Etruscan antiquities,[12] then the term adequately reflects the breadth of Goethe's artistic interests while in Italy.[13] But it is a commonplace—to which Goethe himself lent support by the importance he attached to having seen, in his last weeks in Rome, as much ancient sculpture (and casts of such sculpture) as possible[14]—that his Italian classicism was primarily oriented to Graeco-Roman art, was narrowly Winckelmannian. Yet he also revisited the Borghese Gallery in anticipation of his imminent departure ("1. März [1788]"), and in the *Reise* as a whole art of the Renaissance receives at least twice as much attention—by number of references to it—as that of antiquity.[15] At the end of *Reise III* Goethe's account of his interest in sculpture may thus be less a reaffirmation of Winckelmannian classicism than a last countering of Romantic transcendentalism like that of Mme. de Staël's Friedrich-Schlegelian Corinne, who "disait que la sculpture était l'art du paganisme" (*Corinne, ou l'Italie*, Liv. VIII, Ch. 3). In Rome, however, his interest represented awareness that, unlike paintings, of which by the standards of the time moderately adequate copies existed, classical sculpture and other monuments had to be seen *in situ* and engraved firmly on the visual memory if adequate impressions of them were to be retained for years to come.

Thus *Reise III*, though it differs from *Reise I–II* in the greater use of interpolated documents and sustained passages of narrative, still faithfully records Goethe's Italian experiences and attitudes,[16] and Goethe, writing to

[12] René Michéa, Le "Voyage en Italie" de Goethe (Paris, 1954) 279. For the importance of neoclassicism as an expression of eighteenth-century anti-transcendental secularism cf. von Einem, HA 12:556, who cites Peter Cornelius's condemnation of the late Raphael's secularism.

[13] The account of L.-F. Cassas' drawings of Middle Eastern monuments ("Bericht. September [1787]") is the most striking expression of this breadth of interests; in it items not reproduced in Cassas' Voyage pittoresque. . . (Paris, 1799)—cf. von Einem, HA 11:655—are described, which indicates that it accurately records an Italian, not a later, response to them.

[14] "Bericht, April [1788]" (composed with Heinrich Meyer's help, August, 1829).

[15] For the equal importance to Goethe of Graeco-Roman monuments and Renaissance paintings cf. his letter (7 December 1795) acknowledging Lichtenberg's gift of early fascicles of Ausführliche Erklärung der Hogarthischen Kupferstiche: "Ich leugne nicht daß eine anhaltende Betrachtung der Kunstwerke, die uns das Altertum und die Römische Schule zurückgelassen haben, nicht der neuern Art, die mehr zum Verstande als zu der gebildeten Sinnlichkeit spricht, einigermaßen entfernt hat. . . ."

[16] Cf. Melitta Gerhard, "Die Redaktion der 'Italienischen Reise' im Lichte von Goethes autobiographischem Gesamtwerk," JbFDtHochst., 1930: 131–50 on the use of "Berichte" in Reise III to heighten an effect of objectivity already intended in Reise I–II, and on revisions

Göttling 8 November 1828, could rightly claim that in it was to be seen "wie. . . der Grund meines ganzen nachherigen Lebens sich befestigt und gestaltet hat." Goethe's statement insists that, to the best of his own knowledge and belief, he had by the end of his Italian sojourn established the basic values to which he would henceforth adhere—values no doubt modified or refined by subsequently acquired knowledge and experience, but not repudiated in the course of some "gegenklassische Wandlung."[17] It also draws attention to the easily ignored fact that his "klassisches Weltbild, noch mehr sein klassischer Stil,"[18] did not—as is often implied[9] —evolve solely in Italy.

To the pre-Italian forms of Goethe's classicism that extended back to his youth and were probably first "befestigt" by Oeser in Leipzig,[20] Michéa, Kohlschmidt, von Einem, and others have variously drawn attention,[21] and Robert Weber goes so far as to imply that no change in Goethe's "Kunstanschauungen" is revealed by the *Reise*: "Es ist der Geist der *klassischen*

of and deletions from earlier documents that permit concentration, without biographical or historical distortion, on Goethe's sojourn in Italy.

[17] For the thesis that the Italian years inaugurated a period of extreme neoclassicism extending to Schiller's death or to the time of *West-östlicher Divan* cf. Staiger 299, also 428–48 ("Wandlungen"), and Hans Pyritz, "Humanität und Leidenschaft: Goethes gegenklassische Wandlung 1814/1815," in his *Goethe-Studien* (Köln, 1962) 97–191. But as Victor Lange observes in his introduction to Goethe, *Werke* (München: Winkler, 1972) 1:xxiii: "Nach Schillers Tod hält Goethe an [dem] exemplarisch-bildenden Sinn des lyrischen, die Gestalt der Wirklichkeit erhellenden und bewegenden Sprechens fest, selbst dort, wo er sich der grundsätzlich anderen, die Welt im Subjektiven setzenden Dichtungstheorie der Romantik zu nähern scheint." And with reference to *West-östlicher Divan*, Horst Althaus similarly observes ("Einige Maximen in Goethes Kunstlehre," in his *Ästhetik, Ökonomie und Gesellschaft* [Bern/München: Francke, 1971] 194): "Die Früchte, die Blumen und die Düfte mögen vom Orient kommen, das Gesetz allein geben die Griechen"; cf. also Ingeborg Hillman, *Dichtung als Gegenstand der Dichtung: Zum Problem der Einheit des "West-östlichen Divan"* (Bonn, 1965) 47, n. 23, countering Ernst Beutler, Erich Trunz, and Carl Becker (to whom Konrad Burdach could be added).

[18] Pyritz 126f.

[19] Cf. Vincenzo Errante, "La Fuga di Goethe in Italia e la sua conversione allo stile neoclassico," *Die Mittelschule* I (1941/42), H. 11: 5–21.

[20] In Weimar Goethe was also in contact with Oeser through 1785, although he later regarded Oeser's Winckelmannian ideas negatively.

[21] Michéa 385ff. (and 463), with reference to Goethe's Spinozism; Werner Kohlschmidt, *Geschichte der deutschen Literatur vom Barock bis zur Klassik* (Stuttgart, 1965) 757, apropos of Goethe's interest in the Greek epigram and "antike Kleinkunst"; von Einem, HA 12:554, in connection with Goethe's rejection at the beginning of the 1780's of subjectivity in Maler Müller and Fuseli, who notes: "Hier nun werden wir Zeugen. . . von dem Hinauswachsen der Klassik des Dichters und Denkers über den Klassizismus der bildenden Kunst." (Otto Stelzer, in his excellent *Goethe und die bildende Kunst* [Braunschweig, 1949] 25 also has Goethe return from Italy a "Klassizist.")

Kunst, den der Dichter der 'Iphigenie' aus dem Norden mitbrachte und der ihn wieder heimgeleitete,"[22] although this is overstatement, or statement at best true of Goethe's interpretation of Graeco-Roman art and its history. For in Italy Goethe, despite unwavering admiration of Raphael, does not, like conventional neoclassicists, exclude from his appreciation earlier painters such as Mantegna[23] and Leonardo, avoids depreciation of Michelangelo, soon ceases to be an uncritical admirer of the Bolognese eclectics, and continues to esteem landscape—Dutch as well as (Franco-)Italian—despite its low place in neoclassical rankings of kinds of paintings.[24] And the insight recorded in *Reise III*, "daß die *Form* zuletzt alles einschließe" (letter of 11 April 1788), may have been inspired by Goethe's viewing of casts of classical statues in the French Academy, but it is only a soberer version of his more effusive statement of 1775: "Jede Form, auch die gefühlteste, hat etwas Unwahres; allein sie ist einmal das Glas, wodurch wir die heiligen Strahlen der verbreiteten Natur an das Herz der Menschen zum Feuerblick sammeln."[25]

Not the subject treated, then, but what Goethe—in criticism of the overspecificness (and the psychologism) of a passage in consequence simply omitted from Meyer's essay "Über die Gegenstände der bildenden Kunst" when it was published in *Die Propyläen*—called "das wichtige

---

[22] Festausgabe 17:12 (Weber names Herder, Lessing, Winckelmann, and Oeser as the major influences); Hans Rudolf Vaget, *Dilettantismus und Meisterschaft: Zum Problem des Dilettantismus bei Goethe*. . . (München, 1971) also argues that Italy marked no radical change in Goethe's basic aesthetic concepts.

[23] In her otherwise exemplary "Die Kunstanschauung Goethes in der 'Italienischen Reise' " *Italien* 2 (1929): 317–29 [et seq.] Wanda Kampmann exaggerates the Winckelmannian element in Goethe's criticism of Mantegna's Verona frescoes, the language of which— e.g., "zart"—is not that of Winckelmann's characterization of the archaic Greek style.

[24] In "Goethe und die bildende Kunst," in his *Goethe-Studien* (München, 1972) 116f. von Einem interprets the publication in *Die Propyläen* of Heinrich Meyer's "Über die Gegenstände der bildenden Kunst" (1798) as evidence that after his Storm-and-Stress period Goethe again ranked kinds of painting according to their subjects (similarly, Staiger 34), but as recently as 20 May 1796 (letter to Meyer) Goethe had rejected any ranking of the arts. For evidence that Meyer's essay inadequately represented Goethe's views, see Walther Scheidig, *Goethes Preisaufgaben für bildende Künstler 1799 bis 1805* (Weimar, 1958) 12f., and cf. Kampmann 329: "Daß Goethe dem Gegenstand eine so hohe ästhetische Bedeutung beilegt, wird eher verständlich, wenn man ihn nicht als bloßen Stoff versteht, sondern als den schon geistig irgendwie geprägten Gehalt." In "Einfache Nachahmung der Natur, Manier, Stil," published less than a year after his return from Rom, Goethe's idea that "Stil" ("der höchste Grad, wohin sie [die Kunst] gelangen kann") may be achievable in still life— an even "lower" art than landscape—is antithetical to neoclassical depreciation of what the artist has "gerade von der Natur kopiert" (Lessing, *Laokoon*, Abs. XI, par. 7, preferring imaginary or ideal to real landscape).

[25] "Aus Goethes Brieftasche," HA 12:22.

ästhetische *Interesse der Form* und Behandlung,"[26] was and afterward always remained the central concern of his classicism.[27] Accordingly, to assert "Im allgemeinen bestimmt sich. . . für Goethe der Wert des Bildes nach der Art, wie der Maler das Sukzessive ins Simultane des Raums auflöst,"[28] is to ignore Goethe's interest in landscape and still life and to have read *Italienische Reise* with the preconception that it records a conversion to or reaffirmation of a neoclassicism unmodified—"Grundsätzlich ändert sich aber nichts"[29]— between Goethe's so often quoted expression of admiration for Roman funerary monuments in Verona, 1786, and the end of the stay in Rome. But were this true, the *Reise* would be a monument to futility, and one might better accept Seillière's hostile evaluation of what is to be found in it: "Sous le couvert d'un néo-hellenisme dont le vernis seul sera classique, mais dont l'inspiration demeurera purement romantique à y regarder de près, — puisqu'il s'agit surtout d'une apologie de l'*instinct*, sous prétexte de *naïveté*, de simplicité et de *sérénité* méditerranéennes,—le poète. . . s'étonnera lui-même de se trouver aussi peu modifié dans son fond par douze années d'efforts dans une autre direction morale."[30]

For all its bias, Seillière's comment has the virtue of drawing attention to the disproportionate importance in *Reise I–II* of idealization of primitive-idyllic features of Italian and Sicilian life and landscape. It is significant, however, that such idealization is noticeably less evident in *Reise III*, where it appears most strikingly not in connection with the Italian scene but in a discussion of the effects of works of art:

> Überhaupt aber ist dies die entschiedenste Wirkung aller Kunstwerke, daß sie uns in den Zustand der Zeit und der Individuen versetzen, die sie hervorbrachten. Umgeben von antiken Statuen, empfindet man sich in einem bewegten Naturleben, man wird die Mannigfaltigkeit der Menschen-gestaltung gewahr und durchaus auf den Menschen in seinem reinsten

---

[26] WA I.47:332.

[27] Cf. Goethe's letter to Zelter, 30 October 1808: "Kein Mensch will begreifen, daß die höchste und einzige Operation der Natur und Kunst die Gestaltung sei. . . ."; *Pandora*, l. 676: "einzig veredelt die Form den Gehalt"; letter to A.L. de Chézy, 9 October 1830: "Nun. . . begrüßt Ihre. . . Übersetzung mich in hohen Jahren, wo der *Stoff* eines Kunstwerks. . . für die Betrachtung fast Null wird, und man der *Behandlung* allein, aber in desto höherem Grade, Ehre zu geben sich befähigt fühlt."

[28] Staiger 35, who illustrates this with Goethe's description—written in 1829—of Raphael's cartoon *The Death of Ananias*.

[29] Staiger 34 (but von Einem, HA 12:557: "Die Erfahrung der Geschichtlichkeit der Kunst ist Goethe in Italien aufgegangen").

[30] E. Seillière, "Les Elements romantiques dans l'œuvre de Goethe après 1786," *Revue Germanique* 9 (1913): 529–56, here 531.

Zustand zurückgeführt, wodurch denn der Beschauer selbst lebendig und rein menschlich wird.[31]

Sentimental primitivism did give way to a more objective and more—though not exclusively—historical frame of reference. (That this change in emphasis occurred in Italy and is not a "correction" of a much older Goethe, is confirmed by the similarity of emphasis on the timeless-generic in the final, Ash Wednesday section of "Das Römische Karneval," written in 1788, and by Goethe's earlier, almost Schillerian, rejection of sentimentalized primitivism toward the end of *Reise II* in connection with his analysis—"An Herder, Neapel, den 17. Mai 1787"—of the difference between Homeric and modern-manneristic simplicity.)

Classicism and the Historical Sense

"Der Künstler ist zwar der Sohn seiner Zeit, aber schlimm für ihn, wenn er zugleich ihr Zögling oder gar noch ihr Günstling ist. [...] Den Stoff zwar wird er von der Gegenwart nehmen, aber die Form von einer edleren Zeit, ja jenseits aller Zeit, von der absoluten unwandelbaren Einheit seines Wesens entlehnen."[32] So the universal historian Schiller, in a context in which Graeco-Roman antiquity down to the early first century A.D. alone represents supreme artistic expression of the human spirit. And here Goethe, reflecting in December, 1787, on the monuments of Rome:

> Die Peterskirche ist gewiß so groß gedacht und wohl größer und kühner als einer der alten Tempel, und nicht allein was zweitausend Jahre vernichten sollten, lag vor unserm Augen, sondern zugleich was eine gesteigerte Bildung wieder hervorzubringen vermochte.
> Selbst das Schwanken des Kunstgeschmackes, das Bestreben zum einfachen Großen, das Wiederkehren zum vervielfachten Kleineren, alles deutete auf Leben und Bewegung, Kunst- und Menschengeschichte standen synchronistisch vor unseren Augen.[33]

---

[31] "Bericht. April [1788]." HA 11:545.

[32] Friedrich Schiller, *On the Aesthetic Education of Man. . .* , ed. Elizabeth M. Wilkinson and L.A. Willoughby (Oxford, 1967) 56.

[33] HA 11:456. As early as "Den 28. Januar 1787" Goethe had declared with reference to the rise and fall of art styles: "jeder, dem es Ernst ist, sieht wohl ein, daß auch in diesem Felde kein Urteil möglich ist, als wenn man es historisch entwickeln kann." To say that the historical "ist immer nur Gleichnis des Unvergänglichen" in the *Reise* (von Einem, HA 11: 566—but cf. also n. 29 above) is misleading, since it can also be the non-recurrent (cf. 103, 122, 220, etc.). Goethe can appreciate St. Peter's without condemning its Baroque elements because his architectural mentor is Palladio (Palladianism, which is less Baroque, had been

Goethe's pragmatic reconciliation of aesthetic absolutism with historical relativism is a significant deviation from the elegiac neoclassicism that emerged at the same time as did the Gothic revival (of which his disapproval, being once more unfashionable, has more offended). To say that Goethe's enthusiasm is unhistorical because it permits him to appreciate monuments dating from the sixth or fifth century B.C. to the second A.D.,[34] is to disregard the fact that all the Greek and Roman antiquities he singles out for attention or praise, whether Greek, Hellenistic, or Roman, belong to some part of the long period of idealizing naturalism (the chief basis of Renaissance and later enthusiasm for classical art) which constitutes a homogeneous unit in any large overview of the history of ancient art.[35] Goethe's admiration of Graeco-Roman works both static (or nobly calm) and dynamic (or manneristic) is evidence not of neoclassical blindness to historical differences,[36] but of a catholicity of taste that would not arbitrarily categorize still-life and landscape as inferior branches of painting, that could admire the grandeur of Jesuit Baroque in Southern Germany,[37] and that preferred the delicacy of the seventeenth-century Swanevelt to the sensationalism of a "neoclassical" Piranesi.[38] The often quoted "Jeder sei auf seine Art ein Grieche!" sounds conventionally neoclassical if "auf seine Art" is left unstressed, but the essay in which it occurs ("Antik und Modern," published a year after *Reise II*) subsequently insists, "so ist unser wiederholtes, aufrichtiges Bekenntnis, daß keiner Zeit versagt sei, das schönste Talent hervorzubringen," and concludes: "Der Parnaß ist ein *Montserrat*, der

a pre-Italian enthusiasm—cf. Harald Keller, "Goethe, Palladio und England," Bayerische Akademie der Wissenschaften, Phil.-hist. Kl., *Sitzungsberichte*, 1971, H. 6).

[34] E.g., Staiger 30f.

[35] Idealizing naturalism is the "Methode" that in *Diderots Versuch über die Malerei* (2. Kap., "Von der Harmonie der Farben") explains why Greek art "aus den verschiedenen Zeiten und von verschiedenem Werte" produces "einen gewissen gemeinsamen Eindruck." The beginning of a radically different style c. 200 A.D. is delineated with exceptional clarity by Ranucci Bianchi Bandinelli, *Rom—Das Ende der Antike. Das Universum der Kunst*, vol. 17 (München, 1971).

[36] Kampmann 327 finds in Goethe's awareness that Raphael represents the culmination of a long historical development what fundamentally differentiates his *Klassik* from "Klassizismus."

[37] HA 11:11 (though "hier und da fehlt es auch nicht an etwas Abgeschmacktem"). The commonplace that Goethe "could hardly glance without wincing at medieval pictures, or at gothic, let alone baroque, architecture" (Butler 110) needs correction.

[38] Cf. HA 11:452. The motif of ruined grandeur in Piranesi appealed to the instinct that explains Winckelmann's pleasure in "die fragmentarische, mehr andeutende als darstellende Überlieferung von der Antike" (Kampmann 367, with reference to the end of Winckelmann's *Geschichte* and its "Sehnsucht" motif).

viele Ansiedlungen in mancherlei Etagen erlaubt; ein jeder gehe hin, versuche sich und er wird eine Stätte finden, es sei auf Gipfeln oder in Winkeln!"[39]

Goethe's dependence on the ideas of Winckelmann is an article of faith of those who, at least for art, equate his liberal classicism with conventional neoclassicism.[40] Yet nothing could be further removed from Goethean "Gegenständlichkeit"—that almost painfully obsessive concern with disinterested observation which is a leitmotif of earlier parts of the *Reise*— than the characteristically Winckelmannian view that painting's "größtes Glück" is "die Vorstellung unsichtbarer, vergangener und zukünftiger Dinge."[41] What Winckelmann depreciated in Michelangelo, Goethe esteemed;[42] although both disliked certain themes of Christian art, Goethe did not share Winckelmann's enthusiasm for allegorical painting;[43] unlike Winckelmann, Goethe is not negative on ancient Roman wall-decoration;[44] and the absence in the *Reise* of the criteria "edle Einfalt" and "stille Größe"— and of the beauty of the artist's subjects—is eloquent silence that anticipates by a decade the un- or anti-Winckelmannian elements of "Über Laokoon."[45] What Winckelmann primarily represented for Goethe was historical understanding: "Durch Winckelmann sind wir dringend aufgeregt, die Epochen zu sondern. . ." (28 January 1787 [HA 11:167]), and it is thanks to him that in Catania Goethe could appreciate the numismatic collection of the Prince of Biscari: "Ich. . . half mir an jenem dauerhaften Winckelmannischen Faden, der uns durch die verschiedenen Kunstepochen durchleitet, so ziemlich hin" (291).

---

[39] The punctuation of Goethe's final sentence, whose *Montserrat* recalls the end of *Faust II*, and whose message is that of the verses at the end of my observations, is here modernized.

[40] E.g., H.A. Korff, "Goethe und die bildende Kunst," *ZsfDtkde* 41 (1927): 657–73.

[41] Winckelmann's formulation at the end of *Gedanken über die Nachahmung der griechischen Werke in der Malerei und Bildhauerkunst*. In Goethe's classicism as finally formulated in Italy "bleibt—darin liegt das Neue der Goetheschen Anschauung und sein tiefer Unterschied gegen die Tradition, insbesondere gegen Winckelmann—das Charakteristische immer die Bedingung der Schönheit" (von Einem, HA 11:568).

[42] Cf. Herbert von Einem, "Goethe und Michelangelo," *Goethe Jb.* 92 (1975): 165–93 (Winckelmann, p. 166).

[43] In the *Reise* Goethe acknowledges an indebtedness to Mengs's writing on art, but makes no mention of his *Parnassus* or of his allegories in the Vatican Library, praising instead of these typically neoclassical works the portrait of Clement XIII ("das herrlichste Bild, welches Mengs vielleicht je gemalt hat," HA 11:523) done in a Baroque tradition.

[44] *Reise II* (HA 11:198).

[45] For Winckelmann beauty was inherent in the artist's subject or model (cf. *Geschichte der Kunst des Altertums*, IV, 2—explanation of the beauty of Raphael's Galatea and Guido's angels), for Goethe it was artistic expression or statement.

Goethe pairs "Winckelmann und Mengs" as the pioneers who opened the way his friend Heinrich Meyer was following in 1787 (HA 11:439) only because both represented a historical approach to art. For Mengs's taste in painting was not Goethe's either. Taking Raphael, Correggio, and Titian as criteria of excellence, Mengs regarded the Dutch as "low imitators of Nature," held that Michelangelo "seeking to be great was always vulgar," considered Tintoretto's only merit "pomp of solicitude [i.e., treatment of detail]," and even censured in the late Titian "a Taste low and trivial."[46] He praises Poussin (in his *Schreiben an Herrn Anton Pons* [Wien, 1778]—in Goethe's library), but not Claude Lorrain, whom Goethe preferred, and although he mentions Rembrandt and Dou favorably, he considers them much inferior to Velasquez and Titian. What distinguishes Mengs from Winckelmann is his far greater interest in color—it is immediately after reporting in *Reise III* that he has acquired the new edition of Mengs's works that Goethe first mentions his own "Spekulationen über Farben" ("Rom, den 7. März 1788")—although for Mengs even Titian, his master colorist, takes third place after Raphael and Corregio, respectively representing *expression* and *delight*, "since truth is rather a duty than an ornament."[47]

Color—and Collage

In the preface to his poem on the art of painting, one of the major contributors to Diderot's *Encyclopédie* explains the order of its cantos: "Le Dessein. . . devoit précéder la Couleur, parce qu'on peut étudier & imiter les formes des corps, indépendamment de leurs couleurs."[48] Goethe expressed the antithesis of this neoclassical position as early as 1791, in the first of *Beiträge zur Optik* (Einleitung §1), and restated it in "Entwurf einer Farbenlehre" thus: "Nunmehr behaupten wir. . . , daß das Auge keine Form sehe, indem Hell, Dunkel und Farbe zusammen allein dasjenige ausmachen, was den Gegenstand vom Gegenstand, die Teile des Gegenstandes von einander fürs Auge unterscheidet."[49] Only those who read the *Reise* with the

---

[46] Raphael Mengs, *Works* (London, 1796) 1:136, 149, 189, 189.

[47] Mengs 1:37.

[48] Claude-Henry Watelet, *L'Art de peindre* (Paris, 1760—cf. Goethe's note, WA I.48:236).

[49] HA 13 (München, 1975—7. Aufl.) 323. Similarly, in *Diderots Versuch über die Malerei* (2. Kap., "Eigenschaften eines echten Koloristen"): "Bei allem, was nicht menschlicher Körper ist, bedeutet die Farbe fast mehr als die Gestalt. . . ." The absence of discussion of color in *Die Propyläen* and the fact that color was optional for entries submitted in the Weimarer Kunstfreunde competitions (1799–1805) are sometimes adduced as evidence of a post-Italian period of extreme Goethean neoclassicism. Color was to have been treated in *Die Propyläen* (cf. "Einleitung," HA 12:44f.), but Goethe had not advanced far enough in his color studies to include any of them before the journal ceased publication; for the

preconception that it documents Goethean neoclassicism will fail to find in it evidence of Goethe's interest in (and his occasional judgments of) color. That Goethe made a detour through Cento on his way from Ferrara to Bologna is but partially explained by his guidebook's recommendation that it permits seeing a wealth of paintings by Guercino[50] ("Hauptmeister der bologneser Maler-Schule," esteem for which places "Goethe durchaus in der Tradition der klassischen Kunstlehre"[51]), since neither Mengs nor Winckelmann considered Guercino a major artist. But Guercino was and was recognized even by Mengs and Winckelmann as a great colorist, and Goethe independently discovered Guercino in Padua, for his *Justice and Peace* which there caught Goethe's attention in the church and convent of S. Giustina is not mentioned by Volkmann, who instead recommends paintings by Veronese, Titian, Tintoretto, etc.[52]

What Fuseli termed "the inferior but more alluring charm of colour"[53] was to become an abiding concern of Goethe's by the end of his Roman sojourn, but it may be evidence of a well developed interest in color before Goethe had left Germany that the first artist named in the *Reise* ("München, den 6. September [1786]") is Rubens. Goethe's mentions of Claude Lorrain in all three parts of the *Reise* are usually interpreted only as reflections of his interest in landscape painting,[54] but of Claude's landscapes Goethe was to write (in *Philipp Hackert*): "Was sein Kolorit betrifft, so ist, meiner Meinung nach, keiner dahin gekommen es so vollkommen zu machen."[55] Nevertheless, it has become a commonplace that, in discussing works of art in the *Reise*, "Goethe sich in der Regel über die Farben ausschweigt."

> Nur am Anfang seiner Reise. . . , so bei den Guercinos in Cento und Bologna, ist öfter von Farben die Rede, dann wieder zuletzt, im Frühling

small prizes offered in the competitions works executed in color were hardly to be expected, but in 1802 a landscape in oils—the only such submitted—did win Rohden a prize. Scheidig (n. 24) 492f. thus needlessly interprets as self-criticism Goethe's conclusion to Heinrich Meyer's *Siebente Weimarische Kunstausstellung vom Jahre 1805*: "Für das laufende Jahr bleibt unsere Ausstellung geschlossen. Inzwischen gedenken wir uns mit Freunden der Kunst und Natur über die Farben zu unterhalten. Vielleicht richten wir künftig unsere Preisaufgaben gegen diese nicht genugsam beobachtete Seite der Kunst."

[50] J.J. Volkmann, *Historisch-kritische Nachrichten von Italien*. . . (Leipzig, 1771) 3:481.

[51] H. von Einem, HA 11:598.

[52] Goethe, *Reise-Tagebuch*, "26. September 1786" ("ein schön Bild"). Volkmann 3:650.

[53] Henry Fuseli, *Lectures on Painting* (London, 1801), 2nd lecture (cf. Kant, *Kritik der Urteilskraft*, I. Teil, I, §14: "In der Malerei. . . ist die *Zeichnung* das Wesentliche. . . . Die Farben. . . gehören zum Reiz").

[54] Cf. von Einem, HA 11:622f.

[55] "Über Landschaftsmalerei. Theoretische Fragmente."

1788 in Rom, wo es heißt: "Ferner habe ich allerlei Spekulationen über Farben gemacht. . . ." [...] Er äußert sich lieber über Bilder, in denen die Zeichnung wesentlich ist. . . ."[56]

Indeed Staiger, after citing from *Titan* the description of the sunrise as seen by Albano when his blindfold is removed, asserts, "In der ganzen 'Italienischen Reise' Goethes gibt es keine Schilderung, die es mit dieser Farbenfülle. . . aufnehmen könnte,"[57] although in the passage from Jean Paul only the color blue is mentioned. By contrast, in a descriptive passage no longer than Jean Paul's—"Neapel, den 29. Mai 1787"—Goethe mentions color thirty times with thirteen references to (ten) specific colors or shades.[58] And although in the *Reise* he does not usually discuss color when mentioning paintings, the minimal use of color in James Moore's *The Deluge* is carefully noted and effectively conveyed in his analysis of the work ("Rom, den 9. Juli [1787]").

The poet who as artist studied in Italy its use with Kniep, Dies, and Hackert was thus not indifferent to color (though probably aware then, as later, of the futility of its verbal description unsupported by color charts), but perhaps no single sentence in the *Reise* better conveys the non-neoclassicism of Goethe in Rome than the opening of the letter—to Frau von Stein—"28. September 1787" (*Reise III*): "Ich bin hier sehr glücklich, es wird den ganzen Tag bis in die Nacht gezeichnet, gemalt, getuscht, geklebt, Handwerk und Kunst recht ex professo getrieben." Of the four specific activities mentioned, all but the first (design) involve color, and the last is startlingly un-neoclassical in light of the late eighteenth-century prejudice against regarding collage, then chiefly used for popular devotional pictures, as serious art.[59] That Goethe's collage involved coloring we know, however, from an account in F.I.L. Meyer's *Darstellungen aus Italien* of the "malerische Wirkung dieser. . . Darstellungsart des Mondscheins*, von Herrn PHILIPP HACKERTS eigner Erfindung."

---

[56] Staiger 36f. Cf. Wilhelm Pinder, "Goethe und die bildende Kunst," in his *Gesammelte Aufsätze* (Leipzig, 1938) 162 ("gerade die Farbe hat er [Goethe] selten bei Kunstwerken geschildert").

[57] Staiger 12f.

[58] Another such passage is "Palermo. . . den 7. April 1787" (nine specific colors). In "Amor als Landschaftsmaler," written after Goethe's return to Rome, color is similarly used (with far more frequency than in his earlier poetry), and in "Künstlers Apotheose" (1789) the student expresses a concern for color—and design—lacking in its Storm-and-Stress counterpart "Des Künstlers Vergötterung."

[59] Cf. Herta Wescher, *Die Collage* (Köln, 1968), who mentions neither Goethe nor Hackert.

Die Landschaft selbst wird mit Wasserfarbe auf Papier gemalt, die
großen. . . Massen derselben. . . werden besonders ausgeschnitten, kolorirt,
und dann auf Papier geklebt. Die Stellen im Wasser, worauf die
Mondstrahlen am stärksten wirken, werden mit einem Messer dünne
geschabt, und die übrigen, mehr und minder starken Lichter in der
Landschaft mit einem darauf gebrachten transparenten Spiritus angegeben.
Alles übrige wird kolorirt, das weiße Papier zu den Lichten ausgespart, und
die Mondscheibe ganz weiß gelassen.—Die kolorirte Seite des ganzen
Blattes wird dann mit feinem weißen Papier beklebt, worauf nur die
Mondscheibe ausgeschnitten ist.[60]

Literary Classicism

It should now be possible to assert, without being merely paradoxical,
that Goethe was more neoclassical before 1786 than after, and to understand
why Goethe, despite claims in letters from Italy and in the *Reise* that he had
greatly improved *Iphigenie auf Tauris* in the fall of 1786, later could more
than once speak disparagingly of its sentimentality (which illustrates
neoclassicism rather than "Klassik") and call it, writing to Schiller in 1802,
a "gräzisierendes Schauspiel."[61] He indeed polished his text as he turned it
into blank verse, but he made no radical change in its basic elements, so
that the less sentimental Iphigenie to be modeled on the *St. Agatha* he saw
in Bologna is an intention rather than a realization.[62] (Attempts to use
revisions made for the final text of *Iphigenie auf Tauris* to demonstrate a
substantive "influence" of Goethe's Italian sojourn must accordingly be
fruitless—or erroneous.)[63]

---

[60] Meyer (Berlin, 1792) 304f. Although the collages were lit from behind by two lamps,
Meyer insists they are "keine Guckkastentändelei." To Körner—on 12 September 1790—
Schiller writes that Goethe has "vortreffliche Stücke der Art aus Italien gebracht."

[61] The negative value for Goethe of "gräzisieren" is clearest in "Antik und Modern,"
where the highest praise of Raphael's (Renaissance) style is: "Er gräzisiert nirgends, fühlt,
denkt, handelt aber durchaus wie ein Grieche" (HA 12:175).

[62] The unidentified *St. Agatha* whose "gesunde, sichere Jungfräulichkeit" (HA 11:107)
was to embody qualities Goethe now recognized as wanting in Frau von Stein could well
have been by or in the manner of Guercino (hence possibly the "Raphael" Fritz Stolberg
later saw in Bologna—cf. von Einem's note, p. 602), to whom two days earlier Goethe had
in Cento devoted a whole day.

[63] E.g., R.M. Meyer (n. 2 above). H.G. Haile, *Artist in Chrysalis: A Biographical Study of
Goethe in Italy* (Urbana, 1973) 81f. finds "in the lines given her [Iphigenia] in Rome"—"Von
dem fremden Manne / Entfernete mich ein Schauer; doch es reißt / Mein Innerstes gewaltig
mich zum Bruder" (in Goethe's prose version: "mich schaudert vor dem fremden Mann,
und mich reißt mein Innerstes zum Bruder")—evidence of "rivalry between Orestes and the
king within Iphigenia's heart," although the stranger *is* her brother. On the whole the final
text represents successful neoclassization, though one at times achieved with loss of

In contrast to *Iphigenie auf Tauris*, Goethe's plan of an *Iphigenie von Delphi*[64]—conceived on the way from Cento to Bologna, a fortnight after he had been bored in Venice by a performance of Crébillon's *Electre* (1708) and its double love plot—seems even more sentimentally neoclassical, especially in Electra's recognition of her sister just as she is about to murder her as the priestess reported to have slain Orestes and Pylades on a Taurian altar ("Wenn diese Szene gelingt, so ist nicht leicht etwas Größeres und Rührenderes auf dem Theater gesehen worden"). The tragedy finally entitled *Nausikaa* was also an early Italian conception, first mentioned in Goethe's *Reise-Tagebuch*, 22 October 1786, as *Ulysses auf Phäa*; if it remained almost entirely a plan, this is probably less because interest in the "Urpflanze" diverted Goethe's energies from it ("der Garten des Alcinous war verschwunden, ein Weltgarten hatte sich aufgetan"[65]), than because its Winckelmannian noble simplicity and quiet grandeur—or Homeric idyllicism—came to be seen by an ever more genuinely classical Goethe as sentimental and romantically hellenistic.

The literary works Goethe extensively rewrote or conceived and executed in Italy are largely free of the sentimentality of his Italian letters and his plans from before the "Wiedergeburt" he there sought. The *Faust* scene "Hexenküche" and its "Wald und Höhle" monologue are ironically objective, the former comico-satirically, the latter dramatico-seriously; "Amor als Landschaftsmaler" is the antithesis of Goethe's pre-Italian sentimental lyricism; and as for *Erwin und Elmire* and *Claudine von Villa Bella*—in *Reise III* the latter's "Cupido, loser eigensinniger Knabe" symbolizes Goethe's successful assimilation of all that Rome, where "eine große Anstrengung gefordert ward, sich gegen so vieles aufrechtzuerhalten, in Tätigkeit nicht zu ermüden und im Aufnehmen nicht lässig zu werden,"[66] had to offer him—the Roman revisions of these originally Storm-and-Stress expressions of sentimentality have many classical elements of style and structure that serve to conventionalize the romanticism of their genre.[67]

---

concision and clarity; Kohlschmidt, p. 764, may claim: "[Es] zeigt schon ein Vergleich zwischen der Urfassung des *Parzenliedes* mit der italienischen Fassung, daß über die stilgeschichtlichen Einflüsse der Freunde [Moritz, Wieland] hinaus die ganze römische 'Wiedergeburt' mit im Spiel ist," but even here the price of metrical regularization is repetition (*ewigen* now l. 1729 as well as 1745), meaningless expansion (*können sie brauchen* for *brauchen sie*; the *je* in *Den sie je erheben*; the poetic *Erhebet* for *Erhebt*), generalization (*die Gäste* for *der Gast*), loss of metaphor (*der Atem Erstickter Titanen* for *des Riesen erstickter Mund*), vagueness (*Ein leichtes Gewölke* for *Ein leichter Rauch*, which better described volcanic fumes from Tartarus), and blandness (*meiden* for *hassen*).

[64] HA 11:107f.

[65] HA 11:375 (*Reise III*, "Bericht. Juli [1787]")

[66] HA 11:478f.

[67] How, and how much, Goethe in Rome revised *Egmont* is so uncertain that brief generalization is not possible here; the "musical" element of its opening scene, and the "operatic" of its final act, seem stylizations comparable to those of the *Singspiel* revisions.

Torquato Tasso, however, though chiefly revised and completed after Goethe's return from Rome, is the most significant reflection of his new classicism, both formally and as the expression of a heightened (and by Goethe never before so objectively conveyed) awareness of the ambiguous complexity of human behavior in a world of social-historical realities; although it shares with *Iphigenie auf Tauris* features of what has been called "Seelendrama," its Renaissance world contains elements of light, color, and the pictural—those features that make Goethe's *Römische Elegien* "Bildgedichte"[68]—which clearly mark a great advance beyond the statically Winckelmannian plasticity of the earlier play.[69]

Henceforth Goethe's literary production always in some way conveyed the spirit of the classicism he evolved in Italy, and to label "classical" only those of his works with obvious neoclassical features, e.g., *Hermann und Dorothea* or *Achilleis*, is as unhelpful as to find in later parts of *Wilhelm Meisters Lehrjahre* "das äußerste Stadium des neuklassischen Stilisierungsprozesses der Goetheschen Iphigenie."[70] Goethe's classical ideal as tentatively formulated in the second letter of *Reise III* (though there only with reference to drawing) had been "die Natur abzuschreiben und der Zeichnung gleich eine Gestalt zu geben"—a process that is "wieder ein Gipfel irdischer Dinge." But by the end of *Reise III* it has become the insight already cited, "daß die *Form* zuletzt alles einschließe." Such a classicism alone explains the coexistence (and often nearly simultaneous creation) of works as different as the *Lehrjahre* and *Hermann und Dorothea*, *Die Wahlverwandtschaften* and *Pandora*, *West-östlicher Divan* and *Reise I–II*, or the final *Wilhelm Meisters Wanderjahre* and the "Helena" of *Faust*, and only one who wrote in its spirit could rightly claim, as did Goethe in 1800:

Wir ehren froh mit immer gleichem Muthe
Das Alterthum und jedes neue Gute.[71]

---

[68] Lange (Goethe, *Werke*) 1:xx. That Renaissance painting (not Graeco-Roman sculpture) is important for the visual elements of the elegies has often been noted; Errante, p. 9, also emphasizes the importance of line as "recipiente di colore."

[69] Cf. René Michéa, "L'élément pictural de 'Torquato Tasso,' " *Revue de l'Enseignement des Langues vivantes* 51 (1934): 109–17.

[70] Giuliano Baioni, " 'Märchen'—'Wilhelm Meisters Lehrjahre'—'Hermann und Dorothea.' Zur Gesellschaftsidee der deutschen Klassik," *Goethe Jb.* 92 (1975): 113, interpreting as an injunction to establish social regimentation Natalie's observation that children need discipline.

[71] *Abschied* [zu Faust], Festausgabe 5:588, as dated by Hans Gerhart Gräf, *Goethe über seine Dichtungen*, 2. Teil, II (Frankfurt/Main, 1904) 89ff. On Goethe's perdurable rejection of both "starrer Klassizismus" and "romantische Verflüchtigung," see also Matthijs Jolles (rev. of Emil Staiger, *Goethe, 1786–1814*), *Anzeiger* 89 (1958): 30 and 38.

Goethe's Last Play: *Die Wette*

If by "last" we mean "the last to be conceived and executed," and by "play" a *Schauspiel*—rather than, for example, a *Festspiel* like *Des Epimenides Erwachen* (1814)—then Goethe's last play is *Die Wette* (1812). It is printed only in "complete" editions of Goethe's works,[1] and even in large-scale treatments of Goethe's life and works it is often not mentioned.[2] The circumstances of its composition—at the request of Maria Louisa of Austria—make discussion of the play a necessary part of any account of Goethe and Austria, but in these accounts its literary qualities naturally receive little attention.[3] Critical discussion of the text is thus to be found almost exclusively in remarks of editors whose duty it was to write introductory essays on works by Goethe in volumes they prepared for publication, and only one—very short—separate critical essay on it seems to have appeared in print during the almost 150 years since it was published posthumously, in 1837.

That essay, by August Henneberger, is concerned primarily with the dramatic technique of *Die Wette*, but its conclusion, that the play lacks literary merit, is one variously echoed by all subsequent critics.[4] The most

[1] It was also once printed in the ninth and last volume of *Goethes Theater* (Stuttgart, 1868 [1869]).

[2] *Die Wette* is not mentioned by Brandes, Friedenthal, Gundolf, Haarhaus, Lewes, Heinrich Meyer, R.M. Meyer, Staiger, or Viëtor, who represent a great range of methods and interests; Bielschowski gives an account of its composition, and Emil Ludwig discusses it briefly as a late improvisation which, as improvisation, recalls the much earlier *Clavigo*.

[3] It is thus discussed by August Sauer in his introduction to *Goethe und Österreich*, Schriften der Goethe-Gesellschaft, 17 (Weimar, 1902) xliiif., in Johannes Urzidil, *Goethe in Böhmen* (Zürich: Artemis, 1962) 377ff., and, according to Goedeke, in R.M. Werner, *Goethe und die Gräfin O'Donell* (Berlin, 1888). The eight-line occasional poem "Eleonore" was, as Goethe's note explains, "Zum Schluß einer dramatischen Vorstellung in Teplitz, an Ihre Majestät die Kaiserin von Österreich, gesprochen von Gräfin O'Donell." The countess had the part of Leonore, the heroine of *Die Wette*, whose name in the list of *dramatis personae* and as speaker is Leonore, but who is Eleonore in one stage direction.

[4] Henneberger's article: "Ueber Göthe's Lustspiele. 2. Die Wette," *Archiv* 11 (1852): 140–42. Subsequent critics: Franz Muncker, in Jubiläums-Ausgabe, 11:xxxif.; K.J. Schröer, in *Deutsche National-Litteratur*, 91:333–36; Karl Heinemann, in Goethe, *Werke*, ed. Heinemann (Leipzig: Bibliographisches Institut, 1906) 19:395f.; Robert Riemann, in Goethe,

succinct of these is Zeitler, who terms it "ein äußerliches, unbedeutendes Gelegenheitslustspiel," with "durchaus konventionelle Theaterfiguren," and characterizes it thus: "Ein Liebespaar ist durch einen Türvorhang getrennt; es wird gar keine besondere Verwicklung herbeigeführt, daß sie sich am Ende in die Arme sinken. Die Expositionsszenen sind besonders schwach und bequem. Immerhin sprechen auch Goethesche Elemente aus dem Lustspielchen, z.B. Auseinandersetzungen über weiblichen Charakter und Denkungsart."[5] When Muncker calls the play "recht unbedeutend," he is but restating an already long-received opinion. This opinion has not subsequently been modified in any significant way, and is still that of Kurt May: "Das szenische Geschehen hat nur eine sehr schwache Spannung. . . . Von Anmut ist im Text nicht sehr viel zu bemerken, aber eine *lebendige Aufführung* [emphasis added] könnte den Reiz des kleinen Spieles erhöhen."

It is not my intention to try to demonstrate that *Die Wette* is a hitherto unrecognized masterpiece—I doubt if that could successfully be done—but I hope to show that it can illustrate some important aspects of Goethe's literary development. I am at least partly encouraged to do so by Paul Goodman's observation, "The very same sentence that is a platitude when said by any man is importantly true when said by Goethe,"[6] although there is not, *pace* Zeitler, a great wealth of Goethean wisdom in this text.

Die Wette is the shortest of Goethe's comedies, and is also shorter than any of his farces except *Ein Fastnachtspiel. . . vom Pater Brey*, written some forty years earlier. It consists of five *Auftritte*, the first four of which constitute one scene (*Bild*), taking place, as becomes clear from the expository dialogue, in a room in an inn. The fifth and final *Auftritt*, which constitutes less than a third of the total printed text, is a new *Bild*, "Getheilte Zimmer, wohl möblirt, mit allerlei Gegenständen zur Unterhaltung versehen, als: Pulte, Bücher, Instrumente und dergl. Thüre, Gitter und Vorhang, wie oben [i.e., in the expository dialogue of *1. Auftritt*]." Since the first *Bild* is entirely devoted to (narrative) exposition, the fifth and final scene—in print considerably shorter than the play's *Dritter Auftritt*—is simultaneously the climax of the dramatic action and its dénouement. The five scenes together thus constitute units equivalent to the five acts of neoclassical—analytical— comedy. The first four successively represent (1) exposition of the conditions of the action; (2) a first account of the consequences of these

Werke, ed. Karl Alt et al. (Berlin: Bong, [1910]) 4:xxf.; Kurt May, in Gedenkausgabe 6:1233f. Since all these items are only one to three pages long, quotations from them are not here provided with page-references.

[5] "Die Wette," *Goethe-Handbuch*, ed. Julius Zeitler, vol. 3 (Stuttgart, 1918) 560.

[6] Paul Goodman, "Some Problems of Interpretation: Silence, and Speech as Action," in his *Utopian Essays, and Practical Proposals* (New York: Random House, 1962) 247.

conditions for its hero and heroine, with emphasis on the latter; (3) a full account of the psychological crisis in which hero and heroine find themselves after a week of trial; (4) a moment of "last suspense" which is dramatically the weakest point of the play (a weak point in countless comedies, however, even in those by masters of the well-made piece!), since the non-appearance of hero and heroine before the final scene limits the suspense to modified recapitulation of the already expressed expectations of two other—to be sure the main—actors of the play; and (5) the climax-dénouement. (Like *Pater Brey*, with its first scenes in a small shop and the remainder in Sibylla's garden, the play is also structurally bipartite, in an even simpler way than with the farce, in which, despite the use of one less speaking actor than the six required for *Die Wette*, there are eleven *Auftritte*, and in which dramatic developments appear well before the middle of the text.)[7]

The distribution of parts in *Die Wette* is skillfully handled. All but one of the actors have at least one substantial speech or participate actively in the dialogue. Even the exception, the friend to whom the main character, Dorn, explains the situation in which the play's two lovers find themselves, appears and speaks in all four scenes in which he appears. This role (Förster) accordingly demands an actor able to react—to convey an impression of responsiveness—if, on the stage, the long expository speeches of Dorn are to have any dramatic value. (Although there may not have been an amateur at Teplitz in 1812 up to the part of Förster, it is written as if Goethe had had a professional actor in mind.)

The simplicity of the play's structure is not a defect, as Henneberger concedes, who considers its fundamental weakness to be a lack of "komische Kraft." This he explains as deriving from (1) what he regards as the "weitschweifige, den Zuschauer ermüdende Weise" in which the exposition is handled, pointing out that Förster does not become a participant in the action; and (2) from the use of two conventionally comic servants—Johann and Friederike—to supplement the exposition by Dorn, to whom they report the (non-)events during the week of Dorn's absence. In what might be considered a redeeming comic element, the fact that this pair make their reports "in dem geistvollen Erzählungsstyl eines Bedienten und einer Kammerjungfer," Henneberger takes objection to two features: (a) the play is burdened with a second "selbstständiges Liebesverhältniß" and

---

[7] The structure of *Pater Brey* is actually that of a three-act play according to the stage conventions of the 1770's: the opening three scenes (in the *Krämer*'s shop), the first four scenes in Sibylla's garden, and then—since the stage is briefly empty after this short scene—the remaining *Auftritte*. (There is a sixth actor in *Pater Brey*, the shop boy summoned in its opening verse, but he has no dramatic function and speaks no lines.)

(b) the roles of the two servants are completely stereotyped, deriving from "der längstbegrabenen altfranzösischen Komödie der [Christian Felix] Weiße usw." The negative conclusion that Henneberger believes he must demonstrate, Heinemann simply offers without explanation: "Seinem Werte nach erscheint das Lustspiel des großen Dichters nicht würdig," adding— without specific examples—"doch steht es ja damit in Goethes Werken nicht allein da."

If Bielschowski compares the rapid composition of *Die Wette* to that of a superior *Clavigo*, Schröer chooses as analogue a superior *Die Geschwister*, and like Muncker derives the mediocrity of the comedy—only a "Scherz" and a "Zeichen der Verehrung und Ergebenheit [of Goethe for Maria Louisa]"—from Goethe's poor health in the summer of its writing. Closest to Zeitler in his final remarks—that *Die Wette* does contain some "gehaltvollen, feinen und wahren Bemerkungen"—Muncker nevertheless is in basic agreement with Henneberger; he finds the characters conventional and uninteresting, with partial exception of the pair of young lovers, the exposition unsatisfactory ("besonders bei der Exposition hat es sich der Verfasser recht bequem gemacht"), and the language "trocken und farblos, wiewohl sie die Sicherheit und Gewandtheit des Ausdrucks keinen Augenblick vermissen läßt"—this last despite the fact that it is a work "nirgends von eigenartigem künstlerischem Gepräge."[8]

Although Riemann devotes less than a page to discussion of *Die Wette*, which he also evaluates negatively, his remarks seem to reveal a more genuinely thoughtful (or critical) response to the text than that offered by his predecessors. He suggests that its motif was better suited to farcical than comic treatment: "Hier wies die Idee eigentlich auf eine Posse mit starker Situationskomik. . . . Aber man wartet vergebens darauf, daß die Liebenden irgendwelche Dummheiten begehen, die verbotene und die erlaubte Tür verwechseln. . . usw. Von alledem geschieht in dem vornehmen, aber durchaus witzlosen Lustspiele nichts." His observation that the servants Johann and Friederike talk elegantly is presumably meant as an objection to what Henneberger had already condemned as Goethe's use of an outmoded comic tradition (although there has never been any period in the long history of comedy in which this convention has not been accepted practice!), since he combines with it the negative comment that Dorn and

[8] Both Muncker and Heinemann emphasize the linguistic polish of the play's speeches, the former probably, and the latter explicitly, to counter whole or even partial attribution of the text—as by Kurt May—to Maria Louisa, who was not completely fluent in German. (May's negative conclusion is curiously ambiguous: "Auch wo Goethe flach ist, ist er doch niemals ohne innere Sicherheit und Leichtigkeit." At least technically *Die Wette* does not, as I think I show, lack "Sicherheit.")

Förster talk "in langatmigen Sätzen." (Actually, Förster has only *one* long, thirty-word sentence which is also a complete speech; even his longest speech—thirty-six words—typically consists of three sentences that successively divide into five breathing units of five, six, nine, three, and thirteen words, while the thirty-word sentence divides into easily uttered units of nine, eight, and thirteen words.)[9]

Riemann's most significant observation, it seems to me, comes at the very end of his brief remarks: "Nur eines ist in dem kleinen Stück von Bedeutung. . . . Goethe. . . läßt. . . eine Persönlichkeit, Dorn, über die weibliche Denkungsart sprechen. Recht interessant führt sie Dorn auf eine Mischung von Eitelheit und Scham zurück. Besser hörten wir das freilich von Goethe selbst. [Had illness not prevented the play's performance, the Teplitz audience would have so heard them, since Goethe had rehearsed the part of Dorn.] Besser wäre die 'Wette' eine Erzählung geblieben und etwa in die 'Wanderjahre' eingegangen, in deren Stil sie gehalten ist." Although *Die Wette* does express psychological insights important for Goethe—not only on "die weibliche Denkungsart," but also, for example, on "üble Laune," a Wertherian trait of Leonore, and "Raschheit," a Faustian trait of Eduard, both of which are serious threats to domestic bliss[10]—its central motif of the testing of two young people's power to "entsagen," which Förster, in his longest speech, calls "sonderbar," clearly establishes a close thematic connection with the novellas of *Wilhelm Meisters Wanderjahre oder die Entsagenden* (1821). Except for "Wo steckt der Verräter" (1820), these novellas were begun in 1807 and separately published between 1808 and 1818. Although *Dichtung und Wahrheit* had been Goethe's "Hauptgeschäft" since late 1810, and although he did not return to work on *Die Wanderjahre* until 1820, it was immediately after his return from Bohemia to Weimar in September, 1812, that he completed "Die neue Melusine" (perhaps then intending to use it in *Dichtung und Wahrheit*). *Die Wette* can therefore properly be considered in connection with *Die Wanderjahre*, and might be justified artistically as a novella in the form of dramatic dialogue, as a work to which the normal criteria of drama need not be applied. Read as such, it can bear comparison at least with "Wo steckt der Verräter" and, although it was first published in the final *Wanderjahre* of 1829, with the long-since written "Die gefährliche Wette"; the non-inclusion of *Die Wette*

---

[9] Both sentences occur toward the end of the first scene of the play; the one-sentence speech—Förster's antepenultimate in the scene—begins "Und ich komme gerade recht zu diesem wunderlichen Abenteuer. . ."; the other is his final speech, beginning "Wir wollen das Beste hoffen! Indessen bleibt das Mittel immer sonderbar. . . ."

[10] Cf. *1. Auftritt*, Dorn's penultimate speech, which refers back to his earlier—separate—thumbnail characterizations of the two lovers.

in *Die Wanderjahre* can be most conveniently explained by the fact that two novellas with a wager as their central motif would be reduplicative, although other factors—e.g., differences in tone, the absence of any serious tensions in Eduard and Leonore or between them, etc.—might also explain its non-inclusion.

But I would suggest that *Die Wette* is actually too competently dramatic to be disposed of as a novella in dialogue, and that it is too much a theater-piece to have fitted into the narrative or narrative-reflective context of *Die Wanderjahre*. This is not to claim that it is a work "worthy" of Goethe's best talents, but simply that its shortcomings as a play have been unfairly exaggerated. Indeed, from the fact that Goethe does not mention it in the account of 1812 in his *Tag- und Jahreshefte*, Henneberger—I believe alone of the critics here mentioned—is probably correct to infer that he was not long satisfied with it, although at the time of its composition he had characterized it as "dieses anmuthige Stück."[11] And his failure to print it with his other dramatic writings in the *Ausgabe letzter Hand* would seem further confirmation of the correctness of Henneberger's inference.

On superficial inspection the greatest structural defect of *Die Wette* would seem to be the disproportion between its four *Auftritte* of exposition and narrated action, and its much shorter final *Auftritt* of action and dénouement. On the printed page the final *Auftritt* constitutes, as noted above, less than a third of the text, but the time required for its performance makes it at least equivalent in length to the four preceding scenes, which have no time-consuming stage business and require no rhetorical or other pauses. Whereas Dorn immediately speaks—to himself—when he appears at the beginning of the play, Eduard and Leonore have extended stage-business before the opening soliloquies of the scene in which they appear. (The stage direction reads: "Eduard geht schnell auf und ab, spricht heftig mit sich selbst, sieht bald verwirrt bald unentschlossen aus. Leonore traurig, eine Arbeit in der Hand, blickt halb seufzend nach der Thür, dann besieht sie eine Brieftasche mit Eduards Chiffer und benetzt sie mit heißen Thränen.") Each of their two soliloquies is highly emotional, demanding pauses for reflection, and between them there is further stage-business (e.g., "Er setzt sich an den Schreibtisch, nimmt die Feder, doch statt zu schreiben, vertieft er sich in Gedanken" and "Sie läßt die Arbeit fallen und seufzt").

---

[11] Letter to Josephine O'Donell, 7 Aug. 1812. The value of *anmuthig* is not, as Sauer— emphasizing how Goethe dissociates himself from *Die Wette*, whose "Idee von der Kaiserin herrührt"—claims, laudatory of Maria Louisa, but represents an aesthetic judgment: the play has "classical" qualities. Cf. *Goethe-Wörterbuch*, s.v. "anmuthig, 1c: *bes mBez auf Inhalt, Motiv, Komposition. . . das Strenge, Steife, Heftige ausschließend*." (Goethe's "attributions" of the play to the Empress are in letters to Christiane, 1 and 5 Aug. 1812.)

Even more time-consuming, however, is a song which Leonore sings in the hope it will encourage Eduard to relent, and which brings about the dénouement, but which is not included in the printed text. That the song is sung in its entirety is clear from the stage direction, which has Eduard go to the door and pull back the curtain to Leonore's half of the stage (her room) while she is singing too close to the wall for him to see her; only when she finishes does she go to the door herself, "um zu horchen; sie sieht den Vorhang weggezogen, erblickt den Geliebten; Schrecken, Entzücken spricht sie aus. Die Thüre öffnet sich; sie ist in seinen Armen, ehe sie sich's versieht."

Die Wette is thus structurally better balanced than has been recognized by critics who read it without envisioning its actualized performance. It is not a mere closet drama, but the work of a writer with many decades—the last two with professional actors in a professional theater—of practical experience. The divided stage of the second *Bild*, with its "geheime Oeffnung" in the ceiling of both "Zimmer" through which Dorn and Förster may observe—and hear—the two lovers, represents a degree of theatrical complexity very different from anything demanded by *Pater Brey*, *Clavigo*, or *Die Geschwister*, and suggests, incidentally, a type of stage set more likely to occur in a nineteenth-century comedy or (Viennese) "Lokalposse" than in neoclassical comedy of the kind to which Henneberger's reference to Weiße would assign the play.[12]

But even the much condemned exposition of *Die Wette* is technically more competent than the play's detractors have been willing to recognize. Except for Dorn's opening monologue, which establishes the scene as an uncomfortable inn close to the chateau where Eduard and Leonore have been left to their ordeal, there is no use of soliloquy for plot exposition. This monologue, however, serves primarily to establish a comic tone, and introduces the play's action only with its final sentence, "Doch alles mag hingehen, wenn ich nur meine Absicht erreiche, wenn das junge Paar glücklich wird!" The explanation of Dorn's physical discomforts, and of his (mysterious) wish, then begins at once, with the arrival of his friend Förster. By the end of the first scene the exposition of what has happened before Dorn's week away is complete, and has taken the form of an interrogation.

---

[12] In Weimar a horizontally divided stage had been used two years earlier for Goethe's production of Zacharias Werner's *Der vierundzwanzigste Februar* (première, 24 Feb. 1810). The addition of a simultaneous vertical division—although on a far less ambitious scale than in such a work as Nestroy's *Zu ebener Erde und erster Stock* (1835)—may be intended as parodistic exaggeration of stage devices common to melodrama and farce. Of all who have written about *Die Wette*, only Werner (p. 54—cited H.G. Gräf, *Goethe über seine Dichtungen*, 2. Teil, IV [Frankfurt/Main: Rütten & Loening, 1908] 448) seems to have been aware of the technical difficulties that the staging of this "simple" play presents.

Particularly skillful is Goethe's unobtrusive but emphatic identification by name of all the characters who appear or will appear: Dorn's and Förster's first words to each other are their respective names, and within far less than a minute the "Liebenden" of *Die Wette* have been identified and named ("Leonore und Eduard, festgebannt"), while well before the scene's end "Johann und Friederike, welche ihre Herrschaften aufmerksam bewachen," have also been given emphatic mention.

The remaining three scenes in the inn are chiefly analytical—though narrated—"exposition" of *action*, of what has happened during Dorn's absence. Instead of having Dorn's commissioned observers (*Aufpasser*)—the lovers' respective servants—however, report immediately to him, Goethe breaks the pattern of interrogation by having the two friends leave to settle Dorn in his quarters and by devoting the second *Auftritt* to the two servants alone. Not finding Dorn as expected, Johann and Friederike ("wir gemeinen Leute," as Johann says) represent a healthy contrast to what Johann calls the "Raffinement" of Eduard and Leonore; their own hopes of early marriage—the so-called neoclassical subplot—are disposed of in a few lines incidental to their comments on the states of Eduard and Leonore. Johann's reportorial function in this scene is to say that he has "manches Drollige" to tell Dorn; what Friederike reports about Leonore is thus the scene's main expositional material, and so Goethe achieves (classical) clarity of emphasis at the same time that he varies the pattern of treating, as he had in the first scene, both lovers at the same time (or in immediate alternation).

The third scene returns to the pattern of interrogation as Dorn and Förster join the servants with Dorn's "Willkommen, ihr Leute! Sprecht, was ist vorgefallen?" Now Johann reports how Eduard has behaved until Dorn, having heard enough, dismisses him. (He does not leave, however, but stands aside with Friederike.) Again skillfully breaking the pattern of continuous interrogation, Goethe first lets a discussion of Johann's report by Dorn and Förster intervene before Dorn turns and says "Sprich also, Friederike!" This time the comments of Dorn and Förster accompany—rather than follow—Friederike's report, so that once again there is no repetition of an already employed dramatic pattern by the point when, at the end of the scene, Friederike is also dismissed. Only in the fourth and final scene of the first half of the play, which is also its shortest scene, is there repetition of the pattern of (gentle) disagreement between Dorn and Förster, but even this is not unvaried repetition: in the first scene Förster's objections primarily concerned possible "bedenkliche Folgen" of the trial to which the lovers are subjected; in the third, the general inferences about male and female psychology Dorn drew from the servants' reports; and now, Dorn's paternal confidence that his daughter Leonore will not be the one to give in first.

Conventional elements obviously abound in *Die Wette*, but they are used with a degree of assured technical competence rare in Goethe's writings for the stage. The absence of such competence does not diminish the effectiveness of works which have greater poetic qualities or many other forms of dramatic—and substantive—interest, but as could be shown, for example, by comparison with what Goethe completed of *Elpenor* (its two acts are largely expository, but they fail to make clear what the dramatic interest of its plot is to be), *Die Wette* demonstrates that when Goethe wrote his last "regular" play his sense of theatrical practicalities was, if anything, greater than ever before. *Des Epimenides Erwachen* may exploit theatrical machinery and allegory in ways that anticipate many features of the second part of *Faust*, but *Die Wette* is a reminder that the author of that part of *Faust* had long since become keenly conscious of more fundamental dramaturgical elements, and that it may thus be proper to read even Goethe's greatest poetic drama both as poetry *and* as drama.

What "saves" *Die Wette* from being merely a farce-like *pièce bien faite*, however, is not only the thoughtful analysis of masculine and feminine psychology which is normally considered its one redeeming grace, but also the harmony both of its "classical" dramatic structure and of a stylistic unity of tone in no small part achieved by what Henneberger and others have condemned as a major fault: the clearly deliberate non-use of "naturalistic" language by Friederike and Johann in a text too short to sustain the degree of tonal variety Goethe bravely—and in large measure successfully—risked in *Faust*.

Die Wette thus represents Goethe's farewell to conventional stage-drama, of which he had had more than his fill even five years before he resigned the directorship of the Weimar theater. In light of the ever increasing importance of narrative prose, about to become the dominant literary genre for the rest of the nineteenth century, the fact that it is a dramatization of what was originally conceived as a novella—and had been first narrated orally by Goethe at Teplitz—makes it even more appropriately such a farewell.

"Das Leben ist ein Gänsespiel"
Some Aspects of Goethe's *West-östlicher Divan*

> Talismane werd' ich in dem Buch zerstreuen,
> Das bewirkt ein Gleichgewicht.
> Wer mit gläubiger Nadel sticht
> Ueberall soll gutes Wort ihn freuen. (V,1)

Although H.A. Korff still considered the *West-östlicher Divan* primarily significant as the culmination of a series of groups of personal love lyrics inaugurated by Goethe's poems for Friederike Brion,[1] interpretation had long emphasized other aspects of the *Divan* as well—especially, since Konrad Burdach, its religious and ideological substance.[2] Both before and after Suleika had been identified with Marianne von Willemer, the *Divan* was often depreciated as an artificial exercise and its exoticism condemned as escapist.[3] It was thus perhaps inevitable that poems to which direct biographical and confessional significance could be attached at first enjoyed particular favor among those seeking to redeem the work.[4] In the heyday of "interpretation," the years 1939–1956 covered by the

---

[1] *Die Liebesgedichte des West-östlichen Divans in zeitlicher Folge mit Einführung und entstehungsgeschichtlichem Kommentar.* Zweite Auflage (Stuttgart, 1949—originally Leipzig, etc., 1947).

[2] E.g., Ernst Beutler in his edition, Sammlung Dieterich No. 125, 1956 (1st ed., Leipzig, 1943). On the absurdity of seeing only profundity in the *Divan*, cf. Claude David, "Note sur le 'Divan': D'un prétendu mysticisme," *Etudes Germaniques* 6 (1951): 220–30.

[3] Often by the Young Germans, with the notable exception of Heine, and their immediate successors (e.g., K. Goedeke). In his edition of *Goethe's Poems* (Boston, 1904), Charles Harris could still assert that "The Divan has generally been regarded as among the least successful of Goethe's lyric achievements" and explain this as a consequence of "the feeling of the reader that he is dealing with something artificial, something for the most part made and not lived" (254).

[4] Beutler's negative evaluation of "Kenne wohl der Männer Blicke" (VIII,9—numbering here follows Goethe, *West-östlicher Divan*, Kritische Ausgabe der Gedichte mit text-geschichtlichem Kommentar von Hans Albert Maier, 2 vols. [Tübingen, 1965]) seems to be little more than a consequence of his knowledge that the poem was written December 12, 1817, i.e., not as a part of the Marianne-Suleika series. It is actually a brilliant dramatic lyric, and placed between Hatem's explanation of Suleika's ring dream (VIII,8) and "Gingo biloba" (VIII,10) it also contributes to the dialogue pattern (the almost regular alternation of speakers) that is being established at this point in "Buch Suleika." The further function

Bernhard Blume-Adolf E. Schroeder bibliography "Interpretations of German Poetry," critics concentrated their attention on lyrics of the *Divan* which were to all intents fully understandable without reference to its cyclical character and Eastern elements.[5] Recent criticism has again sought to interpret the *Divan* in the broad context of its original frame of reference, as well as in that of Goethe's other immediate intellectual and literary interests during the years of its composition.[6] Quite properly concerned with making the work accessible to readers indifferent to or alienated from what can be regarded as the romantic-subjective lyric tradition, some interpreters have stressed aspects of form and substance which can be felt to be modern: tones of irony, and the emphatic recurrence of poetry itself as a major theme.[7] Although irony in the lyric is almost as old as Western literature, it implies the modern value "objectivity." As for lyric poetry on the theme of poetry, it is no novelty in Goethe's oeuvre, but in the *Divan* it, as well as what has been called "artistischer Selbstgenuß der Sprache,"[8] is more relevant to developments in the European lyric subsequent to Goethe than to poetic traditions—for poetry as a theme, these were chiefly didactic and allegorical—flourishing immediately before or during his lifetime.

Yet the Western European modernity of the *Divan* should not be uncritically overstressed. Much of its costume is frankly Eastern, and so is much of its "Stoff"—the sources noted by generations of editors and recorded in H.A. Maier's edition as "Antezedenzien." Goethe's chief oriental inspiration was Hafiz, a medieval Persian poet. But there is much in the *Divan* that derives from oriental wisdom literature—and "oriental wisdom" had long been synonymous with "ancient wisdom," a fact from which even

---

of this poem in relating "Buch Suleika" to "Buch des Sängers" has been nicely pointed out by Ingeborg Hillmann in her monograph (see n. 7, below) 33.

[5] "Interpretations of German Poetry (1939–1956): A Bibliography," *Monatshefte* 49 (1957): 241–63.

[6] E.g., Heinrich Meyer, *Goethe: Das Leben im Werk* (Hamburg-Bergedorf, 1951), emphasizing as "die eigentliche Keimzelle des Buches nicht die Suleikalyrik, sondern die Auseinandersetzung mit der Zerstörung" (626), and the renewed concern with what H.A. Maier records in his edition as "Antezedenzien," especially in the studies of Katharina Mommsen (*Goethe und die Moallakat* [Berlin, 1960]; *Goethe und 1001 Nacht* [Berlin, 1960]; *Goethe und Diez* [Berlin, 1961]).

[7] Cf. Henry Hatfield, *Goethe: A Critical Introduction* (Norfolk, 1963) 118 on irony; also Ferdinand Bergenthal, " 'Das Wort ist ein Fächer!' Über Goethes Sprachauffassung im West-östlichen Divan," *Literaturwissenschaftliches Jahrbuch. . . der Görres-Gesellschaft* 5 (1964): 335–44, and Ingeborg Hillmann, *Dichtung als Gegenstand der Dichtung: Untersuchungen zum Problem der Einheit des "West-östlichen Divan"* (Bonn, 1965 = Bonner Arbeiten zur deutschen Literatur, 10).

[8] Carl Becker, "Das Buch Suleika als Zyklus," in *Varia Variorum: Festgabe für Karl Reinhardt* (Münster/Köln, 1952) 225–52, here 225.

the radicals of the Enlightenment sought to profit by presenting what they regarded as timeless truths in the guise of oriental letter, tale, or drama. The unity in duality which is adumbrated by the compound *west-östlich* is thus not only that of East and West, or that of the lyrical (and botanical-biological) moment here and now so effectively symbolized by "Gingo biloba"; it is also the equally important polarity of past and present, of old and new, thematically announced in the very first lines of the *Divan*:

> Nord und West und Süd zersplittern,
> Throne bersten, Reiche zittern,
> Flüchte du, im reinen Osten
> Patriarchenluft zu kosten,
> Unter Lieben, Trinken, Singen,
> Soll dich Chisers Quell verjüngen.
> (I,1—"Hegire")

The rejuvenation that the poet seeks through his flight to the East and to the past is formal as well as substantive, is metamorphosis as well as renascence. Hence the relative richness of forms in Goethe's *Divan*, at least by contrast with the divan of Hafiz, and the almost systematic alternation of style and tone from poem to poem, from book to book, that permits a collection of largely brief, and rarely complex, poems to mirror so fully the polarities and tensions of the multiple place-time coordinates titularly abbreviated in the adjective *west-östlich*.[9]

It is regularly noted with approval in criticism of and commentaries on the *Divan* that in it Goethe only occasionally, and even then never rigorously, imitated the rigid versification or structure of his oriental poetic models. Accordingly, he could limit elaborate metaphor, for Persian poets a chief source of individuation and variation, to occasional use. Although a few metaphors and hyperboles in the *Divan* derive from known oriental writers, the majority of them, and even some that have specific Eastern sources, belong to categories also cultivated by European poets—a point made in the quatrain:

> Herrlich ist der Orient
> Ueber's Mittelmeer gedrungen,

---

[9] The predominance of certain metrical patterns stressed by Wolfgang Kayser, "Beobachtungen zur Verskunst des West-östlichen Divans," *PEGS*, n.s. 23 (1953–54): 74–96 (also in his *Die Vortragsreise* [Bern, 1958] 149–68) makes variations in versification the more emphatic; the attaching of a specific verse form to an individual speaker, noted by Kayser with particular reference to Suleika, is a device dependent upon application of the un-Eastern principle of formal variation.

Nur wer Hafis liebt und kennt
Weiß was Calderon gesungen.
(VI,14c)

A poem like "Nachklang" (VIII,33), however, is "oriental" in feeling less by virtue of its Hafizian "Mondgesicht"[10]—

Laß mich nicht so der Nacht dem Schmerze,
Du allerliebstes, du mein Mondgesicht!
O du mein Phosphor, meine Kerze,
Du meine Sonne, du mein Licht.

—than because it immediately follows "Hochbild" ("Die Sonne, Helios der Griechen"). For by mythologizing a natural phenomenon, and especially by drawing attention to classical antecedent, Goethe is deliberately going contrary to the practice of Persian poets for whom, as he insisted in his *Noten und Abhandlungen zu besserem Verständnis des. . . Divans*, "die Naturgegenstände. . . zum Surrogat der Mythologie [werden]."[11] Despite the word "Mondgesicht," which even a Western poet might simply have invented for the rhyme with "du mein Licht," "Nachklang" in no way represents a deviation from the tradition of the lyric epigram as cultivated in classical antiquity and by Renaissance poets and their successors. If one seeks a counterpart of "Nachklang," there is no need to search the pages of Hafiz; it is sufficient to look in the Palatine Anthology (7.670) or at a neolatin lyric like Pontano's "De Stella,"[12] which I quote not because it might have influenced Goethe's poem (there is no evidence that Goethe read any verse by Pontano, although he may have known the prose work *Charon*), but because its ghazal-like repetitions (of "refulget" and "refert") no less than its metaphors illustrate with a mere three distichs how little Goethe needed to deviate from the classical Western tradition to create a seemingly oriental lyric:

---

[10] In his *Divan* commentary (HA 2 [12. Aufl., München, 1981]), Erich Trunz singles out this borrowing from Hafiz in his general discussion of metaphor (563) and in his notes to "Nachklang" records many occurrences of "Mondgesicht" in Hammer's translation (641).

[11] "Allgemeines," HA 2:165.

[12] *Eridanus*, VIII (Ioannis Ioviani Pontani *Carmina: Ecloghe—Elegie—Liriche* a cura di Johannes Oeschger [Bari, 1948] 389). The poem in the Anthology is a funeral epigram: Ἀστὴρ πρὶν μὲν ἔλαμπες ἐνὶ ζωοῖσιν Ἑῷος· / νῦν δὲ θανὼν λάμπεις Ἕσπερος ἐν φθιμένοις.

Nostra die quod Stella nitet, quod nocte refulget,
Solem Stella die, sidera nocte refert.
Nocte eadem surgente nitet, cedente refulget,
Phosphoron hic, illic Hesperon ipsa refert.
Ergo eadem mihi sol, eadem mihi sidus et una
Lucifer est, eadem Vesper et una mihi.[13]

The line between conventional formulation and personalized expression is hardly clearer in the *Divan* than that between Eastern and Western or ancient and modern types of rhetoric. The verses expressing Hatem's surprise that Suleika has written poems can be read as orientally disguised biographical information, since women poets had hardly been uncommon in Europe since the Renaissance. It is also possible, however, to interpret his astonishment at the discovery of high talent—"Atem. . . / So harmonisch als der meine" (VIII,28)—not as an Eastern fiction, but simply as a Western topos of hyperbolic compliment, properly comparable with the sonnet "I Versi di Nice" of Clemente Bondi (whose collected poems, given him by the Empress Ludovica, Goethe sufficiently appreciated to write, in 1812, the sonnet to Bondi beginning "Aus jenen Ländern echten Sonnenscheines / Beglückten oft mich Gaben der Gefilde. . ."). Bondi is perhaps more transparently flattering than Goethe-Hatem—

Sogno? son desto? e nell' orecchio mio
Suona non finto l'insperato canto?
O pur sedotto da soave incanto
Sè stesso inganna il credulo desío?
Questa che scrive è Nice mia? Son' io
Cuí degna amica il ciel di sì gran vanto?
E queste note armoníose tanto
Su questo foglio la sua man scolpío?
O forse tu per mio piacer dettasti,
Febo, quei versi, e ad onorar te stesso
Poscia il bel nome sotto lor segnasti?

---

[13] The phrasing of Pontano's conclusion may itself be formulaic, for there is a close equivalent of it at the end of Goethe's "Klein ist unter den Fürsten Germaniens freilich der meine" ("Epigramme. Venedig 1790," 34b: ". . . und Er war mir August und Mäcen." The repetition by Pontano of words in end-position is more in the tradition of classical and Neolatin *Anacreontea* than of the elegiac poets; although only a stylistic mannerism (unlike the obligatory repetition of the rhyme word in a ghazal), it remained a striking feature of both unrhymed and rhymed "anacreontic" vernacular verse as long as the Anacreontics were imitated.

Degno è di te lo stil leggiadro e ameno;
Ma deh! se fosser tuoi, Febo, il confesso,
Se fosser tuoi mi piacerebbon meno.[14]

—but the motif of amazement, which he caps with a classical Greek allusion, is as much the core of his poem as it is of Goethe's, with its brief roster of classical Persian poets.

In "Buch Suleika" the use of transparently conventional elements in the tradition of Renaissance occasional poetry may be explained by extraneous biographical reference to Suleika-Marianne's facility—or talent—for occasional verse. Elsewhere in the *Divan*, however, their use can only be regarded as the programmatic demonstration of elements common to Eastern and Western poetry. A nice illustration, if merely because of its brevity and apparent unambiguity, is a poem of "Buch der Betrachtungen":

Das Leben ist ein Gänsespiel:
Je mehr man vorwärts gehet,
Je früher kommt man an das Ziel,
Wo niemand gerne stehet.

Man sagt die Gänse wären dumm,
O! glaubt mir nicht den Leuten:
Denn eine sieht einmal sich rum
Mich rückwärts zu bedeuten.

Ganz anders ist's in dieser Welt
Wo alles vorwärts drücket,
Wenn einer stolpert oder fällt
Keine Seele rückwärts blicket.
(IV,16)

Following Burdach, Erich Trunz explains: "Anknüpfend an ein Gesellschafts-spiel mit Würfeln. Die Gänse-Figuren rücken um die gewürfelte Zahl vor. Kommt man auf ein Feld, wo eine rückwärtsblickende Gans gemalt ist, muß man zurück oder muß warten. Kommt man auf ein Feld, wo eine tote Gans abgebildet ist, so scheidet man aus."[15] It is perhaps also helpful to know

---

[14] *Poesie* (Pisa, 1799) 1:95.
[15] Goethe, *Gedichte* (n. 10, above) 604.

Burdach's explanation of "das Ziel, wo niemand gerne stehet" as "Feld 58 (Bild: Tod mit der Sense oder auch eine tote Gans), dessen Betreten das Ausscheiden aus dem laufenden Spiel bedingt,"[16] although without any of this information, or even erroneously confusing *Gänsespiel* and *Gänse-marsch*, the substantive content of the poem is perfectly clear. Düntzer discursively states it thus: "Das Leben schreitet unaufhaltsam seinem Ende zu; jeder wandelt fürbaß, ohne sich um die Andern zu kümmern, die hinter ihm kommen. Die Spitze des Gedichts liegt gerade darin, daß man immer vorwärts geht, ohne einmal stehn zu bleiben, um rückwärts zu sehn. Das Leben ist aber ein ganz eigener Gänsemarsch, da man nach einem Ziele schreitet, das man nicht gern erreicht. Von den Gänsen dreht sich doch wohl eine einmal um, als ob sie einem etwas sagen wolle." Then, as an afterthought, he adds: "Freilich ist V.8 *mich* auffallend, da man eher an eine andere Gans denken möchte."[17] It is, of course, the *mich* that in part gives Goethe's epigram its personal lyric quality, and this in turn has an important function in the ordering of poems in "Buch der Betrachtungen," since one determining factor is alternation between poems in which personal first and second person forms occur, and others with only impersonal second and third person forms.[18]

Since goose is a European game, it might be thought that the poem qualifies as *west-östlich* only because it takes something familiar and ordinary as the basis for developing in an oriental manner a novel metaphor of serious character. Writing about Persian poets, Goethe declared: "Ein immer bewegtes öffentliches Leben, in welchem alle Gegenstände gleichen Wert haben, wogt vor unserer Einbildungskraft, deswegen uns ihre Vergleichungen oft so sehr auffallend und mißliebig sind. Ohne Bedenken verknüpfen sie die edelsten und niedrigsten Bilder, an welches Verfahren wir uns nicht so leicht gewöhnen."[19] Goose here would thus be simply a substitute, perhaps deliberately inferior, for chess in a poem of Hafiz, permitting "Das Leben ist ein Gänsespiel" to serve in the *Divan* of 1819 as

---

[16] Goethe, Jubiläums-Ausgabe 5:354.

[17] Heinrich Düntzer, *Goethes Westöstlicher Divan* (Leipzig, 1878 = Erläuterungen zu den Deutschen Klassikern, 1. Abth., XXXI–XXXIII) 271.

[18] In the *Divan* of 1819 the "Gänsespiel" poem (personal first, and impersonal second/third, person) followed "Behandelt die Frauen mit Nachsicht!" and preceded "Freygebiger wird betrogen," both in the impersonal second and third person. In the final *Divan* of 1827 the completely third-person "Das Leben ist ein schlechter Spaß" has been inserted before it, and after it "Die Jahre nahmen dir, du sagst, so vieles" (personal first and second person) and "Vor den Wissenden sich stellen" (impersonal second and third person equally distributed) precede "Freygebiger wird betrogen" (whose impersonal second-person forms appear only in the final two lines).

[19] *Noten und Abhandlungen. . .* , "Allgemeines" (HA 2:162).

a stylistic transition from "Behandelt die Frauen mit Nachsicht," a versification of popular wisdom from the "Sunna," to "Freygebiger wird betrogen," which completely lacks any specific Eastern or Western coloring.

In the final *Divan* of 1827 the functions and implications of "Das Leben ist ein Gänsespiel" are more complex. Before it is inserted "Das Leben ist ein schlechter Spaß," whose German colloquial tone provides an immediate Western foil to the Easternism of "Behandelt die Frauen mit Nachsicht." After it is placed the lyric dialogue "Die Jahre nahmen dir, du sagst, so vieles," a more elegiac—yet more affirmative—expression of life's transitoriness; like "Freygebiger wird betrogen," which now follows a new "oriental" poem, "Vor den Wissenden sich stellen," it is neither Eastern nor Western in coloring. Partly because of the unavoidable assimilation of the introductory metaphor of the "Gänsespiel" poem to the German-proverbial sphere of "Das Leben ist ein schlechter Spaß," but also because its four-stress *abab* quatrains, each line of which is a syntactic unit, are now counterposed to the longer, often runover lines of "Die Jahre nahmen dir, du sagst, so vieles" (and so no longer represent as marked a metrical variation as when they stood between equally short and shorter couplets), "Das Leben ist ein Gänsespiel" has lost some of its *lyric* significance.

Although not all of Goethe's additions to the *Divan* of 1827 have been regarded by every critic as felicitously placed, the consensus is clearly that most insertions represent thematic or formal strengthening of one or more of the elements which contribute to the cyclic structure of its separate books. The tone of affirmation of the poems inserted before and after "Das Leben ist ein Gänsespiel" helps clarify the enigmatic "Freygebiger wird betrogen" that originally followed it: after the pessimism of "Wenn einer stolpert oder fällt / Keine Seele rückwärts blicket," the bitterly ironic injunction "Betrogener betrüge!" could too easily be misunderstood as an expression of (very un-Goethean) cynicism.[20] But is this gain worth the attendant partial loss of Eastern *and* lyric qualities that had formerly attached to the "Gänsespiel" poem? Has its function not become less complex? Is it now, as it were, simply a metaphor-bridge between proverbial pessimism and the series of affirmations of life—so greatly strengthened by "Mir bleibt genug! Es bleibt Idee und Liebe!" ("Die Jahre nehmen dir. . .")—which still conclude "Buch der Betrachtungen?"

---

[20] Further reasons for rejecting the traditional interpretation of "Freygebiger wird betrogen" as wholly pessimistic are offered in my "Zum besseren Verständnis einiger Gedichte des *West-östlichen Divan*," *Euphorion* 59 (1965): 178–206, here 185 (reprinted in Edgar Lohner, ed., *Interpretationen zum West-östlichen Divan Goethes* [Darmstadt: Wissenschaftliche Buchgesellschaft, 1973] 95–146, here 108f.).

To answer these questions it is necessary to recall once again that for the *Divan* "west-östlich" is also synonymous with "alt-neu." This is the sense of Goethe's often cited warning, whose time span embraces classical antiquity, "Wer nicht von dreytausend Jahren / Sich weiß Rechenschaft zu geben, / Bleib im Dunkeln unerfahren, / Mag von Tag zu Tage leben" (V,13), as well as of the self-injunction of "Unbegrenzt" (II,6), "Nun töne Lied mit eignem Feuer! / Denn du bist älter, du bist neuer."

The game of goose—its very name already obsolete in England by 1801 according to the Oxford dictionary[21]—apparently ceased to be popular in Germany early in the nineteenth century. Otherwise Düntzer, who also drew from earlier *Divan* commentaries, would surely have been less inexact in his interpretation of Goethe's poem.[22] And the author of the entry "Gänsespiel" in the *Deutsches Wörterbuch*—after describing the board game and citing from Enoch Gläser's *Schäferbelustigung* of 1653 the couplet, entitled "Gansspiel," "Wir sehn durch manches glükk auf gleiches ziel im herzen. / den wunsch verrükt der tod. wer gläubt, das dis ein scherzen?"— would hardly have otherwise added, "In andern spielen stellen die spielenden selber die gänse dar und ein solches musz bei GÖTHE gemeint sein. . . ." For it was certainly the board game that Goethe had in mind when he wrote the *Divan* poem and when, in letters of 1828 and 1831, he used "Gänsespiel" as a metaphor for human life.[23]

Goethe may well have played the game with his young son, especially since it has never ceased to be popular in France—it is also still played in Switzerland—and may, even after a possible decline in German favor toward the latter part of the eighteenth century, have enjoyed a revival in Germany during the period of French emigration. He surely knew its mention as an adult pastime in *L'Avare* of Molière and *Le Joueur* of Regnard, and from emblematic verses on the younger Surugue's engraving of *Le jeu de l'oye*, the genre painting by Chardin, he probably derived—directly or indirectly—the metaphor of life as a game of goose. He is also hardly likely

---

[21] *The Oxford Universal Dictionary on Historical Principles*, 3rd. ed. (Oxford, 1955) 813. (Two decades later, in *Don Juan* [XII, lviii], Byron called "good society. . . / 'The royal game of Goose,' . . . / Where everybody has some separate aim, / An end to answer, or a plan to lay," but his metaphor is revealingly unspecific.)

[22] Düntzer's uncertainty is reflected in his note (loc. cit.) to the word *Gänsespiel*: "Gänsegang, Gänsemarsch. Sanders denkt an ein Würfelspiel, auch Hildebrand will ein Kinderspiel verstehen, bei welchem die Kinder die Gänse gespielt. *Gänsegang* führt schon das Campesche Wörterbuch (1808) in dem Sinne an, wie wir jetzt *Gänsemarsch* brauchen, das nach Hildebrand erst in den dreißiger Jahren in Gebrauch gekommen sein soll."

[23] To Marianne von Willemer, Jan. 3, 1828 (J.J. Riese's death a departure "aus diesem Gänsespiel"); to Zelter, Dec. 14, 1831.

to have been ignorant of the fact that Napoleon played it avidly. But in any event, he clearly knew it better than most explicators of his *Divan*.

The game of goose was invented or became widely popular in the late Renaissance. Known in Italy simply as "Il dilettevole gi(u)oco di l'oca," since 1640 almost every French form of it has borne some variant of the name "Le noble jeu de l'oie renouvelé des Grecs."[24] The pseudo-attribution of a classical antecedent remained normal through the eighteenth century, and it was also sometimes claimed that the number of spaces through which flat pieces (*not* geese!) were moved had been established in light of the classical theory of climacteric years, for the standard board comprises 63 spaces, or seven times nine. These run in a spiral from the outside to the center, where a roast goose is depicted. The pieces, one for each player, were moved according to the total points made on successive throws of a pair of dice, very much as in "Parchisi, the Royal Game of India," with doubled points or repeated throws allowed for doublets, and with extra advances granted a piece reaching spaces with the picture of a goose, which are nos. 5, 9, 14, 18, etc. (Ecclesiastics were provided with a polyhedron that offered equivalent point combinations.) Contrary to the statement of Burdach, the direction in which the geese look seems never to have affected the value of the spaces in which they are depicted, but *other* spaces were unlucky: a piece could be delayed by (falling in) a well (no. 31), charged for passing (landing on) a bridge (no. 6) or staying at an inn (no. 19), and sent back to start over if it landed on space no. 58 (only five spaces short of victory!), on which death was variously represented by a skeleton, a death's-head, a tomb, a grave, etc.—though apparently not yet in Goethe's day by a goose accidentally run over by some vehicle.

For appreciating Goethe's poem, the fact that the "death square"—"das Ziel, / Wo niemand gerne stehet"—does not mean total exclusion from the game, but simply a temporary, though serious reversal of fortune, cannot be too much insisted upon. Goethe never ceased to proclaim the principle formulated for Wilhelm Meister as "Gedenke zu leben," and it is his voice that we hear when the pastor of *Hermann und Dorothea* declares, "Des Todes rührendes Bild steht / Nicht als Schrecken dem Weisen und nicht als Ende dem Frommen. . . ." In the *Divan* death is not absent, but even in

[24] For this and what follows, see Henry-René d'Allemagne's lavishly illustrated *Le noble jeu de l'oie en France, de 1640 à 1950*. . . (Paris, 1950), particularly the section "Histoire des jeux de l'oie" (23–60) contributed by René Poirier. O. Strohmeyer, "Zu Goethes Divan," *Zft. f. d. dt. Unterricht* 18 (1904): 210f., noted that forms of the game with 64 to 100 spaces (with "eine rückwärtssehende Gans" depicted on penalty spaces) were being sold in Kiel in this century. What Goethe knew, however, is the classical form of the gameboard "worauf. . . Gänse und allerlei andere Dinge in 63 Abteilungen abgebildet sind" (1819 edition of Heinsius's dictionary, cited by Strohmeyer).

"Buch Timur" it is primarily important as "Todeskälte" (VII,1) and as the fiery death of "tausend Rosen" to which the destruction of the "Myriaden Seelen [die] / Timurs Herrschaft aufgezehrt" (VII,2) is merely incidental.[25] Elsewhere, from the opening "Hegire" ("Wisset nur, daß Dichterworte / Um des Paradieses Pforte / Immer leise klopfend schweben, / Sich erbittend ew'ges Leben") through the "Wiederfinden" of "Buch Suleika" ("Beyde sind wir auf der Erde / Musterhaft in Freud und Quaal / Und ein zweytes Wort: Es werde! / Trennt uns nicht zum zweytenmal" [VIII,35]), the "Es ist gut" of "Buch der Parabeln" ("Und ruft er uns, wohlan! es sey! / Nur, das beding' ich, alle zwey" [X,10]), the "Vermächtnis alt persischen Glaubens" of "Buch des Parsen" (XI,1), and the entire final "Buch des Paradieses," death is the well-paid price of life lived fully, is even the transcendence of life:

> Und so lang du das nicht hast,
> Dieses: Stirb und werde!
> Bist du nur ein trüber Gast
> Auf der dunklen Erde.
> ("Selige Sehnsucht"—I,17)

Just as there is no whit of depreciation of this life or of this world in "Selige Sehnsucht,"[26] so there is none in "Das Leben ist ein Gänsespiel." Its theme is human indifference in the sundered Europe of "Hegire," in the selfishly competitive and envious society repeatedly satirized throughout the *Divan* (especially in "Buch der Betrachtungen" and in the immediately subsequent "Buch des Unmuths" and "Buch der Sprüche"), and its speaker is the poet who in the person of Hatem originally wrote "Timur spricht" (V,15b) as "Was? Ihr misbilliget den kräftigen Sturm / Des Übermuths? Du Volck von Laffen! / Wenn Allah mich bestimmt zum Wurm / So hätt er mich als Wurm geschaffen."[27] This poet has imaginatively chosen to attach Eastern talismanic value to the direction in which the geese depicted on the game board face, and so he has given renewed significance to an old Western

---

[25] In the secular context of "Buch des Unmuths" the enjoining of suicide upon the enemies of Mohammed (taken almost verbatim from Sura 22 of the Koran) is so weakened as to be little more than an orientalized "Go hang!" or "Schert euch zum Teufel!"

[26] In the article mentioned above, n. 20, I have pointed out (182, n. 17) that "dark earth" may be a classical formula rather than an expression of depreciation of this life; further confirmation seems offered by the ode of Anacreon beginning Ἐ γῆ μέλαινα πίνει. The epithet "dark" meant little to poets who had not *seen*, as Goethe had, the great Mediterranean contrast between land and gleaming sea, and so Ronsard omitted it in his version ("La terre les eaux va boyvant"), while Cowley in his replaced it by "thirsty."

[27] Goethe, *West-östlicher Divan*, ed. H.A. Maier 2:222.

emblem. Instead of the *memento mori* of Enoch Gläser's "Gansspiel" we have a "Gedenke zu leben," and the less pessimistic but still shallow didacticism of the quatrain of Antoine Danchet that "explained" Surugue's engraving of "Le jeu de l'oye"—

Avant que la Carrière à ce jeu soit finie,
Que de risques à craindre et d'écueils à franchir.
Enfants, vous ne pouvez trop tôt y réfléchir,
C'est une image de la vie.[28]

—has been metamorphosed by a poet with a clear eye for visual detail into a self-contained lyric epigram simultaneously extending and elaborating the affirmative vision of life the whole *Divan* embodies.

Because so much emblem poetry represents little more than an intellectual game, it is understandable that "serious" critics either silently ignore "Das Leben ist ein Gänsespiel," or mention the poem only in passing, as if it were a literary trifle. Nevertheless, although in the *Divan* the highest value is "Liebe," to "Spiel" there surely attaches much of the positive significance it has in Schiller's classical aesthetics.[29] The fiction of Hatem-Goethe writing "Eastern" poetry is itself a game. At times it is even played with bits of party costume and the tinsel decorations of masquerade (as in "Buch Suleika": "Die Sonne kommt! Ein Prachterscheinen" and "Komm Liebchen, komm! umwinde mir die Mütze" [VIII,12 and 13]); at others it becomes the precariously serious ball game of passionate devotion (VIII,16, l. 16ff.). Yet tragedy is never permitted to intrude all the way—even the pathos of "Hochbild" is, after all, followed by the rejection of complete renunciation in "Nachklang," and there is no book of the *Divan* which ends on a defeatist tone. The "Gänsespiel" poem may, especially out of context and with its central metaphor imperfectly understood, seem mere negative satire. But "zuletzt ist unerläßlich, / Daß der Dichter manches hasse, / Was unleidlich ist und häßlich / Nicht wie Schönes leben lasse" ("Elemente" [I,7]), and in this sense its function is positive.

---

[28] Cited by Poirier, 28. The name of Danchet (1671–1748) does not occur in Goethe's writings, although he is alluded to (by Diderot) in *Rameaus Neffe*. Chardin was admired by Diderot as a master of color, as Goethe notes in "Diderots Versuch über die Malerei," but there is no evidence that Goethe shared Diderot's admiration.

[29] The word "Spiel" itself is not, however, used for play in this highest sense, but is reserved for erotic play (III,6 l. 9), for activity in general (IV,15 l. 4), for sense response (IV,17 l. 2); its equivalent is the neologism "Lustgebrauch" when, in the "Behramgur" poem (VIII,29 l. 6), the theme is an elevated or spiritual love.

Goethe's creative use of emblematic elements throughout all his works has recently received much attention, and that he conceived of the *Divan* as expressing also the Western emblematic tradition is clear from the vignette he suggested accompany "Lieblich ist des Mädchens Blick" (IV,4) in Gubitz's *Gaben der Milde*—"ein paar Hände, wovon die eine einen reichen Ärmel über einer mit Ringen geschmückt[en] zeigte, welche ein Geldstück in eine nackte Hand fallen läßt, die nur ein Stückchen Leinwand schließt." The same concern with the visually emblematic explains his (abandoned) idea of having individual poems of the printed *Divan* separated not by asterisks, but by "Waffen, Reichsinsignien, Waren, geschliffene Glasflaschen, Rosen, streitbare Nachtigallen, Juwelenketten, Ringe, Perlenschnuren, Spiegel usw. . . ."[30] (In the printing of *Divan* poems in Cotta's *Taschenbuch für Damen* Goethe's suggestion of having vignettes of turbans replace asterisks was actually followed.) "Das Leben ist ein Gänsespiel" thus introduces literarily one of the "Elemente" Goethe wished to incorporate in the *Divan*; it exemplifies, particularly in contrast to the lines of Danchet, the felicitous revitalization of the Renaissance and classical tradition of emblematic poetry. Above all, however, it gives vigorous expression to the sense of the indestructibility of the world of the spirit—of "Idee und Liebe" as a hendiadys rather than as a pair of values[31]—which is the theme of so many *Divan* poems, and thus it properly occupies a modest place beside lyrics that, like "Wiederfinden" and "Sommernacht" (IX,19), more grandiosely express the oneness of Western "past" and Eastern "present" which in the *Divan* is the primary artistic symbol of Goethe's sustaining vision of life as unity in multiplicity.[32]

[30] Full detail and illustrations are provided by E.F. Kossmann, "Drei Vignetten Goethes zu 'Divan'-Gedichten," *Jahrbuch der Goethe-Gesellschaft* 14 (1928): 147–51. For the importance of emblematic elements in Goethe's lyrics, see Arthur Henkel, *Wandrers Sturmlied: Versuch das dunkle Gedicht des jungen Goethe zu verstehen* (Frankfurt/Main, 1962).

[31] My reasons for regarding "Idee und Liebe" as a hendiadys are given in the article mentioned above, n. 20 (185f.—in the reprint 108).

[32] For Hammer—and Goethe in his *Noten und Abhandlungen*—Hafiz was a Persian Horace, and it was thus not incongruous for Düntzer to draw parallels between "Das Leben ist ein schlechter Spaß" and Horace's first satire, or to note that the opening words of "Die Jahre nahmen dir, du sagst, so vieles" echo Horace's "multa [commoda anni] recedentes adimunt" (*Epist.* II,3 l. 176). Momme Mommsen, "Schwan und Schwänchen," *Goethe* 13 (1951): 290–95, has drawn attention to the possible influence of Martial—the distich is cited under Maier's "Antezedenzien," 2:370—on "Heute hast du gut gegessen" (IX,15), and Walter Marg, "Goethes 'Wiederfinden,' " *Euphorion* 46 (1952): 59–79, points out what he regards as patent echoes of Ovid in the earliest preserved draft of "Wiederfinden" (VIII,35, and Maier 2:334), the Platonic and neoplatonic component of which had always been recognized. Ingeborg Hillmann, op. cit. 47, is thus surely right in rejecting the common older view that the *Divan* in any way reveals a repudiation by Goethe of classical aesthetic values.

Goethe's *Novelle* as Pictorial Narrative

Eckermann records as of 15 January 1827 the first critical discussion of Goethe's *Novelle*; in it both speakers comment on pictorial elements in the text, Eckermann reporting:

Ich. . . las bis zu der bedeutenden Stelle, wo alle um den toten Tiger herumstehen und der Wärtel die Nachricht bringt, daß der Löwe oben an der Ruine sich in die Sonne gelegt habe.

Während des Lesens hatte ich die außerordentliche Deutlichkeit zu bewundern, womit alle Gegenstände. . . vor die Augen gebracht waren. Der Auszug zur Jagd, die Zeichnungen der alten Schloßruine, der Jahrmarkt, der Feldweg zur Ruine, alles trat entschieden vor die Anschauung. . . .

Das Gespräch lenkte sich auf den Inhalt. "Eine schöne Situation," sagte ich, "ist die, wo Honorio, der Fürstin gegenüber, am tot ausgestreckten Tiger steht, die klagende weinende Frau mit dem Knaben herzugekommen ist, und auch der Fürst mit dem Jagdgefolge zu der seltsamen Gruppe soeben herbeieilt. Das müßte ein treffliches Bild machen. . . ."

"Gewiß," sagte Goethe, "das wäre ein schönes Bild; — doch," fuhr er nach einigem Bedenken fort, "der Gegenstand wäre fast zu reich und der Figuren zu viele, so daß die Gruppierung und Verteilung von Licht und Schatten sehr schwer werden würde. Allein den früheren Moment, wo Honorio auf dem Tiger kniet und die Fürstin am Pferde gegenüber steht, habe ich mir wohl als Bild gedacht. . . ."

When Goethe ignores his hypothesis that the earlier moment is the text's climax (*Kern*)—and does not point out that there has already been one hunt-scene with massed figures that recalls Wouvermans in Dresden's *Gemäldegalerie* which he especially admired—Eckermann observes

daß diese Novelle von allen übrigen der "Wanderjahre" einen ganz verschiedenen Charakter trage, indem darin alles Darstellung des Äußern, alles real sei. "Sie haben recht," sagte Goethe, "Innerliches finden Sie in dem Gelesenen fast gar nicht, und in meinen übrigen Sachen ist davon fast zuviel."

When Eckermann three days later, having read the rest of *Novelle*, again discussed the work with Goethe, their comments dealt almost exclusively with the denouement, which Eckermann, like many later readers, found not only "zu ideal, zu lyrisch," but also too abrupt. But Goethe, with skillful morphological analogies, soon persuaded him of the "Trefflichkeit dieser wunderbaren Komposition," whose task was to show "wie das Unbändige, Unüberwindliche"—here follows the word conveniently ignored by those who would claim Goethe for pacifism—"oft besser durch Liebe und Frömmigkeit als durch Gewalt bezwungen werde." Only at the end of their long discussion did Goethe again mention the pictorial aspect of his tale, for which prose rather than the "ottava rima" once advised for it by Schiller was best suited, inasmuch as "es kam sehr auf genaue Zeichnung der Lokalität an, wobei man doch in solchen Reimen wäre geniert gewesen." Then Goethe's explanation of the distinctly different "Charakter und Ton" of each story in *Wilhelm Meisters Wanderjahre*—"ich ging dabei zu Werke wie ein Maler, der bei gewissen Gegenständen gewisse Farben vermeidet und gewisse andere dagegen vorwalten läßt"—permits Eckermann again to express admiration of "das Detail. . . , womit besonders das Landschaftliche" is depicted in *Novelle*, and Goethe to observe factually:

> Ich habe niemals die Natur poetischer Zwecke wegen betrachtet. Aber weil mein früheres Landschaftszeichnen und dann mein späteres Naturforschen mich zu einem beständigen genauen Ansehen der natürlichen Gegenstände trieb, so habe ich die Natur bis in ihre kleinsten Details nach und nach auswendig gelernt, dergestalt daß, wenn ich als Poet etwas brauche, es mir zu Gebote steht und ich nicht leicht gegen die Wahrheit fehle.

(Here the conversation shifts, with mention of the indebtedness of the author of *Wilhelm Tell* to Goethe for Swiss local color, to Schiller.)

Despite its title, Goethe's tale is not a novella if, as normally, by that term is understood a narrative continually focusing on one human actor or group of such actors; and like Eckermann many critics—usually, like him, with good grace, although occasionally with evident uneasiness or outright disapproval—have acknowledged this fact. For before the arrival of the tiger's mistress and her son (neither previously mentioned), of the Prince and his attendants, of the lion tamer (also a new figure), and of the castellan who reports that the lion is now calmly resting "hinter der höhern Ringmauer. . . im Sonnenschein," the constellation of figures dominating the text has radically changed with the departure of the Prince's prolix uncle. In the remaining, scant third of *Novelle* the Prince soon hastens away with a few attendants, followed more slowly by the Princess with the others, so that the only character left from earlier parts of the text is Honorio, superfluously ready to shoot the lion should it be necessary to do so (and hence, perhaps, unresponsive to either plea or prophecy from the tiger's—now lion's— mistress); but he too soon disappears from the text, left behind as the mother and castellan move up to where her child will come into view with a lion even more "stumm-freundlich" than any in the scene "Bergschluchten" of *Faust*. None of Goethe's working titles—*Die Jagd, Jagd-Novelle, Die wunderbare Jagd, Die Jagdgeschichte*—fits a text in which no hunting is seen. Two further titles Goethe considered were *Der Tiger und der Löwe* and *Das Kind mit dem Löwen*, but he obviously recognized their inadequacies: they focus attention on only a narrow spectrum of the text's motifs and, what is worse, suggest a moral fable in the tradition of La Fontaine. Even less appropriate a title, since Honorio has not seen the lion by the story's end, is Erwin Wäsche's *Honorio und der Löwe*, preferable to which, although unsatisfactory for reasons already indicated, would be *Honorio und die Fürstin* (inferred from Richard Thieberger's discussion of "Die Fürstin als Heldin von Goethes *Novelle*").

Discontinuity, as shifting from the language of stylized realism to that of affective lyricality, as replacing one group of protagonists by another, and as introducing such a wealth of motifs that on first reading it is impossible to know which are important and which merely tangential, is not so great that most critical readers have the least uncertainty about the purport of *Novelle*, formulated with unrivaled succinctness by E.M. Wilkinson as "the taming of the dionysiac by the apolline." Although no lion is tamed in *Novelle*, its lion has been tamed and, as "der Gezähmte, . . . der dem eigenen friedlichen Willen Anheimgegebene," is properly the symbol of a preference for the apolline present from the first two paragraphs of the text, where it appears as communality, harmony, cooperation, affinity, and order, to the last two, where it is seen as affection of lion for child, child for lion, and mother for child, as harmony between disparate creatures, as oneness with God-Nature, and as ingenuous benevolence. (Interpreters of *Novelle* whose views of it—though sometimes formulated with more caution or less explicitness—are consonant with Wilkinson's and Goethe's own interpretations include Karl-Heinz Hahn, Maurice Marache, Victor Lange, Viktor Žmegač, Gerhard Schulz, and—despite his finding more that is "miraculous" in it than do most of its admirers—David E. Wellbery.)

The unity of *Novelle*, like that of *Faust* and the *comedias* of Calderón Goethe so admired, is thus thematic and does not derive from the conventional elements of narrative used to structure the text—viz., expositional material, direct and indirect characterization, retarding moments, dramatic surprises and reversals, and dialogue ranging from brief questions and answers via courtly and pathetic formality to long stylized speeches that evoke association with heroic and religious poetry. To define the thematic too narrowly leads only to absurdities, however, and does to *Novelle* the kind of injustice done to *Faust* when it is read as a morality play teaching religious, political, social, ecological, and other such lessons.

Nevertheless, important themes critics have discerned in *Novelle* include: "eine Absage an die Jagd als legitime Tätigkeit" (Schulz, disregarding Goethe's approval elsewhere, and as late as 1828, of game control and the "geselligen"—a most positive Goethean epithet—pleasures of the hunt); a turning to Pauline Christianity (K.F. Göschel, A. Lehmann, Ernst Beutler, Benno von Wiese, and—with minimal sectarianism—Düntzer) or to a secularized form of it (Wilhelm Emrich, with the formulation "Umwandlung tierisch wilder Kraft in gebändigt erlöste Heilsfülle," Kurt May, Paul Stöcklein, Herman Meyer, Henry Hatfield, and Schulz); a romantic or oriental-romantic primitivism not consonant with late-Goethean classicism (Emrich, discovering the "Erfüllung und Wiederkehr einer paradiesisch reinen Urzeit," Detlev W. Schumann, Bernhard Seuffert, Emil Staiger, Meyer, and Hiltrud Häntzschel); nationalist allegorico-political symbolism (Hermann Baumgart, Alfred G. Steer); criticism of animal exploitation (David Barry and, with witty irony in his plot summary, Schulz: "Von den Flötentönen des Schaustellerknaben besänftigt, wird der 'Tyrann der Wälder' zum Lamme, vermutlich um auf Jahrmärkten auch fernerhin die Bürger mit exotischem Reiz zu locken und zugleich die Anschauung gezähmter Wildheit zu liefern"); barely covert pacifism (Schumann, Edmund Edel, and Barry, for all of whom Egmont must represent a Goethean aberration and threnodic praise of Euphorion mere irony); humane authority as the antidote to political-social inequities (strengthened, for Wellbery, by drawing from the primordial or moderating, with Hahn, Steer, and Dieter Borchmeyer, Restoration extremism and, for Herbert Lehnert, backwardness as embodied in the reigning Prince's uncle); urgent need to remain in harmony with Nature (Hofmannsthal, Carl Viëtor, P.J. Arnold, and C.A.H. Russ); and earnest warning against asocial self-interest, not least as dishonest advertising that pictures animals as wild when they are not (Barry and, by implication in their plot résumés, others too many to enumerate here).

From the foregoing promiscuous catalogue are noticeably absent the names of several important critics of *Novelle* who have also not hesitated to discern various significant themes in that work. In contrast to those who neglect pictorial elements, and to those who, despite their illuminating of many, often recondite, iconographic details, only interpret them thematico-allegorically rather than as pictorial symbols in their own right (e.g., Düntzer, Beutler, H. Meyer), these critics—notably Oskar Walzel, Wolfgang Staroste, Jane K. Brown, and Rosemary Balfour—strongly emphasize their importance for Goethe's text as expressions of his aesthetic principles. Limits of space prevent my indicating how much of what follows represents agreement with individual members of either group just described or my acknowledging more than general indebtedness to most of them. It is, however, actually a critic named in my first, larger category—Lange, in his introduction to the Winkler edition of Goethe's works—whose formal-aesthetic characterization of *Novelle* as a consistent "System von bedeutenden und bewegenden Bildern" seems to me to identify with unmatched succinctness what makes the text, despite the discontinuities of a narrative perhaps overburdened thematically, an aesthetically satisfying whole, *pace* G.G. Gervinus, Paul Heyse/Hermann Kurz, Richard M. Meyer, Max Herrmann, Friedrich Gundolf, André Gide, Gottfried Benn, Luciano Zagari, Harry Steinhauer, Johannes Klein, and others variously disturbed by its form or its substance, or by both.

That narrative discontinuity and thematic nimiety need not be blemishes in a text primarily comprising a series and system of pictures had already been demonstrated by Goethe—not so brilliantly as in *Novelle*, but with skill and grace—with a work, only slightly shorter than its successor, composed six years earlier: *Wilhelm Tischbeins Idyllen*. It may well be that, because its sixteen fairly substantial poems were detached from their prose context when, supplemented by six brief epigrams, Goethe placed them in the group "Kunst" of his *Gedichte*, this work and its formal and thematic pertinency to *Novelle* have been overlooked by interpreters of the later text, which is usually treated as a pendant to *Die Wahlverwandtschaften*, *Wilhelm Meisters Wanderjahre*, and *Faust*. Written at Tischbein's request—as it were to realize decades later on a small scale the ambitious collaboration on a collection of idylls for which "weder dichtende noch bildende Kunst, jede für sich, zur Darstellung hinreichend wären" (*Italienische Reise*)—the *Idyllen* comprise descriptions of sixteen sketches of a cycle of paintings by Tischbein with verses accompanying all but one of these descriptions; in a brief introduction the circumstances of the work's composition are explained; an even briefer conclusion expresses Goethe's hope that his effort will receive a friendly reception like that earlier accorded "Philostrats Gemälde," which also had the purpose of evoking "Bilder in der Einbildungskraft."

Common to *Idyllen* and *Novelle* are pictorial description; general—sometimes sententious—observations; narrative elements (in *Idyllen* these are primarily historico-biographical, but there also are elements of fictional narrative invented by Goethe in his "readings" of Tischbein's sketches); and lyrical passages in sharp relief—in *Novelle* beginning with the lament for the slain tiger—against sober-prose backgrounds. These common features set *Novelle* apart from both "Philostrats Gemälde" and the late literary works with which it is usually associated in accounts of Goethe for obviously convenient chronological reasons paraded as thematic intertextuality, something which almost any two Goethean texts selected at random could be used to illustrate.

To trace in detail the many elements shared by *Idyllen* and *Novelle* becomes otiose once attention has been drawn to the affinity of the two works. How they happen to be affinitive will, moreover, be obvious if it be remembered that in the planned Italian "Idyllenwerk" of 1786 pictures were to have a narrative function and that in the *Idyllen* descriptions are in a narrative order different from that of the series of sketches sent by Tischbein to Goethe. As Erich Trunz has noted, Goethe's alteration of the pictures' order introduces "Steigerung" into the *Idyllen* as a structuring factor—a factor similarly discerned in *Novelle* by Brown in her nice examination of the aesthetic context of this work's original conception at the time of Goethe/ Meyer's contributions to *Die Propyläen*, but one still lacking in the nine-class arrangement by subjects of "Philostrats Gemälde" that makes the "Gemälde," despite a wealth of narrative, descriptive, and reflective elements of high intrinsic merit, compositionally far inferior to either of its two successors.

In contrast to either of its predecessors, *Novelle* contains—conveyed through words only—pictures in all five pre-cinematic senses of "picture" as defined in *Webster's New Collegiate Dictionary*: "a representation, as of a person or landscape, produced by. . . drawing; . . . a description so vivid as to suggest a mental image. . . ; an image. . . ; . . . an image made by the lens of. . . a telescope; a. . . *tableau vivant*." This maximal "Steigerung" of the pictorial in large part explains how what by normal genre standards would be a discontinuous text is an aesthetically pleasing whole. It permits Goethe to demonstrate by example that his faith in the power of the visual was well justified—the conviction of the rightness of the eye which underlay both his sound optical and his unsound light theories, and which had been incidentally illustrated in the *Idyllen* by an otherwise atypically prosaic explanation of "Centaurenbildung": "Wie der Mensch sich körperlich niemals freier, erhabener, begünstigter fühlt als zu Pferde, wo er. . . die mächtigen Glieder eines so herrlichen Tiers, eben als wären es die eigenen, seinem Willen unterwirft und so über die Erde hin als höheres Wesen"—one is reminded of the lion tamer's steed, created to carry "den Mann. . . , wohin er will"—"zu wallen vermag, ebenso erscheint der Centaur beneidenswert, dessen unmögliche Bildung uns nicht so ganz unwahrscheinlich ent- gegentritt, weil ja der in einiger Ferne hinjagende Reiter mit dem Pferde verschmolzen zu sein scheint."

From the history of its composition as well as from the 107, actually numbered, narrative units of the outline for it dated 8 October 1826 it transpires that in contrast to *Die Jagd*, planned successively for epic and balladic treatments, *Novelle* was conceived as a pictorial work. The point reached by Eckermann when he first discussed *Novelle* with Goethe is unit 102 ("Wächter von der Burg"), which comes three quarters of the way through the text but is followed by only five more units ("Erhöhte Jagdlust," "Einhalt der Familie," "Kapitulation," "Frau Kind und Wächter," and—the crowning flower in the morphological analogy reported by Eckermann— "Idyllische Darstellung"). Goethe subsequently expanded the four units 103– 106 to fourteen, but introduced idyllic elements—they appear with "Der Knabe schien seine Flöte versuchen zu wollen"—sooner than originally planned (now after "Einhalt der Familie"), with the result that the denouement of *Novelle* remains dominated by them. The final unit of the text is thus always as it were its final cause, the pictorial culmination in idyll of a long series of moments/units all of which are pictorial except nos. 8, 9, 20, 28, 32–35, 60, 66, 87–92, 94, 95, and four of the subsequently added ten extra units. As final cause, moreover, it was written in important part before Goethe began dictating *Novelle*—hence Goethe's diary entry of 10 October: "Kleines Gedicht zu Abschluß der projektierten Novelle"—and so provides, as Ilse Graham has noticed, an instance when "die Vorläufigkeit endgültiger Lösungen" happily failed to place obstructions in the way of the swift completion of a work of Goethe's. The high proportion of visual elements in *Novelle* clearly represents the realization of a conscious artistic intention, not a lapse in critical judgment leading Goethe to introduce into narration amounts of description inappropriate to narrative effectiveness.

If "Bildhaftigkeit" is the essence of *Novelle*, as Adolf v. Grolman cogently argued in an unfortunately over-elliptical article insisting on its being the determinant, and literally central, structural factor in the text, it becomes possible to see the work as clearly all of one piece and rightly meriting the praise long heaped on it for often dubiously plausible reasons. Some elements otherwise anomalous, inexplicable, or superfluous then reveal their full significance, something particularly obvious with features of *Novelle* that make it a sequel—to be sure, one far superior—to *Wilhelm Tischbeins Idyllen*. Thus the epithet *wacker*, attached by the uncle of Prince Friedrich to his "Zeichner" (alias "unser Meister"), is that used by Goethe to characterize positively Tischbein's achievements as artist—and is, I think significantly, one that in all he wrote about him Goethe never applies to Philipp Hackert, whose landscapes, no matter how skillfully executed, he considered mere *vedute*. Both "unser Meister" and Tischbein are highly praised for skillfully rendering *das Charakteristische* in nature, which the latter "Gestalt um Gestalt, bis zu den Tieren verfolgte," and for their effective treatment of architectural elements in landscapes that share many common details, including ruins with parts restored. Although the artist of *Novelle*, unlike Tischbein, does not appear as a "Geschichtsmaler," its narrator offers a copious quota of idyllic and non-idyllic landscapes with figures. And even the lion tamer's curious speech that obsequiously begins "Gott hat dem Fürsten Weisheit gegeben"—curious because it is not, despite Schulz and others, a petition motivating narrative action, however structurally functional it may be as the first musically accompanied part of the bridge from prose to verse that has begun with the lament for the slain tiger—recalls by probably unconscious association the drawings for which, as is recounted in *Italienische Reise*, Tischbein also wanted poems by Goethe, amongst them being, besides wild natural scenes, one depicting man as "Pferde-bändiger und allen Tieren. . . , wo nicht an Stärke, doch an List überlegen."

(The lion tamer's speech is also curious as the only important textual element for which there is no corresponding unit in any of Goethe's outlines for *Novelle*. Its function is not merely the formal-structural one already noted, however, since it is also pictorially thematic, providing visually the middle term of a series "*naiv, sentimentalisch, idyllisch*" that connects the secular *pietà* of the woman lamenting her slain tiger—a moment in which man and beast are one *in* nature—via its prophet-like speaker fully aware of nature as *the other* to the "idyllische Darstellung" representing child and beast in a symbiotic coexistence that is harmony *with* nature. Although there may be, as Brown claims, an affinity between the idyllic at the end of *Novelle* and the concept of play in Schiller's "Ästhetische Briefe," I think the formal-thematic pattern of his *Über naive und sentimentalische Dichtung* makes the latter work more immediately relevant to, and more useful for understanding, Goethe's text in its unique individuality.)

The primacy of the pictorial possibly explains certain deviations from strict verisimilitude in *Novelle* which represent more than stylizations of reality reconcilable with Goethe's declaration to Eckermann that he does not "leicht gegen die Wahrheit fehle[n]." Pictorial convention and pictorial license—and their literary counterparts—permit a tiger to bound along like a jaguar, a lion to be so anthropomorphized as to look friendly and grateful (and to be a member of a species with no successfully protected animal enemies), and the lion's habitat to be a South American tropical "Palmen-wald" instead of open range or mixed forest. They also allow iconographic conflations: the Apocryphal singers in the fiery oven with Daniel (Judaic), Pliny on lions with the sculpture "Lion and Eros" (Graeco-Roman), and to the latter added the Androclus motif (Christian). In the lion tamer's largely Goethean paean to Nature mankind is suddenly set outside and above the creation of which it is part, and his exotically oriental family comprises a wife of whose language—Johannes Urzidil identifies it as Czech, Steer as Hebrew, although it is surely Romany—it is said, "Vergebens würde man sie in unsern Mundarten übersetzen wollen," while he himself orates in a fluid biblical German and his son sings a hymn-like Goethean lyric of tremen-dous complexity, soon joined to one's amazement by his broken-German-speaking mother. If conflation be taken as the conceptual equivalent of social accommodation, environmental adaptation, and artistic "correcting" and "compensating," it is an important symbolic expression of the way to harmony within a natural order that in *Novelle*, as elsewhere in Goethe's works, embraces stones and trees, animals and man, the economic and the political, and ethical and cultural values.

In ideal and idyllic circumstances—not always, but as Eckermann faithfully reported, "oft"—the apollonian may indeed tame the dionysiac. This is the pictorial theme of *Novelle*, which as "idyllische Darstellung" is a pendant to the unthreatened idyllic moment when Faust wins Helen and when still "selbst Gefahr erschiene nur als eitles Dräun," for in *Novelle* the only thing to fear are the consequences of the imaginary. In its world of market on fire and of Honorio distressed, passions, threats, and disorders can, as in Goethe's, be courageously faced or quietly dealt with, and it is one of the lesser of such passions—Goethe's disaffection with romanticism—that best explains his ironic declaration to Wilhelm von Humboldt of 22 October 1826 that, since the work he has just completed is in prose, it may pass as a "Novelle. . . , eine Rubrik unter welcher gar vieles wunderliche Zeug kursiert." As Trunz so rightly noted in his edition of the *Idyllen*, Goethe's praise of Tischbein in 1821, after decades of coolness towards him, was in no small part a rear-guard countering of the influence of the romantics' "neu-deutsche, religios-patriotische Kunst," and so *Novelle*, with its Tischbein-like "Zeichner" and its almost always meticulously objective word-painting narrator, demands recognition as a late, highly important, and—I would venture to assert—fully successful expression of Goethean classicism.

Bibliographical Note

Except for *Tischbeins Idyllen*, edited by Trunz (1949; repr. 1961 in his *Studien zu Goethes Alterswerken*), Goethe texts are cited from or in the style of the Hamburger Ausgabe, the bibliographical editor/author entries of which for *Novelle* identify the sources of most of my references/quotations. "Düntzer" is not here cited as editor, but as author of his 1848 article on *Novelle*, for which consult Goedeke's *Grundriß* which, supplemented by still appearing annual bibliographies, will locate other items not in the Hamburger Ausgabe except for: Goethe monographs (Emrich, Hatfield, Graham [*Goethe, Schauen und Glauben*], Gundolf, Marache, Richard M. Meyer, Urzidil, Viëtor, Wilkinson [*Encyclopedia Britannica*, s.v. Goethe]); histories of German literature (Gervinus, Schulz, Žmegač); novella studies/anthologies (Heyse/Kurz, Johannes Klein, Harry Steinhauer [*Twelve German*

Novellas]). Russ is the Clarendon editor of *Goethe: Three Tales*, Häntzschel the author of "Novelle" in *Kindlers Literatur Lexikon*, and Wellbery editor of Vol. 6 of *Goethe's Collected Works* (New York, Suhrkamp; repr. Princeton University Press). For Hofmannsthal, cf. Richard Exner in *Insel-Almanach auf das Jahr 1965*: "Hugo von Hofmannsthal: Fragmente zu Goethes 'Novelle.' " For Benn, cf. his *Briefe an F.W. Oelze* (1977), No. 63.

The Mothers, the Phorcides, and the Cabiri in *Faust*

In a recent interpretation of the *Faust* scene "Finstere Galerie" Friedrich Bruns astutely observes that in connection with the Mothers "die bisherige Faustforschung mit einer wenig beachteten oder als belanglos auf die Seite geschobenen Ausnahme Mütterembryologie getrieben [hat]."[1] Clarifying and developing ideas of Obenauer and Rickert, and eliminating one by one widely accepted interpretations of the Realm of the Mothers which are contradicted by the actual evidence of the text of *Faust* or which cannot be reconciled with Goethe's known aesthetic and philosophico-scientific theories, Bruns comes to the conclusion: "Das Reich der Mütter ist die Vergangenheit, im weiteren Sinn die Geschichte, in der das Vergangene weiter west, nicht ohne Gefahr für das nach neuen Zielen drängende Leben" (378). With this conclusion I can only agree, for it is confirmed—as Bruns himself shows, especially in the final pages of his essay—by the scene "Rittersaal," by the prologue to the Classical Walpurgisnight, and by the transformation of the heroine of the "Helena" from a figure of classical antiquity to a living contemporary of Faust's. Although it seems to me that several of the novel corollaries which Bruns develops in the course of his article are contradicted by textual evidence, they do not invalidate his main conclusion and so shall not be discussed in the following attempt to show the affiliation of the Phorcides and the Cabiri of two later *Faust* scenes with the Mothers of "Finstere Galerie" and "Rittersaal." One of his premises, however, seems to me to be untenable: viz., that the only important dramatic function of the scene "Finstere Galerie" is simply to define the Realm of the Mothers (so that, for instance, in "Rittersaal" Faust may be represented as advancing beyond a dead and dangerous past toward a more living present). This premise, which is, to be sure, implicit rather than explicit in Bruns's discussion, not only allows him to ignore the 42 lines of text that lead up to Mephistopheles' introduction of the Realm of the Mothers (373), but it also causes him to accept, I think somewhat uncritically, the

---

[1] "Die Mütter in Goethes *Faust*: Versuch einer Deutung," *Monatshefte* 43 (1951): 365–89, here 371.

consensus of more recent *Faust* interpreters that the scene "Finstere Galerie" is strictly serious in tone.

"Die Worte Mephistos [i.e., 6212ff.] ergreifen Faust," Bruns declares, "wie jeden aufnahmefähigen Leser. Wer hier Unsinn und Hocus Pocus wittert, darf so wenig über diese Dichtung sprechen wie ein Tontauber über eine Bachsche Fuge" (373). Without denying that I feel something like awe at the passage in question and at some of the passages subsequent to it in the same scene, I am nevertheless persuaded that if anywhere in *Faust II* there are the "sehr ernste Scherze" alluded to by Goethe in his letter to Wilhelm von Humboldt under the date of March 17, 1832, they are to be found in the scene "Finstere Galerie." For it opens with comic motifs already familiar from earlier scenes (6173–76: Mephisto's feigned ignorance of Faust's reason for drawing him aside, as recognized by Faust 6179–80; 6193–6202: Mephisto's feigned impotence to provide something Faust wants, as recognized by Faust 6203) and with the ironico-comic motif that the hero who has in "Anmutige Gegend" resolved "Zum höchsten Dasein immerfort zu streben" and whose great masquerade was largely an allegory representing the desirability of nobler forms of "Tätigkeit" should be "gequält zu tun" by an Emperor who merely wants to be amused by *tableaux vivants* of Helen and Paris. Moreover, as Mephisto becomes eloquent about the Realm of the Mothers, Faust observes "Hier wittert's nach der Hexenküche"—the latter a scene so patently parodistic in its treatment of vulgar superstitions that mention of it can only make doubtful the assumption that we are to fall under the spell of Mephisto's hypnotizing eloquence in the same measure that Faust does. And, finally, the scene ends with Mephisto mildly—and is not Mephistophelean mildness always ironic in *Faust?*—remarking "Wenn ihm der Schlüssel nur zum besten frommt! / Neugierig bin ich ob er wiederkommt?", an exclamation and a question so completely lacking in pathos as to cast doubt upon the reliability of Mephisto's preceding statements and even upon the "heroism" which Faust's descent to the Realm of the Mothers will actually demand.

To suggest that Faust's ordeal is less than dangerous, and perhaps less than important (except in so far as it leads to his "Raub der Helena," to physical unconsciousness, and hence to a Classical Walpurgisnight which will motivate the place of the "Helena" as "Achse" at the center of *Faust II*), is not to minimize Faust's readiness to undergo a dangerous adventure: Faust is certainly awed by the name of the Mothers, and he clearly summons up the courage to face a vague and frightening Unknown. Perhaps the most obvious evidence that Faust's subjective courage is disproportionate to any probable danger to himself is to be found in the fact that he experiences a feeling of hypnotic awe only when Mephisto has just mentioned the Mothers by name—not when Mephisto describes in awesome language the desolate solitude in which the Mothers dwell. Their name is first mentioned in line 6215, but by the end of

Mephisto's "Kein Weg! In's Unbetretene" speech (6222–27), Faust is again ready to doubt the meaningfulness of what Mephisto is asserting (hence "Hier wittert's nach der Hexenküche" [6229] and "Du sprichst als erster aller Mystagogen" [6249]). If Faust nonetheless agrees to pull Mephisto's chestnuts out of the fire for him, he does so largely in the spirit of contradiction: "Nur immer zu! wir wollen es ergründen, / In deinem Nichts hoff' ich das All zu finden" (6256–57). It is only when Mephisto again mentions the Mothers by name (6264) that Faust again assumes a serious, unskeptical tone; but now he has taken the magic key into his hand, is in direct physical rapport with Mephistophelean supernatural-magical forces, and is in any case already committed to his adventure by his earlier "Nur immer zu!" Only at this point, when he has already compromised himself by undertaking to use magic to satisfy the Emperor's ignoble lust for novel amusement, does Faust speak of what he is about to do as a "großes Werk" (6282). And the very fact that he now becomes obviously theatrical—strikes, contrary to his wont throughout the whole of *Faust*, what is specifically described as "eine entschieden gebietende Attitüde mit dem Schlüssel" (6293)—would indicate that he is paying the price of degradation which he regularly pays for the use of magic in the course of his long dramatic career.

Actually, analysis of Mephisto's description of the Realm of the Mothers confirms the supposition that the scene "Finstere Galerie" is comic even more than it is serious. Its comedy is not, of course, of the obvious, grotesque kind that characterizes "Hexenküche," nor is it as unsubtle as that of the mass-suggestion episode which concludes "Kaiserliche Pfalz: Saal des Thrones." The comedy is, however, that of mystagogic delusion, and it is very high comedy because the victim of suggestion is a highly intelligent and unusually skeptical subject. Traditional assertions to the contrary, there is certainly hocuspocus in the use of a magical key and a trapdoor descent in the course of "Finstere Galerie." If, on the other hand, there is no pure nonsense of the "Hexen-einmaleins" variety, that is only because the uncreative Mephistopheles constructs the awesome Void of the Realm of the Mothers as he goes along, meeting Faust's criticisms and objections, and developing suggestions which actually come from Faust himself. The Realm of the Mothers is a brilliant extemporization that Faust fails to recognize as such because the extemporizer unbalances him emotionally by mentioning the Mothers whenever his skeptical faculties seem to be about to make him lose patience with further extempo-rization.[2]

---

[2] It is a matter of indifference to this discussion whether Faust is being audaciously reminded by Mephistopheles of his crimes against the mother of his child and her mother, or whether, as Bruns suggests (373), he is moved by disturbing associations connected with his own experiences as a son.

It is not necessary to credit Mephisto with diabolical omniscience in order to explain the Realm of the Mothers, at least on a psychological dramatic level, as an extension of Faust's own thoughts or elaboration of his own ideas, although Mephistophelean omniscience of what goes on in Faust's mind is a basic assumption of the legend upon which Goethe is elaborating and a regular condition of the development of the dramatic action of *Faust* up to this point and on after it.[3] While Mephisto is still inventing implausible reasons for not fulfilling Faust's request for help—implausible both because in earlier versions of the legend help is forthcoming and because in the course of both Classical Walpurgisnight and "Helena" he occasionally lets slip remarks that show considerable familiarity with classical antiquity (cf. 6979f., 7080ff., 7714ff., 8813–78, etc.)—Faust significantly declares:

Bei dir gerät man stets in's Ungewisse,
Der Vater bist du aller Hindernisse,
Für jedes Mittel willst du neuen Lohn.

[3] Mephisto's remarks in "Prolog im Himmel," his complete dossier on Gretchen when he has just countered "du mußt mir die Dirne schaffen" with a "Nun, welche?" and his preparation of Faust's appearance at the imperial court—when we do not yet know how Faust envisions "das höchste Dasein"—may be regarded as sufficient examples of such omniscience, the last instance of which is the most important dramatically if the action of *Faust II* is not to seem less "plausibly" motivated than that of *Faust I*. One later example of omniscience is Mephisto's entrance in "Innerer Burghof" with a speech ("Buchstabiert in Liebesfibeln. . .") that directly parodies the Calderonesque manner of Faust's and Helen's baroque-romantic rhyme play. One corollary of this assumption of Mephistophelean omniscience might be that he knows that Faust is still disturbed deep within by "des Vorwurfs glühend bittre Pfeile," is to be knocked off his guard by an allusion to Mothers because Faust subconsciously regards himself as guilty of Gretchen's and her mother's deaths. Another might be that he realizes Faust's intense current interest in poetry (the "Schöpfungsgenuß von innen" whose first outlet has been the allegorical masquerade and whose next will be the *Raub der Helena*) and so is simply mocking with a "praise of Nothingness" Faust's quasi-religious, *Deutsche-Klassik* faith in the vital significance of aesthetic creation, or at least his faith in the creative power of the human spirit that can somehow make something where nothing existed before, despite the old saw that nothing can be made from Nothing. (This second corollary would not represent a reading back from the "Rittersaal" variant "Dichter" [for "Magier"] in the manner of B. von Wiese, who in his *Die deutsche Tragödie von Lessing bis Hebbel* [Hamburg, 1948, 1:179] declares: "Mit der Mütterszene betreten wir Faustische Welt als 'Schöpfungsgenuß von innen.' " It is, rather, a reading on from the final words of Faust-Plutus's farewell to the Young Charioteer, ending "Dorthin wo Schönes, Gutes nur gefällt, / Zur Einsamkeit!—Da schaffe deine Welt.")

Although Mephisto continues to protest—"Das Heidenvolk geht mich nichts an"—he concedes, with a "Doch" (6211), that there is a "Mittel" after all. And it is only at this point that he begins to introduce the Mothers in a passage which well represents "das Ungewisse" in an extreme form. For he presents goddesses of whose existence he frankly acknowledges there are no (mortal) witnesses ("ungekannt/ Euch Sterblichen") and who dwell in a timeless Void. May there not be ironic frankness in the ambiguous "Von ihnen sprechen ist Verlegenheit," i.e., genuine embarrassment at having to improvise in order not to be caught openly in lies by a Faust whose sound knowledge of the Devil's powers has already once been demonstrated in the first scene "Studierzimmer"?

When, under the spell of "Mütter," Faust almost automatically asks "Wohin der Weg?" his informant is content to describe *no* way ("Kein Weg! In's Unbetretene, / Nicht zu Betretende; ein Weg an's Unerbetene / Nicht zu Erbittende") and then to ask if Faust is ready to go this "no way" which is barred by no locks or bolts. But a pure "nowhere" is hard to keep inventing, even for a spirit of negation, and so Mephisto compromises by temporarily substituting "Öd' und Einsamkeit" for a pure Void—but not without the impertinence appropriate to a master of suggestive mystification (hence the question "Hast du Begriff von. . ." directed to a Faust, one of whose most memorable earlier scenes was "Wald und Höhle," who has more recently represented the "pure" poet Young Charioteer as best able to create in "Einsamkeit"). Angered, Faust repudiates the imputation that he has not known solitude, even asserting that he had on occasion fled to it even before his meeting with Mephisto because he could not endure "Das Leere lernen, Leeres lehren." Now Mephistopheles develops the concepts of "emptiness" with Schillerian poetic vigor (cf. the general eighteenth-century fascination with the then newly popularized scientific and mathematical concepts of immensity and infinity), but he momentarily relinquishes any effort to describe a pure Void as such, contenting himself with a picture of a limitless ocean before once again returning to the theme of Mephistophelean nothingness. When Faust becomes angry and denies that there can be absolute Nothingness (hence the challenging "In deinem Nichts hoff' ich das All zu finden"), Mephisto forces—at least in the prestidigitator's sense of the verb—the magic key into his hand.

Faust's resistance begins to weaken, and Mephistopheles immediately begins to fill his Void with objects, now turning it into "der Gebilde losgebundene Reiche" and making it, as Bruns rightly insists, into a storehouse of things past and gone ("das nicht mehr Vorhandene," 6278). When the magic of the key makes Faust feel "neue Stärke"—is this pure suggestion?—Mephisto boldly introduces concrete objects such as a tripod and an "allertiefster Grund" on which the Mothers must be imagined as sitting, standing, and walking (6286). What but a moment before was simply a realm of something like Platonic ideas of things past now becomes a realm of "Gestaltung, Umgestaltung," which seems to be a concession to Faust's refusal (6271) to seek his salvation in the merely static ("im Erstarren"). The rest of the scene shows Faust striking his unnatural "Attitüde" and ends with Mephisto's coolly ironic remarks already cited above.

*****

The connection between the Mothers and the Phorcides and Cabiri does not derive solely from the scene "Finstere Galerie," although there the several Mothers—clearly more than three (cf. 6286)—suggest blindfolded or eyeless priestesses who stare into the Unknown, into the realm of abstract and invisible "Schemen," and so offer a vague parallel to the almost eyeless Phorcides with one eye among the three of them. The connection, especially that with the Cabiri, results more from the fact that in "Rittersaal" the Mothers are metamorphosed by Faust, playing the role of "Wunder-mann" (6421) with theatrical grandiloquence (6424: "großartig"), from goddesses of timeless eternals into fate-like powers actually capable of giving and taking away life ("Ihr verteilt zum Zelt des Tages, zum Gewölb' der Nächte, was einmal war"). As Fates they suggest a trinity (cf. Moira, Parcae, Norns, all most frequently represented as trinities), although this is not explicitly stated; yet certainly the physical introduction of a tripod from below the stage also suggests an apparatus at the three sides of which three beings have sat. What seems to me most important, however, is that they are no longer representatives of absolute isolation: Faust corrects his "die ihr. . . ewig einsam wohnt" by adding "Und doch gesellig!" It is as if Faust, tricked into nonsense by Mephistopheles, is compelled to make the nonsense somewhat more plausible than it was originally and therefore adapts it, himself now extemporizing, to the magic pantomime that he feels constrained to produce. Only when he falls under the spell of Helen's beauty does he again become irrational, take his ordeal seriously, confuse theatrical or magical illusion with realities (6553), and invoke the Mothers seriously. In vain, of course, since they were insubstantial extensions of Mephistophelean Nothingness from the moment that they first were mentioned!

The Phorcides (7969–8033) or Graeae of the Classical Walpurgisnight are the Norn-like, weird sisters of the Parcae, as Mephisto explicitly states in the first speech he addresses to them. They themselves emphasize the fact that they live "Versenkt in Einsamkeit und stillste Nacht," which further strengthens the parallel between themselves and the Mothers. But if in their

half-visibility—it is a Walpurgis *Night* and they are in a dimly illuminated
cave at that (7965–66)—they are less remote from us than the purely
hypothetical and, in Goethe's day, still obscure Mothers, they are in one way
more remarkable: they are "Beinah uns selbst, ganz allen unbekannt." This
may be nonsense, since anyone who knows the story of Perseus and
Medusa has heard of them, but it is certainly an even more outrageous
supposition as stated than Mephisto's characterization of the Mothers as
"Göttinnen, ungekannt / Euch Sterblichen, von uns nicht gern genannt."
That it is nonsense seems also to be emphasized by another reminder of
"Hexenküche" now introduced—Mephisto's "Da ging' es wohl auch
mythologisch an / In zwei die Wesenheit der drei zu fassen," which is an
ironic allusion to trinitarianism matched only by his words then: "Denn ein
vollkommner Widerspruch / Bleibt gleich geheimnisvoll für Kluge wie für
Toren. / [...] / Es war die Art zu allen Zeiten, / Durch Drei und Eins, und
Eins und Drei / Irrtum statt Wahrheit zu verbreiten" (2557ff.).

In the light of logic, at least, the poetic aura of the Realm of the Mothers
becomes very largely a "Widerspruch," an antilogy, even as do some of the
things which the Phorcides have been quoted as saying about themselves.
But instead of letting the atmosphere of awe dominate in this episode of the
Classical Walpurgisnight, Goethe has emphasized the comic side of poetic
supernaturalism and cast doubt, for those who have not yet seen its negative
implications, upon the absolute seriousness of "Finstere Galerie." The
humorous side of unknown deities is not yet an exhausted theme in *Faust*,
however, and a few acting minutes later (after thirty lines of text: 8064ff.)
the Nereids and Tritons exit to fetch the Cabiri of Samothrace, and the Sirens
wonderingly ask:

> Was denken sie zu vollführen
> Im Reiche der hohen Kabiren?
> Sind Götter: wundersam eigen,
> Die sich immerfort selbst erzeugen,
> Und niemals wissen was sie sind.

Even if we did not know of the strange fantasies which Romantic
mythologists fabricated on the subject of the significance of the Cabiri in the
early years of the nineteenth century, we would still recognize in the Sirens'
characterization of the Cabiri something contradictory which must remain
"gleich geheimnisvoll für Kluge wie für Toren." The Cabiri are the last
variation on the theme, potentially either serious or comic, of mysterious
deities. When they are triumphantly brought in—conveniently concealed
from view in a giant tortoise shell—they are identified as simultaneously

great and small ("Klein von Gestalt, / Groß von Gewalt"). A trinity of them is present (8186), but now the pattern "Finstere Galerie"-"Rittersaal" is reversed, and a trinity quickly metamorphoses into several more deities as the dialogue begins to echo, not too faintly, the numerological nonsense of the "Hexeneinmaleins" and culminates in the revelation that what for a while seems to be a septad is really an octet whose last member no one has ever thought of before:

> *Nereiden.* . . Drei haben wir mitgenommen,
> Der vierte wollte nicht kommen,
> Er sagte er sei der Rechte,
> Der für alle dächte. . . .
> Sind eigentlich ihrer sieben.
> *Sirenen*   Wo sind die drei geblieben?"
> *Nereiden.* . . Wir wüßten's nicht zu sagen,
> Sind im Olymp zu erfragen;
> Doch wes't auch wohl der Achte,
> An den noch niemand dachte!

Although the Cabiri are the least awesome members of the series "Mothers-Phorcides-Cabiri" (hence Homunculus's observation: "Die Ungestalten seh' ich an / Als irden-schlechte Töpfe," 8219f.), in large part because they simply furnish occasion for the Nereids and Tritons to demonstrate to themselves that they are more than mere fishes (8069), i.e., to satisfy their human pride—

> *Nereiden.* . . Wie unser Ruhm zum höchsten prangt
> Dieses Fest anzuführen!
> *Sirenen*   Die Helden des Altertums
> Ermangeln des Ruhms,
> Wo und wie er auch prangt,
> Wenn sie das goldne Vließ erlangt,
> Ihr die Kabiren.
> (*Wiederholt als Allgesang.*)
> Wenn sie das goldne Vließ erlangt,
> Wir! ihr! die Kabiren.

—the episode of the Cabiri may perhaps nevertheless be regarded as that series' most important member. For the all-too-human pride of the Nereids and Tritons at last places the thrice-introduced motif of mysterious deities in a context which, by virtue of its patently humanistic tone, endows the motif with a universal human significance instead of with a primarily esoteric and intellectual (the Mothers) or with a primarily negative and fantastic one (the Phorcides) only. However comic the Schellingesque formulation "Sehnsuchtsvolle Hungerleider / Nach dem Unerreichlichen" may be as a description of the supposed nature of these obscure divinities, it does endow them with fundamental traits of Faust's and Man's nature as this has been repeatedly revealed and described in the course of the drama. The descent to the Mothers is a path of error demanded by the action of *Faust II* if the "Helena" is to be in any measure dramatically motivated. Mephistopheles' encounter with the Phorcides is frankly fortuitous, but it also serves a purpose: to provide a classical disguise for Faust's antagonist in the same "Helena." Only the Cabiri are introduced without teleological considerations—except that they serve to counteract any lasting "transcendental" spell that the scene "Finstere Galerie" might otherwise continue to cast in a work whose hero in his moment of greatest insight and courage boldly declares: "Nach drüben ist die Aussicht uns verrannt; / Tor! wer dorthin die Augen blinzelnd richtet, / Sich über Wolken seinesgleichen dichtet!" (11442–44)—and so, misshapen and unmysterious as they finally prove to be, they alone of these three groups are positive symbols of the human power to grow and aspire first defined in "Vorspiel auf dem Theater" ("Wer fertig ist, dem ist nichts recht zu machen; / Ein Werdender wird immer dankbar sein," 182f.) and repeatedly acclaimed even unto the concluding lines of *Faust*, where the Chorus mysticus sings its supreme symbol, "Das Ewig-Weibliche."

The Visions of Leda and the Swan in *Faust*

Werner Günther, in a brief essay entitled "Leda und der Schwan," has nicely contrasted the vision of Leda and the swan in the *Faust* scene "Laboratorium" with the later treatment of the same motif in "Klassische Walpurgisnacht."[1] Noting that the first account emphasizes action and is sensually suggestive in tone—"Homunculus entziffert Fausts Traum auf seine Weise"—and that the second is chastely restrained and blends action into "das Landschaftlich-Stimmungshafte," he chooses to see in the second treatment of the motif its "Erhebung ins Künstlerische," a "symbolhafte Vergegenständlichung des Schöpfungsprozesses" which, intentionally or unintentionally, anticipates or prefigures the "Entstehen" of Homunculus and which reflects the aesthetic purification that Faust is undergoing. Although the majority of critics of *Faust* has failed to distinguish clearly between these two very dissimilar treatments of the same motif,[2] Hermann Baumgart partly anticipated Günther's point when he observed that the second vision "verhält sich zu dem früheren Traumgesichte wie das mit Meisterschaft durchgeführte Kunstwerk zu einer ersten Konzeption."[3] Were it not that several distinguished *Faust* interpreters have chosen to single out the first vision, rather than the second, for special praise—and that some of them have even passed over the latter with hardly a word of comment[4]—I should hardly venture to offer a slightly different explanation from Günther's of the contrast which he has so nicely developed. But since able critics have not discerned in the vision described by Homunculus in "Laboratorium" the marks of artistic inferiority that are posited by Günther and Baumgart, an attempt to reconcile with traditional critical opinion Günther's persuasive interpretation of the larger significance of the repetition of the motif of Leda and the swan seems to be in order.

---

[1] *Bemerkungen zu einigen Stellen in Goethes Faust* (University of Neuchatel, Recueil de travaux publié par la Faculté des lettres, Fascicle 24, 1950) 41–48.

[2] E.g., Düntzer, Reinhard Buchwald ("derselbe Traum": *Führer durch Goethes Faustdichtung* [1942] 206), Rickert, Traumann, Stawell and Dickinson (he "sees the swans as he saw them in his swoon": *Goethe & Faust* 179), Trendelenburg, Daur, Böhme, and May.

[3] *Goethes Faust als einheitliche Dichtung* (Königsberg i./Pr., 1902) 2:207.

[4] E.g., Düntzer, Daur, and May; and Petsch, Beutler, Trunz, and Trendelenburg.

The scene which Homunculus attributes to the imagination of the recumbent Faust is in the best tradition of eighteenth-century sensualistic verse: women disrobing, the setting of a grove, beauties bathing in water of crystal-like transparency, a developing erotic situation described in detail up to the point when propriety demands that a curtain be drawn (here: "Auf einmal aber steigt ein Dunst empor, / Und deckt mit dichtgewebtem Flor / Die lieblichste von allen Szenen"), and author's asides like Homunculus's "Das wird immer besser." In the works of Heinse—including his translation from Ariosto—and Wieland (and Wieland's French models) such scenes are anything but rare, and Wieland, with his animated asides, was one of the greatest masters of the well-timed "Schleier" or "Vorhang vor badenden Schönen."[5] How strong an influence the sensualistic tradition could exert is well illustrated by lines from the second of *Gedichte eines Skalden* by Gerstenberg, an author who was surely consciously attempting to get away from neoclassicistic prettiness:

> Wo über bunt beblümte Rasen
> Der See, vom Hauch der Luft bewegt,
> Krystallne Wellen vor sich jägt,
> Sehn wir, mit süßem Duft beladen,
> Die Göttin Blakullur sich baden.
> . . . diamantne Tropfen blitzen, . . .
> Erzitternd, durch das Laub im Hain,
> Indes die Wellen schmeichlerisch sich regen,
> Ihr Bild in die glanzvolle Luft zu prägen. . . .
> Bescheiden schlüpfte sie zur Tiefe nieder;
> Allein das Ebenmaß der weißen Glieder
> Strahlt durch die heitre Fläche wider.
> Es scherzt um ihren Hals ihr blondes Haar. . . .

It is only necessary to read the bathing scenes in Wieland's *Idris und Zenide* (I. Gesang, stanzas 16ff., and IV, 32ff.) to realize that the passage in *Faust* contains every important feature characteristic of such scenes since the *Orlando Furioso*: in the earlier one Wieland's vocabulary even parallels that of Homunculus (common to both are "Hain," "fließend Krystall," "Spiegel-wellen," "plätschern"), and in the later one, in which "die klatschenden Krystallen [wallen] um Arm und Brust" of a bathing girl, the culmination of

---

[5] These are the words used by Wieland himself in the discussion of the preferableness of suggestion to full statement which concludes the "Zweites Buch" of *Die Grazien*.

an erotic episode is suppressed by the fiction of "eine kleine Lücke / Im Manuskript" (corresponding to the "Flor" in *Faust*). What distinguishes the "Laboratorium" passage from its counterparts in older literature is its brevity. But Goethe has not simply parodied in miniature an episode of a kind which his predecessors treated with deliberate longwindedness. For instead of offering a series of successive moments, each of which is equally developed and equally important, he places the emphasis on the culmination of the episode: the swan's conquest of a Leda whose attendants all are fleeing. (The entire passage consists of eighteen lines; eight set the scene, while the remaining ten describe the crisis and its disappearance from view.) By concentrating upon the significant moment Goethe is able to transmute an overfamiliar classicistic motif into a classical one, and the traditional suggestive element, though still retained, is effectively subordinated to the union of a divine and a mortal being whose fruit will be the divinely human beauty of Helen ("Den Gottbetörten," she will later say in reference to a Lynceus infatuated by her beauty, "treffe keinen Schmach"). Surely the first vision of Leda and the swan in *Faust* deserves all the admiration that critics have expressed apropos of it.

The second, however, is even more remarkable—and not simply because Goethe has eliminated the overtones of sensuality traditionally associated with the literary and artistic representation of either bathing beauties or Leda and the Swan.[6] For Goethe actually fails to represent the feminine protagonist of the episode in his version—"Der Blick dringt scharf nach jener Hülle, / Das reiche Laub der grünen Fülle / Verbirgt die hohe Königin"—and even Jupiter's interest in her is only briefly suggested in the lines "Welle selbst auf Wogen wellend, / Dringt er [the boldest of the swans] zu dem heiligen Ort." Whereas the first version culminated in the picture of an all-important symbolic moment, the second is a diptych each half of which is of equal importance and of equal length.[7] These two pictures, young women frolicking in the shallows of a woodland brook, and young women bathers avoiding proximity with swans (the fighting of some of which shows how dangerous they are), posit a third—Leda and the swan—without providing a single suggestive detail for it. A sharp contrast between two natural situations, one an idyll and the other an idyll menaced or destroyed, suggests the supernatural danger to which Leda is exposed, the

---

[6] A characteristic eighteenth-century literary treatment of the latter subject (one almost too familiar in European painting since the Renaissance) is P.-J. Bernard's "Léda" (*Oeuvres* [Paris, 1803] 2:194ff.).

[7] Eighteen lines from "Gewässer schleichen durch die Frische" to "Verbirgt die hohe Königin" and from "Wundersam! auch Schwäne kommen" to "Nur an die eigne Sicherheit."

supernatural force to which she must succumb. The one culminating symbolic moment of "Laboratorium," the one important passage to which "Stil" (as Goethe used the term to contrast with "Einfache Nachahmung der Natur" and "Manier") can be attributed, is replaced in "Klassische Walpurgisnacht" by two pictures each of which represents concretely one and only one situation divested of all unclassical—non-simultaneous or other incongruous—features.

By the simple technical device of abruptly opposing the one picture to the other, by suddenly shifting from iambic meter ("Verbirgt die hohe Königin") to trochaics ("Wundersam! auch Schwäne kommen") when the idyll is intruded upon, Goethe is able to suggest without suggestiveness the motif of Leda and the swan which, at least in Western art and literature, never seems to have been otherwise successfully idealized—even by artists and poets whose power to achieve classic representation is usually equal to Goethe's. What others had done, at least in painting, before him (and what others were to do in poetry after him—Yeats), Goethe does in the scene "Laboratorium," where debased motifs are re-ennobled by being endowed with symbolic value. In the vision of the "Klassische Walpurgisnacht," however, he eliminates the need of idealization or classicization and so does achieve dramatic representation of what must in *Faust*, as in Goethe's own thought, be regarded as a higher form of poetic statement than that of the "Laboratorium" vision or of such earlier conscious artistic efforts of Faust's as the great but too baroque "Mummenschanz" or the stiffly pantomimic "Raub der Helena."

Goethe, Aristophanes, and the Classical Walpurgisnight

I n his comprehensive account of Aristophanes' fame and influence, *Aristophanes und die Nachwelt*, Wilhelm Süss asserts that after his Italian journey "hat Goethe jedes nähere Verhältnis zu Aristophanes verloren."[1] In view of the justness of his strictures upon the merits of Goethe's adaptation of the first part of *The Birds* (1780), one is tempted to be convinced when Süss goes on to declare:

> Bei Wolfs Wolken weiß er nur Format, Druck und Papier zu loben. Gelegentliche Äußerungen zeigen überraschende Lauheit. Vieles davon gehört freilich zu jener Gattung von höchst allgemeinen und recht wohlwollenden Urteilen, wie sie der alte Goethe gelegentlich diesem oder jenem gegenüber aussprach, und wie sie in unserer Zeit, in der Goethezitate zum ständigen Beiwerk fast jedes Buches gehören, immer aufs neue wieder gewichtig kolportiert werden. In der Antike des Neuhumanismus mit ihren kalten, blassen Marmorbildern, ihrer edlen Einfalt und stillen Größe, über der
> ewig klar und spiegelrein und eben
> floß das zephyrleichte Leben
> im Olymp den Seligen dahin,
> ist Aristophanes wiederum ein Fremdling.

Certainly the remarks of Goethe's most frequently cited in discussions of his relation to Aristophanes[2] confirm Süss's view that the lively interest in Aristophanes aroused by Storm and Stress writers was maintained later primarily by virtue of the efforts of the German romanticists and their successors. This does not prove, however, that Aristophanes ceased to be a fructifying influence for the poet Goethe after 1780; "Deutsche Klassik" and "Deutsche

[1] *Das Erbe der Alten*, Hefte 2–3 (Leipzig, 1911): 119.

[2] See Franz Thalmayr, *Goethe und das classische Alterthum* (Leipzig, 1897) 47; Hans Morsch, "Goethe und die griechischen Bühnendichter" (*Programm*, Berlin, 1888) 13; Curt Hille, *Die deutsche Komödie unter der Einwirkung des Aristophanes* (Breslauer Beiträge, N.F., Heft 2, Leipzig, 1907) 123f.; Fritz Hilsenbeck, *Aristophanes und die deutsche Literatur des 18. Jahrhunderts* (Berliner Beiträge, German. Abt., No. 21, Berlin, 1908) 58.

Romantik" are not mutually exclusive worlds. Goethe never ceased to be well informed about the literary and critical enthusiasms of his younger, romantic contemporaries; although he may have ignored Aristophanes in his years of extreme Winckelmannian classicism, he could not have successfully done so after Tieck's inauguration of the genre "Aristophanic comedy" with *Der gestiefelte Kater* (1797). It is therefore not surprising to discover that Goethe read or reread various plays of Aristophanes in 1798, 1790–1800, 1810, 1812, and 1821,[3] and that all his critical opinions of Aristophanes, except for the phrase "der ungezogene Liebling der Grazien" (epilogue to *Die Vögel*), were formulated between 1803 and 1831.[4]

That Goethe repeatedly mentions Aristophanes between March 15, 1778 (diary entry) and March 3, 1832 (conversation with C.W. Göttling) is not of itself a very important fact, although it is perhaps significant that in Grumach's *Goethe und die Antike* as many pages are needed to record his references to Aristophanes as are devoted to his references to the indubitably influential figure of Vergil. Many of Goethe's recorded remarks are little more than responses to situations not of his own creating, and reveal only that he was a man of broad interests, usually willing to contribute politely to conversations and to acknowledge politely in writing the receipt of letters and books. If his interest in Aristophanes is to be considered of literary importance, it must be found reflected in his literary works. *Die Vögel* follows Aristophanes' comedy too closely to stand as an independent poetic creation, and it is therefore probably best ignored in any attempt to evaluate Aristophanes' ultimate importance for Goethe. Even Goethe's quotation of the opening lines of *The Ecclesiazusae* at the end of the second act of *Der Triumph der Empfindsamkeit* (1777), although evidence that he shared the fashionable Storm-and-Stress interest in Aristophanes, cannot plausibly be offered in demonstration of either genuine familiarity with the plays or deep appreciation of the merits of Attic comedy.

Goethe's first truly free literary exploitation or development of something from Aristophanes follows his reading of Wieland's translation of *The Knights* (diary entry, January 11, 1798)—his use of the Boeotian seer Bacis (*Knights*, ll. 122ff.) in the title and text of *Weissagungen des Bakis*. The debt to Aristophanes is not simply the borrowing of a name which Goethe may well have known already from Herodotus, although this is what E. von der Hellen seems to imply in his commentary (Jubiläums-Ausgabe 1:362f.). These oracular distichs are comic verse, half parodistic, half nonsensical; they are products of the same skeptical spirit that allows Aristophanes in

---

[3] Elise von Keudell, *Goethe als Benutzer der Weimarer Bibliothek* (Weimar, 1931) 34; Ernst Grumach, *Goethe und die Antike: Eine Sammlung* (Berlin, 1949) 1:306–8.

[4] Grumach 1:307–9.

The Knights to have Demosthenes ask Nicias if he really believes that there are gods, and Goethe frankly refers to them as "Torheiten" in his letter to A.W. Schlegel of March 20, 1800. Their pompousness is meant to be humorous—a fact of some importance for the understanding of the second part of *Faust*, which is not fully accessible to the reader who approaches its text with the assumption that Goethe uses elevated diction only when in dead earnest. On December 4, 1827, in a period when he was constantly concerned with *Faust II*, Goethe wrote revealingly to Zelter:

> Die Deutschen quälen sich und mich mit den Weissagungen des Bakis, früher mit dem Hexeneinmaleins [*Faust I*] und so manchem andern Unsinn, den man dem schlichten Menschenverstande anzueignen gedenkt.

The *Weissagungen des Bakis* with their double-entendres and deliberate comic obscurity are the work of a writer who admired Aristophanes without feeling the need to imitate his work slavishly; they represent a partial revelation of the profound sympathy with Aristophanic humor that Goethe was later to acknowledge in "Zum Kyklops des Euripides" (1823):

> Von dem Niedrigen, Sittenlosen wendet sich der Gebildete mit Abscheu weg und wird in Erstaunen gesetzt, wenn es ihm dergestalt gebracht wird, daß er es nicht abweisen kann, vielmehr solches mit Behagen aufzunehmen genötigt ist. Aristophanes gibt uns hievon die unverwerflichsten Zeugnisse.

In the *Annalen* for 1820 and 1821 (composed in 1823 and 1825 and in 1822–23, respectively) Goethe mentions Aristophanes once under each year:

> Reisigs Bemerkungen über den Aristophanes erschienen bald darauf; ich eignete mir gleichfalls [as with Wolf's *Prolegomena ad Homerum*], was mir gehörte, daraus zu. . . .
> "Aristophanes" von Voß gab uns neue Ansichten und ein frisches Interesse an dem seltsamsten aller Theaterdichter.

Neither of these statements is remarkably illuminating in itself, but the contexts in which they stand show that for Goethe Aristophanes had become a literary figure of the first importance.

The first quotation comes from a paragraph devoted solely to Homer and Aristophanes, Wolf and Reisig, and its "gleichfalls" refers to what might be called Goethe's faith that apparently discrete parts of a literary work may none the less constitute a coherent whole, to the faith that may well have sustained him as he strove to complete *Faust*:

Beim Studieren des gedachten Werkes [*Prolegomena ad Homerum*] merkt' ich mir selbst und meinen inneren Geistesoperationen auf. Da gewahrt' ich denn, daß eine Systole und Diastole immerwährend in mir vorging. Ich war gewohnt, die beiden Homerischen Gedichte als Ganzheiten anzusehen, und hier wurden sie mir jedes mit großer Kenntnis, Scharfsinn und Geschicklichkeit getrennt und aus einander gezogen, und indem sich mein Verstand dieser Vorstellung willig hingab, so faßte gleich darauf ein herkömmliches Gefühl alles wieder auf *einen* Punkt zusammen, und eine gewisse Läßlichkeit, die uns bei allen wahren poetischen Produktionen ergreift, ließ mich die bekannt gewordenen Lücken, Differenzen und Mängel wohlwollend übersehen.

In his next paragraph Goethe turns to a topic—"die französische Literatur, ältere und neuere"—far removed from Greek literature, but in the one before that on Homer and Aristophanes he treats, also together, two subjects of central importance in the "Hauptgeschäft" of the last years of his life: mythology and geology.

Hermanns Programm über das Wesen und die Behandlung der Mythologie empfing ich mit der Hochachtung, die ich den Arbeiten dieses vorzüglichen Mannes [author of *De mythologica Graecorum antiquissima*, mentioned in the *Annalen* for 1817, the year of its appearance] von jeher gewidmet hatte. . . . Eine Bemerkung konnte mir nicht entgehen: daß die sprach-erfindenden Urvölker, bei Benamung der Naturerscheinungen und deren Verehrung als waltender Gottheiten, mehr durch das Furchtbare als durch das Erfreuliche derselben aufgeregt worden, so daß sie eigentlich mehr tumultuarisch zerstörende als ruhig schaffende Gottheiten gewahr wurden. Mir schienen, da sich denn doch dieses Menschengeschlecht in seinen Grundzügen niemals verändert, die neuesten geologischen Theoristen von eben dem Schlage, die ohne feuerspeiende Berge, Erdbeben, Kluftrisse, unterirdische Druck- und Quetschwerke. . . keine Welt zu erschaffen wissen.

The second reference to Aristophanes in the *Annalen* likewise follows a discussion of Homer (three paragraphs this time, rather than just one), but is separated from it by the following short paragraph:

Die Fragmente Phaethons, von Ritter Hermann mitgeteilt, erregten meine Produktivität. Ich studierte eilig manches Stück des Euripides, um mir den Sinn dieses außerordentlichen Mannes wieder zu vergegenwärtigen. Professor Göttling übersetzte die Fragmente, und ich beschäftigte mich lange mit einer möglichen Ergänzung.

Goethe's "Ergänzung" is "Phaethon, Tragödie des Euripides: Versuch einer Wiederherstellung aus Bruchstücken," *Über Kunst und Altertum* IV, H. 2 (1823), yet it is also the Euphorion scene of *Faust*, as has long been generally recognized. 'Mythology, Homer, Aristophanes' and 'Homer, Euripides, Aristophanes'—with the use of these two groups of concepts both the "Klassische Walpurgisnacht" and the "Helena" can be more than sufficiently illuminated for the needs of a general critical interpretation of Goethe's *Faust*. It may be helpful to mention Aeschylus and Sophocles in connection with the "Helena"; but it is essential to understand that the "Helena," especially in its first and last scenes, deliberately challenges comparison with the dramas of Euripides. And, although it may seem that Vulcanism and Neptunism are almost as important as Greek mythology for the "Pharsalische Felder" section of the "Klassische Walpurgisnacht" (everything before "Felsbuchten des Ägäischen Meers"), these two geological theories are simply modern forms of myth-making anachronistically introduced with Aristophanico-comic effect into the world of classical mythology which is this Walpurgisnight. That Thales is here opposed by a somewhat ridiculous Anaxagoras is a motif worthy of Aristophanes, who never missed an opportunity to ridicule Euripides; for, as Goethe knew from Diogenes Laertius's life of Anaxagoras, Euripides was the pupil of Anaxagoras:

> Von diesem Philosophen wird gemeldet, er habe behauptet, die Sonne sei eine durchglühte Metallmasse. . . , wahrscheinlich, wie der aufmerkende und folgernde Philosoph sie aus der Esse halbgeschmolzen unter den schweren Hämmern gesehen. Bald darauf heißt es, daß er auch den Fall des Steins bei Aigos Potamoi vorausgesagt, und zwar werde derselbe aus der Sonne herunter fallen. Daher habe auch Euripides, der sein Schüler gewesen, die Sonne in der Tragödie *Phaethon* einen Goldklumpen genannt. . . . ("Euripides Phaethon," *Über Kunst und Altertum*, VI, H. 2 [1827])

To assert that Euripides is the most important classical literary model for the "Helena" is to be almost trite. To assert that Aristophanes is similarly important for the "Klassische Walpurgisnacht" may, however, seem to be merely clever. And it may even be objected that to discover an Aristophanic allusion to Euripides in the figure of Anaxagoras is to read into the text of *Faust* something for which no internal evidence exists—to interpret the "Klassische Walpurgisnacht" *ex post facto* in the light of the "Helena," a section of the text entirely different in spirit. But is in the "Helena" there nothing Aristophanic? Phorkyas-Mephistopheles' words on interrupting Faust and Helen in "Innerer Burghof,"

> Buchstabiert in Liebesfibeln,
> Tändelnd grübelt nur am Liebeln,
> Müßig liebelt fort im Grübeln,

are clearly malicious but not unhumorous parody of the language of their serious love scene. The exposition of the scene usually called "Schattiger Hain" is provided by a Mephistopheles whose account of the birth of Euphorion at least opens in a tone of Aristophanic mockery and skepticism, and who even addresses the "Bärtigen" of the audience with Aristophanic disregard of realistic illusion. And is there nothing Euripidean in the "Klassische Walpurgisnacht?" Its prologue is surely without a close counterpart in the works of Aeschylus or Sophocles, let alone of Aristophanes, but it is in the tradition of *Hecuba* (ghost of Polydorus), *Alcestis* (Apollo retreating before death), and the expository prologue primarily associated with the name of Euripides. Because there are serious elements in the "Klassische Walpurgisnacht"—"Felsbuchten des Ägäischen Meers" is obviously not primarily farcical comedy—it is easy for the overearnest reader of *Faust* to ignore its Aristophanic component; to do this, however, is to risk finding it "ungebührlich ausgedehnt" (R. Petsch, Festausgabe 5:678); for only if it is stylistically an Aristophanic counterpart of a Euripidean "Helena" can the length of the "Klassische Walpurgisnacht" be compositionally justified.

The latter part of the first act and the entire second act of *Faust II* together constitute "Helenas Antecedentien." The "Helena" itself, completed in 1825 and 1826, may antedate the execution of these antecedents, but—except for the "Urhelena" passages of 1800—it cannot have been written before Goethe conceived the "Raub der Helena" ("Rittersaal") and the "Klassische Walpurgisnacht." What form these two passages were to take need not have been clear to him, but that there were to be such passages is evident from the "Helena" act: not only does Faust desire Helen (making some such scene as "Rittersaal" necessary), but he tricks her into his presence with the help of a Mephistopheles who has already assumed the shape of Phorkyas. The "Helena-Ankündigung" of December 15–18, 1826 outlines a classical Walpurgisnight much more complex and confusing than the one which Goethe finally wrote; its very wealth of detail indicates, however, that he had already stored up in his memory all the motifs, themes, and mythological and historical figures which were to be used in the "Klassische Walpurgisnacht." The years 1825 and 1826, the years of the completion of the "Helena" and hence almost certainly of the conception of a classical Walpurgisnight, are those of Goethe's greatest interest in Euripides (fifteen of the seventy-one entries covering the years 1773–1832 in Grumach are from 1825 and 1826) and of Goethe's greatest tribute to Aristophanes—at some time between January 1825, when he outlined the contents of the third volume of the *Ausgabe letzter Hand*, and the end of the following year he placed in the group "Gott und Welt" the five poems now entitled "Parabase," "Die Metamorphose der Pflanzen," "Epirrhema," "Metamorphose der Tiere," and "Antepirrhema." Only if Goethe genuinely respected Aristophanes, whose plays *are* Old Comedy, can he have gratuitously added the titles "Parabase," "Epirrhema," and "Antepirrhema" to poems which in 1820, in *Zur Morphologie*, had no titles at all—especially when they are poems used to set in relief two such important statements of Goethe's world outlook as "Die Metamorphose der Pflanzen" and "Metamorphose der Tiere."

Whereas *Die Vögel* is Aristophanic chiefly because it is an imitation of Aristophanes, the three "Gott und Welt" poems with Old Comedy titles are for Goethe Aristophanic because he has come to realize that lightness of tone, certainly not a distinguishing feature of either "Metamorphose," is both perfectly compatible with basic seriousness—

> Das sogenannte Trauerspiel ist eigentlich das wahre Lustspiel und das sogenannte Lustspiel das eigentliche Trauerspiel, wenn man über etwas weinen oder lachen dürfte. Daß Ödipus sich die Augen ausreißt, ist eine Dummheit und nicht *weinerlich*; daß Aristophanes sich über die Menschen moquiert, ist ein Ernst, aber nicht lächerlich (to Riemer, 1803/1814— Biedermann ²2:255)

—and, what is more important, can be advantageously used to set strictly serious materials in effective relief. It is therefore misleading that, in his otherwise excellent commentary on this group of five poems, Emil Staiger should suggest:

> Vermutlich haben die Goethe wohlbekannten "Vögel" des Aristophanes die Überschrift [Parabase] veranlaßt, da dort in der Parabase ein naturgeschichtlicher Mythos erzählt und wenigstens das Leben der gefiederten Tierwelt beschrieben wird.[5]

Since neither "Metamorphose" is a comic myth such as is found in *The Birds*, Staiger surely errs in taking "Parabase" to be the title of the group of poems, rather than that of "Freudig war vor vielen Jahren" only. This first

---

[5] J.W. Goethe, *Gedichte, mit Erläuterungen von Emil Staiger* (n.p., n.d.) 2:474.

poem is a parabasis in the narrowest sense of the term, "der Anfang des Vortrags [the series of speeches that constitute the parabasis of Old Comedy], oder der erste Abschnitt, in dem der Dichter von sich spricht. . . auch Anapästus. . . genannt,"[6] and accordingly it ends on the completely personal note, "Zum Erstaunen bin ich da," while "Epirrhema" ("Müsset im Naturbetrachten. . .") and "Antepirrhema" ("So schauet mit bescheidnem Blick. . .") are both couched in the exhortation or "Volkspredigt"[7] form regularly characteristic of these two sections of the total parabasis.

The foregoing delimitation of the Aristophanic component of the five poems "Parabase"-"Antepirrhema" should make clear that to discern Aristophanic elements in the "Klassische Walpurgisnacht" is not to insist that this part of *Faust* is Aristophanic in any rigidly classicistic or archaizing sense. On the other hand, the close thematic association of these poems with the text of *Faust* and, especially, with its Classical Walpurgisnight[8] is further evidence that Goethe was highly conscious of the form and substance of Old Comedy both when he planned and when he executed the "Klassische Walpurgisnacht." Of greatest total relevance to *Faust* is "Metamorphose der Tiere," which states directly:

Dieser schöne Begriff von Macht und Schranken, von Willkür
Und Gesetz, von Freiheit und Maß, von beweglicher Ordnung,
Vorzug und Mangel erfreue dich hoch! Die heilige Muse
Bringt harmonisch ihn dir, mit sanftem Zwange belehrend.
Keinen höhern Begriff erringt der sittliche Denker,
Keinen der tätige Mann, der dichtende Künstler; der Herrscher,
Der verdient, es zu sein, erfreut nur durch ihn sich der Krone.

Here is the doctrine of one universal law governing all activity, whether in the realm of physical nature or in that of the spirit, which is the great theme of "Felsbuchten des Ägäischen Meers." For it is in connection with

---

[6] P.F. Kannegiesser, *Die alte komische Bühne im Athen* (Breslau, 1817) 360.

[7] Ibid., 366 and 372.

[8] The loom image of "Antepirrhema" is a serious variation of *Faust*, ll. 1922–27. In "Parabase," "gestaltend, umgestaltend" recalls Mephistopheles' "Gestaltung, Umgestaltung" (in the "Finstere Galerie" scene of "Helenas Antecedentien"), while its "Nah und fern und fern und nah" and "Zum Erstaunen" recall the stage direction "Proteus. . . bald nah, bald fern" and Thales' "Trifft man auch Proteus, gleich ist er zerronnen, / Und steht er auch, so sagt er nur zuletzt / Was staunen macht und in Verwirrung setzt" (in "Felsbuchten des Ägäischen Meers"). "Die Metamorphose der Pflanzen," with its "Bildsam ändre der Mensch selbst die bestimmte Gestalt" and its "gedenke denn auch. . . wie Amor zuletzt Blüten und Früchte gezeugt," is echoed in Proteus's "Man wächst so nach und nach heran / Und bildet sich zu höherem Vollbringen" and the Sirens' "So herrsche denn Eros der alles begonnen!"

Homunculus's quest for physical existence that the power of art to make meaningful the apparent disharmonies of finite human life is for the first time asserted in *Faust* since "Vorspiel auf dem Theater" (in Nereus's account of "Trojas Gerichtstag, rhythmisch festgebannt")—and for the first time since the Lord's "Ein guter Mensch. . ." in "Prolog im Himmel," the effort which ethical conduct demands is unqualifiedly declared to be a positive good (Thales' "'s ist auch wohl fein / Ein wackrer Mann zu seiner Zeit zu sein"). If there is, then, a gratuitous tribute to Aristophanes in "Gott und Welt," it is not because Goethe was thinking of *The Birds*, but because he had by 1825 determined that the part of *Faust* in which he would use mytho-poetically his concept of metamorphosis was to contain the Aristophanic counterpart of the Euripidean element already embodied in the "Helena."

Its very title indicates that the "Klassische Walpurgisnacht," like the "Helena," is a phantasmagoria. Loosely analogous to the romantic "Walpur-gisnacht" of *Faust I* both in structure and in its function as dramatic revelation of Faust's feverish inner confusion at a critical moment in his development, it is above all else constructed of motifs from ancient Greek and Roman folklore that correspond to those of Northern folklore and superstition in its romantic counterpart. Since Düntzer, unfortunately, *Faust* commentators and critics have been so concerned with elucidating the classical allusions and the ideological connections with Goethe's total world outlook that they have usually lost sight of the fundamental artistic design of the "Klassische Walpurgisnacht"—what might be called the Aristophanic dramatic pattern of all that falls between Erichtho's opening monologue and Mephistopheles' departure for Hell. Indeed, literal-minded critics and editors have obscured the uninterrupted flow of the action of this, the longer part of the "Klassische Walpurgisnacht," by insisting that it be read as four distinct scenes ("Pharsalische Felder," "Am obern Peneios," "Am untern Peneios," and "Am obern Peneios *wie zuvor*"); and stage directions which reflect their concern with naturalistic geography have even been interpolated in such otherwise reliable editions of *Faust* as those of Erich Schmidt (Jubiläums-Ausgabe), the Welt-Goethe, and Trunz.[9] For some unknown reason the equally natural stage direction "Ein Tempel bei Pydna" has never been added after line 7462—although perhaps only because it is impossible to reconcile the geography of this part of Walpurgisnight with the fact that Pydna is north of Olympus, not south, as Goethe's text would imply.

---

[9] For the textual-critical arguments against these interpolations, see H.G. Fiedler, *Textual Studies of Goethe's Faust* (Oxford, 1946) 57–64.

The first, larger section of the "Klassische Walpurgisnacht" is, then, best thought of as performed with the *mise en scène simultanée* of the Attic stage, with only the simplest theatrical machinery needed to suggest changes of milieu—machinery not very extensive even for a quasi-naturalistic production, in view of the semidarkness in which the action takes place. As in Aristophanic comedy, which in this respect does not differ from Attic tragedy, the scenes are almost exclusively exterior ones, the exception being the glimpse of Manto "inwendig träumend" after line 7470, which is a stage effect as simple as that which Euripides and Aristophanes expected when their texts called for a glimpse into a door of the façade of the *skēnē*, what stage props are visually demanded by the exterior scenes fall into the category of simple ones which even the Attic stage could provide with its eccyclema. (The objection may be raised that in *Faust II*— witness the "Mummenschanz" of the preceding act—Goethe seems to write for a realistic proscenium stage, but it may be countered that, until "Des Gegenkaisers Zelt," the action of the fourth act also demands a simultaneous stage set, as the stage direction after line 10296 makes clear. In any event, "Vorspiel auf dem Theater"—which Goethe did *not* cut out in his greatly abbreviated stage version of Part I—would seem to have among its several functions[10] that of accustoming a *Faust* audience to theatrical variety, including occasionally a stark theatrical simplicity no longer admired by popular taste at the beginning of the nineteenth century but one well illustrated by its own bare stage.)

There is thus evidence that Goethe was much interested in and much admired Aristophanes at the time of the composition of the "Klassische Walpurgisnacht." There is good reason to believe, on the basis of textual-critical arguments and in light of the deliberate compositional variety which characterizes *Faust* as a whole, that an important part of the Walpurgisnight is phantasmagoria—and it is obvious that much of this phantasmagoria is comic and satiric, best staged in an adaptation of the theatrical style of Attic comedy.

Two questions must still be answered, however: Is it probable that Goethe expected the Aristophanic *theatrical* quality of sections of the Walpurgisnight to be recognized as such? (That there are passages quite Aristophanic in tone and substance has long been recognized, though not excessively emphasized.) And is there any evidence that Goethe had reason to expect such recognition as he began to execute this part of the text of *Faust?* The second question can be answered with an unqualified

---

[10] See my "A Reconsideration of some Unappreciated Aspects of the Prologues and Early Scenes in Goethe's 'Faust,' " *MLR* 47 (1952): 362–73, esp. 363–66.

affirmative, not only because of the wide popularity of comedy labeled "Aristophanic" and sometimes even formally Aristophanic (Platen!) during the romantic period, but because Wieland—and no doubt others—had specifically commented on the element of Aristophanic "Unflätigkeit" in the romantic Walpurgisnight.[11] The answer to the first question is also affirmative, for we shall now see that in both theme and motif the "Klassische Walpurgisnacht" is in so many ways directly indebted to Aristophanes that anyone moderately well read in classical literature (in an age when the tyranny of Greece over Germany was still very near its greatest height) would inevitably be reminded again and again of Attic comedy—and of no other "classical" literary form, let alone any post-classical one—as he read it or heard it performed.

Although the stage direction "Pharsalische Felder" can—unfortunately, as we have seen—be interpreted with naturalistic literalness, it in fact describes a land of the dead, a Hades with non-Elysian fields populated by creatures from the underworld and by shades from a vanished past, the neoclassical equivalent of the Christian underworld glimpsed momentarily on the Brocken in *Faust I*. The only classical drama which such a setting evokes is Aristophanes' *Frogs*, rightly described by the classical philologist Karl Reinhardt as "das einzige erhaltene Hadesdrama der Antike";[12] and the analogy between "Klassische Walpurgisnacht" and "Hadesdrama" is hardly to be overlooked if it is felt, as it seems to have been by a majority of *Faust* interpreters, that the function of the "Klassische Walpurgisnacht" is to enable Faust to bring Helen from a deeper part of its underworld to Sparta and renewed existence on earth. A few critics, however, would insist that Faust's descent to Persephone is not sufficiently developed in the final text to warrant drawing much of a parallel—that Goethe's unexecuted intentions should not color our reading of the Walpurgisnight. These critics may rightly point out that in the Walpurgisnight as a whole the ultimate emphasis is upon Homunculus's quest for real existence. But where in classical drama do we find the quixotic quest, the utopian enterprise? In Aristophanic comedy first and foremost!

There are, however, interpreters of *Faust* who point out that even the Homunculus episodes of the Walpurgisnight do not constitute a major part of it—for them the analogy between Goethean fantasy and Aristophanic fantasy cannot be a decisive factor in persuading them to read the first, larger section of the Walpurgisnight as Aristophanic comedy. These interpreters, it seems to me, may all be classed as "serious-minded,"

[11] Letter to Retzer printed in 1815 (see *Faust*, Jubiläums-Ausgabe, note to line 4132).
[12] "Die klassische Walpurgisnacht: Entstehung und Bedeutung," *Antike und Abendland* 1 (Hamburg, 1945): 133–62 (quotation, p. 134).

although they may emphasize such different "serious" aspects of the Walpurgisnight as its mythology (myth as Faustian "Bildungserlebnis," myth as expression of Goethe's Jungian or Bachofenian "Weltbild"), its baroque elements (again "Bildungserlebnis," or else manifestation of Goethe's "Altersstil"), and its scientific ideas ("Natur und Geist," Neptunism as more acceptable to Goethe than Vulcanism, his ideas on the genesis and development of life). Some of these aspects of the Walpurgisnight were certainly very serious concerns of Goethe's; but, as we have seen, Goethe did not find comedy and seriousness incompatible. For a classical dramatic counterpart of the dispute between Thales and Anaxagoras in the Walpurgisnight it is necessary to look at Aristophanes' *Clouds*, in which Socrates is impudently ridiculed, and for a corresponding counterpart to the satiric treatment of the romantic philosophers' and mythologists' speculations on the subject of the Cabiri it is well to recall the burlesque mythology of the parabasis of his *Birds*. For all his impudence and "Unflätigkeit" Aristophanes was more often than not an earnest critic of his age and its beliefs; whatever serious themes Goethe takes up in the Walpurgisnight, he is capable of treating them with a light, Aristophanic touch.

The utopian and fantastic are blended with the comic and the burlesque both in *Faust* and in Aristophanes. Faust, Mephistopheles, and Homunculus arrive in the land of supernatural beings as aeronauts, and Trygaeus reaches the palace of Zeus—in *Peace*—by flying on a dung beetle. The Pharsalian Fields are an underworld, however, through which the three visitors in *Faust* move with rapid changes of place similar to the movements of Dionysus, Xanthias, and Heracles in *The Frogs*; and Faust seeks to recover Helen even as Dionysus wants to recover the incomparable Euripides. If Faust is content to be on Greek soil, Mephisto—like Dionysus's timid servant—is confessedly ill at ease amid classical monsters. These monsters, moreover, are treated in the Walpurgisnight with the same satiric and ironic levity as are supernatural beings in Aristophanic comedy. Griffons, sphinxes, sirens, and Lamiae all condescend to taunt a Mephistopheles whom they admittedly despise. The centaur Chiron condescendingly puts himself at the disposal of a strange barbarian who clearly lacks the Greek view of things Greek. And Nereus and Proteus, with comic reluctance, despite their all-too-human grouchiness and pessimism, further the quest of the novel Homunculus.

The burlesquing of the supernatural and monstrous is, of course, itself a common motif of Aristophanic comedy. The powers of Thessalian witches, represented on the Pharsalian Fields by Erichtho, become a comic motif in *The Clouds* when Strepsiades explains to Socrates that he could avoid paying his debts if he purchased a Thessalian witch to pull the moon out of the sky (interest and debts coming due according to the lunar month); and the same motif appears in the Walpurgisnight when Anaxagoras interprets the fall of a meteor as the result of his summoning Diana-*Luna*-Hecate to his help ("So wär' es wahr, daß sich thessalische Frauen. . ."). In *The Knights* Aristophanes ridicules, among other things, the absurdity of acting on oracles; in the Walpurgisnight the oracular riddle is propounded both by a sphinx and by Mephistopheles, and the apparently favorable oracular utterance is represented by Manto's "Den lieb' ich, der Unmögliches begehrt." The very motif of Chiron's bringing Faust to Manto, "Tochter Äskulaps," so that he may be cured of his mental aberration (his impulse to find Helen) recalls the irreverent treatment of temple cures in *Plutus*. Karl Reinhardt (loc. cit.) has pointed out in connection with *The Frogs* that "offenbar hat Aristophanes vor allem zu den Unterweltsgespenstern die so heiter-greuliche Empuse beigesteuert," and the metamorphosing spectre of that play appears on the Pharsalian Fields to taunt Mephisto; she not only has an abnormal leg, as in *The Frogs*, but is also an unwelcome competitor of the prostitute-like Lamiae—a detail not found in Hederich's *Mythologisches Lexicon*, so often the inspiration of Goethe's satirical touches in the Walpurgisnight, but one easily suggested by the description of an old and ugly prostitute of *The Ecclesiazusae* as "an Empusa with a body covered with blemishes and blotches." Certainly the use of half-human monsters for satirico-comic effect is a basic feature of Aristophanic comedy—hence such titles as *The Wasps*, *The Birds*, and *The Frogs*—and it is surely significant that the least familiar monsters of the Walpurgisnight, the Empusa and the Lamiae (cf. *Wasps*, parabasis), probably came to Goethe's attention through his reading of Aristophanes.

One weakness of modern "Aristophanic" comedies was long the fact that modern standards of propriety inhibited their authors from introducing sexual obscenity. Tieck alludes to dung in *Der gestiefelte Kater*, and for this mild allusion there is the excuse of a long popular-literary tradition; but he ventures nothing of the boldness of certain passages in the Walpurgisnight of *Faust I*. Goethe, on the other hand, lets his Sphinxes maliciously address Mephistopheles with the words,

> Sprich nicht vom Herzen! das ist eitel;
> Ein lederner verschrumpfter Beutel
> Das paßt dir eher zu Gesicht,

and does not hesitate to represent Mephisto in frank pursuit of Lamiae of whom, "Geschnürten Leibs, geschminkten Angesichts," the latter declares: "Nichts haben sie Gesundes zu erwidern." Not to cite further specific lines, it must nevertheless be noted that the motif of Homunculus's hermaphroditism, that of the Sphinxes' double-sexedness, and that of Mephisto's transvestism upon assuming the shape of one of the Phorcides ("Man schilt mich nun, o Schmach! Hermaphroditen") are all in the best—or worst— unadulterated Aristophanic tradition. Not only did Aristophanes' audience expect obscenities and get them: Aristophanes occasionally incorporated motifs which permitted them in the plot structure of his comedies, the best example of this being the disguising of Euripides' father-in-law as a woman so that he may spy on the Thesmophoriazusae.

Two larger aspects of the Walpurgisnight as a whole are not without important Aristophanic analogues: Faust's madness (as both Chiron and, earlier, Mephisto—"Wen Helena paralysiert / Der kommt so leicht nicht zu Verstande"—regard his quest for Helen) and the dispute between Anaxagoras and Thales. In *The Wasps* Philocleon's mad passion for jury duty is the mainspring of the comic action, the rack on which Aristophanes loosely hangs his satire, and so it is comparable to Faust's passion for Helen, which becomes the excuse of all the digressions that the Walpurgisnight admittedly contains. But, since in Aristophanic comedy the digressions often develop the essential themes with which the author is concerned, Goethe's cavalier treatment of dramatic action in the Walpurgisnight is no longer disturbing when the Aristophanic element of that section of *Faust* is recognized for what it is. As for the dispute between Anaxagoras and Thales, it is perhaps a digression in the constructive sense just characterized, and yet without it the Walpurgisnight would lack one of the standard formal features of Attic comedy, namely the agon or debate. In an Aristophanic comedy written in pseudoclassical metrical forms an agon would be little more than one additional obviously Aristophanic feature. In this Walpurgisnight, however, Goethe has used modern meters (as he did in his version of *The Birds*), and so the important place given to a debate on a theoretical issue—and one on which both sides are demonstrated to be partly wrong: appearance of Seismos, fall of meteorite—is not only in the best comic tradition of dramatic irony, but is also a final means of insisting that the fundamental "Aristophanism" of the Walpurgisnight shall not be overlooked.[13]

---

[13] F.E. Hirsch, " 'Aristophanische' Wortfügungen in der Sprache des 19. Jahrhunderts," *Zft. f. dt. Wortforschung* 12 (1910): 241–48, draws his examples chiefly from Nestroy, Glasbrenner, Platen, and Vischer's *Faust III*, although *Faust II*, "Klassische Walpurgisnacht," speech of "Die Kraniche des Ibykus," contains such eminently "Aristophanic" compounds as "Flügelflatterschlagen" and "Fettbauchkrummbeinschelme." F. Förster's report of a conversation with Goethe on Aug. 25, 1831, shows that Goethe felt them to be such: "Die Berliner Sprachverderber sind. . . die einzigen, in denen noch eine nationelle Sprachentwickelung bemerkbar ist, z.B. Butterkellertreppengefalle, das ist ein Wort, wie es Aristophanes nicht gewagter hätte bilden können" (Biedermann [2]4:386, cited by Grumach 1: 308–9).

It would be absurd to claim that ability to recognize the Aristophanic elements of the "Klassische Walpurgisnight" will suddenly make this section of *Faust* transparently simple. In the scene "Felsbuchten des Ägäischen Meers" it is also important, for instance, to recognize Goethe's debt to the tradition of theatrical cantata and to the tradition of theatrical masque and opera.[14] But simply not to read the Walpurgisnight in the expectation of following the personal fortunes of Faust is in large measure to be able to read it with appreciation of what it really is—a phantasmagoria on themes and motifs intimately bound up with the view of life to which Faust in some measure attains and which Goethe is expressing in *Faust*, at this point with the aid of Aristophanic comedy. Even the charge that the "Klassische Walpurgisnacht" is "oppressively learned" (W.H. Bruford, *Theatre, Drama and Audience in Goethe's Germany*) loses much of its weight if it is remembered that pedantry and fantastic speculation are themselves objects of satire in the episode of the Cabiri. It is understandable that E.M. Butler, after having immersed herself in the fine points of Northern folklore and occultism long enough to produce three solid volumes on *Ritual Magic, The Myth of the Magus*, and *The Fortunes of Faust*, should assert on returning to the Walpurgisnight that it "contains so many recondite mythological allusions that one feels bewildered and out of one's depth" (*Fortunes* [Cambridge, 1952] 257); but for one who comes to it from the reading of Aeschylus, Sophocles, Euripides, and, above all, Aristophanes its allusions and figures are almost all completely familiar.[15] A knowledge of Greek drama and moderate familiarity with the *Iliad* and the *Odyssey* make every direct classical allusion *in the dramatic text*—as opposed to those allusions which represent simply stage-direction substitutes for detailed instructions to actor, director, or costumer—comprehensible, with the one important exception of the Cabiri. And, since the Cabiri were the subjects of lively speculation and controversy among philologians, mythologists, and "Naturphilosophen" in Goethe's day, Goethe can hardly be condemned for having failed to realize that they would once again fall into relative obscurity and become as it were the property of classical scholars only. I therefore agree wholeheartedly with

---

[14] Reinhardt 154f. and note 42 points out that the motif of "Doriden als Retterinnen" seems to be the invention of K.W. Ramler (in the cantata *Ino*), and draws attention to Dryden's *Albion and Albanius*, an opera text in which Venus and Albanius appear "in a great scallop-shell. . . drawn by dolphins" (see *Works*, ed. Scott and Saintsbury, 7:279); in a study of Goethe and Calderón (in this volume) I seek to show that Calderonian drama is even more important for this scene than either Witkowski or Beutler has suggested.

[15] This is easily verified by checking them against the "Glossary" of *The Complete Greek Drama*, ed. W.J. Oates and Eugene O'Neill, Jr. (New York, 1938). Allusions familiar from the *Odyssey* (cf. next sentence of text), but none familiar from Greek drama, are recorded by Thalmayr 169.

Henri Lichtenberger's summing up of the question of the "obscurity" of the Classical Walpurgisnight: "le reproche d'obscurité n'est guère mieux fondé que celui d'érudition encombrante et touffue."[16]

For a well-read contemporary of Goethe's, in an age when German Graecophilia was greatest if not most "gründlich," the "Klassische Walpurgisnacht" should have been immediately accessible. But it had the misfortune to find its first readers in decades of very different intellectual concerns from those which had inspired Goethe's choice of form and motifs. What was not understood seemed obscure—intentionally so—and so the myth of the difficulty of understanding the Classical Walpurgisnight became firmly established before subsequent generations, less hostile to Goethe, had a chance to read *Faust II* without prejudice. It is surely ironic that even in the present century, in Hille's account of German comedy under the influence of Aristophanes, Friedrich Theodor Vischer's *Faust III* should be discussed as an Aristophanic comedy without any hint, either in connection with that discussion or elsewhere in Hille's monograph, that there are obviously Aristophanic elements in the work that Vischer Aristophanically parodied.[17]

---

[16] See his edition of *Faust: Deuxième partie* (Paris, n.d.) lxxxix.

[17] It is unfortunate that Georges Dalmeyda (*Goethe et le drame antique*, Paris, 1908), a thoughtful and thorough critic, should have been so concerned with the theme of tragedy as to pass over the "Klassische Walpurgisnacht" with little more than a bare mention in his otherwise excellent study. The tendency to emphasize only Goethe's early interest in Aristophanes, as established by Süss, is still apparent in P. Friedländer, "Aristophanes in Deutschland," *Die Antike* 8 (1932): 229–53 and 9 (1933): 81–104. No light is shed on the theme of the foregoing study either by E. Maass's *Goethe und die Antike* or, more surprising, by V. Valentin's *Die klassische Walpurgisnacht*, a monograph purporting to be "eine litterarhistorisch-ästhetische Untersuchung." How little attention indeed has been paid to the form of the Walpurgisnight—and how much to unconcrete speculation apropos of it—is clear from Ada M. Klett[-Bister], *Der Streit um 'Faust II' seit 1900* [sc. *bis 1938*] (Jena, 1939 = Jenaer Germanistische Forschungen, Bd. 33) 39–41.

Goethe, Calderón, and *Faust: Der Tragödie zweiter Teil*

Although Goethe's profound admiration of Calderón has been public knowledge ever since the first years of the nineteenth century, and although his interest in Calderón has been frequently scrutinized by students of literature in the seven decades between W. von Biedermann's essay "Trauerspiel in der Christenheit" (*Goethe-Forschungen* [1879] 154–90) and F. Strich's "Die theatralische Sendung Spaniens" (*Goethe und die Weltliteratur* [1946] 159–66), the fact that the Second Part of *Faust* contains many Calderonian elements seems not to have been properly emphasized either by "Goethe-Philolog" or by "Faust-Erklärer." It can nevertheless be demonstrated that some acquaintance with Spanish drama of the Golden Age—and Calderón *was* this drama for Goethe's contemporaries—is fully as important for appreciation of *Faust II* as is moderate familiarity with Greek drama of the fifth century B.C. Indeed, the history of *Faust* criticism and interpretation, which have produced no one generally accepted explanation of what principles of dramatic technique (as opposed to "plot content") govern the structure of the Second Part, seems to me to demonstrate that failure to recognize the deliberately Calderonizing features of Goethe's drama has not only favored subjective and digressive speculation hardly warranted by the text but has also resulted in interpretations actually contradicted by it.

But, the reader of these lines will ask, if all these things are true, why it is then that Calderón's importance for *Faust* has not long since been recognized. The answer to this question is so simple, and comes from an authority apparently so unimpeachable, that it will have to be proved misleading before any but the most docile reader would let himself be led to an examination of "Calderonian influences" in the Second Part of *Faust*. For under the date May 12, 1825, Eckermann reports the following pronouncement by Goethe: "Es kommt nur immer darauf an, daß derjenige, von dem wir lernen wollen, unserer Natur gemäß sei. So hat z.B. Calderon, so groß er ist und so sehr ich ihn bewundere, auf mich gar keinen Einfluß gehabt, weder im Guten noch im Schlimmen." It is little wonder that Strich begins his chapter on "Die theatralische Sendung Spaniens" with the denial that Spanish civilization became for Goethe a "Bildungsmacht. . . wie es die italienische und französische wurde," and that he opens his survey of the evidence of Goethe's explicit interest in Calderón (which somehow nevertheless fills five well-packed large-octave pages!) with the above-quoted remarks by Goethe. To explain away the somewhat contradictory evidence that he soon begins to cite, Strich is constrained to preface it with the statement, "Goethe hat Calderon gewiß auch zu spät erst kennengelernt, als daß er ihm noch zu einem wahren Bildner hätte werden können." His "gewiß auch zu spät," like so many scholars' *zwar*'s and *of-course*'s, reveals that he is fitting his data to an apriori theory and is not developing an explanation from the facts. Between 1802 and 1831 Goethe discussed or expressed admiration of Calderón in some twenty recorded conversations; paid tribute to his greatness in the notes to *Rameaus Neffe*; sketched a tragedy in the Calderonian manner;[1] named him with Hafiz in the *West-östlicher Divan*; devoted an essay to his *Tochter der Luft*; had *Der standhafte Prinz Don Fernando von Portugal* performed eleven times, *Das Leben ein Traum* eleven, and *Die große Zenobia* two by the Weimar troupe; and repeatedly mentioned him favorably—on at least ten occasions with critical comment—in his correspondence. In addition to *Die Tochter der Luft* (actually two plays) and the three plays rehearsed and produced under his direction, Goethe also read (I list only those specifically mentioned by title in conversation or in writing, although it is certain[2] that he read several more—plays printed in the same volume as ones mentioned by title) *Die Andacht zum Kreuz, Über allen Zauber Liebe, Die Schärpe und die Blume,*

---

[1] The fragments (1807ff.) are printed WA I.11:335–48 and 53:363–66; in his essay, where they are supplied with the title "Trauerspiel in der Christenheit," Biedermann points out their many Calderonizing features: plot structure, motifs, verse forms and—perhaps more important—"theatrical" decoration. Sp. Wukadinović, "Die Christianer," *Goethe-Probleme* (1926) 67–97, refuses to accept Biedermann's thesis of a strong Calderonian influence on the fragments, chiefly on the grounds—they strike me as feeble ones—that Goethe does not imitate Calderón slavishly and that in using motifs similar to Calderón's he expresses a dissimilar world-view (as if the Classical motifs of *Faust* were meant to express a Greek view of life!); Wukadinović's "metrical" objection (78) to Biedermann's discovery of "liras" (i.e., "silvas") in the fragments is based on a false assumption about the frequency with which lines of seven syllables need be introduced in this verse form (cf. dialogue of Circe and Ulysses quoted later in the text of this article). It seems to me that Walther Rehm, referring to Wukadinović's substitution of Zacharias Werner for Calderón as first source of the for Goethe unusual features of these fragments, rightly asks whether, "angesichts des geplanten Trauerspiels 'Die Christianer' und des Schlusses des *Faust II*. . . der Einfluß Calderons. . . auf Goethe wirklich unwesentlich sei" ("Schiller und das Barockdrama," *Götterstille und Göttertrauer: Aufsätze zur deutsch-antiken Begegnung* [Bern, 1951] 64).

[2] Thus he certainly read Vol. 5 of Gries's Calderón translation (*Dame Kobold* and *Der Richter von Zalamea*), for in a letter of June 11, 1822, he thanks Gries for two days' pleasure; as inspirer of Gries's undertaking, he presumably read all the volumes that appeared during his lifetime.

Der wundertätige Magus, and *Die Locken Absalons*. "Bildner" or not, Calderón was certainly something far more than a mere name to Goethe! Before I explain what the concept "Calderon" meant to Goethe—which is to indicate the general function of Calderonizing elements in *Faust*—I should like to offer two further explanations of why Calderón's importance for the Second Part of *Faust* has not been recognized. (1) Although most interpreters of Goethe's works have approached them biographically and have therefore seen only those features to which Goethe has explicitly drawn their attention, there have been a few critics who have attempted to read them in the larger context which is the history of Western literature. Unfortunately, these critics, who have done much to throw light on the Classical, older Medieval, Renaissance, Reformation, and—latterly—Baroque elements in *Faust*, have without exception been the products of either one or both of two great educational traditions: that of Classical Philology and that of Germanic Philology. The Classical Philologist naturally reads the "Klassische Walpurgisnacht" and the "Helena" as Goethe's direct reworking of Classical sources; it is therefore not surprising that he should be blind to other elements, including even obviously post-Classical treatment of Greek and Roman motifs. For the Germanic Philologist the development of modern European literature is represented almost exclusively by German materials; whatever the merits of German Baroque literature, it produced little or nothing in dramatic form remotely comparable to the plays of Calderón— and certainly nothing that Goethe acknowledged to be comparable—and so it is natural that he should fail to recognize Calderonian features in *Faust II*. Although he may be familiar with Calderón's influence in the Romantic period, he can have become so accustomed to placing Goethe in the category "Klassik" that he automatically disregards the possibility that there might be evidence of such influence in *Faust*. And, finally, even if he has not done this, he has so narrowed the meaning of the word "romantisch" when applied to German literature that he easily forgets that in Goethe's day anything post-Classical was Romantic—a fact of some importance for the proper interpretation of a "Helena" which originally had the descriptive subtitle "klassisch-romantische Phantasmagorie." (2) The fact that Calderón's *El Mágico prodigioso* has as its protagonist one of the forerunners of the figure of Faust has—and this is confirmed by the plethora of essays which have compared Calderón's play with Goethe's—caused critics and scholars to examine with care only the work of which Goethe wrote (to Knebel, October 17, 1812) that it represented "das Sujet vom Doktor Faust mit einer unglaublichen Großheit behandelt." If interpreters of *Faust* had similarly limited themselves to examining only works of Classical literature in which magus-figures appear, they could not have got very far in their elucidations of Classical motifs in *Faust II*.

In a letter to Schiller (January 28, 1804) Goethe reported his reactions to *Der standhafte Prinz*:

> Man wird, wie bei den vorigen Stücken, aus mancherlei Ursachen im Genuß des einzelnen, besonders beim ersten Lesen, gestört; wenn man aber durch ist und die Idee sich wie ein Phönix aus den Flammen vor den Augen des Geistes emporhebt, so glaubt man nichts Vortrefflicher's gelesen zu haben. Es verdient gewiß neben der *Andacht zum Kreuze* zu stehen, ja man ordnet es höher, vielleicht weil man es zuletzt gelesen hat und weil der Gegenstand so wie die Behandlung im höchsten Sinne liebenswürdig ist. Ja ich möchte sagen, wenn die Poesie ganz von der Welt verloren ginge, so könnte man sie aus diesem Stück wieder herstellen.

Two points in this statement deserve emphasis: first, that Calderonian drama—like *Faust II*—has a unity ("die Idee") which is not immediately evident from its separate parts, although the relevance of the parts to the whole does appear when the end of the work is reached; second, that Calderonian drama is poetic in the broadest sense (represents "*die* Poesie"), which I interpret to mean that Goethe approved Calderón's generous use of passages of lyrical and narrative poetry in the larger context of a work of dramatic poetry (his own practice in *Faust II*). This interpretation of Goethe's second point is confirmed by what he wrote (May 1, 1815) to the General Intendant of the Royal Theater in Berlin, Count von Brühl:

> Man hat die höheren Forderungen der Poesie, die sich eigentlich auf dem Theater nur symbolisch oder allegorisch aussprechen können [again *Faust II*], der Tragödie und Komödie durchaus verkümmert, und alles was nur einigermaßen die Einbildungskraft in Anspruch nimmt, in die Oper verwiesen [this might imply, contrary to what is so often asserted, that *Faust II* is not intended to be operatic in the musical sense], und auch hier hat sich die Prosa des Trauer- und Lustspiels, ja des Dramas nach und nach eingeschlichen, daß die Geister selbst oft die prosaischsten Figuren von der Welt sind.
>
> Diese Richtung, in welcher sich Autoren, Schauspieler, Publikum wechselsweise bestärken, ist nicht zu ändern, ja ihr nicht gerade entgegenzuarbeiten; aber sie zu lenken und zu leiten geht doch an, und wenn man es auch nur im Einzelnen tut; hierzu habe ich früher die Masken, später die spanischen Stücke gebraucht.

The Calderonian element in *Faust* is thus at least in large part a reflection of the later Goethe's dislike of "einfache Nachahmung der Natur." Between this and Goethe's ideal of "Stil" comes "Manier," which he also repudiated;

not simple imitation of the Calderonian manner, but adaptation of it to his own style, is what we will find in *Faust II.*

Thanking Gries for his translations of *Das laute Geheimnis* and *Der wundertätige Magus*—"bis in die tiefe Nacht hat mich Ihr Calderon festgehalten"—Goethe wrote (May 29, 1816):

> In ein herrliches, meerumflossenes, blumen- und fruchtreiches, von klaren Gestirnen beschienenes Land versetzen uns diese Werke, und zugleich in die Bildungsepoche einer Nation, von der wir uns kaum einen Begriff machen können. . . . Noch Eins füge ich hinzu, daß mein Aufenthalt im Orient mir den trefflichen Calderon, der seine arabische Bildung nicht verleugnet, nur noch werter macht, wie man edle Stammväter in würdigen Enkeln gern wiederfindet und bewundert.

Calderón has now become a symbol of the ties between Oriental and Western European civilizations, of medieval-baroque lushness and exoticism—which are highly important elements in the *Faust* scene "Innerer Burghof" with its meeting of Classical and Romantic and its survey of world history from Ancient Greece to Medieval-Modern Europe by way of the Migrations of the Peoples. Five years later (Goethe wrote on May 20, 1821, acknowledging Gries's translation of *Die Tochter der Luft*: "das unschätzbare Stück. . . gehört. . . zu einer der vorzüglichsten Productionen dieses einzigen Mannes") Calderonian drama still receives highest praise, and Goethe is able to catalogue what he considers its meritorious features ("seine Verdienste"):

> die geistreichste Konzeption eines bedeutenden Gegenstandes, die Verwandlung des Geschichtlichen in ein Fabelhaftes ["Innerer Burghof"!], die gewandteste Benutzung aller dramatischen und theatralischen Vorteile [think of Phorkyas's entrance at Faust's words to Helen: "Durchgrüble nicht das einzigste Geschick! / Dasein ist Pflicht und wär's ein Augenblick"; of the vanishing of Helen as she embraces Faust for the last time; of Faust's departure in a cloud immediately thereafter!], poetische Gleichnisfülle [Lynceus's "Laß mich knieen, laß mich schauen" speech], rhetorische Dialektik [its concluding "Drohe nur mich zu vernichten, / Schönheit bändigt allen Zorn"]—das alles, in gewissen hohen Punkten zusammentreffend, wahrhaft rührend, obgleich im Ganzen nicht auf's Gemüt angesehen.

What Goethe regarded as peculiarly Calderonian had been clearly established to his own satisfaction well before, on taking up and completing *Faust*, he found it advantageous to use the Calderonian manner in his own work.

A passing mention of Calderón recorded by Eckermann under the date of February 26, 1824, brings us to the eve of the years during which *Faust* was to be Goethe's "Hauptgeschäft": "Dieses Bild eines französischen Künstlers z.B. ist galant wie kein anderes and daher ein Musterstück seiner Art." Goethe is showing Eckermann some engravings, "das Beste in jeder Gattung, damit Sie sehen, daß keine Gattung gering zu achten, sondern daß jede erfreulich ist, sobald ein großes Talent darin den Gipfel erreichte." A rococo scene is described: "Das, dächte ich, sagte Goethe, wäre so galant wie irgendein Stück von Calderon, und Sie haben nun in dieser Art das Vorzüglichste gesehen." Calderón's excellence, which Goethe has so far praised for artistic reasons, is here for the first time specifically associated with what might be called the art of the *galant*—and what could be more *galant* than Faust's wooing of Helen in "Innerer Burghof?" What Goethe in an undated letter to Frau von Stein referred to as "Calderonische Art" and "Spanische Anmut" (WA IV.50, No. 21) is now recognized by him, rightly or wrongly, as the theme or subject which Calderón—Calderonian drama represents a "Gattung" of drama at its best—treated with more skill than any other dramatic writer. We can now understand why, in his essay *Calderons Tochter der Luft* (1822), Goethe should have named Calderón with Shakespeare; the English poet and the Spanish one represent not the same degree of greatness but equal degrees of excellence:

> Die Haupthandlung geht ihren großen poetischen Gang, die Zwischenszenen, welche menuettartig in zierlichen Figuren sich bewegen, sind rhetorisch, dialektisch, sophistisch [Lynceus again!]. Alle Elemente der Menschheit werden erschöpft, und so fehlt auch zuletzt der Narr nicht, dessen hausbackener Verstand, wenn irgend eine Täuschung auf Anteil und Neigung Anspruch machen sollte, sie alsobald [Phorkyas's interruption in "Innerer Burghof"!], wo nicht gar schon im voraus [the comic tone of Phorkyas's announcement of the birth and first hours of the still-to-appear Euphorion!], zu zerstören droht.
>
> Nun gesteht man bei einigem Nachdenken, daß menschliche Zustände, Gefühle, Ereignisse in ursprünglicher Natürlichkeit sich nicht in dieser Art aufs Theater bringen lassen, sie müssen schon verarbeitet, zubereitet, sublimiert sein; und so finden wir sie auch hier: der Dichter steht an der Schwelle der Überkultur, er gibt eine Quintessenz der Menschheit [even as does Goethe in *Faust*].
>
> Shakespeare reicht uns im Gegenteil die volle, reife Traube vom Stock; wir mögen sie nun beliebig Beere für Beere genießen, sie auspressen, keltern, als Most, als gegornen Wein kosten oder schlürfen, auf jede Weise sind wir erquickt. Bei Calderon dagegen ist dem Zuschauer, dessen Wahl und Wollen nichts überlassen; wir empfangen abgezogenen, höchst rektifizierten Weingeist, mit manchen Spezereien geschärft, mit Süßigkeiten gemildert; wir müssen den Trank einnehmen, wie er ist, als schmackhaftes köstliches Reizmittel, oder ihn abweisen.

It is hardly surprising that Eckermann should in 1826 be told (conversation of July 26—"Ich fragte, wie ein Stück beschaffen sein müsse, um theatralisch zu sein"):

> Es muß symbolisch sein. . . . Das heißt: Jede Handlung muß an sich bedeutend sein und auf eine noch wichtigere hinzielen [a condition which *Faust*, its admirers believe, fulfills]. . . . Bei Calderon. . . finden Sie dieselbe theatralische Vollkommenheit [*sc.* wie im *Tartuffe* und in der *Minna von Barnhelm*]. Seine Stücke sind durchaus bretterrecht; es ist in ihnen kein Zug, der nicht für die beabsichtigte Wirkung kalkuliert wäre. Calderon ist dasjenige Genie, was zugleich den größten Verstand hatte. . . . Shakespeare. . . schrieb diese [i.e., seine] Stücke aus seiner Natur heraus, und dann machte seine Zeit und die Einrichtung der damaligen Bühne an ihn keine Anforderungen. . . . Hätte aber Shakespeare für den Hof zu Madrid oder für das Theater Ludwigs des Vierzehnten geschrieben, er hätte sich auch wahrscheinlich einer strengeren Theaterform gefügt.

Sophisticated theatricality in the interest of effective symbolic statement, baroque rhetorical ornateness as the supreme literary expression of the spirit of gallantry—these two elements are harmoniously blended in "Innerer Burghof," the central scene of that "Helena" which Goethe regarded as the axis of his great drama. But the importance of Calderón for *Faust II* is not limited to passages executed in 1825 and 1826. Having found Calderonian devices extremely useful for Act III, Goethe continued to exploit them and adapt them to his needs as he filled in the "Antezedenzien" of "Helena" and as he completed the rest of Part II ("Anmutige Gegend," Act V and Act IV). Before May 12, 1825, Calderón may indeed have exerted no influence on Goethe "weder im Guten noch im Schlimmen." After that date his influence—at times "im Guten," at times "im Schlimmen"—can hardly be explained away. Goethe's utterances on the subject of Calderón become more enthusiastic, praise is no longer balanced with cautious qualification. Thus he writes to Zelter (February 6, 1827)—almost six full years after his first reading of *Die Tochter der Luft* and his essay on it—that this play is "ein grandioses Werk." If in his letter he finds it important to remind Zelter how "im Original ist die Absicht, daß Semiramis and Ninus von Einer Schauspielerin gespielt werden," it is perhaps because he is uncertain whether the role of Helen really demands two actresses, as he had told Eckermann just eight days before.[3] The end of the following month (March 28, 1827) he tells Eckermann, who has mentioned Shakespeare and Calderón, that "Beide sind freilich der Art, daß man über sie nicht Gutes genug sagen kann," and in his next sentence he names as other examples of dramatic greatness Aeschylus and Sophocles: Calderón has finally gained a place in Goethe's estimation that makes him a peer of the indubitably greatest dramatists of all time. And so it is not surprising that, having read *Die Locken Absalons* in Gries's translation, he should write to Zelter on April 28, 1829: "Bei mir ist die alte Wahrheit wieder aufgestanden: daß, wie Natur und Poesie sich in der neueren Zeit vielleicht niemals inniger zusammengefunden haben als bei Shakespeare, so die höchste Kultur und Poesie nie inniger als bei Calderon." Consciousness of Calderón's manneredness has disappeared as Goethe has over the years become acclimated to Calderonian "Manier," and for the Goethe who is completing *Faust* Calderón can represent a "Stil" and hence be worthy of more serious imitation than is found in the obviously manneristic or baroque passages of the "Helena."

In his *Kritische Essays zur europäischen Literatur* (Bern, 1950), E.R. Curtius aptly characterizes "die Welt Calderons" as a "zeitloses Mittelalter" (191). In Goethe's "Helena"—the oldest manuscript is headed "Helena im Mittelalter"—the primary function of Calderonian elements is to suggest such a timeless Middle Ages, which alone can effectively constitute a substantial counterpart to the thousand and more years of Graeco-Roman civilization symbolically represented in the Classical Walpurgisnight and in the first "Helena" scene ("Vor dem Palaste des Menelas zu Sparta"). Although Faust himself is in many ways a "Renaissance Man," as Harold Jantz has helpfully demonstrated in a recent monograph, at this point in Goethe's tragedy he is the symbolic heir both of Classical civilization and of well over a thousand years of post-Classical (Christian-Oriental-Medieval) culture. In the great masquerade at the Emperor's residence it was only fitting that he should represent the spirit of Italianate Humanism, for the Empire ("Saal des Thrones") has represented Medieval society in its period of disintegration only. Now, however, he is the "sentimentive" (*sentimentalisch*), Northern or Romantic spirit seeking to achieve fullness through symbolic union with Helen, the spirit of Classical Antiquity, and so it is the Middle Ages at its best, at its most timeless, which is represented in "Innerer Burghof."

The change of scene from "Vor dem Palaste des Menelas zu Sparta" to "Innerer Burghof" takes place without any interruption of the dramatic action. This is usually explained as a dramatico-technical feature intended

---

[3] In any case, it was Eckermann and not Goethe who asserted that the "Helena" begins as tragedy and ends as opera. (The example of Calderonian drama makes clear enough that an opera singer is not needed to deliver lines against musical backgrounds.)

by Goethe to preserve the unity of action characteristic of Attic tragedy and demanded by the Greek stage. The "Helena," however, is designed for a proscenium stage (stage direction after l. 9954: "Phorkyas. . . tritt ins Proszenium") and for three stage sets, the second of which is completely un-Classical and the third of which is anything but the façade required by Classical drama, and so it may well be doubted that Goethe's dramatico-technical device could have any classicizing function or effect. In Calderonian drama, however, this device is not uncommon, since Calderón wrote for a stage which permitted sudden changes of scenery and since he constructed plays in which startling scenic contrasts (and rapid successions of scenes) heighten the dramatic effect. Inasmuch as Calderón frequently uses several different verse forms in the same scene, and usually begins new scenes in new verse forms (sometimes simply changing the assonance of his *romances*), it is always striking when the same verse form is carried over from one scene to another—usually from one shorter to one longer scene, or vice versa[4]—and is an indication that scene follows scene without pause. In *Eifersucht das große Scheusal* (Gries's translation appeared in 1819) the last two scenes of Act II take place respectively in "Gegend am Meer bei Joppe" and "Abgelegene Waldgegend": the former, short scene ends in *redondillas* (*abba* rhymes), but its last redondilla ("PTOLEMÄUS. Führt mich denn! PHILIPPUS. Ich will's; denn keiner / Darf mit euch mich sprechen sehn. *Beide ab*.") is only completed in the next scene (*"Philippus und Ptolemäus treten wieder auf*. PTOLEMÄUS. Jetzt sind wir allein; erspähn / Wird uns hier gewiß nicht Einer").[5] This practice, which corresponds exactly with the carrying over of the final chorus of "Vor dem Palaste des Menelas" to "Innerer Burghof," is even found with chorus in *Der wundertätige Magus*, where III, i ("Gebirg und Wald; im Hintergrund eine Höhle") ends with *"Gesang hinter der Szene*. EINE STIMME. Welches sind die schönsten Triebe / Dieses Lebens? CHOR. Liebe, Liebe! *Während des Gesanges geht der Dämon ab*," while, after *"Die Bühne verwandelt sich in Justinens Zimmer, Justina tritt auf in heftiger Unruhe*," the same Voice and Chorus are heard as "Dunkles Hirngespinnst" by Justina. From "Vor dem Palaste" to "Innerer Burghof," and from "Innerer Burghof" to "Schattiger Hain" ("Der Schauplatz verwandelt sich durchaus"), are two transitions in a Calderonian theatrical

---

[4] E.g., *Die große Zenobia*, I, i–ii, II, i–ii (16 lines)–iii; *Das laute Geheimnis*, I, ii–iii; *Dame Kobold*, II, v–vi, III, last 3 scenes; *Der Richter von Zalamea*, I, i–ii, II, i–ii, iii–iv, III, ii–iii; *Drei Vergeltungen in Einer*, I, iii–iv, III, last scenes; *Hüte dich vor stillem Wasser*, II, i–ii. (Here, as in the body of this essay, "scene" is used in the English sense, as equivalent to French "tableau.")

[5] The same technique is used in *Die Locken Absalons*, II, iii–iv: "Die Bühne verwandelt sich [from "Anmutige Gegend am Ufer des Jordan"] in einen festlich geschmückten Saal" after the third line of a *redondilla*.

manner which a public made familiar with Calderón by the efforts of the German Romanticists and of Goethe could hardly fail to recognize as such.

Within "Innerer Burghof" the Calderonian element is not only represented, as has been anticipatorily indicated in the first section of this essay, by rhetorical subtlety and extravagance—even before Lynceus speaks Faust has antithetically described him as one "Der, Pflicht verfehlend, mir die Pflicht entwand"—but also by certain purely technical (metrical and theatrical) features of Goethe's text. Biedermann, in his study of the so-called "Trauerspiel in der Christenheit," rightly emphasized not only its unusual rhetoric ("Es ist nicht Goethes natürliche, sondern Calderons berechnete Weise" [181]) but also its "Sprachformen" ("der vierfüßige trochäische Vers fällt uns zuerst auf, welcher eine so entschiedene Eigentümlichkeit der klassischen Bühnendichtung Spaniens ist" [183]). Lynceus's "Laß mich knieen, laß mich schauen" speech is always printed as seven four-line stanzas, a fact that has successfully prevented its being recognized as a passage of *redondillas* (groups of four trochaic tetrameter verses rhyming *abba*), since in many Spanish texts and in all the standard German translations of Calderón's plays such "stanzas" are never marked by indentation or special spacing. (As the quotation from *Eifersucht das große Scheusal* demonstrated, a stanza might be divided between two speakers, making stanzaic printing impracticable; in any case, a passage of lyrical dialogue should not be read with marked pauses between its stanzaic parts, although the dramatist—here Goethe—may have found it helpful to compose a passage in so exotic a form as *redondillas* stanzaically.) That Goethe's spacing between *redondillas* does not separate all of them with a marked lyric pause is evident from the third stanza ("Zog den Blick nach jener Seite"), which must be read or spoken immediately after the second (ending "Ging auf einmal mir die Sonne. Wunderbar im Süden auf.") if its grammatical and logical subject is to be understood, and the same is also evident from the close logical connection between stanzas five and six. In view of Lope de Vega's well known precept (*Arte nuevo de hacer comedias*) that "las redondillas" are for "cosas de amor," it is not surprising that Goethe should use them at a point when through Lynceus Faust gallantly pays homage to Helen, even though in Calderón's time their use was not restricted to love passages: in *Die große Zenobia*, the last play of Calderón's to be produced under Goethe's direction in Weimar, the passage (I, 1) in which Decius arrives to pay homage to the newly acclaimed Emperor Aurelian is composed in *redondillas*.

When Lynceus in his second speech to Helen declares, "Von Osten kamen wir heran," he refers explicitly to the great migrations, but since Helen and Faust shortly thereafter begin to speak in rhymed couplets, it is possible to read into his words the more general thought that the Middle

Age is a period of important oriental influences. "Herzlich ist der Orient," Goethe declares in the *Divan*, "Über's Mittelmeer gedrungen, / Nur wer Hafis liebt und kennt / Weiß was Calderon gesungen," and there also we are reminded that "Behramgur, sagt man, hat den Reim erfunden, / Er sprach entzückt aus reiner Seele Drang; / Dilaram schnell, die Freundin seiner Stunden, / Erwiderte mit gleichem Wort und Klang." The device of having sentences divided between actors, and of having rhymes provided by one speaker for lines already started by another, is one of the most striking features of Calderonian drama. Two examples of the dozens to be found in the plays of Calderón known to Goethe are here cited; the first is from *Das Leben ein Traum* (I, ii—in *décimas*), the second from *Über allen Zauber Liebe* (II, ii—a passage in *silvas* [verses of seven and eleven syllables arranged freely and rhymed in pairs], but taken from a point at which there begins an uninterrupted series of eight pentameter lines).

I. ESTRELLA (*den König begrüßend*). Du, gleich Thales,
    ASTOLF (*eben so*).
                                        Gleich Eukliden,
    E.   Der den Sonnen,
    A.   Der den Sternen,
    E.   Stark als Herrscher,
    A.   Mild im Frieden,
    E.   Licht und Strahlen,
    A.   Bahn und Fernen,
    E.   Hat gemessen,
    A.   Hat beschieden,
    E.   Laß, mit innigem Erwarmen,
    A.   Laß, mit zärtlichem Umarmen,
    E.   Mich an dir, als Epheu, hangen,
    A.   Deine Füße mich umfangen.
    BASILIUS [the king].   Kinder, naht euch meinen Armen!

II. CIRCE.   Wie kannst du meinen Fragen
                        Mit Doppelsinn Antwort zu geben wagen?
    ULYSSES.   Weil ich gedacht, was du mich jetzt beschuldigt,
                        Das wäre schon zuvor bei dir entschuldigt.
    C.   Ach ja! denn mir entfiel—
    U. (*beiseit*)
                                        Ich bin von Sinnen.
    C.   Der heut'ge Streit.
    U. (*beiseit*)
                                        Auch ich hatt' ihn nicht innen.
    C.   Was sagst du?

U.	Daß ich deshalb mich vermessen.
C.	Deshalb?
U.	Ja.
C. (*beiseit*)	O verwünscht der Streit! — Indessen,

Da wir zum Scherz nur diese Sprache wählen,
Erzähl' bloß von der Jagd.

U.	Ich will erzählen.

In "Innerer Burghof" the dividing of rhymed lines between two speakers is more functional than in Calderón, but it is a device whose dramatic effectiveness can well have come to Goethe's attention through the reading and seeing of Calderón's plays.

Although by no means unique in Calderón, constantly recurring motifs of Calderonian heroic drama are the sudden summons to war and battle, and the passing of military processions across the stage to the sound of trumpets, "kriegerische Musik" and "Waffengetöse." The "Durchmarsch gewaltiger Heereskraft"—to the sound of "Signale, Explosionen von den Türmen, Trompeten und Zinken, kriegerische Musik"—in "Innerer Burghof" will strike anyone fresh from Calderón's plays as a typically Calderonian form of theatrical display, but he who has just read *Über allen Zauber Liebe* will be most reminded of the scene (III, ii) in which Arsidas, commanding troops who are to rescue Ulysses from Circe, assures a timid soldier that the "Fußvolk und Reiter, die. . . / Den Eintritt. . . verwehrten / In das Gebirg" are "Phantome nur zu achten, / Ihr Wüten nicht zu scheuen; / Denn ihre Streiche sind nur eitles Dräuen." Military display and insubstantial, "phantom" danger—this is surely the situation of Faust as in "Innerer Burghof" he asserts "Hier ist nicht Gefahr, / Und selbst Gefahr erschiene nur als eitles Dräun." (Also suggestive of Calderonian theatrical machinery is the "Zur Laube wandeln sich die Thronen" ending of "Innerer Burghof," for which the magic feats of Circe in *Über allen Zauber Liebe* could certainly offer a general model: in Act I she releases Flerida and Lysidas from two trees—"Zwei Bäume öffnen sich"—and at her command, II, ii, "Es steigt aus dem Boden eine zierlich angeordnete und erleuchtete Tafel empor" on which an *al fresco* meal is to be eaten.)

Although "Schattiger Hain" begins and ends in Grecizing meters, the Euphorion episode—from the stage direction "Von hier an bis zur bemerkten Pause durchaus mit vollstimmiger Musik" to "Völlige Pause. Die Musik hört auf"—is in rhymed verse appropriate to the Romantic (medievalizing and modernizing) treatment of a Classical motif (the Phaethon motif). Of its 260 lines, 130—including both the first and last thirty-two—are trochaic tetrameters,[6] and these dominate the episode, since all other lines except nine (9870–73, 9876, and 9884–87) have fewer than four stresses. Not only is the dominant meter Calderonian, however, but also the dominant rhyme scheme of these trochaic lines: ninety-six (including the first and last groups of thirty-two lines each) are rhymed *abab*, the "cuarteta" variation of the redondilla. Goethe thus effectively uses a verse form whose close association with the Spanish theater of the Golden Age and with the timeless Middle Ages of Calderonian drama—in which King David (*Die Locken Absalons*), Ulysses, Zenobia, Semiramis (*Die Tochter der Luft*), and Cyprian of Antioch feel and speak like Eusebio (*Die Andacht zum Kreuze*) or Don Fernando of Portugal (*Der standhafte Prinz*)—contributes to the blending of Ancient and Modern which is a main theme of the Euphorion episode. And even if a theater audience does not recognize anything but the unusualness of Goethe's extensive use of trochaic verse, it has at least felt that the episode is in some way exotic or archaic. (And even the metrically deaf can appreciate that the whole episode is emphatically symbolic, thanks to the continuous musical background against which its lines must be spoken. For this is the first and only long dramatic passage in *Faust* with uninterrupted musical accompaniment—and such passages, sometimes with dialogue against a musical background [*Die Locken Absalons*, I, end] and sometimes with choral participation [as in the already cited scene from *Der wundertätige Magus*], are standard in almost all the plays of Calderón known to Goethe and his contemporaries.)

Before turning to Calderonian elements in those parts of *Faust II* where Goethe's debt to Calderón is properly less obtrusive, it should be noted that even after the Euphorion episode there are certain Calderonian features in "Schattiger Hain." The famous "altes Wort"—"Daß Glück und Schönheit dauerhaft sich nicht vereint"—struck E. v. Lippmann (*Goethe-Jahrbuch 24* [1903]: 220–21) as an echo of the words of Ludovicus in *Das Fegfeuer des hl. Patricius* (II, ii): "Der Schönheit Anteil, der gepries'nen, sind / Die größten Leiden immer, / Da Glück und Schönheit sich vertragen nimmer."[7] In view of Goethe's keen interest in Calderón, it is certainly possible that the Calderonian "Sentenz," which he could have read in the translation of A. Jeitteles (1824), may have influenced the form of Helen's farewell. Somewhat more obviously Calderonian (Calderón representing for Goethe the best of the theatrical Baroque)—and certainly not Classical but Baroque—however, is her highly theatrical disappearance, an exit closely

---

[6] Lines 9679–9710; 9785–9810; 9819–22; 9851–62; 9877–83; 9889–94; 9907–38. (Ll. 9881–82 are here read, like 9888–89, as forming one tetrameter with inner rhyme.)

[7] Quoted from the translation of Lorinser. (All other quotations are from the translations of A.W. Schlegel and J.D. Gries.)

analogous to the heavenly ascension by which Julia escapes the dagger of Curcio at the very end of *Die Andacht zum Kreuze*. And truly Calderonian, if it were to be staged in the spirit of the text, would be the display of theatrical machinery needed for the final metamorphoses of the Chorus—metamorphoses of the same class as that already mentioned in connection with Circe's magic in *Über allen Zauber Liebe*.

In the "Helena" Goethe introduces Calderonizing elements both for their value as "content" as well as because they are appropriate—Calderonian drama being for him "symbolic"—to the quintessentially symbolic character of this section of *Faust*. But all poetry is symbolic, and much of *Faust II* very patently so, and so it is not surprising that Goethe should exploit Calderonian techniques where they can enable him to execute more economically, more quickly, the "Hauptgeschäft" of his last, numbered years. In "Anmutige Gegend," probably the first scene to be completed after the "Helena," the symbolic songs of Ariel and the elfin Chorus are in the trochaic tetrameter (rhymed *abab*) of "symbolic" Spanish drama; the succession of darkness and daylight is a symbol of syncopation of time also exploited by Calderón; and Faust speaks in *terza rima*, a verse form the use of which *Faust* commentaries regularly declare to have been inspired by Streckenfuß's translation of Dante—which may be partly true—although in dramatic literature the one passage in *terza rima* known to Goethe at the time of writing[8] was that of eight-five lines at the beginning of I, ii of *Der standhafte Prinz* (landing on the coast of Africa, Fernando expresses heroic confidence in the ultimate success of the invasion which he directs). In the series of scenes "Mitternacht"-"Grablegung," also composed in 1825 and the years immediately following, Goethe makes effective use of Spanish trochaics in the "Litanei" of Sorge, where they set in relief the more nervous iambics of Faust (poetry of symbolic dramatic situation is thus merged with poetry of character tragedy, Calderón-Goethe with Shakespeare-Goethe); and in the burial scene he exploits in highly sophisticated, literary drama both heavenly intervention (*Andacht zum Kreuze*) and the hell-mouth that Calderón took over from medieval drama (*Fegfeuer des hl. Patricius*, where Ludovicus enters its "furchtbarer Schlund" to endure the "Höllenqual" of purgatorial fire).

In the sequence of scenes "Kaiserliche Pfalz"-"Lustgarten," l. 6036, published in 1828 and apparently composed 1826–27, there is also a blending of the Shakespearean ("History") and the Calderonian styles. Although the great masquerade is Italianate in many respects, its motifs

---

[8] *Terza rima* is also found in *Die Locken Absalons* (II, ii), but Gries's translation of this play did not appear until 1829. (Ticknor, who knew Spanish literature well, believed that the passage in *Der standhafte Prinz* was perhaps the only such in Calderón.)

deriving from "Das Römische Karneval" and Grazzini's *Tutti i Trionfi*, the representation of such large-scale spectacle in a regular dramatic context can hardly have been suggested to Goethe otherwise than by Calderón's daring theatrical practice: not only the use of procession and song, but even the introduction of winged dragons (the Demon of *Der wundertätige Magus* hovers on a "Schlange" over the decapitated Cyprianus and Justina) and of a grand catastrophe (in *Faust* the conflagration, in plays of Calderón such events as the sinking of the palace of Circe, to be replaced by a fire-spewing Aetna, in *Über allen Zauber Liebe*) are typical of Spanish literary drama rather than of anything Italian. Clearly Calderonian, moreover, are the two descriptive passages at the opening of "Lustgarten," the Emperor's account of the fiery underworld and Mephistopheles' picture of a submarine wonderland: although Calderón delights in theatrical spectacle, he regularly introduces "purple" passages of considerable length in unspectacular scenes so that the mind's eye may have pictures when the stage does not provide them. Like Goethe here, but with less concern for the advancing of the dramatic action, he demonstrates incontestably that he is both a master of the theatrical stage effect and of vivid poetic description.

During the execution of "Helenas Antezedenzien" Goethe continued to exploit the possibilities of Calderonian theater. The verbal art of "Finstere Galerie" is balanced by the theatrical spectacle of "Rittersaal," in which, as so often in Calderón's plays, the back of a stage set is opened to reveal another, highly contrasting stage set. In "Hochgewölbtes enges gotisches Zimmer" doors spring open, and the Baccalaureus has a descriptive-narrative speech in rhymed Spanish trochaics; in "Laboratorium" a door opens to reveal Faust stretched out on his couch (in both *Der Richter von Zalamea* and *Drei Vergeltungen in Einer* strangled characters are thus made visible); and in both scenes it is highly probable that the paralyzed Faust is supposed to hear, even if he is asleep, all the dialogue: in *Die Tochter der Luft*, II, iv, two characters leave the chamber in which Ninyas sleeps because "manchesmal / Pflegt im Schlummer man zu hören / Was gesagt wird." (If Faust does not hear the dialogue of these two scenes, they are digressive or even superfluous; if he hears it, they represent not only a contribution to the sum total of his broad experience of life but also dramatic moments of impotent anguish.) And in the longest part of the "Antezedenzien," in the "Klassische Walpurgisnacht," Goethe outdoes Calderón in the introduction of theatrical novelties, for they here succeed one another at a much closer interval than in any Calderonian drama. Two stage effects deserve special mention, since they are both to be found in *Über allen Zauber Liebe*: the first is the emergence of Seismos, which is a comic variant of the Aetna that replaces Circe's palace; the other is the more serious Triumph of Galatea ("Felsbuchten des Ägäischen Meers"), in which the sea is "vom Feuer umronnen"—in Calderón's play Circe sets the sea on fire to destroy the fleeing Greeks (stage direction: "Es kommt Feuer aus dem Wasser"), but all ends well when "Das Meer erheitert sich, und es erscheint auf demselben in einem Triumphwagen, von zwei Delphinen gezogen, Galatea, viele Tritonen und Sirenen mit musikalischen Instrumenten um sie her." It is hardly possible that Goethe, without the precedent set by so highly esteemed a dramatist as Calderón, would have concluded the "Klassische Walpurgisnacht" on the grandiose theatrical scale in which we now have it.[9]

At the beginning and end of Act V of *Faust II* Goethe continued to exploit Calderonian techniques. Not only is "Offene Gegend" a scene of symbolic transparency, but it is even composed in *redondillas*. The continuity of the next scenes, which follow each other without pause as Faust appears successively in his garden, on the balcony of his palace, and then within the palace, is in the Calderonian tradition already emphasized in connection with the "Helena." And in "Bergschluchten" Goethe not only uses one of Calderón's favorite stage settings ("Eine wilde Felsgegend" or a variant of this phrase is a stage direction constantly recurring through Calderón's works), exploits supernatural machinery, and has Pater Seraphicus, Chor seliger Knaben, Die jüngeren Engel, and the three Marys speak chiefly in *redondillas*; he also opens the scene with a "Chor Echo" in the best Calderonian tradition and lets the Marys implore of the Mater Gloriosa pardon for Gretchen in one long rhetorical period in which they speak both in unison and separately (cf. the hailing of Basilius in *Das Leben ein Traum*, as quoted above in connection with "Innerer Burghof"). Here, surely, where Goethe's symbolism is visibly indebted to the Catholic tradition, the Calderonian touches are meant to be recognized as such.

The last part of *Faust* to be completed was Part II, Act IV—the act in which, more than any other, drama of character is subordinated to drama of symbolic action. The multiple stage set of this act ("Hochgebirg, starre zackige Felsengipfel," "Sie steigen über das Mittelgebirg herüber" [after l. 10296] and "Auf dem Vorgebirg") permits an uninterrupted succession of campaign scenes in the Calderonian manner (e.g., of *Die Aurora von Copacabana*—with much supernaturalism) and places them in Calderón's

---

[9] The possibility that *Über allen Zauber Liebe* might be a source of this passage in *Faust* was noted by Witkowski (to ll. 8379–90), who however placed far greater emphasis on Goethe's interest in Philostratos and Renaissance art (Raphael, the Caracci); although Beutler (Gedenkausgabe 5:797–99) gives a much more detailed account of Calderón's play and the theater for which it was designed, and although he mentions Goethe's idea of producing it in Weimar ("Briefentwurf," June, 1803), he seems to see Calderonian influence in *Faust* only at the end of the "Klassische Walpurgisnacht."

favorite outdoor setting (mountainous landscape). The opening cloud machinery is indubitably Baroque theater, and Baroque also is the cloud allegory; indeed, the use of the disturbingly artificial phrase "Aurorens Liebe" for "Gretchen" is peculiarly Calderonian, for in passages of highest praise Calderón has a marked predilection for 'Aurora images.' (Can Faust's opening monologue have been written at the same time as his "Anmutige Gegend" soliloquy, and the rest of the act in 1831? His monologue is metrically very close to the Grecizing passages of the "Helena," and in imagery it is very close to the Calderonizing ones.) Thus in *Die Schärpe und die Blume* (I, i), the play which Goethe read aloud on Tuesdays in the first three months of 1808 (Biedermann, *Goethes Gespräche* [1911] 5:71–72), almost two thirds of a 270-line speech of Enrico is an account in terms of dawn allegory of how homage has been paid to the Crown Infant Balthasar, and in it Queen Isabella replaces the dawn ("Aus fuhr an Aurorens Stelle, / Sie an Schönheit übertreffend, / Isabell' ") while the Infant becomes "Kind Aurorens." Although Calderón does not usually develop imagery at quite this length, the dawn metaphor recurs regularly in his plays; in *Die Tochter der Luft* the lovely Irene is as it were inevitably "Göttliche Morgenröte dieser Sonne" (I, i), and in *Die große Zenobia* it is to be expected that where Zenobia—"jene Göttergleiche" to whom "Schönheit gab Cythere"—rules should be "Wo, in Aurorens Mutterarm erzogen, / Glut strömend, früh der junge Tag erscheinet" (I, i).

In "Auf dem Vorgebirg" the Scouts and Heralds give their reports in Calderonian *redondillas*, and at the first critical point in the battle (ll. 10640–63) Mephistopheles and the Emperor fall into the rhymed Spanish trochaic tetrameter which Goethe has used instead of *asonances* for such narrative-descriptive passages ever since Lynceus's second speech in "Innerer Burghof." The military campaign in which magical forces play a large role has, since Max Morris's drawing of attention to Walter Scott's *Letters on Demonology and Witchcraft*, been interpreted as Goethe's direct reworking of folkloristic materials, but the surprising, brief intrusion of Calderonian meters into an overwhelmingly "iambic" context suggests that Goethe has not entirely forgotten the phantom forces deployed by Circe in *Über allen Zauber Liebe* (see above, in connection with "Innerer Burghof" and "eitles Dräun"). Even the end of Act IV, with its Franco-German alexandrines unknown to Spanish drama, is not without its Calderonian hyperboles, for the speeches in which the newly elevated Arch-Marshal, Arch-Chamberlain, Arch-Steward, and Arch-Cupbearer express their thanks to the Emperor are splendid examples of servile adulation couched in antithetical elegance, and their "Baroque" flavor surely is subtle preparation for the Archbishop's "most Catholic" unctuousness during his final private interview with the Emperor. With the help of Calderonian imagery, verse, stage sets, and—for this should be mentioned too—sound and light effects ("Trommeln und kriegerische Musik," "Furchtbarer Posaunenschall," and Mephisto's "Den Feinden dichte Finsternisse"), Goethe was able to complete the "Hauptgeschäft" of his last years just in time; it may well be doubted whether he could have done so had he not made use of the shortcuts of transparent theatrico-dramatic symbolism the high poetic potentialities of which were revealed to him through the dramas of Calderón.[10]

[10] Following Hugo Schuchardt, "Goethe und Calderon" (*Romanisches und Keltisches: Gesammelte Aufsätze*, Berlin, 1886), C.H. Herford ("On Goethe and Calderon," *PEGS* 2, 57–71), Karl Wollf ("Goethe und Calderon," *Goethe-Jb.* 34, 118–40), and others have been content to consider the possibility of Calderonian "influences" in *Faust* only in connection with Lynceus's first speech in "Innerer Burghof" and with the mysticism of "Berg-schluchten." If Herford passes over "Bergschluchten" in silence, Wollf (having accepted uncritically Goethe's "Calderon hat auf mich gar keinen Einfluß gehabt") boldly asserts that on the "Schlußwendung des großen Weltgedichtes Calderon keinerlei Einfluß geübt hat." It seems to me that the mystical content of "Bergschluchten" can be purely Goethean and its formulation nevertheless be somewhat Calderonian. And so, without accepting Schuchardt's main suggestion (that the end of *Faust II* is "ganz katholisch," that "nirgends streift die Bahn Goethes so nahe an die Calderons an wie hier" [147]), I can still be reminded, as he is, of the end of *Das Fegfeuer des hl. Patricius* by "Bergschluchten": "aus wilder Felsgegend," Schuchardt noted (148), "setzt Ludwig [Ludovicus] über den See nach der Insel wo das Kloster, mit dem Eingang zum Fegefeuer. . . im Hintergrunde, sich befindet. Vergl. z.B.:

> Woge nach Woge spritzt. . .

> Wie tausend Bäche strahlend fließen
> Zum grausen Sturz des Schaums der Flut. . .

> Das sind Bäume; das sind Felsen,
> Wasserstrom, der abestürzt. . .

mit:

> Wie auch jetzt die Winde schweigen,
> Regen sich die Wellen doch. . .

> Dorten stürzen rasch die Bäche
> Von dem Felsen grauenvoll. . ."

These echoes may, as Schuchardt diffidently suggested, represent "nur zufällige Überein-stimmung," but I think that the foregoing article has brought evidence enough to warrant their being considered examples of unconscious imitation by a Goethe long steeped in the atmosphere of Calderón's "zeitloses Mittelalter."

Irony and Ambiguity in the Final Scene of Goethe's *Faust*

A s recently as 1931 Konrad Burdach could confidently assert of the final scene of Goethe's *Faust* that it "springt unvermittelt in eine übersinnliche religiöse Welt und gibt in genialer dichterischer Gestaltung tiefste sittlich-religiöse, tröstende, erhebende, Hoffnung einflößende Gedanken und Ahnungen des Dichters, die sein *persönliches* Bekenntnis sind, aber nicht aus dem Drama, aus der Charakterentwicklung des Helden herauswachsen."[1] By 1949 the climate of critical opinion in Germany had changed so completely that Erich Trunz, in what on the dust wrapper is well described as "der Faust-Kommentar, der die gesamte neuere Faust-Forschung verarbeitet und namhaft macht," apparently deemed it proper to ignore as unimportant or irrelevant the once common charge that the scene is an unorganic pendant to the Tragedy of Faust.[2] In view of Burdach's emphasis on drama, on the character development of the dramatic hero, as the criterion by which the relevance of "Bergschluchten" to the whole of *Faust* is to be determined, the best explanation of how a purely positive evaluation of the scene has become acceptable in German critical circles would seem to be simply this: *Faust* is no longer being read as a drama, even though it quite explicitly purports to be "eine Tragödie." To be sure, Heinrich Rickert in his *Faust* book of 1932 and others since have done much to bring out what he called sub-titularly "die dramatische Einheit der Dichtung," but neither he nor they have made as good a case for a positive *dramatic* evaluation of "Bergschluchten" as for many another scene formerly depreciated by severer critics. What might be called the uncritical critical acceptance of the final scene of *Faust* surely does not, however, represent the mere assumption that, because far more parts of the work are dramatically functional than earlier critics realized, every part is auto-

[1] "Die Schluß-Szene in Goethes Faust," *Sitzungsberichte der Preußischen Akademie der Wissenschaften. Jahrgang 1931. Philosophisch-historische Klasse*: 585–604, here 604.

[2] *Goethes Faust*. Herausgegeben und erläutert von Erich Trunz (Hamburg, 1949) 479–83 and 622-26. Ada M. Klett[-Bister], *Der Streit um 'Faust II' seit 1900*, Jenaer Germanistische Forschungen, 33 (Jena, 1939) 78–86 ("Der himmlische Ausgang"), offers a good survey of previous critical opinions.

matically so. The change in critical attitude is rather to be explained as a by-product of the German critics' increased concern with myth and symbolism, as evidenced in G.W. Hertz's influential *Natur und Geist in Goethes Faust* (1931) and in subsequent studies by Kerényi, Danckert, Emrich, and others. It is obvious, I think, that myth and drama are not necessarily identical, that emphasis on the mythico-symbolic (Hertz's interest in Goethe's "Monaden-mythos," for instance) may bring as corollary indifference to the dramatic aspects of the work of dramatic art. And so, without underestimating the very real contributions which "Symbolinterpretation" and "Mythenforschung" have made toward a better understanding of Goethe's *Faust*,[3] I should like to reexamine the final scene of the Tragedy with reference to two age-old dramatic devices exploited in it—the first of which, at least, was never more highly esteemed by critics than in the age of German romanticism—viz., irony and ambiguity.

The terms irony and ambiguity, it may be objected, can be understood in so many senses that their use in a discussion of "Bergschluchten" is not likely to result in any larger clarification of the scene's dramatic function. Nevertheless, I venture to hope that such concepts as dramatic irony, comic irony, tragic irony, and romantic irony present no special semantic difficulties in a context which limits itself to an evaluation of what purports to be a part of a written drama. If I distinguish ambiguity from irony, it is so that there may be no confusion of limitedly plural meaning (irony—as it were, ambiguity on a plane surface) with that multiplicity and complexity of meaning which is the primary characteristic of poetry regardless of genre (ambiguity—as it were, irony in a plurality of dimensions or with overtones to be determined not by the poet's intention but by the sensitivity of the hearer's ear).[4] For an evaluation of the dramatic function of the final scene of *Faust*, it is necessary to separate the wheat of irony from the chaff of ambiguity, the specifically dramatic from the generally poetic, the Faustian from the Goethean and—as the last pair should make clear—one kind of good from another kind of good rather than something good from what, by an ironic figure of speech, might seem at first to have been characterized as something bad.

---

[3] Wilhelm Emrich, author of *Die Symbolik von Faust II* (Berlin, 1943), rightly warns of the danger of reading myths into symbolism in his "Symbolinterpretation und Mythen-forschung: Möglichkeiten und Grenzen eines neuen Goetheverständnisses," *Euphorion* 47 (1953): 38–67, although he himself at times seems to read *Faust* as allegory rather than as drama.

[4] The "romantic irony" of unwitting self-revelation by the apparently completely objective author would by this definition be more akin to ambiguity.

The major representatives of *Faust* criticism in Germany today may seem to agree on the merits of "Bergschluchten," for they are unanimous in finding that scene meritorious. But their agreement is actually ambiguous, for it is difficult to find any two who discern—or, at least, emphasize—the same specific details in their critical writing.[5] Even more ambiguous is the critical status of the scene if we go outside of German criticism to examine the considered opinions of two British scholars. D.J. Enright introduces his remarks on it with "The play is over; but we must submit, just once more, to the poet's fertile imagination and his love of huge pictorial canvases. . . . This progress to Heaven must be received in a spirit of not-too-solemn appreciation." He concludes that the scene is without any significance unless it serves to link the "Protestant" Prologue in Heaven and "the rich Catholic 'Journey to Heaven' . . . since the preceding scenes have done all that is necessary in relating Faust's end to his beginning, and done it with magnificent economy and ease: *their* significance is unmistakable."[6] From Enright's remarks it would be only proper to regard "Bergschluchten" as a scene of negligible dramatic importance and value—ambiguous in its significance, uneconomical in its execution—but as one still to be suffered patiently and half-politely because it has been preceded by much that is better, itself having clearly no dramatic value.

A second voice from England is even less cautious—or ambiguous—than that of the New Directions' writer. Being a less ambiguous voice—the voice is that of E.M. Butler in her compendious *The Fortunes of Faust*—it is one also more ironic in tone, and its author shows far greater sensitivity to the irony of much of *Faust* than most critics have shown recently. But after admiring the tragic irony of Faust's death scene, which "has still to find its equal in the literature of the world," she goes on to a most insensitive and, by German standards, heretical discussion of the rest of the play:

> Time has stopped for Faust; he is on the threshold of eternity.—One would like to leave him there, as certain of his salvation as one was of Gretchen's before the voice from above announced the self-evident fact in *Faust I*. But Goethe has a tradition to contend with which was not broken yet, in spite of the strenuous efforts of Weidmann, Schink, Schöne, Holtei and their like. He also had a reputation to maintain; and he would surely have been not more but less than human if he had not felt it incumbent on him to do better than they. He must therefore dot the i's and cross the t's of a situation it would not do to leave to his readers' imagination; and moreover

---

[5] Space does not permit this point to be documented here, but it will be illustrated later in this essay by a few examples.

[6] *Commentary on Goethe's Faust* (Norfolk, 1949) 153 and 155.

since the blatant Schöne had forestalled the obvious ending by his *Epilogue in Heaven*, he must take a different line. . . . Goethe therefore sent Faust's immortal soul [*sic*] drifting upwards into Roman Catholic skies. . . . Margarete 'clings' (according to the rubric) to the Virgin Mary; and it is an echo from the past which could well be spared; for of all the plagiarisms which Goethe's *Faust I* had to suffer, this seems [*scil.*, to E.M. Butler] the worst.[7]

Both these English critics are scholars of high repute; if they depreciate the final scene of *Faust*, they surely do so in full knowledge of the various merits ambiguously attributed to it by recent German commentators. It may therefore be suspected that their dissatisfaction arises from the same source as Burdach's, although it takes the form of more general condemnation; a scene without dramatic function is profoundly disturbing in a work in which certain passages obviously represent the achievement of great dramatic heights. But is "Bergschluchten" really undramatic? Does it really fail to derive from Faust's dramatic character? (I gladly concede an affirmative answer to the question: Is the physical symbolism of the scene expressive of the same ideas as have been previously expressed in the drama?)[8] One plausible answer to this double question has already been offered by Max Kommerell, who, in contrast to Enright, frankly admits that in the completed *Faust* our scene "nur sehr notdürftig. . . ihre ursprüngliche Aufgabe [erfüllt], mit dem Prolog im Himmel die ganze Dichtung zu umklammern."[9] For Kommerell sees the scene both as a performance for Faust's benefit—"Für wen spielt denn die ganze Szene, wenn nicht für dies Unsterbliche Faustens"—and as the representation of Faust's "Entmaterialisation" in the first moments of his "Nach-Tod." "Die Innerlichkeit Fausts ist nicht an sich, sondern in der Spiegelung durch einen Prozeß dargestellt. . . an den Substraten, die zu dieser transzendenten Welt gehören."[10] This is a reading of "Bergschluchten" which should, if properly supported by textual evidence, redeem the scene for those readers of *Faust* who expect something dramatic in every important part of a tragedy. If Kommerell's reading has nevertheless failed to persuade others of its rightness, it is perhaps because he brings little evidence to support it; for he belongs to that large group of modern *Faust* interpreters prone to read most of the Second Part of the Tragedy as a play performed *for* Faust's benefit—a sort of *Bildungsdrama*—rather than as a drama in which the chief role is acted

---

[7] *The Fortunes of Faust* (Cambridge, 1952) 262, 263.
[8] Cf. the analysis by Trunz, *Goethes Faust* 623ff.
[9] Kommerell, *Geist und Buchstabe der Dichtung* (Frankfurt/Main, 1944) 112.
[10] Kommerell 115 (and cf. 118).

by Faust. As a result, his interpretation of "Bergschluchten" emphasizes less the dramatic role attributed in passing to Faust than it does the poetic idea, for which little or no direct textual evidence can ever be found, that after having absorbed Cosmos up to his death it is inevitable that the reversal of the process should have to begin on Faust's new plane of existence.[11]

The brilliance of Kommerell's aperçu is, as it were, vitiated by his insistence upon what, for want of a better term, I shall call the "heavenly" life or "heavenly" elements in the final scene of *Faust*. For one of the great ambiguities of the scene is the nature of its setting and the nature of its actors. Is Faust on a new plane of existence, or is he only still on this plane, imagining a next one somewhat more sophisticatedly than does the protagonist of Hauptmann's *Hanneles Himmelfahrt?* Trunz sees the scene beginning in the realm of physical Nature, but he quickly comes to what he regards as "unmittelbarere Offenbarungen des Göttlichen" (Pater Seraphicus, Angels, etc.), a view to which quotation has shown both Enright and Butler subscribe, a view which is certainly shared by almost all interpreters of *Faust*. Even Rickert, in so many ways a humanist of the "Deutsche Klassik" tradition, hesitates to call the setting "irdisch," and yet after denying that it is that, he declares, "trotzdem müssen wir den Ausdruck 'himmlisch' für den Schauplatz mit Vorsicht gebrauchen."[12] He compromises on "Der Weg zum Himmel," which, of course, gives the heavenly component of the scene greater weight than the "earthly" one. But examination of the textual evidence will show, I think, that the scene is *not* dominantly characterized by heavenly elements; indeed, it will be possible to adduce evidence of this patiently gathered by critics and scholars who, despite their own gleanings, continue to speak of the scene as if the this-worldly played only a minimal role in it. Such, ironically, is the power of romantic preconception to triumph over evidence.

Perhaps the most interesting demonstration—by a critic, incidentally, who places the action of "Bergschluchten" in a "Vorhimmel"—that this scene does not take place outside the frequently all-too-earthly world of Faust's multifarious experiences, that it does not return to a heaven either corresponding to or complementing the one of the Prologue in Heaven, is offered by Kurt May in his primarily stylistic interpretation of Part Two of the Tragedy. It may be recalled in passing that the Tragedy of Faust begins *after* the Prologue in Heaven, as stated in the text after line 353, whereas there is no textual indication that "Bergschluchten" is not the final scene of the

---

[11] A similar emphasis on Faust's assimilation of Cosmos ("Welt") is found in Dorothea Lohmeyer, *Faust und die Welt* (Potsdam, 1940); it no doubt also reflects the influence of Hertz's monograph.

[12] *Goethes Faust: Die dramatische Einheit der Dichtung* (Tübingen, 1932) 476.

Tragedy of Faust—which does not mean, of course, that it cannot also
ambiguously serve as an epilogue to the whole *Faust* at the same time. May
marshals plentiful evidence forcing him to conclude that "in der Sprach-
gestaltung gibt es zwischen den früheren Szenen und dieser letzten nicht
nur *keinen* Bruch, *keinen* Sprung, sondern ein fließendes Kontinuum," and
he adds in parentheses an observation of more than parenthetical
importance: "So sind ja auch die Versrhythmen dieser letzten Szene *in
keinem einzigen Fall* gegenüber der Versgestalt in den irdischen [*sic*] Szenen
völlig neu gewesen."[13] May's conclusion would not be important were it not
that one of the fundamental stylistic features of *Faust* as a whole is
deliberate stylistic variation, the continual introduction of new verse forms,
of new dramatic techniques, for new states of mind and feeling in *Faust* and
for new types of dramatic situation. Thus we have *ottava rima* in
"Zueignung," *Madrigalverse* for long stretches thereafter, a folk-song manner
for Gretchen's highly symbolic "Es war ein König in Thule," blank verse to
open Faust's "Wald und Höhle" monologue, doggerel for the Walpurgis
Night's Dream, rhythmic prose for "Trüber Tag: Feld," Calderonian *terza
rima* for "Anmutige Gegend," Grecizing meters for the opening of "Klassi-
sche Walpurgisnacht" and much of the "Helena," Romance verse forms
(especially Calderonian ones) for "Innerer Burghof" and several subsequent
scenes, and so forth down to the "baroque" polysyllabically rhyming verses
of "Grablegung." Thus, to turn from verse to dramatic technique, we have
the suggestion of *commedia dell'arte* improvisation of Prelude on the Stage,
the touches of morality play in Prologue in Heaven, of puppet play at the
opening of Faust's first scene, of late medieval farce in the "Schülerszene,"
of middle-class drama in the Gretchen scenes, of revue in the Walpurgis-
night ones, of Baroque allegorical drama in "Anmutige Gegend," of Shake-
spearean or pseudo-Shakespearean "Haupt- und Staatsaktion" in the scenes
at the imperial court, of Renaissance masque in the "Mummenschanz" scene,
of Old Comedy and, later, of Baroque opera or cantata in "Klassische Wal-
purgisnacht," of Greek tragedy in "Helena," and of Calderonian drama in all
final three acts.

   From the foregoing catalogues of examples of stylistic variation in
Faust—catalogues, incidentally, that could be lengthened considerably—it
can be seen that May's conclusion is valid for a larger area than the
"Sprachform" of *Faust* on which his study concentrates. In "Bergschluchten"
May finds "in dichtester Anhäufung" all the stylistic features which are
distinctive of Part Two of the Tragedy, especially those of "Anmutige

---

[13] *Faust II. Teil in der Sprachform gedeutet* (*Neue Forschung* 30: Berlin, 1936) 269 (my
italics).

Gegend" and the Euphorion scene. (I would note in passing the marked absence of the salient stylistic features of Prologue in Heaven.) It is his final observations on "Bergschluchten," however, that lead to the heart of the problem of how that scene should be interpreted:

> Wie oft. . . war für uns beim Eintritt in einen neuen 'Weltenkreis' der Dichtung eine neue Sprache vernehmbar und wie eindeutig haben wir in dieser Tatsache ein—dem Dichter bewußt gewordenes—Gestaltungsprinzip des Werks erkannt. Es kann nicht gleichgültig sein, daß es Goethe nicht in den Sinn gekommen ist, eine letzte, höchste, überlegenste, im *absoluten* Sinn wesentliche Seinsschicht. . . auszuprägen.

And so, constrained to admit that Goethe deliberately avoids raising us to a new dimension ("in eine neue Dimension"), he decides that the scene is "ein dramatisch-theatralischer Allegorismus für ein letztes, großartig unbedingtes Ja zum unendlichen faustischen Streben."[14] This it may well be—or almost be, as my subsequent analysis will attempt to show—but even if it is entirely, unambiguously true, it fails to meet the down-to-earth objections of either Burdach or Butler satisfactorily. A recapitulation of some sort is undoubtedly in order at the end of *Faust*, if only because of the scope of the work; but unless this recapitulation is more than allegorical pageantry, unless it is in some sense a drama involving Faust the dramatic character and not only an allegory of "Faustian striving," it can indeed only vitiate the impression just made so effectively and so forceably by the tragic-ironic scene of his "Grablegung."

Even a cursory survey of the history of *Faust* criticism would show that from 1832 on the great obstacle to clear thinking—as opposed to appropriate and properly appreciative feeling—about "Bergschluchten" is the use of Roman Catholic symbols in it. Although it may be known that Goethe was highly skeptical of organized religion, and although this may be perfectly clear from scene after scene of *Faust* itself, it is extremely difficult for a critic who is the product of a Western Christian civilization, especially since the reestablishment of the intellectual respectability of Christianity beginning with the Romantic movement, not to regard the Catholic symbolism of "Bergschluchten" as somehow more directly literal than, say, the symbols from Greek mythology of the *trionfo di Galatea* that concludes the "Klassische Walpurgisnacht." And this despite the fact that Eckermann honestly reports Goethe's highly objective observation "daß der

---

[14] *Faust II. Teil* 274f.

Schluß. . . sehr schwer zu machen war, und daß ich bei so übersinnlichen, kaum zu ahnenden Dingen mich sehr leicht im Vagen hätte verlieren können, wenn ich nicht meinen poetischen Intentionen durch die scharf umrissenen christlich-kirchlichen Figuren und Vorstellungen eine wohltätig beschränkende Form und Festigkeit gegeben hätte."[15] In a society which professes greater respect for Christianity than it did in the eighteenth century, Christian symbolism easily ceases to be seriously ironic and becomes simply ambiguous. In other words, if the final scene of *Faust* is read, consciously or unconsciously, as the representation of what May called a "new dimension," it will inevitably be misunderstood in one way or another, and its secular mysticism will seem to be a transcendental one.

One representative of what might be called the Christian apologetic school of *Faust* interpreters—and this school still today seems to include members of every Christian persuasion—may stand for all. Joseph von Görres climaxes his analysis of *Faust* thus:

> So hat aller heidnische Apparat zuletzt nur zu einer Huldigung der Wahrheit hingeführt; und was der Mund ein ganzes bewegtes Leben hindurch verschwiegen, das hat im Kunstwerke sich verraten. Aber mehr Licht! möchten wir für den Dichter mit ihm rufen. Wie Luther durch den Glauben, so hat er durch die Liebe die Rechtfertigung zu erwirken geglaubt, aber dabei die ewige Gerechtigkeit verletzt; die Kirche aber lehrt sicherer: nur im *Glauben* und der *Liebe*, denen alsdann auch die Werke nimmer fehlen, wird die *Hoffnung* auf Rechtfertigung realisiert. Dieser Dichterkönig hat also zwar seinen triumphierenden Auszug aus den Pforten der Negation angetreten; aber treu und ehrlich suchend und forschend, hat er immer sein Angesicht der positiven Wahrheit zugewendet; und sein guter Geist hat ihn ihr näher und näher geführt, und ihm zuletzt einen Blick ins Land der Verheißung gestattet.[16]

Others may formulate more cautiously their conviction that Goethe was really less far from the positive truth of the Churches than he himself perhaps thought, but they are, I suspect, as unaware as was Görres that to use Catholic symbolism respectfully and seriously is not necessarily to

---

[15] June 6, 1831. In his introduction to his translation of *Faust deuxième partie* (Paris: Editions Montaigne, n.d.), Henri Lichtenberger properly insists upon the freedom with which Goethe uses Catholic symbols (v. esp. clviii). I should note in passing that Lichtenberger considers the end of *Faust* to differ "nettement par le style des parties qui précèdent" (cxliv), but that he makes this point with reference to the use of medieval Catholic symbolism (instead of classical allusions) and does not use "style" in the more technical sense of May (whose usage I have followed).

[16] *Die Wallfahrt nach Trier* (Regensburg, 1845) 94–95.

subscribe to the traditional views with which it is usually associated. Although Gundolf could regard as anti-Goethean and anti-Faustian the intervention of "Liebe von oben" in "Bergschluchten," Rickert, May, Henri Lichtenberger, and many another critic have had little difficulty in pointing out disparate non-Catholic emphases in the scene's symbolism. Thus, Rickert, unlike those who refer loosely to the figure *Mater gloriosa* as the Virgin Mary (Butler and others) insists humanistically that it is not "die Jungfrau der 'unbefleckten Empfängnis' " who appears, but the "Schutz-herrin der Liebe, wie sie zwischen Mann und Frau besteht."[17] Stawell and Dickinson, who are sufficiently unconfused by the Catholic symbols at the end of *Faust* to be able to remark that "Goethe—one of the most religious spirits in Modern Europe—seems to have recognized that the loss of religious faith might be a necessary stage in growth," make the nice observation apropos the Pater Profundus's prayer that "even in his [Goethe's] heaven, or near it, there returns the struggle with weariness and deadness that was stifling Faust at the beginning of the drama."[18] More such specific points could be illustrated by quotation from the critical literature on *Faust*, but it would be otiose to recall them here. For it is not by isolated details that the poetic significance of "Bergschluchten" as a dramatic scene is determined, but by its total design and by the consonance of that design with the tone and design of *Faust* as a whole.

The first prologues to *Faust* precede "Der Tragödie erster Teil." Whether or not, as I have elsewhere suggested,[19] "Zueignung" is a spoken prologue, the Prelude on the Stage certainly is one, and it is over twice as long as the last of the first prologues, Prologue in Heaven. Even if the Prologue in Heaven were not primarily concerned with things earthly—"der Erde Pracht" and "der kleine Gott der Welt" whose representative is Faust—it would still follow that the primary emphasis of *Faust* was to be recognized as secular, that supernatural machinery and cosmic fictions were to be subordinate to human drama in it. Whereas Prelude on the Stage establishes certain values into which Faust achieves insight only in the long course of his dramatic career,[20] Prologue in Heaven serves chiefly to prepare the audiences of a sophisticated age to accept the use of Mephistopheles, of magic, and of

[17] *Goethes Faust* 481. As will be conceded below in the text of this essay, the *Mater gloriosa* is also "Jungfrau"; Rickert actually overmakes his case.

[18] F.M. Stawell and G. Lowes Dickinson, *Goethe & Faust* (London, 1928) 253 and 257.

[19] "A Reconsideration of Some Unappreciated Aspects of the Prologues and Early Scenes in Goethe's 'Faust,' " *Modern Language Review* 47 (1952): 362–73.

[20] I cannot offer the evidence for this assertion here; a comparison of the ideas of "Lustige Person" and certain passages in "Felsbuchten des Ägäischen Meers" will be profitable if it is accepted that Faust is in some sense or other present at Galatea's triumph.

elemental spirits in the course of the following drama. On the evidence of the first prologues alone, then, it would be unreasonable to approach the final scene of *Faust* in the expectation that it was to be an epilogue primarily in heaven. If it is felt that symmetry demands a counterpart to Prologue in Heaven, that counterpart would have to be sought in the penultimate scene of *Faust* as a whole, viz. in "Grablegung," where heavenly machinery appropriate to the morality play tradition is in fact provided.

But there are other prologues in *Faust*, some of which are in a sense epilogues also. For the closet drama of Faust the thinker is followed by a "new" drama, that of Faust the lover: its prologue is the scene in Auerbach's wine-cellar, a very earthy-earthly place indeed, and in it the potential danger of love become mere sensuality ("Walpurgisnacht") is powerfully antici-pated. At the same time "Auerbachs Keller" is a very earthy-earthly epilogue to the drama of Faust the scholar-teacher, for it gives a final glimpse of the seamier side of that university life to which he had so unhappily devoted himself so long. The Walpurgis Night's Dream takes place in a realm of dream supernaturalism, but it ends with the epilogue on earth of its final eight lines. Before Faust enters the "große Welt" of the imperial court there is another prologue-epilogue, the scene "Anmutige Gegend," which marks the end of the paralyzing effect of self-reproach in connection with Gretchen's death and the reawakening of Faust's impulse to strive; and there can be no doubt, either from stage direction or from text, that this scene insists upon the supreme importance of this earth for man, ending as it does with Faust deliberately turning his eyes from the sun to the earth. The Classical Walpurgisnight opens with a prologue emphasizing its historical-human occasion fully as much as its supernatural premise, and it ends with a hymn to the four elements that once were thought to constitute this world. And even the highly imaginative "Helena" does not end with Faust's baroque cloud-ascension: its Chorus does *not* return to a shadowy underworld, like Helen and Panthalis, but merges—emphatically, in view of the otherwise disproportionate attention given to their fate—with substances of this world.

In "Bergschluchten" the emphasis on the this-worldly that has characterized earlier prologue and epilogue passages in *Faust* is not absent. Whereas "Grablegung" is acted or spoken by supernatural beings alone, if we include Mephistopheles with the group "Lemuren-Dickteufel-Dürrteufel" to which is counterposed the "Chor der Engel," all but 47 of the 268 lines that constitute "Bergschluchten" are spoken solely, except for the final eight-line chorus, by beings who have known earthly existence. The opening chorus of saintly anchorites describes a very concrete setting, an earthly paradise that is the Christian counterpart of Faust's Arcadia at the opening of "Schattiger Hain." The Pater ecstaticus expresses intense longing for a mystic experience which he does not claim to have achieved as yet. Pater profundus describes at length the wild Calderonian landscape which apparently encloses the hermitage, a landscape with "grausen Sturz des Schaums der Flut," with "wildes Brausen" and with lightning performing, as he would persuade himself, a cathartic function; and although he claims that these uncomforting phenomena are "Liebesboten," he is constrained to characterize his "Innres" as "Verquält in stumpfer Sinne Schranken." The opening of "Bergschluchten," it would seem, is far removed from heaven as momentarily glimpsed in the Prologue in Heaven with its closing benedictory "Das Werdende, das ewig wirkt und lebt, / Umfaß' euch mit der Liebe holden Schranken."

The Chorus of Blessed Boys—a cloudlet from which voices emanate—discerned by Pater Seraphicus has, as the apostrophe "Mitternachts-Geborne" insists, at least known a moment of mortal existence. From the kindly words of Pater Seraphicus, "von schroffen Erdewegen / Glückliche! habt ihr keine Spur," it might seem that the blessedness of the Blessed Boys was a corollary of having escaped mundane life, especially since, when they look at the world surrounding the Pater through his eyes, they cry: "Das ist mächtig anzuschauen, / Doch zu düster ist der Ort, / Schüttelt uns mit Schreck und Grauen." When "Faustens Unsterbliches" is entrusted to them by the Angels (figures from "Grablegung," and the only figures in "Bergschluchten" not credited with having known mortal life by living it), they joyously accept the "englisches Unterpfand" as if there were no doubt that it is best to be free of earthly connections. Before the end of the scene, however, it becomes evident that the Blessed Boys were misled by the *vollendeteren Engel*, whose ambiguous "Uns bleibt ein Erdenrest / Zu tragen peinlich" now appears to have been, if not pharisaical, at least an indirect admission of weakness and limitation. For after Gretchen's prayer they are finally heard admitting: "Er überwächst uns schon. . . , / Wird treuer Pflege Lohn / Reichlich erwidern. / . . . Doch dieser hat gelernt, / Er wird uns lehren." In the course of the action—this is dramatic irony in the strictest sense of the term—it transpires that earthly existence is a positive value after all. And such an evaluation of mortal life is certainly in complete consonance with the humanistic tenor of *Faust* up to the present scene; it is in no way "anti-Faustian" or "anti-Goethean" as sometimes has been carelessly asserted.

The very fact that the Blessed Boys are theatrically represented by a cloud should be a hint that they are not going to symbolize values alien to those which Faust himself has held. It is in a cloud that Faust made his exit from the "Helena" and his entrance afterwards in "Hochgebirg," and in that scene clouds represented both Helen and Gretchen, the former symbolizing majestic beauty and the latter "Seelenschönheit." Only by refusing to see the episode of the Blessed Boys in the context of *Faust* as a whole is it possible to miss the irony of their earlier views and so overlook the meaning of their final speech. Indeed, if it be remembered that in Goethe's day the emergence of their voice from a cloud could only be achieved ventriloquistically, a parallel between their passages and the scene in Wagner's laboratory with Mephistopheles providing the voice for Homunculus also suggests itself: if Homunculus was at first a creature of Mephisto's, by the end of the Classical Walpurgisnight he achieved independent existence and truly Faustian impulses; if the Blessed Boys at first share the attitude of Pater Seraphicus, in the end they are expressing observations which they themselves are to be thought to have made independently. That it is proper to discern analogues to the Blessed Boys in earlier episodes of *Faust* would seem to be evident from their "Hände verschlinget / Freudig zum Ringverein" passage, which echoes in substance and meter the opening of the dance section of the Euphorion episode (lines 9745ff.); and if this echo is, as I suspect, for ironic emphasis, there may be reason to take with a grain of salt their assertion, made with the same unqualified confidence as many of those of the ill-fated Euphorion, "Den ihr verehret / Werdet ihr schauen."

Of the 47 lines spoken by purely heavenly beings in "Bergschluchten," the first twenty recapitulate the action of "Grablegung" and state the there dramatically implicit "Wer immer strebend sich bemüht / Den können wir erlösen." Their remaining two choruses are, of course, simply ambiguous unless the earthly component previously stressed in the text itself has been read over. Speaking as they do for the first time after the "dance chorus" of—bodiless—Blessed Boys, they should be expected soon to make statements that can be taken in another sense than that which they themselves in their angelic characters would intend. I have already suggested how there is something too much holier-than-thou in the opening words of the *vollendeteren Engel*; in addition to that bit of dramatic irony, however, there is the irony of their "Kein Engel trennte / Geeinte Zwienatur / Der innigen beiden [i.e., *Geisteskraft* and *Elemente* / *An sich herangerafft*]." For is it desirable that such a separation take place, that a disembodied soul without the imperfect substance which gave it individuality should rise to a heaven? It may be conceded that, as these Angels state, "Die ewige Liebe. . . / Vermag's zu scheiden," but from the course of the scene it becomes evident that body and soul remain together in Faust's heaven, which would seem to mean that a real heavenly existence as defined by the Angels is not seriously posited here. Heaven in "Bergschluchten" remains an extension of earth as Faust has known it.

How much it is Faust's earth which conditions this "Vorhimmel," to use May's rightly cautious term, is evident even from the final speech of the

Jüngeren Engel, a speech primarily serving to advance the dramatic action by putting "Faustens Unsterbliches" into the companionship of the Blessed Boys; for its tying of a newly *regend* "Geisterleben" to the image of a *Sicherlaben* "Am neuen Lenz und Schmuck / Der obern Welt" is exactly in the spirit of Faust's own equation of the rebirth of physical nature with the psychological rebirth of man as he humanistically outlined it for Wagner during their Easter walk. Faust's emergence from a chrysalis as announced by the Blessed Boys repeats the image of Hermes escaping from his swaddling clothes to a life of somewhat Euphorion-like activity as contained in the Trojan Women's chorus at the opening of "Schattiger Hain." And the sky into which the Doctor Marianus turns his gaze is dominated by the figure of the Mater Gloriosa who symbolizes a mystery ("Geheimnis") into which the occupant of the "höchsten, reinlichsten Zelle" does not seem to have penetrated.

If, as more recent critics of *Faust* have insisted, Faust is to be thought of as having somehow experienced the entire "Bildungserlebnis" which was the Classical Walpurgisnight, then through the *trionfo di Galatea* he has been vouchsafed greater insight into this mystery than Doctor Marianus. Be this as it may, the latter's devotion to one who has been "Jungfrau, rein im schönsten Sinn"—the ambiguous apostrophe, without a verb form, permits the supplying of "has been" at this point—and who has been "Mutter" is certainly comparable to Faust's devotion to Gretchen and compatible with Faust's awed reaction to the name "Mütter" in the scene "Finstere Galerie." His devotion to a "Mutter, Ehren würdig" who is also "Uns erwählte Königin" is not without its parallel in Faust's devotion to Helen, queen of his Greek kingdom and mother of Euphorion—especially since the pagan phrase "Göttern ebenbürtig" that modifies "Königin" recalls the "divine" beauty and supposedly divine parentage of Helen as well as the Aphrodite-substitute Galatea. At all events, the exclusive surrounding of the Mater gloriosa by three Marys who are prototypes of the unfortunate Gretchen, and by Gretchen herself, seems to insist that into this "Vorhimmel" may be projected the best which the human spirit can conceive only on the condition that human imperfection always remains perpetually implicated with it. It is as if the heart-felt cry of Faust's "Wald und Höhle" soliloquy were still to be heard echoing: "O daß dem Menschen nichts Vollkommnes wird, / Empfind' ich nun." For the true beyond is yet to be reached: "(*Mater gloriosa.*) Komm! hebe dich zu höhern Sphären! / Wenn er dich ahnet folgt er nach."

Whether Faust actually rises to higher spheres is never stated. *Faust* ends abruptly as Doctor Marianus gives to the Mater gloriosa, now simultaneously "Jungfrau, Mutter, Königin, Göttin," the devotion which is due the simultaneous symbol of the four great symbols of "das Ewig-Weibliche" that have appeared earlier to Faust himself in the two persons of Gretchen and Helen. The three penitents have obtained *for Gretchen* the Mater gloriosa's "Verzeihen angemessen," but it is significant, I think, that *before* this pardon is granted in the two lines already quoted Gretchen permits herself to speak of her happiness, "meinem Glück," which is conditioned solely on the fact that "Der früh Geliebte, / Nicht mehr Getrübte, / Er kommt zurück." In uttering her two lines to Gretchen the Mater gloriosa has pardoned Gretchen unconditionally; Faust is granted only the privilege of continuing to pursue "salvation" by following love if he is still able to do so. If Benno von Wiese rightly interprets Gretchen in the present context as the symbol of the "Erlösung des Menschen durch die Liebe," as the supreme *Faust* symbol of "das Göttliche im weiblichen Symbol,"[21] it does not follow that this insight is attained by Faust only after death. Its partial attainment was already evident in his "Erhabner Geist, du gabst mir, gabst mir alles" soliloquy, and its full attainment was announced in the soliloquy in which he clarified for himself the relative importance of Helen and Gretchen: "Wie Seelen-schönheit," he declared at the opening of "Hochgebirg," "steigert sich die holde Form, / Löst sich nicht auf, erhebt sich in den Äther hin, / Und zieht das Beste meines Innern mit sich fort."

If Faust is "gerettet," it is explicitly because "Wer immer strebend sich bemüht / Den können wir erlösen." That he enjoys a hearty welcome in his "Vorhimmel" is simply an extra benefit accruing from the fact that "an ihm die Liebe gar / Von oben teilgenommen [hat]." This love is Gretchen's "Liebe von oben" because it was given to one not fully aware of its value until too late, and not because it is a transcendent force which somehow penetrates from without into the "Erdenkreis" in which Faust, worshipper of God-Nature, heroically gives sole allegiance in his scene with Care ("Mitter-nacht"). If the ambiguity of "Liebe von oben" is appropriate to a Catholi-cizing scene, its ironic value should nevertheless be evident also; and unless the irony is appreciated, we do indeed have that stylistic anomaly in "Bergschluchten" which would be a *Faust* scene in a new realm of experience not formulated with a new style of its own. The points of view expressed in the final scene of *Faust* are those of Faust himself, not those of Goethe only or, least of all, those of an alien Catholic mythology. Faust's dying words are heard in the scene "Großer Vorhof des Palasts"; the framework established by Prologue in Heaven is closed by "Grablegung"; and with "Bergschluchten" we have Faust's dying insights, his final and most intense poetic vision, one far surpassing in luminosity those of the "Traum-und Zaubersphäre" which was his romantic Walpurgisnight, of the Young

[21] *Die deutsche Tragödie von Lessing bis Hebbel* (Hamburg, 1948) 1:201.

Charioteer episode of his great masquerade, or of the Classical Walpurgis-night's phantasmagoria.

To read "Bergschluchten" as an expression of Faust's ideas, as well as of Goethe's, should make it possible for those critics who expect a scene in a drama to have a dramatic function to reconcile themselves to it. Once it is felt that the whole scene is perhaps rich in deliberate ambiguity, many a detail otherwise "disturbingly" superfluous or seemingly included only for the sake of its Catholic-mythological appropriateness will begin to suggest characteristically Faustian associations. The motherly services of the *Magna peccatrix* will recall Gretchen's care for her infant "Schwesterchen," the well evoked by the *Mulier Samaritana* will recall the various patriarchal motifs of the Gretchen scenes, and the atonement in the desert of *Maria Aegyptiaca* may suggest the flight from society of Gretchen the infanticide. To think specifically of such associations would be to destroy the flow of the final scene, but to be half-aware of them would in no way diminish its immediate lustre. Certainly in a "Vorhimmel" predominantly occupied by former mortal human beings it will be right to wonder whether Gretchen's "Er ahnet kaum das frische Leben / So gleicht er schon der heiligen Schar" does not define "heilige Schar" no less than it does the Faust about to emerge in "erste Jugendkraft." And whether, even, "erste Jugendkraft" does not suggest the rejuvenated Faust whose earlier "new" start led him into a path of error, as well as one of good, no less of an ordeal than that he had formerly followed in his academic study.

There are thus reasons to believe that "Bergschluchten" says less about a Beyond of which Faust had asserted "Nach drüben ist die Aussicht uns verrannt" than has sometimes been claimed, and to believe that his "Vorhimmel" is in many respects an extension of the realm of experience in which he always has existed—the realm of God-Nature and God-Love. The non-reappearance of the God-Father of the Prologue in Heaven in the final scene of *Faust* is consistent with Faust's anti-transcendentalism. So also is the absence of the Holy Ghost, surely an essential concept in any form of trinitarian Christianity.[22] But if any Beyond is only a projection of something "vergänglich," is in itself something "vergänglich," it may nevertheless in some measure rightly symbolize the true Eternal. As the *Chorus mysticus* insists: "Alles Vergängliche / Ist nur ein Gleichnis." For only in the individual, transitory phenomenon—which may include the poetic symbol—can the anti-transcendentalist obtain his only glimpse of whatever eternal verities there are. That this interpretation of these two lines is perfectly

---

[22] I have collected much of the evidence for the negative symbolic value of trinitarianism in *Faust* in "The Mothers, the Phorcides and the Cabiri in Goethe's *Faust*," (see above, pp. 235ff.).

reconcilable with the dramatically demonstrated rightness of Faust's refusal to say unconditionally to any moment "Verweile doch! du bist so schön!" has been nicely set forth by Lichtenberger:

> L'homme peut et doit s'élever au pressentiment que dans le Passager se manifeste à chaque instant l'Eternel, l'Absolu, l'Infini. Tout phénomène individuel est, en soi, éphémère et destitué de toute valeur. Mais il est en même temps un symbole de l'infini et, à ce titre, plein de sens et investi d'une valeur éternelle. L'homme doit donc s'abandonner à la vie *comme si* dans chaque phénomène se trouvait le Tout, l'Infini. . . . Mais dans le tréfonds de sa conscience—et c'est par là seulement qu'il peut échapper à la désillusion et au désespoir—il saura toujours que l'Éphémère n'a pas de valeur en soi, qu'il ne vaut que comme symbole.[23]

Ironically, then, by the very definition of "Alles Vergängliche" which is offered in the *Chorus mysticus*, it is possible to assert that in *Faust* all scenes represent both immanence and transcendence, that no scene, even the final one, may properly be said to belong to a sphere distinctly different from that of all the others.[24] And lest a prejudice against regarding a highly ironic text as appropriate to the admittedly serious substance of the final scene of Goethe's *Faust* should cause my readers to doubt the propriety of all or part of the foregoing interpretation, I would remind them that Goethe himself referred less than a year before his death to that Tragedy as to "diesen ernst gemeinten Scherzen."[25]

---

[23] Lichtenberger, op. cit., clxiif.

[24] As dream-like reprise of earlier *Faust* motifs and elements "Bergschluchten" as it were also offers a projection of a dying Faust's last insights, "Denn am Ende des Lebens," so Goethe is reported to have observed by F.W. Riemer (*Mitteilungen über Goethe* [Berlin, 1841] 1:568), "gehen dem gefaßten Geiste Gedanken auf, welche zu verfolgen und in Ausübung zu bringen, eine Wiederholung des Lebens gar werth wären."

[25] Letter to Sulpiz Boisserée, November 24, 1831.

The Evaluation of Romanticism in Goethe's *Faust*

Subtle discriminations can be made between the many different values of the words "romantic" and "romanticism," but for the purposes of the following discussion only two of their spheres of meaning need be distinguished: (1) that of style and form, of "romantic" artistic techniques, of literary "romanticism" as represented by the works of its best known practitioners at the beginning of the nineteenth century, and (2) that of what, for want of a better word, I shall call world-outlooks, of "romantic" attitudes—of both that parochial "romanticism" which Goethe called "wahnsinnigen, protestantisch-katholischen, poetisch-christlichen Obskurantismus," which his friend Heinrich Meyer labeled "neu-deutsch religiospatriotisch" in *Kunst und Altertum*, and that more cosmopolitan "romanticism" which could achieve profound sympathy with cultures so dissimilar to that of early nineteenth-century Europe as those of ancient Greece and the middle Orient. Failure to differentiate sharply between the category of romantic technique and that of romantic attitude is one reason for the widely diverging interpretations and evaluations of Goethe's *Faust* that have been and continue to be offered by reputable critics and scholars. Other factors have contributed to critical confusion—failure to distinguish between Goethe and Faust, failure to understand the sometimes archaic language of Goethe's text, failure to appreciate the significance of certain of its formal-stylistic features, failure to recognize that the tone as well as the function of passages which survive from *Urfaust* into *Faust, ein Fragment* and from there into *Faust I* changes with their new contexts—but none, I believe, can have obscured the design of *Faust* as a whole to the extent that has the failure to discriminate between romanticisms. If, because *Faust* is a drama in the romantic literary manner, it is read with the expectation of discovering a romantic world-outlook expressed in it, it can be simultaneously seen as a glorification of ruthless egotism (Santayana) and of disinterested selflessness (Ernst Beutler), and—disregarding non-aesthetic judgments—it can be simultaneously regarded as marred by glaring stylistic discrepancies (E.M. Butler) and as distinguished by a grandiose symbolic unity (Trunz).[1] And if it is read with the assumption that at times it expresses a romantic view of life and at others one hostile to romanticism, something which can easily happen because the mature Goethe's world-outlook was admittedly too complex to exclude all romantic values or because it is remembered that parts of the text of *Faust* were composed when Goethe had not yet completed the process of maturation, then the hostile critic may very reasonably condemn its lack of unity of tone while the sympathetic one must seek to discern its true merits in many admirable discrete elements rather than in any fully achieved over-all design such as is normally looked for in a text purporting to be a drama and, specifically, a tragedy.

That *Faust* could serve as a prototype of early German romantic drama is only too obvious, for although only *Faust, ein Fragment* had been published before Tieck wrote his *Leben und Tod der heiligen Genoveva* (1799) and *Kaiser Octavianus* (1804), *Faust* shares with these works such superficially striking features as episodic plot structure, exploitation of chapbook materials, passages in both prose and verse, a great wealth of verse forms, musical interludes, a central figure who appears at widely separated points in his life, an extraordinarily large number of minor *dramatis personae*, supernatural machinery, and allegorical and mythological representations. Empirically, then, the literary romanticism of *Faust* as a whole may reasonably be posited, and from the fact that *Faust* was completed in Goethe's last years it is possible to conclude that when Goethe wrote, "Klassisch ist das Gesunde, romantisch das Kranke," or, "Das Romantische ist schon in seinen Abgrund verlaufen, das Gräßlichste der neueren Produktionen ist kaum noch gesunkener zu denken," he was not denying the positive merits of romantic literary techniques but was simply questioning the viability of common romantic views of life. But if *Faust* is prima facie evidence that Goethe set a high value on literary romanticism, it is also evidence that he was not sympathetic with certain fundamental elements of the romantic world-outlook. This cannot, however, be demonstrated by an analysis of Faust's dramatic character, since for most of *Faust* its titular hero is only too obviously a "romantic hero" (even in such partially classicized scenes as "Innerer Burghof" and "Schattiger Hain," which in any case represent that aspect of romanticism known as "romantic Hellenism"), nor by quotation out of dramatic or lyric context of passages in which Faust expresses views on the nature of man that are pantheistic,

---

[1] One source of such critical divergence is a tendency to evaluate the artistic function of certain superficially classicistic sections of *Faust II* (the "Mummenschanz," the Classical Walpurgisnight and, especially, the "Helena") without taking into consideration their romantic elements and without remembering the evaluation of romanticism already posited previously in *Faust*.

anti-transcendental, or simply not Christian-humanistic. Such passages might show that "Goethes Anschauung vom Menschen" (as Karl Viëtor has admirably expounded it in his *Geist und Form*) is at times Faust's, but they can be and often have been reconciled with interpretations of *Faust* as a theodicistic mystery play (Benno von Wiese) whose hero, "though not in a state of grace," was "in a state in which divine grace could operate."[2] However unambiguously Faust may assert, "Nach drüben ist die Aussicht uns verrannt; / Tor, wer dorthin die Augen blinzelnd richtet, / Sich über Wolken seinesgleichen dichtet!" (11442–44), the supernatural machinery of "Bergschluchten" is sufficient to give his assertion the lie unless it has already long been clear to the reader or spectator that the use of romantic literary and theatrical techniques in *Faust* is never tantamount to approbation of a romantic world-outlook.

To determine the evaluation of romanticism (other than literary romanticism) in *Faust* is to re-examine certain aspects of Goethe's anthropology, but it is to do so without pretensions to intellectual-historical thoroughness. For it is not Goethe but *Faust* as a structure with its own self-contained norms that must be our true concern. If it can be shown that *Faust*—and by *Faust* I mean *Faust I* and *Faust II*, not *Urfaust*, the *Fragment* or even *Helena: klassisch-romantische Phantasmagorie, Zwischenspiel zu Faust*—consistently presents romantic attitudes and romantic behavior in an unfavorable light, and that Faust is drawn again and again into a path of error because his all-too-human enthusiasms are also all-too-romantic, one of the chief sources of confusion in *Faust* interpretation and criticism will have been obviated. And, although by no means all important general considerations that concern critics of *Faust* can be illuminated by determining the evaluation of romanticism in it, clarification of the function of romanticism will, I believe, make it possible to offer better solutions to some vexing problems which *Faust* criticism has raised than could otherwise be offered.

I. Romantic Subjectivism

There are in *Faust* two metaphors for the operation of natural forces, and both derive from what was once a very familiar sphere of domestic activity, that directed toward the production of textiles. Although these metaphors have quite dissimilar values, this fact has been obscured for many readers of the nineteenth and the twentieth centuries because industrialization has taken spinning and weaving from the home to the

---

[2] E.M. Butler, *The Fortunes of Faust* (Cambridge, 1952) 264.

factory, where to all intents and purposes both processes are equally mechanical ones. When *Faust* was written, however, there was probably no one on the continent of Europe who had not seen thread spun and cloth woven in his own household—if not by members of his own family, at least by servants or retainers; and so there was probably also no one who did not know that spinning is an almost entirely mechanical process, one that can be carried on with a bare minimum of attention, whereas weaving requires considerable concentration and even a modicum of intelligence. In the companion piece to Faust's soliloquy beginning, "Erhabner Geist, du gabst mir, gabst mir alles," in the lyric monologue, "Meine Ruh' ist hin, / Mein Herz ist schwer," Gretchen reveals a willingness to surrender to the instinct of love (love largely compounded of irrational physical desire: "Ach dürft ich fassen / Und halten ihn, / Und küssen ihn / So wie ich wollt', / An seinen Küssen / Vergehen sollt'!") that contrasts most strikingly with the fatalistic rationalization of the erotic impulse to which Faust has given expression hardly more than an acting minute before in the impassioned speech ending with the hortatory, "Mag ihr Geschick auf mich zusammen- stürzen / Und sie mit mir zugrunde gehn." That Gretchen's words are spoken mechanically, even unthinkingly, is insisted upon by the assimilation of their rhythm to that of her spinning wheel, itself a visible symbol of the narrow—and intellectually narrow—world to which her existence is normally confined. The conclusion may therefore be drawn that in *Faust* spinning symbolizes the instinctive and the irrational, in definite contrast to the objectively contemplative or the irrational speciously rationalized.

Although the scene with Gretchen at her spinning wheel is the one instance of spinning symbolism in *Faust* the significance of which has been generally remarked upon, there is another and, I think, more important metaphorical reference to spinning in Goethe's text. If it has not received due critical attention (and to the best of my knowledge and belief it has received none whatever), the reason is surely the unwarranted critical assumption that *Faust* either begins with the scene "Prolog im Himmel" or with the scene "Nacht" ("Habe nun, ach! Philosophie"). My reasons for regarding this assumption as not only unjustified but critically disastrous have been stated elsewhere;[3] only my argument that the prologues to *Faust* establish the value of symbols that recur in the text later is relevant here, for it is in "Vorspiel auf dem Theater," third speech of the Poet, that Goethe first introduces an image having to do with textile production. Protesting against the Director's too pragmatic view of drama, the Poet—a romantic egotist

---

[3] "A Reconsideration of some Unappreciated Aspects of the Prologues and Early Scenes in Goethe's *Faust*," *MLR* 47 (1952): 362–73 (esp. 363–67).

only too prone to believe that among all human activities his own poetic activity represents the supreme manifestation of the human spirit ("Wer sichert den Olymp, vereinet Götter? / Des Menschen Kraft im Dichter offenbart") reveals a degree of insight into the nature of life and art far less penetrating, though far more elegantly formulated, than that which the Player immediately offers in the next speech. For while the Player utters the genuinely Goethean remark—one whose "truth" is attested by God in "Prolog im Himmel" and then again and again by other sympathetic characters in the course of the action of *Faust* as well as by the action itself (Faust's "salvation"): "Wer fertig ist, dem ist nichts recht zu machen; / Ein Werdender wird immer dankbar sein"—the Poet cavalierly disposes of Nature (to whose authority he has just appealed, with "Der Dichter sollte wohl das höchste Recht, / Das Menschenrecht, das ihm Natur vergönnt, / Um deinetwillen freventlich verscherzen!") as a mechanical, hardly rational and clearly disharmonious order when he declares:

Wodurch besiegt er [der Dichter] jedes Element?
Ist es der Einklang nicht, der aus dem Busen dringt,
Und in sein Herz die Welt zurücke schlingt?
Wenn die Natur des Fadens ew'ge Länge,
Gleichgültig drehend, auf die Spindel zwingt,
Wenn aller Wesen unharmon'sche Menge
Verdrießlich durch einander klingt;
Wer teilt die fließend immer gleiche Reihe
Belebend ab, daß sie sich rhythmisch regt?

The Poet's view of Nature is obviously not Goethe's, whose scientific studies sufficiently testify to his faith that the physical world represents a cosmic order the complexities of which can at least be partly grasped by human reason and the underlying principles of which can probably be intuited by the scientific observer. Nor is the Poet's view that presented sympathetically in *Faust*, whether in such passages as the Homunculus episodes of the Classical Walpurgisnight or in the series of speeches through which Faust is revealed as gaining an ever greater objectivity of insight into the visible world of natural phenomena. Yet the Poet is certainly a romanticist—a believer in the independent powers of the creative self; a man who, despite physical maturity ("Gib meine Jugend mir zurück!"), is prey to immature emotionalism; a nonthinker who, because he lacks an integrated world-outlook (sees no clearly defined relationship between poet and man or between man and Nature), must in the end tacitly accede to the relative wisdom of the Player and to the pragmatism of his Director. It therefore seems reasonable to conclude that in *Faust* romantic subjectivism is not consciously represented by Goethe in a favorable light. And this conclusion is confirmed by the action of Goethe's drama—or, better, by its actions—and by passages in the text that would seem digressive, did they not help to clarify a negative evaluation of romanticism which the romantic technique of *Faust* and the sympathetic representation of its usually romantic hero might otherwise obscure. Faust's own lack of a harmonious world-outlook brings him to the verge of suicidal death at the very beginning of the tragedy; it drives him into an ambiguous relationship with Mephistopheles not long after; it permits him to destroy Margarete's little world; it allows him to become involved in Mephistophelian chicanery at the Emperor's court; it lets him cherish the fantastic dream of possessing Helen; it renders him indifferent to practical ethical considerations as he seeks to realize the grandiose engineering projects of his final days; and, perhaps the supreme irony, it admits him to an afterlife in which the best prospect held out is one of "höhern Sphären" to which he may perhaps (conditionally: "Wenn er dich ahnet folgt er nach") some time attain. The depreciation of reason ("den Schein des Himmelslichts. . . , Vernunft") by a Mephisto treated by the Lord of "Prolog im Himmel" with sovereign condescension and humiliated after Faust's death by painful physical reminders of his helpless impotence is patent evidence in ironic form that subjective irrationalism represents a negative value in *Faust*. Indeed, coming as it does after the Earth Spirit's self-descriptive "So schaff' ich am sausenden Webstuhl der Zeit, / Und wirke der Gottheit [i.e., Natur—l. 455] lebendiges Kleid," Mephisto's later satiric use of weaving imagery, in his exposition of the defects of academic logic to the Student in the scene "Studierzimmer [II]," is an especially striking illustration, with the aid of dramatic irony, of how the irrationalist can present rational objectivity—*Collegium Logicum* may not represent profound truth in *Faust*, but it clearly represents truth—in an unfavorable light if he wishes to pervert truth (weaving symbolism[4]) for the sake of his own subjective irrationalism.

Evaluation of romanticism in terms of the action of *Faust* has involved the assumption that Goethe thought of his text as a drama which could be recognized as approximately fitting the ancient Aristotelian definition of a tragedy. Not all critics have interpreted *Faust* as drama in this traditional

---

[4] That the metaphor had in Goethe's day a long established positive value is well brought out in J.A. Walz's "Linguistic Notes on Goethe's *Faust*, Part I," *JEGP* 29 (1930): 204–32 (esp. 212–15). Cf. also the weaving imagery of "Antepirrhema" (in "Gott und Welt"), itself a gloss on what is perhaps the most revealing single poetic statement of Goethe's sense of a world meaningful and ordered on all planes (the physical, the ethical, and the aesthetic), his "Metamorphose der Tiere."

sense, if only because the second part has seemed to them very loosely constructed. Although, for reasons largely irrelevant to the present discussion, I incline to interpret the "eine Tragödie" of Goethe's title with an almost narrow literalness, it is equally possible to discover a negative evaluation of romantic subjectivism in *Faust* when interpreting it simply as a series of half-lyric and half-dramatic scenes or groups of scenes most of which have in common the presence of Faust or figures connected with him. If the Poet of "Vorspiel" is not the first (important) cause that he thinks himself to be, if he is no Carlylean hero as poet, neither is Faust ever for very long the master of the particular world in which he happens to be represented. The magus of the first scene "Nacht" is bluntly humiliated by the Earth Spirit; the magician-exorciser of "Studierzimmer [I]" is lulled to sleep by the supernatural being that he thinks is under his control; the rake who accosts Margarete is soon the sentimental victim of her simple virtues, in the end to be the pathetic, helpless bystander at her mortal apotheosis; the would-be statesman at the Emperor's court is the dupe of Mephisto-phelian financial chicanery, then a purveyor of occasional entertainment (a masquerade that does not successfully convey to its audience the "messages" with which Faust has burdened it) and of magical dumbshow which he himself disastrously confuses with literal reality; the wooer and winner of Helen gains his ends with the help of the cruelty of Mephisto and the bombastic eloquence of Lynceus only to play second fiddle to his son Euphorion before losing him and his mother; and the engineer and colonizer who dies heroically confident of the tangible worth of his last mortal achievements is still a plaything in the hands of Mephisto and the creatures of Mephisto (whether or not, as the latter asserts—significantly: "beiseite"—he has simply prepared a feast for Neptune, the "Wasserteufel").

Certainly it is significant that at the end of "Marthens Garten," the scene in which Faust has offered Margarete his Storm-and-Stress religious credo (a completely subjective one, whatever its debt to mystic and other traditions), Mephistopheles is allowed to mock the pseudoscience of Physiognomy, a highly subjective and irrational interpretation of one particular aspect of the visible world of Nature, and to explain Margarete's antipathy towards himself with "Sie fühlt, daß ich ganz sicher ein Genie," a remark at this point gratuitously digressive or even anachronistic, yet also one which sets Storm-and-Stress subjectivism (especially its failure to provide a satisfactory basis for social ethics) in a most unpleasant light. If Storm and Stress represents preromantic subjectivism, the subjective idealism of the Baccalaureus whom Mephisto interviews while Faust lies unconscious in his study is clearly introduced as a theme in *Faust* so that the practical implications of German romantic speculation at its full flower may be unfavorably evaluated. The irony of such a remark as the former

Student's, "Wenn ich nicht will, so darf kein Teufel sein," may be very unsubtle, but the interview as a whole makes perfectly clear both that speculation disjoined from knowledge of empirical reality is to be regarded as folly and that consistent romantic egotism would not only be inhumane but would also produce a perpetual human immaturity unleavened by any inherited practical wisdom (cf. esp. 6774–89). The folly of the Baccalaureus is cruel and ignoble, but it is that of temporary inexperience ("In wenig Jahren wird es anders sein"); if experience never comes, the price of such folly is death and oblivion, the "Vorbei und reines Nicht, vollkommnes Einerlei" which Mephisto (wrongly) uses to describe the sum total of Faust's own mortal striving; and even if inexperience is generous and noble, like that form which the Byronic Euphorion represents, it still can bear no tangible fruit:

> Doch du ranntest unaufhaltsam
> Frei *ins willenlose Netz*,
> So entzweitest du gewaltsam
> Dich mit *Sitte*, mit *Gesetz*;
> Doch zuletzt das höchste Sinnen
> Gab dem reinen Mut Gewicht,
> Wolltest Herrliches gewinnen,
> *Aber es gelang dir nicht*. [Italics mine.][5]

II. Romantic Primitivism

In his monumental study *Geist der Goethezeit* H.A. Korff persuasively demonstrates that one of the most important factors conditioning the relatively short life of Storm and Stress as a significant cultural and literary phenomenon was the fact that no stable world-outlook, no objective criteria of ethical or artistic values, could be derived from a subjective psychology that equated greatness almost exclusively with uniqueness and originality. If Storm-and-Stress writers contributed more toward giving folksong and other forms of popular literature prestige with educated readers than did other eighteenth-century preromanticists, it is because they for a while succeeded in identifying their own uniqueness with the originality of

---

[5] I interpret the "willenlose Netz" of these lines to be insufficient understanding of the autonomous existence of objective reality, as the web of circumstance in which the enthusiast and fatalist is helplessly trapped. (The close connection between determinism and subjectivism is a basic concern of Goethe's thought—see "J.C. Lavater and Goethe: Problems of Psychology and Theology in *Die Leiden des jungen Werthers*," in this volume, esp. 40–48).

primitive genius. Although the later German romanticists hardly regarded themselves as untutored geniuses, they inherited from their preromantic forerunners a respect for popular literature, or at least a willingness to exploit elements from it for serious artistic purposes; and so German folksong and chapbook, German folklore and history furnished important materials to the German romantic writer, who often revealed a genuine talent for sophisticated unsophistication. Theoretically, of course, romantic universalism should have led to sympathetic exploitation of the primitive in art and literature in a great variety of historical and geographical forms, but for all their vaunted universality the German romanticists actually showed less broad an interest in anthropologically primitive cultures than did many of the preceding century's preromanticists. The early German (or Northern) past; contemporary survivals of primitive simplicity and primitive belief in lower social strata; early modern painting in Germany, the Netherlands and Italy; and the primitive origins of classical Greek mythology: these are the four chief spheres of romantic primitivistic interest in the early nineteenth century. The first two—and perhaps the third—of these have an important place in German romantic literature, the third is certainly an important influence on the development of romantic painting and illustration, and the fourth was an important factor in romantic philosophico-religious speculation. At least two of these spheres of romantic primitivistic interest are well represented in *Faust*, and from an analysis of the manner of their representation it is possible to discover in what light one large and important aspect of romanticism is to be evaluated in the context of Goethe's poetic drama.

The fact that untutored simplicity and such widely acknowledged virtues as moral goodness, sound common sense, sincerity and effective verbal self-expression are not incompatible has apparently been appreciated ever since man first became aware of the advantages which may accrue through the acquisition of learning. Nevertheless, for a combination of reasons which it is unnecessary to analyze here, the second half of the eighteenth century saw a wide diffusion of the paradoxical view that the highest virtues are almost exclusively the property of the simple, the common and even the primitive man. Many of the clichés of sentimental romantic literature—the noble savage, the noble prostitute, the noble criminal—owe their currency to the conveniently striking contrasts and conflicts which the primitivistic paradox afforded a would-be author, and the curious mixture of genuinely popular and offensively vulgar elements which is characteristic of some Storm-and-Stress and some romantic writing (the young Goethe, the young Schiller, Bürger; Tieck, Arnim, Brentano) undoubtedly derives from the paradoxical confusion of untutored simplicity with all positive virtues. If *Faust* were simply the sentimental drama of Faust and Margarete, an

"Urfaust" so completed that the main dramatic development highlighted only the fate of Gretchen, it would be impossible to decide on the basis of the evidence afforded by such a text whether its author wished the paradox of romantic primitivism to be accepted uncritically by his readers (either as "truth," or because its "truth" was irrelevant to the achieving of sympathy with the drama's heroine) or whether he wished them to be aware of its insufficiency (Faust becoming involved in a disastrous sentimental attachment and in terrible crimes because he temporarily deludes himself with the belief that in the primitive simplicity of the "kleine Welt" there is lasting happiness for himself). In the final design of *Faust*, however, no room is left for uncertainties of this kind: Margarete may remain an admirable representative of simple virtues, but instead of having to outweigh only Marthe, Valentin, Lieschen, and the students of the scene in Auerbach's wine-cellar, she must also overshadow the cumulative picture of gullible or selfish simplicity which is offered in parts of "Vor dem Tor," "Hexenküche," "Walpurgisnacht," "Kaiserliche Pfalz: Saal des Thrones," the "Mummenschanz," and the "Helena"; and whereas a completed *Urfaust* might suggest a high degree of sympathy with romantic primitivism simply because it was largely popular by virtue of its themes and its formal elements, the *Faust* actually completed is so complex, so sophisticated, and so literarily allusive on other than popular levels that only the most insensitive reader could fail to perceive that Faust's responses to the primitive, and the contrasts between Faust and those *dramatis personae* who represent relatively primitive simplicity, are functional in the over-all design of the drama.

From the "Inszenierungsentwurf" for a production of *Faust* projected sometime after 1810 (cf. WA I.14, 1:314–17) it is clear that the first of the five acts of the performance was to consist of "Zueignung," "Vorspiel auf dem Theater," and "Prolog im Himmel"—certainly a multiplicity of prologues in itself anything but unsophisticated. Each of these three prologues, moreover, contains passages indicating that in *Faust* "das Volkstümliche" cannot properly be regarded as automatically synonymous with the good or the desirable. In "Zueignung" it is said of "der unbekannten Menge" that "Ihr Beifall selbst macht meinem Herzen bang," a statement clearly enough casting doubt on popular judgment. "Vorspiel auf dem Theater" opens with the Director's assurance that he wishes "der Menge zu behagen," a harmless enough statement until such cynical observations as "Ich weiß wie man den Geist des Volks versöhnt" and "Zwar sind sie an das Beste nicht gewöhnt" reveal profound skepticism about popular taste; and lest it be thought that the Director's views are those of an unenlightened mercenary, the very next and very different speaker, the Poet (who has not yet begun to reveal his "romantic" prejudices in all their inconsistency, and who in fact is allowed to employ the elevated *ottava rima* of the more direct prologue "Zueignung"), refers to "jener bunten Menge, / Bei deren Anblick uns der Geist entflieht." And in "Prolog im Himmel" Mephistopheles can assert of mankind in general ("der kleine Gott der Welt") that it uses "Vernunft" merely "tierischer als jedes Tier zu sein" without being contradicted by the Lord as he is when he makes comparably pejorative statements about the complex intellectual, Dr. Faust: a good man may be simple, of course, but there is surely no implication in this scene either that simplicity and goodness stand in any fixed, axiomatic relationship to each other.

In the course of the first scene in which Faust appears it is soon evident that, isolated and discontented, he would like to escape to simplicity (apostrophe to "voller Mondenschein") by returning to nature,[6] but the best that unsophistication can do for him after magical communion with nature has been denied him is to reduce him to sentimental helplessness just as he is about to seek (not without a certain display of rhetorical bombast) harmony in a next world ("Zu neuen Ufern lockt ein neuer Tag"): a simple religious faith in which he does not believe, whose heaven he will repudiate even in his final mortal hour, evokes the memory of hope and hence reawakens hope itself. In "Vor dem Tor" Faust persists in his agnosticism, and at the same time the scene shows "groß und klein"—for the romantic primitivist the latter alone would be important—variously pursuing selfish interests, expressing inhuman indifference to the common welfare, and even inclining to belief in such primitive superstition as is associated with witchcraft. In "Auerbachs Keller" folksong and popular ditty are used to heighten a picture of plebeian vulgarity which as a whole serves to represent the worst and most bestial aspects of human life, the "flache Unbedeutenheit" (Mephisto's monologue just before the "Schülerszene") to which Faust may be degraded unless he justifies the promise of the Lord of "Prolog im Himmel." "Hexenküche," whether or not it be read as alluding to the more disgraceful aspects of the French Revolution, exploits motifs from folklore and vulgar superstition with obviously bitter irony, and represents popular gullibility and the willful irrationalism of the untutored (hence, perhaps, the He-Ape's parental lesson beginning, "Das ist die Welt. . .") most unattractively—especially since apes are patently "man-beasts" (cf. orangutan = wild man).

---

[6] Although Harold Jantz has recently suggested that this is a typical wish of a Renaissance magus, it is hard to regard it as such in a text so characteristic of the great age of European romanticism. Is it not significant that Goethe reintroduces dew imagery here ("In deinem Tau gesund mich baden") as well as when Faust apostrophizes the neat and modest simplicity of Margarete's bedroom ("du süße Liebespein! / Die du vom Tau der Hoffnung schmachtend lebst"), i.e., in a context of patently post-Renaissance primitivistic sentimentality and in a passage strongly marked by the language of that secularized religious eroticism that flourished first and foremost in the sentimental eighteenth century?

Following all these passages of *Faust*, the so-called Gretchen tragedy can hardly be taken as an unqualified paean to the simple life, nor Gretchen, despite critics like Otto Ludwig and Witkowski,[7] as a paragon of the inevitable virtues of primitive or popular ("volkstümlich") simplicity. And as the Gretchen action reaches its climax, it is significantly interrupted—at least stylistically—by Faust's Walpurgisnight in the Harz Mountains, a scene that may open with Faust expressing pleasure in the prospect of a pleasant walk through wooded paths, but one that also presents the primitive wish-dream of a return to nature in a series of distinctly unpleasant fertility-filth images in which sadistic impulses are closely associated with vulgar sensationalism (especially well summed up in the "Bänkelgesang" motifs of the speech of "Trödelhexe"). If the Walpurgisnight intermezzo which concludes Faust's visit to the Brocken represents sophisticates and intellectuals in a comic light, it cannot be said to counteract in any way the far more powerful negative impression furnished by the foregoing episodes: goodness in *Faust*, or the goodness of a good man, is clearly independent of a figure's relative closeness to nature, to the simple, and to the primitive.

This might seem to be Faust's conclusion, for after the death of Margarete his view of Nature changes (the anthropocentric view of his speech "Vom Eise befreit sind Strom und Bäche" in "Vor dem Tor" and the egocentric attitude of the opening monologue of "Wald und Höhle" are replaced by the more objective, distanced symbolism of his soliloquy in "Anmutige Gegend"), and he simultaneously turns from the "kleine Welt" of the Gretchen episodes to the great world of affairs of state, of art ("Mummenschanz"), myth and beauty, and of great social and engineering enterprise in which he remains for the rest of his dramatic mortal existence. Mephisto's role at the Imperial Court is surely an ironic perversion of the German romantic use of the figure of the Fool, for instead of representing common sense licensed by actual or assumed simple-wittedness he is the embodiment of a malicious obscurantism ("Im Finstern sind Mysterien zu Haus") well able to hoodwink both the highest figures of the Empire and the lower orders ("Gemurmel"), whose common sense had first warned them against "ein Schalk." The depiction of successful mass suggestion in "Kaiserliche Pfalz: Saal des Thrones" is succeeded by the equally disheartening picture of mob unruliness and vulgar greed that threaten to disrupt the great masquerade of the next scene, a picture some of whose dramatic significance is finally made clear when Faust himself falls prey to the vulgar confusion of illusion and reality at his "Raub der Helena" and

---

[7] Cf. S. Atkins, "A Reconsideration of Some Misunderstood Passages in the 'Gretchen Tragedy' of Goethe's 'Faust,' " *MLR* 48 (1953): 421–34.

when he, calling both "Wirklichkeiten," falls unconscious with the cry, "Wer sie erkannt der darf sie nicht entbehren."

In the Classical Walpurgisnight, as Faust seeks his indispensable Helen, the uglier monsters of Greek antiquity are passed in review. In their revaluation of primitive Greek mythology the German romanticists had hardly been anticipated by their eighteenth-century predecessors, if only because the generation of the former was the first to enjoy the full benefits of the thorough study of Greek antiquities which earlier neoclassical enthusiasms had inspired. That most of the figures with whom Mephisto exchanges words in this Walpurgisnight are repulsive is a fact not changed by Faust's closer contacts with the more pleasantly human ones; for even Faust, satisfied as he is with seeing antiquities at close hand, adds to his "das Anschaun tut mir G'nüge" the revealing words "Im *Widerwärtigen* große, tüchtige Züge" (italics mine). After Mephisto has exited in the shape of a Phorkyad—that is, after evil has disappeared—the action of the Walpurgis-night shifts to "Felsbuchten des Ägäischen Meers," and the monstrous shapes of the earlier *chiaroscuro* scenes are replaced by "higher" ones, ones more human and more consciously artistic ("*Telchinen*: . . . Wir ersten wir waren's, die Göttergewalt / Aufstellten in würdiger Menschengestalt"). Only the Cabiri still represent the primitive, the earliest (pre-Olympian) deities at this point, and they not only remain invisible but also afford the occasion for passing satiric allusion to (Schelling's) romantic speculations on the transcendental significance of primitive mythology. Even if Goethe's ironic attitude towards primitivism has not been recognized in the Cabiri passages, the whole Homunculus action can leave little doubt that to be one with Nature is not sufficient: Proteus may warn, "Denn bist du erst ein Mensch geworden, / Dann ist es völlig aus mit dir," but Thales's countering, "Nachdem es kommt; 's ist auch wohl fein / Ein wackrer Mann zu seiner Zeit zu sein" (an echo of both the Player's "Die Gegenwart von einem braven Knaben / Ist, dächt' ich, immer auch schon was" in "Vorspiel auf dem Theater" and of the Lord's "Ein guter Mensch" in "Prolog im Himmel") shows that any primitivistic identification of man with beast cannot be countenanced within the frame of reference of *Faust*. The author of *Faust*, also once the author of *Satyros*, recognized (with Voltaire and many others who pointed out that the logical end-result of a Rousseauist return to nature would be to go about on all fours) that romantic primitivism could not have any place in a consistent and constructive world-outlook. At the end of his career Faust is man not at one with Nature, but man, still in harmony with natural law, seeking to wrest from Nature those conditions which will permit a genuine flowering of man's civilizing potentialities.

III. Romantic Parochialism

Although the myth of the magus can be said, loosely speaking, to be universal, and although the dramatic possibilities inherent in the legend of Faust were first recognized by an Elizabethan poet whose treatment of it is acknowledged to have served as ultimate model for many structural elements of Goethe's drama, interpreters of *Faust* have frequently let their critical judgment of the work be influenced by a nationalist bias—either their own, or one which they have assumed to be evident in *Faust* itself. Despite the fact that romantic subjectivism is evaluated negatively in *Faust*, Santayana nevertheless discerned in it a glorification of egotism in the national tradition of German idealistic philosophy. So effective, indeed, has been the romantic glorification of national character—itself a corollary of romantic primitivism and subjectivism, which sought to discover evidence of national uniqueness by examining the development of the nation ("Volk") from its primitive origins on—that since the later eighteenth century an overwhelming majority of critics have (consciously or unconsciously) used nationalism as one of their touchstones when trying to define the individuality of a given work of art. For all their "Humanität," the Storm-and-Stress writers—and for all their "Universalität," the German romanticists—contributed in many ways to the flowering of parochial nationalism in the last century and in this. It is therefore hardly surprising that Albert Daur, whose monograph *Faust und der Teufel* (Heidelberg, 1950) is the latest interpretation of *Faust* in its entirety, should, after recognizing in *Faust* "die Gabe Goethes an die Menschheit, nicht nur an sein Volk," conclude his often sensitive study with the somehow too familiar-sounding words: "Aus diesem Volk aber stieg es empor: denn stets kamen die Weltwerke, der Ruhm der Völker, denen sie gehören, aus deren Wesen und verkörpern, vom Menschlichen kündend, doch auch ihr bestimmtes Volkstum. So stieg aus dem deutschen Wesen, aus der Tiefe deutschen Volkstums Goethe's 'Faust' ans Licht."

As has been indicated above in connection with romantic primitivism, there is a certain justification in regarding the *Urfaust* as an expression of sympathy with the popular in a form exploiting popular elements for the sake of their favorable connotations. The ironic tone of much of the completed *Faust*—especially of the prologues and of such scenes in *Faust I* as "Hexenküche" and "Walpurgisnacht"—as well as the emphasis which it places on the plight of a distinguished intellectual and the use it makes of allusions, classical and modern, literary and historical, beyond the grasp of a naive reader would seem, however, to exclude the possibility of regarding it as a basically popular ("volkstümlich") piece of writing. Since this conclusion does not necessarily mean that *Faust* is also unnationalistic, or even anti-nationalistic, a brief examination of the evaluations of Germanness and nationalism expressed in it is in order. In the first dramatic scene, "Vorspiel auf dem Theater," the Director not only speaks with condescension of popular taste, but he opens his remarks with a question implying that German popular taste may well be worse than that of other nations:

> Ihr beiden die ihr mir so oft,
> In Not und Trübsal, beigestanden,
> Sagt was ihr wohl, in deutschen Landen,
> Von unsrer Unternehmung hofft?

In Auerbach's wine-cellar the Leipzig students whose unattractive behavior helps limit Faust's utterances to a greeting of welcome and the remark, "Ich hätte Lust nun abzufahren," are the spokesmen of chauvinistic nationalism; it is not enough that Frosch should want Rhine wine because "Das Vaterland verleiht die allerbesten Gaben," but Brander must bluntly explain that xenophobia, in principle a good thing, cannot always be consistent:

> Man kann nicht stets das Fremde meiden,
> Das Gute liegt uns oft so fern.
> Ein echter deutscher Mann mag keinen Franzen leiden,
> Doch ihre Weine trinkt er gern.

That Frosch of "Auerbachs Keller" should have earlier sung the opening words of a satiric "Das liebe, heil'ge röm'sche Reich, / Wie hält's nur noch zusammen?" and given occasion for Brander to disparage that ancient political institution is not a significant fact for the evaluation of nationalism in *Faust*, if only because the theme of the weakness of the Empire represents banal humor, rather than humor pure and simple, in this scene. In the frequently anachronistic contexts of *Faust*, of which this is one, the Empire can no more be a symbol of national unity than it was in Goethe's own day, when a nationalistic romanticist like Görres could cheerfully compose a comic obituary on its demise. At the beginning of *Faust II*, however, the action clearly takes place at a late medieval or, at latest, early modern Imperial Court at a moment when the welfare of all German lands is dependent upon the success with which the Emperor and his counselors meet a political crisis; but there is not the slightest suggestion ever offered that evil conditions can be remedied by any appeal to national feeling—the desiderata that will alone re-establish order are such international virtues as justice, economy, labor, incorruption and cooperation. And although it is not specifically stated that a nation cannot raise itself by its own national bootstraps in political-social affairs, the scene which follows the analysis of "Kaiserliche Pfalz: Saal des Thrones" opens with a clear hint that indigenous culture is not necessarily the highest imaginable: "*Herold*: Denkt nicht, ihr seid in deutschen Grenzen / Von Teufels-, Narren- und Totentänzen: / Ein heitres Fest erwartet euch" The following masquerade, with its sage allegories, is visibly Italianate in character; if, as Faust's important role suggests, it is an expression of Faustian wisdom, it is impossible not to draw the conclusion that in *Faust* the good and the national are not romantically confused.

If a reader of the interview between Mephistopheles and the Baccalaureus regards subjective idealism as there expounded as an especially German form of philosophy (it was certainly very German by virtue of the linguistic origin of its chief exponents at the time of the writing of *Faust*), the unfavorable light in which it is allowed to appear is evidence of anything but chauvinistic nationalism. In the subsequent Walpurgisnight national pride is exclusively represented by Mephisto, whose depreciation of the ancient monsters of classical mythology does *not* successfully make those of Northern folklore (in Goethe's day a clear differentiation between German or Germanic and other non-Southern mythologies had hardly become general) in the least bit more admirable. When Faust does use the word "Vaterland," it is not applied to Germany but to an Arcadian Greece which, as the land of supreme beauty, is to be preferred by Helen to "Dem Erdkreis, der dir angehöret" (because beauty is a suzerain power), to all other lands. And so it is not surprising that Euphorion's Byronic enthusiasm for a war of national liberation is represented as a tragic, though noble, aberration to be condemned by Chorus, Helen, and Faust, or that its immediate, visible result should be Euphorion's death and the dissolution of the harmonious ties that have momentarily bound Faust and Helen together. The evaluation of romantic nationalism which is implicit, and occasionally almost explicit, in *Faust* is a negative one: neither in Faust's last great vision of a free people on free soil nor in any passage that prepares for it is there any indication that the good and the parochial are necessarily identical.

IV. Romantic Utopianism

Since by definition a utopia exists nowhere, it is legitimate, though perhaps unconventional, to consider as aspects of romantic utopianism not only visions of ideal societies which are projected into the future but also those which are projected into the past. Romantic Hellenism and romantic

Medievalism are the two most important manifestations of this utopianism in German literature, with romantic exoticism (romantic Orientalism would be a sufficiently broad term for what flourished after 1800) occupying a much smaller place in popular favor despite Goethe's *West-östlicher Divan* and the literary efforts of various amateur and professional Orientalists.[8] Whereas romantic primitivism isolates certain concrete aspects of contemporary society so that they seem to represent survivals of a patriarchal simplicity somehow tinged with the aura of a Garden of Eden (or of its secular equivalent, Arcadia: the short-lived "Schattiger Hain" of the "Helena"), backward-looking romantic utopianism sees in highly complex and sophisticated civilizations only those aspects that theoretically might produce stability and harmony and willfully ignores quite concrete evidence not confirming its historical idealizations. With the aid of a sort of vicarious parochialism it was possible for many German romanticists of the early nineteenth century (Schiller, Hölderlin) to conceive of the glory that was Greece or (Wackenroder, Novalis) of a medieval synthesis (to use a more modern romantic term) as self-contained perfections and to think of them as destroyed solely by hostile external forces, although close historical inspection certainly indicates that at no time did either of these civilizations simultaneously enjoy static internal political, cultural, religious *and* social conditions that could have perpetuated themselves indefinitely even if the pressure of external factors had been negligible. But these romanticists, confident of the validity of their subjective historical analyses, could nonetheless all too easily draw inspiration and moral support for their own utopian dreams from the two great visions of golden ages past which they had inherited from their eighteenth-century forerunners.

The newer of these visions, that of a glorious medieval civilization (perversely depreciated by the rationalistic Enlightenment), is well represented by certain literary-historically famous works of Wackenroder, Tieck, Novalis, and Fouqué which offer, at best, idealized but diffuse pictures of the medieval scene and, at worst, prettified and confused ones. Inasmuch as our concept today of what is medieval is quite different from the popular concept of a century and a quarter ago (thanks in large part to the genuine enthusiasm for medieval studies inspired by the preromanticists and their romantic successors), the evaluation of romantic medievalism in *Faust* can only be determined to the mutual satisfaction of the present writer and his individual readers if they are willing to agree that Goethe has consciously represented the medieval European scene in various parts of his

---

[8] The validity of these generalizations is nicely confirmed by an analysis of the elements of popularized romanticism in Heine's verse: not only folkloristic-medieval motifs but also Greek-classical ones occupy a much larger place than do oriental ones.

drama; this means that they must accept as medieval certain historical phenomena now regarded as modern (as characteristic of such post-medieval ages as those of the Reformation or the Baroque) because they were popularly accepted as such at the time of the completion of *Faust*. *Faust* as a whole may not be a historical drama, even though Faust may well be in many ways a Renaissance man, but it does contain scenes that represent aspects of what Goethe's contemporaries would have recognized as the medieval European world; both what is represented, and the way in which it is represented, must be interpreted in the light of romantic historical knowledge and romantic literary convention if the larger significance of romantic medievalism in *Faust* is to be properly appreciated.

In the early scenes of *Der Tragödie erster Teil*—scenes chiefly set "in einem hochgewölbten, engen, gotischen Zimmer"—the hero with whom the audience is expected partially to identify itself repudiates a tradition of formal learning symbolized by the Gothic environment from which he first seeks to escape through magical vision and from which he in the end does escape by associating himself with Mephistopheles. Although this tradition is not purely "medieval," having assimilated to itself certain traits of eighteenth-century analytical rationalism (the famulus Wagner!), it is unambiguously represented as something completely outdated; neither magic nor alchemy is a uniquely medieval phenomenon, but by the end of the Enlightenment both were popularly regarded as late medieval phenomena (cf. Arnim's *Isabella von Ägypten*). It is thus significant that in "Vor dem Tor" Faust describes at length his father's and his own youthful alchemical medical practices, for it leaves the impression that the father's "modern" scientific inclinations—"Mein Vater war ein dunkler Ehrenmann, / Der über die Natur und ihre heil'gen Kreise, / In Redlichkeit, jedoch auf seine Weise, / Mit grillenhafter Mühe sann"—bore no good fruit because he could not break with medieval methods. And similar misdirection, nicely designed to associate all error with medieval survivals, is certainly characteristic of Mephisto's interview with the Student: although Mephistopheles is describing eighteenth-century university studies (the passage beginning "Der Geist der Medizin ist leicht zu fassen" has no medieval-alchemical allusions), he allows himself a survey of the faculties (such a survey itself being in a late medieval satiric tradition) that makes "Collegium Logicum" sound like little more than what was once regarded as arid scholastic logic and that by the allotment of more space to this than to any other subject makes it seem to loom disproportionally large in any "modern" curriculum; and it describes theological instruction of a medieval Catholic strictness despite the fact that liberalism had infected some Catholic and countless Protestant theologians of the eighteenth century.

The representation of things medieval in *Faust I* does not constitute a sufficiently large element in the text to warrant any general conclusions about the evaluation of romantic medievalism in *Faust* as a whole. *Faust II*, however, is in large part a historical drama whose setting is Germany at the end of the middle ages (Acts I and IV); and, in connection with the depiction of medieval political institutions, medieval art, and medieval Christianity (the medieval ecclesiastic) in it, a clearly unromantic attitude towards things medieval is ultimately established as normative for *Faust*. Its first dramatic scene, "Kaiserliche Pfalz: Saal des Thrones," might well be regarded as a bold challenging of the romantic medievalist's articles of faith: a scene of medieval pomp and ceremony is used to depict the German middle ages as a period of disastrous factionalism, of war and poverty, of mass hysteria (dancing madness) and clerical intolerance, of venal justice and aristocratic extravagance, and to represent the theoretical head of the largest political entity of the period as an irresponsible, pleasure-loving prince whose personal concerns are so important that he interrupts state ceremony for their sake (opening address from the throne interrupted after three lines with a question about the absence of the imperial jester). After such a scene the Renaissance motifs of the great court masquerade must be felt as modern and preferable to medieval ones ("Denkt nicht, ihr seid in deutschen Grenzen, / Von Teufels-, Narren- und Totentänzen. . ."), and the allegorical wisdom of the "Mummenschanz" must seem a theoretical advance beyond medieval superstition (the Chancellor's "Natur ist Sünde, Geist ist Teufel"). The convention of the grand historical tableau—a standard feature of romantic historical drama—is thus employed two times in immediate succession to suggest, first by negative example and then by positive one, that the romantic picture of a medieval golden age is false and foolish.

The impotence of the Holy Roman Emperor and the opportunistic policies of his advisers continue to be treated satirically in Acts I and IV of *Faust II*, to reach their culmination in the scene "Des Gegenkaisers Zelt," in which the Emperor achieves supreme vainglory ("Jedoch zum höchsten Preis wend' ich den frommen Blick, / Das selten sonst geschah, zur eignen Brust zurück") in taking all credit for a victory that still leaves him at the mercy of the Chancellor-Archbishop (hence the curtain line: "So könnt' ich wohl zunächst das ganze Reich verschreiben"), and in which the promulgation of a historically fateful Golden Bull—again grand historical tableau—is first and foremost the occasion for the greatest princes of the Empire to reveal themselves as sycophants and sybarites. Such consistently unworthy representatives of medieval society as dominate these two acts must inevitably assimilate to themselves all uncritical exponents of romantic medievalism, and so when, shortly before Faust's visit to Greece, the

Architect of "Rittersaal" depreciates classical architecture at the expense of the medieval gothic style, the irony is transparent:

Das wär' antik! Ich wüßt' es nicht zu preisen,
Es sollte plump und überlästig heißen.
Roh nennt man edel, unbehülflich groß.
Schmalpfeiler lieb' ich, strebend, grenzenlos;
Spitzbögiger Zenit erhebt den Geist;
Solch ein Gebäu erbaut uns allermeist.

In *Faust*, at least, romantic Medievalism is an illusion more dangerous than romantic Hellenism.

But romantic Hellenism, however preferable to romantic Medievalism, is also an illusion. The world of the Classical Walpurgisnight is populated with monsters conveniently ignored in the works of Hölderlin and Schiller; in the scene "Vor dem Palaste des Menelas zu Sparta" not only the horrors of the Trojan War but also the cruelty of Greek toward Greek (motif of human sacrifice) are insistently represented; and, above all, in the "Helena" as a whole it appears that a return to the past—a wedding of the modern-romantic to the ancient-classical—can only be impermanent and that the fruit of such a union can only be the imbalance, the instability, symbolized by Euphorion. More substantial than the vision of Helen is the reality of Margarete, for in Faust's soliloquy at the opening of Act IV the cloud which is "Junonen ähnlich, Leden, Helenen," soon becomes "formlos breit," while the one which is "Aurorens Liebe" rises into the ether, retaining its form ("Löst sich nicht auf"). By the standards of *Faust* romantic Hellenism remains something inferior to appreciation of contemporary reality, and yet is always superior to romantic Medievalism. Even in the idealized "timeless" middle ages of "Innerer Burghof,"[9] in the "wundersam aus vielen einsge-wordnen Burg," Faust does not long remain with Helen; the setting of their brief idyll is a "schattiger Hain" of "Arkadien in Spartas Nachbarschaft."

To the utopia of the past can be contrasted the utopia of the future, which is partially realized in the new world that Faust seeks to create at the end of his mortal career. A world built on the sacrifice of human life—if Baucis' "Menschenopfer mußten bluten" should be an exaggeration of superstitious incomprehension, it is still certain that she, her husband and

---

[9] It should be noted that the Baroque features of this scene are for Goethe medieval—not only because, through Spanish influence, Baroque art and literature acquired medieval ingredients absent in the Renaissance style (E.R. Curtius), but also because, as I point out in "Goethe, Calderón and *Faust: Der Tragödie zweiter Teil*" (in this volume), Calderonian drama was consciously regarded by Goethe as Catholic-medieval.

the traveler whom they are sheltering are sacrificed to Faust's desire to make all he surveys part of his paradise (Philemon's "ein paradiesisch Bild" and Faust's "Im Innern hier ein paradiesisch Land")—and a world built with forced labor ("die Menge, die mir frönet" and "Bezahle, locke, presse bei!"), at the moment of Faust's death it bears striking resemblances to totalitarian orders inspired by such principles as equality of sacrifice and equality of benefit. But it differs from historical totalitarian societies in several important respects: it is not national, it is not hierarchical, it is not consciously classless, and—most important—its leader does not offer a vision of static security as its justification: "Räume vielen Millionen, / Nicht sicher zwar doch tätig-frei zu wohnen. / . . . / Nur der verdient sich Freiheit wie das Leben, / Der täglich sie erobern muß." Mephistopheles is surely right when he prophesies "Vernichtung" for the physical world that Faust has had created, for there is no historical evidence that there was ever a utopia in the past or that, accordingly, there might be one in the future. There is historical evidence, however, that a vision of a better world on this earth can change the course of history when that vision looks forward rather than backwards, as the example of the rise of two world powers so different in their ideologies as the U.S.A. and the U.S.S.R. indicates. The ideology of the latter state is very close to being romantically utopian—and it is a totalitarian state. That of the former hardly envisages any form of ultimate static perfection, but it does posit a faith in human autonomy like that to which Faust confesses when he declares that he would like to stand "auf freiem Grund mit freiem Volke."

In *Faust*, certainly, no romantic golden age, past or future, is represented either as an enduring reality or as a reality potentially capable of enduring long. Romantic utopianism is an illusion of no positive value, to which in the end is opposed the prophetic vision of free men cooperating ever anew as circumstances which threaten their very existence always continue to arise: "Das ist der Weisheit letzter Schluß: / Nur der verdient sich Freiheit wie das Leben, / Der täglich sie erobern muß." After Faust's heroic triumph over Care and in the light of Mephistopheles' defeated efforts to claim his soul, his final vision can only be regarded as more realistic than utopian, as a final insight into truth rather than a last pursuit of error. If Faust's actual politico-social achievement is unworthy of this vision, that is but the tragic irony of a finite and imperfect reality in which, as has always been the case in *Faust*, the word holds true: "Es irrt der Mensch so lang' er strebt."

V. Romantic Supernaturalism

In my analysis of Faust's last hours I have interpreted "frei" as meaning primarily "autonomous," that is, determined by man himself with no reference to any posited higher, supernatural authority. For it is clearly important that Faust's one moment of true heroism—his defiance of Care—after many dramatic crises at which he has stood by ineffectual or even helpless comes when he has renounced the use of magic ("Nimm dich in acht und sprich kein Zauberwort"). The machinery of *Faust* has been supernatural up to this point, and will remain supernatural until the very end of the concluding "Chorus mysticus," and so it is easy for those who confuse romantic techniques with romantic attitudes to forget the significant words which the hero of *Faust* utters in the moment when he has every claim to our fullest sympathy: "Nach drüben ist die Aussicht uns verrannt; / Tor, wer dorthin die Augen blinzelnd richtet, / Sich über Wolken seinesgleichen dichtet!" In the light of these words the supernatural machinery of the remainder of the text can hardly be meant to demonstrate symbolically that Faust's life has been justified by "good works"[10] (what good works does Faust have to his credit? a cynic might well ask) or by unwitting faith in some higher power. Only if a positive value had been attached to romantic supernaturalism before Faust's unconditional "Dem Tüchtigen ist diese Welt nicht stumm; / Was braucht er in die Ewigkeit zu schweifen! / . . . / Wenn Geister spuken geh' er seinen Gang" would there be any justification for disregarding his repudiation of it. But, as we shall see, the evidence of *Faust* as a whole is overwhelmingly unfavorable to any apologetic interpretation of the supernatural elements in it.

The already noted fact that the "Tragödie" is preceded by two profane prologues, the second of which ("Vorspiel auf dem Theater") is rich in strongly anti-romantic irony, causes its third prologue ("Prolog im Himmel") to be partially assimilated to the realm of finite physical reality, of practical theater, which they have represented. The Prologue in Heaven is highly ironic, for it employs an adaptation of the heaven of the Christian morality play to announce the heretical doctrine that "Ein guter Mensch in seinem dunklen Drange / Ist sich des rechten Weges wohl bewußt"—the doctrine that man's goodness is independent of any faith of which he may be conscious. An anthropomorphic Lord who expresses ideas of the deistic and even atheistic Enlightenment is surely a sophisticated theatrical invention; the scene in which he appears in large measure exists to guarantee that the supernatural machinery of the Faust legend—and other supernatural

---

[10] Lily B. Campbell, *"Doctor Faustus*: A Case of Conscience," *PMLA* 67 (1952): 223.

machinery employed in the play that follows—will not be misunderstood as symbolic of transcendental forces. To take as an illustration the first example of supernaturalism within the Tragedy: in his first scene Faust seeks occult experience, and momentarily enjoys the mystic transports that the sign of the macrocosm induces; soon discontented with "ein Schauspiel nur," he summons the Earth Spirit, who magically appears and, by his crushing words, puts an end to the search for occult experience; Faust subsequently recognizes that man is really only an "Erdensohn," and although this insight drives him to the verge of suicide, memories of earlier religious experience evoked by a Christian gospel in which he does not believe ("Die Botschaft hör' ich wohl, allein mir fehlt der Glaube") cause him to renounce his fatal resolution. The dramatic function of the supernatural appearance of the Earth Spirit is thus to eliminate the possibility that through contact with higher forces Faust might be able to guide his career more wisely than he actually does: neither untraditional nor traditional forms of conscious religious experience can in *Faust* make a good man "des rechten Weges wohl bewußt."

In contrast to the *Urfaust*, written, as it was, by a man of pantheistic beliefs who might not have objected to being called a liberal Christian (by the Goethe who corresponded with Lavater in the 1770's), *Faust I* is conspicuously non-Christian. Christ is absent from the Prologue in Heaven; mention of his crucifixion is perhaps carefully avoided in the Easter hymn at the end of Faust's first scene; Faust regards his response to the hearing of the hymn as a conditioned reflex (adolescent religious emotionalism reawakened when the faith that made it possible is long since abandoned); it is implied that the prayers and fasting of one firm in his faith can have no value ("Vor dem Tor," ll. 1024ff., where Faust takes for granted that prayer can have no magical efficacy); in Faust's consideration of "Im Anfang war das *Wort*" the fact that the Word is Christ is completely ignored; trinitarianism is ridiculed as nonsense in "Hexenküche" (directly by Mephistopheles, but with the confirmation of Faust's reaction to the "Hexen-Einmaleins": "Mich dünkt, die Alte spricht im Fieber"). After such preparation, Mephisto's allusions to superstitious piety and clerical greed in "Spaziergang" have a negative-critical function which they may lack in the *Urfaust*, and Faust's remarks about God in "Marthens Garten" seem more obviously evasive than they would otherwise; the heartless cruelty of the vainglorious Valentin becomes a criticism of the effectiveness of Christian ethical instruction when he dies with the words, "Ich gehe durch den Todesschlaf / Zu Gott ein als Soldat und brav," and the concept of perfect justice meted out to imperfect souls on a day of judgment appears as sadistic perversion in the next scene, "Dom."

In *Faust II* the representatives of Christianity and their practices continue to be represented in a one-sidedly unfavorable light until the final scene. The Chancellor-Archbishop represents bigotry, superstition (as opposed to "Natur und Geist"), and greed; Northern-Christian prudishness is generously elaborated upon in the Classical Walpurgisnight; a very unpleasant pagan trinity—the "Dreigetüm" of the Phorcides—seems to be introduced with deliberately parodistic echoes of Christian theological language; in the representation of the "timeless middle ages," of medieval civilization at its poetic best, in the scene "Innerer Burghof," mention of Christianity is somehow avoided, although in the previous scene Mephistopheles-Phorkyas has ironically declared that polished Gothic architecture—surely best represented by cathedrals—leaves no room for thought ("ja selbst der Gedanke gleitet ab"—a plainly ironic remark if "Vernunft" is man's highest attribute, a God-given "Schein des Himmelslichts" as asserted in "Prolog im Himmel"); and in Act V Mephistopheles can finally bring Faust to the point of evicting Philemon and Baucis by associating their chapel and devotions with the Church's "verfluchte[s] Bim-Baum-Bimmel, / Umnebelnd heitern Abendhimmel." Even in "Grablegung," a scene in which Christian symbols (angels) are employed with positive values, we are not allowed to forget that "Das Schändlichste was wir [die Teufel] erfunden / Ist ihrer Andacht eben recht." After all this, "Bergschluchten" can only strike the sensitive observer as patently ironic in its use of traditional Christian materials, however unironic it may be as a final summation of the themes and motifs of *Faust* as a whole: Father, Son, and Holy Ghost are ignored so that created beings, the great majority of whom were once mortals on this earth (anchorites, infants who have died at birth, Church fathers, Mary mother of Jesus, Mary Magdalene, the Samaritan woman, Mary of Egypt, Margarete), may state that if there is a "beyond," it can only be part of the non-transcendental continuum in which Faust's mortal existence was lived.

The repudiation of supernatural Christianity in *Faust* is in itself consistent, but recognition of its repudiation is not made dependent upon analysis out of context of widely separated passages. Although romantic supernaturalism as a technical device is repeatedly used with serious purpose in *Faust*, it is, more often than not, treated with ironic overtones that are, as it were, transferred to romantic supernaturalism as an attitude. If theatrical hocus-pocus plays a considerable role in such scenes as "Auerbachs Keller," "Hexenküche," the two Walpurgisnights, the great masquerade, "Rittersaal" and the campaign scenes of Part II, Act IV, it is to emphasize that supernaturalism is never to merit our completely suspended disbelief. The supernatural is associated with the error of occultism, with that of naive or sentimental Christian religious experience (Part I, first two scenes, as analyzed above), with that of gullible belief in spirits summoned to perform at séances (the rigmarole of sounding glasses in "Hexenküche," bluntly called nonsense by Faust), and with that of taking poetic illusion for literal reality (actions of the mob in the masquerade scene; reaction of Faust to the *tableau vivant* of Helen in "Rittersaal"). Faust's successive paths of error are all littered with the debris of magic; the great master of magical illusions throughout *Faust* is Mephistopheles, the symbol of evil and Faust's "Helfershelfer" in the investigation of these paths; only when Faust renounces magic and forfeits the loyalty of Mephistopheles does he achieve true heroic stature. And so the conclusion seems inescapable: only a negative evaluation of romantic supernaturalism as a potential basis for establishing a viable world-outlook is posited in Goethe's *Faust*.

VI. Larger Implications

It has long been impossible to discuss the cultural-historical phenomenon of romanticism without remarking that "Sehnsucht" is a fundamental romantic experience. In the externally romantic context of *Faust* both the naive reader and the careless one will naturally assimilate to a romantic world-outlook a sententious utterance such as that of the Angels in the scene "Bergschluchten": "Wer immer strebend sich bemüht / Den können wir erlösen." So to do, however, is arbitrarily to disregard the insistently anti-romantic tenor of *Faust* as a whole and—more important—is to disregard the fact that "Streben" has by this point long since been defined as something which does not equal "Sehnsucht." For "Streben" is not effortless longing, nor is it longing for the impossible. Man (Faust) is unable to achieve self-fulfillment in isolation (in the "Studierzimmer") or in effortlessness (i.e., without Mephistopheles: "Des Menschen Tätigkeit kann allzuleicht erschlaffen, / Er liebt sich bald die unbedingte Ruh; / Drum geb' ich gern ihm den Gesellen zu, / Der reizt, und wirkt, und muß, als Teufel schaffen"). Faust realizes the first impossibility before his first adventures in the little world and the great, and in the course of these adventures he comes to recognize the second one. If full insight—insight which is affirmed heroically in action—is only achieved by Faust in his scene with Care when he repudiates both the effortlessness which magic has symbolized and the spiritual paralysis which is Care herself (the attitude of *taedium vitae*, the spiritual disease of what in *Die Leiden des jungen Werthers* was called "Trägheit"), the dramatic moment is not one of theatrical surprise. For the action of *Faust* has shown its hero both repeatedly defeated in his aspirations for the impossible and also achieving ever greater insight into the necessity of limiting aspirations to the realm of the humanly possible.

Although his love for Margarete cannot be literally "ewig," and although it ends tragically for her, Faust is able to cherish her memory even after Helen has taken her place. The cosmic aspirations of Faust the magician-philosopher are replaced by contentment with ability to observe the external phenomenal world—at first somewhat egocentrically in the "Erhabner Geist" soliloquy of "Wald und Höhle," then far more objectively in the monologue of "Anmutige Gegend." In this latter scene, in which supernatural machinery from the Baroque operatic tradition is employed for the symbolic representation of Faust's physical recovery from the paralyzing shock of realizing that he has been responsible for Margarete's destruction, the Chorus describing Faust's regeneration speaks for his subconscious mind when it concludes with the words:

> Säume nicht, dich zu erdreisten
> Wenn die Menge zaudernd schweift;
> Alles kann der Edle leisten,
> Der versteht und rasch ergreift.

Faust later demonstrates his increased understanding of the importance of wisely directed activity in the great masquerade (Victoria allegory), although he is still incapable of not toying with longing for impossible ideals (hence, perhaps, the Young Charioteer episode, with Faust's very un-*Faust*-like—and very un-Goethean—dichotomization of the "poetic" and the "real"). As Manto will tolerantly observe, the quest for Helen is an "Unmögliches," and it is Faust the romanticist who seeks Helen: "Und sollt' *ich* nicht," he declares in an outburst of romantic subjectivism (hence the "Sperrdruck" of the first person pronoun), "sehnsüchtigster Gewalt, / Ins Leben ziehn die einzigste Gestalt?" (the bombastic superlative of "einzig" is also revealing!). After the Classical Walpurgisnight, culminating in a hymn to elemental reality (life and eros), the word "Sehnsucht" appears for the second and last time in *Faust*, and even though its context is romantic-medieval (dialogue of Calderonian lyrical virtuosity—"oriental" rhyme play) and hence in itself suspect in the light of the anti-utopianism of *Faust*, the hero carefully insists that the value of "Sehnsucht" is for him something like "anticipation of actual enjoyment in the here and now" ("Nun schaut der Geist nicht vorwärts nicht zurück, / Die Gegenwart allein"—here Helen affirms his view—"ist unser Glück"). And in a few moments he makes clear that his

"Sehnsucht" *is* capable of fulfillment: "Durchgrüble nicht das einzigste Geschick! / Dasein ist Pflicht und wär's ein Augenblick."[11]

The last project of Faust, the creating of a new land, is nothing "Unmögliches," although the means which are employed for its execution are still tainted with magic (the supernatural campaign of Act IV, supernatural workers among those under Mephisto's overseership in Act V). As Faust's "Streben" has become more and more realistic, the possibility of its confusion with "Sehnsucht" has been eliminated. Perfect balance between will and the achievable is the proper goal of human striving, despite the known fact that "dem Menschen nichts Vollkommnes wird" ("Wald und Höhle"). Faust is a "romantic" hero who becomes ever less "romantic," a fact overlooked by critics who find it disturbing that Euphorion's "parents wring their hands at his recklessness, and Faust (of all people!) implores him to be moderate."[12] The ideal is unattainable, but it can be approached concretely: this is not what Goethe or Schiller would have regarded as an ancient classical view—in "Shakespeare und kein Ende" Goethe declared that "Ein Wollen, das über die Kräfte eines Individuums hinausgeht, ist modern. . . denn alle Helden des dichterischen Altertums wollen nur das, was Menschen möglich ist, und daher entspringt das schöne Gleichgewicht zwischen Wollen, Sollen und Vollbringen"—but it is the view of "Deutsche Klassik" as the fullest possible antithesis to "Deutsche Romantik" or even to Romanticism in general. It is man's destiny "zum höchsten Dasein immerfort zu streben" within the earthly sphere where we have life "am farbigen Abglanz." Or as Goethe wrote to Sulpiz Boisserée on February 25, 1832:

> Ich habe immer gesucht, das möglichst Erkennbare, Wißbare, Anwendbare zu ergreifen, und habe es zu eigener Zufriedenheit, ja auch zur Billigung anderer darin weit gebracht. Hiedurch bin ich für mich an die Grenze gelangt, dergestalt daß ich da anfange zu glauben, wo andere verzweifeln, und zwar diejenigen, die vom Erkennen zu viel verlangen und, wenn sie nur ein gewisses dem Menschen Beschiedenes erreichen können, die größten Schätze der Menschheit für nichts achten.

Goethe could "believe" because he saw, as have seen later scientists whose concept of the nature of the physical world is profoundly different from his, an ordered design in all things about him. "Streben" in *Faust* is

---

[11] It is noteworthy that in *Faust* superlative forms of "einzig" are used only in passages in which "Sehnsucht" ("sehnsüchtigst") occurs or is understood (line 9628: Euphorion a symbol of romantic aspiration), and that all are marked by the same tone of ironic exaggeration of romantic elements.

[12] E.M. Butler, *The Fortunes of Faust*, 236.

"Sehnsucht" that can be harmonized with the known, the knowable, and the possible; it is romanticism reduced to the barest minimum consonant with the fact that men are capable of being romantic as Faust is romantic. The scene "Bergschluchten" is a last reminder that the "classical" ideal, however important man's striving toward it, is but an ideal; finite existence must include romanticism, but romanticism is one aspect of that objective reality, ever imperfect, which is symbolized by Mephistopheles and in working against which man's highest positive powers are exercised and developed. To assert that *Faust* is not tragic (D.J. Enright and many others) is to take the romantic supernaturalism of "Bergschluchten" literally despite the negative evaluation of such supernaturalism throughout Goethe's drama: a process of salvation which never leads to perfection, but only to (ever) "höhern Sphären," is only an "Erlösen" in the weakened eighteenth-century sense of the term. So to assert is also to ignore the fact that Faust conditionalizes with a "dürft' ich sagen" the satisfaction of his dying "Verweile doch, du bist so schön! / Es kann die Spur von meinen Erdetagen / Nicht in Äonen untergehn." *Faust* may indeed be the last great literary creation of the European Enlightenment (Geneviève Bianquis, "Goethe et Voltaire"[13]), but it is also a product of the Enlightenment in its last, most mature development: shallow optimism has given way to a renewed sense of tragedy (as Cassirer's *Philosophie der Aufklärung* makes clear) and, as in Lessing's *Nathan der Weise*, the earthly utopia is postponed for all finite human time (the "tausend tausend Jahre" of the ring parable is a historically inconceivable time span). Man is doomed to failure, error, and frustration; only in struggling against this doom does he achieve tragic dignity. Neither on earth nor elsewhere is there to be some utopia for him, and so *Faust* is no romantic martyr drama in which suffering is untragically counterbalanced by certain redemption but is, as the title page indeed asserts, "eine Tragödie."

If the reader of these pages will recall to mind the many different scenes from every part of *Faust* that have been adduced in connection with this examination of the evaluation of romanticism in Goethe's text, he will realize that there is hardly a scene in *Faust* as a whole which is not directly relevant to this sphere of ideas, to this basic problem of Faust's dramatic career. If drama is character in action and the illumination of character through action, *Faust* is far freer of irrelevancies and digressions than many critics, even those sympathetic and admiring, have appreciated. From "Zueignung" to "Bergschluchten" the fundamental issue of Faust's

---

[13] This essay is included in her *Études sur Goethe*, Publications de l'Université de Dijon, VIII (Paris: Société Les Belles Lettres, 1951) 91–98.

romanticism is never lost sight of; if it is recognized that romanticism is Faust's problem, even those scenes in which he plays a passive role or from which he is strikingly absent take on a heightened significance and are seen to be structurally important. To assume a profound difference in the design and dramatic method of *Faust II*, as opposed to *Faust I*, is to ignore the sophisticated irony which distinguishes *Faust I* from the *Urfaust*. *Faust* is a drama of anti-romanticism in a romantic form, and the supreme irony of all is that in it romantic motifs and techniques should be masterfully employed—this is romantic irony—to express the last great poetic statement of the world-outlook of "Deutsche Klassik."

Stuart Atkins Bibliography

I. Books and Editions

The Testament of Werther in Poetry and Drama. Cambridge, Mass.: Harvard University Press, 1949.

The German Quarterly (Managing Editor): 25, No. 4 (1952)–30, No. 3 (1957).

Goethe's "Faust": A Literary Analysis. Cambridge, Mass.: Harvard University Press, 1958, ²1964, ³1969.

Goethe's "Faust": The Prologues and Part One/Two. The Bayard Taylor Translation Revised and Edited, with a New Introduction. New York: Collier Books, 1962, ²1964, ³1967.

Goethe's "Faust": The Prologues and Part One. Bilingual Edition. New York: Collier Books, 1963, ²1966.

The Age of Goethe: An Anthology of German Literature. Boston: Houghton Mifflin, 1969.

Heinrich Heine, *Werke.* 2 volumes. München: Beck, 1973, 1977.

Johann Wolfgang von Goethe, *Faust I & II.* Ed. and Translation. Boston: Suhrkamp/Insel, 1984. Republished: Princeton University Press, 1994.

II. Articles and Notes

"A Note on Fritz Nettenmair (Otto Ludwig's 'Zwischen Himmel und Erde')," *Monatshefte* 31 (1939): 349–52.

"*Urfaust* l. 309," *Modern Language Notes* 55 (1940): 201–4.

"Some Misunderstood Passages in Otto Ludwig's 'Zwischen Himmel und Erde,' " *Monatshefte* 33 (1941): 308–20.

"Again on the Modern Languages in Colleges," *Modern Language Journal* 25 (1941): 473–76.

"Addison's *Cato*: I. i. 47–53," *Philological Quarterly* 21 (1942): 430–33.

"Many Misunderstood Passages," *German Quarterly* 25 (1942): 134–46.

"Vestis Virum Reddit (Gottfried Keller's 'Kleider machen Leute')," *Monatshefte* 35 (1943): 95–102.

"An Early Translation from 'Hermann und Dorothea,' " *Modern Language Review* 38 (1943): 40–43.

"Some Notes to Kleist's *Der zerbrochene Krug*," *Philological Quarterly* 22 (1943): 278–83.

"Sir Herbert Croft and German Literature," *Modern Language Quarterly* 5 (1944): 193–200.

"The American Language," *Modern Language Notes* 59 (1944): 335–36.

"*Peter Schlemihl* in Relation to the Popular Novel of the Romantic Period," *Germanic Review* 21 (1946): 191–208.

"Germany Through French Eyes After the Liberation," *German Quarterly* 20 (1947): 166–82.

"A Possible Dickens Influence in Zola," *Modern Language Quarterly* 8 (1947): 302–8.

"La Réforme de l'Enseignement universitaire aux États-Unis," *Les Études Américaines* (Paris) 5 (1947): 35–37.

"J.C. Lavater and Goethe: Problems of Psychology and Theology in *Die Leiden des jungen Werthers*," *PMLA* 63 (1948): 520–76.

"Some Problems of Literary Interpretation," *New England MLA Bulletin* 10 (1948): 21–29.

"Werther's 'Misfallen an uns selbst, das immer mit einem Neide verknüpft ist,' " *Modern Language Review* 43 (1948): 96–98.

"On the Opening Lines of Goethe's *Iphigenie*," *Germanic Review* 24 (1949): 116–23.

"The Apprentice Novelist—Goethe's Letters, 1765–1767," *Modern Language Quarterly* 10 (1949): 290–306.

"Werther's 'Neid'—A Reply," *Modern Language Review* 44 (1949): 385–86.

"My Debt to Goethe," *Books Abroad* 23 (1949): 349.

"*Mirages français*—French Literature in German Eyes," *Yale French Studies* 6 (1950): 35–44.

"The Parable of the Rings in Lessing's *Nathan der Weise*," *Germanic Review* 26 (1951): 259–67.

"Karl Viëtor: November 29, 1892–June 7, 1951," *Germanic Review* 26 (1951): 171–72.

" 'Geistes Kraft und Mund,' " *Modern Language Notes* 66 (1951): 331.

"A Humanistic Approach to Literature: Critical Interpretation of Two Sonnets by Platen," *German Quarterly* 25 (1952): 259–76.

"An 'Ur-Urmeister?' " *Modern Language Notes* 67 (1952): 368–76.

"A Reconsideration of Some Unappreciated Aspects of the Prologues and Early Scenes in Goethe's 'Faust,' " *Modern Language Review* 47 (1952): 362–73.

"Karl Viëtor" (with H.M. Jones, T. Starck), *Harvard University Gazette* 47 (1952): 103–4.

"A Reconsideration of Some Misunderstood Passages in the 'Gretchen Tragedy' of Goethe's 'Faust,' " *Modern Language Review* 48 (1953): 421–34.

"Again on 'Pythonissa. Faust II,' L. 9135," *Modern Language Notes* 68 (1953): 216.

"The Visions of Leda and the Swan in Goethe's *Faust*," *Modern Language Notes* 68 (1953): 340–44.

"Goethe, Calderon and *Faust: Der Tragödie zweiter Teil*," *Germanic Review* 28 (1953): 83–98.

"The Mothers, the Phorcides and the Cabiri in Goethe's *Faust*," *Monatshefte* 45 (1953): 289–96.

"Some Lexicographical Notes on Goethe's *Faust,*" *Modern Language Quarterly* 14 (1953): 82–97.

"The Prologues to Goethe's 'Faust,' and the Question of Unity: A Partial Reply," *Modern Language Review* 48 (1953): 193–94.

"Goethe, Aristophanes, and the Classical Walpurgisnight," *Comparative Literature* 6 (1954): 64–78.

"F.W.C. Lieder," *German Quarterly* 27 (1954): 126.

"The Evaluation of Romanticism in Goethe's *Faust,*" *Journal of English and Germanic Philology* 54 (1955): 9–38.

"Irony and Ambiguity in the Final Scene of Goethe's *Faust,*" in *On Romanticism and the Art of Translation: Studies in Honor of Edwin Hermann Zeydel,* ed. Gottfried F. Merkel. Princeton: Princeton University Press, 1956, pp. 7–27.

"The Evaluation of Heine's *Neue Gedichte,*" in *Wächter und Hüter: Festschrift für Hermann J. Weigand zum 17. November 1957,* ed. Curt v. Faber du Faur et al. Yale University, Department of Germanic Languages, pp. 99–107.

"A *Faust* Miscellany," *Modern Language Notes* 72 (1957): 286–87.

"An Editorial Farewell," *German Quarterly* 30 (1957): 143–44.

" 'Adulterism,' " *Modern Language Review* 54 (1959): 654.

"Gestalt als Gehalt in Schillers 'Braut von Messina,' " *Deutsche Vierteljahrsschrift für Literaturwissenschaft und Geistesgeschichte* 33 (1959): 529–64.

"The First Draft of Heine's 'Für die Mouche,' " *Harvard Library Bulletin* 13 (1959): 415–43.

"Heine's Letter to Bocage, September 11, 1855," *Modern Language Quarterly* 20 (1959): 74–76.

"*Faust*forschung und *Faust*deutung seit 1945," *Euphorion* 53 (1959): 422–40.

"Ristiana," *Journal of English and Germanic Philology* 59 (1960): 70–75.

"Heine and the Wreck of the *Amphitrite,*" *Harvard Library Bulletin* 14 (1960): 395–99.

"The Unpublished Passages of Heine's Letter to Charlotte Embden, July 11, 1844," *Modern Language Notes* 76 (1961): 824–26.

"Corrigenda to the 'Nationalausgabe': Notes to Schiller's *Kabale und Liebe,*" *Modern Language Notes* 79 (1964): 554–55.

"The Function of the Exotic in Heine's Later Poetry," in *Connaissance de l'étranger: mélanges offerts à la mémoire de Jean-Marie Carré.* Paris: Didier, 1965, pp. 119–30.

"Zum besseren Verständnis einiger Gedichte des *West-östlichen Divan,*" *Euphorion* 59 (1965): 178–206.

"Preromanticism," in *Encyclopedia of Poetry and Poetics.* Princeton: Princeton University Press, 1965, pp. 662–63.

"Rococo," in *Encyclopedia of Poetry and Poetics,* p. 712.

"Sturm und Drang," in *Encyclopedia of Poetry and Poetics,* p. 813.

"Zeitalter der Aufklärung," in *Das Fischer-Lexikon: Literatur* II/1. Fischer-Bücherei. Frankfurt/Main: Fischer, 1965, pp. 58–78.

"Zeitalter der Entdeckung," in *Das Fischer-Lexikon: Literatur* II/2. Fischer-Bücherei. Frankfurt/Main: Fischer, 1965, pp. 617–39.

"The Interpretation of Goethe's *Faust* since 1958," *Orbis Litterarum* 20 (1965): 239–67.

"Studies and Interpretations of Goethe's *Faust* since 1959," *German Quarterly* 39 (1966): 303–10.

"Goethe und die Tradition der Renaissancelyrik," in *Tradition und Ursprünglichkeit*, hrsg. vom Internationalen Germanistenkongreß. Bern: Francke, 1965, pp. 176–77.

"The First Draft of Heine's Newsletter from Paris, May 30, 1840," *Harvard Library Bulletin* 15 (1967): 353–67.

"The Sense of Guilt and the Compulsion to Atone," in *Goethe's Faust Part One: Essays in Criticism*, ed. J.B. Vickery and J'nan Sellery. Belmont, Calif.: Wadsworth, 1969, pp. 124–35.

" 'Das Leben ist ein Gänsespiel': Some Aspects of Goethe's *West-östlicher Divan*," in *Festschrift für Bernhard Blume*, ed. Egon Schwarz et al. Göttingen: Vandenhoeck & Ruprecht, 1967, pp. 90–102.

"The French Text of Eleven Letters from Heine to His Wife (1844)," *Harvard Library Bulletin* 18 (1970): 267–81.

"Faust," in *Encyclopedia Americana* (International Edition), vol. 11. New York, 1971, pp. 56–58.

"Goethe," in *Encyclopedia Americana*, vol. 13. New York, 1971, pp. 1–5.

"*Wilhelm Meisters Lehrjahre*: Novel or Romance?" In *Essays on European Literature in Honor of Liselotte Dieckmann*, ed. P.U. Hohendahl et al. St. Louis: Washington University Press, 1972, pp. 45–52.

"Goethe und die Renaissancelyrik," in *Goethe und die Tradition*, ed. Hans Reiss. Frankfurt/Main: Athenäum, 1972, pp. 102–29.

"Notes (Chiefly Lexical) to Goethe's *Faust*," in *Traditions and Transitions: Studies in Honor of Harold Jantz*, ed. L.E. Kurth et al. München: Delp, 1972, pp. 132–41.

"Remarks Suggested by Fascist Humanism and the Enemy Enlightenment," *PMLA* 88 (1973): 400–7.

"Zum besseren Verständnis einiger Gedichte des 'West-östlichen Divan,' " in *Interpretationen zum West-östlichen Divan Goethes*, ed. Edgar Lohner. Darmstadt: Wissenschaftliche Buchgesellschaft, 1973, pp. 95–146.

" 'Schlecht und modern?' Englische *Faust*-Übersetzungen seit 1949," in *Ansichten zu Faust*, ed. Günther Mahal. Stuttgart: Kohlhammer, 1973, pp. 219–26.

"Observations on Goethe's *Torquato Tasso*," in *Husbanding the Golden Grain: Studies in Honor of Henry W. Nordmeyer*, ed. Luanne T. Frank and Emery E. George. Ann Arbor, Department of Germanic Languages and Literatures, University of Michigan, pp. 5–23.

"Motif in Literature: The Faust Theme," in *Dictionary of the History of Ideas*, vol. 3. New York: Scribners, 1973, pp. 244–53.

"Observations on Goethe's *Torquato Tasso*," *Carleton Germanic Papers* 2 (1973): 41–59.

"Neue Überlegungen zu einigen mißverstandenen Passagen der 'Gretchentragödie,' " in *Aufsätze zu Goethes "Faust I*," ed. Werner Keller. Darmstadt: Wissenschaftliche Buchgesellschaft, 1974, pp. 496–520.

"Negation, Pflege oder Aufhebung? Einstellungen zum literarischen 'Erbe,' " in *American Association of Teachers of German: Proceedings of the 42nd Annual Meeting* (Bonn), ed. Reinhold Grimm. Philadelphia, 1975, pp. 12–16.

"Preromanticism," in *Princeton Encyclopedia of Poetry and Poetics*. Princeton: Princeton University Press, 1974, pp. 662–63.

"Rococo," in *Princeton Encyclopedia of Poetry and Poetics*, p. 712.

"Sturm und Drang," in *Princeton Encyclopedia of Poetry and Poetics*, p. 813.

"Taught by Success—Kleist's Prince of Homburg," *German Quarterly* 50 (1977): 1–9.

"*Italienische Reise* and Goethean Classicism," in *Aspekte der Goethezeit*, ed. S.A. Corngold et al. Göttingen: Vandenhoeck & Ruprecht, 1977, pp. 81–96.

"*Torquato Tasso* Kommentar," in *Goethes Werke* (Hamburger Ausgabe), 5:499–577. München: Beck, 8., neub. Aufl. 1977.

"Heinrich von Kleist and the Fine Arts—Kleist and Bury, or Kleist and Lethière?" *German Life and Letters* 31 (1978): 166–74.

"Anhang: *Torquato Tasso*," in Johann Wolfgang Goethe, *Die großen Weimarer Dramen*. München: Deutscher Taschenbuch Verlag, 1979, pp. 346–415.

"Der Miniaturmaler der 'Italienischen Reise': Ein Nachtrag zum Thema Goethe und Leonardo," *Goethe Jahrbuch* 96 (1979): 258–60.

"Probleme der deutschen Klassik," *Jahrbuch für Internationale Germanistik* 11 (1979): 158–60.

"Codicils to 'The Testament of Werther in Poetry and Drama,' " in *Literatur als Dialog*, ed. Reingard Nethersole. Johannesburg: Ravan, 1979, pp. 195–205.

"For Professor Karl Thiens," in *Hommage für Karl Thiens* (catalogue of exhibition "Meinungen zu Faust," Goethe-Museum, Düsseldorf, February, 1979). Stuttgart: Lichtpauserei Spannagel, 1979.

"*Die Wahlverwandtschaften*: Novel of German Classicism," *German Quarterly* 53 (1980): 1–45 and 347.

"Goethe's Nausicaa: A Figure in Fresco," in *Studien zur Goethezeit, Erich Trunz zum 75. Geburtstag*, ed. Hans-Joachim Mähl and Eberhard Mannack. Heidelberg: Carl Winter Universitätsverlag, 1981, pp. 33–44.

"Goethe's Last Play, *Die Wette*," *Modern Language Notes* 97 (1982): 546–55.

"Die Ringparabel in Lessings 'Nathan der Weise,' " in *Lessings "Nathan der Weise,"* ed. Klaus Bohnen. Darmstadt: Wissenschaftliche Buchgesellschaft, 1984, pp. 155–67.

"On Translating *Faust*," in *Johann Wolfgang Goethe: One Hundred and Fifty Years of Continuing Vitality*, ed. Ulrich Goebel, Wolodymyr T. Zyla. Lubbock: Texas Tech Press, 1984, pp. 21–39.

"Of Curious Readers," *Carleton Germanic Papers* 12 (1984): 1–9.

"On Goethe's Classicism," in *Goethe Proceedings: Essays Commemorating the Goethe Sesquicentennial at the University of California, Davis*, ed. Clifford A. Bernd et al. Columbia, SC: Camden House, 1984, pp. 1–21.

" 'Ins Wasser wirf deine Kuchen': Dankrede," in Deutsche Akademie für Sprache und Dichtung, *Jahrbuch 1984* (Heidelberg: Lambert Schneider) 51–55.

"Über Goethes Klassik," in *Goethe Jahrbuch* 103 (1986): 278–301.

"Goethes 'Faust' auf englisch: Übersetzung als Interpretation," in *Goethe Jahrbuch* 104 (1987): 253–69.

"Aesthetic Qualities," in *Approaches to Teaching Goethe's Faust*, ed. Douglas J. McMillan. New York: The Modern Language Association, 1987, pp. 66–69.

"Vorwort," in Wolodomyr T. Zyla: *Johann Wolfgang Goethe in der ukrainischen Literatur*. München: Ukrainische Freie Universität, 1989, pp. 5–6.

"Preromanticism"; "Rococo"; "Sturm und Drang" (revised), in *The New Princeton Encyclopedia of Poetry and Poetics*. Princeton: Princeton University Press, 1993, pp. 974–75; 1074–75; 1224–25.

"Goethe's *Novelle* as Pictorial Narrative," in *Poetry Poetics Translation: Festschrift in Honor of Richard Exner*, ed. Ursula Mahlendorf and Laurence Rickels. Würzburg: Königshausen & Neumann, 1994, pp. 73–81.

"Goethe's *Faust* at the Hands of Its Translators: Some Recent Developments," in *Interpreting Goethe's Faust Today*, ed. Jane K. Brown et al. Columbia, SC: Camden House, 1994, pp. 231–38.

"Evaluating a *Faust* Translation. On the Occasion of Martin Greenberg's Version of Part One," *Goethe Yearbook* 7 (1994): 210–21.

III. Reviews

L.J. Russon and M.A. London, eds., *Vier Abenteuergeschichten. Modern Language Journal* 26 (1942): 388.

C.M. Purin et al., *Conversational Approach to German. German Quarterly* 21 (1948): 134–35.

Paul Reiff, *Die Ästhetik der deutschen Frühromantik. Germanic Review* 23 (1948): 302–3.

Edith Amelie Runge, *Primitivism and Related Ideas in Sturm und Drang Literature. Modern Language Quarterly* 9 (1948): 376–77.

Carlo Rudino, *Il Dramma di Margherita: Interpretazione dal Goethe. Modern Language Quarterly* 10 (1949): 101.

Maurice Boucher, *Le Sentiment national en Allemagne. Journal of English and Germanic Philology* 48 (1949): 158–59.

Jean-Marie Carré, *Les Écrivains français et le mirage allemand 1800–1940. Comparative Literature* 1 (1949): 91–92.

Hermann Schneider, *Urfaust? Eine Studie. Germanic Review* 24 (1949): 228–29.

Bayard Quincy Morgan and A.R. Hohlfeld, eds., *German Literature in British Magazines, 1750–1860. Modern Language Quarterly* 11 (1950): 377.

Isaac Tabak, *Judaic Lore in Heine: the Heritage of a Poet. Modern Language Forum* 35 (1950): 157–58.

Hans Heinrich Borcherdt, *Der Roman der Goethezeit. Germanic Review* 26 (1951): 153–54.

Werner Danckert, *Goethe: Der mythische Urgrund seiner Weltschau. Germanic Review* 27 (1952): 59–61.

Hans M. Wolff, *Goethes Weg zur Humanität. Modern Language Notes* 67 (1952): 190–92.

G.H. Needler, *Goethe and Scott. Journal of English and Germanic Philology* 51 (1952): 278–79.

Paul Holyrod Curts, *Basic German: A Brief Introduction to the German Language. German Quarterly* 26 (1953): 75.

Werner F. Leopold, *Bibliography of Child Language. German Quarterly* 26 (1953): 76.

Richard A. Williams et al., *Annotated Bibliography of Modern Language Methodology. German Quarterly* 26 (1953): 79.

Johann Wolfgang von Goethe, *Die Schriften zur Naturwissenschaft*, I 3, ed. Rupprecht Matthaei. *Erasmus* 6 (1953): 28–29.

Georg Ticknor, *The Sorrows of Young Werther. German-American Review* 19, No. 3 (1953): 38.

Geneviève Bianquis, *Études sur Goethe. Erasmus* 6 (1953): 143–45.

Merrill C. Hill, *Graphic German Grammar. German Quarterly* 26 (1953): 220.

Wilton W. Blancke, ed., *General Principles of Language and Experiences in Language. German Quarterly* 27 (1954): 71.

Ronald Gray, *Goethe the Alchemist. Modern Language Review* 49 (1954): 101–3.

John B. Carroll, *The Study of Language. German Quarterly* 27 (1954): 131.

Klaus Günther Just, ed., Lohenstein: *Türkische Trauerspiele. German Quarterly* 27 (1954): 216–17.

R.B. Farrell, *Dictionary of German Synonyms. German Quarterly* 27 (1954): 217–18.

Oskar Loerke, ed., *Deutscher Geist: Ein Lesebuch aus zwei Jahrhunderten. German Quarterly* 27 (1954): 266–67.

B.Q. Morgan, transl.: Goethe, *Faust: Part One. Yearbook of Comparative and General Literature* 4 (1955): 92–93.

August Closs, *Woge im Westen. German Quarterly* 28 (1955): 68.

Erich Trunz, ed., *Goethes Werke* (Hamburger Ausgabe), vol. 3: *Faust. German Quarterly* 28 (1955): 73–74.

Erich Trunz, ed., *Goethes Werke* (Hamburger Ausgabe), vol. 8: Romane und Novellen, III. *German Quarterly* 28 (1955): 206–7.

Edward C. Breitenkamp, *The U.S. Information Control Division and Its Effect on German Publishers and Writers 1945 to 1949. German Quarterly* 28 (1955): 218.

Herbert von Einem, ed., *Goethes Werke* (Hamburger Ausgabe), vol. 11: Autobiographische Schriften, III (*Italienische Reise*). *German Quarterly* 28 (1955): 289–90.

Goethes Werke (Hamburger Ausgabe), vol. 6: Romane und Novellen, I. *German Quarterly* 29 (1956): 208–9.

Louis DeVries and Alfred P. Kehlenbeck, *Essentials of Reading German: Grammar and Usage*. *German Quarterly* 29 (1956): 212.

Edgar Hederer, ed., *Deutsche Dichtung des Barock*. *German Quarterly* 29 (1956): 289–90.

Klaus Günther Just, ed., Lohenstein: *Römische Trauerspiele*. *German Quarterly* 29 (1956): 292.

Wildhagen-Heraucourt, *English-German & German-English Dictionary*. *German Quarterly* 29 (1956): 292.

Hugh Powell, ed., Gryphius: *Carolus Stuardus*. *Modern Language Notes* 71 (1956): 618–19.

William Rose, ed., *Last Poems [of Heine]*. *German Quarterly* 29 (1956): 56–57.

Heinz Griesbach and Dora Schulz, *Deutsche Sprachlehre für Ausländer*. *German Quarterly* 30 (1957): 68.

Erich Trunz, ed., *Goethes Werke* (Hamburger Ausgabe), vol. 2: Gedichte und Epen, II. *German Quarterly* 30 (1957): 141–42.

Fritz Bergemann, ed., Eckermann: *Gespräche mit Goethe*. *German Quarterly* 30 (1957): 228.

Hermann Tiemann, ed., Meta Klopstock, geborene Moller: *Briefwechsel mit Klopstock, ihren Verwandten und Freunden*, 3 vols. *Erasmus* 10 (1957): 329–30.

Vincenzo Errante, *Il mito di Faust*. *Comparative Literature* 9 (1957): 372–75.

Bayard Quincy Morgan, transl. *The Sufferings of Young Werther*. *German Quarterly* 31 (1958): 249.

August Closs, *Medusa's Mirror*. *German Quarterly* 31 (1958): 245–46.

Klaus Günther Just, ed., Lohenstein: *Afrikanische Trauerspiele*. *German Quarterly* 31 (1958): 246–47.

Robert Lado, *Linguistics Across Cultures*. *German Quarterly* 31 (1958): 254.

Eduard Berend, ed., *Jean Pauls Sämtliche Werke*, Ergänzungsband: *J.-P.'s Persönlichkeit in Berichten der Zeitgenossen*. *Erasmus* 11 (1958): 501–3.

August von Platen, *Dichtungen*, ed. Günther Voigt. *Journal of English and Germanic Philology* 58 (1959): 173–76.

Josef Strelka, *Der burgundische Renaissancehof Margarethes von Österreich und seine literarhistorische Bedeutung*. *German Quarterly* 32 (1959): 173–74.

Curt von Faber du Faur, *German Baroque Literature: A Catalogue*. *German Quarterly* 32 (1959): 174–75.

Jahrbuch der schlesischen Friedrich-Wilhelms-Universität zu Breslau, III. *German Quarterly* 32 (1959): 178.

Erna Merker, *Wörterbuch zu Goethes Werther* (Erste Lieferung). *German Quarterly* 32 (1959): 185.

E.M. Butler, *Heinrich Heine*. *Modern Language Notes* 74 (1959): 766–68.

Goethes Werke (Hamburger Ausgabe), vol. 10: Autobiographische Schriften, II. *German Quarterly* 32 (1959): 385–86.

The Era of Goethe: Essays Presented to James Boyd. Monatshefte 52 (1960): 87–89.

Emil Staiger, *Goethe 1814–1832. Germanic Review* 35 (1960): 311–15.

Ernst Grumach, ed., *Beiträge zur Goetheforschung. Journal of English and Germanic Philology* 59 (1960): 782–84.

Jacob Steiner, *Sprache und Stilwandel in Goethes Wilhelm Meister. Modern Language Review* 56 (1961): 614–15.

Elizabeth Sewall, *The Orphic Voice: Poetry and Natural History. Germanistik* 2 (1961): 206–8.

Maurice Marache, *Le Symbole dans la pensé et l'œuvre de Goethe. Monatshefte* 54 (1962): 131–32.

Heinrich Heine, *Werke und Briefe*, vols. I, II, ed. Hans Kaufmann. *Journal of English and Germanic Philology* 61 (1962): 130–31.

Gottfried Wilhelm and Eberhard Galley, *Heine-Bibliographie*, Teil I, II. *Modern Language Review* 57 (1962): 287–88.

S.S. Prawer, *Heine the Tragic Satirist. Modern Language Review* 57 (1962): 289–91.

Heine-Jahrbuch 1962. *Modern Language Review* 58 (1963): 137–38.

Hans Reiss, *Goethes Romane. German Quarterly* 37 (1964): 266–68.

Laura Hofrichter, *Heinrich Heine. Journal of English and Germanic Philology* 63 (1964): 734–36.

Eduard Berend, *Jean-Paul-Bibliographie. Erasmus* 16 (1964): 394–96.

Erich Trunz, ed., *Goethes Werke* (Hamburger Ausgabe), vol. 1: Gedichte. *German Quarterly* 38 (1965): 219–21.

Fritz Strich, *Goethes Faust. German Quarterly* 39 (1966): 239–40.

Charles E. Passage, transl., *Faust, Part One & Part Two. German Quarterly* 39 (1966): 387–89.

Hanna Fischer-Lamberg, ed., *Der junge Goethe: Neubearbeitete Ausgabe in fünf Bänden*, I, II. *Modern Language Review* 61 (1966): 726–29.

Ernst and Renate Grumach, eds., Goethe, *Begegnungen und Gespräche*, I. *Modern Language Review* 61 (1966): 729–32.

Johann Rist, *Sämtliche Werke*, Bd. I: *Dramatische Dichtungen*, ed. Eberhard Mannack. *Journal of English and Germanic Philology* 67 (1968): 117–19.

Harold Jantz, *The Soothsayings of Bakis: Goethe's Tragi-Comic Observations on Life, Time and History. Monatshefte* 60 (1968): 297–99.

André Dabezies, *Visages de Faust au XXe siècle: Literature, idéologie et mythes. Germanic Review* 43 (1968): 290–91.

Goethe Wörterbuch. . . (A–abrufen) (Bd. I, 1. Lieferung). *Modern Language Review* 63 (1968): 751–52.

Ernst and Renate Grumach, eds., Goethe, *Begegnungen und Gespräche*, II. *Modern Language Review* 63 (1968): 752–53.

Ernst Loeb, *Die Symbolik des Wasserzyklus bei Goethe. Erasmus* 20 (1968): 550–53.

Ronald Gray, *Goethe: A Critical Introduction. Modern Language Review* 64 (1969): 452–59.

Albert Fuchs, *Goethe-Studien. German Quarterly* 42 (1969): 735–36.

Goethe Wörterbuch (Bd. I, 2. Lieferung). *Modern Language Review* 64 (1969): 935–36.

Manfred Windfuhr, *Heinrich Heine: Revolution und Reflexion. Journal of English and Germanic Philology* 69 (1970): 346–48.

Hanna Fischer-Lamberg, ed., *Der junge Goethe*, III, IV. *Modern Language Review* 65 (1970): 213–16.

Werner Vortriede and Uwe Schweikert, *Heine-Kommentar* (2 vols.). *Monatshefte* 63 (1971): 171–72.

Lessing Yearbook II, 1970. *Modern Language Notes* 87 (1972): 523–24.

Klaus Scherpe, *Werther und Wertherwirkung. Germanic Review* 47 (1972): 297–300.

Johann Wolfgang Goethe, *Gedenkausgabe: Registerband. Monatshefte* 64 (1972): 306–7.

Johann Rist, *Sämtliche Werke*, Bd. II: *Dramatische Dichtungen*, ed. Eberhard Mannack. *Journal of English and Germanic Philology* 71 (1972): 574–75.

Gerhard Storz, *Heinrich Heines lyrische Dichtung. Modern Language Quarterly* 33 (1972): 341–43.

Wolfgang Herwig, ed., *Goethes Gespräche*, III, 1. Teil: *1817–1825. Monatshefte* 64 (1972): 393–94.

Herman Meyer, *Natürlicher Enthusiasmus: Das Morgenländische in Goethes "Novelle." Journal of English and Germanic Philology* 73 (1974): 288–90.

Heinrich Heine, *Historisch-kritische Gesamtausgabe der Werke*, ed. Manfred Windfuhr, VI. *Journal of English and Germanic Philology* 73 (1974): 406–9.

Albert Fuchs, *Le "Faust" de Goethe: Mystère, Document humain, Confession personnelle. German Quarterly*, AATG Membership Directory 1974: 136–39.

Hanna Fischer-Lamberg, ed., *Der junge Goethe*, V. *Modern Language Review* 70 (1975): 698–702.

Hanna Fischer-Lamberg, ed., *Der junge Goethe*, Registerband. *Modern Language Review* 70 (1975): 702–4.

Helmut Koopman, ed., *Heinrich Heine. Monatshefte* 69 (1977): 213.

Liselotte Dieckmann, *Johann Wolfgang Goethe. Philological Quarterly* 54 (1975): 948–49.

Gertrud Waseem, *Das kontrollierte Herz: Die Darstellung der Liebe in Heinrich Heines "Buch der Lieder." Seminar* 13 (1977): 283–84.

Hans Henning, *Faust Bibliographie Teil III: Das Faust-Thema neben und nach Goethe. German Quarterly* 50 (1977): 561–62.

Jost Hermand, *Streitobjekt Heine: Ein Forschungsbericht 1945–1975. Journal of English and Germanic Philology* 76 (1977): 96–97.

Renate Grumach, ed., *Goethe, Begegnungen und Gespräche*, III. *German Quarterly* 51 (1978): 369–70.

Harold Jantz, *The Form of Faust: The Work of Art and Its Intrinsic Structures.* *Journal of English and Germanic Philology* 78 (1979): 295–99.

Marvin Carlson, *Goethe and the Weimar Theatre.* *German Quarterly* 52 (1979): 413–15.

Meredith Lee, *Studies in Goethe's Lyric Cycles.* *German Quarterly* 52 (1979): 539–40.

Goethe-Wörterbuch, I. (A–azurn). *Modern Language Notes* 95 (1980): 705–6.

H.G. Haile, *Invitation to Goethe's Faust.* *Thought* (Fordham University) 54 (1979): 220–22.

Karl Robert Mandelkow, ed., *Goethe im Urteil seiner Kritiker: Dokumente zur Wirkungsgeschichte Goethes in Deutschland*, III: *1870–1918. The Eighteenth Century*, n.s. 6 (1984): 459–60.

Barker Fairley, *Selected Essays on German Literature.* *Seminar* 22 (1986): 186–88.

Wolfgang Herwig, ed., *Goethes Gespräche*, III, 2. Teil; IV (Kommentar). *Monatshefte* 78 (1986): 235–37.

Fritz Mende, ed., Heinrich Heine Säkularausgabe, vol. 7: *Über Frankreich 1831–1837: Berichte über Kunst und Politik. Journal of English and Germanic Philology* 85 (1986): 79–81.

André von Gronicka, *The Russian Image of Goethe*, vol. 2. *Yearbook of Comparative and General Literature* 35 (1986): 167–68.

Review Article: "Recent Books about Goethe," *Monatshefte* 78 (1986): 369–76.

Rosemary Ashton, *Little Germany: Exile and Asylum in Victorian England.* *Victorian Studies* 30 (1987): 544–45.

Brigitte Peucker, *Lyric Descent in the German Romantic Tradition.* *Studies in Romanticism* 29 (1990): 161–65.

Jutta Van Selm, *Zwischen Bild und Text: Goethes Werdegang zum Klassizismus.* *Goethe Yearbook* 5 (1990): 327–30.

Steven P. Sondrup and David Chisholm, *Verskonkordanz zu Goethes "Faust, Erster Teil."* *Goethe Yearbook* 5 (1990): 354–55.

Martin Bidney, *Blake and Goethe: Psychology, Ontology, Imagination.* *Blake Illustrated Quarterly* 24 (Winter 1990/91): 99–101.

Faust through Four Centuries: Retrospect and Analysis, ed. Peter Boerner and Sidney Johnson. *Journal of English and Germanic Philology* 90 (1991): 291–93.

Ilse Graham, *Schauen und Glauben.* *Goethe Yearbook* 6 (1992): 211–15.

Helmut Ammerlahn, *Aufbau und Krise der Sinn-Gestalt: Tasso und die Prinzessin im Kontext der Goetheschen Werke.* *Goethe Yearbook* 7 (1994): 253–54.

Karl-Heinz Hahn and Irmtraut Schmid, eds., *Briefe an Goethe. . . in Regestform*, vols. 1–2. *Goethe Yearbook* 7 (1994): 239–41.